# THE VICTORIAN AGE

*The Victorian Age* introduces students of nineteenth-century literary and cultural history to the main areas of intellectual debate in the Victorian period. Bringing together for the first time in one volume a wide range of primary source material, this anthology gives readers a unique insight into the ways in which different areas of Victorian intellectual debate were interconnected.

*The Victorian Age* covers developments in social and political theory, economics, science and religion, aesthetics, and sexuality and gender, and provides access to a range of documents which have hitherto been highly inaccessible – both difficult to locate and difficult to interpret and understand. This authoritative anthology contains a general introduction which explains the various ways in which the relationship between literary and intellectual culture can be theorised; essays describing the background to the areas of debate illustrated by the selected source documents; bibliographical notes on all the documents included; and brief accounts of the reputation and career of the documents' authors.

This volume will enable humanities students, as well as the general reader, to understand complex areas of debates in an unusually wide range of disciplines, several of which will be unfamiliar.

**Josephine M. Guy** is Senior Lecturer in Victorian Studies at the University of Nottingham.

D1350306

# THE
# VICTORIAN AGE

An anthology of sources and documents

*Josephine M. Guy*

Routledge
Taylor & Francis Group

LONDON AND NEW YORK

First published 1998
by Routledge
2 Park Square, Milton Park, Abingdon, Oxon, OX14 4RN

Simultaneously published in the USA and Canada
by Routledge
270 Madison Ave, New York NY 10016

First published in paperback 2002

Transferred to Digital Printing 2005

*Routledge is an imprint of the Taylor & Francis Group*

© 1998, 2002 Josephine M. Guy, editorial matter and selection

The right of Josephine M. Guy to be identified as the Author of this Work has been
asserted by her in accordance with the Copyright, Designs and Patents Act 1988

Typeset in Baskerville by Routledge

*British Library Cataloguing in Publication Data*
A catalogue record for this book is available from the British Library

*Library of Congress Cataloging in Publication Data*
Guy, Josephine M., 1963–
The Victorian Age: an anthology of sources and documents / Josephine M. Guy.
Includes bibliographical references and index.
1. Great Britain–History–Victoria, 1837–1901–Sources. 2. Great Britain–Intellectual
life–19th century–Sources. I. Title.
DA550.G965 1998                   97–46664
941.081–dc21                       CIP

ISBN 0–415–18555–6 (Hbk)
ISBN 0–415–27114–2 (Pbk)

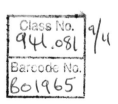

# CONTENTS

*Acknowledgements*                                                                    ix

INTRODUCTION                                                                           1
A note on the texts                                                                    7
A note on annotation                                                                   8

### Part I
### Defining society: ethics, economics and politics

INTRODUCTION                                                                          11

1 THEORIES OF SOCIAL LIFE: UTILITARIANISM,                                            27
COMMUNITARIANISM, ORGANICISM
From Jeremy Bentham, *An Introduction to the Principles of*
*Morals and Legislation* (1789; 1838) *27*
From John Stuart Mill, 'Utilitarianism' (1861) *39*
From John Grote, *An Examination of the Utilitarian Philosophy* (1870) *56*
From Robert Owen, *Report to the County of Lanark* (1821) *68*
From Herbert Spencer, 'Art IV. – The Social Organism' (1860) *83*

2 THEORIES OF THE MARKET: POLITICAL ECONOMY,
MARGINAL UTILITY THEORY, SOCIALIST ECONOMICS                                          93
From David Ricardo, *On the Principles of Political Economy, and*
*Taxation* (1817; 1821) *93*
From John Stuart Mill, 'On the Definition of Political
Economy' (1836) *108*
From Walter Bagehot, 'The Postulates of English Political
Economy No. 1' (1876) *115*
From William Stanley Jevons, *The Theory of Political Economy* (1871) *129*
From Henry Mayers Hyndman, *England for All: The Text-Book*
*of Democracy* (1881) *142*

CONTENTS

3  POLITICS AND REPRESENTATION: AUTHORITARIANISM,      155
   LIBERALISM, SOCIALISM
   *From* Thomas Carlyle, *Chartism* (1840)  *155*
   *From* Matthew Arnold, 'Anarchy and Authority' (1868)  *167*
   *From* John Stuart Mill, *On Liberty* (1859)  *183*
   William Morris *et al.*, 'The Manifesto of the Socialist League' (1885)  *193*

## Part II
## Science and religion

INTRODUCTION                                              199

4  GOD AND NATURE: EVOLUTIONARY THEORY                   213
   *From* Charles Lyell, *Principles of Geology. Volume I* (1830)  *213*
   *From* Charles Darwin, *On the Origin of Species by Means of Natural Selection*
      (1859)  *227*
   *From* Thomas Henry Huxley, *Evidence as to Man's Place
      in Nature* (1863)  *254*
   *From* Samuel Wilberforce, 'Art VII. – *On the Origin of
      Species . . .*' (1860)  *272*
   *From* Herbert Spencer, 'The Study of Sociology. XIV. –
      Preparation in Biology' (1873)  *278*

5  GOD AND REASON: BIBLICAL SCHOLARSHIP                  289
   *From* Benjamin Jowett, 'On the Interpretation of Scripture' (1860)  *289*
   *From* John William Colenso, *The Pentateuch and Book of Joshua Critically
      Examined* (1862)  *299*

## Part III
## Art and culture

INTRODUCTION                                              313

6  ART AS MORALITY                                       325
   *From* John Ruskin, *The Stones of Venice. Volume II* (1853)  *325*
   *From* Matthew Arnold, 'Art VIII.–The Functions of Criticism at the
      Present Time' (1864)  *351*

7  ART FOR ART'S SAKE                                    369
   *From* Algernon Swinburne, *Notes on Poems and Reviews* (1866)  *369*
   *From* Walter Pater, *Studies in the History of the Renaissance* (1873)  *383*
   *From* Oscar Wilde, 'The Decay of Lying: A Dialogue' (1889)  *390*
   *From* Arthur Symons, *The Symbolist Movement in Literature* (1899)  *410*

8  ART AS PATHOLOGY                                      415
   *From* Max Nordau, *Degeneration* (1895)  *415*

9  ART AND THE STATE                                                    433
   *From* William Morris, 'Art Under Plutocracy' (1884)  *433*
   *From* William John Courthope, *Life in Poetry: Law in Taste* (1901)  *446*


                             **Part IV**
                          **Sex and gender**

   INTRODUCTION                                                         463

10  DEFINING THE NORM                                                   473
   *From* William Acton, *The Functions and Disorders of the Reproductive*
      *Organs* (1857)  *473*
   *From* Henry Havelock Ellis, *Man and Woman: A Study of Human*
      *Secondary Sexual Characters* (1894)  *486*

11  DEFINING WOMEN                                                      495
   *From* Sarah Stickney Ellis, *The Women of England: Their Social*
      *Duties, and Domestic Habits* (n.d. 1843?)  *495*
   *From* John Ruskin, *Sesame and Lilies* (1865)  *505*
   *From* John Stuart Mill, *The Subjection of Women* (1869)  *520*

12  DEFINING MEN                                                        535
   *From* Edward Carpenter, *Homogenic Love and its Place in a*
      *Free Society* (1894)  *535*
   *From* John Addington Symonds, *A Problem in Modern Ethics* (1896)  *549*


   *Notes*                                                              557
   *Index*                                                              616

# ACKNOWLEDGEMENTS

I would like to thank my employers, the University of Nottingham, for a research grant, and the Department of English Studies at the University of Nottingham for a sabbatical semester; both helped towards the completion of this work. I am also grateful to Brian Read for permission to reprint the Introduction from Arthur Symons' *The Symbolist Movement in Literature*, and to Professor François Lafitte for permission to reprint the conclusion of Havelock Ellis' *Man and Woman*. All efforts to trace the heirs to the estate of Edward Carpenter have been unsuccessful; I therefore invite the owners of the copyright of his pamphlet, *Homogenic Love*, to contact either me or the publisher.

# INTRODUCTION

The aim of this anthology, to provide for students of Victorian literature a 'context' for some of the contemporary intellectual issues which inform it, may seem simple and straightforward. In fact it represents an ambition which is more complicated than it appears, and needs a word of explanation. The general idea of reading literature 'in context' will probably be familiar enough to most students and readers. Indeed few will be naïve enough to think that Victorian literature was produced in a social or intellectual vacuum. At the same time, though, to define the nature and limits of the social and intellectual environment in which works are produced is no easy task. Furthermore the relevance of such information to the ways in which we judge or value individual works has been for some time a matter of considerable dispute among critics.

A basic point of contention among cultural critics has been the *nature* of the relationship between historical knowledge and aesthetic or literary judgements. Broadly speaking, there have been three ways of understanding that relationship. The first argues that literary value is essentialist: that is, judgements about it are not contingent on historical circumstances. Such a view is no longer fashionable, although it is perhaps worth noting that it does have a long and distinguished pedigree.[1] The second approach (and one much more popular with modern critics) asserts that all literary judgements are politically or ideologically determined or conditioned and that the study of history permits us (and indeed should be employed to permit us) to uncover those political or ideological concerns.[2] For example, history might be used to show how valuing Tennyson's poetry (at the expense of the work of, say, Adelaide Anne Procter) is based upon the politics of gender. It is worth pointing out that in recent years a focus on the ideological determination of literary value has led some critics to erase the distinction between 'text' and 'context', or between 'literature' and 'historical background', to the extent that literary works come to be seen as one among many 'signifying practices' or 'discourses'. The task of the critic (in this view) is therefore to resituate the text within its 'discursive milieu' in order better to understand the nature of its contemporary (and modern) significance.[3] The third view points out that most cultures (and certainly all modern European cultures) mark out a special *category* of written works as literature, but goes on to suggest that the values which are used to define that category are in their turn historically contingent and culturally specific.[4] Practically speaking, this amounts to asserting that the Victorians, like us, identified a special *class* of literary works, but that they differed from us in their choice of the values used to define that class, and therefore in their choice of the members which comprise it. So, for example, we would not necessarily concur with our Victorian forebears about the *kinds* of works which would count as literature. Thus today 'our' definition of literature might include the Bible but exclude certain works of history; by contrast, for the Victorians (certainly in the early and middle decades of the nineteenth century), these categories were not so distinct. It is perhaps worth pointing out that the second and third ways of thinking about the relationship between historical knowledge and literary judgements are not wholly incompatible with each other: they are, after all, both using history to investigate the construction of 'literariness'. Their overall aims, though, are rather different, for where one uses history to 'deconstruct' the notion of literary identity, the other preserves literariness as a distinct (although not essentialist) category.

The arguments underlying these three positions are complex and subtle. It is obviously beyond the scope of this anthology to enter into the disputes between their various advocates, but it is nevertheless useful to locate its ambitions in terms of them. The present anthology has, then, been put together with the third (and, in part, the second) way of thinking about literary value in mind. That is, its principal aim is to help the modern reader understand how Victorian readers arrived at *their* judgements about *their own* literary and intellectual culture.

Of necessity, however, this anthology attempts to document only some aspects of that culture. I have identified four main areas of debate: discussions about the nature of social life (including attempts to define the social basis of ethics, the nature of the market and the relationship between power and representation); the contest between science and religion (which centred on competing definitions of the natural world and man's place in it); theories of art and literature (including moral theories, the divorce of art from morality and attempts to politicise and pathologise these categories); and finally debates about sex and gender, or human nature and social norms (where discussion centres on the relationship between biology and behaviour). There are of course many areas of Victorian intellectual life which it has proved impossible to cover: they include, for example, the fascination with technology and machinery, developments within medicine (such as germ-theory or eugenics), as well as the whole area of race and the politics of imperialism. There are also many areas of knowledge which will seem under-represented, such as anthropology, philology, developments in philosophy and psychology, as well as in mathematics and the physical sciences. There are several reasons for these omissions. My main criterion of inclusion (given the inevitable restrictions of space) has been based on my sense of those debates most relevant to understanding the connections between Victorian literature and intellectual culture. So although specific issues, such as contemporary developments in germ-theory, may illuminate the work of a particular author, they are not nearly so fundamental as the impact of evolutionary theory on a whole range of writers. Moreover, the present anthology unavoidably makes a judgement about which issues in Victorian intellectual life were central and which were marginal. In this sense it is worth pointing out that many aspects of the debates in the areas I have omitted turn out to be parasitic upon those areas of intellectual life which I do document (for example, eugenics and anthropology, together with arguments about racial superiority and primitivism, were dependent upon interpretations of Darwin's work).

One general way of thinking about the nature of the relationship between literary and intellectual culture, and therefore of the ways in which literary judgements were made, is in terms of intertextuality: that is, in terms of the way a text makes references to other texts or establishes textual relationships and resonances with literary and intellectual norms and traditions. In this respect we need to consider the general intellectual climate in which writers worked in order to discern dominant intellectual trends against which their concerns (and the concerns of their works) can be explained and evaluated. There are many models which critics use to understand such intellectual activity; some of the most popular have derived from the writing of the French cultural theorist Michel Foucault and the concepts of 'discourse' and the 'episteme' which he formulates.[5] Equally productive has been the notion of ideology (understood in a whole variety of ways) which emphasises the power-relations (or the politics) of knowledge – the way, that is, ideas come to be authorised, and norms established, within a culture.[6] Moreover, some political theorists have suggested that authority itself is a normative issue, in that the social mechanisms by which texts come to be authorised are themselves by no means universal. So trying to define which texts were seen to 'matter' at a particular moment in time – that is, which texts were orthodox and which heterodox – also involves uncovering the criteria by which a culture assigns status to works.[7] Furthermore, we also need to be aware that different kinds of works may be authorised in different ways. To take an obvious example, a culture may value both poetry and science, but the way status is assigned to a poem will be very different from the way status is assigned to a scientific paper.

In this respect one particularly important element of an intellectual context of literary works involves understanding the normative nature of definitions of literary value. This in turn entails attempting to uncover the criteria which define literariness within a particular culture, and therefore the concept of literary identity under which authors 'create' particular works, and under which a reading community in turn comes to label them as literature. This kind of information has proved fundamental for investigating phenomena such as avant-gardism, where the most fruitful way of understanding certain writers and artists is in terms of their attempt to challenge or change normative aesthetic concepts. It is also worth pointing out that, in this view, a 'context' is not something which is separate from, or inferior to, the 'text'. That is, the 'context' does not simply explain a text; rather, it also identifies it for our attention – it 'labels' it for us.

Another aspect of Victorian intellectual and literary culture is more prosaic, but it is no less important; it is the role played by printing technologies and publishing practices. One of the main issues here is the nature of what we can call an 'authorial process'. We need to be aware that textual production may involve a number of people and a number of institutions: they vary from a patron, a periodical owner and editor, to a typesetter, or a theatre-manager. Other issues concern the forms in which a text was published – whether it was in a magazine, periodical, single or multi-volume book, pamphlet, broadsheet, and so on – and the relationship between the form of publication, its social prestige and its readership.[8] We also have to be alert to the fact that single works often appeared in a variety of forms or media. It is well known that nineteenth-century novels were often published serially before being produced in book form; but many other kinds of writing were also published in this way. Much criticism – such as the essays which make up Matthew Arnold's *Culture and Anarchy* or Oscar Wilde's *Intentions* – was first read in magazines. So was the social science and economics (of, say, Walter Bagehot, John Stuart Mill and Herbert Spencer) and much of the popular scientific writing of Thomas Huxley.

Paying attention to publishing practices should alert us to the importance of *how* works were read: that is, who read them, and for what purposes. Of considerable importance here is the role of censorship – both formal (in state censorship, for example), and informal (the censoring authority of, say, a magazine owner or editor). We could also extend this line of inquiry to consider questions about the wider economy: that is, the relationship between a country's wealth and the number of people who could afford to read, had the time to read, and who would have seen reading as relevant to their lives. In other words, we might consider the sociology of reading, and this consideration would have to involve the economics of the book trade – an issue which in turn bears upon the number of markets for literature and on the interest groups in society who defined or controlled literary taste. In recent years some critics have gone so far as to suggest that attention to such a sociology should be extended to include the materiality of a text's embodiments. The kind of paper it is printed on, the quality of the binding, the colour of the ink, the size of the margins – all such details, it is suggested, have a bearing on how texts are identified, interpreted and valued.[9]

It has been argued that all of the diverse information which I have mentioned forms part of the 'context' which explains how literary works and literary meanings are produced. That diversity inevitably brings problems of its own. How is all that information to be organised and handled? Of course it is the attempt to answer just these sorts of questions – to discriminate between contingency and causality – which makes historical inquiry so challenging. Indeed, our concern will always be not simply the uncovering of new information or data, but also the establishing of new ways of connecting and explaining the information which we already possess. Moreover, it is in relation to precisely these two tasks that anthologies must define themselves: so the anthologist either concentrates on bringing to the reader's attention hitherto unknown or little-read works, or presents familiar works, but juxtaposes them in new and fruitful ways. The present book is designed with both ambitions in mind. In this respect, it is worth acknowledging that at the present time there are already some anthologies which focus on single aspects of Victorian intellectual culture. There are, however, a number of distinct advantages in bringing together various areas of debate within a single volume. When we see different debates juxtaposed we are encouraged to examine the interconnections between them – to view nineteenth-century intellectual culture as a complex whole, rather than as a series of debates about discrete issues. For example, we see how developments in economics affect both arguments in biology and disputes in art and literature. Indeed, one of the most distinctive characteristics of Victorian intellectual life was that it was much less specialised than today's equivalent. There were many overlapping areas in different sorts of debates; moreover, different debates had participants in common. This in turn partly explains the phenomenon of the Victorian 'sage' – figures such as John Stuart Mill or Thomas Carlyle who felt able (and were seen to be able) to comment authoritatively on a whole variety of issues – on art, politics, economics, and so on. In other words, the diversity of the present anthology is in part designed to exhibit certain fundamental characteristics of Victorian intellectual culture.

An attentive reader will notice the overwhelming predominance of male writers. I make no apology for this. The aim of the anthology is to present to the reader the work of those figures who dominated intellectual debate at the time; and as many women have noted with regret, in the nineteenth century these figures were overwhelmingly male. Of course women did write on the issues I discuss, and the new breed of professional women writers who began to emerge in the second half of the century developed an increasingly important public voice. But their work was still relatively marginal compared to the status enjoyed by figures such as Herbert Spencer or John Stuart Mill. Equally absent from this volume (and for the same kind of reasons) are the voices of the working classes and ethnic and racial minorities. In this respect, it is inevitable that this anthology will appear to some modern eyes as conservative and orthodox. In short, when I suggest that this collection is concerned with figures whom the Victorians considered important, I am referring of course to a narrow and very privileged group of Victorians – to an intellectual culture which was defined and controlled by an educated, mainly metropolitan, middle- and upper middle-class male élite. My reason for focusing on this group is simply that the norms of intellectual authority and literary taste in the nineteenth century were largely under their control. Of course this is not to deny that there were any number and kind of dissenting voices in the Victorian period. Indeed documenting Victorian radicalism is as complex and large a subject as documenting the Victorian intellectual élite; it could run to many anthologies and would present acute problems of selection of its own. However, to understand heterodoxy we need to know orthodoxy. That is, in order to understand the whole concept of 'radicalism' or 'dissent' we need to understand their targets. And it is to this primary task which the present anthology is largely addressed.

## A NOTE ON THE TEXTS

Broadly speaking, this anthology has adopted the principle of documentary editing. I have printed those texts which I judge to have possessed the greatest social currency or had the greatest social impact at the time. Generally this has involved choosing periodical essays over books, popular editions over more specialised publications and first rather than second or subsequent editions. In most cases these decisions have been straightforward, but some have involved difficulties which are discussed in the appropriate explanatory notes. I have tried wherever possible to preserve the integrity of texts by producing complete essays or, in the case of extracts from books, complete chapters. Inevitably, though, the competing demands of representing a debate and representing a particular author's argument has led to some compromises and omissions. In such cases, I have tried to limit the omitted matter to what I judge to be digressions or examples. In all cases I have attempted to preserve the clarity of a writer's argument. Omissions are indicated in the text thus: '[ ... ]', and every omission has been fully described in an appropriate note. Full bibliographical details of each piece are given in the first note.

This anthology covers a period during which there were considerable changes in printing and publishing practices and conventions. In order to give the modern reader some flavour of the range of styles to be found in nineteenth-century documents, I have not tried to impose a uniformity of presentation upon the texts I have selected. In practice this means that spelling and individual house-styles (such as the -ize or -ise forms of verbs, or to-day for today), punctuation (for example, what now appears to be an idiosyncratic use of semi-colons or the practice of placing a final quotation mark outside other punctuation marks) and styles (such as the use of 100*l*. for £100) have not been standardised; nor have references to old forms of currency (£.s.d.) been changed to post-decimal forms. For purposes of clarity, however, I have made two exceptions to this practice. I have imposed a uniformity on the use of double and single quotation marks; and I have indented all quoted material. As a rule, typography in early nineteenth-century periodicals and books did not indent quotations but used quotation marks at the beginning of each line, a practice which I judge to be unnecessarily confusing for the modern reader. I have, nevertheless, maintained the nineteenth-century custom of surrounding all quoted matter with quotation marks. Obvious errors, either by printer or author (such as John Addington Symonds' spelling of 'Gomorrha' for 'Gomorrah' in *A Problem in Modern Ethics*), have been silently corrected. A feature of nineteenth-century scholarship is the increasingly systematic use of footnotes. In general these have been faithfully reproduced. The exceptions are those few occasions when the reader is directed to a page number in the original text; all these omissions, however, have been indicated in an appropriate editorial note. Finally, non-authorial marginal glosses have been omitted.

## A NOTE ON ANNOTATION

As I have indicated in 'A note on the texts', some of the anthologised texts have authorial notes. These are indicated by superscript letters. Editorial notes are indicated by superscript numbers. On the rare occasions where an authorial note has required explanation, the information is given in the appropriate place in square brackets. On one occasion an author (Max Nordau) uses square brackets; to avoid confusion, these have been replaced by swung brackets.

The editorial notes give a full bibliographical history of each anthologised piece. The few exceptions to the principles for the choice of copy-text described in 'A note on the texts' are explained in the first note. Any omitted material is indicated by a footnote and the reasons for its omission are described fully. The annotation attempts to provide the following information: contemporary references are identified; foreign phrases and quotations are translated and (where possible) their sources are identified. For the most part I have not attempted to use the annotation to refer to the rest of a writer's *oeuvre*, principally because I am not interested in the writer for his or her own sake, and therefore the place which a piece of work has in a writer's development.

# Part I

# DEFINING SOCIETY
## Ethics, economics and politics

## CONTENTS

INTRODUCTION                                                    11

1 THEORIES OF SOCIAL LIFE: UTILITARIANISM,                     27
  COMMUNITARIANISM, ORGANICISM
  *From* Jeremy Bentham, *An Introduction to the Principles of
    Morals and Legislation* (1789; 1838) *27*
  *From* John Stuart Mill, 'Utilitarianism' (1861) *39*
  *From* John Grote, *An Examination of the Utilitarian Philosophy* (1870) *56*
  *From* Robert Owen, *Report to the County of Lanark* (1821) *68*
  *From* Herbert Spencer, 'Art IV. – The Social Organism' (1860) *83*

2 THEORIES OF THE MARKET: POLITICAL ECONOMY,                   93
  MARGINAL UTILITY THEORY, SOCIALIST ECONOMICS
  *From* David Ricardo, *On the Principles of Political Economy, and
    Taxation* (1817; 1821) *93*
  *From* John Stuart Mill, 'On the Definition of Political
    Economy' (1836) *108*
  *From* Walter Bagehot, 'The Postulates of English Political
    Economy No. 1' (1876) *115*
  *From* William Stanley Jevons, *The Theory of Political Economy* (1871) *129*
  *From* Henry Mayers Hyndman, *England for All: The Text-Book of
    Democracy* (1881) *142*

3 POLITICS AND REPRESENTATION: AUTHORITARIANISM,              155
  LIBERALISM, SOCIALISM
  *From* Thomas Carlyle, *Chartism* (1840) *155*
  *From* Matthew Arnold, 'Anarchy and Authority' (1868) *167*
  *From* John Stuart Mill, *On Liberty* (1859) *183*
  William Morris *et al.*, 'The Manifesto of the Socialist League' (1885) *193*

# INTRODUCTION

In her memorable 'Author's Introduction' to *Felix Holt the Radical* (1866), George Eliot uses the device of a coach journey across the English Midlands to trace the social and demographic contours of early Victorian Britain. The landscape we are invited to cross, with its contrast between village and manufacturing town, meadow and coal-pit, health and sickness, together with Eliot's pointed references to rick-burners, trade unions and riots, dissenting religion, reform and radicalism, contains many of what have become the clichés of nineteenth-century social history: urbanisation, industrialism, secularism and social unrest. In the novel the landscape of the Midlands provides the backdrop for Eliot's concern with social change; or, more precisely, with what she sees as the disruption to traditional patterns of sociability brought about by changes both in work-practices and in political and moral life. For the Victorians in general this interest in the grounds of social life and the nature of social cohesion proved to be both central and compelling, uniting what otherwise appear to be disparate areas of thought and activity. So whether debate was about the workings of the free market, the right to political representation, or the ethical basis of criminal legislation, at its heart lay the vexed question of defining the nature of civil society – what can usefully be termed the nature of the 'social'.

However, while we should acknowledge the pervasiveness of this concern, we also need to recognise that social theory *as theory* (that is, social theory as it is understood by modern sociologists) was largely absent from early and mid-Victorian intellectual life. Although it was widely recognised that there *were* fundamental problems in contemporary society (perhaps illustrated most dramatically in that sub-genre of Victorian fiction which we call the 'social-problem' or 'industrial' novel), it was not until the 1880s that we find in (say) socialist thought systematic attempts to retheorise the basis of social life – to reconstruct society wholesale in order to permit different kinds of social relationships and different ways of living. Why was this so? Or, to put the question around the other way, Why was it that so many of those who were critical of society were nevertheless able to retain their faith in the basic soundness of British social structures and institutions?

Answers to this question have taken several forms. It has been noted that in contrast to the political and social upheavals in Europe (and particularly in France) Victorian Britain, for all its manifest social problems, was in practice a surprisingly stable and well-ordered society: in other words social disorder was simply not violent nor sustained enough to provoke the kind of unease which had motivated the flowering of French social theory in the early nineteenth century.[1] Significantly, the kinds of social problems typically presented in mid-Victorian fiction – those associated with mechanised industry and urban overcrowding – were not in practice very typical. So during the early and mid-Victorian period much of the population continued to live in rural areas; large-scale factories, such as cotton-mills, were relatively rare when compared to the incidence of small-scale industries and traditional artisan production. Indeed, in trying to account for the relative stability of nineteenth-century Britain, economic historians have emphasised the centrality of the performance of the British economy. Described as the 'dominant' (or even the 'super-dominant'[2]) economy of the nineteenth century, wealth creation in 'the first industrial nation', to borrow Peter Mathias's term,[3] was steady enough to withstand the pressures brought about by dramatic demographic changes (the population of Britain quadrupled between 1801 and 1911 and more than doubled during Victoria's reign). The relationship between a country's wealth and the size of its population had been a source of controversy in Britain since the apocalyptic warnings sounded by Thomas Malthus in his *Essay on the Principle of Population* (first published anonymously in 1798, and subsequently revised and reprinted many times). Malthus claimed that while the population was increasing geometrically, productive capacity increased only arithmetically – a discrepancy which he predicted would lead to widespread suffering and eventual starvation for a large sector of society. That Malthus' pessimism was not borne out in practice was largely due to his underestimate of the productive efficiency achieved by technological innovation and the accompanying transformation in the structure of industry and the organisation of labour.

These developments, together with changes in agriculture, transport and finance, and the trading opportunities supplied by Britain's newly acquired colonies, led to the emergence of a new type of economy. It was characterised by high productivity, largely driven by industrial production, and by sustained and relatively rapid growth. Historians estimate that in nineteenth-century Britain the annual growth in gross domestic product averaged 2 per cent. Although modest by modern standards, it did in fact amount to more than a threefold increase in sixty years, and more than a sevenfold increase in the century. Perhaps the most important result was a steady increase in overall national wealth. At the same time, though, the annual rate of growth per capita was less impressive, averaging between 1 and 1.4 per cent; moreover, the distribution of wealth remained highly unequal. Paradoxically, then, although *average* wages and average living standards did increase and improve, a large proportion of the population was still impoverished at the end of Victoria's reign (estimates put the figure at between 25 and 30 per cent). Furthermore at particular moments in the century, the figure for those in distress was considerably higher.[4] Clearly, then, any simple equation of economic growth with the maintenance of social order needs to be treated with caution.

In contrast to economic historians, some cultural historians have stressed the role of British political and legal institutions in suppressing social unrest: that is, they have attributed social stability to the operation of power rather than to consent. It is certainly undeniable that in the early decades of the century, with memories of Revolutionary excesses in France still fresh, Britain saw a significant increase in repressive legislation aimed at restricting rights of free assembly and public protest. It is worth remembering that throughout the nineteenth century the instruments of state control were used much more frequently and blatantly than nowadays. For example, there was a systematic attempt to improve the policing of social disorder, initially through the use of militias, then through reform of the criminal justice system and prison building, and finally through the establishment of a professional police force. On the other hand, there was also a great deal of legislation aimed at removing social ills and ameliorating inequities – legislation to reduce working hours, to increase political representation, to control child labour, and so forth. Indeed it has been suggested that the origins of the British welfare state can (in part at least) be traced back to the interventionist character of Victorian social legislation.[5] From this perspective, then, it was not power and repressiveness, but rather the adaptability and flexibility of British institutions in responding to demands for reform which explain their durability. (To say as much, however, is not to deny that what we now consider to be self-evident rights of the individual – to political representation, to membership of a trade union, to health and safety at work – were only achieved in a piecemeal way and after considerable struggle.)

A further complication to which the modern reader should be alert is the local quality of much nineteenth-century political activity. Regional loyalty, coupled with the regional nature of much of the Victorian economy, produced an uneven response to what we now tend to understand as national issues. So, for example, some commentators have attributed the patchy appeal of Chartism and the unequal impact of electoral reform to exactly this local pattern of domestic politics.[6] Finally, it is perhaps worth noting that those economic analyses which point to consent and those political analyses which in turn point to coercion are not necessarily incompatible with each other. So those who were politically enfranchised were also economically empowered. Moreover, there was a significant time-lag between economic expansion and political and social reform; for example, although wealth creation tended to become more urban (shifting from the agrarian sector to the industrial and then the financial sectors) the ruling-class was still largely drawn from its traditional land-owning base. At the same time, that time-lag between economic and social change was not great enough to produce total social breakdown, although it *was* sufficient to produce continued social unrest.

The precise relationship between actual social unrest, the perception of social disorder and proposals for social restructuring is clearly a complicated one. Although nineteenth-century Britain was in general terms an ordered and peaceful society, and (until the late decades of the century) produced comparatively little systematic social theorising, by the same token the discontents and suffering which did exist in Victorian Britain should not be understated; nor should the voices of protest be overlooked. The Chartist movement, the Hyde Park riots, the recurring strikes and lockouts, the growth of trade-unionism, as well as the findings of Royal Commissions on poverty and disease, the squalor of urban overcrowding, agitation for women's rights – all of these were a highly visible and highly vocal testimony to a fundamental and persistent malaise in British social life. They produced considerable anxiety (albeit basically a self-interested one) on the part of middle-class intellectuals. Thomas Carlyle, for example, caught the mood perfectly when he addressed the 'condition and disposition of the working classes' by arguing that it was 'the most ominous of all practical matters whatever; a matter in regard to which if something be not done, something will *do* itself one day, and in a fashion that will please nobody.' So what was to be done? How did commentators respond to those inequalities and dissatisfactions identified by Carlyle?

In practice those problems were enormously varied, but we can usefully identify three large and related areas of contention. While they certainly do not exhaust all the issues involved, they do give some indication of the character and dimensions of the debate about what I have termed the 'social'. The first centres on attempts to define a principle of social cohesion, or the theoretical basis of sociability. The second (which is an aspect of the first) focuses on what many Victorians saw as the determining factor in the social relationships which *could* be formed: namely the operation of the market. Thirdly, there was a very specific debate about power and representation – about how the interests of the individual relate to the social interest. Perhaps a simpler way of describing these three areas is in terms of a concern with the ethical or moral basis of society, its economic basis, and its political basis. As we shall see, one of the great difficulties for Victorian commentators was synthesising these areas and explaining how exactly they related to each other.

Up until the 1860s the dominant way of thinking about sociability in Victorian Britain was, paradoxically, not properly social at all in the sense that social life tended to be theorised from the activities of the individual. The nature of individual behaviour was held to determine social behaviour (rather than, as modern sociologists have tended to argue, the other way round). Such a perspective in turn depended upon the prevalence of an essentialist view of human nature – that as human beings we have certain basic motivations and desires in common with each other, and that these in turn allow our behaviour to be predicted. What was disputed was the nature of those motivations and desires, and therefore the particular kinds of behaviour (and social life) they typically gave rise to. Utilitarianism, known best by its succinct formula, 'the greatest happiness of the greatest number' offered one particularly useful (if always controversial) understanding of these issues.

The origins of utilitarian thought can be traced to the middle of the eighteenth century and the work of philosophers such as Thomas Hobbes and David Hume. However, it was Jeremy Bentham who was responsible for bringing utilitarianism to prominence. Although his most famous work, *An Introduction to the Principles of Morals and Legislation*, was published in 1789, it did not gain a wide readership until the early 1800s. Assessing Bentham's reputation in 1877, the philosopher Henry Sidgwick commented that as an 'active force' Benthamism belonged to the nineteenth rather than to the eighteenth century. He went on: 'no extinction has yet overtaken Bentham: his system is even an important element of our current political thought; hardly a decade – though an eventful one – has elapsed since it might almost have been called a predominant element'.[7] Bentham's enduring reputation was due in part to his lasting influence on social reform; but it was also due to his many disciples, particularly James Mill and the Philosophic Radicals and, later in the century, James Mill's son, John Stuart Mill. Whatever prestige utilitarianism enjoyed among legislators, however, was matched by a profound unpopularity with the general public: Dickens' well-known caricature of utilitarian ways of thinking in *Hard Times* found a ready and sympathetic audience.[8]

Utilitarianism began with the premise that all human behaviour was governed by a desire to seek pleasure and avoid pain, and that a recognition of this fundamental law could provide the foundation for a theory of morals. Bentham argued that it was possible to calculate *quantities* of pleasure or pain produced by particular actions, and that such calculations could form an objective basis for a system of legislation. The aim of that legislation was to ensure a right or 'good' society where 'good' was defined in terms of the principle of utility or 'the greatest happiness of the greatest number'. In drawing up his 'felicific calculus' Bentham assumed that pleasure is measurable, that any particular person's pleasure is as desirable as that of any other person, and that this equality of treatment allowed individuals to conform to the principle of utility – to accept that right or good actions at an individual level always correlate with (and are conducive to) the greatest happiness. There were (and are) any number of objections to this line of argument: fundamentally, as the philosopher George Grote later argued, Bentham never properly explained what pleasure is; nor did he adequately prove that pleasure and happiness are indeed identical; nor did he take any account of the *experience* of pleasure. It is not simply that a certain pleasure may be 'felt' differently according to the experiencing subject, but that pleasure itself may take many different forms. Benthamite utilitarianism took no account of different *qualities* of pleasure, and therefore seemed to its detractors to be an exceptionally unsophisticated and inhumane doctrine.

John Stuart Mill's recharacterisation of utilitarianism in 1861 was an attempt to rescue it from such criticism. He conceded that there were different kinds of pleasure, and that some individuals preferred some pleasures to others. Mill went on to argue that some pleasures were superior to others. He claimed that in the case of any two pleasures, if

> one of the two, by those who are completely acquainted with both, [is] placed so far above the other that they prefer it, even though knowing it to be attended with a greater amount of discontent, and [if] they would not resign it for any quantity of the other pleasure which their nature is capable of, we are justified in ascribing to the preferred enjoyment a superiority in quality, so far outweighing quantity as to render it, in comparison, of small account.

He further suggested that in practice superior pleasures were those which employed the 'higher faculties': 'better to be a human dissatisfied than a pig satisfied; better to be a Socrates dissatisfied than a fool satisfied' was his memorable phrase. But Mill's distinction did not really rescue utilitarianism. The difficulty was that his criterion of 'superiority' was not fully explained. For example, what constituted the 'higher faculties'? And how could any one person claim to 'know' about any other person's experience of pleasure? More fundamentally the concession that pleasures are *qualitatively* different made any comparison of their *quantities* impossible. Thus Mill ironically (and unwittingly) appeared to destroy the very guarantee of objectivity – the felicific calculus – which had recommended Bentham's system in the first instance.[9]

To commentators such as Robert Owen, utilitarianism's emphasis on the individual as the basic unit of analysis, and on individual behaviour as basically selfish or pleasure-seeking, appeared as a symptom, rather than the resolution, of current social conflict; utilitarianism, that is, appeared to embody precisely the centripetal or atomistic tendencies which Owen considered to be destructive of social life. Moreover Owen also disagreed with utilitarian models of human behaviour, believing that human character was learned rather than innate. Hence appropriate moral (or social) behaviour was fundamentally a matter of appropriate education. At a basic level, however, Owen conceded the utilitarian formula of the 'greatest happiness of the greatest number', but he had different views about how such an aim could be achieved. At the heart of his concept of social life was the proposition that proper or healthy human relationships depended upon co-operation rather than competition, and upon community rather than individualism – principles which in turn could only operate, Owen argued, under a completely different kind of social system, one based on the common ownership of property. Owen's life and writing were devoted to explaining how such a system would work, both in practice (in his management of the New Lanark Mills in Scotland and his involvement in experimental communities in America) and in his theorising (which is to be found in his extensive *oeuvre*, including *A New View of Society* [1813–14], *Report to the County of Lanark* [1820] and the *Book of the New Moral World* [1836–44]). Like Bentham, Owen had many followers, and the 'Owenites', as they became known, disseminated their ideas through an impressive array of publications, including several periodicals which they had founded. Owenism, though, was not nearly so influential as Benthamism, and by the mid-1840s the movement had virtually collapsed. There were various reasons for this decline: most importantly Owen's model society was basically agrarian, and his concept of social change was small-scale and gradualist. For commentators in the 1830s and 1840s, who were faced with the permanence and increasing complexity of the institutions of industrialism, Owenite communities simply seemed irrelevant; they seemed inadequate as an answer to contemporary social ills. Moreover, Owen had also failed to provide a coherent economic account of his new society. This weakness was serious for it enabled him to be virtually dismissed by one of the most influential bodies of Victorian social and political theory, that of political economy. (Significantly, political economists' view of the market – as I shall explain below – exactly coincided with, and helped to reinforce, the atomistic individualism of utilitarian conceptions of social life.) Lastly, in his critique of Christian marriage and his endorsement of divorce and birth control, Owen also offended the moral sensibility of many Victorians.[10]

It is tempting to see in Owenism a precursor of socialist thought. However (as I explain below), socialism did not become an intellectual force in Britain until the 1880s. Up to that time, the main alternative to utilitarian conceptions of social life was organicism. Like utilitarianism and unlike Owenism, organicism was not an invention of the nineteenth century. Moreover, even if we confine our interest to that period, it is difficult to summarise for it is not easily identified with a single writer or a single school. Broadly speaking (and as the term implies) organicism conceived of society as an organism with functionally interdependent units. The stress in organicism was thus on the hierarchical (but also mutually dependent) relationship between the individual parts and the whole: if one part is damaged or at fault then the whole organism suffers. Organicism did not necessarily implicate any particular political or economic organisation, although it was generally conservative in that it emphasised stability or very gradual change (rather than revolution).

In the nineteenth century, one of the most able literary advocates of organic views of social life was George Eliot. Eliot in turn was indebted to the ideas of her partner, George Henry Lewes, and of her friend, Herbert Spencer. Spencer's exposition of organicism, outlined initially in his article in the *Westminster Review* and subsequently elaborated in his *Principles of Sociology*, is particularly interesting for it brings out what is arguably the nineteenth century's most significant contribution to organic theories of society. Spencer drew upon current developments in science (particularly evolutionary biology) to lend to organicism a new authority. The result was the introduction of a new kind of vocabulary into explanations of social behaviour – one of health and disease, of progress and degeneration. Importantly, such a vocabulary implied that existing social structures (with all their inequalities) were in some sense 'natural' and inevitable; and consequently that deviation from these structures – social unrest or political agitation – was in some sense 'unnatural' and therefore, in the long term, pointless. Such arguments in turn provided strong ammunition for critiques of non-normative activities and lifestyles, including those of artists and writers.

In organicism, then, there was a basic conservatism in that its account of social life more or less precluded radical social change or social engineering. A similar sort of conservatism is also to be found in political economy. Strictly speaking, political economy was a theory of the market rather than a theory of social life. However, the way in which political economy defined the market made economic activity the primary determinant of social relationships. In this respect the authority which political economy enjoyed in the early and middle decades of the century had a direct influence on how the Victorians responded to problems of social unrest and disorder.

The origins of political economy (like utilitarianism) are to be found in the late eighteenth century and particularly in Adam Smith's *Wealth of Nations* (1776). Smith coined the term to define a new way of understanding the relationship between the political and economic affairs of the state. He claimed first that the economic sphere could be separated from other spheres, and secondly that it constituted the primary explanation of human conduct. He then went on to describe how the economic sphere – or the market – operated. His key concept was the proposition that the market was self-regulating and that it operated according to its own internal laws or logic – what he famously called the 'invisible hand'. These laws in turn were based on the principle of competition. As Bentham was later to emphasise, Smith argued that individuals were basically selfish and profit-seeking, and that the market was the unintended result of a multitude or aggregate of individuals' competitive actions carried out for purely private purposes – for, that is, the satisfaction of purely private wants. In other words, the market was not 'planned'; nor was it the result of decisions by any particular political bodies, such as the state. It followed that attempts by government to intervene in order to control the market or regulate economic activity were simply misplaced. It is at this point that the association between political economy and the principles of laissez-faire, so often noted by nineteenth-century novelists, becomes visible and understandable.

The main avenue for the dissemination of Smith's work in the nineteenth century was David Ricardo's *Principles of Political Economy, and Taxation* (1817). Ricardo changed the emphasis of political economy from a concern with wealth creation to that of wealth distribution. Consequently he developed new ideas on issues such as value, labour, price and taxation. Among his most important and controversial contributions were: (i) the labour theory of value (which argued that the exchange value of a product was regulated by the quantity of the labour needed to produce it); and (ii) what was known as 'the iron law of wages'. Ricardo claimed that labour had a 'natural' price – 'that price which is necessary to enable the labourers, one with another, to subsist and perpetuate their race without either increase or diminution'; and that it had a 'market price' – the amount which was actually paid for labour. Moreover, natural price was regulated by the price of 'food, necessaries, and conveniences' while market price was regulated by the proportion of the supply to the demand for labour. Ricardo argued that although market price might deviate from natural price, over the long term it tended to 'conform' to it. His reasoning was broadly as follows: when the country was prosperous and production increased, the demand for labour meant that the market price exceeded the natural price and wages were high. The work-force would subsequently increase through the labourer's improved ability to rear a family. Eventually, though, this increase in the supply of labour would outstrip demand and lead wages to fall again to their natural price, or even below it. The result was the suffering and contraction of the work-force. The details of Ricardo's law were complex, but in general terms it seemed to justify poverty as an inevitable consequence of the market; moreover, the law absolved the government from any need to intervene to control wages.

It was precisely a concern with the apparent social irresponsibility of political economy, together with an acute awareness of its limitations, which distinguished John Stuart Mill's *Principles of Political Economy*. Published in 1848, and revised and reprinted many times, it became the standard work of reference on the topic until the turn of the century. Mill had become interested in some aspects of socialist thought, particularly that of French social theorists such as Auguste Comte. He was impressed by socialist analyses of the unequal relationship which the market imposed upon employer and employee, and in distinction to Ricardo, he argued that the laws of distribution (unlike the laws of production) were not fixed – a circumstance which appeared to allow for more flexibility in alleviating poverty and distress. Mill also drew attention to the limited nature of the explanations of society to be found in political economy: he stressed that its model of 'economic man' was an artificial (if necessary) abstraction which only dealt with some aspects of human behaviour; and that its tenets did not necessarily apply to all countries. These points were also taken up by Walter Bagehot. A banker by trade, and therefore someone intensely concerned with the *practice* (as opposed to the theory) of business, Bagehot was also deeply critical of political economy's excessive abstraction and its parochialism. At the same time, though, it is important to point out that both Mill and Bagehot were redefining rather than contesting political economy. Mill's interpretation of this body of thought may have been more sensitive and humane than those of his predecessors, but he never abandoned political economy's emphasis on competition and private property, nor was he ever really comfortable with the idea of state intervention.

Political economy was not a particularly unified body of thought and there were many profound disagreements between individual political economists. Nevertheless the influence of political economy remained surprisingly consistent through the early and middle decades of the century. Although many commentators criticised its basic tenets and many deplored its apparent endorsement of laissez-faire policies, none was able to formulate a coherent alternative economic doctrine. The ruthless and competitive individualism of the market was typically countered by an appeal to altruism which in turn was based on the notion (familiar in the social-problem novels of the

1840s and 1850s) of a 'brotherhood of interests'. But whether such appeals came from the radical Owen or the bourgeois Mrs Gaskell, they were always compromised by their inability to explain what a theory of economic activity not based on self-interest would actually entail. All of this was to change, however, in the 1870s when two new and quite different critiques of political economy began to emerge: those proposed by marginal utility theory and by Marxism.

Marginal utility theory was developed simultaneously and independently in three different countries: by William Stanley Jevons in Britain, Léon Walras in Switzerland and Carl Menger in Austria.[11] Jevons began to formulate his ideas in the 1860s, but it was the publication of his *Theory of Political Economy* in 1871 which consolidated his reputation. The title is significant for it indicated that Jevons was working within the same broad tradition as Smith, Ricardo and Mill; he was attempting to revise political economy – to explain better the workings of the market, rather than to repudiate it. The most original element of Jevons' work concerned his use of utilitarian accounts of pleasure and pain in order to critique the labour theory of value. Jevons argued that the exchange value of a commodity was determined not by the amount of labour needed to produce it, but rather by the demands and wishes of individual consumers. Moreover, the utility (or value) which an individual obtained from a homogeneous stock of goods was determined by the usefulness of the last unit; that is, the marginal utility of a stock diminished as the quantity of that stock increased. For Jevons, then, utility, far from being an intrinsic quality of particular goods (as it had been for Ricardo), was defined through an act of evaluation, where that act was performed by an individual in relation to the specificity of his or her own wants. In simple terms, Jevons radically shifted the grounds of political economy from a concern with production to that of consumption; so the central question for economics was no longer the productivity of the economy as a whole, but how the economy might best provision the individual. Some modern critics have seen in Jevons' work the beginning of modern theories of consumerism. It took some time for Jevons' ideas to gain acceptance in Britain; none the less by the turn of the century marginal utility theory had largely superseded traditional (or classical) political economy to become the new academic orthodoxy. The fate of socialist or Marxist economics was very different.

I have suggested that one reason for the demise of Owenism in the 1840s was its failure to develop a coherent economic analysis; by the same token, the seriousness with which socialist polemic was treated in the 1880s owed much to the detail and sophistication of Karl Marx's analysis of the market. None the less it is important to point out that Marx's views first became widely known in Britain, not through his own works, but through British writers who popularised his ideas. Marx's main works were not translated into English until the late 1880s and 1890s – that is, several years after his death; and even then the quality and accessibility of those translations were very varied.[12] In this respect an important early disseminator of Marxist polemic in Britain was H. M. Hyndman, particularly through his popular *England for All: The Text-Book of Democracy* (1881) which borrowed generously from Marx in its chapters on labour and capital. One of the most striking features distinguishing the Marxist critique of classical political economy from that of Jevons was the wholesale rejection of the market as destructive of human relationships. While Jevons had focused on how the market might best satisfy individual needs, Marx was concerned with the *social* cost of such provisioning. As Hyndman argues, the fundamental objection to the market concerned the division of labour which separated workers from their produce and concentrated power in the hands of a small group of capitalists who owned the means of production. The capitalists' control over 'land, machinery, and currency' allowed them to exploit the work-force in order that they might live 'in luxury and idleness'. The result was the alienation of the working classes and conflict between classes. Hyndman's (and of course Marx's) solution to such conflict and inequity was a completely different economic system, one based on communal ownership, both of property and of the means of production. As Hyndman rather simplistically put it: 'between the workers of all civilized countries there is no real difference: they create the wealth and produce the food, and, under proper conditions, all would live in moderation, all would have enough.' Those 'proper conditions' were naturally the structures and institutions of socialism or communism, rather than those of capitalism. For Marx, the main vehicle for the social and economic transformation of society was violent struggle; by contrast, Hyndman (in keeping with Owenite traditions) emphasised 'voluntary combination and peaceful endeavour'. This issue of the mechanism and pace of social change – whether evolutionary or revolutionary – was a contentious one in late nineteenth-century British socialism, and disagreements led to two rival socialist organisations: Hyndman's Social Democratic Federation (accused by its detractors of advocating 'state socialism') and the more radical Socialist League led by William Morris.

23

During the nineteenth century understanding the market was certainly the central feature of attempts to understand and define social life. A dominant element in social theory, stretching from Smith through to Marx, was the proposition that economic activity was the primary determinant of social relationships. At the same time, however, economics was by no means the only issue of concern. Indeed the very conditions which had foregrounded the market in the public mind – social distress and social unrest – also pointed to the need to rethink political life. In Victorian Britain, debate about politics or the operation of power centred on the issue of political representation and parliamentary democracy. The best known (and most visible) element of this debate was the Chartist movement and agitation for the extension of the franchise from the 1820s onwards. Also important were the theoretical issues which underlay debates about political representation. The most urgent of these was the fairly abstract question of the relationship between the individual and the state, or the individual interest and the social interest (as it was defined by the state).

Opponents of democracy, such as Carlyle or Arnold, generally pointed to the alleged ignorance or 'rudeness' of the general populace; in their view the majority of people were not sufficiently sophisticated or disinterested to vote or act in ways which would maximise the social good. Carlyle and Arnold identified fundamental conflicts of interest between different groups or classes in society, and they argued that representative government would merely exacerbate rather than resolve those conflicts. Carlyle went so far as to claim that the social good was best protected by what we would now see as a form of dictatorship – by a strong leader (or hero) whose perception of the social interest would be so self-evidently correct as to command a natural allegiance from the populace. Arnold, by contrast, argued for a strong state as the guarantor of the social good. Arnold's state was to be a kind of umpire between conflicting interests by embodying and promoting what he termed our 'best self'; the state represented that realm of 'disinterested' value which raises individuals above factional interests and therefore makes for social cohesion. One consequence of Arnold's and Carlyle's definition of the social good as a realm of absolute value was to turn political questions into moral ones. Such a tactic in turn permitted them to ignore the possibility that there might be competing definitions of the social good, and thus an inevitable element of coercion to social order. Those who dissented from Carlylean heroism or Arnoldian disinterestedness simply nominated themselves as ill-educated; indeed, as I have suggested, Carlyle's and

Arnold's opposition to democracy was largely on the grounds that it enfranchised such ignorance.

John Stuart Mill's approach to the role of the state, developed out of his sympathy for a utilitarian definition of morality, was – unsurprisingly, perhaps – very different. As I indicated earlier, Mill's re-examination of the concepts of pleasure and pain had led him to see that people not only have uniquely human attributes, but also uniquely individual ones. Importantly, if the experience of pleasure varied according to the individual, then it followed that the route to happiness was self-development. It is precisely the conditions for such self-development which is one of the central concerns of *On Liberty* (1859). Influenced by Alexis de Tocqueville's *Democracy in America* (1835), Mill noted that the identification of rulers with the wishes of the majority did not necessarily avoid abuses of power. On the contrary, democracy could lead to what he termed the 'tyranny of the majority'. Moreover, the tendency of majority views to oppress minority opinions threatened the principle of individual liberty which underwrote Mill's utilitarian conception of the social good. *On Liberty* thus centres on defending the proposition that 'the sole end' for which men 'are warranted individually or collectively, in interfering with the liberty of action of any of their number, is self-protection'. Mill continues, 'the only purpose for which power can be rightly exercised over any member of a civilised community, against his will, is to prevent harm to others.' In distinction to Arnold, such an argument implied a very limited role for the state: in Mill's view, the state should not seek to determine for the individual the nature of his or her own good. Instead the state was restricted to defining (and enforcing) the limits of behaviour considered harmful to others. Mill argued that freedom of thought and discussion was fundamental and was always outside state interference; he therefore saw no need to legislate against, say, blasphemy. By contrast, he conceded that freedom of action could on occasions be curtailed by the state, but only if a certain course of conduct would bring actual harm or hurt or injury to others. Mill's arguments were central in establishing what we now understand as a liberal democracy, but it is as well to recall that what constitutes harm, hurt or injury is a very contentious point.

Given Mill's distrust of democracy, it may seem surprising that he was a supporter of a representative parliament. However, he believed that democracy, for all its attendant dangers, was still the best form of government. Like Arnold, Mill was not optimistic about the average person's capacity to participate successfully in such a system, and he argued for the importance of educating the electorate. At the same time (and in distinction to Arnold) Mill saw the participation in democracy as possessing an educative value in encouraging active citizenship. Moreover, if individuals (rather than the state) were the best defenders of their own rights, then it followed that as many individuals as possible (including, for Mill, women) should influence the government which acts to secure those rights.

Where Arnold's state implied coercion (as perhaps by definition all states do), and where Mill tried to limit the state's power in order to guarantee the conditions for individual freedom, in socialist theory the state is abolished altogether. As the Socialist League Manifesto claimed, 'Absolutism, Constitutionalism, Republicanism have all been tried in our day and under our present social system, and all alike have failed in dealing with the real evils of life.' For socialists, then, both political conflict and the machinery to resolve it (that is, the state, in whatever way it is defined) was part of the problem of modern society; hence the futility of attempting to bring about social change by political reform (as Hyndman had been accused of doing). It also follows from this argument that under socialism, politics *must* be absent; indeed it was precisely the economic efficiency of socialist society (rather than any political institutions) which was held to guarantee the replacement of politics by consent, and thus the abolition of the state. It is worth noting in passing that in one respect socialist arguments for the abolition of the state were uncomfortably similar to propositions for a strong state: that is, Morris and his colleagues (like Arnold and Carlyle) did not admit of the possibility in a socialist society that there could be any real conflict of interest between the social good and the individual good. Hence (again like Arnold and Carlyle) they were able to collapse the distinction between consent and coercion by asserting the self-evident moral 'rightness' of socialist organisation.

What emerges from this picture is once again the complexity of Victorian debates about power, representation, individual liberty and civil society. In that complexity, however, we can discern a narrative which distinguishes between writers such as Carlyle, Arnold, Hyndman and Morris, whose prescriptions for the social good gave them the confidence to define the individual good, and the liberal tradition of Mill, who was much more interested in the right of individuals to determine for themselves their own good. Interestingly, it is exactly this contrast which reverberates through the literature of the period, from the prescription for a just society in Gaskell's 'brotherhood' of interests or from Eliot's web of communal life to Thomas Hardy's or Oscar Wilde's celebration of the uniqueness of the individual and their fear for its vulnerability.

1

# THEORIES OF SOCIAL LIFE

Utilitarianism, communitarianism, organicism

### JEREMY BENTHAM, *AN INTRODUCTION TO THE PRINCIPLES OF MORALS AND LEGISLATION* (1789; 1838)

The name of Jeremy Bentham (1748–1832) is synonymous with utilitarianism, but he was not the originator of utilitarian principles. He was, however, utilitarianism's most influential spokesman, inspiring many disciples and establishing a distinctive school of thought. He was much more a reformer than a philosopher, applying utilitarian principles to a variety of practical problems – political, administrative and particularly legal. His first published work, *A Fragment on Government* (1776), was an attack on Sir William Blackstone and the idea, central to Whig politics, that society depends on a social compact. In 1785 Bentham travelled to Russia to stay with his brother; while he was there William Paley's *Principles of Moral and Political Philosophy* (1785) was published. At the urging of some friends, who recognised similarities between Paley's work and his own, Bentham returned to England in 1788 to further his career as a writer. The result was his most famous work, *An Introduction to the Principles of Morals and Legislation* (1789). Between 1788 and 1790 Bentham wrote a number of works addressed specifically to a French readership. In the early 1790s he gave his attention once more to domestic issues, devoting his time to a scheme he had devised for a model prison, published in 1791 as the *Panopticon; or, The Inspection House*. Although it was officially approved by an Act of Parliament in 1794, nothing came of the scheme in Bentham's lifetime. In the early 1800s the editorial work of Etienne Dumont established Bentham's reputation not only in Britain but also in America and the Continent. Bentham was invited to provided a Code of Law for Russia, Geneva and Portugal and in 1822 published his *Codification Proposal*. In the meantime his friendship with James Mill had led to the publication of a long pamphlet *Plan of Parliamentary Reform, in the Form of a Catechism* (1817), a defence of democracy. Bentham's last project, his enormous *Constitutional Code* (the first part of which was published in 1830), was unfinished when he died.

**From Jeremy Bentham, *An Introduction to the Principles of Morals and Legislation*, *The Works of Jeremy Bentham, Vol I*, ed. John Bowring (Edinburgh: William Tait, 1838)[1]**

*Chapter I: Of the Principle of Utility.*

Nature has placed mankind under the governance of two sovereign masters, *pain* and *pleasure*. It is for them alone to point out what we ought to do, as well as to determine what we shall do. On the one hand the standard of right and wrong, on the other the chain of causes and effects, are fastened to their throne. They govern us in all we do, in all we say, in all we think: every effort we can make to throw off our subjection, will serve but to demonstrate and confirm it. In words a man may pretend to abjure their empire: but in reality he will remain subject to it all the while. The *principle of utility*[a] recognises this subjection, and assumes it for the foundation of that system, the object of which is to rear the fabric of felicity by the hands of reason and of law. Systems which attempt to question it, deal in sounds instead of sense, in caprice instead of reason, in darkness instead of light.

But enough of metaphor and declamation: it is not by such means that moral science is to be improved.

II. The principle of utility is the foundation of the present work: it will be proper therefore at the outset to give an explicit and determinate account of what is meant by it. By the principle[b] of utility is meant that principle which

---

a    Note by the Author, July 1822 –

To this denomination has of late been added, or substituted, the *greatest happiness* or *greatest felicity* principle: this for shortness, instead of saying at length *that principle* which states the greatest happiness of all those whose interest is in question, as being the right and proper, and only right and proper and universally desirable, end of human action: of human action in every situation, and in particular in that of a functionary or set of functionaries exercising the powers of Government. The word *utility* does not so clearly point to the ideas of *pleasure* and *pain* as the words *happiness* and *felicity* do: nor does it lead us to the consideration of the *number*, of the interests affected; to the *number*, as being the circumstance, which contributes, in the largest proportion, to the formation of the standard here in question; the *standard of right and wrong*, by which alone the propriety of human conduct, in every situation, can with propriety be tried. This want of a sufficiently manifest connexion between the ideas of *happiness* and *pleasure* on the one hand, and the idea of *utility* on the other, I have every now and then found operating, and with but too much efficiency, as a bar to the acceptance, that might otherwise have been given, to this principle.

approves or disapproves of every action whatsoever, according to the tendency which it appears to have to augment or diminish the happiness of the party whose interest is in question: or, what is the same thing in other words, to promote or to oppose that happiness. I say of every action whatsoever; and therefore not only of every action of a private individual, but of every measure of government.

III. By utility is meant that property in any object, whereby it tends to produce benefit, advantage, pleasure, good, or happiness (all this in the present case comes to the same thing), or (what comes again to the same thing) to prevent the happening of mischief, pain, evil, or unhappiness to the party whose interest is considered: if that party be the community in general, then the happiness of the community: if a particular individual, then the happiness of that individual.

IV. The interest of the community is one of the most general expressions that can occur in the phraseology of morals: no wonder that the meaning of it is often lost. When it has a meaning, it is this. The community is a fictitious *body*, composed of the individual persons who are considered as constituting as it were its *members*. The interest of the community then is, what? – the sum of the interests of the several members who compose it.

V. It is in vain to talk of the interest of the community, without understanding what is the interest of the individual.[c] A thing is said to promote the interest, or to be *for* the interest, of an individual, when it tends to add to the sum total of his pleasures: or, what comes to the same thing, to diminish the sum total of his pains.

VI. An action then may be said to be conformable to the principle of utility, or, for shortness sake, to utility (meaning with respect to the community at large), when the tendency it has to augment the happiness of the community is greater than any it has to diminish it.

VII. A measure of government (which is but a particular kind of action, performed by a particular person or persons) may be said to be conformable to or dictated by the principle of utility, when in like manner the tendency which it has to augment the happiness of the community is greater than any which it has to diminish it.

VIII. When an action, or in particular a measure of government, is supposed

---

b   (Principle.) The word principle is derived from the Latin principium: which seems to be compounded of the two words *primus*, first, or chief, and *cipium*, a termination which seems to be derived from *capio*, to take, as in *mancipium*, *municipium*; to which are analogous *auceps*, *forceps*, and others. It is a term of very vague and very extensive signification: it is applied to any thing which is conceived to serve as a foundation or beginning to any series of operations: in some cases, of physical operations: but of mental operations in the present case.

    The principle here in question may be taken for an act of the mind; a sentiment; a sentiment of approbation; a sentiment which, when applied to an action, approves of its utility, as that quality of it by which the measure of approbation or disapprobation bestowed upon it ought to be governed.

c   (Interest, &c.) Interest is one of those words, which not having any superior *genus*, cannot in the ordinary way be defined.

by a man to be conformable to the principle of utility, it may be convenient, for the purposes of discourse, to imagine a kind of law or dictate, called a law or dictate of utility: and to speak of the action in question, as being conformable to such law or dictate.

IX. A man may be said to be a partizan of the principle of utility, when the approbation or disapprobation he annexes to any action, or to any measure, is determined by, and proportioned to the tendency which he conceives it to have to augment or to diminish the happiness of the community: or in other words, to its conformity or unconformity to the laws or dictates of utility.

X. Of an action that is conformable to the principle of utility, one may always say either that it is one that ought to be done, or at least that it is not one that ought not to be done. One may say also, that it is right it should be done; at least that it is not wrong it should be done: that it is a right action; at least that it is not a wrong action. When thus interpreted, the words *ought*, and *right* and *wrong*, and others of that stamp, have a meaning: when otherwise, they have none.

XI. Has the rectitude of this principle been ever formally contested? It should seem that it had, by those who have not known what they have been meaning. Is it susceptible of any direct proof? It should seem not: for that which is used to prove everything else, cannot itself be proved: a chain of proofs must have their commencement somewhere. To give such proof is as impossible as it is needless.

XII. Not that there is or ever has been that human creature breathing, however stupid or perverse, who has not on many, perhaps on most occasions of his life, deferred to it. By the natural constitution of the human frame, on most occasions of their lives men in general embrace this principle, without thinking of it: if not for the ordering of their own actions, yet for the trying of their own actions, as well as of those of other men. There have been, at the same time, not many, perhaps, even of the most intelligent, who have been disposed to embrace it purely and without reserve. There are even few who have not taken some occasion or other to quarrel with it, either on account of their not understanding always how to apply it, or on account of some prejudice or other which they were afraid to examine into, or could not bear to part with. For such is the stuff that man is made of: in principle and in practice, in a right track and in a wrong one, the rarest of all human qualities is consistency.

XIII. When a man attempts to combat the principle of utility, it is with reasons drawn, without his being aware of it, from that very principle itself. [d] His arguments, if they prove any thing, prove not that the principle is *wrong*, but that,

---

d    'The principle of utility (I have heard it said) is a dangerous principle: it is dangerous on certain occasions to consult it.' This is as much as to say, what? that it is not consonant to utility, to consult utility; in short, that it is *not* consulting it, to consult it.

Addition by the Author, July 1822 –

Not long after the publication of the Fragment on Government, anno 1776, in which, in the character of an all-comprehensive and all-commanding principle, the principle of *utility* was brought to view, one person by whom observation to the above effect was made was *Alexander*

according to the applications he supposes to be made of it, it is *misapplied*. Is it possible for a man move the earth? Yes; but he must first find out another earth to stand upon.

XIV. To disprove the propriety of it by arguments is impossible; but, from the causes that have been mentioned, or from some confused or partial view of it, a man may happen to be disposed not to relish it. Where this is the case, if he thinks the settling of his opinions on such a subject worth the trouble, let him take the following steps, and at length, perhaps, he may come to reconcile himself to it.

1. Let him settle with himself, whether he would wish to discard this principle altogether; if so, let him consider what it is that all his reasonings (in matters of politics especially) can amount to?

2. If he would, let him settle with himself, whether he would judge and act without any principle, or whether there is any other he would judge and act by?

3. If there be, let him examine and satisfy himself whether the principle he thinks he has found is really any separate intelligible principle; or whether it

*Wedderburn*, at that time Attorney or Solicitor General, afterwards successively Chief Justice of the Common Pleas, and Chancellor of England, under the successive titles of Lord Loughborough and Earl of Rosslyn. It was made – not indeed in my hearing, but in the hearing of a person by whom it was almost immediately communicated to me. So far from being self-contradictory, it was a shrewd and perfectly true one. By that distinguished functionary, the state of the Government was thoroughly understood: by the obscure individual, at that time not so much as supposed to be so: his disquisitions had not been as yet applied, with any thing like a comprehensive view, to the field of Constitutional Law, nor therefore to those features of the English Government, by which the greatest happiness of the ruling *one* with or without that of a favoured few, are now so plainly seen to be the only ends to which the course of it has at any time been directed. The *principle of utility* was an appellative, at that time employed – employed by me, as it had been by others, to designate that which, in a more perspicuous and instructive manner, may, as above, be designated by the name of the *greatest happiness principle*. 'This principle (said Wedderburn) is a dangerous one.' Saying so, he said that which, to a certain extent, is strictly true: a principle, which lays down, as the only *right* and justifiable end of Government, the greatest happiness of the greatest number – how can it be denied to be a dangerous one? dangerous it unquestionably is, to every government which has for its *actual* end or object, the greatest happiness of a certain *one*, with or without the addition of some comparatively small number of others, whom it is matter of pleasure or accommodation to him to admit, each of them, to a share in the concern, on the footing of so many junior partners. *Dangerous* it therefore really was, to the interest – the sinister interest – of all those functionaries, himself included, whose interest it was, to maximize delay, vexation, and expense, in judicial and other modes of procedure, for the sake of the profit, extractable out of the expense. In a Government which had for its end in view the greatest happiness of the greatest number, Alexander Wedderburn might have been Attorney General and then Chancellor: but he would not have been Attorney General with £15,000 a-year, nor Chancellor, with a peerage, with a veto upon all justice, with £25,000 a-year, and with 500 sinecures at his disposal, under the name of Ecclesiastical Benefices, besides *et cæteras*. [Alexander Wedderburn (1733–1805) met Bentham at the house of John Lind, Bentham's friend; see Bentham's account of the issue in the 1828 edn. of the *Fragment on Government*.]

be not a mere principle in words, a kind of phrase, which at bottom expresses neither more nor less than the mere averment of his own unfounded sentiments; that is, what in another person he might be apt to call caprice?

4. If he is inclined to think that his own approbation or disapprobation, annexed to the idea of an act, without any regard to its consequences, is a sufficient foundation for him to judge and act upon, let him ask himself whether his sentiment is to be a standard of right and wrong, with respect to every other man, or whether every man's sentiment has the same privilege of being a standard to itself?

5. In the first case, let him ask himself whether his principle is not despotical, and hostile to all the rest of human race?

6. In the second case, whether it is not anarchical, and whether at this rate there are not as many different standards of right and wrong as there are men? and whether even to the same man, the same thing, which is right to-day, may not (without the least change in its nature) be wrong to-morrow? and whether the same thing is not right and wrong in the same place at the same time? and in either case, whether all argument is not at an end? and whether, when two men have said, 'I like this,' and 'I don't like it,' they can (upon such a principle) have any thing more to say?

7. If he should have said to himself, No: for that the sentiment which he proposes as a standard must be grounded on reflection, let him say on what particulars the reflection is to turn? If on particulars having relation to the utility of the act, then let him say whether this is not deserting his own principle, and borrowing assistance from that very one in opposition to which he sets it up: or if not on those particulars, on what other particulars?

8. If he should be for compounding the matter, and adopting his own principle in part, and the principle of utility in part, let him say how far he will adopt it?

9. When he has settled with himself where he will stop, then let him ask himself how he justifies to himself the adopting it so far? and why he will not adopt it any farther?

10. Admitting any other principle than the principle of utility to be a right principle, a principle that it is right for a man to pursue; admitting (what is not true) that the word *right* can have a meaning without reference to utility, let him say whether there is any such thing as a *motive* that a man can have to pursue the dictates of it: if there is, let him say what that motive is, and how it is to be distinguished from those which enforce the dictates of utility: if not, then lastly let him say what it is this other principle can be good for?

*Chapter III: Of the Four$^e$ Sanctions or Sources of Pain and Pleasure*

I. It has been shown that the happiness of the individuals, of whom a community is composed, that is, their pleasures and their security, is the end and the sole end which the legislator ought to have in view: the sole standard, in conformity to which each individual ought, as far as depends upon the legislator, to be *made* to fashion his behaviour. But whether it be this or any thing else that is to be *done*, there is nothing by which a man can ultimately be *made* to do it, but either pain or pleasure. Having taken a general view of these two grand objects (*viz.* pleasure, and what comes to the same thing, immunity from pain) in the character of *final* causes; it will be necessary to take a view of pleasure and pain itself, in the character of *efficient* causes or means.

II. There are four distinguishable sources from which pleasure and pain are in use to flow: considered separately, they may be termed the *physical*, the *political*, the *moral*, and the *religious*: and inasmuch as the pleasures and pains belonging to each of them are capable of giving a binding force to any law or rule of conduct, they may all of them be termed *sanctions*.[f]

III. If it be in the present life, and from the ordinary course of nature, not purposely modified by the interposition of the will of any human being, nor by any extraordinary interposition of any superior invisible being, that the pleasure or the pain takes place or is expected, it may be said to issue from, or to belong to, the *physical sanction*.

IV. If at the hands of a *particular* person or set of persons in the community,

e    The following is an extract from a letter of Bentham's to Dumont, dated Oct. 28, 1821: –

'*Sanctions*. Since the Traités, others have been discovered. There are now, I. Human: six, viz. 1. Physical; 2. Retributive; 3. Sympathetic; 4. Antipathetic; 5. Popular, or Moral; 6. Political, including Legal and Administrative.

'II. Superhuman *vice* Religious: all exemplifiable in the case of drunkeness; viz. the punitory class.

'*Note* – Sanctions *in genere* duae, punitoriae et remuneratoriae; *in serie*, septem ut super; seven multiplied by two, equal fourteen.

'The Judic story of the popular or moral sanction has two Sanctions: that of the few, and that of the many: Aristocratical and Democratical: their laws, their decisions, are to a vast extent opposite.'

f    Sanctio, in Latin, was used to signify the *act of binding*, and, by a common grammatical transition, *any thing which serves to bind a man*: to wit, to the observance of such or such a mode of conduct. According to a Latin grammarian,* the import of the word is derived by rather a far-fetched process (such as those commonly are, and in a great measure indeed must be, by which intellectual ideas are derived from sensible ones) from the word *sanguis*, blood: because among the Romans, with a view to inculcate into the people a persuasion that such or such a mode of conduct would be rendered obligatory upon a man by the force of what I call the religious sanction (that is, that he would be made to suffer by the extraordinary interposition of some superior being, if he failed to observe the mode of conduct in question) certain ceremonies were contrived by the priests: in the course of which ceremonies the blood of victims was made use of.

A sanction then is a source of obligatory powers or *motives*: that is, of *pains* and *pleasures*; which, according as they are connected with such or such modes of conduct, operate, and are indeed the only things which can operate, as *motives*. See Ch. x (Motives).

*Servius. See Ainsworth's Dict. ad verbum *Sanctio* [Bentham's own note to his notes; Robert Ainsworth (1660–1743) published a Latin dictionary between 1714 and 1736. Bentham's reference to it is inaccurate.]

who under names correspondent to that of *judge*, are chosen for the particular purpose of dispensing it, according to the will of the sovereign or supreme ruling power in the state, it may be said to issue from the *political sanction*.

V. If at the hands of such *chance* persons in the community, as the party in question may happen in the course of his life to have concerns with, according to each man's spontaneous disposition, and not according to any settled or concerted rule, it may be said to issue from the *moral* or *popular sanction*.[g]

VI. If from the immediate hand of a superior invisible being, either in the present life, or in a future, it may be said to issue from the *religious sanction*.

VII. Pleasures or pains which may be expected to issue from the *physical, political*, or *moral* sanctions, must all of them be expected to be experienced, if ever, in the *present* life: those which may be expected to issue from the *religious* sanction, may be expected to be experienced either in the *present* life or in a *future*.

VIII. Those which can be experienced in the present life, can of course be no others than such as human nature in the course of the present life is susceptible of: and from each of these sources may flow all the pleasures or pains of which, in the course of the present life, human nature is susceptible. With regard to these, then (with which alone we have in this place any concern), those of them which belong to any one of those sanctions, differ not ultimately in kind from those which belong to any one of the other three: the only difference there is among them lies in the circumstances that accompany their production. A suffering which befalls a man in the natural and spontaneous course of things, shall be styled, for instance, a *calamity*; in which case, if it be supposed to befall him through any imprudence of his, it may be styled a punishment issuing from the physical sanction. Now this same suffering, if inflicted by the law, will be what is commonly called a *punishment*; if incurred for want of any friendly assistance, which the misconduct, or supposed misconduct, of the sufferer has occasioned to be withholden, a punishment issuing from the *moral* sanction; if through the immediate interposition of a particular providence, a punishment issuing from the religious sanction.

IX. A man's goods, or his person, are consumed by fire. If this happened to him by what is called an accident, it was a calamity: if by reason of his own imprudence (for instance, from his neglecting to put his candle out), it may be styled a punishment of the physical sanction: if it happened to him by the sentence of the political magistrate, a punishment belonging to the political sanction – that is, what is commonly called a punishment: if for want of any assistance which his *neighbour* withheld from him out of some dislike to his *moral*

---

g    Better termed *popular*, as more directly indicative of its constituent cause; as likewise of its relation to the more common phrase *public opinion*, in French *opinion publique*, the name there given to that tutelary power, of which of late so much is said, and by which so much is done. The latter appellation is however unhappy and inexpressive; since if *opinion* is material, it is only in virtue of the influence it exercises over action, through the medium of the affections and the will.

character, a punishment of the *moral* sanction: if by an immediate act of *God's* displeasure, manifested on account of some *sin* committed by him, or through any distraction of mind, occasioned by the dread of such displeasure, a punishment of the *religious* sanction.[h]

X. As to such of the pleasures and pains belonging to the religious sanction, as regard a future life, of what kind these may be, we cannot know. These lie not open to our observation. During the present life they are matter only of expectation: and, whether that expectation be derived from natural or revealed religion, the particular kind of pleasure or pain, if it be different from all those which lie open to our observation, is what we can have no idea of. The best ideas we can obtain of such pains and pleasures are altogether unliquidated in point of quality. In what other respects our ideas of them *may* be liquidated, will be considered in another place.[i]

XI. Of these four sanctions, the physical is altogether, we may observe, the ground-work of the political and the moral: so is it also of the religious, in as far as the latter bears relation to the present life. It is included in each of those other three. This may operate in any case (that is, any of the pains or pleasures belonging to it may operate) independently of *them*: none of *them* can operate but by means of this. In a word, the powers of nature may operate of themselves; but neither the magistrate, nor men at large, *can* operate, nor is God in the case in question *supposed* to operate, but through the powers of nature.

XII. For these four objects, which in their nature have so much in common, it seemed of use to find a common name. It seemed of use, in the first place, for the convenience of giving a name to certain pleasures and pains, for which a name equally characteristic could hardly otherwise have been found: in the second place, for the sake of holding up the efficacy of certain moral forces, the influence of which is apt not to be sufficiently attended to. Does the political sanction exert an influence over the conduct of mankind? The moral, the religious sanctions, do so too. In every inch of his career are the operations of the political magistrate liable to be aided or impeded by these two foreign powers: who, one or other of them, or both, are sure to be either his rivals or his allies. Does it happen to him to leave them out in his calculations? he will be sure almost to find himself mistaken in the result. Of all this we shall find abundant proofs in the sequel of this work. It behoves him, therefore, to have them continually before his eyes; and that under such a name as exhibits the relation they bear to his own purposes and designs.

---

h   A suffering conceived to befall a man by the immediate act of God, as above, is often, for shortness sake, called a *judgement*: instead of saying, a suffering inflicted on him in consequence of a special judgement formed, and resolution thereupon taken, by the Deity.

i   See Ch. xv. (Cases unmeet), par. 2, Note.

*Chapter IV: Value of a Lot of Pleasure or Pain, How to be Measured*

I. Pleasures then, and the avoidance of pains are the *ends* which the legislator has in view: it behoves him therefore to understand their *value*. Pleasures and pains are the *instruments* he has to work with: it behoves him therefore to understand their force, which is again, in another point of view, their value.

II. To a person considered *by himself*, the value of a pleasure or pain considered *by itself*, will be greater or less, according to the four following circumstances:[j]

1. Its *intensity*.
2. Its *duration*.
3. Its *certainty* or *uncertainty*.
4. Its *propinquity* or *remoteness*.

III. These are the circumstances which are to be considered in estimating a pleasure or a pain considered each of them by itself. But when the value of any pleasure or pain is considered for the purpose of estimating the tendency of any *act* by which it is produced, there are two other circumstances to be taken into the account; these are,

5. Its *fecundity*, or the chance it has of being followed by sensations of the *same* kind: that is, pleasures, if it be a pleasure: pains, if it be a pain.
6. Its *purity*, or the chance it has of *not* being followed by sensations of the *opposite* kind: that is, pains, if it be a pleasure: pleasures, if it be a pain.

These two last, however, are in strictness scarcely to be deemed properties of the pleasure or the pain itself; they are not, therefore, in strictness to be taken into the account of the value of that pleasure or that pain. They are in strictness to be deemed properties only of the act, or other event, by which such pleasure or pain has been produced; and accordingly are only to be taken into the account of the tendency of such act or such event.

IV. To a *number* of persons, with reference to each of whom the value of a

---

j   These circumstances have since been denominated *elements* or *dimensions* of *value* in a pleasure or a pain.

　　Not long after the publication of the first edition, the following memoriter verses were framed, in the view of lodging more effectually, in the memory, these points, on which the whole fabric of morals and legislation may be seen to rest.

> *Intense, long, certain, speedy, fruitful, pure* –
> Such marks in *pleasures* and in *pains* endure.
> Such pleasures seek, if *private* be thy end:
> If it be *public*, wide let them *extend*.
> Such *pains* avoid, whichever be thy view:
> If pains *must* come, let them *extend* to few.

36

pleasure or a pain is considered, it will be greater or less, according to several circumstances: to wit, the six preceding ones; *viz.*

1. Its *intensity*.
2. Its *duration*.
3. Its *certainty* or *uncertainty*.
4. Its *propinquity* or *remoteness*.
5. Its *fecundity*.
6. Its *purity*.

And one other; to wit:

7. Its *extent*; that is, the number of persons to whom it *extends*; or (in other words) who are affected by it.

V. To take an exact account, then, of the general tendency of any act, by which the interests of the community are affected, proceed as follows. Begin with any one person of those whose interests seem most immediately to be affected by it: and take an account,

1. Of the value of each distinguishable *pleasure* which appears to be produced by it in the *first* instance.
2. Of the value of each *pain* which appears to be produced by it in the *first* instance.
3. Of the value of each pleasure which appears to be produced by it *after* the first. This constitutes the *fecundity* of the first *pleasure* and the *impurity* of the first pain.
4. Of the value of each *pain* which appears to be produced by it after the first. This constitutes the *fecundity* of the first *pain*, and the *impurity* of the first pleasure.
5. Sum up all the values of all the *pleasures* on the one side, and those of all the pains on the other. The balance, if it be on the side of pleasure, will give the *good* tendency of the act upon the whole, with respect to the interests of that *individual* person; if on the side of pain, the *bad* tendency of it upon the whole.
6. Take an account of the *number* of persons whose interests appear to be concerned; and repeat the above process with respect to each. *Sum up* the numbers expressive of the degrees of *good* tendency, which the act has, with respect to each individual, in regard to whom the tendency of it is *good* upon the whole: do this again with respect to each individual, in regard to whom the tendency of it is *good* upon the whole: do this again with respect to each individual, in regard to whom the tendency of it is *bad* upon the whole. Take the *balance*; which, if on the side of *pleasure*, will give the general *good tendency* of the act, with respect to the total number or community of individuals

37

concerned; if on the side of pain, the general *evil tendency*, with respect to the same community.

VI. It is not to be expected that this process should be strictly pursued previously to every moral judgment, or to every legislative or judicial operation. It may, however, be always kept in view: and as near as the process actually pursued on these occasions approaches to it, so near will such process approach to the character of an exact one.

VII. The same process is alike applicable to pleasure and pain, in whatever shape they appear; and by whatever denomination they are distinguished: to pleasure, whether it be called *good* (which is properly the cause or instrument of pleasure), or *profit* (which is distant pleasure, or the cause or instrument of distant pleasure), or *convenience*, or *advantage*, *benefit*, *emolument*, *happiness*, and so forth: to pain, whether it be called *evil* (which corresponds to *good*), or *mischief*, or *inconvenience*, or *disadvantage*, or *loss*, or *unhappiness*, and so forth.

VIII. Nor is this a novel and unwarranted, any more than it is a useless theory. In all this there is nothing but what the practice of mankind, wheresoever they have a clear view of their own interest, is perfectly conformable to. An article of property, an estate in land, for instance, is valuable: on what account? On account of the pleasures of all kinds which it enables a man to produce, and, what comes to the same thing, the pains of all kinds which it enables him to avert. But the value of such an article of property is universally understood to rise or fall according to the length or shortness of the time which a man has in it: the certainty or uncertainty of its coming into possession: and the nearness or remoteness of the time at which, if at all, it is to come into possession. As to the *intensity* of the pleasures which a man may derive from it, this is never thought of, because it depends upon the use which each particular person may come to make of it; which cannot be estimated till the particular pleasures he may come to derive from it, or the particular pains he may come to exclude by means of it, are brought to view. For the same reason, neither does he think of the *fecundity* or *purity* of those pleasures.

## JOHN STUART MILL, 'UTILITARIANISM' (1861)

John Stuart Mill (1806–73) was one of the most influential writers in Victorian Britain, and certainly its most distinguished philosopher. Mill wrote on literary, political, philosophical and economic topics, an *oeuvre* which is impressive in both its range and authority. His work typically had a synthesising quality with the result that many of his books became standard works in the nineteenth century, a status which history has largely confirmed. After a precocious childhood under the watchful and often overbearing tutelage of his father (the philosopher James Mill), his career began with regular periodical contributions to utilitarian debates, and his editing (at the age of 19) of Jeremy Bentham's *Rationale of Judicial Evidence* (published in 1827). Two years earlier he had joined the East India Company as a junior clerk; much later, at the age of 50, he would be appointed its Chief Examiner. Mill's precocity, however, had a price: in 1826, he suffered a mental breakdown brought on in part by the rigours of his upbringing and in part by his growing doubts about the validity of his father's intellectual enthusiasms. The rest of Mill's long career can be seen as an extended engagement with, and rewriting of, the educational programme instilled in him by his father. In the late 1820s Mill became interested in the ideas of the French social theorist, Henri de Saint-Simon, and those of his disciple, Auguste Comte, and in 1830 he travelled to Paris and began to write extensively on French affairs. In 1833 he contributed his first critical article on Bentham's philosophy, condemning Bentham but not utilitarianism. From 1837 to 1840 he took over the proprietorship of the *London and Westminster Review*, a newly established journal set up from the amalgamation of the *Westminster Review* and *London Review* to promote the radical cause. His first major work, *System of Logic*, appeared in 1843, and was followed by *Essays on Some Unsettled Questions of Political Economy* (1844) and *Principles of Political Economy* (1848). In between, Mill wrote a series of leaders for the *Morning Chronicle*, a paper with an interest in social issues. In 1858 Parliament took over the administration of India and Mill retired from his post of Chief Examiner in the East India Company. The same year also saw the death of his wife, Harriet Taylor, whom he had married in 1851. In the late 1850s and early 1860s Mill produced three of his best-known works: *On Liberty* (1859), *Utilitarianism* (serialised in *Fraser's Magazine* in 1861) and *Considerations On Representative Government* (1861). In 1865 he was elected as MP for Westminster and in 1867 campaigned unsuccessfully for the extension of the suffrage to women. He lost his seat in 1868, and the following year published *The Subjection of Women*, a work which had been written eight years earlier. The 1860s also saw the publication of works on the philosophy of William Hamilton and on Auguste Comte. Mill died in 1873; his *Autobiography* was published posthumously later that year, and in 1879, the 'Chapters on Socialism', edited by his step-daughter, Helen Taylor, was published in the *Fortnightly Review*.

## *From* John Stuart Mill, 'Utilitarianism', *Fraser's Magazine*, LXIV (October 1861), pp. 391–406[1]

*Chapter II: What Utilitarianism Is*

A passing remark is all that needs be given to the ignorant blunder of supposing that those who stand up for utility as the test of right and wrong, use the term in that restricted and merely colloquial sense in which utility is opposed to pleasure. An apology is due to the philosophical opponents of utilitarianism, for even the momentary appearance of confounding them with any one capable of so absurd a misconception; which is the more extraordinary, inasmuch as the contrary accusation, of referring everything to pleasure, and that too in its grossest form, is another of the common charges against utilitarianism; and, as has been pointedly remarked by an able writer, the same sort of persons, and often the very same persons, denounce the theory 'as impracticably dry when the word utility precedes the word pleasure, and as too practicably voluptuous when the word pleasure precedes the word utility.' Those who know anything about the matter are aware that every writer, from Epicurus to Bentham,[2] who maintained the theory of utility, meant by it, not something to be contradistinguished from pleasure, but pleasure itself, together with exemption from pain; and instead of opposing the useful to the agreeable or the ornamental, have always declared that the useful means these, among other things. Yet the common herd, including the herd of writers, not only in newspapers and periodicals, but in books of weight and pretension, are perpetually falling into this shallow mistake. Having caught up the word utilitarian, while knowing nothing whatever about it but its sound, they habitually express by it the rejection, or the neglect, of pleasure in some of its forms; of beauty, of ornament, or of amusement. Nor is the term thus ignorantly misapplied solely in disparagement, but occasionally in compliment; as though it implied superiority to frivolity and the mere pleasures of the moment. And this perverted use is the only one in which the word is popularly known, and the one from which the new generation are acquiring their sole notion of its meaning. Those who introduced the word, but who had for many years discontinued it as a distinctive appellation, may well feel themselves called upon to resume it, if by doing so they can hope to contribute anything towards rescuing it from this utter degradation.[a]

The creed which accepts as the foundation of morals, Utility, or the Greatest Happiness Principle, holds that actions are right in proportion as they tend to promote happiness, wrong as they tend to produce the reverse of happiness. By happiness is intended pleasure, and the absence of pain; by unhappiness, pain, and the privation of pleasure. To give a clear view of the moral standard set up by the theory, much more requires to be said; in particular, what things it includes in the ideas of pain and pleasure; and to what extent this is left an open question. But these supplementary explanations do not affect the theory of life on which this theory of morality is grounded – namely, that pleasure, and freedom from pain, are the only things desirable as ends; and that all desirable things (which are as numerous in the utilitarian as in any other scheme) are desirable either for the pleasure inherent in themselves, or as means to the promotion of pleasure and the prevention of pain.

Now, such a theory of life excites in many minds, and among them in some of the most estimable in feeling and purpose, inveterate dislike. To suppose that life has (as they express it) no higher end than pleasure – no better and nobler object of desire and pursuit – they designate as utterly mean and grovelling; as a doctrine worthy only of swine, to whom the followers of Epicurus were, at a very early period, contemptuously likened; and modern holders of the doctrine are occasionally made the subject of equally polite comparisons by its German, French, and English assailants.

When thus attacked, the Epicureans have always answered, that it is not they, but their accusers, who represent human nature in a degrading light; since the accusation supposes human beings to be capable of no pleasures except those of which swine are capable. If this supposition were true, the charge could not be gainsaid, but would then be no longer an imputation; for if the sources of pleasure were precisely the same to human beings and to swine, the rule of life which is good enough for the one would be good enough for the other. The comparison of the Epicurean life to that of beasts is felt as degrading, precisely because a beast's pleasures do not satisfy a human being's conceptions of happiness.

---

a    The author of this essay has reason for believing himself to be the first person who brought the word utilitarian into use. He did not invent it, but adopted it from a passing expression in Mr Galt's *Annals of the Parish*. After using it as a designation for several years, he and others abandoned it from a growing dislike to anything resembling a badge or watchword of sectarian distinction. But as a name for one single opinion, not a set of opinions – to denote the recognition of utility as a standard, not any particular way of applying it – the term supplies a want in the language, and offers, in many cases, a convenient mode of avoiding tiresome circumlocution. [John Galt (1779–1839) wrote with very mixed success on a variety of topics and in a variety of genres, including essays, dramatic works, travel writing and novels. His best known work was *Annals of the Parish*, a portrait of rural Scotland, written in 1809 and published in 1821. Galt records the term 'Utilitarians' being used in 1794.]

Human beings have faculties more elevated than the animal appetites, and when once made conscious of them, do not regard anything as happiness which does not include their gratification. I do not, indeed, consider the Epicureans to have been by any means faultless in drawing out their scheme of consequences from the utilitarian principle. To do this in any sufficient manner, many Stoic,[3] as well as Christian elements require to be included. But there is no known Epicurean theory of life which does not assign to the pleasures of the intellect, of the feelings and imagination, and of the moral sentiments, a much higher value as pleasure than to those of mere sensation. It must be admitted, however, that utilitarian writers in general have placed the superiority of mental over bodily pleasures chiefly in the greater permanency, safety, uncostliness, &c., of the former – that is, in their circumstantial advantages rather than in their intrinsic nature. And on all these points utilitarians have fully proved their case; but they might have taken the other, and, as it may be called, higher ground, with entire consistency. It is quite compatible with the principle of utility to recognize the fact, that some *kinds* of pleasure are more desirable and more valuable than others. It would be absurd that while, in estimating all other things, quality is considered as well as quantity, the estimation of pleasures should be supposed to depend on quantity alone.

If I am asked, what I mean by difference of quality in pleasures, or what makes one pleasure more valuable than another, merely as a pleasure, except its being greater in amount, there is but one possible answer. Of two pleasures, if there be one to which all or almost all who have experience of both give a decided preference, irrespective of any feeling of moral obligation to prefer it, that is the more desirable pleasure. If one of the two is, by those who are competently acquainted with both, placed so far above the other that they prefer it, even though knowing it to be attended with a greater amount of discontent, and would not resign it for any quantity of the other pleasure which their nature is capable of, we are justified in ascribing to the preferred enjoyment a superiority in quality, so far outweighing quantity as to render it, in comparison, of small account.

Now it is an unquestionable fact that those who are equally acquainted with, and equally capable of appreciating and enjoying, both, do give a most marked preference to the manner of existence which employs their higher faculties. Few human creatures would consent to be changed into any of the lower animals, for a promise of the fullest allowance of a beast's pleasures; no intelligent human being would consent to be a fool, no instructed person would be an ignoramus, no person of feeling and conscience would be selfish and base, even though they should be persuaded that the fool, the dunce, or the rascal is better satisfied with his lot than they are with theirs. They would not resign what they possess more than he, for the most complete satisfaction of all the desires which they have in common with him. If they ever fancy they would, it is only in cases of unhappiness so extreme, that to escape from it they would exchange their lot for almost any other, however undesirable in their own eyes. A being of higher faculties

42

requires more to make him happy, is capable probably of more acute suffering, and is certainly accessible to it at more points, than one of an inferior type; but in spite of these liabilities, he can never really wish to sink into what he feels to be a lower grade of existence. We may give what explanation we please of this unwillingness; we may attribute it to pride, a name which is given indiscriminately to some of the most, and to some of the least estimable feelings of which mankind are capable: we may refer it to the love of liberty and personal independence, an appeal to which was with the Stoics one of the most effective means for the inculcation of it; to the love of power, or to the love of excitement, both of which do really enter into and contribute to it; but its most appropriate appellation is a sense of dignity, which all human beings possess in one form or other, and in some, though by no means in exact, proportion to their higher faculties, and which is so essential a part of the happiness of those in whom it is strong, that nothing which conflicts with it could be, otherwise than momentarily, an object of desire to them. Whoever supposes that this preference takes place at a sacrifice of happiness – that the superior being, in anything like equal circumstances, is not happier than the inferior – confounds the two very different ideas, of happiness, and content. It is indisputable that the being whose capacities of enjoyment are low, has the greatest chance of having them fully satisfied; and a highly endowed being will always feel that any happiness which he can look for, as the world is constituted, is imperfect. But he can learn to bear its imperfections, if they are at all bearable; and they will not make him envy the being who is indeed unconscious of the imperfections, but only because he feels not at all the good which those imperfections qualify. It is better to be a human being dissatisfied than a pig satisfied; better to be Socrates dissatisfied than a fool satisfied. And if the fool, or the pig, are of a different opinion, it is because they only know their own side of the question. The other party to the comparison knows both sides.[4]

It may be objected, that many who are capable of the higher pleasures, occasionally, under the influence of temptation, postpone them to the lower. But this is quite compatible with a full appreciation of the intrinsic superiority of the higher. Men often, from infirmity of character, make their election for the nearer good, though they know it to be the less valuable; and this no less when the choice is between two bodily pleasures, than when it is between bodily and mental. They pursue sensual indulgences to the injury of health, though perfectly aware that health is the greater good. It may be further objected, that many who begin with youthful enthusiasm for everything noble, as they advance in years sink into indolence and selfishness. But I do not believe that those who undergo this very common change, voluntarily choose the lower description of pleasures in preference to the higher. I believe that before they devote themselves exclusively to the one, they have already become incapable of the other. Capacity for the nobler feelings is in most natures a very tender plant, easily killed, not only by hostile influences, but by mere want of sustenance; and in the majority of young persons it speedily dies away if the occupations to which their

43

position in life has devoted them, and the society into which it has thrown them, are not favourable to keeping that higher capacity in exercise. Men lose their high aspirations as they lose their intellectual tastes, because they have not time or opportunity for indulging them; and they addict themselves to inferior pleasures, not because they deliberately prefer them, but because they are either the only ones to which they have access, or the only ones which they are any longer capable of enjoying. It may be questioned whether any one who has remained equally susceptible to both classes of pleasures, ever knowingly and calmly preferred the lower; though many, in all ages, have broken down in an ineffectual attempt to combine both.

From this verdict of the only competent judges, I apprehend there can be no appeal. On a question which is the best worth having of two pleasures, or which of two modes of existence is the most grateful to the feelings, apart from its moral attributes and from its consequences, the judgment of those who are qualified by knowledge of both, or, if they differ, that of the majority among them, must be admitted as final. And there needs be the less hesitation to accept this judgment respecting the quality of pleasures, since there is no other tribunal to be referred to even on the question of quantity. What means are there of determining which is the acutest of two pains, or the intensest of two pleasurable sensations, except the general suffrage of those who are familiar with both? Neither pains nor pleasures are homogeneous, and pain is always heterogeneous with pleasure. What is there to decide whether a particular pleasure is worth purchasing at the cost of a particular pain, except the feelings and judgment of the experienced? When, therefore, those feelings and judgment declare the pleasures derived from the higher faculties to be preferable *in kind*, apart from the question of intensity, to those of which the animal nature, disjoined from the higher faculties, is susceptible, they are entitled on this subject to the same regard.

I have dwelt on this point, as being a necessary part of a perfectly just conception of Utility or Happiness, considered as the directive rule of human conduct. But it is by no means an indispensable condition to the acceptance of the utilitarian standard; for that standard is not the agent's own greatest happiness, but the greatest amount of happiness altogether; and if it may possibly be doubted whether a noble character is always the happier for its nobleness, there can be no doubt that it makes other people happier, and that the world in general is immensely a gainer by it. Utilitarianism, therefore, could only attain its end by the general cultivation of nobleness of character, even if each individual were only benefited by the nobleness of others, and his own, so far as happiness is concerned, were a sheer deduction from the benefit. But the bare enunciation of such an absurdity renders refutation superfluous.

According to the Greatest Happiness Principle, as above explained, the ultimate end, with reference to and for the sake of which all other things are desirable (whether we are considering our own good or that of other people), is an existence exempt as far as possible from pain, and as rich as possible in enjoyments, both in point of quantity and quality; the test of quality, and the rule for measuring it against quantity, being the preference felt by those who in their opportunities of experience, to which must be added their habits of self-consciousness and self-observation, are best furnished with the means of comparison. This being, according to the utilitarian opinion, the end of human action, is necessarily also the standard of morality; which may accordingly be defined, the rules and precepts for human conduct, by the observance of which an existence such as has been described might be, to the greatest extent possible, secured to all mankind; and not to them only, but, so far as the nature of things admits, to the whole sentient creation.

Against this doctrine, however, arises another class of objectors, who say that happiness, in any form, cannot be the rational purpose of human life and action; because, in the first place, it is unattainable: and they contemptuously ask, what right hast thou to be happy? a question which Mr Carlyle[5] clenches by the addition, What right, a short time ago, hadst thou even *to be*? Next, they say, that men can do *without* happiness; that all noble human beings have felt this, and could not have become noble but by learning the lesson of Entsagen, or renunciation; which lesson, thoroughly learnt and submitted to, they affirm to be the beginning and necessary condition of all virtue.

The first of these objections would go to the root of the matter were it well founded; for if no happiness is to be had at all by human beings, the attainment of it cannot be the end of morality, or of any rational conduct. Though, even in that case, something might still be said for the utilitarian theory; since utility includes not solely the pursuit of happiness, but the prevention or mitigation of unhappiness; and if the former aim be chimerical, there will be all the greater scope and more imperative need for the latter, so long at least as mankind think fit to live, and do not take refuge in the simultaneous act of suicide recommended under certain conditions by Novalis.[6] When, however, it is thus positively asserted to be impossible that human life should be happy, the assertion, if not something like a verbal quibble, is at least an exaggeration. If by happiness be meant a continuity of highly pleasurable excitement, it is evident enough that this is impossible. A state of exalted pleasure lasts only moments, or in some cases, and with some intermissions, hours or days, and is the occasional brilliant flash of enjoyment, not its permanent and steady flame. Of this the philosophers who have taught that happiness is the end of life were as fully aware as those who taunt them. The happiness which they meant was not a life of rapture, but moments of such, in an existence made up of few and transitory pains, many and various pleasures, with a decided predominance of the active over the passive, and having as the foundation of the whole, not to expect more from life than it is capable of bestowing. A life thus composed, to those who have been fortunate enough to obtain it, has always appeared worthy of the name of happiness. And such an existence is even now the lot of many during some considerable portion of their lives. The present wretched education, and wretched social arrangements, are the only real hindrance to its being attainable by almost all.

45

The objectors perhaps may doubt whether human beings, if taught to consider happiness as the end of life, would be satisfied with such a moderate share of it. But great numbers of mankind have been satisfied with much less. The main constituents of a satisfied life appear to be two, either of which by itself is often found sufficient for the purpose: tranquillity, and excitement. With much tranquillity, many find that they can be content with very little pleasure: with much excitement, many can reconcile themselves to a considerable quantity of pain. There is assuredly no inherent impossibility in enabling even the mass of mankind to unite both; since the two are so far from being incompatible that they are a natural alliance, the prolongation of either being a preparation for, and exciting a wish for, the other. It is only those in whom indolence amounts to a vice, that do not desire excitement after an interval of repose: it is only those in whom the need of excitement is a disease, that feel the tranquillity which follows excitement dull and insipid, instead of pleasurable in direct proportion to the excitement which preceded it. When people who are tolerably fortunate in their outward lot do not find in life sufficient enjoyment to make it valuable to them, the cause generally is, caring for nobody but themselves. To those who have neither public nor private affections, the excitements of life are much curtailed, and in any case dwindle in value as the time approaches when all selfish interests must be terminated by death: while those who leave after them objects of personal affection, and especially those who have also cultivated a fellow-feeling with the collective interests of mankind, retain as lively an interest in life on the eve of death as in the vigour of youth and health. Next to selfishness, the principal cause which makes life unsatisfactory is want of mental cultivation. A cultivated mind – I do not mean that of a philosopher, but any mind to which the fountains of knowledge have been opened, and which has been taught, in any tolerable degree, to exercise its faculties – finds sources of inexhaustible interest in all that surrounds it; in the objects of nature, the achievements of art, the imaginations of poetry, the incidents of history, the ways of mankind, past and present, and their prospects in the future. It is possible, indeed, to become indifferent to all this, and that too without having exhausted a thousandth part of it; but only when one has had from the beginning no moral or human interest in these things, and has sought in them only the gratification of curiosity.

Now there is absolutely no reason in the nature of things why an amount of mental culture sufficient to give an intelligent interest in these objects of contemplation, should not be the inheritance of every one born in a civilized country. As little is there an inherent necessity that any human being should be a selfish egotist, devoid of every feeling or care but those which centre in his own miserable individuality. Something far superior to this is sufficiently common even now, to give ample earnest of what the human species may be made. Genuine private affections, and a sincere interest in the public good, are possible, though in unequal degrees, to every rightly brought up human being. In a world in which there is so much to interest, so much to enjoy, and so much also to correct and improve, every one who has this moderate amount of moral and intellectual requisites is capable of an existence which may be called enviable; and unless such a person, through bad laws, or subjection to the will of others, is denied the liberty to use the sources of happiness within his reach, he will not fail to find this enviable existence, if he escape the positive evils of life, the great sources of physical and mental suffering – such as indigence, disease, and the unkindness, worthlessness, or premature loss of objects of affection. The main stress of the problem lies, therefore, in the contest with these calamities, from which it is a rare good fortune entirely to escape; which, as things now are, cannot be obviated, and often cannot be in any material degree mitigated. Yet no one whose opinion deserves a moment's consideration can doubt that most of the great positive evils of the world are in themselves removable, and will, if human affairs continue to improve, be in the end reduced within narrow limits. Poverty, in any sense implying suffering, may be completely extinguished by the wisdom of society, combined with the good sense and providence of individuals. Even that most intractable of enemies, disease, may be indefinitely reduced in dimensions by good physical and moral education, and proper control of noxious influences; while the progress of science holds out a promise for the future of still more direct conquests over this detestable foe. And every advance in that direction relieves us from some, not only of the chances which cut short our own lives, but, what concerns us still more, which deprive us of those in whom our happiness is wrapt up. As for vicissitudes of fortune, and other disappointments connected with worldly circumstances, these are principally the effect either of gross imprudence, of ill-regulated desires, or of bad or imperfect social institutions. All the grand sources, in short, of human suffering are in a great degree, many of them almost entirely, conquerable by human care and effort; and though their removal is grievously slow – though a long succession of generations will perish in the breach before the conquest is completed, and this world becomes all that, if will and knowledge were not wanting, it might easily be made – yet every mind sufficiently intelligent and generous to bear a part, however small and unconspicuous, in the endeavour, will draw a noble enjoyment from the contest itself, which he would not for any bribe in the form of selfish indulgence consent to be without.

And this leads to the true estimation of what is said by the objectors concerning the possibility, and the obligation, of learning to do without happiness. Unquestionably it is possible to do without happiness; it is done involuntarily by nineteen-twentieths of mankind, even in those parts of our present world which are least deep in barbarism; and it often has to be done voluntarily by the hero or the martyr, for the sake of something which he prizes more than his individual happiness. But this something, what is it, unless the happiness of others, or some of the requisites of happiness? It is noble to be capable of resigning entirely one's own portion of happiness, or chances of it: but, after all, this self-sacrifice must be for some end; it is not its own end; and if we are told that its end is not happiness, but virtue, which is better than happiness, I ask, would the sacrifice be made if the hero or martyr did not believe that it would earn for others immunity from similar sacrifices? Would it be made if he thought that his renunciation of happiness for himself would produce no fruit for any of his fellow creatures, but to make their lot like his, and place them also in the condition of persons who have renounced happiness? All honour to those who can abnegate for themselves the personal enjoyment of life, when by such renunciation they contribute worthily to increase the amount of happiness in the world; but he who does it, or professes to do it, for any other purpose, is no more deserving of admiration than the ascetic mounted on his pillar. He may be an inspiriting proof of what men *can* do, but assuredly not an example of what they *should.*

Though it is only in a very imperfect state of the world's arrangements that any one can best serve the happiness of others by the absolute sacrifice of his own, yet so long as the world is in that imperfect state, I fully acknowledge that the readiness to make such a sacrifice is the highest virtue which can be found in man. I will add, that in this condition of the world, paradoxical as the assertion may be, the conscious ability to do without happiness gives the best prospect of realizing such happiness as is attainable. For nothing except that consciousness, can raise a person above the chances of life, by making him feel that, let fate and fortune do their worst, they have not power to subdue him; which, once felt, frees him from excess of anxiety concerning the evils of life, and enables him, like many a Stoic in the worst times of the Roman Empire, to cultivate in tranquillity the sources of satisfaction accessible to him, without concerning himself about the uncertainty of their duration, any more than about their inevitable end.

Meanwhile, let utilitarians never cease to claim the morality of self-devotion as a possession which belongs by as good a right to them, as either to the Stoic or to the Transcendentalist.[7] The utilitarian morality does recognise in human beings the power of sacrificing their own greatest good for the good of others. It only refuses to admit that the sacrifice is itself a good. A sacrifice which does not increase, or tend to increase, the sum total of happiness, it considers as wasted. The only self-renunciation which it applauds, is devotion to the happiness, or to some of the means of happiness, of others; either of mankind collectively, or of individuals within the limits imposed by the collective interests of mankind.

I must again repeat, what the assailants of utilitarianism seldom have the justice to acknowledge, that the happiness which forms the utilitarian standard of what is right in conduct, is not the agent's own happiness, but that of all concerned. As between his own happiness and that of others, utilitarianism requires him to be as strictly impartial as a disinterested and benevolent spectator. In the golden rule of Jesus of Nazareth, we read the complete spirit of the ethics of utility. To do as you would be done by, and to love your neighbour as yourself, constitute the ideal perfection of utilitarian morality. As the means of making the nearest approach to this ideal, utility would enjoin, first, that laws and social arrangements should place the happiness, or (as speaking practically it may be called) the interest, of every individual, as nearly as possible in harmony with the interest of the whole; and secondly, that education and opinion, which

have so vast a power over human character, should so use that power as to establish in the mind of every individual an indissoluble association between his own
happiness and the good of the whole; especially between his own happiness and
the practice of such modes of conduct, negative and positive, as regard for the
universal happiness prescribes; so that not only he may be unable to conceive the
possibility of happiness to himself, consistently with conduct opposed to the
general good, but also that a direct impulse to promote the general good may be
in every individual one of the habitual motives of action, and the sentiments
connected therewith may fill a large and prominent place in every human
being's sentient existence. If the impugners of the utilitarian morality represented it to their own minds in this its true character, I know not what
recommendation possessed by any other morality they could possibly affirm to
be wanting to it; what more beautiful or more exalted developments of human
nature any other ethical system can be supposed to foster, or what springs of
action, not accessible to the utilitarian, such systems rely on for giving effect to
their mandates.

The objectors to utilitarianism cannot always be charged with representing it
in a discreditable light. On the contrary, those among them who entertain
anything like a just idea of its disinterested character, sometimes find fault with
its standard as being too high for humanity. They say it is exacting too much to
require that people shall always act from the inducement of promoting the
general interests of society. But this is to mistake the very meaning of a standard
of morals, and confound the rule of action with the motive of it. It is the business of ethics to tell us what are our duties, or by what test we may know them;
but no system of ethics requires that the sole motive of all we do shall be a
feeling of duty; on the contrary, ninety-nine hundredths of all our actions are
done from other motives, and rightly so done, if the rule of duty does not
condemn them. It is the more unjust to utilitarianism that this particular misapprehension should be made a ground of objection to it, inasmuch as utilitarian
moralists have gone beyond almost all others in affirming that the motive has
nothing to do with the morality of the action, though much with the worth of
the agent. He who saves a fellow creature from drowning does what is morally
right, whether his motive be duty, or the hope of being paid for his trouble; he
who betrays the friend that trusts him, is guilty of a crime, even if his object be
to serve another friend to whom he is under greater obligations. But to speak
only of actions done from the motive of duty, and in direct obedience to principle: it is a misapprehension of the utilitarian mode of thought, to conceive it as
implying that people should fix their minds upon so wide a generality as the
world, or society at large. The great majority of good actions are intended not
for the benefit of the world, but for that of individuals, of which the good of the
world is made up; and the thoughts of the most virtuous man need not on these
occasions travel beyond the particular persons concerned, except so far as is
necessary to assure himself that in benefiting them he is not violating the rights,
that is, the legitimate and authorized expectations, of any one else. The multipli-

cation of happiness is, according to the utilitarian ethics, the object of virtue; the occasions on which any person (except one in a thousand) has it in his power to do this on an extended scale, in other words, to be a public benefactor, are but exceptional; and on these occasions alone is he called on to consider public utility; in every other case, private utility, the interest or happiness of some few persons, is all he has to attend to. Those alone the influence of whose actions extends to society in general, need concern themselves habitually about so large an object. In the case of abstinences indeed – of things which people forbear to do from moral considerations, though the consequences in the particular case might be beneficial – it would be unworthy of an intelligent agent not to be consciously aware that the action is of a class which, if practised generally, would be generally injurious, and that this is the ground of the obligation to abstain from it. The amount of regard for the public interest implied in this recognition, is no greater than is demanded by every system of morals, for they all enjoin to abstain from whatever is manifestly pernicious to society.

The same considerations dispose of another reproach against the doctrine of utility, founded on a still grosser misconception of the purpose of a standard of morality, and of the very meaning of the words right and wrong. It is often affirmed that utilitarianism renders men cold and unsympathizing; that it chills their moral feelings towards individuals; that it makes them regard only the dry and hard consideration of the consequences of actions, not taking into their moral estimate the qualities from which those actions emanate. If the assertion means that they do not allow their judgment respecting the rightness or wrong-ness of an action to be influenced by their opinion of the qualities of the person who does it, this is a complaint not against utilitarianism, but against having any standard of morality at all; for certainly no known ethical standard decides an action to be good or bad because it is done by a good or a bad man, still less because done by an amiable, a brave, or a benevolent man, or the contrary. These considerations are relevant, not to the estimation of actions, but of persons; and there is nothing in the utilitarian theory inconsistent with the fact that there are other things which interest us in persons besides the rightness and wrongness of their actions. The Stoics, indeed, with the paradoxical misuse of language which was part of their system, and by which they strove to raise them-selves above all concern about anything but virtue, were fond of saying that he who has that has everything; that he, and only he, is rich, is beautiful, is a king. But no claim of this description is made for the virtuous man by the utilitarian doctrine. Utilitarians are quite aware that there are other desirable possessions and qualities besides virtue, and are perfectly willing to allow to all of them their full worth. They are also aware that a right action does not necessarily indicate a virtuous character, and that actions which are blameable often proceed from qualities entitled to praise. When this is apparent in any particular case, it modi-fies their estimation, not certainly of the act, but of the agent. I grant that they are, notwithstanding, of opinion, that in the long run the best proof of a good character is good actions; and resolutely refuse to consider any mental disposition as good, of which the predominant tendency is to produce bad conduct. This makes them unpopular with many people; but it is an unpopularity which they must share with every one who regards the distinction between right and wrong in a serious light; and the reproach is not one which a conscientious utilitarian need be anxious to repel.

If no more be meant by the objection than that many utilitarians look on the morality of actions, as measured by the utilitarian standard, with too exclusive a regard, and do not lay sufficient stress upon the other beauties of character which go towards making a human being loveable or admirable, this may be admitted. Utilitarians who have cultivated their moral feelings, but not their sympathies, nor their artistic perceptions, do fall into this mistake; and so do all other moralists under the same conditions. What can be said in excuse for other moralists is equally available for them, namely, that if there is to be any error, it is better that it should be on that side. As a matter of fact, we may affirm that among utilitarians as among adherents of other systems, there is every imaginable degree of rigidity and of laxity in the application of their standard: some are even puritanically rigorous, while others are as indulgent as can possibly be desired by sinner or by sentimentalist. But on the whole, a doctrine which brings prominently forward the interest that mankind have in the repression and prevention of conduct which violates the moral law, is likely to be inferior to no other in turning the sanctions of opinion against such violations. It is true, the question, What does violate the moral law? is one on which those who recognise different standards of morality are likely now and then to differ. But difference of opinion on moral questions was not first introduced into the world by utilitarianism, while that doctrine does supply, if not always an easy, at all events a tangible and intelligible mode of deciding such differences.

It may not be superfluous to notice a few more of the common misapprehensions of utilitarian ethics, even those which are so obvious and gross that it might appear impossible for any person of candour and intelligence to fall into them; since persons, even of considerable mental endowments, often give themselves so little trouble to understand the bearings of any opinion against which they entertain a prejudice, and men are in general so little conscious of this voluntary ignorance as a defect, that the vulgarest misunderstandings of ethical doctrines are continually met with in the deliberate writings of persons of the greatest pretensions both to high principle and to philosophy. We not uncommonly hear the doctrine of utility inveighed against as a *godless* doctrine. If it be necessary to say anything at all against so mere an assumption, we may say that the question depends upon what idea we have formed of the moral character of the Deity. If it be a true belief that God desires, above all things, the happiness of his creatures, and that this was his purpose in their creation, utility is not only not a godless doctrine, but more profoundly religious than any other. If it be meant that utilitarianism does not recognise the revealed will of God as the supreme law of morals, I answer, that an utilitarian who believes in the perfect goodness and wisdom of God, necessarily believes that whatever God has thought fit to reveal on the subject of morals, must fulfil the requirements of utility in a supreme degree. But others besides utilitarians have been of opinion that the Christian revelation was intended, and is fitted, to inform the hearts and minds of mankind with a spirit which should enable them to find for themselves what is right, and incline them to do it when found, rather than to tell them, except in a very general way, what it is; and that we need a doctrine of ethics, carefully followed out, to *interpret* to us the will of God. Whether this opinion is correct or not, it is superfluous here to discuss; since whatever aid religion, either natural or revealed, can afford to ethical investigation, is as open to the utilitarian moralist as to any other. He can use it as the testimony of God to the usefulness or hurt-fulness of any given course of action, by as good a right as others can use it for the indication of a transcendental law, having no connexion with usefulness or with happiness.

Again Utility is often summarily stigmatized as an immoral doctrine by giving it the name of Expediency, and taking advantage of the popular use of that term to contrast it with Principle. But the Expedient, in the sense in which it is opposed to the Right, generally means that which is expedient for the particular interest of the agent himself; as when a Minister sacrifices the interests of his country to keep himself in place. When it means anything better than this, it means that which is expedient for some immediate object, some temporary purpose, but which violates a rule whose observance is expedient in a much higher degree. The Expedient, in this sense, instead of being the same thing with the useful, is a branch of the hurtful. Thus, it would often be expedient, for the purpose of getting over some momentary embarrassment, or attaining some object immediately useful to ourselves or others, to tell a lie. But inasmuch as the cultivation in ourselves of a sensitive feeling on the subject of veracity, is one of the most useful, and the enfeeblement of that feeling one of the most hurtful things to which our conduct can be instrumental; and inasmuch as any, even unintentional, deviation from truth, does that much towards weakening the trust-worthiness of human assertion, which is not only the principal support of all present social well-being, but the insufficiency of which does more than any one thing that can be named to keep back civilization, virtue, everything on which human happiness on the largest scale depends; we feel that the violation, for a present advantage, of a rule of such transcendent expediency, is not expedient, and that he who, for the sake of a convenience to himself or to some other indi-vidual, does what depends on him to deprive mankind of the good, and inflict upon them the evil, involved in the greater or less reliance which they can place in each other's word, acts the part of one of their worst enemies. Yet that even this rule, sacred as it is, admits of possible exceptions, is acknowledged by all moralists; the chief of which is when the withholding of some fact (as of infor-mation from a malefactor, or of bad news from a person dangerously ill) would save an individual (especially an individual other than oneself) from great and unmerited evil, and when the withholding can only be effected by denial. But in order that the exception may not extend itself beyond the need, and may have the least possible effect in weakening reliance on veracity, it ought to be recognised, and, if possible, its limits defined; and if the principle of utility is good for anything, it must be good for weighing these conflicting utilities against one another, and marking out the region within which one or the other preponderates.

Again, defenders of utility often find themselves called upon to reply to such objections as this – that there is not time, previous to action, for calculating and weighing the effects of any line of conduct on the general happiness. This is exactly as if any one were to say that it is impossible to guide our conduct by Christianity, because there is not time, on every occasion of which anything has to be done, to read through the Old and New Testaments. The answer to the objection is, that there has been ample time, namely, the whole past duration of the human species. During all that time mankind have been learning by experience the tendencies of actions; on which experience all the prudence, as well as all the morality of life, are dependent. People talk as if the commencement of this course of experience had hitherto been put off, and as if, at the moment when some man feels tempted to meddle with the property or life of another, he had to begin considering for the first time whether murder and theft are injurious to human happiness. Even then I do not think that he would find the question very puzzling; but, at all events, the matter is now done to his hand. It is truly a whimsical supposition that if mankind were agreed in considering utility to be the test of morality, they would remain without any agreement as to what *is* useful, and would take no measures for having their notions on the subject taught to the young, and enforced by law and opinion. There is no difficulty in proving any ethical standard whatever to work ill, if we suppose universal idiocy to be conjoined with it; but on any hypothesis short of that, mankind must by this time have acquired positive beliefs as to the effects of some actions on their happiness; and the beliefs which have thus come down are the rules of morality for the multitude, and for the philosopher until he has succeeded in finding better. That philosophers might easily do this, even now, on many subjects; that the received code of ethics is by no means of divine right; and that mankind have still much to learn as to the effects of actions on the general happiness, I admit, or rather, earnestly maintain. The corollaries from the principle of utility, like the precepts of every practical art, admit of indefinite improvement, and, in a progressive state of the human mind, their improvement is perpetually going on. But to consider the rules of morality as improvable, is one thing; to pass over the intermediate generalizations entirely, and endeavour to test each individual action directly by the first principle, is another. It is a strange notion that the acknowledgment of a first principle is inconsistent with the admission of secondary ones. To inform a traveller respecting the place of his ultimate destination, is not to forbid the use of landmarks and direction-posts on the way. The proposition that happiness is the end and aim of morality, does not mean that no road ought to be laid down to that goal, or that persons going thither should not be advised to take one direction rather than another. Men really ought to leave

53

off talking a kind of nonsense on this subject, which they would neither talk nor listen to on other matters of practical concernment. Nobody argues that the art of navigation is not founded on astronomy, because sailors cannot wait to calculate the Nautical Almanack.[8] Being rational creatures, they go to sea with it ready calculated; and all rational creatures go out upon the sea of life with their minds made up on the common questions of right and wrong, as well as on many of the far more difficult questions of wise and foolish. And this, as long as foresight is a human quality, it is to be presumed they will continue to do. Whatever we adopt as the fundamental principle of morality, we require subordinate principles to apply it by; the impossibility of doing without them, being common to all systems, can afford no argument against any one in particular; but gravely to argue as if no such secondary principles could be had, and as if mankind had remained till now, and always must remain, without drawing any general conclusions from the experience of human life, is as high a pitch, I think, as absurdity has ever reached in philosophical controversy.

The remainder of the stock arguments against utilitarianism, mostly consist in laying to its charge the common infirmities of human nature, and the general difficulties which embarrass conscientious persons in shaping their course through life. We are told that an utilitarian will be apt to make his own particular case an exception to moral rules, and, when under temptation, will see an utility in the breach of a rule, greater than he will see in its observance. But is utility the only creed which is able to furnish us with excuses for evil doing, and means of cheating our own conscience? They are afforded in abundance by all doctrines which recognise as a fact in morals the existence of conflicting considerations; which all doctrines do, that have been believed by sane persons. It is not the fault of any creed, but of the complicated nature of human affairs, that rules of conduct cannot be so framed as to require no exceptions, and that hardly any kind of action can safely be laid down as either always obligatory or always condemnable. There is no ethical creed which does not temper the rigidity of its laws, by giving a certain latitude, under the moral responsibility of the agent, for accommodation to peculiarities of circumstances; and under every creed, at the opening thus made, self-deception and dishonest casuistry get in. There exists no moral system under which there do not arise unequivocal cases of conflicting obligation. These are the real difficulties, the knotty points both in the theory of ethics, and in the conscientious guidance of personal conduct. They are overcome practically with greater or with less success according to the intellect and virtue of the individual; but it can hardly be pretended that any one will be the less qualified for dealing with them, from possessing an ultimate standard to which conflicting rights and duties can be referred. If utility is the ultimate source of moral obligations, utility may be invoked to decide between them when their demands are incompatible. Though the application of the standard may be difficult, it is better than none at all: while in other systems, the moral laws all claiming independent authority, there is no common umpire entitled to interfere between them; their claims to precedence one over another rest on little better than sophistry, and unless determined, as they generally are, by the unacknowledged influence of considerations of utility, afford a free scope for the action of personal desires and partialities. We must remember that only in these cases of conflict between secondary principles is it requisite that first principles should be appealed to. There is no case of moral obligation in which some secondary principle is not involved; and if only one, there can seldom be any real doubt which one it is, in the mind of any person by whom the principle itself is recognised.

## JOHN GROTE, *AN EXAMINATION OF THE UTILITARIAN PHILOSOPHY* (1870)

The philosopher John Grote (1813–66) was the younger brother of George Grote, the historian of ancient Greece. After studying classics at Cambridge, Grote was ordained as a deacon in 1842 and a priest in 1844. He succeeded to a college living at Trumpington, near Cambridge, and in 1855 was elected to the Knightbridge Chair of Moral Philosophy at Cambridge. That same year he published an essay, *Old Studies and New*; with the exception of a few pamphlets, nothing else appeared in his lifetime, except for the first volume of his major philosophical project, *Exploratio Philosophica* (1865). He died the following year before completing the second volume. A fastidious worker and a man of a rather nervous temperament, Grote found it difficult to bring his work to completion, and it was his literary executor, Joseph Mayor, who was responsible for three major posthumous publications: *An Examination of the Utilitarian Philosophy* (1870), *Sermons* (1872) and *A Treatise on the Moral Ideals* (1876).

**From John Grote, *An Examination of the Utilitarian Philosophy* (Cambridge: Deighton, Bell, and Co., 1870)[1]**

*Chapter II: What Does Happiness Consist In?*

Is there such a thing as happiness? Is it attainable, and is it describable, so as to lend itself to be an object of action, such as utilitarianism would make it? And what is the bearing of these questions on the question whether utilitarianism is or is not the right moral philosophy?

These are the general questions which are partially touched on, so far as Mr Mill's papers suggest them,[2] in this chapter.

The utilitarian stands firm on the ground of positivism, of *what is*, so far as that will carry him. Happiness, whether we mean by it welfare or pleasure, is a real thing, which we do desire for ourselves, and more or less for others also: it is to a certain extent attainable, and to a certain extent describable. To how great an extent?

In reality this question does not belong to utilitarianism more than to any other philosophy. The important question about a system of philosophy is not whether it is (apparently) easy and simple, but whether it is true. Happiness might be an exceedingly difficult thing both to describe and to attain, and yet utilitarianism be true, if in other ways we were led to consider so. Human nature and life are large things, and I do not see why we should really presume beforehand that moral philosophy would be easy. But utilitarians have been much in the habit of recommending their philosophy on the ground of its easiness.

Hence the common effort on their part to show that happiness is easily describable, and easily attainable.

Taking Bentham and Paley[3] as representatives of the old utilitarianism, the former had the mind of a legislator, the latter of a man of prudential good sense. The former looked at the manner in which happiness could be best provided for by institutions, the latter showed how life could be best lived with a view to it.

In view of legislation, what is to be considered 'the desirable' or happiness must be to some extent agreed upon and described, and Bentham did good service by his attempt to do this systematically. And prudential rules for the conduct of life, such as Paley had given, and Mr Mill in these papers, are the oldest part of moral philosophy.

Against utilitarianism it has been argued, that it cannot furnish a proper rule of human conduct on account of the imperfect manner in which, after all, happiness can be understood and described. This argument does not disprove utilitarianism, for it is open to the utilitarian to say that no *more* proper rule is furnished by any other philosophy, and that it is not his business to show that a rule proper to the degree which the argument supposes, exists at all: but it meets any claims which the utilitarian may make, not on the ground of his rule being the right, or the only, or the best, rule, but on the ground of its being a satisfactory one. And the argument is valid, from various considerations about happiness, such as the following.

1.  Happiness is very different for different people.
2.  We as yet, at least, know very little how far a man, by the power of his own will and imagination on his thoughts and feelings, can make his own happiness under any circumstances.
3.  Nor how far, under any circumstances again, his constitution and temper may have settled the question of happiness or unhappiness for him.
4.  We have no means of deciding whether we shall best spend our efforts in trying to be happy under existing circumstances, or in trying to improve the circumstances.
5.  Nor of deciding, if there are different qualities or heights of happiness, whether we had best rest in the lower quality or strive to attain to the higher.

I might go on with many more difficulties like these, and I have called utilitarianism, in what follows, superficial, because instead of facing the real questions, it rests so much on mere prudentialisms. Of the above, the first difficulty is the most salient; and is so great, that it furnishes a ready retort against the utilitarian who urges against other moral theories, as, for instance, those which dwell much on duty, the uncertainty of the rules which they give. There are wants of our animal nature the satisfaction of which is happiness in the view of the economist: but human life develops wants and feelings much beyond all this, and *here* it is as hard to find universally accepted pleasures as it is to find universally accepted notions of duty.

It is a commonplace that happiness is not the same thing for every one in such a sense that it can be, in any detail, particularized and described. Utilitarians have the voice of mankind and of literature *with* them when they say that all action is, naturally, aimed at happiness, but *against* them when they go on from this to say that we may lay down on paper what happiness is, and so have an easy or ready way of directing our action, and that in the best manner.

A positivism thoroughly carried out would recognize in the utilitarian notion of happiness one of the unreal ideas, whether metaphysical, imaginative, or of whatever kind, which are to be discarded. Such an extreme positivism brings us in many respects to the same point to which a thorough idealism would. Utilitarianism and other partial moral systems present to us a partial view of life, and say, Live according to an ideal of life, but one which goes *thus* far only. The positivism which I have spoken of would say, Live, taking life itself in all its fulness as your guide, and beware that you do not let the singleness and simplicity of your view be altered by an ideal, which after all is not life itself, but only something of your own construction. Such thorough positivism quarrels with idealism more on the ground of the necessary imperfection and incompleteness of it than on any other. It says, There can be no true and complete ideal of life but such as we unconsciously form in *living*. As against partial idealisms, this is thoroughly true. And as against idealism of any kind, in so far as this is necessarily in some degree partial, it is worthy to be borne in mind.

The two passages in which Mr Mill seems to state most distinctly the utilitarian theory without reference to objections are in pp. 9, 10, 17. 'The creed,' it is said in the former of these passages, 'which accepts as the foundation of morals, utility, holds that actions are right in proportion as they tend to produce happiness, wrong as they tend to produce the reverse of happiness. By happiness is intended pleasure, and the absence of pain: by unhappiness, pain, and the privation of pleasure.'

The utilitarian theory of life is, 'that pleasure and freedom from pain are the only things desirable as ends: and that all desirable things (which are as numerous in the utilitarian as in any other scheme) are desirable either for the pleasure inherent in themselves, or as means to the promotion of pleasure and the prevention of pain.'

The utilitarian τέλος, or the ultimate end of life, is described by Mr Mill in the second passage which I have referred to: calling it roughly happiness, it gives, in Mr Mill's view, the standard of morality; which (standard) 'may accordingly be defined, the rules and precepts for human conduct, by the observance of which an existence such as has been described might be, to the greatest extent possible, secured to all mankind; and not to them only, but, so far as the nature of things admits, to the whole sentient creation.'[4]

Now from the beginning of moral philosophy to the present day, whenever the question of an action being right or wrong has been considered as depending upon the end to which it conduced, that end has been of necessity such as might be described as some kind of happiness of somebody. Nothing is acted for except as in some way desirable. And since the very notion of reasonable action is that it is for a purpose, no system of morality could entirely neglect to take account of the purpose or end of actions. And so far as it does this, it determines morality by the consideration of conduciveness to happiness: or is so far what Mr Mill would call utilitarian.

It is evident however that we are advanced but a little way towards answering the questions of morality when we have got only to this: and there are some particulars of the complicated feelings of mankind in relation to morality, which this consideration of the conduciveness of actions to an end does not seem likely to be able to account for.

The specific differences of Mr Mill's utilitarianism as above described, among other systems which refer action to an end, seem to be that by happiness he would understand pleasure and absence of pain, describing the circumstances of these with reference to actual human life: and again, that he would make this conduciveness to an end (namely, pleasure as thus understood) the *sole* test of rightness.

If we are to suppose happiness and pleasure to be different *notions*, so that the saying that happiness consists in pleasure is any explanation of the former, we must mean by pleasure not merely well-being, or any indefinite idea of that kind, but something of which we have distinct consciousness and experience. And so Mr Mill, in clear and in fact beautiful language, explains [what] he does mean. It is here that there comes in the difference between Mr Mill's utilitarianism and other moral systems which may attribute no less importance to the conduciveness of actions to happiness. Let Mr Mill, if he will, make the great scheme of morality utilitarian, in this sense, that he supposes the happiness of whatever can feel happiness to be the proper object of all the action which can go on in the universe;[a] and as we know that the action of God is directed to this purpose, let us consider that the rightness or valuableness of human action is only another word for the conformity of *it* also to this same purpose. But the knowledge how we are to act in the complicated relations of human life cannot be gained by a summary transference of this leading idea to another region of thought, and understanding by happiness simply recognized or experienced pleasure: even supposing we were certain that no accompanying ideas, besides that of the universal end to be attained, were needed.

I hope I may be able to avoid, in controverting Mr Mill, any disposition to value less than he does human happiness, or even human pleasure, and the action which is conducive to it. I recognize fully the worth, not only of *his* utilitarianism, but of the older and inferior, as aiding the study, than which nothing can be more important, of the manner in which human happiness may be promoted. I do not very much believe in *a science* of human happiness, for reasons which we may perhaps see presently; but we all might be made much

a    *Util.* p. 31.

wiser in regard to ourselves, and much less helpless and more serviceable in respect of others, by intelligent thought as to what happiness is: and if utilitarianism furnishes us with this, we may afford to pardon it some theoretical error. But it appears to me that the attempt of utilitarianism, as it shows itself in these papers, to make itself at once into the whole of morality, and to proclaim that, as to action, there is noting worthy of human thought but happiness, will hinder rather than injure the good work which in a restricted sphere it might do, namely, making us better understand what man's happiness really is.

The difficulty of utilitarianism in regard of its claims exclusively to determine action, arises not so much from the supposition of the *unattainableness* of happiness, which is what Mr Mill in the main sets himself to controvert (for few would doubt but that, whether attainable or not, it is a thing worth striving after), as from the difficulty of determining, after we have passed the narrow limits of food and raiment, of health, peace, and competence, what, for different people, it consists in, and of comparing the supposed happiness of one person with that of another. The question is not, Have we a clear enough view of what it is, to stimulate our own action so far as we want such stimulus, and to guide our benevolence; but, Have we a clear enough view of it to be able to balance and calculate the different ingredients of it, the different pleasures, as Bentham did, or in any similar way, so that our reason may be able to determine the desirablenss of actions in *this* way to the exclusion of all others?

Perhaps we shall be able to form a presumption as to the probability of mankind being agreed in regard of the happiness to be aimed at, by seeing how far we agree with Mr Mill's own view of happiness as expressed in these papers. One passage in which he describes it is the following: 'The happiness which they' (some philosophers) 'meant was not a life of rapture, but moments of such, in an existence made up of few and transitory pains, many and various pleasures, with a decided predominance of the active over the passive, and having as the foundation of the whole, not to expect more from life than it is capable of bestowing. A life thus composed . . . has always appeared worthy of the name of happiness.'[b]

Let us take any feature of this picture, as for instance the last: 'not to expect more from life than it is capable of bestowing.' (How, by the way, are we to know how much it is capable of bestowing?) This is supposedly a point of happiness. I will not say it is not, but I am not very clear about it, if we are to look at life as we really think and talk about it, and not in that rather conventional way which we may perhaps call the moralistic,[c*] and which is used for exemplar stories and for advice to others, in which strong elements are evaporated, and strong features

---

b    *Util.* p. 18. [See page 45.]

c*  Perhaps the best way in which I can obviate misapprehension as to what I mean by this term, is to mention what a view of happiness like that given in Paley suggests to me. It is very valuable and useful, on the supposition that we understand it simply as a corrective, and are sure (as we may be sure) that it will not be attended to more than in a certain, and that a limited, degree. Just as the advice of parents to their children is given with the feeling, on the part of the parent,

toned down. I can hardly think Nature was wrong in filling us, as she does, especially in earlier days, with hope and unlimited expectation, even though perhaps much of bitter disappointment should follow. At least we cannot accept it as a general fact of human nature that this absence of hopefulness, this want of sanguiness, is a feature of happiness: and the same I think of the other features assigned by Mr Mill, as for instance variety of pleasures: can we hope then for much general agreement in the future?

So far as the maxim that we should not expect too much from life, goes in company with the religious idea of another life to which we may transfer our expectations, it is well; but so far as it stands independent of this, both it and the theory of life to which it belongs are surely questionable. Mr Mill has wisely pointed out the difference between happiness and content, but he scarcely seems, in his own view of life, sufficiently to bear it in mind. After saying 'It is better to be Socrates dissatisfied than a fool satisfied,'d it is not consistent to write, as he

that there is sure to be enough in the child of strong passion, hopefulness, enterprize, and other elements of this kind, which he only fears lest there should be too much of, but the absence of which, though they make no part of his advice, he understands would be quite as great a calamity as disregard of his advice. Mr Mill's prescription for happiness, not to expect too much from life, is of this character. Considering the exceeding likelihood that we shall form utterly unreasonable expectations, the advice, in this point of view, is most sensible. But if Mr Mill's view were, not simply to correct and restrain a temper of mind which he knows is sure to exist in spite of all that may be said against it, but to describe the temper which he thinks should be, I would take, for happiness, what seems to me to be the side of nature against him. And so as to Paley: if his description of what will make us happy is intended as a portrait of a happy life, without the supposition of there existing besides a mass of strong emotion, impulse, imagination, and other such elements, of which what he gives is really only a chastening or correction, I must say that in my view, setting aside (as he too must set aside) casualty and misfortune, human life as it exists is not only better but happier than he would make it.

If we *are* to think of a happiness greater and better than nature provides for us already, the soberer elements of it correcting, but not supplanting the more energetic, let us take a better and worthier ideal than that of Paley; an ideal really worth striving after. Of this the reader will find more in the sequel.

By the 'moralistic' view of life, in a sense slightly depreciatory, I mean such a view of it as is taken by Juvenal in the tenth Satire, and by Johnson in his imitation of it, 'The Vanity of Human Wishes.' When that which is very well as simple correction is carried out into a real criticism of human life with its enterprize and its action, I can only say that the philosophic view seems to me both less true, and lower, than the vulgar.

Johnson's view as to what we should expect from life may appear from such lines as

Condemn'd to hope's delusive mine
As on we toil from day to day,

and similar ones. Johnson was the opposite of a superficial and commonplace man, and was led to views of this kind partly by his century, and partly by his temperament. [There had been several verse renderings of Juvenal's tenth satire prior to the *Vanity of Human Wishes*, but Samuel Johnson's poem, published in 1749, was the best known; the quotation is from the opening lines of Johnson's poem 'On the death of Dr Robert Levet'.]

d    *Util.* p. 14. [See page 43.]

61

does in a subsequent page, as if a happy life and a satisfied one were the same.[e]*
The fact is, that Mr Mill's notion of the difference in *quality* between one sort of
happiness and another is difficult to reconcile, not only with the utilitarian
theory to which he applies it, but with any idea of happiness being at all readily
attainable and consisting, to any important degree, in satisfaction. Are we, or are
we not, to try to make our happiness and pleasures of the highest quality of
which our nature is capable? And if we admit this idea of *highest* quality, have we
not got, not only an idea not belonging to utilitarianism, but also a very
disturbing idea? Is life to be an effort after the higher happiness, or a satisfaction
in the nearer and lower; a well-adjusted balancing, as Mr Mill describes it, of
tranquillity and excitement?

In reality, Mr Mill upon his utilitarian principles, in spite of his saying that
happiness is not contentment, or the merely being satisfied, is obliged to come to
what amounts to saying that it *is*, having no choice except to do this or to put it
in the other Epicurean idea of indulgence.[5] It is thus that utilitarianism, by
making a general theory of human life and human happiness of too *immediate*
importance to morals, is likely *not* to be of use in furthering our knowledge what
that serious and complicated thing, human life, is. Utilitarians *must have* general
rules of human happiness for their system, and they can hardly help assuming as
such what are at best most imperfectly made out to be so, rules, for instance,
which would make happiness for one person, but not for another. Mr Mill's
remarks upon human happiness in the papers before us are full of interest, and
full of true feeling and happy expression, as regards the particular points
touched, but I think it will be considered, on examination, that the theory they
involve is superficial. It is very well, as practical advice, to tell us that happiness
consists in mental cultivation, in working so much and allowing ourselves just so
much excitement as will render rest pleasant, and resting no longer than till we
get an appetite for excitement again:[f] but the springs of human happiness and
unhappiness lie deeper than all this, and Mr Mill goes surely nearer to touching
them in his incidental remarks which have no dependence on utilitarianism,
(such as those on egotism[g]) than he does in his theory.

I do not think that moral philosophy can be of the use of which it should be,
unless it struggles, at least, to cope with the greatness and complexity of the
problem which there is before it, and to face the difficulty of the variableness
and vastness of the nature of man. Whether it ever can do much in this way, I
do not say: but at least the most important thing it can do is to try. With all its
failings hitherto, whatever they may have been, of laying its foundations here
and there in different places, so as to make everything perhaps doubtful in it and
much necessarily wrong, there is one failing at least as great as any, namely the

e*   *Ib.* p. 19. 'The main constituents of a satisfied life appear to be two,' &c. [See page 46.]
f    *Ib.* p. 19, 20.
g    *Ib.* p. 20.

way in which, led by its various hypotheses, it has taken views of human nature manifestly partial and incomplete even to the eyes of those who are no philosophers, if only they think a moment. When people feel, as they must, the variety of thought and feeling even in their own minds, multiplied infinitely in the society of men around them, they must wonder, one would think, what moral philosophy can be for, when they read its hasty hypotheses and summary generalizations; as, that they really do everything by deliberate selfishness, that all ideas of honour are something fantastic and absurd, or whatever else it may be. The moral philosopher must to some extent make *himself* the measure of human nature: the more real-minded he is, and the less he is the mere echo of others, the more is there danger of his failing to take account of moral facts as to human nature, which his own disposition does not lead him to enter into: and when to the promptings of individuality there are added the exigencies of theory, portraits of human nature (for such every moral philosophy must be) arise, which are most unsatisfactory and incomplete.

Utilitarianism I think does not help at all that most important object, in regard of moral philosophy, the widening of its range and view. Obliged by its principles to assume a definiteness or describability as to happiness, which, in my notion, does not exist, utilitarianism can hardly help being hasty and premature in fixing what happiness is, and calling that happiness, which, if we are to have the idea, really seems not worthy of the name. I only, in this respect, demur to the *claims* of utilitarianism when compared with what it *does*: I welcome what it does, but cannot think that it is *much*, that it is much better than what *has* been done by other systems before it, or that it promises much in the future.

To return to Mr Mill's description of happiness: the same thing, it seems to me, is to be said of this, which is to be said of that of Paley[h]* and perhaps of

---

h*  Paley, B. I. ch. 6, describes happiness as *not* consisting in (1) self-indulgence, (2) idleness, (3) greatness; and *as* consisting in (1) sociality, (2) occupation, (3) what we may call moderation, (4) health. If his account had been given in perfect good faith, I do not see why he should not have added competent livelihood or fortune, for that is not more a matter out of our own power than health is, and in the importance of it for happiness Aristotle and an English tradesman would alike agree. But Paley wished to establish that happiness is pretty equally distributed amongst the different orders of civil society. The fact is, that happiness is distributed among *all*, rich and poor, sick and healthful, old and young, in a manner very ill represented by the above superficial statement, and according to complicated laws which such generalities only tend to obscure.

Paley's account of happiness is very interesting, but more so, I think, as showing his own mind than in any other view. That it does so, that it is thus *first-hand*, is a great merit. But the moralist, in describing happiness, *must be* in a difficulty. If he takes the picture from his own feeling and experience, it must be most incomplete. If he takes it from his thought, intercourse with others, and general judgement, it is very likely to be most vague and mistaken.

Paley's third character of happiness, which I have called 'moderation,' is in reality 'the prudent constitution of the habits.' Like much of Paley, it is so practical as to be in fact unpractical. 'Set the habits in such a manner that every change may be a change for the better.' To use the illustration which Paley himself gives: Inure yourself to books of science and argumentation,

*[continued]*

many others: namely, that as views of life, practical and interesting so far as they go, no fault is to be found with them: but that in the character of descriptions of happiness such as must be required to make significant and effective the utilitarian axiom, that actions are right as they promote happiness and wrong as they do the reverse, they are altogether insufficient and incomplete. Utilitarianism requires us not only to admit its axiom, but to confess that it is the single moral maxim that is of value, and that any others, as that actions are right so far as they are kind, so far as they are fair or just, or whatever it may be, are only derivative from this. We ask for a description of the happiness. Sometimes utilitarianism, as in Bentham, may make the attempt to methodize and systematize pleasures in a sort of scientific manner: but I apprehend that the more practical and thoughtful of the school, as perhaps Mr Mill, do not like this. They *then* have to give us, as happiness, either what their own individual disposition prompts, or else a repetition, more or less, of that rude and manifestly incomplete human *practical* observation about happiness which has always existed, but which, merely repeated, is little more than common-place. True, fresh, and original observations as to human life and happiness *may* be made by utilitarians as by others: but there is nothing I think in their system to lead them specially to make it.

The three most noticeable features of Mr Mill's description of happiness are perhaps, first that he goes far, as we have seen, to resolve happiness into content-

because then any other book which may fall in your way will be a change for the better: they (the books of science) will give you an appetite for novels, well-written pamphlets, and articles of news, and you will sit down to these latter with relish, till the habitual feeling acts again to send you to your graver reading. It seems to me odd that Paley should have taken this merely business view of the science and argumentation of which he was such a master: but what is of more consequence, I think it shows how the looking at things only in the point of view of happiness and pleasure obscures our notion of their relative importance: and I think what Paley here says of books belongs to his whole view of life. He thinks of life as an alternation of work and play, much in the way that a schoolboy thinks of *his* life, with the same absence of notion of the work being for any purpose, except that it must be, and with the same notion that it is the play or enjoyment which is the real life. But even the schoolboy would hardly understand being told to go into school only in order that he might enjoy his play the more, and the telling us, deliberately, to set our habits so that changes in them may be for the better, seems to me the same kind of advice.

What is wanted is the thought of life as directed upon other views than this conscious thought of the happiness of it: either simply natural views, such as that we have our bread to get, our family to support, our position to secure or improve, our plans and enterprizes to carry out, the interests of our neighbourhood or our country, or of science, or of the human race, to further as we may; and happiness to us will then mean the degree in which we are able to succeed in these things, and to bear want of success with patience: or more ideal views, in which it will be rather the worthier of these purposes which suggest themselves to us, and other purposes as well, such as the improvement of our own and others' character, the higher interests of the human race, the glory of God. Here too, it is in *living*, that we shall find, if we find, our happiness.

The same unpracticalness arising from an attempt at being over-practical belongs to what Paley says as to occupation, or 'the exercise of our faculties to some engaging end.'

ment, and changes his term from a 'happy life' into a 'satisfied' one:[i] then that he considers a very great element of happiness to be wideness of interest and intellectual cultivation:[j*] and last that he disagrees with the often repeated couplet which tells us that the portion of human woe which kings and laws can cure is very small, and thinks that better laws would cure a very great deal of it.[k]

The first of these is something which I wonder at seeing brought into so much prominence by a political economist like Mr Mill, since in that science aspiration after improvement of economical condition appears as the principle of all progress, and contentment with a low condition the thing most to be dreaded. Nor is the praise of contentment, one would think, very utilitarian in *principle*, for contentment depends upon the mind as well as the condition. And if we think much of what the mind of itself can do in this respect, we drift away from the idea of assignable happiness being the only good thing, and come towards the idea which Mr Mill does not like, of its being possible, if we may say so, to be something as good as happy without apparent means of happiness. As a commonplace, the praise of contentment has the sort of truth which such things have; a truth, that is, partial, and admitting the opposite to be said with equal truth. When Mr Mill says, for instance, as we have seen, that it is a great thing for happiness to expect little from life, I apprehend that with at least an equal degree of truth we might say, that it was a great thing for happiness to expect a great deal from it. But really, whether we do well to be satisfied depends (and in this Mr Mill will agree with me) on what it is we are satisfied with. To be satisfied with what ought not to satisfy us is as great a misfortune as to be dissatisfied and restless when there is no reason for being so: *i.e.* we come away from happiness into the region of 'ought,' the right, the fitting. *Right* dissatisfaction is the spring of all human progress and improvement.

About the value for happiness of mental cultivation and wide-spreading intellectual interest I will not speak. Mr Mill corrects what there might be of superficiality in the notion as he first gives it, and as is involved, to my view, in the word *cultivation*, by saying, at the conclusion of the passage, that it is not for the gratification of curiosity only that these things should be regarded, but that 'a moral and a human interest' should be taken in them. And no one can doubt but that in the mind thus exercised is to be found one of the best and most real sources of happiness.[l*]

i    p. 19. [See page 46.]

j*    The necessity, for happiness, of social and loving emotion, which Mr Mill puts forward very prominently, should perhaps be added as a separate feature.

k    p. 21. [See page 47.]

l*    'Nam sive oblectatio quaeritur animi, requiesque curarum: quae conferri cum eorum studiis potest, qui semper aliquid anquirunt, quod spectet et valeat ad bene beateque vivendum?' Cic. *de Off.* 2. 2. Cicero here gives us at once an ingredient of happiness, and the proper place of happiness itself in the investigations which he speaks of. It is to be hoped that the noble and liberal tone of mind which he speaks of is more abundant in our time and country than on the surface it would appear to be. [I.e. Cicero, *De Officiis*, II. 2: 'For if we are looking for mental enjoyment and relaxation, what pleasure can be compared with the pursuits of those who are always studying something that will tend toward and effectively promote a good and happy life?']

Nor will I say anything, at least just now, about the manner in which Mr Mill thinks we ought all to be happy now, if it were not for 'bad laws and subjection to the will of others.'[m] I wish laws were better, and whatever I may think myself, I rejoice to see others full of faith in the improvability of them, and would not say a word to produce hopelessness or wrong satisfaction with what is not good. Mr Mill's language is not indeed altogether encouraging: he anticipates this world becoming some day, 'all that, if will and knowledge were not wanting, it might easily be made.'[n] If will and knowledge both are wanting, if we neither care for the thing nor know anything about it, no wonder the task is not easy, but it may be possible.

Mr Mill goes on to say, after describing the kind of life which is worthy of the name of happiness, that 'such an existence is even now the lot of many during some considerable portion of their lives. The present wretched education, and wretched social arrangements, are the only real hindrance to its being attainable by almost all.'[o]

Then, showing more in detail how this may be, he says that 'most of the great positive evils of the world' (of which he takes as examples poverty, disease, and vicissitudes of fortune,) 'are in a great degree, many of them almost entirely, conquerable by human care and effort.'

Now here of course the question, What *are* better social arrangements, is as difficult as the question, What *is* happiness. And while heartily agreeing with Mr Mill in his hopefulness for the future, and only wishing to be able to agree with him still more, I am compelled to feel that the question is one which must very speedily arise, and which even the few and general words which he has said suggest. For instance, in regard of poverty we read, 'Poverty, in any sense implying suffering, may be completely extinguished by the wisdom of society, combined with the good sense and providence of individuals.' I do not think I am doing injustice to Mr Mill in considering that these words point at that cutting of the knot which many political economists recommend in the case of the difficulty of poverty, the taking care that numbers shall not be too great. This proposed remedy, coming from those who value as highly as Mr Mill does human happiness, of which the first and great element is surely life and existence itself, has always surprised me. It is indeed a ready remedy for poverty, but how, if it is to go to such an extent as to change the character of human society, it is to escape being a selfishness *en grand* of the human race (increasing individual enjoyment only by diminishing the number of enjoyers) I do not see. Not however to discuss this: in the same way as some of Mr Mill's prospective social arrangements seem questionable, some of his views of the present seem superficial; as where he says, 'As for vicissitudes of fortune, and other disappointments

---

m   p. 21. [See above, page 47.]

n   p. 22. [See above, page 47.]

o   p. 19. [See above, page 45.]

connected with worldly circumstances, these are principally the effect either of gross imprudence, or of ill-regulated desires, or of bad and imperfect social institutions.'

Is this so? and is our hope of amendment for the future to depend on our forming as to the present such views as this?

This observation of Mr Mill's suggests to me to close the chapter with saying that in writing about human happiness, while we must get rid of superstition, I do not think we can get rid, or ought to do so, of a feeling something like awe. The word itself, so far as its history is concerned, implies in almost every language something *not* in our own power. It is both unfeeling and unreal to talk of it as being so, except so far as we recognize an inward force, which may be supplemented by religious feeling, rising above adverse circumstances. The contemplation with a steady eye of the possible vicissitudes of life, in the midst of which our course is to be steered towards such happiness as may be possible for us, is something very different from Mr Mill's view of vicissitudes here. And for myself, there is something more terrible in the idea of such fearful alternations as these 'vicissitudes' represent being in our own power and resting upon us, considering our ignorance, than there is in the supposition of their being out of our power, so long as we may hope and trust the universe is not for evil.

## ROBERT OWEN, *REPORT TO THE COUNTY OF LANARK* (1821)

Robert Owen (1771–1858) began his career as a successful entrepreneur. As partner and manager of the New Lanark Mills in Scotland (from 1800 to 1829) he became one of the wealthiest cotton spinners of his time. Through a programme of education, improved living conditions and lowered working hours, Owen attempted to create in New Lanark a model society, one similar to the rural communities he had known as a child in Wales. The success of New Lanark led him to extend his ideas to society as a whole, and much of his life was spent in energetically urging his proposals for social reform on governments in Britain, Europe and America. In particular, he campaigned vigorously for a national education system, for factory reform, and for state-aided unemployment relief. Owen sank much of his fortune into the setting up of model communities, the most ambitious of which was New Harmony in Indiana (which he was involved with from 1825 to 1828); all, however, failed within a few years. Between 1829 and 1834 he enjoyed national celebrity when he became the figurehead of a general trade-union movement. By the 1840s, though, his reputation had declined, and by 1846 the Owenite movement had more or less collapsed. Owen was a prolific (if repetitive) author, and together with his supporters he produced an impressive array of publications, including books, pamphlets, lectures, tracts and several periodicals. His first major work was the four essays published in 1813 which made up *A New View of Society*. In them Owen argued for the social and environmental determination of character, a circumstance which through education permitted the rational and peaceful reconstruction of society. In *Report to the County of Lanark* (1821), Owen extended his ideas, emphasising the destructive role of machinery in modern life and the importance of a society based on co-operation and the communal ownership of property, rather than competition. The most mature statement of these views appeared in the seven part *Book of the New Moral World* (1836–44). Owen continued writing and publishing up until his death in 1858.

## From Robert Owen, *Report to the County of Lanark* (Glasgow: Wardlaw & Cunninghame, 1821)[1]

From *Part III: Details of the Plan*[2]

3rd – *The arrangement for feeding, lodging, and clothing the population, and for training and educating the children.*

It being always most convenient for the workman to reside near to his employment, the site for the dwellings of the cultivators will be chosen as near to the centre of the land, as water, proper levels, dry situation, etc., etc., may admit; and as courts, alleys, lanes, and streets create many unnecessary inconveniences, are injurious to health, and destructive to almost all the natural comforts of human life, they will be excluded, and a disposition of the buildings free from these objections and greatly more economical will be adopted.

As it will afterwards appear that the food for the whole population can be provided better and cheaper under one general arrangement of cooking, and that the children can be better trained and educated together under the eye of their parents than under any other circumstances, a large square, or rather parallelogram, will be found to combine the greatest advantages in its form for the domestic arrangements of the association.

This form, indeed, affords so many advantages for the comfort of human life, that if great ignorance respecting the means necessary to secure good conduct and happiness among the working classes had not prevailed in all ranks, it must long ago have become universal.

It admits of a most simple, easy, convenient, and economical arrangement for all the purposes required.

The four sides of this figure may be adapted to contain all the private apartments or sleeping and sitting rooms for the adult part of the population; general sleeping apartments for the children while under tuition; store-rooms, or warehouses in which to deposit various products; an inn, or house for the accommodation of strangers; an infirmary; etc., etc.

In a line across the centre of the parallelogram, leaving free space for air and light and easy communication, might be erected the church, or places for worship; the schools; kitchen and apartments for eating; all in the most convenient situation for the whole population, and under the best possible public superintendence, without trouble, expense, or inconvenience to any party.

The advantages of this general domestic arrangement can only be known and appreciated by those who have had great experience in the beneficial results of extensive combinations in improving the condition of the working classes, and whose minds, advancing beyond the petty range of individual party interest, have been calmly directed to consider what may now be attained by a well-devised association of human powers for the benefit of all ranks. It is such individuals only who can detect the present total want of foresight in the conduct of society, and its gross misapplication of the most valuable and abundant means of securing prosperity. They can distinctly perceive that the blind are leading the blind from difficulties to dangers, which they feel to increase at every step.

The parallelogram being found to be the best form in which to dispose the dwelling and chief domestic arrangements for the proposed associations of cultivators, it will be useful now to explain the principles on which those arrangements have been formed.

The first in order, and the most necessary, are those respecting food.

It has been, and still is, a received opinion among theorists in political economy, that man can provide better for himself, and more advantageously for the public, when left to his own individual exertions, opposed to and in competition with his fellows, than when aided by any social arrangement which shall unite his interest individually and generally with society.

This principle of individual interest, opposed as it is perpetually to the public good, is considered, by the most celebrated political economists, to be the corner-stone to the social system, and without which, society could not subsist.

Yet when they shall know themselves, and discover the wonderful effects which combination and union can produce, they will acknowledge that the present arrangement of society is the most anti-social, impolitic, and irrational, that can be devised; that under its influence all the superior and valuable qualities of human nature are repressed from infancy, and that the most unnatural means are used to bring out the most injurious propensities; in short, that the utmost pains are taken to make that which by nature is the most delightful compound for producing excellence and happiness, absurd, imbecile, and wretched.

Such is the conduct now pursued by those who are called the best and wisest of the present generation, although there is not one rational object to be gained by it.

From this principle of individual interest have arisen all the divisions of mankind, the endless errors and mischiefs of class, sect, party, and of national antipathies, creating the angry and malevolent passions, and all the crimes and misery with which the human race have been hitherto afflicted.

In short, if there be one closet doctrine more contrary to truth than another, it is the notion that individual interest, as that term is now understood, is a more advantageous principle on which to found the social system, for the benefit of all, or of any, than the principle of union and mutual cooperation.

The former acts like an immense weight to repress the most valuable faculties and dispositions, and to give a wrong direction to all human powers. It is one of those magnificent errors, (if the expression may be allowed), that when enforced in practice brings ten thousand evils in its train. The principle on which these economists proceed, instead of adding to the wealth of nations or of individuals, is itself the sole cause of poverty; and but for its operation wealth would long ago have ceased to be a subject of contention in any part of the world. If, it may be asked, experience has proved that union, combination and extensive arrangement among mankind, are a thousand times more powerful to destroy, than the efforts of an unconnected multitude, where each acts individually for himself, – would not a similar increased effect be produced by union, combination, and extensive arrangement, to *create and conserve*? Why should not the result be the same in the one case as in the other? But it is well known that a combination of men and of interests can effect that which it would be futile to attempt, and impossible to accomplish, by individual exertions and separate interests. Then why, it may be inquired, have men so long acted individually, and in opposition to each other? This is an important question, and merits the most serious attention.

Men have not yet been trained in principles that will permit then *to act in union*, except to defend themselves or to destroy others. For self-preservation they were early compelled to unite for these purposes in war. A necessity, however, equally powerful will now compel men to be trained to act together to *create and conserve*, that, in like manner, they may preserve life in peace. Fortunately for mankind the system of individual opposing interests has now reached the extreme point of error and inconsistency; – in the midst of the most ample means to create wealth, all are in poverty, or in imminent danger from the effects of poverty upon others.

The reflecting part of mankind have admitted, in theory, that the characters of men are formed chiefly by the circumstances in which they are placed; yet the science of the influence of circumstances, which is the most important of all the sciences, remains unknown for the great practical business of life. When it shall be fully developed it will be discovered that to unite the mental faculties of men for the attainment of pacific and civil objects will be a far more easy task than it has been to combine their physical powers to carry on extensive war-like preparations.

The discovery of the distance and movements of the heavenly bodies, – of the time-piece, – of a vessel to navigate the most distant parts of the ocean, – of the steam-engine, which performs under the easy control of one man the labour of many thousands, – and of the press, by which knowledge and improvement may be speedily given to the most ignorant in all parts of the earth, – these have, indeed, been discoveries of high import to mankind; but, important as these and others have been in their effects on the condition of human society, their combined benefits in practice will fall short of those which will be speedily attained by the new intellectual power which men will acquire through the knowledge of 'the science of the influence of circumstances over the whole conduct, character, and proceedings of the human race.' By this latter discovery more will be accomplished in one year, for the well-being of human nature, including, without any exceptions, all ranks and descriptions of men, than has ever yet been effected in one or in many centuries. Strange as this language many seem to those whose minds have not yet had a glimpse of the real state in which society now is, it will prove to be not more strange than true.

Are not the mental energies of the world at this moment in a state of high effervescences? – Is not society at a stand, incompetent to proceed in its present course? – And do not all men cry out that 'something must be done'? – That

71

'something,' to produce the effect desired, must be a complete renovation of the whole social compact; one not forced on prematurely, by confusion and violence; not one to be brought about by futile measures of the Radicals, Whigs, or Tories, of Britain, – the Liberals or Royalists of France, – the Illuminati of Germany,[3] or the mere party proceedings of any little local portion of human beings, trained as they have hitherto been in almost every kind of error, and without any true knowledge of themselves.

No! The change sought for must be preceded by the clear development of a great and universal principle which shall unite in one all the petty jarring interests, by which, till now, human nature has been made a most inveterate enemy to itself.

No! Extensive, – nay, rather, universal, – as the rearrangement of society must be, to relieve it from the difficulties with which it is now overwhelmed, it will be effected in peace and quietness, with the goodwill and hearty concurrence of all parties, and of every people. It will necessarily commence by common consent, on account of its advantage, almost simultaneously among all civilized nations; and, once begun, will daily advance with an accelerating ratio, unopposed, and bearing down before it the existing systems of the world. The only astonishment then will be that such systems could so long have existed.

Under the new arrangements which will succeed them, no complaints of any kind will be heard in society. The causes of the evils that exist will become evident to every one, as well as the natural means of easily withdrawing those causes. These, by common consent, will be removed, and the evils, of course, will permanently cease, soon to be known only by description. Should any of the causes of evil be irremovable by the new powers which men are about to acquire, they will then know that they are necessary and unavoidable evils; and childish unavailing complaints will cease to be made. But your Reporter[4] has yet failed to discover any which do not proceed from the errors of the existing system, or which, under the contemplated arrangements are not easily removable.

Of the natural effects of this language and these sentiments upon mankind in general, your Reporter is, perhaps, as fully aware as any individual can be; but he knows that the full development of these truths is absolutely necessary to prepare the public to receive and understand the practical details which he is about to explain, and to comprehend those enlarged measures for the amelioration of society, which the distress of the times, arising from the errors of the present arrangements, now renders unavoidable. He is not now, however, addressing the common public, but those whose minds have had all the benefit of the knowledge which society at present affords; and it is from such individuals that he hopes to derive the assistance requisite to effect the practical good which he has devoted all the powers and faculties of his mind to obtain for his fellow-creatures.

Your Reporter has stated that this happy change will be effected through the knowledge which will be derived from the science of the influence of circumstances over human nature.

Through this science, new mental powers will be created, which will place all those circumstances that determine the misery or happiness of men under the immediate control and direction of the present population of the world, and will entirely supersede all necessity for *the present truly irrational system of individual rewards and punishments*: – a system which has ever been opposed to the most obvious dictates of common sense and of humanity, and which will be no longer permitted than while men continue unenlightened and barbarous.

The first rays of knowledge will show, to the meanest capacity, that all the tendencies of this system are to degrade men below the ordinary state of animals, and to render them more miserable and irrational.

The science of the influence of circumstances over human nature will dispel this ignorance, and will prove how much more easily men may be trained by other means to become, without exception, active, kind, and intelligent, – devoid of those unpleasant and irrational feelings which for ages have tormented the whole human race.

This science may be truly called one whereby ignorance, poverty, crime, and misery, may be prevented; and will indeed open a new era to the human race; one in which real happiness will commence, and perpetually go on increasing through every succeeding generation.

And although the characters of all have been formed under the existing circumstances, which are together unfavourable to their habits, dispositions, mental acquirements, and happiness, – yet, by the attainment of this new science, those of the present day will be enabled to place themselves, and more especially the rising generation, under circumstances so agreeable to human nature, and so well adapted to all the acknowledged ends of human life, that those objects of anxious desire so ardently sought for through past ages will be secured to everyone with the certainty of a mathematical procedure.

Improbable as this statement must seem to those who have necessarily been formed, by existing circumstances, into the creatures of the place in which they happen to live; which circumstances, to speak correctly, and with the sincerity and honesty which the subject now demands, could not form them into anything but mere local animals; still, even they must be conscious that the time is not long passed when their forefathers would have deemed it far more improbable that the light cloudy mist which they saw arise from boiling water could be so applied, by human agency, that under the easy control of one of themselves it should be made to execute the labour of thousands. Yet, by the aid of mechanical and chemical science, this and many other supposed impossibilities have been made familiar certainties. In like manner, fearful as men may now be to allow themselves to hope that the accumulated evils of ages are not permanent in their nature, probably many now live who will see the science introduced, that, in their days, will rapidly diminish, and, in the latter days of their children, will entirely remove these evils.

It is now time to return to the consideration of the preparatory means by which these important results are to be accomplished.

Your Reporter now uses the terms 'preparatory,' because the present state of

73

society, *governed by circumstances*, is so different, in its several parts and entire combination, from that which will arise when society shall be taught to *govern circumstances*, that some temporary intermediate arrangements, to serve as a step whereby we may advance from the one to the other, will be necessary.

The long experience which he has had in the practice of the science now about to be introduced has convinced him of the utility, nay, of the absolute necessity, of forming arrangements for a temporary intermediate stage of existence, in which we, who have acquired the wretched habits of the old system, may be permitted, without inconvenience, gradually to part with them, and exchange them for those requisite for the new and improved state of society. Thus will the means be prepared, by which, silently and without contest, all the local errors and prejudices which have kept men and nations strangers to each other and to themselves, will be removed. The habits, dispositions, notions, and consequent feelings, engendered by old society, will be thus allowed, without disturbance of any kind, to die a natural death; but as the character, conduct, and enjoyment of individuals formed under the new system will speedily become living examples of the vast superiority of the one state over the other, the natural death of old society and all that appertains to it, although gradual, will not be lingering. Simple inspection, when both can be seen together, will produce motives sufficiently strong to carry the new arrangements as speedily into execution as practice will admit. The change, even in those who are now the most tenacious supporters of 'things as they are,' though left entirely to the influence of their own inclinations, will be so rapid, that they will wonder at themselves.

This intermediate change is the one, the details of which your Reporter has in part explained, and to which he now again begs to direct your attention.

Under the present system there is the most minute division of mental power and manual labour in the individuals of the working classes; private interests are placed perpetually at variance with the public good; and in every nation men are purposely trained from infancy to suppose that their well-being is incompatible with the progress and prosperity of other nations. Such are the means by which old society seeks to obtain the desired objects of life. The details now to be submitted have been devised upon principles which will lead to an opposite practice; to the combination of extensive mental and manual powers in the individuals of the working classes; to a complete identity of private and public interest; and to the training of nations to comprehend that their power and happiness cannot attain their full and natural development but through an equal increase of the power and happiness of all other states. These, therefore, are the real points at variance between that which *is* and that which *ought to be*.

It is upon these principles that arrangements are now proposed for the new agricultural villages, by which the food of the inhabitants may be prepared in one establishment, where they will eat together as one family.

Various objections have been urged against this practice; but they have come from those only, who, whatever may be their pretensions in other respects, are mere children in the knowledge of the principles and economy of social life.

By such arrangements the members of these new associations may be supplied with food at far less expense and with much more comfort than by any individual or family arrangements; and when the parties have been once trained and accustomed, as they easily may be, to the former mode, they will never afterwards feel any inclination to return to the latter.

If a saving in the quantity of food, – the obtaining of a superior quality of prepared provisions from the same materials, – and the operation of preparing them being effected in much less time, and with far less fuel, and with greater ease, comfort, and health, to all the parties employed, – be advantages, these will be obtained in a remarkable manner by the new arrangements proposed.

And if to partake of viands so prepared, served up with every regard to comfort, in clean, spacious, well-lighted, and pleasantly ventilated apartments, and in the society of well-dressed, well-trained, well-educated, and well-informed associates, possessing the most benevolent dispositions and desirable habits, can give zest and proper enjoyment to meals, then will the inhabitants of the proposed villages experience all this in an eminent degree.

When the new arrangements shall become familiar to the parties, this superior mode of living may be enjoyed at far less expense and with much less trouble than are necessary to procure such meals as the poor are now compelled to eat, surrounded by every object of discomfort and disgust, in the cellars and garrets of the most unhealthy courts, alleys, and lanes, in London, Dublin, and Edinburgh, or Glasgow, Manchester, Leeds, and Birmingham.

Striking, however, as the contrast is in this description, and although the actual practice will far exceed what words can convey, yet there are many closet theorists and inexperienced persons, probably, who still contend for individual arrangements and interests, in preference to that which they cannot comprehend.

These individuals must be left to be convinced by the facts themselves.

We now proceed to describe the interior accommodations of the private lodging-houses, which will occupy three sides of the parallelogram.

As it is of essential importance that there should be abundance of space within the line of the private dwellings, the parallelogram, in all cases, whether the association is intended to be near the maximum or the minimum in numbers, should be of large dimensions; and to accommodate a greater or less population, the private dwellings should be of one, two, three, or four stories, and the interior arrangements formed accordingly.

These will be very simple.

No kitchen will be necessary, as the public arrangements for cooking will supersede the necessity for any.

The apartments will always be well-ventilated, and, when necessary, heated or cooled on the improved principles lately introduced in the Derby Infirmary.

The expense and trouble, to say nothing of the superior health and comforts which these improvements will give, will be very greatly less than attach to the present practice.

To heat, cool, and ventilate their apartments, the parties will have no further

75

trouble than to open or shut two slides, or valves, in each room, the atmosphere of which, by this simple contrivance, may always be kept temperate and pure.

One stove of proper dimensions, judiciously placed, will supply the apartments of several dwellings, with little trouble and at a very little expense, when the buildings are originally adapted for this arrangement.

Thus will all the inconveniences and expense of separate fires and fire-places, and their appendages, be avoided, as well as the trouble and disagreeable effects of mending fires and removing ashes, etc., etc.

Good sleeping apartments looking over the gardens in the country, and sitting-rooms of proper dimensions fronting the square, will afford as much lodging-accommodation, as, with the other public arrangements, can be useful to, or desired by, these associated cultivators.

Food and lodging being thus provided for, the next consideration regards dress.

This, too, is a subject, the utility and disadvantages of which seem to be little understood by the Public generally; and, in consequence, the most ridiculous and absurd notions and practices have prevailed respecting it.

Most persons take it for granted, without thinking on the subject, that to be warm and healthy it is necessary to cover the body with thick clothing and to exclude the air as much as possible; and first appearances favour this conclusion. Facts, however, prove, that under the same circumstances, those who from infancy have been the most lightly clad, and who, by their form of dress, have been the most exposed to the atmosphere, are much stronger, more active, in better general health, warmer in cold weather, and far less incommoded by heat, than those who from constant habit have been dressed in such description of clothing as excludes the air from their bodies. The more the air is excluded by clothing, although at first the wearer feels warmer by each additional covering he puts on, yet in a few weeks, or months at most, the less capable he becomes of bearing cold than before.

The Romans and the Highlanders of Scotland appear to be the only two nations who adopted a national dress on account of its utility, without however neglecting to render it highly becoming and ornamental. The form of the dress of these nations was calculated first to give strength and manly beauty to the figure, and afterwards to display it to advantage. The time, expense, thought, and labour, now employed to create a variety of dress, the effects of which are to deteriorate the physical powers, and to render the human figure an object of pity and commiseration, are a certain proof of the low state of intellect among all classes in society. The whole of this gross misapplication of the human faculties serves no one useful or rational purpose. On the contrary, it essentially weakens all the physical and mental powers, and is, in all respects, highly pernicious to society.

All other circumstances remaining the same, sexual delicacy and virtue will be found much higher in nations among whom the person, *from its infancy*, is the most exposed than among those people who exclude from sight every part of the body except the eyes.

Although your Reporter is satisfied that the principle now stated is derived from the unchanging laws of nature, and is true to the utmost extent to which it can be carried; yet mankind must be trained in different habits, dispositions, and sentiments, before they can be permitted to act rationally on this, or almost any other law of nature.

The intermediate stage of society which your Reporter now recommends, admits, however, of judicious practical approximations towards the observance of these laws.

In the present case he recommends that the male children of the new villagers should be clothed in a dress somewhat resembling the Roman and Highland garb, in order that the limbs may be free from ligatures, and the air may circulate over every part of the body, and that they may be trained to become strong, active, well-limbed, and healthy.

And the female should have a well-chosen dress to secure similar important advantages.

The inhabitants of these villages, under the arrangements which your Reporter has in view, may be better dressed, for all the acknowledged purposes of dress, at much less than the one-hundredth part of the labour, inconvenience, and expense, that are now required to clothe the same number of persons in the middle ranks of life; while the form and material of the new dress will be acknowledged to be superior to any of the old.

If your Reporter should be told that all this waste of thought, time, labour, and capital is useful, inasmuch as it affords employment for the working classes; he replies, that no waste of any of these valuable means can be of the slightest benefit to any class; and that it would be far better, if superior occupations cannot be found for human beings, to resort to a Noble Lord's expedient, and direct them to make holes in the earth and fill them up again, repeating the operation without limit, rather than suffer a very large proportion of the working classes to be immured all their lives in unhealthy atmospheres, and toil at wretched employments, merely to render their fellow-creatures weak and absurd, both in body and mind.

The new villages having adopted the best form and material of dress, permanent arrangements will be made to produce it with little trouble or expense to any party; and all further considerations respecting it will give them neither care, thought, nor trouble, for many years, or perhaps centuries.

The advantages of this part of the Plan will prove to be so great in practice that fashions will exist but for a very short period, and then only among the most weak and silly part of the creation.

Your Reporter has now to enter upon the most interesting portion of this division of the subject, and, he may add, the most important part of the economy of human life, with reference to the science of the influence of circumstances over the well-being and happiness of mankind, and to the full power and control which men may now acquire over those circumstances, and by which they may direct them to produce among the human race, with ease and certainty, either universal good or evil.

77

No one can mistake the application of these terms to the training and education of the children.

Since men began to think and write, much has been thought and written on this subject; and yet all that has been thought and written has failed to make the subject understood, or to disclose the principles on which we should proceed. Even now, the minds of the most enlightened are scarcely prepared to begin to think rationally respecting it. The circumstances of the times, however, require that a substantial advance should now be made in this part of the economy of human life.

Before any rational plan can be devised for the proper training and education of children, it should be distinctly known what capabilities and qualities infants and children possess, or, in fact, what they really are by nature.

If this knowledge is to be attained, as all human knowledge has been acquired, through the evidence of our senses, then is it evident that infants receive from a source and power over which they have no control, all the natural qualities they possess, and that from birth they are naturally subjected to impressions derived from the circumstances around them; which impressions, combined with their natural qualities (whatever fanciful speculative men may say to the contrary), do truly determine the character of the individual through every period of life.

The knowledge thus acquired will give to men the same kind of control over the combination of the natural powers and faculties of infants, as they now possess over the formation of animals; and although, from the nature of the subject, it must be slow in its progress and limited in extent, yet the time is not perhaps far distant when it may be applied to an important rational purpose, that is, to improve the breed of men, more than men have yet improved the breed of domestic animals.

But, whatever knowledge may be attained to enable man to improve the breed of his progeny at birth, facts exist in endless profusion to prove to every mind capable of reflection, that men may now possess a most extensive control over those circumstances which affect the infant after birth; and that, as far as such circumstances can influence the human character, the day has arrived when the existing generation may so far control them, that the rising generations may become in character, without any individual exceptions, whatever men can now desire them to be, that is not contrary to human nature.

It is with reference to this important consideration that your Reporter, in the forming of these new arrangements, has taken so much pains to exclude every circumstance that could make an evil impression on the infants and children of this new generation.

And he is prepared, when others can follow him, so to combine new circumstances, that real vice, or that conduct which creates evil and misery in society, shall be utterly unknown in these villages, to whatever number they may extend.

Proceeding on these principles, your Reporter recommends arrangements by which the children shall be trained together as though they were literally all of one family.

For this purpose two schools will be required within the interior of the square, with spacious play and exercise grounds.

The schools may be conveniently placed in the line of buildings to be erected across the centre of the parallelograms, in connexion with the church and places of worship.

The first school will be for the infants from two to six years of age. The second for children from six to twelve.

It may be stated, without fear of contradiction from any party who is master of the subject, that the whole success of these arrangements will depend upon the manner in which the infants and children shall be trained and educated in these schools. Men are, and ever will be, what they are and shall be made in infancy and childhood. The apparent exceptions to this law are the effects of the same causes, combined with subsequent impressions, arising from the new circumstances in which the individual showing these exceptions have been placed.

One of the most general sources of error and of evil to the world is the notion *that infants, children, and men, are agents governed by a will formed by themselves and fashioned after their own choice.*

It is, however, as evident as any fact can be made to man, that he does not possess the smallest control over the formation of any of his own faculties or powers, or over the peculiar and ever-varying manner in which those powers and faculties, physical and mental, are combined in each individual.

Such being the case, it follows that human nature up to this period has been misunderstood, vilified, and savagely ill-treated; and that, in consequence, the language and conduct of mankind respecting it form a compound of all that is inconsistent and incongruous and most injurious to themselves, from the greatest to the least. All at this moment suffer grievously in consequence of this fundamental error.

To those who possess any knowledge on this subject it is known, that 'man is the creature of circumstances,' and that he really is, at every moment of his existence, precisely what the circumstances in which he has been placed, combined with his natural qualities, make him.

Does it then, your Reporter would ask, exhibit any sign of real wisdom to train him as if he were a being who created himself, formed his individual will, and was the author of his own inclinations and propensities?

Surely if men ever become wise – if they ever acquire knowledge enough to know themselves and enjoy a happy existence, it must be from discovering that they are not subjects for praise or blame, reward or punishment; but are beings capable, by proper treatment, of receiving unlimited improvement and knowledge; and, in consequence, of experiencing such uninterrupted enjoyment through this life as will best prepare them for an after-existence.

This view of human nature rests upon facts which no one can disprove. Your

Reporter now challenges all those who, from imagined interest, or from the notions which they have been taught to suppose true, are disposed to question its solidity, to point out one of his deductions on this subject which does not immediately follow from a self-evident truth. He is satisfied that the united wisdom of old society will fail in the attempt.

Why, then, may your Reporter be permitted to ask, should any parties tenaciously defend these notions? Are they, although false, in any manner beneficial to man? Does any party, or does a single individual, derive any real advantage from them?

Could your Reporter devise the means effectually to dispel the impressions so powerfully made on the human mind through early life, by the locality of the circumstances of birth and education, he would be enabled thoroughly to convince those who now suppose themselves the chief gainers by the present popular belief on those points and the order of things which proceeds from such belief, that they are themselves *essential* sufferers in consequence, – that they are deceived and deceive others greatly to their own cost. Superior knowledge of the subject will one day convince all that every human being, of every rank or station in life, has suffered and is now suffering a useless and grievous yoke by reason of these fallacies of the imagination.

Your Reporter is well aware that for ages past the great mass of mankind have been so placed as to be compelled to believe that all derived incalculable benefits from them. Yet there is no truth more certain than that these same individuals might have been placed under circumstances which would have enabled them not only to discover the falsehood of these notions, but to see distinctly the innumerable positive evils which they alone have inflicted upon society. While these fallacies of the brain shall be taught and believed by any portion of mankind, *in them* charity and benevolence, in their true sense, can never exist. Such men have imbibed notions that must make them, whatever be their language, haters and opposers of those who contend for the truth in opposition to their errors; nor can men so taught bear to be told that they have been made the mere dupes of the most useless and mischievous fantasies. Their errors, having been generated by circumstances over which they had no control, and for which, consequently, they cannot be blameable, are to be removed only by other circumstances sufficiently powerful to counteract the effects of the former.

From what has been said it is obvious that to produce such a total change among men as the one now contemplated by your Reporter will require the arrangement of new circumstances, that, in each part, and in their entire combinations, shall be so consistent with the known laws of nature, that the most acute mind shall fail to discover the slightest deviation from them.

It is upon these grounds that your Reporter, in educating the rising generation within his influence, has long adopted principles different from those which are usually acted upon.

He considers all children as beings whose dispositions, habits, and sentiments are to be formed *for* them; that these can be well-formed only by excluding all notions of reward, punishment, and emulation; and that, if their characters are not such as they ought to be, the error proceeds from their instructors and the other circumstances which surround them. He knows that principles as certain as those upon which the science of mathematics is founded may be applied to the forming of any given general character, and that by the influence of other circumstances, not a few individuals only, but the whole population of the world, may in a few years be rendered a very far superior race of beings to any now upon the earth, or which has been made known to us by history.

The children in these new schools should be therefore trained systematically to acquire useful knowledge through the means of sensible signs, by which their powers of reflection and judgement may be habituated to draw accurate conclusions from the facts presented to them. This mode of instruction is founded in nature, and will supersede the present defective and tiresome system of book learning, which is ill-calculated to give either pleasure or instruction to the minds of children. When arrangements founded on these principles shall be judiciously formed and applied to practice, children will, with ease and delight to themselves, acquire more real knowledge in a day, than they have yet attained under the old system in many months. They will not only thus acquire valuable knowledge, but the best habits and dispositions will be at the same time imperceptibly created in every one; and they will be trained to fill every office and to perform every duty that the well-being of their associates and the establishments can require. It is only by education, rightly understood, that communities of men can ever be well governed, and by means of such education every object of human society will be attained with the least labour and the most satisfaction.

It is obvious that training and education must be viewed as intimately connected with the employments of the association. The latter, indeed, will form an essential part of education under these arrangements. Each association, generally speaking, should create for itself a full supply of the usual necessaries, conveniences, and comforts of life.

The dwelling-houses and domestic arrangements being placed as near the centre of the land to be cultivated as circumstances will permit, it is concluded that the most convenient situation for the gardens will be adjoining the houses on the outside of the square; that these should be bounded by the principal roads; and that beyond them, at a sufficient distance to be covered by a plantation, should be placed the workshops and manufactory.

All will take their turn at *some one or more* of the occupations in this department, aided by every improvement that science can afford, alternately with employment in agriculture and gardening.

It has been a popular opinion to recommend a minute division of labour and a division of interests. It will presently appear, however, that this minute division of labour and division of interests are only other terms for poverty, ignorance, waste of every kind, universal opposition throughout society, crime, misery, and great bodily and mental imbecility.

To avoid these evils, which, while they continue, must keep mankind in a most degraded state, each child will receive a general education, early in life, that will fit him for the proper purposes of society, make him the most useful to it, and the most capable of enjoying it.

Before he is twelve years old he may with ease be trained to acquire a correct view of the outline of all the knowledge which men have yet attained.

By this means he will early learn what he is in relation to past ages, to the period in which he lives, to the circumstances in which he is placed, to the individuals around him, and to future events. *He will then only have any pretensions to the name of a rational being.*

His physical powers may be equally enlarged, in a manner as beneficial to himself as to those around him. As his strength increases he will be initiated in the practice of all the leading operations of his community, by which his services, at all times and under all circumstances, will afford a great gain to society beyond the expense of his subsistence; while at the same time he will be in the continual possession of more substantial comforts and real enjoyments than have ever yet appertained to any class in society.

The new wealth which one individual, by comparatively light and always healthy employment, may create under the arrangements now proposed, is indeed incalculable. They would give him giant powers compared with those which the working class or any other now possesses. There would at once be an end of all mere animal machines, who could only follow a plough, or turn a sod, of make some insignificant part of some insignificant manufacture or frivolous article which society could better spare than possess. Instead of the unhealthy pointer of a pin, – header of a nail, – piecer of a thread – or clodhopper,[5] senselessly gazing at the soil around him, without understanding or rational reflection, there would spring up a working class full of activity and useful knowledge, with habits, information, manners, and dispositions, that would place the lowest in the scale many degrees above the best of any class which has yet been formed by the circumstances of past or present society.

Such are a few only of the advantages which a rational mode of training and education, combined with the other parts of this system, would give to all the individuals within the action of its influence.

## HERBERT SPENCER, 'ART IV. – THE SOCIAL ORGANISM' (1860)

Although he is little read today, Herbert Spencer (1820–1903) was the dominant writer on social theory in Britain in the Victorian period. Together with the French social theorist, Auguste Comte, Spencer is credited by historians with founding sociology; indeed it was on his death that the British Sociological Society was founded at the London School of Economics. The enormous range of his influence is difficult to appreciate; he wrote scholarly treatises on philosophy, biology and sociology, numerous essays and reviews, as well as popular books designed to bring his ideas to the attention of a general audience. His first major work was *Social Statics* (1851); it was followed by the ambitious *System of Synthetic Philosophy* which grew out of Spencer's belief in the theoretical and methodological unity of all science. It comprised five works: *The Principles of Psychology* (1855), *First Principles* (1862), *The Principles of Biology* (1864–7), *The Principles of Sociology* (1876–96) and *The Principles of Ethics* (1892). Drawing on examples from all areas of knowledge – from linguistics to chemistry and physics – Spencer attempted to demonstrate the universality of what he saw as a basic evolutionary process of increasing differentiation (or specialisation of functions) followed by integration (that is, the mutual interdependence and co-ordination of those functions). Spencer also produced *Education* (1861), *The Man Versus the State* (1884) and several collections of essays, as well as classifying and arranging the multi-volume *Descriptive Sociology* – a series of studies of different societies around the world commissioned from a variety of scholars. After his death, responsibility for the series was taken over by the Herbert Spencer Trustees, and volumes continued to be produced up until the early 1930s.

*From* Herbert Spencer, 'Art IV. – The Social Organism', *Westminster Review*, XVII (January 1860), pp. 90–121[1]

*Art IV – The Social Organism*[2]

Sir James Macintosh[3] got great credit for the saying, that 'constitutions are not made, but grow.' In our day the most significant thing about this saying is, that it was ever thought so significant. As from the surprise displayed by a man at some familiar fact you may judge of his general culture; so from the admiration which an age accords a new thought, its average degree of enlightenment may be safely inferred. That this apophthegm of Macintosh should have been quoted and requoted as it has, shows how profound has been the ignorance of social science – how a small ray of truth has seemed brilliant, as a distant rushlight looks like a star in the surrounding darkness.

Such a conception could not indeed fail to be startling when let fall in the midst of a system of thought to which it was utterly alien. Universally in Macintosh's day, as by an immense majority in our own day, all things were explained on the hypothesis of manufacture, rather than that of growth. It was held that the planets were severally projected round the sun from the Creator's hand, with exactly the velocity required to balance the sun's attraction. The formation of the earth, the separation of sea from land, the production of animals, were mechanical works from which God rested as a labourer rests. Man was supposed to be moulded after a manner somewhat akin to that in which a modeller makes a clay figure. And of course, in harmony with such ideas, societies were tacitly assumed to be arranged thus or thus by direct interposition of Providence; or by the regulations of law-makers; or by both.

Yet that societies are not artificially put together, is a truth so manifest, that it seems wonderful men should have ever overlooked it. Perhaps nothing more clearly shows the small value of historical studies as they have been commonly pursued. You need but to look at the changes going on around, or observe social organization in its leading peculiarities, to see that these are neither supernatural, nor are determined by the wills of individual men, as by implication historians commonly teach; but are consequent on general natural causes. The one case of the division of labour suffices to show this. It has not been by the command of any ruler that some men have become manufacturers, while others have remained cultivators of the soil. In Lancashire, millions have devoted themselves to the making of cotton fabrics; in Yorkshire, perhaps another million live by producing woollens; and the pottery of Staffordshire, the cutlery of Sheffield, the hardware of Birmingham, severally occupy their hundreds of thousands. These are large facts in the structure of English society; but we can ascribe them neither to miracle, nor to legislation. It is not by 'the hero as king,' any more than by 'collective wisdom,' that men have been segregated into producers, wholesale distributors, and retail distributors. The whole of our industrial organization, from its most conspicuous features down to its minutest details, has become what it is, not only without legislative guidance, but, to a considerable extent, in spite of legislative hindrances. It has arisen under the pressure of human wants and activities. While each citizen has been pursuing his individual welfare, and none taking thought about division of labour, or indeed conscious of the need for it, division of labour has yet been ever becoming more complete. It has been doing this slowly and silently; scarcely any having observed it until quite modern times. By steps so small, that year after year the industrial arrangements have seemed to men just what they were before – by changes as insensible as those through which a seed passes into a tree; society has become the complex body of mutually dependent workers which we now see. And this economic organization, mark, is the all-essential organization. Through the combination thus spontaneously evolved it is, that every citizen is supplied with daily necessaries, at the same time that he yields some product or aid to others. That we are severally alive to-day, we owe to the regular working of this combination during the past week; and could it be suddenly abolished, a great proportion of us would be dead before another week was ended. If these most conspicuous and vital arrangements of our social structure have arisen without the devising of any one, but through the individual efforts of citizens severally to satisfy their own wants, we may be tolerably certain that all the other less important social arrangements have similarly arisen.

'But surely,' it will be said, 'the social changes directly produced by law cannot be classed as spontaneous growths. When parliaments or kings dictate this or that thing to be done, and appoint officials to do it, the process is clearly artificial; and society to this extent becomes a manufacture rather than a growth.' No, not even these changes are exceptions, if they be real and permanent changes. The true sources of such changes lie deeper than the acts of legislators. To take first the simplest instance: – we all know that the enactments of representative governments ultimately depend on the national will: they may for a time be out of harmony with it, but eventually they have to conform to it. And to say that the national will is that which finally determines them, is to say that they result from the average of individual desires; or in other words – from the average of individual natures. A law so initiated, therefore, really grows out of the popular character. In the case of a Government representing but a limited class, the same thing still holds, though not so manifestly. For the very existence of a supreme class monopolizing all power, is itself due to certain sentiments in the commonality. But for the feeling of loyalty on the part of retainers, a feudal system could not exist. We see in the protest of the Highlanders[4] against the abolition of heritable jurisdictions, that they preferred that kind of local rule. And if thus to the popular nature must be ascribed the growth of an irresponsible ruling class; then to the popular nature must be ascribed the social arrangements which that class creates in the pursuit of its own ends. Even where the Government is despotic, the doctrine still holds. It is not simply that the existence of such a form of government is consequent on the character of the people, and that, as we have abundant proof, other forms suddenly created will not act, but rapidly retrograde to the old form; but it is that such regulations as a despot makes, if really operative, are so because of their fitness to the social state. Not only are his acts very much swayed by general opinion – by precedent, by the feeling of his nobles, his priesthood, his army – and are so in part results of the national character; but when they are out of harmony with the national character, they are soon practically abrogated. The utter failure of Cromwell permanently to establish a new social condition, and the rapid revival of suppressed institutions and practices after his death, show how powerless is a monarch to change the type of the society he governs. He may disturb, he may retard, or he may aid the natural process of organization; but the general course of this process is beyond his control.[5]

85

Thus that which is so obviously true of the industrial structure of society, is true of its whole structure. The fact that 'constitutions are not made but grow,' is simply a fragment of the much larger fact, that under all its aspects and through all its ramifications, society is a growth and not a manufacture.

A dim perception that there exists some analogy between the body politic and a living individual body, was early reached, and from time to time re-appeared in literature. But this perception was necessarily vague and more or less fanciful. In the absence of physiological science, and especially of those comprehensive generalizations which it has but recently reached, it was impossible to discern the real parallelisms.

The central idea of Plato's model Republic,[6] is the correspondence between the parts of a society and the faculties of the human mind. Classifying these faculties under the heads of Reason, Will, and Passion, he classifies the members of his ideal society under what he regards as the three analogous heads: – councillors, who are to exercise government; military or executive, who are to fulfil their behests; and the commonality bent on gain and selfish gratification. In other words, the ruler, the warrior, and the craftsman, are, according to him, the analogues of our reflective, volitional, and emotional powers. Now even were there truth in the implied assumption of a parallelism between the structure of a society and that of a man, this classification would be indefensible. It might more truly be contended that, as the military power obeys the commands of the Government, it is the Government which answers to the Will; while the military power is simply an agency set in motion by it. Or, again, it might be contended that whereas the Will is a product of predominant desires, to which the reason serves merely as an eye, it is the craftsmen, who, according to the alleged analogy, ought to be the moving power of the warriors.

Hobbes[7] sought to establish a still more definite parallelism; not, however, between a society and the human mind, but between a society and the human body. In the introduction to the work in which he develops this conception, he says –

'For by art is created that great LEVIATHAN called a COMMONWEALTH, or STATE, in Latin CIVITAS, which is but an artificial man; though of greater stature and strength than the natural, for whose protection and defence it was intended, and in which the *sovereignty* is an artificial *soul*, as giving life and motion to the whole body; the *magistrates* and other *officers* of judicature and execution artificial *joints*; *reward* and *punishment*, by which, fastened to the seat of the sovereignty, every joint and member is moved to perform his duty, are the *nerves*, that do the same in the body natural; the *wealth* and *riches* of all the particular members are the *strength*; *salus populi*, the *people's safety*, its *business*; *counsellors*, by whom all things needful for it to know are suggested unto it, are the *memory*; *equity* and *laws* an artificial *reason* and *will*; *concord*, *health*; *sedition*, *sickness*; *civil war*, *death*.'

86

And Hobbes carries this comparison so far as actually to give a drawing of the Leviathan – a vast human-shaped figure, whose body and limbs are made up of multitudes of men. Just noting that these different analogies asserted by Plato and Hobbes, serve to cancel each other (being, as they are, so completely at variance), we may say that on the whole those of Hobbes are the more plausible. But they are full of inconsistencies. If the sovereignty is the *soul* of the body politic, how can it be that magistrates, who are a kind of deputy sovereigns, should be comparable to *joints*? Or, again, how can the three mental functions, memory, reason, and will, be severally analogous, the first to counsellors, who are a class of public officers; and the other two to equity and laws, which are not classes of officers, but abstractions? Or, once more, if magistrates are the artificial joints of society, how can reward and punishment be its nerves? Its nerves must surely be some class of persons. Reward and punishment must in societies, as in individuals, be *conditions* of the nerves, and not the nerves themselves.

But the errors of these comparisons made by Plato and Hobbes, lie much deeper than appears at a glance. In the first place, both thinkers assume that the organization of a society is comparable, not simply to the organization of a living body in general, but to the organization of the human body in particular. This is an assumption for which there is no warrant whatever. It is in no way implied by the evidence, and is simply one of those fancies which we commonly find mixed up with the truths of early speculation. Still more erroneous, however, are the two conceptions in this, that they both regard a society as an artificial structure. Plato's model republic – his ideal of a healthful body politic – is to be consciously put together by men; just as a watch might be; and he manifestly thinks of societies in general as originated in this manner. Still more specifically does Hobbes express this view. 'For by *art*,' he says, 'is created that great Leviathan called a COMMONWEALTH.' And he even goes so far as to compare the supposed social compact from which a society suddenly originates, to the creation of a man by the divine fiat. Thus they both fall into the extreme inconsistency of considering a community as similar in structure to a human being, and yet, as produced in the same way as an artificial mechanism – in nature, an organism; in history, a machine.

Notwithstanding errors, however, these speculations have considerable significance. That such analogies, however crudely conceived, should have arrested the attention, not only of Plato and Hobbes, but of many others, is a reason for suspecting that *some* analogy exists. The untenableness of the particular comparisons above instanced is no ground for denying an essential parallelism; for early ideas are usually but vague adumbrations of the truth. Lacking the great generalizations of biology, it was, as we have said, impossible to trace out the real relations of social organizations to organizations of another order. We propose here to show what are the analogies which modern science discloses to us.

Let us set out by succinctly stating the points of similarity and the points of difference. Societies agree with individual organisms in three conspicuous peculiarities: -

87

1. That commencing as small aggregations they insensibly augment in mass; some of them reaching eventually perhaps a hundred thousand times what they originally were.
2. That while at first so simple in structure as to be almost considered structureless, they assume, in the course of their growth, a continually increasing complexity of structure.
3. That though in their early undeveloped state there exists in them scarcely any mutual dependence of parts, these parts gradually acquire a mutual dependence, which becomes at last so great, that the activity and life of each part is made possible only by the activity and life of the rest.

These three parallelisms will appear the more significant the more we contemplate them. Observe that, while they are points in which societies agree with individual organisms, they are points in which all individual organisms agree with each other, and disagree with everything else. In the course of its existence, every plant and animal increases in mass, which, with the exception of crystals, can be said of no inorganic objects. The orderly progress from simplicity to complexity displayed by societies in common with every living body whatever, is a characteristic which substantially distinguishes living bodies from the inanimate bodies amid which they move. And that functional dependence of parts, which is scarcely more manifest in animals or plants than in societies, has no counterpart elsewhere. Moreover, it should be remarked, not only that societies and organisms are alike in these peculiarities, in which they are unlike all other things; but, further, that the highest societies, like the highest organisms, exhibit them in the greatest degree. Looking at the facts in their ensemble, we may observe that the lowest types of animals do not increase to anything like the size of the higher ones; and similarly we see that aboriginal societies are comparatively limited in their growths. In complexity, our large civilized nations as much exceed the primitive savage ones, as a vertebrate animal does a zoophyte.[8] And while in simple communities, as in simple creatures, the mutual dependence of parts is so slight, that subdivision or mutilation causes but little inconvenience; in complex communities as in complex creatures, you cannot remove or injure any considerable organ without producing great disturbance or death of the rest.

On the other hand, the leading differences between societies and individual organisms are these: -

1. That they have no specific external forms. This, however, is a point of contrast which loses much of its importance, when we remember that throughout the entire vegetal kingdom, as well as in some lower divisions of the animal kingdom, the forms are very indefinite, and are manifestly in part determined by surrounding physical circumstances, as the forms of societies are. If, too, it should eventually be shown, as we believe it will, that the form of every species of organism has resulted from the average play of the external forces to which it has been subject during its evolution as a

species; then, that the external forms of societies should depend, as they do, on surrounding conditions, will be a further point of continuity.

2. That whereas the living tissue whereof an individual organism consists, forms one continuous mass, the living elements which make up a society, do not form a continuous mass, but are more or less widely dispersed over some portion of the earth's surface. This, which at first sight appears to be a fundamental distinction, is one which yet to a great extent disappears when we contemplate all the facts. For, in the lower divisions of the animal and vegetal kingdoms, there are forms of organization much more nearly allied, in this respect, to the organization of a society, than might be supposed – forms in which the living units of which the mass is essentially composed, are dispersed through an inert substance, that can scarcely be called living in the full sense of the word. It is thus with some of the *Protococci*, and with the *Nostoceae*, which exist as cells, imbedded in a viscid matter. It is so with the *Thalassicollae* – bodies that are made up of differentiated parts, dispersed through an undifferentiated jelly.[9] And throughout considerable portions of their bodies, some of the *Acalephae*[10] exhibit more or less distinctly this type of structure. Indeed, it may be contended that this is the primitive form of all organization; seeing that, even in the highest creatures, as in ourselves, every tissue develops out of what physiologists call a nucleated blastema[11] – an unorganized though organizable substance, through which organic points are distributed. Now this is very much the case with a society. For we must remember that though the men who make up a society are more or less dispersed, as well as physically separate; yet that the surface over which they are dispersed is not one devoid of life, but is covered by life of a lower order which ministers to their life. The clothing of vegetation which covers the face of a country, makes possible the animal life in that country; and only through its animal and vegetal products can such a country support a human society. Hence the members of the body politic are not to be regarded as wholly separated by wide intervals of mere dead space; but as dispersed through a space occupied by life of a lower order. In our conception of a social organism, we must include all that lower organic existence on which human existence and therefore social existence depends. And when we do this, we see that the citizens who make up a community, may be considered as highly vitalized units surrounded by substances of lower vitality, from which they draw their nutriment; much as in the cases above instanced. Thus, when examined, this apparent distinction in great part disappears.

3. That while the ultimate living elements of an individual organism are mostly fixed in their relative positions, those of the social organism are capable of moving from place to place, seems a marked point of disagreement. But here, too, the disagreement is much less than would be supposed. For while citizens are locomotive in their private capacities, they are fixed in their public capacities. As farmers, manufacturers, or traders, men carry on

their businesses at the same spots, often throughout their whole lives; and if they go away for a time, they leave behind others to discharge their functions in their absence. Not only does each great centre of production, each manufacturing town or district, continue always in the same place; but many of the firms in such town or district are for generations carried on either by the descendants or successors of those who founded them. Just as in a living body, the individual cells that make up some important organ, severally perform their functions for a time and then disappear, leaving others to supply their vacant places; so in each part of a society, while the organ remains, the persons who compose it change. Thus, in social life, as in the life of an animal, the units as well as the larger agencies composed of them, are in the main stationary as respects the places where they discharge their duties and obtain their sustenance. So that the power of individual locomotion does not practically affect the analogy.[a]

4. That while in the body of an animal only a special tissue is endowed with feeling, in a society all the members are endowed with feeling, is the last and perhaps most important distinction. Even this distinction, however, is by no means a complete one. For in some lower divisions of the animal kingdom, characterized by the absence of a nervous system, such sensitiveness as exists is possessed by all parts. It is only in the more organized forms that feeling is monopolized by one particular class of the vital elements. Moreover, we must not forget that societies, too, are not without a certain differentiation of this kind. Though the units of a community are all sensitive, yet they are so in unequal degrees. The classes engaged in agriculture and laborious occupations in general, are far less susceptible, intellectually and emotionally, than the rest; and especially less so than the classes of highest mental culture. Still we have here a tolerably decided contrast between bodies politic and individual bodies. And it is one which we should keep constantly in view. For it reminds us that while in individual bodies the welfare of all other parts is rightly subservient to the welfare of the nervous system, whose pleasurable or painful activities make up the good or evil of life; in bodies politic the same thing does not hold good, or holds good to but a very slight extent. It is well that the lives of all parts of an animal should be merged in the life of the whole, because the whole has a corporate consciousness capable of happiness or misery. But it is not so with a society; since its living units do not and cannot lose individual consciousness; and since the community as a whole has no general or corporate consciousness distinct from those of its components. And this is an everlasting reason why the

---

a    To which let us add the significant fact, that in those communities which are more fully organized than our own, though on a lower type (for it is in the nature of low types to organize more
rapidly), the locomotion of citizens is much more restricted. They cannot move, even from their
own towns, without a permit, sometimes difficult to obtain.

welfare of citizens cannot rightly be sacrificed to some supposed benefit of the State; but why, on the other hand, the State must be regarded as existing solely for the benefit of citizens. The corporate life must here be subservient to the life of the parts, instead of the life of the parts being subservient to the corporate life.

Such, then, are the points of analogy and the points of difference. May we not say that the points of difference serve but to bring into clearer light the points of analogy. While comparison makes definite the obvious contrasts between organisms commonly so called, and the social organism, it shows that even these contrasts are not nearly so decided as was to be expected. The indefiniteness of form, the discontinuity of the parts, the mobility of the parts, and the universal sensitiveness, are not only peculiarities of the social organism which have to be stated with considerable qualifications; but they are peculiarities to which the inferior classes of animals present approximations. Thus we find but little to conflict with the all-important analogies. That societies slowly augment in mass; that they progress in complexity of structure; that at the same time their parts become more mutually dependent; and further, that the extent to which they display these peculiarities is proportionate to their vital activity; are traits that societies have in common with all organic bodies. And these traits in which they agree with all organic bodies and disagree with all other things – these traits which in truth constitute the very essence of organization, entirely subordinate the minor distinctions: such distinctions being scarcely greater than those which separate one half of the organic kingdom from the other. The *principles* of organization are the same; and the differences are simply differences of application.

Thus a general survey of the facts seems quite to justify the comparison of a society to a living body.

# THEORIES OF THE MARKET

Political economy, marginal utility theory, socialist economics

### DAVID RICARDO, *ON THE PRINCIPLES OF POLITICAL ECONOMY, AND TAXATION* (1817; 1821)

David Ricardo (1772–1823) was the main disseminator of the ideas of political economy in the early nineteenth century. His major work, *On the Principles of Political Economy, and Taxation*, grew out of his earlier *Essay on the Influence of a Low Price of Corn on the Profits of Stock* (1815). Initially Ricardo intended simply to revise and enlarge the *Essay*, but was persuaded by his friend James Mill to undertake a much more comprehensive project, a detailed exposition of his differences with Adam Smith and Thomas Malthus over the issues of rent, profit, wages and value. After much doubt and hesitation on Ricardo's behalf, *On the Principles of Political Economy, and Taxation* finally appeared in 1817, and through the work of enthusiastic disciples such as Mill, J. R. McCulloch and Robert Torrens, Ricardian theory came to dominate economic thought for the next forty years or so. Following the *Principles*, Ricardo's main preoccupation was with compiling extensive 'Notes' on Malthus's *Principles of Political Economy* (1820). Although unpublished, some elements of the 'Notes' were incorporated into his revisions to the third edition of *On the Principles of Political Economy, and Taxation*. Ricardo also published several pamphlets and papers on various economic issues. In 1819 he took up a seat in the House of Commons where he remained an active member until his death.

## From David Ricardo, *On the Principles of Political Economy, and Taxation* (London: John Murray, 1821)[1]

From *Chapter I: On Value*

### Section I

*The value of a commodity, or the quantity of any other commodity for which it will exchange, depends on the relative quantity of labour which is necessary for its production, and not on the greater or less compensation which is paid for that labour.*

It has been observed by Adam Smith, that 'the word Value has two different meanings, and sometimes expresses the utility of some particular object, and sometimes the power of purchasing other goods which the possession of that object conveys. The one may be called *value in use*; the other *value in exchange*. The things,' he continues, 'which have the greatest value in use, have frequently little or no value in exchange; and, on the contrary, those which have the greatest value in exchange, have little or no value in use.'[2] Water and air are abundantly useful; they are indeed indispensable to existence, yet, under ordinary circumstances, nothing can be obtained in exchange for them. Gold, on the contrary, though of little use compared with air or water, will exchange for a great quantity of other goods.

Utility then is not the measure of exchangeable value, although it is absolutely essential to it. If a commodity were in no way useful, – in other words, if it could in no way contribute to our gratification, – it would be destitute of exchangeable value, however scarce it might be, or whatever quantity of labour might be necessary to procure it.

Possessing utility, commodities derive their exchangeable value from two sources: from their scarcity, and from the quantity of labour required to obtain them.

There are some commodities, the value of which is determined by their scarcity alone. No labour can increase the quantity of such goods, and therefore their value cannot be lowered by an increased supply. Some rare statues and pictures, scarce books and coins, wines of a peculiar quality, which can be made only from grapes grown on a particular soil, of which there is a very limited quantity, are all of this description. Their value is wholly independent of the quantity of labour originally necessary to produce them, and varies with the varying wealth and inclinations of those who are desirous to possess them.

These commodities, however, form a very small part of the mass of commodities daily exchanged in the market. By far the greatest part of those goods which are the objects of desire, are procured by labour; and they may be multiplied, not in one country alone, but in many, almost without any assignable limit, if we are disposed to bestow the labour necessary to obtain them.

In speaking then of commodities, of their exchangeable value, and of the laws which regulate their relative prices, we mean always such commodities only

94

as can be increased in quantity by the exertion of human industry, and on the production of which competition operates without restraint.

In the early stages of society, the exchangeable value of these commodities, or the rule which determines how much of one shall be given in exchange for another, depends almost exclusively on the comparative quantity of labour expended on each.

'The real price of every thing,' says Adam Smith, 'what every thing really costs to the man who wants to acquire it, is the toil and trouble of acquiring it. What every thing is really worth to the man who has acquired it, and who wants to dispose of it, or exchange it for something else, is the toil and trouble which it can save to himself, and which it can impose upon other people.' 'Labour was the first price – the original purchase-money that was paid for all things.' Again, 'in that early and rude state of society, which precedes both the accumulation of stock and the appropriation of land, the proportion between the quantities of labour necessary for acquiring different objects seems to be the only circumstance which can afford any rule for exchanging them for one another. If among a nation of hunters, for example, it usually cost twice the labour to kill a beaver which it does to kill a deer, one beaver should naturally exchange for, or be worth two deer. It is natural that what is usually the produce of two days', or two hours' labour, should be worth double of what is usually the produce of one day's, or one hour's labour.'[a]

That this is really the foundation of the exchangeable value of all things, excepting those which cannot be increased by human industry, is a doctrine of the utmost importance in political economy; for from no source do so many errors, and so much difference of opinion in that science proceed, as from the vague ideas which are attached to the word value.

If the quantity of labour realized in commodities, regulate their exchangeable value, every increase of the quantity of labour must augment the value of that commodity on which it is exercised, as every diminution must lower it.

Adam Smith, who so accurately defined the original source of exchangeable value, and who was bound in consistency to maintain, that all things became more or less valuable in proportion as more or less labour was bestowed on their production, has himself erected another standard measure of value, and speaks of things being more or less valuable, in proportion as they will exchange for more or less of this standard measure. Sometimes he speaks of corn, at other times of labour, as a standard measure; not the quantity of labour bestowed on the production of any object, but the quantity which it can command in the market: as if these were two equivalent expressions, and as if because a man's labour had become doubly efficient, and he could therefore produce twice the quantity of a commodity, he would necessarily receive twice the former quantity in exchange for it.

a   Book i. chap. 5 [i.e., of Adam Smith's *Wealth of Nations*].

95

If this indeed were true, if the reward of the labourer were always in proportion to what he produced, the quantity of labour bestowed on a commodity, and the quantity of labour which that commodity would purchase, would be equal, and either might accurately measure the variations of other things: but they are not equal; the first is under many circumstances an invariable standard, indicating correctly the variations of other things; the latter is subject to as many fluctuations as the commodities compared with it. Adam Smith, after most ably showing the insufficiency of a variable medium, such as gold and silver, for the purpose of determining the varying value of other things, has himself, by fixing on corn or labour, chosen a medium no less variable.

Gold and silver are no doubt subject to fluctuations, from the discovery of new and more abundant mines; but such discoveries are rare, and their effects, though powerful, are limited to periods of comparatively short duration. They are subject also to fluctuation, from improvements in the skill and machinery with which the minds may be worked; as in consequence of such improvements, a greater quantity may be obtained with the same labour. They are further subject to fluctuation from the decreasing produce of the mines, after they have yielded a supply to the world, for a succession of ages. But from which of these sources of fluctuation is corn exempted? Does not that also vary, on one hand, from improvements in agriculture, from improved machinery and implements used in husbandry, as well as from the discovery of new tracts of fertile land, which in other countries may be taken into cultivation, and which will affect the value of corn in every market where importation is free? Is it not on the other hand subject to be enhanced in value from prohibitions of importation, from increasing population and wealth, and the greater difficulty of obtaining the increased supplies, on account of the additional quantity of labour which the cultivation of inferior lands requires? Is not the value of labour equally variable; being not only affected, as all other things are, by the proportion between the supply and demand, which uniformly varies with every change in the condition of the community, but also by the varying price of food and other necessaries, on which the wages of labour are expended?

In the same country double the quantity of labour may be required to produce a given quantity of food and necessaries at one time, that may be necessary at another, and a distant time; yet the labourer's reward may possibly be very little diminished. If the labourer's wages at the former period, were a certain quantity of food and necessaries, he probably could not have subsisted if that quantity had been reduced. Food and necessaries in this case will have risen 100 per cent. if estimated by the *quantity* of labour necessary to their production, while they will scarcely have increased in value, if measured by the quantity of labour for which they will *exchange*.

The same remark may be made respecting two or more countries. In America and Poland, on the land last taken into cultivation, a year's labour of any given number of men, will produce much more corn than on land similarly circumstanced in England. Now, supposing all other necessaries to be equally cheap in those three countries, would it not be a great mistake to conclude, that the quantity of corn awarded to the labourer, would in each country be in proportion to the facility of production?

If the shoes and clothing of the labourer, could, by improvements in machinery, be produced by one fourth of the labour now necessary to their production, they would probably fall 75 per cent.; but so far is it from being true, that the labourer would thereby be enabled permanently to consume four coats, or four pair of shoes, instead of one, that it is probable his wages would in no long time be adjusted by the effects of competition, and the stimulus to population, to the new value of the necessaries on which they were expended. If these improvements extended to all the objects of the labourer's consumption, we should find him probably at the end of a very few years, in possession of only a small, if any, addition to his enjoyments, although the exchangeable value of those commodities, compared with any other commodity, in the manufacture of which no such improvement were made, had sustained a very considerable reduction; and though they were the produce of a very considerably diminished quantity of labour.

It cannot then be correct, to say with Adam Smith, 'that as labour may sometimes *purchase* a greater, and sometimes a smaller quantity of goods, it is their value which varies, not that of the labour which purchases them;' and therefore, 'that labour *alone never varying in its own value*, is alone the ultimate and real standard by which the value of all commodities can at all times and places be estimated and compared;'[3] – but it is correct to say, as Adam Smith had previously said, 'that the proportion between the quantities of labour necessary for acquiring different objects seems to be the only circumstance which can afford any rule for exchanging them for one another;'[4] or in other words, that it is the comparative quantity of commodities, which labour will produce, that determines their present or past relative value, and not the comparative quantities of commodities, which are given to the labourer in exchange for his labour.

Two commodities vary in relative value, and we wish to know in which the variation has really taken place. If we compare the present value of one, with shoes, stockings, hats, iron, sugar, and all other commodities, we find that it will exchange for precisely the same quantity of all these things as before. If we compare the other with the same commodities, we find it has varied with respect to them all: we may then with great probability infer that the variation has been in this commodity, and not in the commodities with which we have compared it. If on examining still more particularly into all the circumstances connected with the production of these various commodities, we find that precisely the same quantity of labour and capital are necessary to the production of the shoes, stockings, hats, iron, sugar, &c.; but that the same quantity as before is not necessary to produce the single commodity whose relative value is altered, probability is changed into certainty, and we are sure that the variation is in the single commodity: we then discover also the cause of its variation.

If I found that an ounce of gold would exchange for a less quantity of all the commodities above enumerated, and many others; and if, moreover, I found that by the discovery of a new and more fertile mine, or by the employment of machinery to great advantage, a given quantity of gold could be obtained with a less quantity of labour, I should be justified in saying that the cause of the alteration in the value of gold relatively to other commodities, was the greater facility of its production, or the smaller quantity of labour necessary to obtain it. In like manner, if labour fell very considerably in value, relatively to all other things, and if I found that its fall was in consequence of an abundant supply, encouraged by the great facility with which corn, and the other necessaries of the labourer, were produced, it would, I apprehend, be correct for me to say that corn and necessaries had fallen in value in consequence of less quantity of labour being necessary to produce them, and that this facility of providing for the support of the labourer had been followed by a fall in the value of labour. No, say Adam Smith and Mr Malthus,[5] in the case of the gold you were correct in calling its variation a fall of its value, because corn and labour had not then varied; and as gold would command a less quantity of them, as well as of all other things, than before, it was correct to say that all things had remained stationary, and that gold only had varied; but when corn and labour fall, things which we have selected to be our standard measure of value, notwithstanding all the variations to which we acknowledge they are subject, it would be highly improper to say so; the correct language will be to say, that corn and labour have remained stationary, and all other things have risen in value.

Now it is against this language that I protest. I find that precisely, as in the case of the gold, the cause of the variation between corn and other things, is the smaller quantity of labour necessary to produce it, and therefore, by all just reasoning, I am bound to call the variation of corn and labour a fall in their value, and not a rise in the value of the things with which they are compared. If I have to hire a labourer for a week, and instead of ten shillings I pay him eight, no variation having taken place in the value of money, the labourer can probably obtain more food and necessaries, with his eight shillings, than he before obtained for ten: but this is owing, not to a rise in the real value of his wages, as stated by Adam Smith, and more recently by Mr Malthus, but to a fall in the value of the things on which his wages are expended, things perfectly distinct; and yet for calling this a fall in the real value of wages, I am told that I adopt new and unusual language, not reconcileable with the true principles of the science. To me it appears that the unusual and, indeed, inconsistent language, is that used by my opponents.

Suppose a labourer to be paid a bushel of corn for a week's work, when the price of corn is 80s. per quarter, and that he is paid a bushel and a quarter when the price falls to 40s. Suppose, too, that he consumes half a bushel of corn a-week in his own family, and exchanges the remainder for other things, such as fuel, soap, candles, tea, sugar, salt, &c. &c.; if the three-fourths of a bushel which will remain to him, in one case, cannot procure him as much of the above commodities as half a bushel did in the other, which it will not, will labour have risen or fallen in value? Risen, Adam Smith must say, because his standard is corn, and the labourer receives more corn for a week's labour. Fallen, must the same Adam Smith say, 'because the value of a thing depends on the power of purchasing other goods which the possession of that object conveys,'[6] and labour has a less power of purchasing such other goods.

## Section II

*Labour of different qualities differently rewarded. This no cause of variation in the relative value of commodities.*

In speaking, however, of labour, as being the foundation of all value, and the relative quantity of labour as almost exclusively determining the relative value of commodities, I must not be supposed to be inattentive to the different qualities of labour, and the difficulty of comparing an hour's or a day's labour, in one employment, with the same duration of labour in another. The estimation in which different qualities of labour are held, comes soon to be adjusted in the market with sufficient precision for all practical purposes, and depends much on the comparative skill of the labourer, and intensity of the labour performed. The scale, when once formed, is liable to little variation. If a day's labour of a working jeweller be more valuable than a day's labour of a common labourer, it has long ago been adjusted, and placed in its proper position in the scale of value.[b]

In comparing therefore the value of the same commodity, at different periods of time, the consideration of the comparative skill and intensity of labour, required for that particular commodity, needs scarcely to be attended to, as it operates equally at both periods. One description of labour at one time is compared with the same description of labour at another; if a tenth, a fifth, or a fourth, has been added or taken away, an effect proportioned to the cause will be produced on the relative value of the commodity.

---

b   'But though labour be the real measure of the exchangeable value of all commodities, it is not that by which their value is commonly estimated. It is often difficult to ascertain the proportion between two different quantities of labour. The time spent in two different sorts of work will not always alone determine this proportion. The different degrees of hardship endured, and of ingenuity exercised, must likewise be taken into account. There may be more labour in an hour's hard work, than in two hours' easy business; or, in an hour's application to a trade which it costs ten years' labour to learn, than in a month's industry at an ordinary and obvious employment. But it is not easy to find any accurate measure, either of hardship or ingenuity. In exchanging, indeed, the different productions of different sorts of labour for one another, some allowance is commonly made for both. It is adjusted, however, not by any accurate measure, but by the higgling and bargaining of the market, according to that sort of rough equality, which though not exact, is sufficient for carrying on the business of common life.' – *Wealth of Nations*, book i. chap. 10. [Sraffa notes that the passage in fact occurs in Book I, chapter 5, although Book I, chapter 10 also contains a discussion of the same subject.]

If a piece of cloth be now of the value of two pieces of linen, and if, in ten years hence, the ordinary value of a piece of cloth should be four pieces of linen, we may safely conclude, that either more labour is required to make the cloth, or less to make the linen, or that both causes have operated.

As the inquiry to which I wish to draw the reader's attention, relates to the effect of the variations in the relative value of commodities, and not in their absolute value, it will be of little importance to examine into the comparative degree of estimation in which the different kinds of human labour are held. We may fairly conclude, that whatever inequality there might originally have been in them, whatever the ingenuity, skill, or time necessary for the acquirement of one species of manual dexterity more than another, it continues nearly the same from one generation to another; or at least, that the variation is very inconsiderable from year to year, and therefore, can have little effect, for short periods, on the relative value of commodities.

'The proportion between the different rates both of wages and profit in the different employments of labour and stock, seems not to be much affected, as has already been observed, by the riches or poverty, the advancing, stationary, or declining state of the society. Such revolutions in the public welfare, though they affect the general rates both of wages and profit, must in the end affect them equally in all different employments. The proportion between them therefore must remain the same, and cannot well be altered, at least for any considerable time, by any such revolutions.'[c]

### From *Chapter V: On Wages*

Labour, like all other things which are purchased and sold, and which may be increased or diminished in quantity, has its natural and its market price. The natural price of labour is that price which is necessary to enable the labourers, one with another, to subsist and to perpetuate their race, without either increase of diminution.

The power of the labourer to support himself, and the family which may be necessary to keep up the number of labourers, does not depend on the quantity of money which he may receive for wages, but on the quantity of food, necessaries, and conveniences become essential to him from habit, which that money will purchase. The natural price of labour, therefore, depends on the price of the food, necessaries, and conveniences required for the support of the labourer and his family. With a rise in the price of food and necessaries, the natural price of labour will rise; with the fall in their price, the natural price of labour will fall.

With the progress of society the natural price of labour has always a tendency to rise, because one of the principal commodities by which its natural price is regulated, has a tendency to become dearer, from the greater difficulty of

---

c    *Wealth of Nations*, book i. chap. 10.

producing it. As, however, the improvements in agriculture, the discovery of new markets, whence provisions may be imported, may for a time counteract the tendency to a rise in the price of necessaries, and may even occasion their natural price to fall, so will the same causes produce the correspondent effects on the natural price of labour.

The natural price of all commodities, excepting raw produce and labour, has a tendency to fall, in the progress of wealth and population; for though, on one hand, they are enhanced in real value, from the rise in the natural price of the raw material of which they are made, this is more than counterbalanced by the improvements in machinery, by the better division and distribution of labour, and by the increasing skill, both in science and art, of the producers.

The market price of labour is the price which is really paid for it, from the natural operation of the proportion of the supply to the demand; labour is dear when it is scarce, and cheap when it is plentiful. However much the market price of labour may deviate from its natural price, it has, like commodities, a tendency to conform to it.

It is when the market price of labour exceeds its natural price, that the condition of the labourer is flourishing and happy, that he has it in his power to command a greater proportion of the necessaries and enjoyments of life, and therefore to rear a healthy and numerous family. When, however, by the encouragement which high wages give to the increase of population, the number of labourers is increased, wages again fall to their natural price, and indeed from a re-action sometimes fall below it.

When the market price of labour is below its natural price, the condition of the labourers is most wretched: then poverty deprives them of those comforts which custom renders absolute necessaries. It is only after their privations have reduced their number, or the demand for labour has increased, that the market price of labour will rise to its natural price, and that the labourer will have the moderate comforts which the natural rate of wages will afford.

Notwithstanding the tendency of wages to conform to their natural rate, their market rate may, in an improving society, for an indefinite period, be constantly above it; for no sooner may the impulse, which an increased capital gives to a new demand for labour be obeyed, than another increase of capital may produce the same effect; and thus, if the increase of capital be gradual and constant, the demand for labour may give a continued stimulus to an increase of people.

Capital is that part of the wealth of a country which is employed in production, and consists of food, clothing, tools, raw materials, machinery, &c. necessary to give effect to labour.

Capital may increase in quantity at the same time that its value rises. An addition may be made to the food and clothing of a country, at the same time that more labour may be required to produce the additional quantity than before; in that case not only the quantity, but the value of capital will rise.

Or capital may increase without its value increasing, and even while its value is actually diminishing; not only may an addition be made to the food and clothing of a country, but the addition may be made by the aid of machinery, without any increase, and even without an absolute diminution in the proportional quantity of labour required to produce them. The quantity of capital may increase, while neither the whole together, nor any part of it singly, will have a greater value than before, but may actually have a less.

In the first case, the natural price of labour, which always depends on the price of food, clothing, and other necessaries, will rise; in the second, it will remain stationary, or fall; but in both cases the market rate of wages will rise, for in proportion to the increase of capital will be the increase in the demand for labour; in proportion to the work to be done will be the demand for those who are to do it.

In both cases too the market price of labour will rise above its natural price; and in both cases it will have a tendency to conform to its natural price, but in the first case this agreement will be most speedily effected. The situation of the labourer will be improved, but not much improved; for the increased price of food and necessaries will absorb a large portion of his increased wages; consequently a small supply of labour, or a trifling increase in the population, will soon reduce the market price to the then increased natural price of labour.

In the second case, the condition of the labourer will be very greatly improved; he will receive increased money wages, without having to pay any increased price, and perhaps even a diminished price for the commodities which he and his family consume; and it will not be till after a great addition has been made to the population, that the market price of labour will again sink to its then low and reduced natural price.

Thus, then, with every improvement of society, with every increase in its capital, the market wages of labour will rise; but the permanence of their rise will depend on the question, whether the natural price of labour has also risen; and this again will depend on the rise in the natural price of those necessaries on which the wages of labour are expended.

It is not to be understood that the natural price of labour, estimated even in food or necessaries, is absolutely fixed and constant. It varies at different times in the same country, and very materially differs in different countries.[d] It essentially depends on the habits and customs of the people. An English labourer would consider his wages under their natural rate, and too scanty to support a family, if

d   'The shelter and the clothing which are indispensable in one country may be no way necessary in another; and a labourer in Hindostan may continue to work with perfect vigour, though receiving, as his natural wages, only such a supply of covering as would be insufficient to preserve a labourer in Russia from perishing. Even in countries situated in the same climate, different habits of living will often occasion variations in the natural price of labour, as considerable as those which are produced by natural causes.' – p. 68. *An Essay on the External Corn Trade* [1815], *by R. Torrens, Esq* [i.e., the political economist, Robert Torrens (1780–1864)]. The whole of this subject is most ably illustrated by Colonel Torrens.

they enabled him to purchase no other food than potatoes, and to live in no better habitation than a mud cabin; yet these moderate demands of nature are often deemed sufficient in countries where 'man's life is cheap', and his wants easily satisfied. Many of the conveniences now enjoyed in an English cottage, would have been thought luxuries at an earlier period of our history.

From manufactured commodities always falling, and raw produce always rising, with the progress of society, such a disproportion in their relative value is at length created, that in rich countries a labourer, by the sacrifice of a very small quantity only of his food, is able to provide liberally for all his other wants.

Independently of the variations in the value of money, which necessarily affect money wages, but which we have here supposed to have no operation, as we have considered money to be uniformly of the same value, it appears then that wages are subject to a rise or fall from two causes:

> 1st. The supply and demand of labourers.
> 2dly. The price of the commodities on which the wages of labour are
>     expended.

In different stages of society, the accumulation of capital, or of the means of employing labour, is more or less rapid, and must in all cases depend on the productive powers of labour. The productive powers of labour are generally greatest when there is an abundance of fertile land: at such periods accumulation is often so rapid, that labourers cannot be supplied with the same rapidity as capital.

It has been calculated, that under favourable circumstances population may be doubled in twenty-five years;[7] but under the same favourable circumstances, the whole capital of a country might possibly be doubled in a shorter period. In that case, wages during the whole period would have a tendency to rise, because the demand for labour would increase still faster than the supply.

In new settlements, where the arts and knowledge of countries far advanced in refinement are introduced, it is probable that capital has a tendency to increase faster than mankind: and if the deficiency of labourers were not supplied by more populous countries, this tendency would very much raise the price of labour. In proportion as these countries become populous, and land of a worse quality is taken into cultivation, the tendency to an increase of capital diminishes; for the surplus produce remaining, after satisfying the wants of the existing population, must necessarily be in proportion to the facility of production, viz. to the smaller number of persons employed in production. Although, then, it is probable, that under the most favourable circumstances, the power of production is still greater than that of population, it will not long continue so; for the land being limited in quantity, and differing in quality, with every increased portion of capital employed on it, there will be a decreased rate of production, whilst the power of population continues always the same.

In those countries where there is abundance of fertile land, but where, from the ignorance, indolence, and barbarism of the inhabitants, they are exposed to all the evils of want and famine, and where it has been said that population presses against the means of subsistence, a very different remedy should be applied from that which is necessary in long settled countries, where, from the diminishing rate of the supply of raw produce, all the evils of a crowded population are experienced. In the one case, the evil proceeds from bad government, from the insecurity of property, and from a want of education in all ranks of the people. To be made happier they require only to be better governed and instructed, as the augmentation of capital, beyond the augmentation of people, would be the inevitable result. No increase in the population can be too great, as the powers of production are still greater. In the other case, the population increases faster than the funds required for its support. Every exertion of industry, unless accompanied by a diminished rate of increase in the population, will add to the evil, for production cannot keep pace with it.[8]

With a population pressing against the means of subsistence, the only remedies are either a reduction of people, or a more rapid accumulation of capital. In rich countries, where all the fertile land is already cultivated, the latter remedy is neither very practicable nor very desirable, because its effect would be, if pushed very far, to render all classes equally poor. But in poor countries, where there are abundant means of production in store, from fertile land not yet brought into cultivation, it is the only safe and efficacious means of removing the evil, particularly as its effect would be to elevate all classes of the people.

The friends of humanity cannot but wish that in all countries the labouring classes should have a taste for comforts and enjoyments, and that they should be stimulated by all legal means in their exertions to procure them. There cannot be a better security against a superabundant population.[9] In those countries, where the labouring classes have the fewest wants, and are contented with the cheapest food, the people are exposed to the greatest vicissitudes and miseries. They have no place of refuge from calamity; they cannot seek safety in a lower station; they are already so low, that they can fall no lower. On any deficiency of the chief article of their subsistence, there are few substitutes of which they can avail themselves, and dearth to them is attended with almost all the evils of famine.

In the natural advance of society, the wages of labour will have a tendency to fall, as far as they are regulated by supply and demand; for the supply of labourers will continue to increase at the same rate, whilst the demand for them will increase at a slower rate. If, for instance, wages were regulated by a yearly increase of capital, at the rate of 2 per cent., they would fall when it accumulated only at the rate of 1½ per cent. They would fall still lower when it increased only at the rate of 1, or ½ per cent., and would continue to do so until the capital became stationary, when wages also would become stationary, and be only sufficient to keep up the numbers of the actual population. I say that, under these circumstances, wages would fall, if they were regulated only by the supply and demand of labourers; but we must not forget, that wages are also regulated by the prices of the commodities on which they are expended.

As population increases, these necessaries will be constantly rising in price, because more labour will be necessary to produce them. If, then, the money wages of labour should fall, whilst every commodity on which the wages of labour were expended rose, the labourer would be doubly affected, and would be soon totally deprived of subsistence. Instead, therefore, of the money wages of labour falling, they would rise; but they would not rise sufficiently to enable the labourer to purchase as many comforts and necessaries as he did before the rise in the price of those commodities. If his annual wages were before 24*l.*, or six quarters of corn when the price was 4*l.* per quarter, he would probably receive only the value of five quarters when corn rose to 5*l.* per quarter. But five quarters would cost 25*l.*; he would therefore receive an addition in his money wages, though with that addition he would be unable to furnish himself with the same quantity of corn and other commodities, which he had before consumed in his family.[10]

Notwithstanding, then, that the labourer would be really worse paid, yet this increase in his wages would necessarily diminish the profits of the manufacturer; for his goods would sell at no higher price, and yet the expense of producing them would be increased. This, however, will be considered in our examination into the principles which regulate profits.[11]

It appears, then, that the same cause which raises rent, namely, the increasing difficulty of providing an additional quantity of food with the same proportional quantity of labour, will also raise wages; and therefore if money be of an unvarying value, both rent and wages will have a tendency to rise with the progress of wealth and population.

But there is this essential difference between the rise of rent and the rise of wages. The rise in the money value of rent is accompanied by an increased share of the produce; not only is the landlord's money rent greater, but his corn rent also; he will have more corn, and each defined measure of that corn will exchange for a greater quantity of all other goods which have not been raised in value. The fate of the labourer will be less happy; he will receive more money wages, it is true, but his corn wages will be reduced; and not only his command of corn, but his general condition will be deteriorated, by his finding it more difficult to maintain the market rate of wages above their natural rate. While the price of corn rises 10 per cent., wages will always rise less than 10 per cent., but rent will always rise more; the condition of the labourer will generally decline, and that of the landlord will always be improved. [ . . . ][12]

In proportion as corn became dear, he would receive less corn wages, but his money wages would always increase, whilst his enjoyments, on the above supposition, would be precisely the same. But as other commodities would be raised in price in proportion as raw produce entered into their composition, he would have more to pay for some of them. Although his tea, sugar, soap, candles, and house rent, would probably be no dearer, he would pay more for his bacon, cheese, butter, linen, shoes, and cloth; and therefore, even with the above increase of wages, his situation would be comparatively worse. But it may be said that I have been considering the effect of wages on price, on the supposition that gold, or the metal from which money is made, is the produce of the country in which wages varied; and that the consequences which I have deduced agree little with the actual state of things, because gold is a metal of foreign production. The circumstance, however, of gold being a foreign production, will not invalidate the truth of the argument, because it may be shewn, that whether it were found at home, or were imported from abroad, the effects ultimately and, indeed, immediately would be the same.

When wages rise, it is generally because the increase of wealth and capital have occasioned a new demand for labour, which will infallibly be attended with an increased production of commodities. To circulate these additional commodities, even at the same prices as before, more money is required, more of this foreign commodity from which money is made, and which can only be obtained by importation. Whenever a commodity is required in greater abundance than before, its relative value rises comparatively with those commodities with which its purchase is made. If more hats were wanted, their price would rise, and more gold would be given for them. If more gold were required, gold would rise, and hats would fall in price, as a greater quantity of hats and of all other things would then be necessary to purchase the same quantity of gold. But in the case supposed, to say that commodities will rise, because wages rise, is to affirm a positive contradiction; for we first say that gold will rise in relative value in consequence of demand, and secondly, that it will fall in relative value because prices will rise, two effects which are totally incompatible with each other. To say that commodities are raised in price, is the same thing as to say that money is lowered in relative value; for it is by commodities that the relative value of gold is estimated. If then all commodities rose in price, gold could not come from abroad to purchase those dear commodities, but it would go from home to be employed with advantage in purchasing the comparatively cheaper foreign commodities. It appears, then, that the rise of wages will not raise the prices of commodities, whether the metal from which money is made be produced at home or in a foreign country. All commodities cannot rise at the same time without an addition to the quantity of money. This addition could not be obtained at home, as we have already shewn; nor could it be imported from abroad. To purchase any additional quantity of gold from abroad, commodities at home must be cheap, not dear. The importation of gold, and a rise in the price of all home-made commodities with which gold is purchased or paid for, are effects absolutely incompatible. The extensive use of paper money does not alter this question, for paper money conforms, or ought to conform, to the value of gold, and therefore its value is influenced by such causes only as influence the value of that metal.

These then are the laws by which wages are regulated, and by which the happiness of far the greatest part of every community is governed. Like all other contracts, wages should be left to the fair and free competition of the market, and should never be controlled by the interference of the legislature.

The clear and direct tendency of the poor laws, is in direct opposition to these obvious principles: it is not, as the legislature benevolently intended, to amend the condition of the poor, but to deteriorate the condition of both poor and rich; instead of making the poor rich, they are calculated to make the rich poor; and whilst the present laws are in force, it is quite in the natural order of things that the fund for the maintenance of the poor should progressively increase, till it has absorbed all the net revenue of the country, or at least so much of it as the state shall leave to us, after satisfying its own never failing demands for public expenditure.[e]

---

e   With Mr Buchanan in the following passage, if it refers to temporary states of misery, I so far agree, that 'the great evil of the labourer's condition is poverty, arising either from a scarcity of food or of work; and in all countries, laws without number have been enacted for his relief. But there are miseries in the social state which legislation cannot relieve; and it is useful therefore to know its limits, that we may not, by aiming at what is impracticable, miss the good which is really in our power.' – *Buchanan*, p. 61. [The reference is to Buchanan's edition of the *Wealth of Nations*.]

# JOHN STUART MILL, 'ON THE DEFINITION OF POLITICAL ECONOMY' (1836)

## From John Stuart Mill 'On the Definition of Political Economy; and on the Method of Philosophical Investigation in that Science', *London and Westminster Review*, IV and XXVI (October 1836), pp. 1–29[1]

[ ... ] What is now commonly understood by the term 'Political Economy' is not the science of speculative politics, but a branch of that science. It does not treat of the whole of man's nature as modified by the social state, nor of the whole conduct of man in society. It is concerned with him solely as a being who desires to possess wealth, and who is capable of judging of the comparative efficacy of means for obtaining that end. It predicts only such of the phenomena of the social state as take place in consequence of the pursuit of wealth. It makes entire abstraction of every other human passion or motive; except those which may be regarded as perpetually antagonizing principles to the desire of wealth, namely, aversion to labour, and desire of the present enjoyment of costly indulgences. These it takes, to a certain extent, into its calculations, because these do not merely, like other desires, occasionally conflict with the pursuit of wealth, but accompany it always as a drag, or impediment, and are therefore inseparably mixed up in the consideration of it. Political Economy considers mankind as occupied solely in acquiring and consuming wealth; and aims at showing what is the course of action into which mankind, living in a state of society, would be impelled, if that motive, except in the degree in which it is checked by the two perpetual counter-motives above adverted to, were absolute ruler of all their actions. Under the influence of this desire, it shows mankind accumulating wealth, and employing that wealth in the production of other wealth; sanctioning by mutual agreement the institution of property; establishing laws to prevent individuals from encroaching upon the property of others by force or fraud; adopting various contrivances for increasing the productiveness of their labour; settling the division of the produce by agreement, under the influence of competition (competition itself being governed by certain laws, which laws are therefore the ultimate regulators of the division of the produce); and employing certain expedients (as money, credit, &c.) to facilitate the distribution. All these operations, though many of them are really the result of a plurality of motives, are considered by Political Economy as flowing solely from the desire of wealth. The science then proceeds to investigate the laws which govern these several operations, under the supposition that man is a being who is determined, by the necessity of his nature, to prefer a greater portion of wealth to a smaller in all cases, without any other exception than that constituted by the two counter-motives already specified. Not that any political economist was ever so absurd as to suppose that mankind are really thus constituted, but because this is the mode in which science must necessarily proceed. When an effect depends upon a concurrence of causes, those causes must be studied one at a time, and their laws separately investigated, if we wish, through the causes, to obtain the power of either predicting or controlling the effect; since the law of the effect is compounded of the laws of all the causes which determine it. The law of the centripetal and that of the centrifugal force must have been known before the motions of the earth and planets could be explained, or many of them predicted. The same is the case with the conduct of man in society. In order to judge how he will act under the variety of desires and aversions which are concurrently operating upon him, we must know how he would act under the exclusive influence of each one in particular. There is, perhaps, no action of a man's life in which he is neither under the immediate nor under the remote influence of any impulse but the mere desire of wealth. There are many parts of human conduct of which wealth is not even the principal object, and to these Political Economy does not pretend that its conclusions are applicable. But there are also certain departments of human affairs, in which the acquisition of wealth is the main and acknowledged end. It is only of these that Political Economy takes notice. The manner in which it necessarily proceeds is that of treating the main and acknowledged end as if it were the sole end; which, of all hypotheses equally simple, is the nearest to the truth. The political economist inquires, what are the actions which would be produced by this desire, if, within the departments in question, it were unimpeded by any other. In this way a nearer approximation is obtained than would otherwise be practicable, to the real order of human affairs in those departments. This approximation has then to be corrected by making proper allowance for the effects of any impulses of a different description, which can be shown to interfere with the result in any particular case. Only in a few of the most striking cases (such as that important one of the principle of population) are these corrections interpolated into the expositions of Political Economy itself; the strictness of purely scientific arrangement being thereby somewhat departed from, for the sake of practical utility. So far as it is known, or may be presumed, that the conduct of men in the pursuit of wealth is under the collateral influence of any other of the properties of our nature than the desire of obtaining the greatest quantity of wealth with the least labour and self-denial, the conclusions of Political Economy will so far fail of being applicable to the explanation or prediction of real events, until they are modified by a correct allowance for the degree of influence exercised by the other cause.

Political Economy, then, may be defined as follows; and the definition seems to be complete: –

'The science which traces the laws of such of the phenomena of society as arise from the combined operations of mankind for the production of wealth, in so far as those phenomena are not modified by the pursuit of any other object.'

But while this is a correct definition of Political Economy as a portion of the field of science, the didactic writer on the subject will naturally combine in his exposition, with the truths of the pure science, as many of the practical modifi-

cations as will, in his estimation, conduce to the greatest increase of the usefulness of his work.

The above attempt to frame a stricter definition of the science than what are
commonly received as such, may be thought to be of little use; or, at best, to be
chiefly useful in a general survey and classification of the sciences, rather than as
conducing to the more successful pursuit of the particular science in question.
We think otherwise, and for this reason; that, with the consideration of the definition of a science, is inseparably connected that of the *philosophic method* of the
science; the nature of the process by which its investigations are to be carried on,
its truths to be arrived at.

Now, in whatever science there are systematic differences of opinion – which
is as much as to say, in all the moral or mental sciences, and in Political Economy
among the rest; in whatever science there exist, among those who have attended
to the subject, what are commonly called *differences of principle*, as distinguished
from differences of matter-of-fact or detail, – the cause will be found to be, a
difference in their conceptions of the *philosophic method* of the science. The parties
who differ are guided, either knowingly or unconsciously, by different views
concerning the nature of the evidence appropriate to the subject. They differ not
solely in what they believe themselves to see, but in the quarter from which they
obtained the light by which they think they see it.

The most universal of the forms in which this difference of method is accustomed to present itself, is the ancient feud between what is called *theory*, and what
is called *practice* or *experience*. There are two *kinds*, – if we did not see strong objections to the word we would say two *schools* – of inquirers into truth: one of these
sets of people term themselves practical men, and call the others theorists; a title
which the latter do not reject, though they by no means recognise it as peculiar
to them. The distinction between the two is a very broad one, though it is one of
which the language employed is a most incorrect exponent. It has been again
and again demonstrated, that those who are accused of despising facts and disre-
garding experience build and profess to build wholly upon facts and experience;
while those who disavow theory cannot make one step without theorizing. But,
although both classes of inquirers do nothing but theorize, and both of them
consult no other guide than experience, there is this difference between them,
and a most important difference it is: that those who are called practical men
require *specific* experience, and argue wholly *upwards* from particular facts to a
general conclusion; while those who are called theorists aim at embracing a
wider field of experience, and, having argued upwards from particular facts to a
general principle including a much wider range than that of the question under
discussion, then argue *downwards* from that general principle to a variety of
specific conclusions.

Suppose, for example, that the question were, whether absolute kings were
likely to employ the powers of government for the welfare or for the oppression
of their subjects. The practicals would endeavour to determine this question by a
direct induction from the conduct of particular despotic monarchs, as testified

to us by history. The theorists would refer the question to be decided by the test not solely of our experience of kings, but of our experience of man. They would contend that an observation of the tendencies which human nature has manifested in the variety of situations in which human beings have been placed, and especially observation of what passes in our own bosoms, warrants us in inferring that a human being in the situation of a despotic king will make a bad use of power; and that this conclusion would lose nothing of its certainty even if absolute kings had never existed, or if history furnished us with no information of the manner in which they had conducted themselves.

The first of these methods is a method of induction, merely; the last a mixed method of induction and ratiocination. The first may be called the method *à posteriori;* the latter, the method *à priori*. We are aware that this last expression is sometimes used to characterize a supposed mode of philosophizing, which does not profess to be founded upon experience at all. But we are not acquainted with *any* mode of philosophizing which makes such a pretension. By the method *à posteriori* we mean that which requires, as the basis of its conclusions, not *experience* merely, but *specific* experience. By the method *à priori* we mean (what has commonly been meant) reasoning from an assumed hypothesis; which is not a practice confined to mathematics, but is of the essence of all science which admits of general reasoning at all. To verify the hypothesis itself *à posteriori*, that is, to examine whether the facts of any actual case are in accordance with it, is no part of the business of science at all, but of the *application* of science.

In the definition which we have attempted to frame of the science of Political Economy, we have characterized it as essentially an *abstract* science, and its method as the method *à priori*. Such is undoubtedly its character as it has been understood and taught by all its most distinguished teachers. It reasons, and, as we contend, must necessarily reason, from assumptions, not from facts. It is built upon hypotheses, strictly analogous to the hypotheses which, under the name of definitions, are the foundation of the other abstract sciences. Geometry presupposes an arbitrary definition of a line, 'that which has length but not breadth.' Just in the same manner does Political Economy presuppose an arbitrary definition of man, as a being who invariably does that by which he may obtain the greatest amount of necessaries, conveniences, and luxuries, with the smallest quantity of labour and physical self-denial with which they can be obtained in the existing state of knowledge. It is true that this definition of man is not formally prefixed to any work on Political Economy, as the definition of a line is prefixed to Euclid's Elements; and in proportion as by being so prefixed it would be less in danger of being forgotten, we may see ground for regret that this is not done. It is proper that what is assumed in every particular case, should once for all be bought before the mind in its full extent, by being somewhere formally stated as a general maxim. Now, no one who is conversant with systematic treatises on Political Economy will question, that whenever a political economist has shown that, by acting in a particular manner, a labourer may obviously obtain higher wages, a capitalist larger profits, or a landlord higher rent, he concludes, as a matter of course, that they will certainly act in that manner. Political Economy, therefore, reasons from *assumed* premises – from premises which *might* be totally without foundation in fact, and which are not pretended to be universally in accordance with it. The conclusions of Political Economy, therefore, like those of geometry, are only true, as the common phrase is, *in the abstract*; that is, they are only true under certain suppositions, in which none but general causes – causes common to the *whole class* of cases under consideration – are taken into the account.

This ought not to be denied by the political economist. If he deny it, then, and then only, he places himself in the wrong. The *à priori* method which is laid to his charge, as if his employment of it proved his whole science to be worthless, is, as we shall presently show, the only method by which truth can possibly be attained in the moral sciences. All that is requisite is, that he be on his guard not to ascribe to conclusions which are grounded upon an hypothesis a different kind of certainty from that which really belongs to them. They would be true without qualification, only in a case which is purely imaginary. In proportion as the actual facts recede from the hypothesis, he must allow a corresponding deviation from the strict letter of his conclusion; otherwise it will be true only of things such as he has arbitrarily supposed, not of such things as really exist. That which is true in the abstract, is always true in the concrete with proper *allowances*. When a certain cause really exists, and if left to itself would infallibly produce a certain effect, that same effect, *modified* by all the other concurrent causes, will correctly correspond to the result really produced.

The conclusions of geometry are not strictly true of such lines, angles, and figures, as human hands can construct. But no one, therefore, contends that the conclusions of geometry are of no utility, or that it would be better to use Euclid's Elements as waste paper, and content ourselves with 'practice' and 'experience'.

No mathematician ever thought that his definition of a line corresponded to an actual line. As little did any political economist ever imagine that real men had no object of desire but wealth, or none which would not give way to the slightest motive of a pecuniary kind. But they were justified in assuming this, for the purposes of their argument; because they had to do only with those parts of human conduct which have pecuniary advantage for their direct and principal object; and because, as no two individual cases are exactly alike, no *general* maxims could ever be laid down unless *some* of the circumstances of the particular case were left out of consideration.

But we go further than to affirm that the method *à priori* is a legitimate *mode* of philosophical investigation in the moral sciences: we contend that it is the *only* mode. We affirm that the method *à posteriori*, or that of specific experience, is altogether inefficacious in those sciences, as a means of arriving at any considerable body of valuable truth; though it admits of being usefully applied in aid of the method *à priori*, and even forms an indispensable supplement to it. [ . . . ][2]

Having now shown that the method *à priori* in Political Economy, and in all the other branches of moral science, is the only certain or scientific mode of investigation, and that the *à posteriori* method, or that of specific experience, as a means of arriving at truth, is inapplicable to these subjects, we shall yet be able to show that the latter method is notwithstanding of great value in the moral sciences; namely, not as a means of discovering truth, but of verifying it, and reducing to the lowest point that uncertainty before alluded to as arising from the complexity of every particular case, and from the difficulty (not to say impossibility) of our being assured *à priori* that we have taken into account all the material circumstances.

If we could be quite certain that we know all the facts of the particular case, we could derive no additional advantage from specific experience. The causes being given, we know what will be their effect, without an actual trial of every possible combination; since the causes are human feelings, and outward circumstances fitted to excite them: and, as these for the most part are, or at least might be, familiar to us, we can more surely judge of their combined effect from that familiarity, than from any evidence which can be elicited from the complicated and entangled circumstances of an actual experiment. If the knowledge what are the particular causes operating in any given instance were revealed to us by infallible authority, then, if our abstract science were perfect, we should become prophets. But the causes are not so revealed: they are to be collected by observation; and observation in circumstances of complexity is apt to be imperfect. Some of the causes may lie *beyond* observation; many are apt to escape it, unless we are on the look-out for them; and it is only the habit of long and accurate observation which can give us so correct a preconception what causes we are likely to find, as shall induce us to look for them in the right quarter. But such is the nature of the human understanding, that the very fact of attending with intensity to one part of a thing, has a tendency to withdraw the attention from the other parts. We are consequently in great danger of adverting to a portion only of the causes which are actually at work. And if we are in this predicament, the more accurate our deductions and the more certain our conclusions *in the abstract*, (that is, making abstraction of all circumstances except those which form part of hypothesis), the less we are likely to suspect that we are in error: for no one can have looked closely into the sources of fallacious thinking without being deeply conscious that the coherence, and neat concatenation of our philosophical systems, is more apt than we are commonly aware to pass with us as evidence of their truth.

We cannot, therefore, too carefully endeavour to verify our theory, by comparing, in the particular cases to which we have access, the results which it would have led us to predict, with the most trustworthy accounts we can obtain of those which have been actually realized. The discrepancy between our anticipations and the actual fact is often the only circumstance which would have drawn our attention to some important *disturbing cause* which we had overlooked. Nay, it often discloses to us errors in thought, still more serious than the omission of what can with any propriety be termed a disturbing cause. It often reveals to us that the basis itself of our whole argument is insufficient; that the data, from

113

which we had reasoned, comprise only a part, and not the most important part, of the circumstances by which the result is really determined. Such oversights are committed by very good reasoners, and even by a still rarer class, that of good observers. It is a kind of error to which those are peculiarly liable whose views are the largest and most philosophical: for exactly in that ratio are their minds more accustomed to dwell upon those laws, qualities, and tendencies, which are common to large classes of cases, and which belong to all place and all time; while it often happens that circumstances almost peculiar to the particular case or era have a far greater share in governing that one case.

Although, therefore, a philosopher be convinced that no general truths can be attained in the affairs of nations by the *à posteriori* road, it does not the less behove him, according to the measure of his opportunities, to sift and scrutinize the details of every specific experiment. Without this, he may be an excellent professor of abstract science; for a person may be of great use who points out correctly what effects will follow from certain combinations of possible circumstances, in whatever tract of the extensive region of hypothetical cases those combinations may be found. He stands on the same relation to the legislator, as the astronomical geographer to the practical navigator; telling him the latitude and longitude of all sorts of places, but not how to find whereabouts he himself is sailing. If, however, he does no more than this, he must rest contented to take no share in practical politics; to have no opinion, or to hold it with extreme modesty, on the applications which should be made of his doctrines to existing circumstances.

No one who has to think of mankind, however perfect his scientific acquirements, can dispense with a practical knowledge of the actual modes in which the affairs of the world are carried on, and an extensive personal experience of the actual ideas, feelings, and intellectual and moral tendencies of his own country and of his own age. The true practical statesman is he who combines this experience with a profound knowledge of abstract political philosophy. Either acquirement, without the other, leaves him lame and impotent if he is sensible of the deficiency; renders him obstinate and presumptuous if, as is more probable, he is entirely unconscious of it. Knowledge of what is called history, so commonly regarded as the sole fountain of political experience, is useful only in the third degree. History, by itself, if we knew it ten times better than we do, could, for the reasons already given, prove little or nothing: but the study of it is a corrective to the narrow and exclusive views which are apt to be engendered by observation on a more limited scale. Those who never look backwards, seldom look far forwards: their notions of human affairs, and of human nature itself, are circumscribed within the conditions of their own country and their own times. But the uses of history, and the spirit in which it ought to be studied, are subjects which have never yet had justice done them, and which involve considerations more multifarious than can be pertinently introduced in this place.

Such, then, are the respective offices and uses of the *à priori* and the *à posteriori* methods – the method of abstract science, and that of specific experiment – as well in Political Economy, as in all the other branches of social philosophy.

## WALTER BAGEHOT, 'THE POSTULATES OF ENGLISH POLITICAL ECONOMY NO. I' (1876)

Walter Bagehot (1826–77) was a pattern Victorian polymath. He initially intended a career at the Bar and his name was entered as a member of Lincoln's Inn in 1847. However, he left in 1851, and went on to pursue a successful career in banking (he was the inventor of treasury bills) which he managed to combine with the editorship of two periodicals. He also wrote prodigiously on political, economic and literary topics. Bagehot's first essays were published in the late 1840s and his output increased in the 1850s when he began to write on literary issues. In 1855, with Richard Holt Hutton, he co-founded and co-edited the *National Review*; when Hutton resigned in 1862, followed shortly by his successor, Charles Pearson, Bagehot became sole editor until the magazine ceased publication in 1864. In the meantime he became joint director in 1859 of the *Economist* and took over the editorship in 1861. He remained in post at the *Economist* until his death in 1877. From 1859 to 1877 Bagehot contributed around two articles a week on current affairs. His first major work, *The English Constitution*, was published in 1867; other important works included *Physics and Politics* (1872) and the posthumous *Economic Studies* (1880), a collection of essays edited by Hutton. The one conspicuously unsuccessful element of Bagehot's career was his failure to win a seat in the Commons.

### *From* Walter Bagehot, 'The Postulates of English Political Economy No. I.', *Fortnightly Review*, CX n.s. (February 1876), pp. 215–42[1]

*The Postulates of English Political Economy No. I: I*

Adam Smith completed the Wealth of Nations in 1776, and our English political economy is therefore just a hundred years old. In that time it has had a wonderful effect. The life of almost everyone in England – perhaps of everyone – is different and better in consequence of it. The whole commercial policy of the country is not so much founded on it as instinct with it. Ideas which are paradoxes everywhere else in the world are accepted axioms here as results of it. No other form of political philosophy has ever had one thousandth part the influence on us; its teachings have settled down into the common sense of the nation, and have become irreversible.

We are too familiar with the good we have thus acquired to appreciate it properly. To do so we should see what our ancestors were taught. The best book on Political Economy published in England before that of Adam Smith is Sir James Stewart's Inquiry,[2] a book full of acuteness, and written by a man of travel and cultivation. And its teaching is of this sort: –

> 'In all trade two things are to be considered in the commodity sold. The first is the matter; the second is the labour employed to render this matter useful.
>
> 'The matter exported from a country is what the country loses; the price of the labour exported is what it gains.
>
> 'If the value of the matter imported be greater than the value of what is exported the country gains. If a greater value of labour be imported than exported the country loses. Why? Because in the first case strangers must have paid *in matter* the surplus of labour exported; and in the second place because the strangers must have paid to strangers *in matter* the surplus of labour imported. It is therefore a general maxim to discourage the importation of work, and to encourage the exportation of it.'

It was in a world where *this* was believed that our present Political Economy began.

Abroad the influence of our English system has of course not been nearly so great as in England itself. But even there it has had an enormous effect. All the highest financial and commercial legislation of the Continent has been founded upon it. [ . . . ][3]

But notwithstanding these triumphs, the position of our Political Economy is not altogether satisfactory. It lies rather dead in the public mind. Not only it does not excite the same interest as formerly, but there is not exactly the same confidence in it. Younger men either do not study it, or do not feel that it comes home to them, and that it matches with their most living ideas. New sciences have come up in the last few years with new modes of investigation, and they want to know what is the relation of economical science, as their fathers held it, to these new thoughts and these new instruments. They ask, often hardly knowing it, will this 'science,' as it claims to be, harmonize with what we now know to be sciences, or bear to be tried as we now try sciences? And they are not sure of the answer.

Abroad, as is natural, the revolt is more avowed. Indeed, though the Political Economy of Adam Smith penetrated deep into the continent, what has been added in England since has never done so equally; though if our 'science' is true, the newer work required a greater intellectual effort, and is far more complete as a scientific achievement than anything which Adam Smith did himself. Political Economy, as it was taught by Ricardo,[4] has had in this respect much the same fate as another branch of English thought of the same age, with which it has many analogies – jurisprudence as it was taught by Austin and Bentham;[5] it has remained insular. I do not mean that it was not often read and understood, of course it was so, though it was often misread and misunderstood. But it never at all reigned abroad as it reigns here; never was really fully accepted in other countries as it was here where it arose. And no theory, economical or political, can now be both insular and secure; foreign thoughts come soon and trouble us; there will always be doubt here as to what is only believed here.

There are, no doubt, obvious reasons why English Political Economy should be thus unpopular out of England. It is known everywhere as the theory 'of Free Trade,' and out of England free trade is almost everywhere unpopular. Experience shows that no belief is so difficult to create, and no one so easy to disturb. The protectionist creed rises like a weed in every soil. 'Why,' M Thiers[6] was asked, 'do you give these bounties to the French sugar refiners?' 'I wish,' replied he, 'the tall chimneys to smoke.' Every nation wishes prosperity for some conspicuous industry. At what cost to the consumer, by what hardship to less conspicuous industries, that prosperity is obtained, it does not care. Indeed, it hardly knows, it will never read, it will never apprehend the refined reasons which prove those evils and show how great they are; the visible picture of the smoking chimneys absorbs the whole mind. And, in many cases, the eagerness of England in the free-trade cause only does that cause harm. Foreigners say, 'Your English traders are strong and rich; of course you wish to under-sell our traders, who are weak and poor. You have invented this Political Economy to enrich yourselves and ruin us; we will see that you shall not do so.'

And that English political economy is more opposed to the action of government in all ways than most such theories, brings it no accession of popularity. All governments like to interfere; it elevates their position to make out that they can cure the evils of mankind. And all zealots wish they should interfere, for such zealots think they can and may convert the rulers and manipulate the state control: it is a distinct object to convert a definite man, and if he will not be convinced there is always a hope of his successor. But most zealots dislike to appeal to the mass of mankind; they know instinctively that it will be too opaque and impenetrable for them.

But I do not believe that these are the only reasons why our English political economy is not estimated at its value abroad. I believe that this arises from its special characteristic, from that which constitutes its peculiar value, and, paradoxical as it may seem, I also believe that this same characteristic is likewise the reason why it is often not thoroughly understood in England itself. The science of political economy as we have it in England may be defined as the science of business, as business is in large productive and trading communities. It is an analysis of that world so familiar to many Englishmen – the 'great commerce' by which England has become rich. It assumes the principal facts which make that commerce possible, and as is the way of an abstract science, it isolates and simplifies them; it detaches them from the confusion with which they are mixed in fact. And it deals too with the men who carry on that commerce, and who make it possible. It assumes a sort of human nature such as we see it everywhere

117

around us, and again it simplifies that human nature; it looks at one part of it only. Dealing with matters of 'business,' it assumes that man is actuated only by motives of business. It assumes that every man who makes anything, makes it for money, that he always makes that which brings him in most at least cost, and that he will make it in the way that will produce most and spend least; it assumes that every man who buys, buys with his whole heart, and that he who sells, sells with his whole heart, each wanting to gain all possible advantage. Of course we know that this is not so, that men are not like this; but we assume it for simplicity's sake, as an hypothesis. And this deceives many excellent people, for from deficient education they have very indistinct ideas what an abstract science is.

More competent persons, indeed, have understood that English political economists are not speaking of real men, but of imaginary ones; not of men as we see them, but of men as it is convenient to us to suppose they are. But even they often do not understand that the world which our political economists treat of is a very limited and peculiar world also. They often imagine that what they read is applicable to all states of society, and to all equally, whereas it is only true of – and only proved as to – states of society in which commerce has largely developed, and where it has taken the form of development, or something near the form, which it has taken in England.

This explains why abroad the science has not been well understood. Commerce, as we have it in England, is not so full-grown anywhere else as it is here – at any rate, is not so out of the lands populated by the Anglo-Saxon race. Here it is not only a thing definite and observable, but about the most definite thing we have, the thing which it is most difficult to help seeing. But on the continent, though there is much that is like it, and though that much is daily growing more, there is nowhere the same pervading entity – the same patent, pressing, and unmistakable object.

And this brings out too the inherent difficulty of the subject – a difficulty which no other science, I think, presents in equal magnitude. Years ago I heard Mr Cobden say at a League Meeting,[7] that 'Political Economy was the highest study of the human mind, for that the physical sciences required by no means so hard an effort.' An orator cannot be expected to be exactly precise, and of course political economy is in no sense the highest study of mind – there are others which are much higher, for they are concerned with things much nobler than wealth or money; nor is it true that the effort of mind which political economy requires is nearly as great as that required for the abstruser theories of physical science, for the theory of gravitation, or the theory of natural selection; but, nevertheless, what Mr Cobden meant had – as was usual with his first-hand mind – a great fund of truth. He meant that political economy – effectual political economy, political economy which in complex problems succeeds – is a very difficult thing; something altogether more abstruse and difficult, as well as more conclusive, than that which many of those who rush in upon it have a notion of. It is an abstract science which labours under a special hardship. Those who are conversant with its abstractions are usually without a true contact with its facts;

those who are in contact with its facts have usually little sympathy with and little cognizance of its abstractions. Literary men who write about it are constantly using what a great teacher calls 'unreal words' – that is, they are using expressions with which they have no complete vivid picture to correspond. They are like physiologists who have never dissected; like astronomers who have never seen the stars; and, in consequence, just when they seem to be reasoning at their best, their knowledge of the facts falls short. Their primitive picture fails them, and their deduction altogether misses the mark – sometimes, indeed, goes astray so far, that those who live and move among the facts, boldly say that they cannot comprehend 'how any one can talk such nonsense.' While, on the other hand, these people who live and move among the facts often, or mostly, cannot of themselves put together any precise reasonings about them. Men of business have a solid judgment – a wonderful guessing power of what is going to happen – each in his own trade; but they have never practised themselves in reasoning out their judgments and in supporting their guesses by argument; probably if they did so some of the finer and correcter parts of their anticipations would vanish. They are like the sensible lady to whom Coleridge said, 'Madam, I accept your conclusion, but you must let me find the logic for it.' Men of business can no more put into words much of what guides their life than they could tell another person how to speak their language. And so the 'theory of business' leads a life of obstruction, because theorists do not see the business, and the men of business will not reason out the theories. Far from wondering that such a science is not completely perfect, we should rather wonder that it exists at all.

Something has been done to lessen the difficulty by statistics. These give tables of facts which help theoretical writers and keep them straight, but the cure is not complete. Writers without experience of trade are always fancying that these tables mean something more than, or something different from, that which they really mean. A table of prices, for example, seems an easy and simple thing to understand, and a whole literature of statistics assumes that simplicity; but in fact there are many difficulties. At the outset there is a difference between the men of theory and the men of practice. Theorists take a table of prices as facts settled by unalterable laws; a stockbroker will tell you such prices can be 'made.' In actual business such is his constant expression. If you ask him what is the price of such a stock, he will say, if it be a stock at all out of the common, 'I do not know, sir; I will go on to the market and get them to *make* me a price.' And the following passage from the Report of the late Foreign Loans' Committee shows what sort of process 'making' a price sometimes is: –

'Immediately,' they say, 'after the publication of the prospectus' – the case is that of the Honduras Loan – 'and before any allotment was made, M Lefevre authorised extensive purchases and sales of loans on his behalf, brokers were employed by him to deal in the manner best calculated to maintain the price of the stock; the brokers so employed instructed jobbers to purchase the stock when the market required to be strengthened, and to sell it if the market was sufficiently firm. In consequence of the market thus created dealings were carried on to a very large amount. Fifty or a hundred men were in the market dealing with each other and the brokers all round. One jobber had sold the loan (£2,500,000) once over.'

Much money was thus abstracted from credulous rural investors; and I regret to say that book statists are often equally, though less hurtfully, deceived. They make tables in which artificial tables run side by side with natural ones; in which the price of an article like Honduras scrip,[8] which can be indefinitely manipulated, is treated just like the price of Consols,[9] which can scarcely be manipulated at all. In most cases it never occurs to the maker of the table that there could be such a thing as an artificial – a *malâ fide* – price at all. He imagines all prices to be equally straightforward. – Perhaps, however, this may be said to be an unfair sample of price difficulties, because it is drawn from the Stock Exchange, the most complex market for prices; – and no doubt the Stock Exchange has its peculiar difficulties, of which I certainly shall not speak lightly; – but on the other hand, in one cardinal respect, it is the simplest of markets. There is no question in it of the physical quality of commodities: one Turkish bond of 1858 is as good or bad as another; one ordinary share in a railway exactly the same as any other ordinary share; but in other markets each sample differs in quality, and it is a learning in each market to judge of qualities, so many are they, and so fine their gradations. Yet mere tables do not tell this, and cannot tell it. Accordingly in a hundred cases you may see 'prices' compared as if they were prices of the same thing, when in fact they are prices of different things. The *Gazette* average of corn is thus compared incessantly, yet it is hardly the price of the same exact quality of corn in any two years. It is an average of all the prices in all the sales in all the markets. But this year the kind of corn mostly sold may be very superior, and last year very inferior – yet the tables compare the two without noticing the difficulty. And when the range of prices runs over many years, the figures are even more treacherous, for the names remain, while the quality, the thing signified, is changed. And of this persons not engaged in business have no warning. Statistical tables, even those which are most elaborate and careful, are not substitutes for an actual cognizance of the facts: they do not, as a rule, convey a just idea of the movements of a trade to persons not *in* the trade.

It will be asked, why do you frame such a science if from its nature it is so difficult to frame it? The answer is that it is necessary to frame it, or we must go without important knowledge. The facts of commerce, especially of the great commerce, are very complex. Some of the most important are not on the surface; some of those most likely to confuse *are* on the surface. If you attempt to solve such problems without some apparatus of method, you are as sure to fail as if you try to take a modern military fortress – a Metz or a Belfort[10] – by common assault; you must have guns to attack the one, and method to attack the other.

The way to be sure of this is to take a few new problems, such as are for ever presented by investigation and life, and to see what by mere common sense we can make of them. For example, it is said that the general productiveness of the earth is less or more in certain regular cycles, corresponding with perceived changes in the state of the sun, – what would be the effect of this cyclical variation in the efficiency of industry upon commerce? Some hold, and as I think hold justly, that, extraordinary as it may seem, these regular changes in the sun have much to do with the regular recurrence of difficult times in the money market. What common sense would be able to answer these questions? Yet we may be sure that if there be a periodical series of changes in the yielding power of this planet, that series will have many consequences on the industry of men, whether those which have been suggested or others.

Or to take an easier case, who can tell without instruction what is likely to be the effect of the new loans of England to foreign nations? We press upon half-finished and half-civilised communities incalculable sums; we are to them what the London money-dealers are to students at Oxford and Cambridge. We enable these communities to read in every newspaper that they can have ready money, almost of any amount, on 'personal security.' No incipient and no arrested civilizations ever had this facility before. What will be the effect on such civilizations now, no untutored mind can say.

Or again: since the Franco-German War an immense sum of new money has come to England; England has become the settling-place of international bargains much more than it was before; but whose mind could divine the effect of such a change as this, except it had a professed science to help it?

There are indeed two suggested modes of investigation, besides our English Political Economy, and competing with it. One is the Enumerative, or, if I may coin such a word, the 'All-case method'. One school of theorists say, or assume oftener than they say, that you should have a 'complete experience;' that you should accumulate all the facts of these subjects before you begin to reason. A very able German writer[11] has said, in this very Review,[a] of a great economical topic, banking, –

> 'I venture to suggest that there is but one way of arriving at such knowl-edge and truth' (that is absolute truth and full knowledge), 'namely, a thorough investigation of the facts of the case. By the facts, I mean not merely such facts as present themselves to so-called practical men in the common routine of business, but the facts which a complete historical and statistical inquiry would develop. When such a work shall have been accomplished, German economists may boast of having restored

a   *Fortnightly Review* for September, 1873.

the principles of banking, that is to say, of German banking, but not even then of banking in general. To set forth principles of banking in general, it will be necessary to master in the same way the facts of English, Scotch, French, and American banking, in short, every country where banking exists. The only,' he afterwards continues, 'but let us add also, the safe ground of hope for political economy is, following Bacon's exhortation to recommence afresh the whole work of economic enquiry. In what conditions would chemistry, physics, geology, zoology be, and the other branches of natural science which have yielded such prodigious results, if their students had been linked to their chains of deduction from the assumptions and speculations of the last century.'

But the reply is that the method which Mr Cohn suggests was tried in physical science and failed. And it is very remarkable that he should not have remembered it as he speaks of Lord Bacon,[12] for the method which he suggests is exactly that which Lord Bacon himself followed, and owing to the mistaken nature of which he discovered nothing. The investigation into the nature of heat in the *Novum Organum* is exactly such a collection of facts as Mr Cohn suggests, – but nothing comes of it. As Mr Jevons[13] well says, 'Lord Bacon's notion of scientific method was that of a kind of scientific book-keeping. Facts were to be indiscriminately gathered from every source, and posted in a kind of ledger from which would emerge in time a clear balance of truth. It is difficult to imagine a less likely way of arriving at discoveries.' And yet it is precisely that from which, mentioning Bacon's name, but not forewarned by his experience, Mr Cohn hopes to make them.

The real plan that has answered in physical science is much simpler. The discovery of a law of nature is very like the discovery of a murder. In the one case you arrest a suspected person, and in the other you isolate a suspected cause. When Newton,[14] by the fall of the apple, or something else, was led to think that the attraction of gravitation would account for the planetary motions, he took that cause by itself, traced out its effects by abstract mathematics, and so to say found it 'guilty,' – he discovered that it would produce the phenomenon under investigation. In the same way Geology has been revolutionized in our own time by Sir Charles Lyell.[15] He for the first time considered the effects of one particular set of causes by themselves. He showed how large a body of facts could be explained on the hypothesis 'that the forces now operating upon and beneath the earth's surface are the same both in kind and degree as those which, at remote epochs, have worked out geological changes.' He did not wait to begin his inquiry till his data about all kinds of strata, or even about any particular kind, were complete; he took palpable causes as he knew them, and showed how many facts they would explain; he spent a long and most important life in fitting new facts into an abstract and youthful speculation. Just so in an instance which has made a literature and gone the round of the world. Mr Darwin,[16] who is a disciple of Lyell, has shown how one *vera causa*, 'natural selection,' would account for an immense number of the facts of nature; for how many, no doubt, is controverted, but, as is admitted, for a very large number. And this he showed by very difficult pieces of reasoning which very few persons would have thought of, and which most people found at first not at all easy to comprehend. The process by which physical science has become what it is, has not been that of discarding abstract speculations, but of working out abstract speculations. The most important known laws of nature – the laws of motion – the basis of the figures in the Nautical Almanac[17] by which every ship sails, – are difficult and abstract enough, as most of us found to our cost in our youth.

There is no doubt a strong tendency to revolt against abstract reasoning. Human nature has a strong 'factish' element in it. The reasonings of the Principia are now accepted. But in the beginning they were 'mere crotchets of Mr Newton's;' Flamsteed,[18] the greatest astronomical discoverer of his day – the man of facts, *par excellence* – so called them; they have irresistibly conquered, but at first even those most conversant with the matter did not believe them. – I do not claim for the conclusions of English Political Economy the same certainty as for the 'laws of motion.' But I say that the method by which they have been obtained is the same, and that the difference in the success of the two investigations largely comes from this – that the laws of wealth are the laws of a most complex phenomenon which you can but passively observe, and on which you cannot try experiments for science's sake, and that the laws of motion relate to a matter on which you can experiment, and which is comparatively simple in itself.

And to carry the war into the enemy's country, I say also that the method proposed by Mr Cohn, the 'all case' method, is impossible. When I read the words 'all the facts of English banking,' I cannot but ask of what facts is Mr Cohn thinking. Banking in England goes on growing, multiplying, and changing, as the English people itself goes on growing, multiplying, and changing. The facts of it are one thing to-day and another to-morrow; nor at any one moment does any one know them completely. Those who best know many of them will not tell them or hint at them; gradually and in the course of years they separately come to light, and by the time they do so, for the most part, another crop of unknown ones has accumulated. If we wait to reason till the 'facts' are complete, we shall wait till the human race has expired. I think that Mr Cohn and those that think with him are too 'bookish' in this matter. They mean by having all the 'facts' before them, having all the printed facts, all the statistical tables. But what has been said of Nature is true of Commerce. 'Nature,' says Sir Charles Lyell, 'has made it no part of her concern to provide a record of her operations, for the use of men;' nor does trade either – only the smallest of fractions of actual transactions is set down, so that investigation can use it. Literature has been called the 'fragment of fragments,' and in the same way statistics are the 'scrap of scraps.' In real life scarcely any one knows more than a small part of what his neighbour is doing, and he scarcely makes public any of that little, or of what he does himself. A complete record of commercial facts, or even of one kind of such facts, is the completest of dreams. You might as well hope for an entire record of human conversation.

There is also a second antagonistic method to that of English Political Economy, which, by contrast, I will call the 'single case' method. It is said that you should analyse each group of facts separately – that you should take the panic of 1866 separately, and explain it; or, at any rate, the whole history of Lombard Street[19] separately, and explain it. And this is very good and very important; but it is no substitute for a preliminary theory. You might as well try to substitute a corollary for the proposition on which it depends. The history of a panic is the history of a confused conflict of many causes; and unless you know what sort of effect each cause is likely to produce, you cannot explain any part of what happens. It is trying to explain the bursting of a boiler without knowing the theory of steam. Any history of similar phenomena like that of Lombard Street could not be usefully told, unless there was a considerable accumulation of applicable doctrine before existing. You might as well try to write the 'life' of a ship, making as you went along the theory of naval construction. Clumsy dissertations would run all over the narrative; and the result would be a perfect puzzle.

I have been careful not to use in this discussion of methods the phrase which is oftenest used, viz. the Historical method, because there is an excessive ambiguity in it. Sometimes it seems what I have called the Enumerative, or 'all case' method; sometimes the 'single case' method; a most confusing double meaning, for by the mixture of the two, the mind is prevented from seeing the defects of either. And sometimes it has other meanings, with which, as I shall show, I have no quarrel, but rather much sympathy. Rightly conceived, the Historical method is no rival to the abstract method rightly conceived. But I shall be able to explain this better and less tediously at the end of these papers than I can at the beginning.

This conclusion is confirmed by a curious circumstance. At the very moment that our Political Economy is objected to in some quarters as too abstract, in others an attempt is made to substitute for it one which is more abstract still. Mr Jevons of Manchester, and M Walras of Lausanne,[20] without communication, and almost simultaneously, have worked out a 'mathematical' theory of Political Economy; – and any one who thinks what is ordinarily taught in England objectionable, because it is too little concrete in its method, and looks too unlike life and business, had better try the new doctrine, which he will find to be much worse on these points than the old.

But I shall be asked, Do you then say that English Political Economy is perfect? – Surely it is contrary to reason that so much difficulty should be felt in accepting a real science properly treated? At the first beginning no doubt there are difficulties in gaining a hearing for all sciences, but English Political Economy has long passed out of its first beginning? Surely, if there were not some intrinsic defect, it would have been firmly and coherently established, just as others are?

In this reasoning there is evident plausibility, and I answer that, in my judgment, there are three defects in the mode in which Political Economy has been treated in England, which have prevented people from seeing what it really is, and from prizing it at its proper value.

First. It has often been put forward, not as a theory of the principal causes affecting wealth in *certain* societies, but as a theory of the principal, sometimes even of all, the causes affecting wealth in *every* society. And this has occasioned many and strong doubts about it. Travellers fresh from the sight, and historians fresh from the study of peculiar and various states of society, look with dislike and disbelief on a single set of abstract propositions which claims, as they think, to be applicable to all such societies, and to explain a most important part of most of them. I cannot here pause to say how far particular English economists have justified this accusation; I only say that, taking the whole body of them, there is much ground for it, and that in almost every one of them there is some ground. No doubt almost every one – every one of importance – has admitted that there is a 'friction' in society which counteracts the effect of the causes they treat of. But in general they leave their readers with the idea that, after all, this friction is but subordinate; that probably in the course of years it may be neglected; and, at any rate, the causes assigned in the science of Political Economy, as they treat it, are the main and principal ones. Now I hold that these causes are only the main ones in a single kind of society – a society of grown-up competitive commerce, such as we have in England; that it is only in such societies that the other and counteracting forces can be set together under the minor head of 'friction;' but that in other societies these other causes – in some cases one, and in some another – are the most effective ones, and that the greatest confusion arises if you try to fit on *un*-economical societies the theories only true of, and only proved as to, economical ones. In my judgment, we need not that the authority of our Political Economy should be impugned, but that it should be *minimized*; that we should realise distinctly where it is established and where not; that its sovereignty should be upheld, but its frontiers marked. And until this is done, I am sure that there will remain the same doubt and hesitation in many minds about the science that there is now.

Secondly, I think it in consequence of this defect of conception economists have been far more abstract, and in consequence much more dry, than they need have been. If they had distinctly set before themselves that they were dealing only with the causes of wealth in a single set of societies, they might have effectively pointed their doctrines with facts from those societies. But, so long as the vision of universal theory vaguely floated before them, they shrank from particular illustrations. Real societies are plainly so many and so unlike that an instance from one kind does not show that the same thing exists in other societies – it rather raises in the mind a presumption that it does not exist there; and therefore speculators aiming at an all-embracing doctrine refrain from telling cases, because those cases are apt to work in ways, and to raise up the image not only of the societies in which the tenet illustrated is true, but also of the opposite group in which it is false.

Thirdly, it is also in consequence, as I imagine, of this defective conception of their science, that English Economists have not been as fertile as they should have been in verifying it. They have been too content to remain in the 'abstract,' and to shrink from concrete notions, because they could not but feel that much of the most obvious phenomena of many nations did not look much like their abstractions. Whereas in the societies with which the science is really concerned, an almost infinite harvest of verification was close at hand, ready to be gathered in; and because it has not been used, much confidence in the science has been lost, and it is thought 'to be like the stars which give no good light because they are so high.'

Of course this reasoning implies that the boundaries of this sort of Political Economy are arbitrary, and might be fixed here or there. But this is already implied when it is said that Political Economy is an abstract science. All abstractions are arbitrary; they are more or less convenient fictions made by the mind for its own purposes. An abstract idea means a concrete fact or set of facts *minus* something thrown away. The fact or set of facts were made by nature; but how much you will throw aside of them and how much you will keep for consideration you settle for yourself. There may be any number of political economies according as the subject is divided off in one way or in another, and in this way all may be useful if they do not interfere with one another or attempt to rule further than they are proved.

The particular political economy which I have been calling the English Political Economy, is that of which the first beginning was made by Adam Smith. But what he did was much like the rough view of the first traveller who discovers a country; he saw some great outlines well, but he mistook others and left out much. It was Ricardo who made the first map; who reduced the subjects into consecutive shape, and constructed what you can call a science. Few greater efforts of mind have been made, and not many have had greater fruits. From Ricardo the science passed to a whole set of minds – James Mill, Senior, Torrens, MacCulloch,[21] and others, who busied themselves with working out his ideas, with elaborating and with completing them. For five-and-twenty years the English world was full of such discussions. Then Mr J. S. Mill[22] – the Mr Mill whom the present generation know so well, and who has had so much influence, – shaped with masterly literary skill the confused substance of those discussions into a compact whole. He did not add a great deal which was his own, and some of what is due to him does not seem to me of great value. But he pieced the subjects together, showed where what one of his predecessors had done had fitted on to that of another, and adjusted this science to other sciences according to the notions of that time. To many students his book is the Alpha and Omega of Political Economy; they know little of what was before, and imagine little which can come after in the way of improvement. But it is not given to any writer to occupy such a place. Mr Mill would have been the last to claim it for himself. He well knew that taking his own treatise as the standard, what he added to Political Economy was not a ninth of what was due to Ricardo, and that for much of what is new in his book he was rather the *Secrétaire de la Rédaction*, expressing and formulating the current views of a certain world, than producing by original thought from his own brain. And his remoteness from mercantile life, and I should say his enthusiastic character, eager after things far less sublunary than money, made him little likely to give finishing touches to a theory of 'the great commerce.' In fact he has not done so; much yet remains to be done in it as in all sciences. Mr Mill, too, seems to me open to the charge of having widened the old Political Economy either too much or not enough. If it be, as I hold, a theory proved of and applicable to particular societies only, much of what is contained in Mr Mill's book should not be there; if it is, on the contrary, a theory holding good for all societies, as far as they are concerned with wealth, much more ought to be there, and much which is should be guarded and limited. English Political Economy is not a finished and completed theory, but the first lines of a great analysis which has worked out much, but which still leaves much unsettled and unexplained.

There is nothing capricious, we should observe, in this conception of Political Economy, nor though it originated in England is there anything specially English in it. It is the theory of commerce, as commerce tends more and more to be when capital increases and competition grows. England was the first – or one of the first – countries to display these characteristics in such vigour and so isolated as to suggest a separate analysis of them, but as the world goes on, similar characteristics are being evolved in one society after another. A similar money-market, a similar competing trade based on large capital, gradually tends to arise in all countries. As 'men of the world' are the same everywhere, so the great commerce is the same everywhere. Local peculiarities and ancient modifying circumstances fall away in both cases; and it is of this one and uniform commerce which grows daily, and which will grow, according to every probability, more and more, that English Political Economy aspires to be the explanation.

And our Political Economy does not profess to prove this growing world to be a good world – far less to be the best. Abroad the necessity of contesting socialism has made some writers use the conclusions brought out by our English science for that object. But the aim of that science is far more humble; it says these and these forces produce these and these effects, and there it stops. It does not profess to give a moral judgment on either; it leaves it for a higher science, and one yet more difficult, to pronounce what ought and what ought not to be.

The first thing to be done for English Political Economy, as I hold, is to put its aim right. So long as writers on it do not clearly see, and as readers do not at all see, the limits of what they are analysing, the result will not satisfy either. The science will continue to seem what to many minds it seems now, proved perhaps but proved *in nubibus*; true, no doubt, somehow and somewhere, but that somewhere a *terra incognita*,[23] and that somehow an unknown quantity. – As a help in this matter I propose in the present series of papers to take the principal assumptions of Political Economy one by one, and to show, not exhaustively, for that would require a long work, but roughly, where each is true and where it is not. We shall then find that our Political Economy is not a questionable thing of unlimited extent, but a most certain and useful thing of limited extent. By marking the frontier of our property we shall learn its use, and we shall have a positive and reliable basis for estimating its value.

## WILLIAM STANLEY JEVONS, *THE THEORY OF POLITICAL ECONOMY* (1871)

William Stanley Jevons (1835–82) was the architect in Britain of what economic historians have termed the 'marginal revolution'. His early interests were divided between logic and economics, and his first main work was *Pure Logic* (1864). This was followed in 1865 by *The Coal Question*, a publication which brought him prominence in economic circles and established his interest in economic subjects. The book which made his reputation, however, was *The Theory of Political Economy*, published in 1871. In it Jevons elaborated ideas which he had presented some years earlier to the British Association, but which had been largely ignored. Jevons attempted to overturn the orthodoxy of Ricardian economics by suggesting that the origin of value was not labour but utility (or consumption). He produced a mathematical theory of economics based on a calculus of pleasure and pain. Known today as 'marginal utility theory', it is seen as the foundation of modern economic thought. Unlike Ricardo or Bentham, Jevons had no disciples, his work produced no school and his controversial *Theory* took some time to be accepted in orthodox economic circles. Plagued by frequent bouts of ill-health and exhaustion, in 1876 Jevons left his post as Professor of Logic and Political Economy at Owens College, Manchester to take up the Professorship of Political Economy at University College, London. He resigned in 1880, partly over ill-health, and partly over his desire to spend more time on what he considered his major work, provisionally entitled *The Principles of Economics*. Jevons died from drowning in 1882 before completing it. The 'fragments' of the projected work were published by Macmillan in 1905.

*From* **William Stanley Jevons,** *The Theory of Political Economy* **(London: Macmillan, 1871)**[1]

*Preface*

The contents of the following pages can hardly meet with ready acceptance among those who regard the Science of Political Economy as having already acquired a nearly perfect form. I believe it is generally supposed that Adam Smith laid the foundations of this science; that Malthus, Anderson, and Senior added important doctrines; that Ricardo systematised the whole; and, finally, that Mr J. S. Mill filled in the details and completely expounded this branch of knowledge.[2] Mr Mill appears to have had a similar notion; for he distinctly asserts that there was nothing in the Laws of Value which remained for himself or any future writer to clear up. Doubtless it is difficult to help feeling that opinions adopted and confirmed by such eminent men have much weight of probability in their favour. Yet, in the other sciences this weight of authority has not been allowed to restrict the free examination of new opinions and theories; and it has often been ultimately proved that authority was on the wrong side.

There are many portions of Economical doctrine which appear to me as scientific in form as they are consonant with facts. I would especially mention the Theories of Population and Rent, the latter a theory of a distinctly mathematical character which seems to give a clue to the correct mode of treating the whole science. Had Mr Mill contented himself with asserting the unquestionable truth of the Laws of Supply and Demand, I should have agreed with him. As founded upon facts, those laws cannot be shaken by any theory; but it does not therefore follow, that our conception of Value is perfect and final. Other generally accepted doctrines have always appeared to me purely delusive, especially the so-called Wage Fund Theory. This theory pretends to give a solution of the main problem of the science – to determine the wages of labour; yet, on close exami-nation, its conclusion is found to be a mere truism, namely, that the average rate of wages is found by dividing the whole amount appropriated to the payment of wages by the number of those between whom it is divided. Some other supposed conclusions of the science are of a less harmless character, as, for instance, those regarding the advantage of exchange. [ . . . ][3]

In this work I have attempted to treat Economy as a Calculus of Pleasure and Pain, and have sketched out, almost irrespective of previous opinions, the form which the science, as it seems to me, must ultimately take. I have long thought that as it deals throughout with quantities, it must be a mathematical science in matter if not in language. I have endeavoured to arrive at accurate quantitative notions concerning Utility, Value, Labour, Capital, &c., and I have often been surprised to find how clearly some of the most difficult notions, especially that most puzzling of notions *Value*, admit of mathematical analysis and expression. The Theory of Economy thus treated presents a close analogy to the science of Statistical Mechanics, and the Laws of Exchange are found to resemble the Laws of Equilibrium of a lever as determined by the principle of virtual velocities. The nature of Wealth and Value is explained by the consideration of indefinitely small amounts of pleasure and pain, just as the Theory of Statics is made to rest upon the equality of indefinitely small amounts of energy. But I believe that dynamical branches of the Science of Economy may remain to be developed, on the consideration of which I have not at all entered.

Mathematical readers may perhaps think that I have explained some elemen-tary notions, that of the Degree of Utility, for instance, with unnecessary prolixity. But it is to the neglect of Economists to obtain clear and accurate notions of quantity and degree of utility that I venture to attribute the present difficulties and imperfections of the science; and I have purposely dwelt upon the point at full length. Other readers will perhaps think that the occasional introduction of mathematical symbols obscures instead of illustrating the subject. But I must request all readers to remember that, as Mathematicians and Political Economists have hitherto been two nearly distinct classes of persons, there is no slight difficulty in preparing a mathematical work on Economy with which both classes of readers may not have some grounds of complaint.

It is very likely that I have fallen into errors of more or less importance, which I shall be glad to have pointed out; and I may say that the cardinal difficulty of the whole theory is alluded to in the section of Chapter IV upon the 'Ratio of Exchange' [ . . . ]. So able a mathematician as my friend Professor Barker, of Owens College, has had the kindness to examine some of the proof sheets carefully; but he is not, therefore, to be held responsible for the correctness of any part of the work.

My enumeration of the previous attempts to apply mathematical language to Political Economy does not pretend to completeness even as regards English writers; and I find that I forgot to mention a remarkable pamphlet 'On Currency' published anonymously in 1840 (London, Charles Knight and Co.) in which a mathematical analysis of the operations of the Money Market is attempted. The method of treatment is not unlike that adopted by Dr Whewell,[4] to whose Memoirs a reference is made; but finite or occasionally infinitesimal differences are introduced. On the success of this anonymous theory I have not formed an opinion; but the subject is one which must some day be solved by mathematical analysis. Garnier, in his treatise on Political Economy, mentions several continental mathematicians who have written on the subject of Political Economy; but I have not been able to discover even the titles of their Memoirs.[5]

### From *Chapter III: Theory of Utility. Definition of Terms*

Pleasure and pain are undoubtedly the ultimate objects of the Calculus of Economy. To satisfy our wants to the utmost with the least effort – to procure the greatest amount of what is desirable at the expense of the least that is undesirable – in other words, to maximise comfort and pleasure, is the problem of Economy. But it is convenient to transfer our attention as soon as possible to the physical objects or actions which are the source to us of pleasures or pains. A very large part of the labour of any community is spent upon the production of the ordinary necessaries and conveniences of life, food, clothing, buildings, utensils, furniture, ornaments, &c.; and the aggregate of these objects constitute, therefore, the immediate object of our attention.

It will be convenient at once to introduce and define some terms which will facilitate the expression of the Principles of Economy. By a *commodity* we shall understand any object, or, it may be, any action or service, which can afford pleasure or ward off pain. The name was originally abstract, and denoted the quality of anything by which it was capable of serving man. Having acquired, by a common process of confusion, a concrete signification, it will be well to retain it entirely for that signification, and employ the word *utility* to denote the abstract quality whereby an object serves our purposes, and becomes entitled to rank as a commodity. Whatever can produce pleasure or prevent pain *may* possess utility. M Say has correctly and briefly defined utility as 'la faculté qu'ont les choses de pouvoir servir à l'homme, de quelque manière que ce soit.'[6] The food which prevents the pangs of hunger, the clothes which fend off the cold of winter, possess incontestable utility; but we must beware of restricting the meaning of the word by any moral considerations. Anything which an individual is found to desire and to labour for must be assumed to possess for him utility. In the science of Economy we treat men not as they ought to be, but as they are. Bentham, in establishing the foundation of Moral Science in his great 'Introduction to the Principles of Morals and Legislation' (p. 3), thus comprehensively defines the term in question: - 'By utility is meant that property in any object, whereby it tends to produce benefit, advantage, pleasure, good, or happiness (all this, in the present case, comes to the same thing), or (what comes again to the same thing) to prevent the happening of mischief, pain, evil, or unhappiness to the party whose interest is considered.'[7]

This perfectly expresses the meaning of the word in Economy, provided that the will or inclination of the person concerned is taken as the sole criterion, for the time, of what is good and desirable, or painful and evil.

### The Laws of Human Want the Basis of Economy

Political Economy must be founded upon a full and accurate investigation of the conditions of utility; and, to understand this element, we must necessarily examine the character of the wants and desires of man. We, first of all, need a theory of the consumption of wealth. Mr J. S. Mill, indeed, has given an opinion inconsistent with this. 'Political Economy,' he says,[a] 'has nothing to do with the consumption of wealth, further than as the consideration of it is inseparable from that of production, or from that of distribution. We know not of any laws of the consumption of wealth, as the subject of a distinct science; they can be no other than the laws of human enjoyment.'

But it is surely obvious that Political Economy does rest upon the laws of human enjoyment; and that, if those laws are developed by no other science, they must be developed by economists. We labour to produce with the sole object of consuming, and the kinds and amounts of goods produced must be governed entirely by our requirements. Every manufacturer knows and feels how closely he must anticipate the tastes and needs of his customers: his whole success depends upon it; and, in like manner, the whole theory of Economy depends upon a correct theory of consumption. Many economists have had a clear perception of this truth. Lord Lauderdale[8] distinctly states,[b] that 'the great

a    'Essays on some Unsettled Questions of Political Economy,' p. 132.
b    'Inquiry into the Nature and Origin of Public Wealth,' second edition, 1819, p. 306.

and important step towards ascertaining the causes of the direction which industry takes in nations ... seems to be the discovery of what dictates the proportion of demand for the various articles which are produced.' Mr Senior, in his admirable treatise, has also recognised this truth, and pointed out what he calls the *Law of Variety* in human requirements. The necessaries of life are so few and simple, that a man is soon satisfied in regard to these, and desires to extend his range of enjoyment. His first object is to vary his food; but there soon arises the desire of variety and elegance in dress; and to this succeeds the desire to build, to ornament, and to furnish – tastes which are absolutely insatiable where they exist, and seem to increase with every improvement in civilisation.[c]

Bastiat[9] has also observed that human wants are the ultimate object of Economy; and in his 'Harmonies of Political Economy,' he says,[d] '*Wants, Efforts, Satisfaction* – this is the circle of Political Economy.'

In still later years, M Courcelle-Seneuil[10] actually commenced his treatise with a definition of *want* – 'Le besoin économique est un désir qui a pour but la possession et la jouissance d'un objet matériel.'[e] And I conceive that he has given the best possible statement of the problem of Economy when he expresses its object as 'à satisfaire nos besoins avec la moindre somme de travail possible.'[f]

Professor Hearn[11] also commences his excellent treatise, entitled 'Plutology, or the Theory of Efforts to supply Human Wants,' with a chapter in which he considers the nature of the wants impelling man to exertion.

The writer, however, who seems to me to have reached the deepest comprehension of the foundation of Economy, is Mr T. E. Banfield.[12] His course of Lectures delivered in the University of Cambridge in 1844, and published under the title of 'The Organization of Labour,' is highly interesting, but perhaps not always correct. In the following passage[g] he profoundly points out that the scientific basis of Economy is in a theory of consumption: I need make no excuses for quoting this passage at full length.

'The lower wants man experiences in common with brutes. The cravings of hunger and thirst, the effects of heat and cold, of drought and damp, he feels with more acuteness than the rest of the animal world. His sufferings are doubtless sharpened by the consciousness that he has no right to be subject to such inflictions. Experience, however, shows that privations of various kinds affect men differently in degree, according to the circumstances in which they are placed. For some men the privation of certain enjoyments is intolerable, whose loss is not even

c   'Encyclopaedia Metropolitana,' art. *Political Economy*, p. 133. Fifth edition of Reprint, p. 11.
d   'Harmonies of Political Economy,' translated by P. J. Stirling, 1860, p. 65.
e   'Traité Théorique et Pratique d'Economie Politique,' par J. G. Courcelle-Seneuil, 2me ed. Paris, 1867, tom. i. p. 25.
f   *Ib.* p. 33.
g   Second edition, p. 11.

felt by others. Some, again, sacrifice all that others hold dear for the gratification of longings and aspirations that are incomprehensible to their neighbours. Upon this complex foundation of low wants and high aspirations the Political Economist has to build the theory of production and consumption.

'An examination of the nature and intensity of man's wants shows that this connection between them gives to Political Economy its scientific basis. The first proposition of the theory of consumption is, that *the satisfaction of every lower want in the scale creates a desire of a higher character*. If the higher desire existed previous to the satisfaction of the primary want, it becomes more intense when the latter is removed. The removal of a primary want commonly awakens the sense of more than one secondary privation: thus a full supply of ordinary food not only excites to delicacy in eating, but awakens attention to clothing. The highest grade in the scale of wants, that of pleasure derived from the beauties of nature and art, is usually confined to men who are exempted from all the lower privations. Thus the demand for, and the consumption of, objects of refined enjoyment has its lever in the facility with which the primary wants are satisfied. This, therefore, is the key to the true theory of value. Without relative values in the objects to the acquirement of which we direct our power, there would be no foundation for Political Economy as a science.'

## Utility not an Intrinsic Quality

My principal work now lies in tracing out the exact nature and conditions of utility. It seems strange indeed that economists have not bestowed more minute attention on a subject which doubtless furnishes the true key to the problem of Economy.

In the first place, utility, though a quality of things, is *no inherent quality*. It might be more accurately described, perhaps, as *a circumstance of things* arising out of their relation to man's requirements. As Mr Senior most accurately says, 'Utility denotes no intrinsic quality in the things which we call useful; it merely expresses their relations to the pains and pleasures of mankind.' We can never, therefore, say absolutely that some objects have utility and others have not. The ore lying in the mine, the diamond escaping the eye of the searcher, the wheat lying unreaped, the fruit ungathered for want of consumers, have not utility at all. The most wholesome and necessary kinds of food are useless unless there are hands to collect and mouths to eat them. Nor, when we consider the matter closely, can we say that all portions of the same commodity possess equal utility. Water, for instance, may be roughly described as the most useful of all substances. A quart of water per day has the high utility of saving a person from dying in a most distressing manner. Several gallons a day may possess much utility for such purposes as cooking and washing; but after an adequate supply is secured for these uses, any additional quantity is a matter of indifference. All that we can say, then, is, that water, up to a certain quantity, is indispensable; that further quantities will have various degrees of utility; but that beyond a certain point the utility appears to cease.

Exactly the same considerations apply more or less clearly to every other article. A pound of bread per day supplied to a person saves him from starvation, and has the highest conceivable utility. A second pound per day has also no slight utility: it keeps him in a state of comparative plenty, though it be not altogether indispensable. A third pound would begin to be superfluous. It is clear, then, that *utility is not proportional to commodity*: the very same articles vary in utility according as we already possess more or less of the same article. The like may be said of other things. One suit of clothes per annum is necessary, a second convenient, a third desirable, a fourth not unacceptable; but we, sooner or later, reach a point at which further supplies are not desired with any perceptible force, unless it be for subsequent use.

### Law of the Variation of Utility

Let us now investigate this subject a little more closely. Utility must be considered as measured by, or even as actually identical with, the addition made to a person's happiness. It is a convenient name for the aggregate of the favourable balance of feeling produced – the sum of the pleasure created and the pain prevented. We must now carefully discriminate between the *total utility* belonging to any commodity and the utility belonging to any particular portion of it. Thus the total utility of the food we eat consists in maintaining life, and may be considered as infinitely great; but if we were to subtract a tenth part from what we eat daily, our loss would be but slight. It might be doubtful whether we should suffer any harm at all. Let us imagine the whole quantity of food which a person consumes on an average during twenty-four hours to be divided into ten equal parts. If his food be reduced by the last part, he will suffer but little; if a second tenth part be deficient, he will feel the want distinctly; the subtraction of the third tenth part will be decidedly injurious; with every subsequent subtraction of a tenth part his sufferings will be more and more serious, until at length he will be upon the verge of starvation. Now, if we call each of the tenth parts *an increment*, the meaning of these facts is, that each increment of food is less necessary, or possesses less utility, than the previous one. [ . . . ][13]

But the division of the food into ten equal parts is an arbitrary supposition. If we had taken twenty or a hundred or more equal parts, the same general principle would hold true, namely, that each small portion would be less useful and necessary than the last. The law may be considered to hold true theoretically, however small the increments are made; and in this way we shall at last reach a figure which is undistinguishable from a continuous curve. The notion of infinitely small quantities of food may seem absurd as regards one individual; but, when we come to consider the consumption of nations as a whole, the consumption may well be conceived to increase or diminish by quantities which are, practically speaking, infinitely small compared with the whole consumption. [ ... ]

### The Final Degree of Utility and the Law of its Variation

The final degree of utility is that function upon which the whole Theory of Economy will be found to turn. Political Economists, generally speaking, have failed to discriminate between this function and the total utility. From this confusion has arisen much perplexity. Many of those commodities which are the most useful to us are esteemed and desired the least. We cannot live a day without water, and yet in ordinary circumstances we set no value on it. Why is this? Simply because we usually have so much of it that its final degree of utility is reduced nearly to zero. We enjoy, every day, the almost infinite utility of water, but then we do not need to consume more than we have. Let the supply run short by drought, and we begin to feel the higher degree of utility, of which we think but little at other times.

The variation of the function expressing the final degree of utility is the all-important point in all economical problems. We may state, as a general law, that *it varies with the quantity of commodity, and ultimately decreases as that quantity increases.* No commodity can be named which we continue to desire with the same force, whatever be the quantity already in use or possession. All our appetites are capable of *satisfaction* or *satiety* sooner or later, both these words meaning, etymologically, that we have had *enough*, so that more is of no use to us. It does not follow, indeed, that the degree of utility will always sink to zero. This may be the case with many things, especially the simple animal requirements, food, water, air, &c. But the more refined and intellectual our needs become, the less are they capable of satiety. To the desire for articles of taste, science, or curiosity, when once excited, there is hardly a limit.

This great principle of the ultimate decrease of the final degree of utility of any commodity is implied in the writings of many economists, though seldom distinctly stated. It is the real law which lies at the basis of Senior's so-called 'Law of Variety.' Indeed, Senior states the law itself. He says:

'It is obvious that our desires do not aim so much at quantity as at diversity. Not only are there limits to the pleasure which commodities of any given class can afford, but the pleasure diminishes in a rapidly increasing ratio long before those limits are reached. Two articles of the same kind will seldom afford twice the pleasure of one, and still less will ten give five times the pleasure of two. In proportion, therefore, as any article is abundant, the number of those who are provided with it, and do not wish, or wish but little, to increase their provision, is likely to be great; and, so far as they are concerned, the additional supply loses all, or nearly all, its utility. And, in proportion to its scarcity, the number of those who are in want of it, and the degree in which they want it, are likely to be increased; and its utility, or, in other words, the pleasure which the possession of a given quantity of it will afford, increases proportionally.'[h]

Banfield's 'Law of the Subordination of Wants' also rests upon the same basis. It cannot be said, with accuracy, that the satisfaction of a lower want *creates* a higher want; it merely permits the higher want to manifest itself. We distribute our labour and possessions in such a way as to satisfy the more pressing wants first. If food runs short, the all-absorbing question is, how to obtain more, because, at the moment, more pleasure or pain depends upon food than upon any other commodity. But, when food is moderately abundant, its final degree of utility falls very low, and wants of a much more complex and less satiable nature become comparatively prominent.

The writer, however, who appears to me to have most clearly appreciated the nature and importance of the law of utility, is Mr Richard Jennings,[14] who, in 1855, published a small book called 'The Natural Elements of Political Economy.'[i] This work treats of the physical groundwork of Economy, showing its dependence on physiological laws. It appears to me to display a great insight into the real basis of Economy; yet I am not aware that economists have bestowed the slightest attention on Mr Jennings' views.[j] I take the liberty, therefore, of giving a full extract from his remarks on the nature of utility. It will thus be seen that the law, as I state it, is no novelty, and that it is only careful deduction from principles in our possession that is needed to give us a correct Theory of Economy.

'To turn from the relative effect of commodities, in producing sensations, to those which are absolute, or dependent only on the quantity of each commodity, it is but too well known to every condition of men, that the degree of each sensation which is produced, is by no means commensurate with the quantity of the commodity applied to the senses. . . . These effects require to be closely observed, because they are the foundation of the changes of money price, which valuable objects command in times of varied scarcity and abundance; we shall therefore direct out attention to them for the purpose of ascertaining the nature of the law according to which the sensations that attend on

---

h   'Encyclopaedia Metropolitana,' p. 133. Reprint, p. 12.

i   London: Longmans.

j   Professor Cairnes is, however, an exception. See his 'Lectures on the Character and Logical Method of Political Economy.' London, 1857, p. 81. [John Elliot Cairnes (1823–1878); in 1866 he was appointed Professor of Political Economy at University College, London. His *Essays in Political Economy, Theoretical and Applied*, first published in *Fraser's Magazine*, and then in book form in 1873, were seen as confirming Jevons' work.]

consumption vary in degree with changes in the quantity of the commodity consumed.

'We may gaze upon an object until we can no longer discern it, listen until we can no longer hear, smell until the sense of odour is exhausted, taste until the object becomes nauseous, and touch until it becomes painful; we may consume food until we are fully satisfied, and use stimulants until more would cause pain. On the other hand, the same object offered to the special senses for a moderate duration of time, and the same food or stimulants consumed when we are exhausted or weary, may convey much gratification. If the whole quantity of the commodity consumed during the interval of these two states of sensation, the state of satiety and the state of inanition, be conceived to be divided into a number of equal parts, each marked with its proper degrees of sensation, the question to be determined will be, what relation does the difference in the degrees of the sensation bear to the difference in the quantities of the commodity? First, with respect to all commodities, our feelings show that the degrees of satisfaction do not proceed *pari passu*[15] with the quantities consumed; they do not advance equally with each instalment of the commodity offered to the senses, and then suddenly stop; but diminish gradually, until they ultimately disappear, and further instalments can produce no further satisfaction. In this progressive scale the increments of sensation resulting from equal increments of the commodity are obviously less and less at each step, – each degree of sensation is less than the preceding degree. Placing ourselves at that middle point of sensation, the *juste milieu*, the *aurea mediocritas*, the ἄριστον μέτρον[16] of sages, which is the most usual status of the mass of mankind, and which, therefore, is the best position that can be chosen for measuring deviations from the usual amount, we may say that the law which expresses the relation of degrees of sensation to quantities of commodities is of this character: if the average or temperate quantity of commodities be increased, the satisfaction derived is increased in a less degree, and ultimately ceases to be increased at all; if the average or temperate quantity be diminished, the loss of more and more satisfaction will continually ensue, and the detriment thence arising will ultimately become exceedingly great.'[k]

From *Chapter IV: Theory of Exchange. On The Origin of Value*

The preceding pages contain, if I am not mistaken, an explanation of the nature of value which will, for the most part, harmonise with previous views upon the subject. Ricardo has stated, like most other economists, that utility is absolutely

k    pp. 96–99.

essential to value; but that 'possessing utility, commodities derive their exchange-able value from two sources: from their scarcity, and from the quantity of labour required to obtain them.'[l] Senior, again, has admirably defined wealth, or objects possessing value, as 'those things, and those things only, which are transferable, are limited in supply, and are directly or indirectly productive of pleasure or preventive of pain.' Speaking only of things which are transferable, or capable of being passed from hand to hand, we find that the two clearest statements of the nature of value available, recognise *utility* and *scarcity* as the requisites. But the moment that we distinguish between the total utility of a mass of commodity and the degree of utility of different portions, we may say that the scarcity is that which prevents the fall in the final degree of utility. Bread has the almost infinite utility of maintaining life, and when it becomes a question of life or death, a small quantity of food exceeds in value all other things. But when we enjoy our ordinary supplies of food, a loaf of bread has little value, because the utility of an additional loaf is small, our appetite being satiated by our customary meals.

I have pointed out the excessive ambiguity of the word Value, and the apparent impossibility of safely using it. When used to express the mere fact of certain articles exchanging in a particular ratio, I have proposed to substitute the unequivocal expression – *ratio of exchange*. But I am inclined to believe that a ratio is not the meaning which most persons attach to the word Value. There is a certain sense of esteem, of desirableness, which we may have with regard to a thing apart from any distinct consciousness of the ratio in which it would exchange for other things. I may suggest that this distinct feeling of value is probably identical with the final degree of utility. While Adam Smith's often-quoted *value in use* is the total utility of a commodity to us, the *value in exchange* is defined by the *terminal utility*, the remaining desire which we or others have for possessing more.

There remains the question of labour as an element of value. There have not been wanting economists who put forward labour as the *cause of value*, asserting that all objects derive their value from the fact that labour has been expended on them; and it is even implied, if not stated, that value will be exactly proportional to labour. This is a doctrine which cannot stand for a moment, being directly opposed to facts. Ricardo disposes of such an opinion when he says:[m]

'There are some commodities, the value of which is determined by their scarcity alone. No labour can increase the quantity of such goods, and therefore their value cannot be lowered by an increased supply. Some rare statues and pictures, scarce books and coins, wines of a peculiar quality, which can only be made from grapes grown on a particular soil, of which there is a very limited quantity, are all of this

l  'Principles of Political Economy and Taxation,' third edition, p. 2. [See page 94.]
m  'Principles of Political Economy and Taxation,' third edition, p. 2. [See page 94.]

description. Their value is wholly independent of the quantity of labour originally necessary to produce them, and varies with the varying wealth and inclinations of those who are desirous to possess them.'

The mere fact that there are many things, such as rare ancient books, coins, antiquities, which have high values, and which are absolutely incapable of production now, disperses the notion that value depends on labour. Even those things which are producible in any quantities by labour seldom exchange exactly at the corresponding values. The market price of corn, cotton, iron, and most other things is, in the prevalent theories of value, allowed to fluctuate above or below its natural or cost value. There may, again, be any discrepancy between the quantity of labour spent upon an object and the value ultimately attaching to it. A great undertaking like the Great Western Railway, or the Thames Tunnel, may embody a vast amount of labour, but its value depends entirely upon the number of persons who find it useful. If no use could be found for the Great Eastern steamship, its value would be *nil*, except for the utility of some of its materials. On the other hand, a successful undertaking, which happens to possess great utility, may have a value for a time, at least, far exceeding what has been spent upon it, as in the case of the Atlantic cable. The fact is, that *labour once spent has no influence on the future value of any article*: it is gone and lost for ever. In commerce by-gones are for ever by-gones; and we are always starting clear at each moment, judging the values of things with a view to future utility. Industry is essentially prospective, not retrospective; and seldom does the result of any undertaking exactly coincide with the first intentions of its founders.

But though labour is never the cause of value, it is in a large proportion of cases the determining circumstance, and in the following way: – Value depends solely on the final degree of utility. How can we vary this degree of utility? – By having more or less of the commodity to consume. And how shall we get more or less of it? – By spending more or less labour in obtaining a supply. According to this view, then, there are two steps between labour and value. Labour affects supply, and supply affects the degree of utility, which governs value, or the ratio of exchange.

But it is easy to go too far in considering labour as the regulator of value; it is equally to be remembered that labour is itself of unequal value. Ricardo, by a violent assumption, founded his theory of value on quantities of labour considered as one uniform thing. He was aware that labour differs infinitely in quality and efficiency, so that each kind is more or less scarce, and is consequently paid at a higher or lower rate of wages. He regarded these differences as disturbing circumstances which would have to be allowed for; but his theory rests on the assumed equality of labour. This theory rests on a wholly different ground. I hold labour to be *essentially variable*, so that *its value must be determined by the value of the produce, not the value of the produce by that of the labour*. I hold it to be impossible to compare *à priori* the productive powers of a navvy, a carpenter, an ironpuddler,[17] a schoolmaster, and a barrister. Accordingly, it will be found that not one of my equations represents a comparison between one man's labour and another's. The equation, if there is one at all, is between the same person in two or more different occupations. The subject is one in which complicated action and re-action takes place, and which we must defer until after we have described, in the next chapter, the Theory of Labour.

## HENRY MAYERS HYNDMAN, *ENGLAND FOR ALL: THE TEXT-BOOK OF DEMOCRACY* (1881)

Henry Mayers Hyndman (1842–1921) was a key figure in introducing Marxist ideas into Britain in the nineteenth century. He was the leader and founder (in 1881) of the Democratic (later Social Democratic) Federation (the SDF), the first socialist organisation in Britain. That same year also saw the publication of *England for All: The Text-Book of Democracy*. In it Hyndman plagiarised elements of Marx's *Capital*, provoking Marx's anger and instigating a lasting rift with the circle of Engels and Marx. In the 1880s Hyndman published a number of pamphlets on socialism, and in 1883 his next major work, *The Historical Basis of Socialism in England*, appeared. This time the debt to Marx was explicitly acknowledged. Hyndman's domineering leadership of the SDF together with internal disagreements over issues such as the nature of social reform, eventually led to the departure of a substantial proportion of the executive (including William Morris) to set up a rival socialist organisation, the Socialist League. Hyndman continued as leader of the SDF, and remained actively involved in socialist politics well into the next century. However, his dismissal of trade unionism, his antipathy to working-class activism and his anti-Semitism ensured that he remained a controversial figure in British political life.

### From Henry Mayers Hyndman, *England for All: The Text-Book of Democracy* (London: E. W. Allen, 1881)[1]

#### From *Chapter II: Labour*[2]

That natural objects are of no value unless human labour is expended on them is a truth as old as the world. That labour is the real basis, not only of value but of all civilized society, needs no elaborate demonstration at this time of day. Yet it is precisely from this generally admitted but little regarded truth that consequences follow of the highest importance to our modern society. Here come in those 'differences of value,' those strange manipulations of the worth of commodities, which go to the root of all business.

A merchant has a sum of money, say a hundred pounds sterling. Therewith he buys on the market say a hundred pounds' worth of cotton. So far the exchange may be perfectly fair and exact. The merchant has given his labour as expressed in a hundred pounds sterling for another man's labour as embodied in a mass of cotton. But, having bought, he goes away and sells his purchased cotton to another person for 110*l.*, making, as it is said, 10*l.* by the transaction. His 100*l.* was turned into its equivalent in merchandise, and then appeared again as 110*l.* Not only is the original sum replaced, but more is added, and the merchant's money becomes capital. The merchant buys not for himself, or to work up for the use of others, but merely to sell the cotton again at an enhanced price. This is something very different from the use of money as the measure of the value of commodities, or as the means of facilitating exchange. It is commercial capital, which its owner takes upon the market for the purpose of increasing it. Money to start with; then, after a longer or a shorter interval, more money – that, leaving out the intermediate process of buying the cotton, is the process. But the amount of value in circulation at any given moment – that is, the quantity of human labour on the average embodied in commodities – cannot increase of itself. If a merchant has in his possession a commodity whose value is expressed in money by 10*l.*, this value can only be increased absolutely, and made say 11*l.*, by the addition of more labour to the labour-value represented in the first instance – as by making a coat of cloth. The coat is worth more than the cloth, but the value of the cloth remains the same. Thus then all conditions remaining the same, the owner of the money to start with must buy a piece of merchandise at its exact value, and sell it again for what it is worth, and yet have at the end more value than he had at the beginning.

Now the problem begins to take shape.

The increase of value by which money becomes more money and is turned into capital, obviously cannot arise from the money itself. It follows then that the conversion of money into merchandise, and then of that same merchandise into more money, is due to the merchandise. But how? Commodities can no more increase their own exchangeable value than money. In order to obtain an additional exchangeable value from a commodity a sort of merchandise must be found which possesses the remarkable quality of being itself the source of exchangeable value, so that to consume it would be to obtain that labour-force embodied in value, and consequently to create value.

Now it so happens that the capitalist in embryo does find on the market a purchasable commodity endowed with this specific virtue. This is called labour, or force of labour. Under that name is comprised the entire capacities, physical and intellectual, which exist in the body of a man, and which he must set in motion in order to produce articles of utility. Evidently the force of labour cannot present itself on the market for sale, unless it is offered by its owner; he must be able to dispose of it – that is, be the free owner of his labour, of the force of his own body. The moneyed man and he meet on the market; one buys, and the other sells, and both are quits. But the owner of this labour-force must only sell it for a definite time; if he sells it for an indefinite time, from being a merchant, he himself, his force of labour and all, becomes a mere commodity. He is a slave or serf at the command of his master as a chattel. The essential condition for the capitalist to be able to buy the force of labour is, that the owner of the labour instead of being able to keep himself by work on his own land, or to sell goods on which he has himself expended his labour, should be obliged to sell the labour-force in his body pure and simple. A man in order to sell goods of his own making, must of course command the means of production – tools, raw material, &c. Then he is master of his own labour, an independent man; he has the means of exchanging his own labour as embodied in useful articles for other men's labour also embodied in useful articles upon equal terms. But in order that money should be converted into capital the workman himself must be free in a very different sense; not only must he be ready to sell his labour as a commodity, but further, he must be *free* – so very free that he has nothing else in the world but his power of labour to sell – that he should be completely destitute of the means of realizing his own force of labour in commodities by himself, having neither tools, nor land, nor raw materials wherewith to do so.

How does this free labourer thus find himself on the market, ready to enter into free contract? That does not concern the owner of the money, who looks upon the labour-market as a mere branch of the rest of the market for commodities, and governed by the same laws. The appearance of this destitute labourer there is nevertheless, as has been seen, the outcome of a long series of economical evolutions and revolutions extending over centuries. Driven from the land, deprived of the possibility of earning a living, the mass of the people find themselves concentrated in the towns. Nature most assuredly does not turn out possessors of money or goods on the one side, and owners of their pure labour-force, and nothing else, on the other; nor is such a social state common to most periods of history. So long, for example, as the produce of labour is used to supply the needs of the labourer, it does not, as has been seen, become merchandise; in the same way, the production and circulation of commodities may take place under many forms of society. It is not so with capital; that only makes its appearance when that part of the wealth of a country which is employed in production, consisting of food, clothing, tools, raw materials, machinery, &c., necessary to give effect to labour, is found in the hands of an owner, who meets on the market the destitute free labourer come thither sell his labour.

Capital then forms an epoch in social production.

What, however, is this force of labour, which the free owner of it comes on to the market to sell? Clearly it is a human force, physical, moral, intellectual, which requires certain material, food, and clothing and lodging – all at the command of the moneyed man, and not of the labourer – to keep it in order and supplied, so that the waste of one day may be made good, and it may return with equal vigour the next. These necessaries vary, of course, with different climates, and with different degrees of civilization; but in any given country and period the average needs of the labourers are known. Nor is this fact altered by the other fact that, as pointed out by Mill,[3] a series of circumstances may reduce the standard of supposed necessaries. The amount of average necessaries thus ascertained is called by Ricardo,[4] the 'natural price of labour,' and is 'that price which is necessary to enable the labourers one with another to subsist, and to perpetuate their race without either increase or diminution.' In this way we have that amount of average daily necessaries which will maintain the present race of destitute bargainers, and provide them with equally destitute successors.

Assume then that the cost of this amount of daily foods, the natural price of human labour comprised in the necessaries for existence for the twenty-four hours – representing by rights only the quantity of human labour expended in their production – is six hours' work. Half a day's average work is needed then to reproduce the average amount of labour-force expended. Take this at three shillings as expressed in money. Then the owner of the labour who sells its work for six hours at three shillings, sells it for its exact value. 'It is when the market price of labour exceeds its natural price that the condition of the labourer is flourishing and happy – that he has it in his power to command a greater proportion of the necessaries and enjoyments of life. When the market price of labour is below its natural price, the condition of the labourers is most wretched; then poverty deprives them of comforts which custom renders absolute necessaries.' So far Ricardo again. But the natural price of labour reaches its minimum when it is reduced to the value of the means of subsistence physiologically indispensable. When it falls to this minimum, the price has reached a level below the value of the labour-force, which then only just maintains itself without immediate deterioration. For example, a man who sells his labour for just enough to keep himself and his family without making any provision for old age, or future ill-health from which he may suffer, is clearly going down hill. The natural price of his labour has not in this case taken a sufficiently wide range.

When also the capitalist buys the labour, it is the owner of that labour who sells on credit. He advances his labour to the capitalist; the capitalist advances nothing to him without having been previously paid for it. In every country where the capitalist system prevails, the labourer is only paid after he has worked for a certain period – a week, a fortnight, a month – on credit. This enables the capitalist to 'turn round.' If the employer fails, the labourers suffer: they are not paid; for the labour has been sold beforehand, and duly delivered by the expenditure of force from the labourer's body. An illustration of this occurred not long since in the great strike of colliers in the north against the masters, who wished to make their men break the law by contracting out of the Employers' Liability Act.[5] Once out on strike they insisted most strongly upon the reduction of the length of the advance of their labour to the capitalist, from the fortnight to the week. This point they carried. Fortnightly or monthly wages are a hardship to the labourer, which, like many others, can only be removed by resolute combination; for that value in use which the owner of the labour advances to the buyer, only shows itself in employment. And this consumption of force of labour produces, not only commodities, but surplus value besides. Everything else needed for the purposes of production – raw materials, machinery, &c. – have been bought by the capitalist at their actual value, and paid for at their actual price. It is labour only, the labour-force of human beings, from which he derives his surplus value. Out of this, his last purchase, bought on credit, the capitalist makes his capital breed. This labour, bought in the open market, and realized in the commodity – this it is which gives the capitalist the additional value he hungers for.

Now we begin to see how it comes about that 10*l.* turns into 11*l.*, that 100*l.* swells into 110*l.*, without additional value. Now, too, the admirable working of 'freedom of contract' and 'supply and demand' in our modern society appears. Hear, too, William Cobbett[6] for a moment: 'To those who labour, we who labour not with our hands owe all that we eat and drink and wear, all that shades us by day and that shelters us by night, all the means of enjoying health and pleasure; and therefore if we possess talent for the task, we are ungrateful or cowardly, or both, if we omit any effort within our power to prevent them from being slaves. What is a slave? For let us not be amused by a name. A slave is in the first place a man who has no property; and property means something that he has, and that nobody can take from him without his leave or consent. A slave has *no property in his labour*, and any man who is compelled to give up the fruit of his labour to another at the arbitrary will of that other, has no property in his labour, and is therefore a slave, whether the fruit of his labour be taken from him directly or indirectly. If it be said that he gives up the fruit of his labour by his own will, and that it is not forced from him, I answer, To be sure he *may* avoid eating and drinking, and may go naked; but then he must die; and on this condition, and this condition only, can he refuse to give up the fruit of his labour. "Die, wretch, or surrender as much of your income or the fruit of your labour as your masters choose to take."'

To return. The working man who has sold his labour works, of course, under the control of the capitalist to whom his labour thus belongs, and whose object it is that he should work hard and continuously. Besides, the product in which his force of labour is embodied is the property of the capitalist, and in no sense that of the labourer. The capitalist merely pays him his wages, just as he would pay for the hire of a horse or a mule. Then the employer applies the human merchandise he has thus bought to his raw materials and machinery. The result is a value in use to be passed on to others; and not only such value, but a surplus value for the capitalist himself, derived from this purchased labour.

Take, for example, cotton yarns. The capitalist buys, say, ten pounds of raw cotton for 10*s.* In that price there is already expressed the average labour needed for the production, transport, and marketing of the raw cotton. Now put the wear and tear of the spindles, machinery, &c., in working up the raw material into yarn at 2*s.* If a piece of gold of the value of 12*s.* is the output of twenty-four hours' work, it follows that there are, apart from the labour in the factory, two full days of work (at the assumed natural rate of 3*s.* for six hours' work) embodied in the yarn. This accounts for the original labour needed to raise and transport the raw cotton, as well as the labour needed to replace the wear and tear.

It has already been assumed that the workman must give six hours' labour in order to earn 3*s.*, the natural price of his labour required to supply him socially with his absolute necessaries. Now assume further that it takes six hours' labour to turn ten pounds of cotton into ten pounds of yarn; then the workman has added to the raw cotton a value of 3*s.*, a half-a-day's work. So at the end the ten pounds of yarn contain altogether two days and a half of labour; raw cotton and wear and tear of spindles stand for two days; and half-a-day has been absorbed by the cotton in the process of spinning. This quantity of labour is therefore reckoned in a piece of gold of the value of 15s.; that is to say, the price of the yarn worked up from the cotton is 1s. 6d. a pound. Here obviously is no gain to the capitalist. His raw material, his wear and tear of machinery, his wages paid for the labour which he has purchased, eat up the whole of the capital advanced, and yet the ten pounds of yarn only fetch 1s. 6d. a pound, which is the value of the average quantity of labour contained in it. This shows no profit whatever, much to the horror of the capitalist if he stopped there.

But the employer has bought the labourer's whole day's work upon the market. He can make him work therefore not merely the six hours required to produce the return of the 3s. paid, but twelve hours – a day's work. Now if six hours' work produces ten pounds of yarn from ten pounds of cotton, twelve hours' work will give twenty pounds of yarn from twenty pounds of cotton. These twenty pounds of yarn will thus contain five days' labour, of which four are contained in the raw cotton and the wear and tear of machinery and spindles, and one day is absorbed by the yarn during the process of spinning. The expression in money then of these five days' work is 30s. That, therefore, is the price of the twenty pounds of yarn. Thus the yarn is sold now as it was before at 1s. 6d. a pound. But the sum of the values of the merchandise (including labour in the factory) embodied in the yarn does not exceed 27s.; that is to say, 20s. for the raw cotton, 4s. for the wear and tear, and 3s. for the labour in the factory. The value of the product has therefore increased. The 27s. have become 30s. Those 27s. advanced by the capitalist have begotten a surplus value of 3s., and the trick is done. The capitalist has used a certain amount of another man's labour for his own behoof without paying for it, and the trick is done at that man's expense. That free labour which is sold in the open market enables the capitalist to sell the twenty pounds of yarn he has made at the regular price of 1s. 6d. a pound, and, nevertheless, to increase his capital by 3s. on the output of twenty pounds. Labour thus used is the origin of surplus value, and all's well.

Once more it is permissible to look back to the 10l. made into 11l., to the 100l. swollen to 110l. The 1l. like the 10l. is obtained from that free labour which is bound to be sold for less than its worth, in order that its possessor may continue to keep body and soul together. And the surplus value so produced the capitalist, the merchant, the shopkeeper, divide among themselves.

In existing conditions of agricultural production, the agricultural labourer in the same way provides on his part the surplus value which the landowner, the rent-charger, the farmer, the mortgagee, divide, in the shape of rent, settlement, profit on capital, and interest on money lent. The labourer himself, earning his 10s. to 12s. a week, is the man upon whom all these worthy people live, though they do so in a more indirect manner than the capitalist of the large towns, and have perhaps a trifle more conscience left to appeal to. [ . . . ][7]

What, however is this day's work, necessary labour and extra labour together, which the capitalist buys on the market? Obviously there must be some limit to it. A man can't work twenty-four hours on end every day in the week, that is clear. But the limits of the day's work are very elastic. We find ten hours, twelve hours, fourteen, sixteen, even eighteen hours, given as the amount of a day's work. And this limit, however loose already, capitalists, from the shirt-sweaters up to the railway companies, are always striving to extend. They invoke the sacred laws of supply and demand and freedom of contract, to sanction an amount of daily toil which leaves a man or a woman utterly exhausted at its close, which weakens health, reduces vitality, and hands on a broken constitution to the progeny. And all for what? In order to swell that surplus value which 'society' depends upon for its excessive luxury and continued laziness. 'But,' say the labourers when adjured not to endanger society, 'that is all very well; but society is shamefully wronging us. It is society which, having entire command of the police and military forces of the country, enables the capitalist class thus to violate every law of exchange with impunity. These are they who pay us only one-half or one-third or one-quarter of the real value of our day's work. They then are the people who are endangering society, of which we form by far the most important part – not the working men, who ask only that their labour should not be taken for nothing.'

There is a comparison at hand which philanthropizing capitalists – and there are many of them – will understand, if they do not appreciate. Under the old system of *corvée*[8] a man was obliged to give say one day's work in the week, or at most two, to his feudal lord without any payment. Such a man, though he had the remaining five or six days wholly to himself, was thought little better than a slave. Nor was he. English capitalists would, of all men, subscribe largely to relieve human beings from continuing in such a shameful and degraded position. But here at home, we have men, women, and children, who are obliged to give four, five, six hours a day to the capitalist for nothing, and yet are thought free. A factory hand who, as in the instance given above, provides six hours a day of extra labour, makes the capitalist a present of three days' work in the week for nothing. He gives, in fact, three times as much labour for nothing in the week to his employer, as the serf who works one day in the week under *corvée* is obliged to offer in unpaid labour to his lord. But in the one case, under the system of daily or weekly wages, the necessary labour and the extra labour are lumped together as so much paid-for labour; in the other, they are divided. Thus the forced, extra, unpaid labour for the capitalist – the industrial *corvée* – escapes notice, though it is three times greater than the other, and the capitalist is thrice as heavy a master as the feudal lord.

Moreover, the capitalist class has ever been on the look-out to increase the hours of labour beyond measure, in order that they may obtain more extra labour, and thus secure more surplus value. We in England have had sad experience of the baneful effects upon the working population of the never-ceasing endeavours to increase the number of working hours. The reports of the Factory Inspectors up to a comparatively recent date, are positively filled to overflowing with instances of the efforts made by the capitalists to crowd extra labour on men, on women, and, above all, on children. A little is filched from the meal times; the mill is opened a trifle earlier, closed something later, than the prescribed hour. Always this persistent scheming for extra labour.[a] Not only up to the passing of the Factory Acts,[9] but ever since, the same tendency has been relentlessly displayed. Free Trade, by reducing the natural price of labour, increased the profit of capitalists and the number of hours on which they could depend for the production of surplus value. Women and children have, of course, suffered fearfully. They were used up as so much food for surplus value, without the slightest regard to humanity, or to the interest of the country at large. The average age of the working classes was fearfully shortened by the excessive toil. The cotton industry of Lancashire alone in ninety years, or three generations of ordinary men, devoured *nine* generations of work-people. What mattered that to the manufacturers? There were more where they came from. The poor bargainers reproduced themselves, and supply and demand goes merrily on as before. The Factory Acts themselves, still by no means so stringent nor so rigidly administered as they ought to be, were carried against the bitterest opposition of the capitalist class, because the nation had gradually roused itself to the truth that the whole population was rapidly deteriorating, owing to the systematic overwork of women and children. There are even still economists of liberal views, who hold that women in particular ought to be allowed to work in factories as long as they choose, and that the State has no right to interfere to protect the coming generation. Argument after argument is put forward also that longer hours than those to which the Trade Unions have happily reduced the working day are essential, because otherwise capitalists cannot compete with foreign nations.[b]

a   Mr Watherston, a jeweller, who has grown rich on other men's labour, wrote not long ago to the *Economist* to complain of the miserably short hours of work Englishmen now have. They must work more, or trade – his profits, he meant – would suffer. Of course this was the very man for the capitalist party. They got him at once as chairman of the Westminster caucus. How long will working men be gulled by landlords and capitalists into providing them with more unpaid labour, under the pretence of improving trade?

b   To show how impossible it is for the capitalist class to shake themselves clear of the prejudices in which they have been brought up, it is almost enough to say that Mr Bright – a man surely distinguished for his humanity in general concerns – opposed the Factory Acts, which may fairly be regarded as the most beneficent measures of this century, with all his might; that when President of the Board of Trade he declared that adulteration was a legitimate form of competition; and that to this hour he cannot see that interference with freedom of contract as between the capitalist and the labourer may be absolutely essential in the interests of the community at large. Sir Thomas Brassy, as Professor Cairnes has pointed out, could not understand that a reduction of profits might be quite as desirable as a reduction of wages. It is amusing, too, to see Mr Joseph Chamberlain, a capitalist who has taken 700,000*l.* out of the working classes by extra labour, and owns a rigid monopoly, posing as a leader of the democracy. Doubtless they all think

*[continued]*

149

There is, unfortunately, no need to go back to the horrible details contained in the Health Reports[10] of a few years ago, as to the condition of the working classes, whilst wealth is being piled up by their labour all round them. In spite of a little permissive legislation – well-intended, but by no means effectual – things are almost as bad to-day. Some there are of course who, rejoicing in the fact that our population has consumed on the average .001lb. per head more of bacon in the last ten years, or .002lb. per head more cheese, decline to look to that portion of the people who bring down the average.

Such a speech as that delivered by the Bishop of Manchester in June, 1880,[11] ought to awaken the nation to the mischief which is still being done. He, worthy man, wrings his hands in despair at the state of affairs in his own diocese. People living in the most miserable poverty, from which there seems no escape. Misery, filth, starvation, overcrowding, followed by inevitable deterioration. Sadness and hopelessness brood over the streets, and alleys, and cellars, he has explored. What can education do with children living in such conditions as those which he has so graphically described? The men and the women work hard enough when they can get the chance – work endless hours too – do enough in short to feed, and lodge, and clothe themselves in comfort. Yet in Manchester and Salford, in Stockport and Altrincham, in Oldham and Macclesfield, throughout the whole of these great industrial districts, thousands on thousands of labourers exist in good times in squalor, whilst bad times drive them at once to the wall. Dr Fraser himself had shown a few years before what the condition of the agricultural labourer was in this respect, how hard he too works, how little he gets, how foully he is lodged in many cases. Even orthodox economists show further how farmers and manufacturers alike combine to keep down the rate of wages to the bare natural price, or below it, whilst exacting the longest possible hours of toil.

Admitting that in some respects matters have improved, owing to the determination of the working classes no longer to submit to such neglect and oppression

themselves thoroughly in earnest; but *how can* hunters after surplus value, men who are every day engaged in putting wages at a lower level than they ought to be in order to enhance their own profits from unpaid labour, really lead or benefit them by pretending to lead, the working class? The Liberal benches in the House of Commons at this very time are closely packed with plutocrats, who have made all their wealth, and mean to make more, out of the unpaid labour of their own countrymen. The Conservative benches seat a growing proportion of men of the like kidney. What wonder that working men who really understand what is going on around them, almost despair of success in carrying measures which are absolutely essential to the welfare of their class, when the power of capitalism is increasing in every direction, when there is not a single daily newspaper in existence which represents their interests or advocates their claims, and when only three of their class sit in Parliament? [John Bright (1811–89), MP for Manchester and then Birmingham, and a radical activist for free trade and franchise reform; he was a member of the Anti-Corn Law League and founder in 1864 of the Reform League. Thomas Brassey (1805–70), a railway contractor whose undertakings included the Great Northern Railway, which employed 6,000 labourers. For Cairnes, see note j, page 137. Joseph Chamberlain (1836–1911), MP for Birmingham, and president of the Board of Trade, 1880–5.]

as of old, the very last report of the Factory Inspectors shows how much remains to be done, and how little machinery there is to do it. The long weary struggle which has been carried on by the working class, without even proper representation, against *laissez-faire*, political economy, and selfish ideas of freedom, seems still far from being successful.

A mere list of the provisions of the Factory Acts to restrict tyranny by the masters and injury resulting to the hands, proves conclusively that, but for State intervention a condition of slavery of the worst kind would exist now, as it did forty years ago. Meals for instance are not allowed now to be taken in rooms where the atmosphere is poisonous, and some restrictions are even imposed upon keeping men, women, and children employed in the poisonous atmosphere. In Bradford, a city which has long lived in the full and rather greasy odour of Liberal sanctity, the wool-sorting has for years been carried on in such a manner as directly to involve the loss of the lives of many of the hands. Not a single improvement did the capitalists – Mr Coercion-Act Forster[12] is a Bradford man – introduce, till forced to do so by law, and by public opinion following upon the verdict of coroners' juries as to the infamous state of things which brought about the death of the wool-sorters. Children still go to work full time in the collieries when they are twelve years old, though in factories they, fortunately, may not do so until they are thirteen or fourteen. The parents, eager to get their children's wages, take advantage of this, and the capitalist colliery owner of course is always ready to employ cheap child-labour for his engines or other purposes.

In the dangerous trades great improvements have been made by the Factory Acts, but still it is evident far more stringent inspection and regulation is required. In the brickworks we read of a girl carrying to and fro eleven tons of clay in the day for 2s. 3d. a day. Brickmaking, to which women are wholly unsuited, fell into their hands, we are told, 'because masters at one time got wages down very low' – wanted to work women on the cheap in fact. In the great cotton and iron industries years must still elapse before the people recover from the deteriorating effects of unrestricted competition. The best factories and ironworks are not yet controlled sufficiently in the interest of the men, women, and children who work in them. But those who wish to understand what capitalism is capable of, and what is its natural bent, should read the reports of the factory inspectors, Messrs Lakeman and Gould, on the sweating system at the East End of London, and the dens in which the unfortunate milliners and dressmakers work at the West End.[13] 'Workshops,' says Inspector Lakeman, 'are generally small, over-crowded, very dirty, overheated, badly ventilated; and when half a dozen gas burners are alight for five or six hours in a twelve-feet square room, one can imagine that the term "sweater" is not inappropriate. . . . So gigantic has the sweating system become, so rapid the production (for the division of labour is strictly carried out), so varied are the wants of each occupier, that one despairs of making any impression upon these people except by compulsion. *They are bound to a system which excludes freedom*, and from long habit it seems impossible to move them out of it. Now when we see a cloth coat made, lined, braided by hand, the silk and thread found by sweater, all for 2s. 3d., and if the total number be not returned to the clothier completed by the time specified, then a fine of sixpence (I have seen one shilling) levied for each garment, one cannot wonder at the desire of the sweater to keep his team late at night to complete his task.' Coats are sometimes 'finished in this style,' however, as low as 2s. 1d. 'When one thinks that there are about 18,000 to 20,000 people toiling at this one trade of making ready-made clothing, can we wonder at beholding the palace-like premises of merchant tailors who can advertise garments at a very low price, which to them is the cost of material, and say 2s. 1d. for the making of a coat? It does not require much depth of reasoning to judge where the profit comes from.'ᶜ No, worthy Mr Inspector, it does not. The profit of the merchant tailor, like the profit of his noble allies the cotton lords and the wool factors, comes out of the unpaid labour of others, whom he throws upon the streets when they have served his turn of providing surplus value according to the universal law of supply and demand and freedom of contract.

But again; hear Mr Inspector Gould: – 'There is, however, one branch of work, giving employment to thousands of girls and women, which, although entirely harmless in itself, is yet, unfortunately, solely by reason of the conditions under which it is carried on, a typically unhealthy business. I need hardly say that I refer to the making of all articles of ladies' clothing, and principally to the dressmaking section of the trade. Of the thousands of young and delicate girls who are engaged in trying to earn a bare subsistence in a deleterious atmosphere, no one can tell how many go down in the struggle. No statistics can be formed of the percentage of deaths, of enfeebled constitutions, of the amount of disease engendered in the first instance by the deadly atmosphere of the workrooms in second and third class establishments devoted to the dressmaking and ladies' clothing trade in the West End of London. I know of no class of female workers whose vital interests are so entirely neglected, and who labour under such disadvantageous conditions, as the unlucky victims of the dressmaking industry. Nothing is more surprising than to hear the advocates of "women's rights" of both sexes, in full knowledge *apparently* of the hardships undergone by the very class whose battle they profess to fight, cry out for absolute liberty of action to all females employed in labour!' Evidently Mr Gould is quite ignorant of the real bigotry of the advocates of freedom, and had better look to himself. In the shops themselves things are little better. Men and women are kept at work from thirteen to fourteen hours a day for five days in the week, and for sixteen hours on the sixth day.

c    Lord Salisbury [i.e., Robert, 3rd Marquess of Salisbury (1830–1903), three times Prime Minister between 1885 and 1902] spoke at the Merchant Tailors' Hall not long since, of the absurdity of 'plate-hunger.' It seemed more ridiculous to his aristocratic mind than even the earth-hunger of the Irish. Had he by chance a Conservative sweater at his elbow?

As to the accommodation of the labouring class, out of whose unpaid toil the capitalist makes his profit and society waxes fat, the Reports on Artisans' Dwellings, give deplorable facts. Two and three families pigged together into one or two small rooms; streets of houses torn down for improvements, and their occupiers forced to crowd in upon the already overcrowded streets adjoining. This is the rule throughout all our great cities. London is no worse than Glasgow, nor Glasgow worse than Birmingham, Bradford, Leeds, Manchester, or Newcastle. The latter city, indeed, is perhaps the worst of all in this respect in comparison to its population. Hitherto the mere Permissive Acts to remedy this state of things have been almost useless. Yet the homes of the poor are not cheap; they are dear. Cubic space for cubic space, the dens of the East and West End cost more than the mansions of the rich, who have good air, good light, plentiful supply of water, and all that's needed for healthy existence. Those who provide them with all these benefits are left to take care of themselves. No compulsion: that would be too serious. What? force the municipalities to tear down foul, unhealthy dwellings, at the expense of the rich, and build up proper accommodation for the poor? 'Never,' say the ratepayers; 'that would touch us: it is communism, confiscation, the overturn of society.'

We are now in a brief cycle of rising prosperity for the moneyed and manufacturing class. Now is their opportunity to endeavour to remedy in their turn some of the mischiefs below and around them. They justly denounce the selfishness of landlords; let them, too, look at home. But the working class should rely on their own power and peaceful strength – they must trust to themselves alone.

To them, then, I say: - All wealth is produced by labour, and goods exchange in proportion to the quantity of human labour which is embodied in them. Between the workers of all civilized countries there is no real difference: they create the wealth and produce the food, and, under proper conditions, all would live in moderation all would have enough. But landowners, capitalists, merchants, money-lenders, have possessed themselves of the land, of the machinery, of the currency, of the credit. They therefore compel the workers to labour long and live hardly for their benefit; they take of the time, and the life, and the labour of their fellows for nothing. Those who own the soil, and those who manufacture – those who live on interest, and those who trade on differences of value, live alike in luxury and in idleness out of the sweat and the misery of others. They, therefore, are the enemies of the great mass of the people, to be overcome by voluntary combination and peaceful endeavour. You, then, who produce the wealth in every country, consider where you stand; you, men who have seen your homes broken up, your health destroyed, have beheld your wives and children fade away under the tyranny of capitalism, stop and think. Let all who are made poor and miserable for the advantage of others, take heed to themselves. And having thus considered, thus thought, and thus looked at home, stretch out your hands, now powerless, to the workers of the world as your friends, and begin a new and better social epoch for humanity. Working men and working women of Great Britain and Ireland, who now toil and suffer

153

that others may be lazy and rich – Unite! Working men and working women of Europe and America, who now rejoice in the gleam of a transient prosperity, only to be cast into deeper despair on the next stagnation – Unite! Unite! In union alone is safety and happiness for the future, as in difference and selfishness have been danger and misery in the past. Therefore, once more, working men and working women, ye who live hardly to-day, to pass on sadness and poverty to your children to-morrow, Unite! Unite! Unite!

3

# POLITICS AND REPRESENTATION

Authoritarianism, liberalism, socialism


## THOMAS CARLYLE, *CHARTISM* (1840)

As with many 'eminent Victorians', the reputation which Thomas Carlyle (1795–1881) enjoyed among his contemporaries is difficult to appreciate today. His declamatory style, his authoritarian politics and the self-confidence of an autodidact have all proved uncongenial to modern tastes. For his Victorian readers, however, Carlyle was something of a prophet – a commanding if irascible voice calling for action on a variety of social problems. His early career was marked by a succession of false starts: he wrote a long and undistinguished series of essays and reviews for the radical periodical the *Edinburgh Review*. The *Life of Friedrich Schiller* followed in 1825: it enjoyed only modest success. With the anonymous publication in 1829 of 'Signs of the Times' (ostensibly another review) Carlyle established an interest in social topics. It was followed by the semi-autobiographical, semi-mystical satire, *Sartor Resartus*, serialised in *Fraser's Magazine* in 1833–4 and published as a book in England in 1838. Although it later enjoyed considerable success, *Sartor Resartus* was also initially a failure. Approaching his fortieth birthday, Carlyle had yet to make his mark. All this changed, however, with a move to London and the completion of a much more ambitious project – *The French Revolution: A History* (1837). This work made Carlyle's reputation, bringing him almost immediate celebrity among critics and the general reading public alike. It was followed by several other works exploring social and political themes: *Chartism* (1840), *Past and Present* (1843), *On Heroes, Hero-Worship and the Heroic in History* (1841) and *Latter-day Pamphlets* (1850). Carlyle's interest in authoritarian leadership led to two large biographical undertakings: *Oliver Cromwell's Letters and Speeches* (1845) and the massive *History of*

*Friedrich II of Prussia, called Frederick the Great* (1858–65). He also published a biography of a close friend, *The Life of John Sterling* (1851), a more personal and accessible work. Alongside these major projects, Carlyle continued to publish essays and pamphlets, the most notorious of which were *The Nigger Question* (1853) (first published in *Fraser's Magazine* in 1849) and 'Shooting Niagara: and After?' (published in *Macmillan's Magazine* in 1867). Because of their explicit racism, today both works make for uncomfortable reading. In the last fifteen years of his life Carlyle produced very little work. *Reminiscences*, edited by his biographer, J. A. Froude, appeared in 1881, the year of his death.

## *From* Thomas Carlyle, *Chartism* (London: James Fraser, 1840)[1]

### Chapter I: Condition-of-England Question

A feeling very generally exists that the condition and disposition of the Working Classes is a rather ominous matter at present; that something ought to be said, something ought to be done, in regard to it. And surely, at an epoch of history when the 'National Petition' carts itself in waggons along the streets, and is presented 'bound with iron hoops, four men bearing it,' to a Reformed House of Commons;[2] and Chartism numbered by the million and half, taking nothing by its iron-hooped Petition, breaks out into brickbats, cheap pikes, and even into splutterings of conflagration,[3] such very general feeling cannot be considered unnatural! To us individually this matter appears, and has for many years appeared, to be the most ominous of all practical matters whatever; a matter in regard to which if something be not done, something will *do* itself one day, and in a fashion that will please nobody. The time is verily come for acting in it; how much more for consultation about acting in it, for speech and articulate inquiry about it!

We are aware that, according to the newspapers, Chartism is extinct; that a Reform Ministry has 'put down the chimera of Chartism' in the most felicitous effectual manner. So say the newspapers; – and yet, alas, most readers of newspapers know withal that it is indeed the 'chimera' of Chartism, not the reality, which has been put down. The distracted incoherent embodiment of Chartism, whereby in late months it took shape and became visible, this has been put down; or rather has fallen down and gone asunder by gravitation and law of nature: but the living essence of Chartism has not been put down. Chartism means the bitter discontent grown fierce and mad, the wrong condition therefore or the wrong disposition, of the Working Classes of England. It is a new name for a thing which has had many names, which will yet have many. The matter of Chartism is weighty, deep-rooted, far-extending; did not begin yesterday; will by no means end this day or to-morrow. Reform Ministry, constabulary rural police, new levy of soldiers, grants of money to Birmingham; all this is well, or is not well; all this will put down only the embodiment or 'chimera' of Chartism.[4] The essence continuing, new and ever new embodiments, chimeras madder or less mad, have to continue. The melancholy fact remains, that this thing known at present by the name Chartism does exist; has existed; and, either 'put down,' into secret treason, with rusty pistols, vitriol-bottle and match-box, or openly brandishing pike and torch[5] (one knows not in which case *more* fatal-looking), is like to exist till quite other methods have been tried with it. What means this bitter discontent of the Working Classes? Whence comes it, whither goes it? Above all, at what price, on what terms, will it probably consent to depart from us and die into rest? These are questions.

To say that it is mad, incendiary, nefarious, is no answer. To say all this, in never so many dialects, is saying little. 'Glasgow Thuggery,' 'Glasgow Thugs;' it is a witty nickname: the practice of 'Number 60' entering his dark room, to contract for and settle the price of blood with operative assassins, in a Christian city, once distinguished by its rigorous Christianism, is doubtless a fact worthy of all horror:[6] but what will horror do for it? What will execration; nay at bottom, what will condemnation and banishment to Botany Bay[7] do for it? Glasgow Thuggery, Chartist torch-meetings, Birmingham riots, Swing conflagrations,[8] are so many symptoms on the surface; you abolish the symptom to no purpose, if the disease is left untouched. Boils on the surface are curable or incurable, – small matter which, while the virulent humour festers deep within; poisoning the sources of life; and certain enough to find for itself ever new boils and sore issues; ways of announcing that it continues there, that it would fain not continue there.

Delirious Chartism will not have raged entirely to no purpose, as indeed no earthly thing does so, if it have forced all thinking men of the community to think of this vital matter, too apt to be overlooked otherwise. Is the condition of the English working people wrong; so wrong that rational working men cannot, will not, and even should not rest quiet under it? A most grave case, complex beyond all others in the world; a case wherein Botany Bay, constabulary rural police, and such like, will avail but little. Or is the discontent itself mad, like the shape it took? Not the condition of the working people that is wrong; but their disposition, their own thoughts, beliefs and feelings that are wrong? This too were a most grave case, little less alarming, little less complex than the former one. In this case too, where constabulary police and mere rigour of coercion seems more at home, coercion will by no means do all, coercion by itself will not even do much. If there do exist general madness of discontent, then sanity and some measure of content must be brought about again, – not by constabulary police alone. When the thoughts of a people, in the great mass of it, have grown mad, the combined issue of that people's workings will be a madness, an incoherency and ruin! Sanity will have to be recovered for the general mass; coercion itself will otherwise cease to be able to coerce.

157

We have heard it asked, Why Parliament throws no light on this question of the Working Classes, and the condition or disposition they are in? Truly to a remote observer of Parliamentary procedure it seems surprising, especially in late Reformed times, to see what space this question occupies in the Debates of the Nation. Can any other business whatsoever be so pressing on legislators? A Reformed Parliament, one would think, should inquire into popular discontents *before* they get the length of pikes and torches! For what end at all are men, Honourable Members and Reform Members, sent to St Stephen's,[9] with clamour and effort; kept talking, struggling, motioning and counter-motioning? The condition of the great body of people in a country is the condition of the country itself: this you would say is a truism in all times; a truism rather pressing to get recognised as a truth now, and be acted upon, in these times. Yet read Hansard's Debates,[10] or the Morning Papers, if you have nothing to do! The old grand question, whether A is to be in office or B, with the innumerable subsidiary questions growing out of that, courting paragraphs and suffrages for a blessed solution of that: Canada question, Irish Appropriation question, West India question, Queen's Bedchamber question; Game Laws, Usury Laws; African Blacks, Hill Coolies, Smithfield cattle, and Dog-carts,[11] – all manner of questions and subjects, except simply this the alpha and omega of all! Surely Honourable Members ought to speak of the Condition-of-England question too. Radical members, above all; friends of the people; chosen with effort, by the people, to interpret and articulate the dumb deep want of the people! To a remote observer they seem oblivious to their duty. Are they not there, by trade, mission, and expresss appointment of themselves and others, to speak for the good of the British Nation? Whatsoever great British interest can the least speak for itself, for that beyond all they are called to speak. They are either speakers for that great dumb toiling class which cannot speak, or they are nothing that one can well specify.

Alas, the remote observer knows not the nature of Parliaments: how Parliaments, extant there for the British Nation's sake, find that they are extant withal for their own sake; how Parliaments travel so naturally in their deep-rutted routine, common-place worn into ruts axle-deep, from which only strength, insight and courageous generous exertion can lift any Parliament or vehicle; how in Parliaments, Reformed or Unreformed, there may chance to be a strong man, an original, clear-sighted, great-hearted, patient and valiant man, or to be none such; – how, on the whole, Parliaments, lumbering along in their deep ruts of common-place, find, as so many of us otherwise do, that the ruts *are* axle-deep, and the travelling very toilsome of itself, and for the day the evil thereof sufficient! What Parliaments ought to have done in this business, what they will, can or cannot yet do, and where the limits of their faculty and culpability may lie, in regard to it, were a long investigation; into which we need not enter at this moment. What they have done is unhappily plain enough. Hitherto, on this most national of questions, the Collective Wisdom of the Nation has availed us as good as nothing whatever.

And yet, as we say, it is a question which cannot be left to the Collective Folly of the Nation! In or out of Parliament, darkness, neglect, hallucination must contrive to cease in regard to it; true insight into it must be had. How inexpressibly useful were true insight into it; a genuine understanding by the upper classes of society what it is that the under classes intrinsically mean; a clear interpretation of the thought which at heart torments these wild inarticulate souls, struggling there, with inarticulate uproar, like dumb creatures in pain, unable to speak what is in them! Something they do mean; some true thing withal, in the centre of their confused hearts, – for they are hearts created by Heaven too: to the Heaven it is clear what thing; to us not clear. Would that it were! Perfect clearness on it were equivalent to remedy of it. For, as is well said, all battle is misunderstanding; did the parties know one another, the battle would cease. No man at bottom means injustice; it is always for some obscure distorted image of a right that he contends: an obscure image diffracted, exaggerated, in the wonderfullest way, by natural dimness and selfishness; getting tenfold more diffracted by exasperation of contest, till at length it become all but irrecognisable; yet still the image of a right. Could a man own to himself that the thing he fought for was wrong, contrary to fairness and the law of reason, he would own also that it thereby stood condemned and hopeless; he could fight for it no longer. Nay independently of right, could the contending parties get but accurately to discern one another's might and strength to contend, the one would peaceably yield to the other and to Necessity; the contest in this case too were over. No African expedition now, as in the days of Herodotus, is fitted out *against the South-wind*.[12] One expedition was satisfactory in that department. The South-wind Simoom[13] continues blowing occasionally, hateful as ever, maddening as ever; but one expedition was enough. Do we not all submit to Death? The highest sentence of the law, sentence of death, is passed on all of us by the fact of birth; yet we live patiently under it, patiently undergo it when the hour comes. Clear undeniably right, clear undeniable might: either of these once ascertained puts an end to battle. All battle is a confused experiment to ascertain one and both of these.

What are the rights, what are the mights of the discontented Working Classes in England at this epoch? He were an Oedipus,[14] and deliverer from sad social pestilence, who could resolve us fully! For we may say beforehand, The struggle that divides the upper and lower in society over Europe, and more painfully and notably in England than elsewhere, this too is a struggle which will end and adjust itself as all other struggles do and have done, by making the right clear and the might clear; not otherwise than by that. Meantime, the questions, Why are the Working Classes discontented; what is their condition, economical, moral, in their houses and their hearts, as it is in reality and as they figure it to themselves to be; what do they complain of; what ought they, and ought they not to complain of? – these are measurable questions; on some of these any common mortal, did he but turn his eyes to them, might throw some light. Certain researches and considerations of ours on the matter, since no one else will undertake it, are now to be made public. The researches have yielded us little, almost nothing; but the considerations are of old date, and press to have utterance. We are not without hope that our general notion of the business, if we can get it uttered at all, will meet some assent from many candid men.

### Chapter VI: Laissez-faire

From all which enormous events, with truths old and new embodied in them, what innumerable practical inferences are to be drawn! Events are written lessons, glaring in huge hieroglyphic picture-writing, that all may read and know them: the terror and horror they inspire is but the note of preparation for the truth they are to teach; a mere waste of terror if that be not learned. Inferences enough; most didactic, practically applicable in all departments of English things! One inference, but one inclusive of all, shall content us here; this namely: That Laissez-faire has as good as done its part in a great many provinces; that in the province of the Working Classes, Laissez-faire having passed its New Poor-Law,[15] has reached the suicidal point, and now, as felo-de-se,[16] lies dying there, in torchlight meetings and such like; that, in brief, a government of the under classes by the upper on a principle of Let alone is no longer possible in England in these days. This is the one inference inclusive of all. For there can be no acting or doing of any kind, till it be recognised that there is a thing to be done; the thing once recognised, doing in a thousand shapes becomes possible. The Working Classes cannot any longer go on without government; without being *actually* guided and governed; England cannot subsist in peace till, by some means or other, some guidance and government for them is found.

For, alas, on us too the rude truth has come home. Wrappages and speciosities all worn off, the haggard naked fact speaks to us: Are these millions taught? Are these millions guided? We have a Church, the venerable embodiment of an idea which may well call itself divine; which our fathers for long ages, feeling it to be divine, have been embodying as we see: it is a Church well furnished with equipments and appurtenances; educated in universities; rich in money; set on high places that it may be conspicuous to all, honoured of all. We have an Aristocracy of landed wealth and commercial wealth, in whose hands lies the law-making and the law-administering; an Aristocracy rich, powerful, long secure in its place; an Aristocracy with more faculty put free into its hands than was ever before, in any country or time, put into the hands of any class of men. This Church answers: Yes, the people are taught. This Aristocracy, astonishment in every feature, answers: Yes, surely the people are guided! Do we not pass what Acts of Parliament are needful; as many as thirty-nine for the shooting of the partridges alone? Are there not tread-mills, gibbets; even hospitals, poor-rates, New Poor-Law?[17] So answers Church; so answers Aristocracy, astonishment in every feature. – Fact, in the meanwhile, takes his lucifer-box,[18] sets fire to wheat-stacks; sheds an all-too dismal light on several things. Fact searches for his third-rate potato, not in the meekest humour, six-and-thirty weeks each year; and does not find it. Fact passionately joins Messiah Thom of Canterbury, and has himself shot for a new fifth-monarchy brought in by Bedlam.[19] Fact holds his fustian-jacket *Femgericht* in Glasgow City.[20] Fact carts his Petition over London streets, begging that you would simply have the goodness to grant him universal suffrage, and 'the five points,' by way of remedy. These are not symptoms of teaching and guiding.

Nay, at bottom, is it not a singular thing this of *Laissez-faire*, from the first origin of it? As good as an *abdication* on the part of governors; an admission that they are henceforth incompetent to govern, that they are not there to govern at all, but to do – one knows not what! The universal demand of *Laissez-faire* by a people from its governors or upper classes, is a soft-sounding demand; but it is only one step removed from the fatallest. '*Laissez-faire*,' exclaims a sardonic German writer,[21] 'What is this universal cry for *Laissez-faire*? Does it mean that human affairs require no guidance; that wisdom and forethought cannot guide them better than folly and accident? Alas, does it not mean: "*Such* guidance is worse than none! Leave us alone of *your* guidance; eat your wages, and sleep!"' And now if guidance have grown indispensable, and the sleep continue, what becomes of the sleep and its wages? – In those entirely surprising circumstances to which the Eighteenth Century had brought us, in the time of Adam Smith,[22] *Laissez-faire* was a reasonable cry; – as indeed, in all circumstances, for a wise governor there will be meaning in the principle of it. To wise governors you will cry: 'See what you will, and will not, let alone.' To unwise governors, to hungry Greeks throttling down hungry Greeks on the floor of a St Stephen's,[23] you will cry: 'Let *all* things alone; for Heaven's sake, meddle ye with nothing!' How *Laissez-faire* may adjust itself in other provinces we say not: but we do venture to say, and ask whether events everywhere, in world-history and parish-history, in all manner of dialects are not saying it, That in regard to the lower orders of society, and their governance and guidance, the principle of *Laissez-faire* has terminated, and is no longer applicable at all, in this Europe of ours, still less in this England of ours. Not misgovernment, nor yet no-government; only government will now serve. What is the meaning of the 'five-points,' if we will understand them? What are all popular commotions and maddest bellowings, from Peterloo to the Place-de-Grève itself?[24] Bellowings, *in*articulate cries as of a dumb creature in rage and pain; to the ear of wisdom they are inarticulate prayers: 'Guide me, govern me! I am mad, and miserable, and cannot guide myself!' Surely of all 'rights of man,'[25] this right of the ignorant man to be guided by the wiser, to be, gently or forcibly, held in the true course by him, is the indisputablest. Nature herself ordains it from the first; Society struggles towards perfection by enforcing and accomplishing it more and more. If Freedom have any meaning, it means enjoyment of this right, wherein all other rights are enjoyed. It is a sacred right and duty, on both sides; and the summary of all social duties whatsoever between the two. Why does the one toil with his hands, if the other be not to toil, still more unweariedly, with heart and head? The brawny craftsman finds it no child's play to mould his unpliant rugged masses;

neither is guidance of men a dilettantism: what it becomes when treated as a dilettantism, we may see! The wild horse bounds homeless through the wilderness, is not led to stall and manger; but neither does he toil for you, but for himself only.

Democracy, we are well aware, what is called 'self-government' of the multitude by the multitude, is in words the thing everywhere passionately clamoured for at present. Democracy makes rapid progress in these latter times, and ever more rapid, in a perilous accelerative ratio; towards democracy, and that only, the progress of things is everywhere tending as to the final goal and winning-post. So think, so clamour the multitudes everywhere. And yet all men may see, whose sight is good for much, that in democracy can lie no finality; that with the completest winning of democracy there is nothing yet won, – except emptiness, and the free chance to win! Democracy is, by the nature of it, a self-cancelling business; and gives in the long-run a net-result of *zero*. Where no government is wanted, save that of the parish-constable, as in America with its boundless soil, every man being able to find work and recompense for himself, democracy may subsist; not elsewhere, except briefly, as a swift transition towards something other and farther. Democracy never yet, that we heard of, was able to accomplish much work, beyond that same cancelling of itself. Rome and Athens are themes for the schools; unexceptionable for that purpose. In Rome and Athens, as elsewhere, if we look practically, we shall find that it was not by loud voting and debating of many, but by wise insight and ordering of a few that the work was done. So is it ever, so will it ever be. The French Convention[26] was a Parliament elected 'by the five points,' with ballot-boxes, universal suffrages, and what not, as perfectly as Parliament can hope to be in this world; and had indeed a pretty spell of work to do, and did it. The French Convention had to cease from being a free Parliament, and become more arbitrary than any Sultan Bajazet,[27] before it could so much as subsist. It had to purge out its argumentative Girondins, elect its Supreme Committee of *Salut*,[28] guillotine into silence and extinction all that gainsayed it, and rule and work literally by the sternest despotism ever seen in Europe, before it could rule at all. Napoleon was not president of a republic; Cromwell tried hard to rule in that way, but found that he could not. These, 'the armed soldiers of democracy,' had to chain democracy under their feet, and become despots over it, before they could work out the earnest obscure purpose of democracy itself! Democracy, take it where you will in our Europe, is found by us as a regulated method of rebellion and abrogation; it abrogates the old arrangement of things; and leaves, as we say, *zero* and vacuity for the institution of a new arrangement. It is the consummation of No-government and *Laissez-faire*. It may be natural for our Europe at present; but cannot be the ultimatum of it. Not towards the impossibility, 'self-government' of a multitude by a multitude; but towards some possibility, government by the wisest, does bewildered Europe struggle. The blessedest possibility: not misgovernment, not *Laissez-faire*, but veritable government! Cannot one discern too, across all democratic turbulence, clattering of ballot-boxes and infinite sorrowful jangle, needful or not, that this at bottom is the wish and prayer of all human hearts, every-where and at all times: 'Give me a leader; a true leader, not a false sham-leader; a true leader, that he may guide me on the true way, that I may be loyal to him, that I may swear fealty to him and follow him, and feel that it is well with me!' The relation of the taught to their teacher, of the loyal subject to his guiding king, is, under one shape or another, the vital element of human Society; indis-pensable to it, perennial in it; without which, as a body reft of its soul, it falls down into death, and with horrid noisome dissolution passes away and disap-pears.

But verily in these times, with their stern Evangel, that Speciosities which are not Realities can no longer be, all Aristocracies, Priesthoods, Persons in Authority, are called upon to consider. What is an Aristocracy? A corporation of the Best, of the Bravest. To this joyfully, with the heart-loyalty, do men pay the half of their substance, to equip and decorate their Best, to lodge them in palaces, set them high over all. For it is of the nature of men, in every time, to honour and love their Best; to know no limits in honouring them. Whatsoever Aristocracy *is* still a corporation of the Best, is safe from all peril, and the land it rules is a safe and blessed land. Whatsoever Aristocracy does not even attempt to be that, but only to wear the clothes of that, is not safe; neither is the land it rules in safe! For this now is our sad lot, that we must find a *real* Aristocracy, that an apparent Aristocracy, how plausible soever, has become inadequate for us. One way or other, the world will absolutely need to be governed; if not by this class of men, then by that. One can predict, without gift of prophecy, that the era of routine is nearly ended. Wisdom and faculty alone, faithful, valiant, ever-zealous, not pleasant but painful, continual effort, will suffice. Cost what it may, by one means or another, the toiling multitudes of this perplexed, over-crowded Europe, must and will find governors. '*Laissez-faire*, Leave them to do?' The thing they will *do*, if so left, is too frightful to think of! It has been *done* once, in sight of the whole earth, in these generations: can it need to be done a second time?

For a Priesthood, in like manner, whatsoever its titles, possessions, professions, there is but one question: Does it teach and spiritually guide this people, yea or no? If yea, then all is well. But if no, then let it strive earnestly to alter, for as yet there is nothing well! Nothing, we say: and indeed is not this that we call spiritual guidance properly the soul of the whole, the life and eyesight of the whole? The world asks of its Church in these times, more passionately than of any other Institution any question, 'Canst thou teach us or not?' – A Priesthood in France, when the world asked, 'What canst thou do for us?' answered only, aloud and ever louder, 'Are we not of God? Invested with all power?' – till at length France cut short this controversy too, in what frightful way we know. To all men who believed in the Church, to all men who believed in God and the soul of man, there was no issue of the French Revolution half so sorrowful as that. France cast out its benighted blind Priesthood into destruction; yet with what a loss to France also! A solution of continuity, what we may well call such; and this where conti-nuity is so momentous: the New, whatever it may be, cannot now *grow* out of the

Old, but is severed sheer asunder from the Old, – how much lies wasted in that gap! That one whole generation of thinkers should be without a religion to believe, or even to contradict; that Christianity, in thinking France, should as it were fade away so long into a remote extraneous tradition, was one of the saddest facts connected with the future of that country. Look at such Political and Moral Philosophies, St-Simonisms, Robert-Macairisms,[29] and the 'Literature of Desperation'! Kingship was perhaps but a cheap waste, compared with this of the Priestship; under which France still, all but unconsciously, labours; and may long labour, remediless the while. Let others consider it, and take warning by it! France is a pregnant example in all ways. Aristocracies that do not govern, Priesthoods that do not teach; the misery of that, and the misery of altering that, – are written in Belshazzar fire-letters[30] on the history of France.

Or does the British reader, safe in the assurance that 'England is not France,' call all this unpleasant doctrine of ours ideology, perfectibility, and a vacant dream? Does the British reader, resting on the faith that what has been these two generations was from the beginning, and will be to the end, assert himself that things are already as they can be, as they must be; that on the whole, no Upper Classes did ever 'govern' the Lower, in this sense of governing? Believe it not, O British reader! Man is man everywhere; dislikes to have 'sensible species' and 'ghosts of defunct bodies' foisted on him, in England even as in France. How much the Upper Classes did actually, in any the most perfect Feudal time, return to the Under by way of recompense, in government, guidance, protection, we will not undertake to specify here. In Charity-Balls, Soup-Kitchens, in Quarter-Sessions,[31] Prison-Discipline and Tread-mills, we can well believe the old Feudal Aristocracy not to have surpassed the new. Yet we do say that the old Aristocracy were the governors of the Lower Classes, the guides of the Lower Classes; and even, at bottom, that they existed as an Aristocracy because they were found adequate for that. Not by Charity-Balls and Soup-Kitchens; not so; far otherwise! But it was their happiness that, in struggling for their own objects, they *had* to govern the Lower Classes, even in this sense of governing. For, in one word, *Cash Payment* had not then grown to be the universal sole nexus of man to man; it was something other than money that the high then expected from the low, and could not live without getting from the low. Not as buyer and seller alone, of land of what else it might be, but in many senses still as soldier and captain, as clansman and head, as loyal subject and guiding king, was the low related to the high. With the supreme triumph of Cash, a changed time has entered; there must a changed Aristocracy enter. We invite the British reader to meditate earnestly on these things.

Another thing, which the British reader often reads and hears in this time, is worth his meditating for a moment: That Society 'exists for the protection of property.' To which it is added, that the poor man also has property, namely, his 'labour,' and the fifteen-pence or three-and-sixpence a-day he can get for that. True enough, O friends, 'for protecting *property*,' most true: and indeed if you will once sufficiently enforce that Eighth Commandment, the whole 'rights of man' are well cared for; I know no better definition of the rights of man. *Thou shalt not steal, thou shalt not be stolen from*: what a Society were that; Plato's Republic, More's Utopia[32] mere emblems of it! Give every man what is his, the accurate price of what he has done and been, no man shall any more complain, neither shall the earth suffer any more. For the protection of property, in very truth, and for that alone! – And now what is thy property? That parchment title-deed, that purse thou buttonest in thy breeches-pocket? Is that thy valuable property? Unhappy brother, most poor solvent brother, I without parchment at all, with purse oftenest in the flaccid state, imponderous, which will not fling against the wind, have quite other property than that! I have the miraculous breath of Life in me, breathed into my nostrils by Almighty God. I have affectations, thoughts, a god-given *capability* to be and do; rights, therefore, – the right for instance to thy love if I love thee, to thy guidance if I obey thee: the strangest rights, whereof in church-pulpits one still hears something, though almost unintelligible now; rights, stretching high into Immensity, far from Eternity! Fifteen-pence a-day; three-and-sixpence a-day; eight hundred pounds and odd a-day, dost thou call that my property? I value that little; little all I could purchase with that. For truly, as is said, what matters it? In torn boots, in soft-hung carriages-and-four, a man gets always to his journey's end. Socrates walked barefoot, or in wooden shoes, and yet arrived happily. They never asked him, *What* shoes or conveyance? never, What wages hadst thou? but simply, What work didst thou? – Property, O brother? 'Of my very body I have but a life-rent.' As for this flaccid purse of mine, 'tis something, nothing; has been the slave of pickpockets, cutthroats, Jew-brokers, gold-dust-robbers; 'twas his, 'tis mine; – 'tis thine, if thou care much to steal it. But my soul, breathed into me by God, my *Me* and what capability is there; that is mine, and I will resist the stealing of it. I call that mine and not thine; I will keep that, and do what work I can with it: God has given it me, the Devil shall not take it away! Alas, my friends, Society exists and has existed for a great many purposes, not so easy to specify!

Society, it is understood, does not in any age prevent a man from being what he *can be*. A sooty African *can* become a Toussaint L'ouverture,[33] a murderous Three-fingered Jack, let the yellow West Indies say to it what they will. A Scottish Poet 'proud of his name and country,' *can* apply fervently to 'Gentlemen of the Caledonian Hunt,'[34] and become a gauger of beer-barrels, and tragical immortal broken-hearted Singer; the stifled echo of his melody audible through long centuries, one other note in 'that sacred *Miserere*'[35] that rises up to Heaven, out of all times and lands. What I *can be* thou decidedly will not hinder me from being. Nay even for being what I *could be*, I have the strangest claims on thee, – not convenient to adjust at present! Protection of breeches-pocket property? O reader, to what shifts is poor Society reduced, struggling to give still some account of herself, in epochs when Cash Payment has become the sole nexus of man to men! On the whole, we will advise Society not to talk at all about what she exists for; but rather with her whole industry to exist, to try how she can keep existing! That is her best plan. She may depend upon it, if she ever, by cruel chance, did come to exist only for protection of breeches-pocket property, she would lose very soon the gift of protecting even that, and find her career in our lower world on the point of terminating! –

For the rest, that in the most perfect Feudal Ages, the Ideal of Aristocracy nowhere lived in vacant serene purity as an Ideal, but always as a poor imperfect Actual, little heeding or not knowing at all that an Ideal lay in it, – this too we will cheerfully admit. Imperfection, it is known, cleaves to human things; far is the Ideal departed from, in most times; very far! And yet so long as an Ideal (any soul of Truth) does, in never so confused a manner, exist and work within the Actual, it is a tolerable business. Not so, when the Ideal has entirely departed, and the Actual owns to itself that it has no Idea, no soul of Truth any longer: at that degree of imperfection human things cannot continue living; they are obliged to alter or expire, when they attain to that. Blotches and diseases exist on the skin and deeper, the heart continuing whole; but it is another matter when the heart itself becomes diseased; when there is no heart, but a monstrous gangrene pretending to exist there as heart!

On the whole, O reader, thou wilt find everywhere that things which have had an existence among men have first of all had to have a truth and worth in them, and were not semblances but realities. Nothing not a reality ever yet got men to pay bed and board to it for long. Look at Mahometanism itself! Dalai-Lamaism, even Dalai-Lamaism, one rejoices to discover, may be worth its victuals in this world;[36] not a quackery but a sincerity; not a nothing but a something! The mistake of those who believe that fraud, force, injustice, whatsoever untrue thing, howsoever cloaked and decorated, was ever or can ever be the principle of man's relations to man, is great, and the greatest. It is the error of the infidel; in whom the truth as yet is *not*. It is an error pregnant with mere errors and miseries; an error fatal, lamentable, to be abandoned by all men.

## MATTHEW ARNOLD, 'ANARCHY AND AUTHORITY' (1868)

Matthew Arnold (1822–88) was one of the foremost critics in the Victorian period, writing copiously and authoritatively on a wide range of literary and cultural topics. He was also an accomplished poet. A winner of the Newdigate prize for poetry at Oxford, Arnold went on to publish a number of well-received volumes of poetry, the most significant of which were *The Strayed Reveller, and Other Poems* (1849) and *Empedocles on Etna, and Other Poems* (1852). Later collections were largely made up of new editions of earlier work, although there were some notable additions such as 'The Scholar Gipsy' and 'Sohrab and Rustum' in *Poems: A New Edition* (1853), *Merope* (1857) and 'Thyrsis', published in *Macmillan's Magazine* in 1866. In 1857 Arnold was elected Professor of Poetry at Oxford; he was twice renominated in 1877 and 1885, but refused the position on both occasions. Ironically the appointment appeared to mark the decline of his poetic career, and in the late 1850s Arnold turned his talents towards criticism – a genre which better suited his growing interest in public affairs, and in which he established a lasting reputation both at home and abroad. In 1859 he published *England and the Italian Question*, followed in 1861 by *On Translating Homer* and *The Popular Education of France*. *On Translating Homer: Last Words* appeared in 1862. In 1864 Arnold continued his interest in educational issues with *A French Eton*. His most successful work, *Essays in Criticism*, was published in 1865; and one of his most controversial, *Culture and Anarchy*, as a series of essays between 1867–8 and as a book in 1869. The year 1871 saw the publication of *Friendship's Garland*, a more light-hearted treatment of some of the themes in *Culture and Anarchy*. In the early 1870s Arnold devoted himself to religious topics, beginning in 1870 with *St Paul and Protestantism* and continuing with *Literature and Dogma* (1873) and *God and the Bible* (1875). In the last years of his life Arnold returned to literary subjects, undertaking a variety of projects, including contributions to T. H. Ward's *The English Poets* and editions of the poetry of Wordsworth and Byron. Among his last published works were *Irish Essays* (1882) and *Discourses in America* (1885) which followed a lecture tour of the United States undertaken from autumn 1883 to spring 1884. The range and quantity of Arnold's prose writing is even more impressive when set alongside the public offices he held: apart from the Chair at Oxford, he was also appointed an Inspector of schools in 1851. He was promoted to Senior Inspector in

1870, and Chief Inspector in 1884. The work involved extensive travel both at home and in Europe. In 1883 Arnold accepted a Civil List Pension of £250 a year. He died suddenly from heart failure in 1888.

### *From* Matthew Arnold, 'Anarchy and Authority', *Cornhill Magazine*, XVII (January 1868), pp. 30–47[1]

#### *Anarchy and Authority*

I spoke lately of Culture, and tried to show that it was, or ought to be, the study and pursuit of perfection; and that of perfection, as pursued by culture, beauty and intelligence, or, in other words, sweetness and light, were the main characters. But from special reasons springing out of the occasion on which I spoke, I insisted chiefly on beauty, or sweetness, as a character of perfection. To complete rightly my design, it evidently remains to speak also of intelligence, or light, as a character of perfection; and this I had always the intention, at some convenient time, to do. Meanwhile, both here and on the other side of the Atlantic, all sorts of objections have been raised against the 'religion of culture,' as the objectors mockingly call it, which I am supposed to be promul-gating.[2] It is said to be a religion proposing parmaceti,[3] or some scented salve or other, as a cure for human miseries; a religion breathing a spirit of culti-vated inaction, making its believer refuse to lend a hand at uprooting the definite evils on all sides of us, and filling him with antipathy against the reforms and reformers which try to extirpate them. In general, it is summed up as being not practical, or – as some critics more familiarly put it – all moon-shine. That Alcibiades, the editor of the *Morning Star*, taunts me, as its promulgator, with living out of the world and knowing nothing of life and men.[4] That great austere toiler, the editor of the *Daily Telegraph*, upbraids me, but kindly, and more in sorrow than in anger, for trifling with aesthetics and poetical fancies, while he himself, in that arsenal of his in Fleet Street, is bearing the burden and heat of the day.[5] An intelligent American newspaper, the *Nation*, says that it is very easy to sit in one's study and find fault with the course of modern society, but the thing is to propose practical improvements for it;[6] while Mr Frederick Harrison,[7] in a very good-tempered and witty rejoinder, which makes me quite understand his having apparently achieved such a conquest of my young Prussian friend, Arminius,[8] at last gets moved to an almost stern moral impatience, to behold, as he says, 'Death, sin, cruelty stalk among us, filling their maws with innocence and youth,' and me, in the midst of the general tribulation, handing out my pouncet-box.[9]

It is impossible that all these remonstrances and reproofs should not affect me, and I shall try my very best, in completing my design and in speaking of light as one of the characters of perfection, and of culture as giving us light, to profit by the objections I have heard and read, and to drive at practice as much as I can, by showing the communications and passages into practical life from the doctrine which I am inculcating. [ . . . ][10]

It is said that a man with my theories of sweetness and light is full of antipathy against the rougher or coarser movements going on around him, that he will not lend a hand to the humble operation of uprooting evil by their means, and that therefore the believers in action grow impatient with him. But what if rough and coarse action, ill-calculated action, action with insufficient light, is, and has for a long time been, our bane? What if our urgent want now is, not to act at any price, but rather to lay in a stock of light for our difficulties? In that case, to refuse to lend a hand to the rougher and coarser movements going on round us, to make the primary need, both for oneself and others, to consist in enlightening ourselves and qualifying ourselves to act less at random, is surely the best, and in real truth the most practical line, our endeavours can take. So that if I can show what my opponents call rough or coarse action, but what I would rather call random and ill-regulated action – action with insufficient light, action pursued because we like to be doing something and doing it as we please, and do not like the trouble of thinking, and the severe constraint of any kind of rule – if I can show this to be, at the present moment, a practical mischief and danger to us, then I have found a practical use for light in correcting this state of things, and have only to exemplify how, in cases which fall under everybody's observation, it may deal with it.

When last I spoke of culture, I insisted on our bondage to machinery, on our proneness to value machinery as an end in itself, without looking beyond it to the end for which alone, in truth, it is valuable. Freedom, I said, was one of those things which we thus worshipped in itself, without enough regarding the ends for which freedom is to be desired. In our common notions and talk about freedom, we eminently show our idolatry of machinery. Our prevalent notion is – and I quoted a number of instances to prove it – that it is a most happy and important thing for a man merely to be able to do as he likes. On what he is to do when he is thus free to do as he likes, we do not lay so much stress. Our familiar praise of the British Constitution under which we live, is that it is a system of checks – a system which stops and paralyses any power in interfering with the free action of individuals. To this effect Mr Bright, who loves to walk in the old ways of the Constitution, said forcibly in one of his great speeches, what many other people are every day saying less forcibly, that the central idea of English life and politics is *the assertion of personal liberty*.[11] Evidently this is so; but evidently, also, as feudalism, which with its ideas and habits of subordination was for many centuries silently behind the British Constitution, dies out, and we are left with nothing but our system of checks, and our notion of its being the great right and happiness of an Englishman to do as far as possible what he likes, we are in danger of drifting towards anarchy. We have not the notion, so familiar on the Continent and to antiquity, of *the State* – the nation in its collective and corporate character, entrusted with stringent powers for the general advantage, and controlling individual wills in the name of an interest wider than that of individuals. We say, what is very true, that this notion is often made instrumental to tyranny; we say that a State is in reality made up of the individuals who compose it, and that every individual is the best judge of his own interests. Our leading class is an aristocracy, and no aristocracy likes the notion of a State-authority greater than itself, with a stringent administrative machinery superseding the decorative inutilities of lord-lieutenancy, deputy-lieutenancy, and the *posse comitatus*,[12] which are all in its own hands. Our middle-class, the great representative of trade and dissent, with its maxims of every man for himself in business, every man for himself in religion, dreads a powerful administration which might somehow interfere with it; and besides, it has its own decorative inutilities of vestrymanship and guardianship,[13] which are to this class what lord-lieutenancy and the country magistracy are to the aristocratic class, and a stringent administration might either take these functions out of its hands, or prevent its exercising them in its own comfortable, independent manner, as at present.

Then as to our working-class. This class, pressed constantly by the hard daily compulsion of material wants, is naturally the very centre and stronghold of our national idea, that it is man's ideal right and felicity to do as he likes. I think I have somewhere related how Monsieur Michelet[14] said to me of the people of France, that it was 'a nation of barbarians civilized by the conscription.' He meant that through their military service the idea of public duty and of discipline was brought to the mind of these masses, in other respects so raw and uncultivated. Our masses are quite as raw and uncultivated as the French; and, so far from their having the idea of public duty and of discipline, superior to the individual's self-will, brought to their mind by a universal obligation of military service, such as that of the conscription – so far from their having this, the very idea of a conscription is so at variance with our English notion of the prime right and blessedness of doing as one likes, that I remember the manager of the Clay Cross works[15] in Derbyshire told me during the Crimean war, when our want of soldiers was much felt and some people were talking of a conscription, that sooner than submit to a conscription the population of that district would flee to the mines, and lead a sort of Robin Hood life under ground.

For a long time, as I have said, the strong feudal habits of subordination and deference continued to tell upon this class. The modern spirit has now almost entirely dissolved those habits, and the anarchical tendency of our worship of freedom in and for itself, of our superstitious faith, as I say, in machinery, is becoming very manifest. More and more, because of this our blind faith in machinery, because of our want of light to enable us to look beyond machinery to the end for which machinery is valuable, this and that man, and this and that body of men, all over the country, are beginning to assert and put in practice an Englishman's right to do what he likes; his right to march where he likes, meet where he likes, enter where he likes, hoot as he likes, threaten as he likes, smash as he likes.[16] All this, I say, tends to anarchy; and though a number of excellent people, and particularly my friends of the liberal or progressive party, as they call themselves, are kind enough to reassure us by saying that these are trifles, that a few transient outbreaks of rowdyism signify nothing, that our system of liberty is one which itself cures all the evils which it works, that the educated and intelligent classes are in overwhelming strength and majestic repose, ready, like our military force in riots, to act at a moment's notice – yet one finds that one's liberal friends generally say this because they have such faith in themselves and their nostrums, when they shall return, as the public welfare requires, to place and power. But this faith of theirs one cannot exactly share, when one has so long had them and their nostrums at work, and sees that they have not prevented our coming to our present embarrassed condition; and one finds, also, that the outbreaks of rowdyism tend to become less and less trifles, to become more frequent rather than less frequent; and that meanwhile our educated and intelligent classes remain in their majestic repose, and that somehow or other, whatever happens, their overwhelming strength, like our military force in riots, never does act.

How, indeed, *should* their overwhelming strength act, when the man who gives an inflammatory lecture, or breaks down the Park railings, or invades a Secretary of State's office,[17] is only following an Englishman's impulse to do as he likes; and our own conscience tells us that we ourselves have always regarded this impulse as something primary and sacred? Mr Murphy lectures at Birmingham, and showers on the Catholic population of that town 'words,' says Mr Hardy, 'only fit to be addressed to thieves or murderers.'[18] What then? Mr Murphy has his own reasons of several kinds. He suspects the Roman Catholic Church of designs upon Mrs Murphy; and he says, if mayors and magistrates do not care for their wives and daughters, he does. But, above all, he is doing as he likes, or, in worthier language, asserting his personal liberty. 'I will carry out my lectures if they walk over my body as a dead corpse; and I say to the Mayor of Birmingham that he is my servant while I am in Birmingham, and as my servant he must do his duty and protect me.' Touching and beautiful words, which find a sympathetic chord in every British bosom! The moment it is plainly put before us that a man is asserting his personal liberty, we are half disarmed; because we are believers in freedom, and not in some dream of a right reason to which the assertion of our freedom is to be subordinated. Accordingly, the Secretary of State had to say that although the lecturer's language was 'only fit to be addressed to thieves or murderers,' yet 'I do not think he is to be deprived – I do not think that anything I have said could justify the inference that he is to be deprived – of the right of protection in a place built by him for the purpose of these lectures; because the language was not language which afforded grounds for a criminal prosecution.' No, nor to be silenced by Mayor, or Home Secretary, or any administrative authority on earth, simply on their notion of what is discreet and reasonable. This is in perfect consonance with our public opinion, and with our national love for the assertion of personal liberty.

In quite another department of affairs, Sir William Page Wood[19] relates an incident which is just to the same effect as this of Mr Murphy. A testator bequeathed 300*l.* a year, to be for ever applied as a pension to some person who had been unsuccessful in literature, and whose duty should be to support and diffuse, by his writings, the testator's own views, as enforced in the testator's publications. This bequest was appealed against in the Court of Chancery, on the ground of its absurdity; but, being only absurd, it was upheld, and the so-called charity was established. Having, I say, at the bottom of our English hearts a very strong belief in freedom, and a very weak belief in right reason, we are soon silenced when a man pleads the prime right to do as he likes, because this is the prime right for ourselves too; and even if we attempt now and then to mumble something about reason, yet we have thought so little about this and so much about liberty, that we are in conscience forced, when our brother Philistine[20] with whom we are meddling turns boldly round upon us and asks: *Have you any light?* to shake our heads ruefully, and to let him go his own way after all.

There are many things to be said on behalf of this exclusive attention of ours to liberty, and of the relaxed habits of government which it has engendered. It is very easy to mistake or to exaggerate the sort of anarchy from which we are in danger through them. We are not in danger from Fenianism,[21] fierce and turbulent as it may show itself; for against this our conscience is free enough to let us act resolutely and put forth our overwhelming strength the moment there is any real need for it. In the first place, it never was any part of our creed that the great right and blessedness of an Irishman, or, indeed, of anybody on earth except an Englishman, is to do as he likes; and we can have no scruple at all about abridging, if necessary, a non-Englishman's assertion of personal liberty. The British Constitution, its checks, and its prime virtues, are for Englishmen. We may extend them to others out of love and kindness; but we find no real divine law written on our hearts constraining us so to extend them. And then the difference between an Irish Fenian and an English rough is so immense, and the case, in dealing with the Fenian, so much more clear! He is so evidently desperate and dangerous, a man of a conquered race, a Papist, with centuries of ill-usage to inflame him against us, with an alien religion established in his country by us at his expense, with no admiration of our institutions, no love of our virtues, no talents for our business, no turn for our comfort! Show him our symbolical Truss Manufactory on the finest site in Europe,[22] and tell him that British industrialism and individualism can bring a man to that, and he remains cold. Evidently, if we deal tenderly with a sentimentalist like this, it is out of pure philanthropy. But with the Hyde Park rioter how different! He is our own flesh and blood; he is a Protestant; he is framed by nature to do as we do, hate what we hate, love what we love; he is capable of feeling the symbolical force of the Truss Manufactory; the question of questions, for him, is a wages' question. That beautiful sentence Sir Daniel Gooch[23] quoted to the Swindon workmen, and which I treasure as Mrs Gooch's Golden Rule – or the Divine Injunction 'Be ye Perfect' done into British – the sentence Sir Daniel Gooch's mother repeated to him every morning when he was a boy going to work: '*Ever remember, my dear Dan, that you should look forward to being some day manager of that concern*' – this fruitful maxim is perfectly fitted to shine forth in the heart of the Hyde Park rough also, and to be his guiding-star through life. He has no visionary schemes of revolution and transformation, though of course he would like his class to rule, as the aristocratic class like theirs to rule, and the middle-class theirs. Meanwhile, our social machine is a little out of order; there are a good many people in our paradisiacal centres of industrialism and individualism taking the bread out of one another's mouths; the rioter has not yet quite found his groove and settled down to his work, and so he is just asserting his personal liberty a little, going where he likes, assembling where he likes, bawling as he likes, hustling as he likes. Just as the rest of us – as the country squires in the aristocratic class, as the political dissenters in the middle-class – he has no idea of a *State*, of the nation in its collective and corporate controlling, as government, the free swing of this or that one of its members in the name of the higher reason of all of them, his own as well as that of others. He sees the rich, the aristocratic class, in occupation of the executive government, and if he is stopped from making Hyde Park a bear-garden[24] or the streets impassable, he says he is being butchered by the aristocracy.

His apparition is embarrassing, because too many cooks spoil the broth; because, while the aristocratic and middle classes have long been doing as they like with great vigour, he has been too undeveloped and submissive to join in the game; and now, when he comes, he comes in immense numbers, and is rather raw and rough. But he does not break many laws, or not many at one time; and, as our laws were made for very different circumstance from our present (but always with an eye to Englishmen doing as they like), and as the clear letter of the law must be against our Englishman who does as he likes and not only the spirit of the law and public policy, and as Government must neither have any discretionary power nor act resolutely on its own interpretation of the law if any one disputes it, it is evident our laws give our playful giant, in doing as he likes, considerable advantage. Besides, even if he can be clearly proved to commit an illegality in doing as he likes, there is always the resource of not putting the law in force, or of abolishing it. So he has his way, and if he has his way, he is soon satisfied for the time; however, he falls into the habit of taking it oftener and oftener, and at last begins to create by his operations a confusion of which mischievous people may take advantage, and which at any rate, by troubling the common course of business throughout the country, tends to cause distress, and so to increase the sort of anarchy and social disintegration which had previously commenced. And thus that profound sense of settled order and security, without which a society like ours cannot live and grow at all, is beginning to threaten us with taking its departure.

Now, if culture, which simply means trying to perfect oneself, and one's mind as part of oneself, brings us light, and if light shows us that there is nothing so very blessed in merely doing as one likes, that the worship of the mere freedom to do as one likes is worship of machinery, that the really blessed thing is to like what right reason ordains, and to follow her authority, then we have got a practical benefit out of culture. We have got a much wanted principle, a principle of authority, to counteract the tendency to anarchy which seems to be threatening us.

But how to organize this authority, or to what hands to entrust the wielding of it? How to get your *State*, summing up the right reason of the community, and giving effect to it, as circumstances may require, with vigour? And here I think I see my enemies waiting for me with a hungry joy in their eyes. But I shall elude them.

The *State*, the power most representing the right reason of the nation, and most worthy, therefore, of ruling – of exercising, when circumstances require it, authority over us all – is for Mr Carlyle[25] the aristocracy. For Mr Lowe,[26] it is the middle-class with its incomparable Parliament. For the Reform League, it is the working-class, with its 'brightest powers of sympathy and readiest powers of action.'[27] Now, culture, simply trying to see things as they are, in order to seize on the best and to make it prevail, is surely well fitted to help us to judge rightly, by all the aids of observing, reading, and thinking, these three candidates for authority, and can thus render us a practical service of no mean value.

So when Mr Carlyle, a man of genius to whom we have all at one time or other been indebted for refreshment and stimulus, says we should give rule to the aristocracy, mainly because of its dignity and politeness,[28] surely culture is useful in reminding us, that in our idea of perfection the characters of beauty and intelligence are both of them present, and sweetness and light, the two noblest of things, are united. Allowing, therefore, with Mr Carlyle, the aristocratic class to possess sweetness, culture insists on the necessity of light also, and shows us that aristocracies being, by the very nature of things, inaccessible to ideas, unapt to see how the world is going, must be wanting in light, and must therefore be, at a moment when light is our great requisite, helpless. Aristocracies, those children of the established fact, are for epochs of concentration; in epochs of expansion, epochs such as that in which we now live, epochs when always the warning voice is again heard: *Now is the judgment of this world* – in such epochs aristocracies, with their natural clinging to the established fact, their want of sense for the flux of things, for the inevitable transitoriness of all human institutions, are bewildered and helpless. Their serenity, their high spirit, their power of haughty resistance – the great qualities of an aristocracy, and the secret of its distinguished manners and dignity – these very qualities, in an epoch of expansion, turn against their possessors. Again and again I have said how the refinement of an aristocracy may be precious and educative to a raw nation as a kind of shadow of true refinement; how its serenity and dignified freedom from petty cares may serve as a useful foil to set off the vulgarity and hideousness in the type of life which a hard middle-class tends to establish, and to help people to see this vulgarity and hideousness in their true colours. From such an ignoble spectacle as that of poor Mrs Lincoln[29] – a spectacle to vulgarize a whole nation – aristocracies undoubtedly preserve us. But the true grace and serenity is that of which Greece and Greek art suggest the admirable ideals of perfection – a serenity which comes from having made order among ideas and harmonized them; whereas the serenity of aristocracies, at least the peculiar serenity of aristocracies of Teutonic origin, appears to come from their never having had any ideas to trouble them. And so, in a time of expansion like the present, a time for ideas, one gets, perhaps, in regarding an aristocracy, even more than the idea of serenity, the idea of futility and sterility. I have often wondered whether upon the whole earth there is anything so unintelligent, so unapt to perceive how the world is really going, as an ordinary young Englishman of our upper class. Ideas he has not, and neither has he that seriousness of our middle-class which is, as I have often said, the great strength of this class, and may become its salvation. Why, you will hear a young Dives[30] of the aristocratic class, when the whim takes him to sing the praises of wealth and material comfort, sing them with a cynicism from which the conscience of the veriest Philistine of our industrial middle-class would recoil in affright. And when, with the natural sympathy of aristocracies for firm dealing with the multitude, and his uneasiness at our feeble dealing with it at home, an unvarnished young Englishman of our aristocratic class applauds the absolute rulers on the Continent, he manages completely to miss the grounds of reason and intelligence which alone can give any colour of justification, any possibility of existence, to those rulers, and applauds them on grounds which it would make their own hair stand on end to listen to.

And all this while we are in an epoch of expansion; and the essence of an epoch of expansion is a movement of ideas, and the one salvation of an epoch of expansion is a harmony of ideas. The very principle of the authority which we are seeking as a defence against anarchy is right reason, ideas, light. The more, therefore, an aristocracy calls to its aid its innate forces – its impenetrability, its high spirit, its power of haughty resistance – to deal with an epoch of expansion, the graver is the danger, the greater the certainty of explosion, the surer the aristocracy's defeat; for it is trying to do violence to nature instead of working along with it. The best powers shown by the best men of an aristocracy at such an epoch are, it will be observed, non-aristocratical powers, powers of industry, powers of intelligence; and these powers, thus exhibited, tend really not to strengthen the aristocracy, but to take their owners out of it, to expose them to the dissolving agencies of thought and change, to make them men of the modern spirit and of the future. If, as sometimes happens, they add to their non-aristocratical qualities of labour and thought, a strong dose of aristocratical qualities also – of pride, defiance, turn for resistance – this truly aristocratical side of them, so far from adding any strength to them, really neutralizes their force and makes them impracticable and ineffective.

Knowing myself to be sadly to seek, as Mr Frederick Harrison says, in 'a philosophy with coherent, interdependent, subordinate and derivative principles,'[31] I continually have recourse to a plain man's expedient of trying to make what few simple notions I have, clearer and more intelligible to myself by means of example and illustration. And having been brought up at Oxford in the bad old times, when we were stuffed with Greek and Aristotle,[32] and thought nothing of preparing ourselves – as after Mr Lowe's recent great speech we shall do – to

175

fight the battle of life with the German waiters, my head is still full of a lumber of phrases we learnt at Oxford from Aristotle, about virtue being in a mean, and about excess and defect, and so on.[33] Once when I had had the advantage of listening to the Reform debates in the House of Commons, having heard a number of interesting speakers, and among them Lord Elcho and Sir Thomas Bateson,[34] I remember it struck me, applying Aristotle's machinery of the mean to my ideas about our aristocracy, that Lord Elcho was exactly the perfection, or happy mean, or virtue, of aristocracy, and Sir Thomas Bateson the excess; and I fancied that by observing these two we might see both the inadequacy of aristocracy to supply the principle of authority needful for our present wants, and the danger of its trying to supply it when it was not really competent for the business. On the one hand, in Lord Elcho, showing plenty of high spirit, but remarkable, far above and beyond his gift of high spirit, for the fine tempering of his high spirit, for ease, serenity, politeness – the great virtues, as Mr Carlyle says, of aristocracy; in this beautiful and virtuous mean, there seemed evidently some insufficiency of light; while, on the other hand, Sir Thomas Bateson, in whom the high spirit of aristocracy, its impenetrability, defiant courage, and pride of resistance, were developed even in excess, was manifestly capable, if he had his way given him, of causing us great danger, and, indeed, of throwing the whole commonwealth into confusion. Then I reverted to that old fundamental notion of mine about the grand merit of our race being really our honesty; and the very helplessness of our aristocratic or governing class in dealing with our perturbed social state gave me a sort of pride and satisfaction, because I saw they were, as a whole, too honest to try and manage a business for which they did not feel themselves capable.

Surely, now, it is no inconsiderable boon culture confers upon us, if in embarrassed times like the present it enables us to look at the ins and the outs of things in this way, without hatred and without partiality, and with a disposition to see the good in everybody all round. And I try to follow just the same course with our middle-class as with our aristocracy. Mr Lowe talks to us of this strong middle part of the nation, of the unrivalled deeds of our liberal middle-class Parliament, of the noble, the heroic work it has performed in the last thirty years; and I begin to ask myself if we shall not, then, find in our middle-class the principle of authority we want, and if we had not better take administration as well as legislation away from the weak extreme which now administers for us, and commit both to the strong middle part. I observe, too, that the heroes of middle-class liberalism, such as we have hitherto known it, speak with a kind of prophetic anticipation of the great destiny which awaits them, and as if the future was clearly theirs. The advanced party, the progressive party, the party in alliance with the future, are the names they like to give themselves. 'The principles which will obtain recognition in the future,' says Mr Miall, a personage of deserved eminence among the political Dissenters,[35] as they are called, who have been the backbone of middle-class liberalism – 'the principles which will obtain recognition in the future are the principles for which I have long and zealously laboured. I qualified myself for joining in the work of harvest by doing to the best of my ability the duties of seed-time.' These duties, if one is to gather them from the works of the great liberal party in the last thirty years, are, as I have elsewhere summed them up, the advocacy of free trade, of parliamentary reform, of abolition of church-rates, of voluntaryism in religion and education, of non-interference of the State between employers and employed, and of marriage with one's deceased wife's sister.[36]

I know, when I object that all this is machinery, the great liberal middle-class has now grown cunning enough to answer, that it always meant more by these things than meets the eye; that it has had that within which passes show, and that we are soon going to see, in a Free Church[37] and all manner of good things, what it was. But I have learned from Bishop Wilson[38] (if Mr Frederick Harrison will forgive my again quoting that poor old hierophant of a decayed superstition): 'If we would really know our heart let us impartially view our actions;' and I cannot help thinking that if our liberals had had so much sweetness and light in their inner minds as they allege, more of it must have come out in their sayings and doings. An American friend[39] of the English liberals says, indeed, that their dissidence of dissent has been a mere instrument of the political Dissenters for making reason and the will of God prevail (and no doubt he would say the same of marriage with one's deceased wife's sister); and that the abolition of a State Church is merely the Dissenter's means to this end, just as culture is mine. Another American defender of theirs says just the same of their industrialism and free-trade; indeed, this gentleman, taking the bull by the horns, proposes that we should for the future call industrialism culture, and the industrialists the men of culture, and then of course there can be no longer any misapprehension about their true character; and besides the pleasure of being wealthy and comfortable, they will have authentic recognition as vessels of sweetness and light.[40] All this is undoubtedly specious; but I must remark that the culture of which I talked was an endeavour to come at reason and the will of God by means of reading, observing, and thinking; and that whoever calls anything else culture, nay, indeed, call it so if he likes, but then he talks of something quite different from what I talked of. And, again, as culture's way of working for reason and the will of God is by directly trying to know more about them, while the dissidence of dissent is evidently in itself no effort of this kind, nor is its Free Church, in fact, a church with worthier conceptions of God and the ordering of the world than the State Church professes, but with mainly the same conceptions of these as the State Church has, only that every man is to comport himself as he likes in professing them – this being so, I cannot at once accept the Nonconformity any more than the industrialism and the other great works of our liberal middle-class as proof positive that this class is in possession of light, and that here is the true seat of authority for which we are in search; but I must try a little further, and seek for other indications which may enable me to make up my mind.

Why should we not do with the middle-class as we have done with the aristocratic class – find in it some representative men who may stand for the virtuous mean of this class, for the perfection of its present qualities and mode of being, and also for the excess of them. Such men must clearly not be men of genius like Mr Bright;[41] for, as I have formerly said, so far as a man has genius he tends to take himself out of the category of class altogether, and to become simply a man. Mr Bright's brother, Mr Jacob Bright,[42] would, perhaps, be more to the purpose; he seems to sum up very well in himself, without disturbing influences, the general liberal force of the middle-class, the force by which it has done its great works of free-trade, parliamentary reform, voluntaryism, and so on, and the spirit in which it has done them. Now it is clear, from what has already been said, that there has been at least an apparent want of light in the force and spirit through which these great works have been done, and that the works have worn in consequence too much a look of machinery. But this will be clearer still if we take, as the happy mean of the middle-class, not Mr Jacob Bright, but his colleague in the representation of Manchester, Mr Bazley.[43] Mr Bazley sums up for us, in general, the middle-class, its spirit and its works, at least as well as Mr Jacob Bright; and he has given us, moreover, a famous sentence, which bears directly on the resolution of our present question – whether there is light enough in our middle-class to make it the proper seat of the authority we wish to establish. When there was a talk some little while ago about the state of middle-class education, Mr Bazley, as the representative of that class, spoke some memorable words: – 'There had been a cry that middle-class education ought to receive more attention. He confessed himself very much surprised by the clamour that was raised. He did not think that class need excite the sympathy either of the legislature or the public.' Now this satisfaction of Mr Bazley with the mental state of the middle-class was truly representative, and enhances his claim (if that were necessary) to stand as the beautiful and virtuous mean of that class. But it is obviously at variance with our definition of culture, or the pursuit of light and perfection, which made light and perfection consist, not in resting and being, but in growing and becoming, in a perpetual advance in beauty and wisdom. So the middle-class is by its essence, as one may say, by its incomparable self-satisfaction decisively expressed through its beautiful and virtuous mean, self-excluded from wielding an authority of which light is to be the very soul.

Clear as this is, it will be made clearer still if we take some representative man as the excess of the middle-class, and remember that the middle-class, in general, is to be conceived as a body swaying between the qualities of its mean and of its excess, and on the whole, of course, as human nature is constituted, inclining rather towards the excess than the mean. Of its excess no better representative can possibly be imagined than the Rev. W. Cassel,[44] a Dissenting minister from Walsall, who came before the public in connection with the proceedings at Birmingham of Mr Murphy, already mentioned. Speaking in the midst of an irritated population of Catholics, the Rev. W. Cassel exclaimed: – 'I say, then, away with the mass! It is from the bottomless pit; and in the bottomless pit shall all liars have their part, in the lake that burneth with fire and brimstone.' And again: 'When all the praties were black in Ireland, why didn't the priests say the hocus-pocus over them, and make them all good again?'[45] He shared, too, Mr Murphy's fears of some invasion of his domestic happiness: 'What I wish to say to you as Protestant husbands is, *Take care of your wives!*' And, finally, in the true vein of an Englishman doing as he likes, a vein of which I have at some length pointed out the present dangers, he recommended for imitation the example of some churchwardens at Dublin, among whom, said he, 'there was a Luther and also a Melanchthon,'[46] who had made very short work with some ritualist or other, handed him down from his pulpit, and kicked him out. Now it is manifest, as I said in the case of Sir Thomas Bateson, that if we let this excess of the sturdy English middle-class, this conscientious Protestant Dissenter, so strong, so self-reliant, so fully persuaded in his own mind, have his way, he would be capable, with his want of light – or, to use the language of the religious world, with his zeal without knowledge – of kindling a fire which neither he nor any one else could easily quench.

And then comes in, as it did also with the aristocracy, the honesty of our race, and by the voice of another middle-class man, Alderman Wilson, Alderman of the City of London and Colonel of the City of London Militia,[47] proclaims that it has twinges of conscience, and that it will not attempt to cope with our social disorders, and to deal with a business which it feels to be too high for it. Every one remembers how this virtuous Alderman-Colonel, or Colonel-Alderman, led his militia through the London streets; how the bystanders gathered to see him pass; how the London roughs, asserting an Englishman's best and most blissful right of doing what he likes, robbed and beat the bystanders; and how the blameless warrior-magistrate refused to let his troops interfere. 'The crowd,' he touchingly said afterwards, 'was mostly composed of fine healthy strong men, bent on mischief; if he had allowed his soldiers to interfere they might have been overpowered, their rifles taken from them and used against them by the mob; a riot, in fact, might have ensued, and been attended with bloodshed, compared with which the assaults and loss of property that actually occurred would have been as nothing.' Honest and affecting testimony of the English middle-class to its own inadequacy for the authoritative part one's admiration would sometimes incline one to assign to it! 'Who are we,' they say by the voice of their Alderman-Colonel, 'that we should not be overpowered if we attempt to cope with social anarchy, our rifles taken from us and used against us by the mob, and we, perhaps, robbed and beaten ourselves? Or what right have we, beyond a free-born Englishman's impulse to do as he likes, which could justify us in preventing, at the cost of bloodshed, other free-born Englishmen from doing as they like, and robbing and beating us as much as they please?'

This distrust of themselves as an adequate centre of authority does not mark the working-class, as was shown by their readiness the other day in Hyde Park to take upon themselves all the functions of government. But this comes from the working-class being, as I have often said, still an embryo, of which no one can yet quite foresee the final development; and from its not having the same experience and self-knowledge as the aristocratic and middle classes. Honesty it no doubt has, just like the other classes of Englishmen, but honesty in an inchoate and untrained state; and meanwhile its powers of action, which are, as Mr Frederick Harrison says, exceedingly ready, easily run away with it.[48] That it cannot at present have a sufficiency of light which comes by culture – that is, by reading, observing, and thinking – is clear from the very nature of its condition; and, indeed, we saw that Mr Frederick Harrison, in seeking to make a free stage for its bright powers of sympathy and ready powers of action, had to begin by throwing overboard culture, and flouting it as only fit for a professor of belles-lettres. Still, to make it perfectly manifest that no more in the working-class than in the aristocratic and middle classes can one find an adequate centre of authority – that is, as culture teaches us to conceive our required authority, of light – let us again follow, with this class, the method we have followed with the aristocratic and middle classes, and try to bring before our minds representative men, who may figure to us its virtue and its excess. We must not take, of course, Colonel Dickson or Mr Beales; because Colonel Dickson, by his martial profession and dashing exterior, seems to belong properly, like Julius Ceasar and Mirabeau[49] and other great popular leaders, to the aristocratic class, and to be carried into the popular ranks only by his ambition or his genius; while Mr Beales belongs to our solid middle-class, and, perhaps, if he had not been a great popular leader, would have been a Philistine. But Mr Odger,[50] whose speeches we have all read, and of whom his friends relate, besides, much that is favourable, may very well stand for the beautiful and virtuous mean of our present working-class; and I think everybody will admit that in Mr Odger, as in Lord Elcho, there is manifestly, with all his good points, some insufficiency of light. The excess of the working-class, in its present state of development, is perhaps best shown in Mr Bradlaugh,[51] the iconoclast, who seems to be almost for baptizing us all in blood and fire into his new social dispensation, and to whose reflections, now that I have once been set going on Bishop Wilson's track, I cannot forbear commending this maxim of the good old man: 'Intemperance in talk makes a dreadful havoc in the heart.'[52] Mr Bradlaugh, like Sir Thomas Bateson and the Rev. W. Cassel, is evidently capable, if he had his head given him, of running us all into great dangers and confusion. I conclude, therefore – what, indeed, few of those who do me the honour to read this disquisition are likely to dispute – that we can as little find in the working-class as in the aristocratic or in the middle-class our much-wanted source of authority, as culture suggests it to us.

Well, then, what if we tried to rise above the idea of class to the idea of the whole community, the State, and to find our centre of light and authority there? Every one of us has the idea of country, as a sentiment; hardly any one of us has the idea of the State, as a working power. And why? Because we habitually live in our ordinary selves, which do not carry us beyond the ideas and wishes of the class to which we happen to belong. And we are all afraid of giving to the State too much power, because we only conceive of the State as something equivalent to the class in occupation of the executive government, and are afraid of that class abusing power to its own purposes. If we strengthen the State with the aristocratic class in occupation of the executive government, we imagine we are delivering ourselves up captive to the ideas and wishes of Sir Thomas Bateson; if with the middle-class in occupation of the executive government, to those of the Rev. W. Cassel; if with the working-class, to those of Mr Bradlaugh. And with much justice; owing to the exaggerated notion which we English, as I have said, entertain of the right and blessedness of the mere doing as one likes, of the affirming oneself, and oneself just as it is. People of the aristocratic class want to affirm their ordinary selves, their likings and dislikings; people of the middle-class the same, people of the working-class the same. By our everyday selves we are separate, personal, at war; we are only safe from one another's tyranny when no one has any power; and this safety, in its turn, cannot save us from anarchy. And when, therefore, anarchy presents itself as a danger to us, we know not where to turn.

But by our *best self* we are united, impersonal, at harmony. We are in no peril from giving authority to this, because it is the truest friend we all of us can have; and when anarchy is a danger to us, to this authority we may turn with sure trust. Well, and this is the very self which culture seeks to develop in us; at the expense of our old untransformed self, taking pleasure only in doing what it likes or is used to do, and exposing us to the risk of clashing with every one else who is doing the same! So that our poor culture, which is flouted as so unpractical, leads us to the very ideas capable of meeting the great want of our present embarrassed times! We want an authority, and we find nothing but jealous classes, checks, and a dead-lock; culture suggests the idea of *the State*. We find no basis for a firm State-power in our ordinary selves; culture suggests one to us in our *best self*.

It cannot but acutely try a tender conscience to be accused, in a practical country like ours, of keeping aloof from the work and hope of a multitude of earnest-hearted men, and of merely toying with poetry and aesthetics. So it is with no little sense of relief that I find myself thus in the position of one who makes a contribution in aid of the practical necessities of our times. The great thing, it will be observed, is to find our *best* self, and to seek to affirm nothing but that; not – as we English with our over-value for merely being free and busy have been so accustomed to do – resting satisfied with a self which comes uppermost long before our best self, and affirming that with blind energy. In short – to go back yet once more to Bishop Wilson – of these two excellent rules of Bishop Wilson's for a man's guidance: 'Firstly, never go against the best light you have; secondly, take care that your light be not darkness,'[53] we English have followed with praiseworthy zeal the first rule, but we have not given so much heed to the second. We have gone manfully, the Rev. W. Cassel and the rest of us, according to the best light we have; but we have not taken enough care that this should be really the best light possible for us, that it should not be darkness. And, our honesty being very great, conscience has whispered to us that the light we were following, our ordinary self, was indeed, perhaps, only an inferior self, only darkness; and that it would not do to impose this seriously on all the world.

But our best self inspires faith, and is capable of affording a serious principle of authority. For example. – We are on our way to what the late Duke of Wellington, with his strong sagacity, foresaw and admirably described as 'a revolution by due course of law.'[54] This is undoubtedly – if we are still to live and grow and this famous nation is not to stagnate and dwindle away on the one hand, or, on the other, to perish miserably in mere anarchy and confusion – what we are on the way to. Great changes there must be, for a revolution cannot accomplish itself without great changes; yet order there must be, for without order a revolution cannot accomplish itself by due course of law. So whatever brings risk of tumult and disorder, multitudinous processions in the streets of our crowded towns, multitudinous meetings in their public places and parks – demonstrations perfectly unnecessary in the present course of our affairs – our best self, or right reason, plainly enjoins us to prohibit. It enjoins us to encourage and uphold the occupants of the executive power, whoever they may be, in firmly prohibiting them. But it does this clearly and resolutely, and is thus a real principle of authority, because it does it with a free conscience; because in thus provisionally strengthening the executive power, it knows that it is not doing this merely to enable Sir Thomas Bateson to affirm himself as against Mr Bradlaugh, or the Rev. W. Cassel to affirm himself as against both. It knows that it is stablishing *the State*, or organ of our collective best self, of our national right reason; and it has the testimony of conscience that it is establishing the State on behalf of whatever great changes are needed, just as much as on behalf of order; establishing it to deal just as stringently, when the time comes, with Sir Thomas Bateson's Protestant ascendancy, or with the Rev. W. Cassel's sorry education of his children, as it deals with Mr Bradlaugh's street-processions.

But I know that in these humble speculations of mine I am watched by redoubtable adversaries; and – not having the safeguard of a philosophy with principles coherent, interdependent, subordinate, and derivative – it behoves me to walk with great caution. So I must take a little more time to show in somewhat fuller detail the different ways in which light, that new principle of authority which culture supplies to us, may have a real practical operation upon our national life and society.

182

## JOHN STUART MILL, *ON LIBERTY* (1859)

*From* John Stuart Mill, *On Liberty* (London: Parker, 1859)[1]

From *Chapter I: Introductory*

The subject of this Essay is not the so-called Liberty of the Will, so unfortunately opposed to the misnamed doctrine of Philosophical Necessity; but Civil, or Social Liberty: the nature and limits of the power which can be legitimately exercised by society over the individual. A question seldom stated, and hardly ever discussed, in general terms, but which profoundly influences the practical controversies of the age, by its latent presence, and is likely soon to make itself recognised as the vital question of the future. It is so far from being new, that, in a certain sense, it has divided mankind, almost from the remotest ages; but in the stage of progress into which the more civilized portions of the species have now entered, it presents itself under new conditions, and requires a different and more fundamental treatment.

The struggle between Liberty and Authority is the most conspicuous feature in the portions of history with which we are earliest familiar, particularly in that of Greece, Rome, and England. But in old times this contest was between subjects, or some classes of subjects, and the government. By liberty, was meant protection against the tyranny of the political rulers. The rulers were conceived (except in some of the popular governments of Greece) as in a necessarily antagonistic position to the people whom they ruled. They consisted of a governing One, or a governing tribe or caste, who derived their authority from inheritance or conquest, who, at all events, did not hold it at the pleasure of the governed, and whose supremacy men did not venture, perhaps did not desire, to contest, whatever precautions might be taken against its oppressive exercise. Their power was regarded as necessary, but also as highly dangerous; as a weapon which they would attempt to use against their subjects, no less than against external enemies. To prevent the weaker members of the community from being preyed upon by innumerable vultures, it was needful that there should be an animal of prey stronger than the rest, commissioned to keep them down. But as the king of the vultures would be no less bent upon preying on the flock than any of the minor harpies, it was indispensable to be in a perpetual attitude of defence against his beak and claws. The aim, therefore, of patriots was to set limits to the power which the ruler should be suffered to exercise over the community; and this limitation was what they meant by liberty. It was attempted in two ways. First, by obtaining a recognition of certain immunities, called political liberties or rights, which it was to be regarded as a breach of duty in the ruler to infringe, and which, if he did infringe, specific resistance, or general rebellion, was held to be justifiable. A second, and generally a later expedient, was the establishment of constitutional checks, by which the consent of the community, or of a body of some sort, supposed to represent its interests, was made a necessary condition to some of the more important acts of the governing power. To the first of these modes of limitation, the ruling power, in most European countries, was compelled, more or less, to submit. It was not so with the second; and, to attain this, or when already in some degree possessed, to attain it more completely, became everywhere the principle object of the lovers of liberty. And so long as mankind were content to combat one enemy by another, and to be ruled by a master, on condition of being guaranteed more or less efficaciously against his tyranny, they did not carry their aspirations beyond this point.

A time, however, came, in the progress of human affairs, when men ceased to think it a necessity of nature that their governors should be an independent power, opposed in interest to themselves. It appeared to them much better that the various magistrates of the State should be their tenants or delegates, revocable at their pleasure. In that way alone, it seemed, could they have complete security that the powers of government would never be abused to their disadvantage. By degrees this new demand for elective and temporary rulers became the prominent object of the exertions of the popular party, wherever any such party existed; and superseded, to a considerable extent, the previous efforts to limit the power of rulers. As the struggle proceeded for making the ruling power emanate from the periodical choice of the ruled, some persons began to think that too much importance had been attached to the limitation of the power itself. *That* (it might seem) was a resource against rulers whose interests were habitually opposed to those of the people. What was now wanted was, that the rulers should be identified with the people; that their interest and will should be the interest and will of the nation. The nation did not need to be protected against its own will. There was no fear of its tyrannizing over itself. Let the rulers be effectually responsible to it, promptly removable by it, and it could afford to trust them with power of which it could itself dictate the use to be made. Their power was but the nation's own power, concentrated, and in a form convenient for exercise. This mode of thought, or rather perhaps of feeling, was common among the last generation of European liberalism, in the Continental section of which it still apparently predominates. Those who admit any limit to what a government may do, except in the case of such governments as they think ought not to exist, stand out as brilliant exceptions among the political thinkers of the Continent. A similar tone of sentiment might by this time have been prevalent in our own country, if the circumstances which for a time encouraged it, had continued unaltered.

But, in political and philosophical theories, as well as in persons, success discloses faults and infirmities which failure might have concealed from observation. The notion, that the people have no need to limit their power over themselves, might seem axiomatic, when popular government was a thing only dreamed about, or read of as having existed at some distant period of the past. Neither was that notion necessarily disturbed by such temporary aberrations as those of the French Revolution, the worst of which were the work of an usurping few, and which, in any case, belonged, not to the permanent working of popular institutions, but to a sudden and convulsive outbreak against monarchical and aristocratic despotism. In time, however, a democratic republic[2] came to occupy a large portion of the earth's surface, and made itself felt as one of the most powerful members of the community of nations; and elective and responsible government became subject to the observations and criticisms which wait upon a great existing fact. It was now perceived that such phrases as 'self-government,' and 'the power of the people over themselves,' do not express the true state of the case. The 'people' who exercise the power are not always the same people with those over whom it is exercised; and the 'self-government' spoken of is not the government of each by himself, but of each by all the rest. The will of the people, moreover, practically means the will of the most numerous or the most active *part* of the people; the majority, or those who succeed in making themselves accepted as the majority; the people, consequently, *may* desire to oppress a part of their number; and precautions are as much needed against this as against any other abuse of power. The limitation, therefore, of the power of government over individuals loses none of its importance when the holders of power are regularly accountable to the community, that is, to the strongest party therein. This view of things, recommending itself equally to the intelligence of thinkers and to the inclination of those important classes in European society to whose real or supposed interests democracy is adverse, has had no difficulty in establishing itself; and in political speculations 'the tyranny of the majority'[3] is now generally included among the evils against which society requires to be on its guard.

Like other tyrannies, the tyranny of the majority was at first, and is still vulgarly, held in dread, chiefly as operating through the acts of the public authorities. But reflecting persons perceived that when society is itself the tyrant – society collectively, over the separate individuals who compose it – its means of tyrannizing are not restricted to the acts which it may do by the hands of its political functionaries. Society can and does execute its own mandates: and if it issues wrong mandates instead of right, or any mandates at all in things with which it ought not to meddle, it practises a social tyranny more formidable than many kinds of political oppression, since, though not usually upheld by such extreme penalties, it leaves fewer means of escape, penetrating much more deeply into the details of life, and enslaving the soul itself. Protection, therefore, against the tyranny of the magistrate is not enough: there needs protection also against the tyranny of the prevailing opinion and feeling; against the tendency of society to impose, by other means than civil penalties, its own ideas and practices as rules of conduct on those who dissent from them; to fetter the development, and, if possible, prevent the formation, of any individuality not in harmony with its ways, and compel all characters to fashion themselves upon the model of its own. There is a limit to the legitimate interference of collective opinion with individual independence: and to find that limit, and maintain it against encroachment, is as indispensable to a good condition of human affairs, as protection against political despotism.

But though this proposition is not likely to be contested in general terms, the practical question, where to place the limit – how to make the fitting adjustment between individual independence and social control – is a subject on which nearly everything remains to be done. All that makes existence valuable to any one, depends on the enforcement of restraints upon the actions of other people. Some rules of conduct, therefore, must be imposed, by law in the first place, and by opinion on many things which are not fit subjects for the operation of law. What these rules should be, is the principal question in human affairs; but if we except a few of the most obvious cases, it is one of those which least progress has been made in resolving. No two ages, and scarcely any two countries, have decided it alike; and the decision of one age or country is a wonder to another. Yet the people of any given age and country no more suspect any difficulty in it, than if it were a subject on which mankind had always been agreed. The rules which obtain among themselves appear to them self-evident and self-justifying. This all but universal illusion is one of the examples of the magical influence of custom, which is not only, as the proverb says, a second nature, but is continually mistaken for the first. The effect of custom, in preventing any misgiving respecting the rules of conduct which mankind impose on one another, is all the more complete because the subject is one on which it is not generally considered necessary that reasons should be given, either by one person to others, or by each to himself. People are accustomed to believe, and have been encouraged in the belief by some who aspire to the character of philosophers, that their feelings, on subjects of this nature, are better than reasons, and render reasons unnecessary. The practical principle which guides them to their opinions on the regulation of human conduct, is the feeling in each person's mind that everybody should be required to act as he, and those with whom he sympathizes, would like them to act. No one, indeed, acknowledges to himself that his standard of judgment is his own liking; but an opinion on a point of conduct, not supported by reasons, can only count as one person's preference; and if the reasons, when given, are a mere appeal to a similar preference felt by other people, it is still only many people's liking instead of one. To an ordinary man, however, his own preference, thus supported, is not only a perfectly satisfactory reason, but the only one he generally has for any of his notions of morality, taste, or propriety, which are not expressly written in his religious creed; and his chief guide in the interpretation even of that. Men's opinions, accordingly, on what is laudable or blameable, are affected by all the multifarious causes which influence their wishes in regard to the conduct of others, and which are as numerous as those which determine their wishes on any other subject. Sometimes their reason – at other times their prejudices or superstitions: often their social affections, not seldom their antisocial ones, their envy or jealousy, their arrogance or contemptuousness: but most commonly, their desires or fears for themselves – their legitimate or illegitimate self-interest. Wherever there is an ascendant class, a large portion of the morality of the country emanates from its class interests, and its feelings of class superiority. The morality between Spartans and Helots,[4]

186

between planters and negroes, between princes and subjects, between nobles and roturiers,[5] between men and women, has been for the most part the creation of these class interests and feelings: and the sentiments thus generated, react in turn upon the moral feelings of the members of the ascendant class, in their relations among themselves. Where, on the other hand, a class, formerly ascendant, has lost its ascendancy, or where its ascendancy is unpopular, the prevailing moral sentiments frequently bear the impress of an impatient dislike of superiority. Another grand determining principle of the rules of conduct, both in act and forbearance, which have been enforced by law or opinion, has been the servility of mankind towards the supposed preferences or aversions of their temporal masters, or of their gods. This servility, though essentially selfish, is not hypocrisy; it gives rise to perfectly genuine sentiments of abhorrence; it made men burn magicians and heretics. Among so many baser influences, the general and obvious interests of society have of course had a share, and a large one, in the direction of the moral sentiments: less, however, as a matter of reason, and on their own account, than as a consequence of the sympathies and antipathies which grew out of them: and sympathies and antipathies which had little or nothing to do with the interests of society, have made themselves felt in the establishment of moralities with quite as great force.

The likings and dislikings of society, or of some powerful portion of it, are thus the main thing which has practically determined the rules laid down for general observance, under the penalties of law or opinion. And in general, those who have been in advance of society in thought and feeling, have left this condition of things unassailed in principle, however they may have come into conflict with it in some of its details. They have occupied themselves rather in inquiring what things society ought to like or dislike, than in questioning whether its likings or dislikings should be a law to individuals. They preferred endeavouring to alter the feelings of mankind on the particular points on which they were themselves heretical, rather than make common cause in defence of freedom, with heretics generally. The only case in which the higher ground has been taken on principle and maintained with consistency, by any but an individual here and there, is that of religious belief: a case instructive in many ways, and not least so as forming a most striking instance of the fallibility of what is called the moral sense: for the *odium theologicum*,[6] in a sincere bigot, is one of the most unequivocal cases of moral feeling. Those who first broke the yoke of what called itself the Universal Church,[7] were in general as little willing to permit difference of religious opinion as that church itself. But when the heat of the conflict was over, without giving a complete victory to any party, and each church or sect was reduced to limit its hopes to retaining possession of the ground it already occupied; minorities, seeing that they had no chance of becoming majorities, were under the necessity of pleading to those whom they could not convert, for permission to differ. It is accordingly on this battle field, almost solely, that the rights of the individual against society have been asserted on broad grounds of principle, and the claim of society to exercise authority over dissentients, openly controverted. The great writers to whom the world owes what religious liberty it possesses, have mostly asserted freedom of conscience as an indefeasible right, and denied absolutely that a human being is accountable to others for his religious belief. Yet so natural to mankind is intolerance in whatever they really care about, that religious freedom has hardly anywhere been practically realized, except where religious indifference, which dislikes to have its peace disturbed by theological quarrels, has added its weight to the scale. In the minds of almost all religious persons, even in the most tolerant countries, the duty of toleration is admitted with tacit reserves. One person will bear with dissent in matters of church government, but not of dogma; another can tolerate everybody, short of a Papist or an Unitarian;[8] another, every one who believes in revealed religion; a few extend their charity a little further, but stop at the belief in a God and a future state. Wherever the sentiment of the majority is still genuine and intense, it is found to have abated little of its claim to be obeyed.

In England, from the peculiar circumstances of our political history, though the yoke of opinion is perhaps heavier, that of law is lighter, than in most other countries of Europe; and there is considerable jealousy of direct interference, by the legislative or the executive power, with private conduct; not so much from any just regard for the independence of the individual, as from the still subsisting habit of looking on the government as representing an opposite interest to the public. The majority have not yet learnt to feel the power of the government their power, or its opinions their opinions. When they do so, individual liberty will probably be as much exposed to invasion from the government, as it already is from public opinion. But, as yet, there is a considerable amount of feeling ready to be called forth against any attempt of the law to control individuals in things in which they have not hitherto been accustomed to be controlled by it; and this with very little discrimination as to whether the matter is, or is not, within the legitimate sphere of legal control; insomuch that the feeling, highly salutary on the whole, is perhaps quite as often misplaced as well grounded in the particular instances of its application. There is, in fact, no recognised principle by which the propriety or impropriety of government interference is customarily tested. People decide according to their personal preferences. Some, whenever they see any good to be done, or evil to be remedied, would willingly instigate the government to undertake the business; while others prefer to bear almost any amount of social evil, rather than add one to the departments of human interests amenable to governmental control. And men range themselves on one or the other side in any particular case, according to this general direction of their sentiments; or according to the degree of interest which they feel in the particular thing which it is proposed that the government should do, or according to the belief they entertain that the government would, or would not, do it in the manner they prefer; but very rarely on account of any opinion to which they consistently adhere, as to what things are fit to be done by a government. And it seems to me that in consequence of this absence of rule or principle, one side is at present as often wrong as the other; the interference of government is, with about equal frequency, improperly invoked and improperly condemned.

The object of this Essay is to assert one very simple principle, as entitled to govern absolutely the dealings of society with the individual in the way of compulsion and control, whether the means used be physical force in the form of legal penalties, or the moral coercion of public opinion. That principle is, that the sole end for which mankind are warranted, individually or collectively, in interfering with the liberty of action of any of their number, is self-protection. That the only purpose for which power can be rightfully exercised over any member of a civilized community, against his will, is to prevent harm to others. His own good, either physical or moral, is not a sufficient warrant. He cannot rightfully be compelled to do or forbear because it will be better for him to do so, because it will make him happier, because, in the opinions of others, to do so would be wise, or even right. These are good reasons for remonstrating with him, or reasoning with him, or persuading him, or entreating him, but not for compelling him, or visiting him with any evil in case he do otherwise. To justify that, the conduct from which it is desired to deter him, must be calculated to produce evil to some one else. The only part of the conduct of any one, for which he is amenable to society, is that which concerns others. In the part which merely concerns himself, his independence is, of right, absolute. Over himself, over his own body and mind, the individual is sovereign.

It is, perhaps, hardly necessary to say that this doctrine is meant to apply only to human beings in the maturity of their faculties. We are not speaking of children, or of young persons below the age which the law may fix as that of manhood or womanhood. Those who are still in a state to require being taken care of by others, must be protected against their own actions as well as against external injury. For the same reason, we may leave out of consideration those backward states of society in which the race itself may be considered as in its nonage. The early difficulties in the way of spontaneous progress are so great, that there is seldom any choice of means for overcoming them; and a ruler full of the spirit of improvement is warranted in the use of any expedients that will attain an end, perhaps otherwise unattainable. Despotism is a legitimate mode of government in dealing with barbarians, provided the end be their improvement, and the means justified by actually effecting that end. Liberty, as a principle, has no application to any state of things anterior to the time when mankind have become capable of being improved by free and equal discussion. Until then, there is nothing for them but implicit obedience to an Akbar or a Charlemagne,[9] if they are so fortunate as to find one. But as soon as mankind have attained the capacity of being guided to their own improvement by conviction or persuasion (a period long since reached in all nations with whom we need here concern ourselves), compulsion, either in the direct form or in that of pains and penalties for non-compliance, is no longer admissible as a means to their own good, and justifiable only for the security of others.

It is proper to state that I forego any advantage which could be derived to my argument from the idea of abstract right, as a thing independent of utility. I regard utility as the ultimate appeal on all ethical questions; but it must be utility in the largest sense, grounded on the permanent interests of man as a progressive being. Those interests, I contend, authorize the subjection of individual spontaneity to external control, only in respect to those actions of each, which concern the interest of other people. If any one does an act hurtful to others, there is a *primâ facie* case for punishing him, by law, or, where legal penalties are not safely applicable, by general disapprobation. There are also many positive acts for the benefit of others, which he may rightfully be compelled to perform; such as, to give evidence in a court of justice; to bear his fair share in the common defence, or in any other joint work necessary to the interest of the society of which he enjoys the protection; and to perform certain acts of individual beneficence, such as saving a fellow-creature's life, or interposing to protect the defenceless against ill-usage, things which whenever it is obviously a man's duty to do, he may rightfully be made responsible to society for not doing. A person may cause evil to others not only by his actions but by his inaction, and in either case he is justly accountable to them for the injury. The latter case, it is true, requires a much more cautious exercise of compulsion than the former. To make any one answerable for doing evil to others, is the rule; to make him answerable for not preventing evil, is, comparatively speaking, the exception. Yet there are many cases clear enough and grave enough to justify that exception. In all things which regard the external relations of the individual, he is *de jure* amenable to those whose interests are concerned, and if need be, to society as their protector. There are often good reasons for not holding him to the responsibility; but these reasons must arise from the special expediencies of the case: either because it is a kind of case in which he is on the whole likely to act better, when left to his own discretion, than when controlled in any way in which society have it in their power to control him; or because the attempt to exercise control would produce other evils, greater than those which it would prevent. When such reasons as these preclude the enforcement of responsibility, the conscience of the agent himself should step into the vacant judgment seat, and protect those interests of others which have no external protection; judging himself all the more rigidly, because the case does not admit of his being made accountable to the judgment of his fellow-creatures.

But there is a sphere of action in which society, as distinguished from the individual, has, if any, only an indirect interest; comprehending all that portion of a person's life and conduct which affects only himself, or if it also affects others, only with their free, voluntary, and undeceived consent and participation. When I say only himself, I mean directly, and in the first instance: for whatever affects himself, may affect others *through* himself; and the objection which may be grounded on this contingency, will receive consideration in the sequel. This, then, is the appropriate region of human liberty. It comprises, first, the inward domain of consciousness; demanding liberty of conscience, in the most comprehensive sense; liberty of thought and feeling; absolute freedom of opinion and sentiment on all subjects, practical or speculative, scientific, moral, or theological. The liberty of expressing and publishing opinions may seem to fall under a different principle, since it belongs to that part of the conduct of an individual which concerns other people; but, being almost of as much importance as the liberty of thought itself, and resting in great part on the same reasons, is practically inseparable from it. Secondly, the principle requires liberty of tastes and pursuits; of framing the plan of our life to suit our own character; of doing as we like, subject to such consequences as may follow: without impediment from our fellow-creatures, so long as what we do does not harm them, even though they should think our conduct foolish, perverse, or wrong. Thirdly, from this liberty of each individual, follows the liberty, within the same limits, of combination among individuals; freedom to unite, for any purpose not involving harm to others: the persons combining being supposed to be of full age, and not forced or deceived.

No society in which these liberties are not, on the whole, respected, is free, whatever may be its form of government; and none is completely free in which they do not exist absolute and unqualified. The only freedom which deserves the name, is that of pursuing our own good in our own way, so long as we do not attempt to deprive others of theirs, or impede their efforts to obtain it. Each is the proper guardian of his own health, whether bodily, or mental and spiritual. Mankind are greater gainers by suffering each other to live as seems good to themselves, than by compelling each to live as seems good to the rest.

Though this doctrine is anything but new, and, to some persons, may have the air of a truism, there is no doctrine which stands more directly opposed to the general tendency of existing opinion and practice. Society has expended fully as much effort in the attempt (according to its lights) to compel people to conform to its notions of personal, as of social excellence. The ancient commonwealths thought themselves entitled to practise, and the ancient philosophers countenanced, the regulation of every part of private conduct by public authority, on the ground that the State had a deep interest in the whole bodily and mental discipline of every one of its citizens; a mode of thinking which may have been admissible in small republics surrounded by powerful enemies, in constant peril of being subverted by foreign attack or internal commotion, and to which even a short interval of relaxed energy and self-command might so easily be fatal, that they could not afford to wait for the salutary permanent effects of freedom. In the modern world, the greater size of political communities, and above all, the separation between spiritual and temporal authority (which placed the direction of men's consciences in other hands than those which controlled their worldly affairs), prevented so great an interference by law in the details of private life; but the engines of moral repression have been wielded more strenuously against divergence from the reigning opinion in self-regarding, than even in social matters; religion, the most powerful of the elements which have entered into the formation of moral feeling, having almost always been governed either by the ambition of a hierarchy, seeking control over every department of human conduct, or by the spirit of Puritanism. And some of these modern reformers who have placed themselves in strongest opposition to the religions of the past, have been noway behind either churches or sects in their assertion of the right of spiritual domination. M Comte,[10] in particular, whose social system, as unfolded in his *Traité de Politique Positive*, aims at establishing (though by moral more than by legal appliances) a despotism of society over the individual, surpassing anything contemplated in the political ideal of the most rigid disciplinarian among the ancient philosophers.

Apart from the peculiar tenets of individual thinkers, there is also in the world at large an increasing inclination to stretch unduly the powers of society over the individual, both by the force of opinion and even by that of legislation: and as the tendency of all the changes taking place in the world is to strengthen society, and diminish the power of the individual, this encroachment is not one of the evils which tend spontaneously to disappear, but, on the contrary, to grow more and more formidable. The disposition of mankind, whether as rulers or as fellow-citizens, to impose their own opinions and inclinations as a rule of conduct on others, is so energetically supported by some of the best and by some of the worst feelings incident to human nature, that it is hardly ever kept under restraint by anything but want of power; and as the power is not declining, but growing, unless a strong barrier of moral conviction can be raised against the mischief, we must expect, in the present circumstances of the world, to see it increase.

It will be convenient for the argument, if, instead of at once entering upon the general thesis, we confine ourselves in the first instance to a single branch of it, on which the principle here stated is, if not fully, yet to a certain point, recognised by the current opinions. This one branch is the Liberty of Thought: from which it is impossible to separate the cognate liberty of speaking and of writing.

# WILLIAM MORRIS *ET AL.*, 'THE MANIFESTO OF THE SOCIALIST LEAGUE' (1885)

William Morris *et al.*, 'The Manifesto of the Socialist League', *The Commonweal*, I (February 1885), pp. 1–2[1]

*The Manifesto Of The Socialist League*

Fellow Citizens,

We come before you as a body advocating the principles of Revolutionary International Socialism; that is, we seek a change in the basis of Society – a change which would destroy the distinctions of classes and nationalities.

As the civilised world is at present constituted, there are two classes of Society – the one possessing wealth and the instruments of its production, the other producing wealth by means of those instruments but only by the leave and for the use of the possessing classes.

These two classes are necessarily in antagonism to one another. The possessing class, or non-producers, can only live as a class on the unpaid labour of the producers – the more unpaid labour they can wring out of them, the richer they will be; therefore the producing class – the workers – are driven to strive to better themselves at the expense of the possessing class, and the conflict between the two is ceaseless. Sometimes it takes the form of open rebellion, sometimes of strikes, sometimes of mere widespread mendicancy and crime; but it is always going on in one form or other, though it may not always be obvious to the thoughtless looker-on.

We have spoken of unpaid labour: it is necessary to explain what that means. The sole possession of the producing class is the power of labour inherent in their bodies; but since, as we have already said, the rich classes possess all the instruments of labour, that is, the land, capital, and machinery, the producers or workers are forced to sell their sole possession, the power of labour, on such terms as the possessing class will grant them.

These terms are, that after they have produced enough to keep them in working order, and enable them to beget children to take their places when they are worn out, the surplus of their products shall belong to the possessors of property, which bargain is based on the fact that every man working in a civilised community can produce more than he needs for his own sustenance.

This relation of the possessing class to the working class is the essential basis of the system of producing for a profit, on which our modern Society is founded. The way in which it works is as follows. The manufacturer produces to sell at a profit to the broker or factor, who in his turn makes a profit out of his dealings with the merchant, who again sells for a profit to the retailer, who must make his profit out of the general public, aided by various degrees of fraud and adulteration and the ignorance of the value and quality of goods to which this system has reduced the consumer.

The profit-grinding system is maintained by competition, or veiled war, not only between the conflicting classes, but also within the classes themselves: there is always war among the workers for bare subsistence, and among their masters, the employers and middle-men, for the share of the profit wrung out of the workers; lastly, there is competition always, and sometimes open war, among the nations of the civilised world for their share of the world-market. For now, indeed, all the rivalries of nations have been reduced to this one – a degrading struggle for their share of the spoils of barbarous countries to be used at home for the purpose of increasing the riches of the rich and the poverty of the poor.

For, owing to the fact that goods are made primarily to sell, and only secondarily for use, labour is wasted on all hands; since the pursuit of profit compels the manufacturer competing with his fellows to force his wares on the markets by means of their cheapness, whether there is any real demand for them or not. In the words of the Communist manifesto of 1847:[2] –

> 'Cheap goods are their artillery for battering down Chinese walls and for overcoming the obstinate hatred entertained against foreigner by semi-civilised nations: under penalty of ruin the Bourgeoisie compel by competition the universal adoption of their system of production; they force all nations to accept what is called civilisation – to become Bourgeois – and thus the middle-class shapes the world after its own image.'

Moreover, the whole method of distribution under this system is full of waste; for it employs whole armies of clerks, travellers, shopmen, advertisers, and what not, merely for the sake of shifting money from one person's pocket to another's; and this waste in production and waste in distribution, added to the maintenance of the useless lives of the possessing and non-producing class, must all be paid for out of the products of the workers, and is a ceaseless burden on their lives.

Therefore the necessary results of this so-called civilisation are only too obvious in the lives of its slaves, the working-class – in the anxiety and want of leisure amidst which they toil, in the squalor and wretchedness in those parts of our great towns where they dwell; in the degradation of their bodies, their wretched health, and the shortness of their lives; in the terrible brutality so common among them, and which is indeed but the reflection of the cynical selfishness found among the well-to-do classes, a brutality as hideous as the other; and lastly, in the crowd of criminals who are as much manufacturers of our commercial system as the cheap and nasty wares which are made at once for the consumption and the enslavement of the poor.

What remedy, then, do we propose for this failure of our civilisation, which is now admitted by almost all thoughtful people?

We have already shown that the workers, although they produce all the wealth of society, have no control over its production or distribution: the *people*, who are the only really organic part of society, are treated as a mere appendage to capital – as a part of its machinery. This must be altered from the foundation: the land, the capital, the machinery, factories, workshops, stores, means of transit, mines, banking, all means of production and distribution of wealth, must be declared and treated as the common property of all. Every man will then receive the full value of his labour, without deduction for the profit of a master, and as all will have to work, and the waste now incurred by the pursuit of profit will be at an end, the amount of labour necessary for every individual to perform in order to carry on the essential work of the world will be reduced to something like two or three hours daily; so that every one will have abundant leisure for following intellectual or other pursuits congenial to his nature.

This change in the method of production and distribution would enable every one to live decently, and free from the sordid anxieties for daily livelihood which at present weigh so heavily on the greatest part of mankind.

But, moreover, men's social and moral relations would be seriously modified by this gain of economical freedom, and by the collapse of the superstitions, moral and other, which necessarily accompany a state of economical slavery: the test of duty would now rest on the fulfilment of clear and well-defined obligations to the community rather than on the moulding of the individual character and actions to some preconceived standard outside social responsibilities.

Our modern bourgeois property-marriage, maintained as it is by its necessary complement, universal venal prostitution, would give place to kindly and human relations between the sexes.

Education freed from the trammels of commercialism on the one hand and superstition on the other, would become a reasonable drawing out of men's varied faculties in order to fit them for a life of social intercourse and happiness; for mere work would no longer be proposed as the end of life, but happiness for each and all.

Only by such fundamental changes in the life of man, only by the transformation of Civilisation into Socialism, can those miseries of the world before-mentioned be amended.

As to mere politics, Absolutism, Constitutionalism, Republicanism, have all been tried in our day and under our present social system, and all have alike failed in dealing with the real evils of life.

Nor, on the other hand, will certain incomplete schemes of social reform now before the public solve the question.

Co-operation so-called – that is, competitive co-operation for profit – would merely increase the number of small joint-stock capitalists, under the mask of creating an aristocracy of labour, while it would intensify the severity of labour by its temptations to overwork.

Nationalisation of the land alone, which many earnest and sincere persons are now preaching, would be useless so long as labour was subject to the fleecing of surplus value inevitable under the Capitalist system.

No better solution would be that State Socialism,[3] by whatever name it may be called, whose aim it would be to make concessions to the working class while leaving the present system of capital and wages still in operation: no number of merely administrative changes, until the workers are in possession of all political power, would make any real approach to Socialism.

The Socialist League therefore aims at the realisation of complete Revolutionary Socialism, and well knows that this can never happen in any one country without the help of the workers of all civilisation. For us neither geographical boundaries, political history, race, nor creed makes rivals or enemies; for us there are no nations, but only varied masses of workers and friends, whose mutual sympathies are checked or perverted by groups of masters and fleecers whose interest it is to stir up rivalries and hatreds between the dwellers in different lands.

It is clear that for all these oppressed and cheated masses of workers and their masters a great change is preparing: the dominant classes are uneasy, anxious, touched in conscience even, as to the condition of those they govern; the markets of the world are being competed for with an eagerness never before known; everything points to the fact that the great commercial system is becoming unmanageable, and is slipping from the grasp of its present rulers.

The one change possible out of all this is Socialism. As chattel-slavery passed into serfdom, and serfdom into the so-called free-labour system, so most surely will this latter pass into social order.

To the realisation of this change the Socialist League addresses itself with all earnestness. As a means thereto it will do all in its power towards the education of the people in the principles of this great cause, and will strive to organise those who will accept this education, so that when the crisis comes, which the march of events is preparing, there may be a body of men ready to step into their due places and deal with and direct the irresistible movement.

Close fellowship with each other, and steady purpose for the advancement of the Cause, will naturally bring about the organisation and discipline amongst ourselves absolutely necessary to success; but we shall look to it that there shall be no distinctions of rank or dignity amongst us to give opportunities for the selfish ambition of leadership which has so often injured the cause of the workers. We are working *for* equality and brotherhood for all the world, and it is only *through* equality and brotherhood that we can make our work effective.

Let us all strive, then, towards this end of realising the change towards social order, the only cause worthy the attention of the workers of all that are proffered to them: let us work in that cause patiently, yet hopefully, and not shrink from making sacrifices to it. Industry in learning its principles, industry in teaching them, are most necessary to our progress; but to these we must add, if we wish to avoid speedy failure, frankness and fraternal trust in each other, and single-hearted devotion to the religion of Socialism, the only religion which the Socialist League professes.

# Part II

# SCIENCE AND RELIGION

## CONTENTS

INTRODUCTION                                                          199

4  GOD AND NATURE: EVOLUTIONARY THEORY                               213
   *From* Charles Lyell, *Principles of Geology. Volume I* (1830)  *213*
   *From* Charles Darwin, *On the Origin of Species by Means of
      Natural Selection* (1859)  *227*
   *From* Thomas Henry Huxley, *Evidence as to Man's Place
      in Nature* (1863)  *254*
   *From* Samuel Wilberforce, 'Art VII. – *On the Origin of
      Species . . .* ' (1860)  *272*
   *From* Herbert Spencer, 'The Study of Sociology. XIV. –
      Preparation in Biology' (1873)  *278*

5  GOD AND REASON: BIBLICAL SCHOLARSHIP                             289
   *From* Benjamin Jowett, 'On the Interpretation of
      Scripture' (1860)  *289*
   *From* John William Colenso, *The Pentateuch and Book of
      Joshua Critically Examined* (1862)  *299*

# INTRODUCTION

The intellectual history of the nineteenth century has been most consistently understood in terms of the rise of science. Indeed, when it is set against any earlier period of human history, the Victorian age seems to be one of unprecedented scientific discovery and technological innovation. Nineteenth-century science and technology determined the shape and nature of the modern age. Those technologies which we tend to think of as distinguishing our lives as modern – the motor-car, the telephone, moving pictures, and so on – were all in fact nineteenth-century inventions. A second commonplace of the intellectual history of the nineteenth century is that the age of science brought about the decline of religion. In this sense a further dominant feature of contemporary Western life – secularism – also had its origins in the Victorian period. The complex set of values attaching to both Victorianism and modernity – the excitement and fear engendered by technology, the benefit of science weighed against its social cost, the anomie associated with the loss of the certainties of religion – these make our relationship with the Victorian age a particularly familiar one, and they also make it possible to characterise this period of history in terms which still resonate today.

The changed nature of the relationship between science and religion in the nineteenth century is exemplified by Thomas Huxley's curt dismissal of religion as 'the deadly enemy of science.'[1] Huxley's image of two domains of knowledge locked in rivalry is of course reductive, but in many ways it remains an essentially true one. The event which seems best to symbolise it is the famous meeting in Oxford in 1860 of the British Association for the Advancement of Science in which Huxley mounted a vigorous defence of Darwinian theories of evolution against the criticism of them made by the Bishop of Oxford, Samuel Wilberforce. Unfortunately there is no reliable account of this historic meeting, and the eye-witness reports which have survived are predictably partisan. Nevertheless the general consensus was that Huxley was the clear winner. It has been tempting to see in this 'victory' a defining moment in the historic contest between science and religion, for after the 1860s it was science rather than religion which dictated the terms of the debate. Most importantly, the gradual displacement of religion by science was not simply a matter of the substitution of one authority for another; rather, it involved a whole new way of thinking about the ways in which knowledge was to be made authoritative. And it was the persuasiveness of what we now call the 'scientific' method, underwritten by the unprecedented number and undoubted efficacy of scientific theories and technological innovations, which lay behind Huxley's confidence.

Medicine, physics, chemistry, biology, geology, mathematics – all these areas of knowledge underwent fundamental and systematic changes in the nineteenth century. The understanding of the body (particularly via immunology and germ-theory, comparative anatomy, embryology and sexology), a new understanding of the atomic theory of matter (which underlies the periodic table), an equally new understanding of the forms of energy (particularly Michael Faraday's work on electricity, and James Maxwell's on light-waves and electromagnetism), the development of inorganic chemistry, evolutionary theories of development, the discovery of set theory in mathematics, and so on – these represented great moments in Victorian science. When we add to them the enormous leaps made in Victorian technology – for example, the perfection of steam-powered locomotion, the extensive use of iron and steel (particularly in naval and civil engineering), the development of electric lighting, photography, the telegraph, the use of anaesthetics and antiseptics and, at the very end of the century, the internal combustion engine and early cinematography – it becomes clear that one of the outstanding features of Victorian science and technology was their immediate, large-scale and irreversible impact on everyday life. Perhaps the four main areas where that impact was most dramatically experienced were in transport, communications, health and in work. In contrast to earlier centuries, then, the authority of science in Victorian Britain and its consequent equation with 'progress' owed much to its conspicuous success. Of course the social benefits of science were felt very unevenly, and that unevenness was itself a source of considerable disquiet; however, in general terms, it is only the undeniable efficacy and utility of Victorian science which can explain the intellectual normalising of what we would now loosely term a scientific epistemology: that is, the belief that scientific knowledge, to all intents and purposes, *is* knowledge.

In the nineteenth century, scientific authority meant rational enquiry, an emphasis on empirical research, the careful testing of evidence and rigour in argument. Actually none of these requirements was new; what had changed, though, was the perception that they should be properly codified, regulated and standardised. Such a need arose mainly from the sheer volume and complexity of knowledge produced in the second half of the century, and also from the increasing internationalisation of knowledge made possible by dramatic improvements in communication technology. The rise of Victorian science is thus inseparable from (and was almost certainly a causal factor in) a larger set of changes in the social organisation of knowledge, particularly the ways in which knowledge became specialised and professionalised. In order to be competent in a particular field it became increasingly necessary for Victorian intellectuals, scientists or scholars to narrow their interests: to specialise. These specialists subsequently introduced new standards of scholarly rigour to protect their specialised knowledge and confirm their status as experts. Indeed, many historians have discussed the social history of nineteenth-century Britain in terms of the decline of the 'sage' and the accompanying rise of the 'expert'. Ensuring expert standards in turn required a system of formal qualifications, and as knowledge became specialised, so in the late nineteenth century it also became professionalised and institutionalised. Simply put, knowledge increasingly passed into the hands of the universities and learned societies (and their equally learned journals). What we now understand as academic life is largely another nineteenth-century invention (so too were many of the civic universities in which it is practised). One consequence of these developments was that universities themselves were forced to become more professional, and one important function of the far-reaching university reforms set in motion in the middle of the nineteenth century was formally to dissociate academic success from religious orthodoxy. (The Oxford University Act of 1854 and Cambridge University Act of 1856 permitted nonconformists to enter without a religious test to take a BA degree and removed the obligation for fellows to take holy orders; religious tests were abolished altogether in 1871.) Another consequence was that scientific authority became intimately bound up with a scientific 'establishment', and it is no accident that the dominant figures in Victorian science, including Charles Lyell, Charles Darwin and Thomas Huxley, were all institutional men: they all were active members of organisations such as the Royal Society and the Geological Society, and many also held university posts. Most importantly, perhaps, the intellectual paradigms established by science themselves became institutionalised, defining what was to count as authoritative knowledge, rather than simply as scientific knowledge. As a result other knowledge – particularly that of non-scientific subjects, such as history – came under increasing pressure to adopt scientific methods of proof and scientific standards of evidence if it wished to be considered authoritative. In addition whole new areas of study were mapped out. For example, the study of the mind in the late nineteenth century became the province of the new scientific discipline of psychology, rather than being a part of philosophy. Moreover psychology itself was conceived of as an empirical science, grounded in a materialist study of the brain and its physiology. Similarly the study of natural history passed from the hands of amateur zoologists and botanists (zoology and botany were traditional pastimes of gentlemen in the early Victorian period) into those of professionally qualified experts. The career of one of the century's most famous scientists, Charles Darwin, usefully epitomises such a change: the amateur collector of beetles at Cambridge became Secretary of one of the century's most important learned bodies, the Geological Society, and aired his first thoughts on natural selection to the Linnean Society.

Most importantly, theology itself was not immune from these developments. The 'crisis in faith' (as it is sometimes termed) in Victorian Britain was the result of many factors. In the first place, religious controversy was not confined to a series of conflicts with the scientific community. In addition there were significant doctrinal disputes within the Anglican Church, of which the most important was the Oxford Movement, or Tractarianism – an attempt led by John Keble, John Henry Newman, and Edward Pusey to reintroduce High Church ideals into the Church of England. Behind these doctrinal disputes was a much larger question of the relationship of the Church to the State and therefore the relationship of religious to secular authority: in the eyes of the Tractarians, the Liberal or Broad Church conception of a partnership between Church and State made theological doctrine subordinate and thereby ceded too much authority to secular power. The Oxford Movement lost much of its impetus in the mid-1840s when some of its members (in the words of the time) 'went over to Rome' or converted to Roman Catholicism. The debate about the role of an established church, however, continued. It was, for example, taken up in the 1860s by Matthew Arnold who in *Culture and Anarchy* identified the anarchic tendencies of modern society with the divisions between the Anglican Church and various dissenting groups. The status of nonconformists was a source of controversy throughout the century, exacerbated as it was by falling church attendance. The prestige of the Established Church was also undermined by the increasing influence of Dissenters in rural and mining communities, and groups such as the Unitarians among urban élites. Agitation about the political and educational rights of Catholics (which were considerably improved during the nineteenth century) was also a source of conflict. All these dilemmas, brought about by a variety of complex social and doctrinal factors, worked together to problematise religious authority. At the same time, however, they were contained within a conventional religious framework in that they were largely about the nature and role of belief, rather than its possibility. It was this last and more fundamental question which was brought sharply into focus by the dominance of Victorian science, and in two ways.

First, there was a growing incompatibility between scientific and religious explanations of the natural world and man's place in it. Traditionally in what was called 'natural theology' (as it was practised by figures such as William Paley in his widely read *Natural Theology* [1802]), science and religion were in harmony as the goal of science was perceived to be the revelation of divine order – of the Creator's design exhibited in the natural world. In Paley's view the function and rationale of science was to confirm or demonstrate the existence of God. Importantly the appeal to empiricism – the scientific appeal to material evidence – was a strategy used to support rather than to undermine faith, and a mechanistic explanation of the universe was accommodated to the notion of an originary cause: a mechanistic universe merely pointed to a divine mechanic. However, the growth of evolutionary theories of development in geology, natural history and biology gradually eroded this concept of a perfect design. As a result the relationship between scientific methodology and religious faith was also undermined. Most significantly, Darwin's radical speculations about the randomness of nature completely severed it, turning science (as Huxley acknowledged) against religion.

In the nineteenth century the idea of evolution was not in itself new; nor was it necessarily controversial. It had for example formed the orthodox narrative of much Victorian historiography: the notion of a gradual evolution in social and political organisation was both familiar and comforting for whose who believed in the superiority of Western (and particularly of British) civilisation. Moreover a concept of development also underwrote much natural theology: the acknowledgement of continuous change in the natural world led to a revised concept of creation as a slow and gradual process rather than a singular and fixed event. Importantly, however, this notion of evolution was always in the service of a particular teleology in that it was assumed to be controlled by final causes: thus the natural world developed according to a predetermined divine plan, and was evolving towards perfection. The best known literary expression of such a view is probably *In Memoriam*, Alfred Tennyson's long elegy for his friend Arthur Hugh Hallam. Tennyson and the natural theologians would have been content with Leibniz's formula, that the world we live in is the best of all possible worlds. Evolutionary ways of thinking only became controversial when they seemed to hint that the original plan or design was in some sense imperfect, and that the powers of the divine Creator were therefore limited or flawed; or, more radically (as in Darwin's work), when they suggested that there was no plan at all – no final causes, no goal, no 'end' for development. How did this change in perspective come about? How did evolutionary thinking become divorced from teleology?

Broadly speaking, as empirical data about the natural world increased, so it became more difficult to accommodate it to the notion of a purposeful and beneficent design. A particular problem was posed by the discovery (by the French scientist, Georges Cuvier) of large fossil remains in the Tertiary of the Paris Basin which pointed to the extinction of a whole sequence of mammalian fauna. If evolution was directed towards some divinely ordained end, why should whole species and genera die? Initially in Britain it was geologists (rather than naturalists) who attempted to explain this illogicality. As in natural history, geological evidence tended to be interpreted in relation to the Bible: that is, the Bible was used to authorise or support geological findings and strict proponents of this principle (commonly called 'Mosaic' or 'Scriptural' geologists) claimed that the Book of Genesis was literally true and therefore scientifically accurate. When geological evidence began to strain such literalism, geologists (unwilling to relinquish their scientific method, and thus empiricism) tried to establish a new kind of relationship between science and religion. It was based upon a more liberal interpretation of the Bible and a revised view of creation. For example, the Cambridge scientist Adam Sedgwick argued that manifest changes in the organic world, including those revealed by the fossil record, *could* be reconciled to traditional religious thought if they were seen as the result of occasional, sudden and violent events brought about by divine intervention: they were evidence, that is, of a series of successive and progressive creative acts. Such a view maintained William Paley's idea of a fixed creation but at the same time it optimistically hinted at God's continued and active curatorship of the natural order.

For the geologist Charles Lyell, however, such an argument – known as 'catastrophism' – was unsatisfactory not least because it was fundamentally unscientific. In his *Principles of Geology* (1830–3) Lyell attacked the positions of both the Mosaicists and the Catastrophists for failing to understand what constituted a scientific methodology. The key issue, he argued, was the concept of causation; scientifically understood, causation meant the consideration only of true causes: that is, causes which can be observed. Applied to geology, Lyell's argument held that the entire history of the earth could be understood in terms of causes observable in present-day geological formations; these causes were the same both in kind and degree as the causes which had acted in the past – a proposition which in turn required the postulating of a vast geological time-scale. Lyell's thesis (which was referred to as 'uniformitarianism') amounted to a 'steady-state' (as opposed to a directed or progressive) view of geological development. In uniformitarianism there was no obvious movement towards a predetermined or 'perfect' end. It was this anti-teleological element of his theory which was important in the development of evolutionary thinking, particularly the work of Darwin. At the same time, though, it is worth pointing out that Lyell, although initially alone among geologists, never considered himself to be an intellectual revolutionary or iconoclast. A devout Christian, he never accepted the more radical aspects of Darwin's work, although the two men remained friends. Indeed his account of the fossil record was a conservative one: in line with his gradualist view of geological change, he claimed that individual species went extinct one by one as conditions in the environment changed. The subsequent 'gaps' in nature were then filled by the introduction of new species already adapted to occupy those changed conditions. Imaginative as it was, in one obvious way this 'saltationist' view of biological evolution was no more satisfactory than that of the catastrophists, for the question of precisely how new species appeared was once again attributed to a mysterious creative agency.

Lyell's conservatism over biological change was largely prompted by his reading of the work of the French zoologist, Jean-Baptiste Lamarck. Published at the beginning of the century, Lamarck's *Philosophie zoologique* (1809) had been virtually ignored in Britain, certainly until Lyell devoted a considerable portion of the second volume of *Principles of Geology* to rebutting its thesis. Lamarck was the first thoroughgoing biological evolutionist. Opposing creationist arguments, he claimed that the world's flora and fauna were the result of a long and continuous process of development whereby organisms adapted to their environment and then passed on to their offspring these newly acquired traits. In one sense Lamarck was a traditionalist; working within the Renaissance concept of the 'great chain of being', he assumed a teleological development from simple organisms through to complex ones, and so from imperfection to perfection. Where his theory was unacceptable (for Lyell and most of Lyell's contemporaries) was in its insistence on a *vertical* line of development: that is, all lines of evolution originated from the spontaneous generation of simple cellular organisms: it was only through time that these organisms evolved to their present complexity. Lamarck's transformational theory, in other words, had no really functional concept of speciation, and in particular no concept of the uniqueness of *homo sapiens* as a species set apart from the rest of creation. By contrast, for figures such as Lyell (as well as natural theologians and catastrophists) the discrete and objective reality of species was the starting-point of all theories of biological development – species were the basic taxonomic unit of inquiry. Hence to ignore them not only threatened the dignity of man but it was also fundamentally unscientific: without a fixed object of inquiry, Lyell argued, science has nothing to study. Furthermore by ignoring the concept of species Lamarck could have nothing to say about extinction. In his view, it was simply that transformations were sometimes so dramatic that types from earlier points in the evolutionary scale were no longer recognisable.

A fundamentally different but equally controversial explanation of the fossil record was offered by the British amateur geologist, Robert Chambers. Published anonymously in 1844, his *Vestiges of the Natural*

*History of Creation* caused a sensation, becoming an overnight best-seller. It galvanised the scientific establishment at the same time as proving a success with the general reading public. Its title announced the work to be in the tradition of natural theology, but it was Lamarckian evolution rather than creationism which appeared to be Chambers' main source of inspiration. Opposed to the idea of a fixed creation, Chambers accepted the principle of the transformation of organisms, and thus of the animal origins of man; however he rejected Lamarck's theory of acquired traits as wholly inadequate. For Chambers the variety and complexity of species could only be explained by divine intervention – by what he termed a 'Law of Development' which was impressed on matter by the Creator. The law operated through embryological change which was brought about by changes in the environment; this process caused one species to give birth to another in an ascending scale of complexity and perfection. The origins of life in turn were explained in terms of spontaneous generation. Chambers' attempt to accommodate a theory of development to religious orthodoxy was attacked from all sides: geologists ridiculed him for his populism and for the absence of anything which might amount to scientific evidence; theologians attacked his deism – his notion of a Creator so distant from his creation and so impersonal as to have virtually ceased to have any agency. Ironically, then, Chambers' attempt to reconcile science and religion succeeded in alienating both sides. Nevertheless *Vestiges* remained popular and continued to sell well.

To recognise the impact of Darwin's *On the Origin of Species* (1859) we need to appreciate how his understanding of evolution differed from both the transformational view of Lamarck and Chambers on the one hand, and the saltationist thesis of figures such as Lyell on the other. Although controversial, transformation and saltation were both based within traditional patterns of thought: transformation implied a teleology – a progress towards perfection; saltation implied an essentialist view of the constancy and autonomy of types or species. Both transformation and saltation, then, saw metaphysical elements in the history of life – it is worth remembering that teleology and essentialism were both fundamental to nineteenth-century Christianity. Darwin's notion of evolution, by contrast, was both anti-essentialist and anti-teleological. At its centre was his most original and radical insight, the principle of natural selection.

For Darwin, both transformation (which explained organic diversity as the result of differential rates of development or adaptation) and saltation (which assumed the number of species to be fixed, new ones only replacing extinct ones) failed to account adequately for the enormous variety in the natural world which he had experienced at first hand during his five-year voyage on HMS Beagle. A completely new way of thinking was required. Described by Ernst Myer as 'horizontal' evolution, Darwin's critical insight explained species diversity in terms of space, rather than (as with Lamarck) simply in terms of time.[2] Darwin argued that new species could develop from adaptations in existing populations which had become isolated geographically – on the Galapagos Islands, for example. His second and related insight was to realise a principle of common descent: that such diversity of species could be traced back to a common ancestor, to the original isolated species which had produced the 'daughter' species. Ultimately the origin of all species could be traced back to a single ancestor with the result that man, no longer a special creation, became firmly part of the same order of creation as all other animals. Taken together these two concepts – of common descent and geographical isolation – implied a *branching* model of evolution in which species evolve and multiply through time and by dint of spatial isolation. Such a theory was fundamentally different from the linear scale which had characterised earlier developmental theories.

The third and most controversial element in Darwin's thinking was his concept of adaptation: that is, his theory of natural selection. Rejecting both Lamarck's notion of acquired traits and Chambers' idea of embryological development, Darwin offered a revolutionary two-step theory of adaptation based on a gradualist view of change. The theory of natural selection first posits the existence of abundant variability within every generation of a species or population. Today such variation is attributed to random genetic differentiation, but for Darwin its mechanisms remained a theoretical concept only. Secondly, adaptation works on individuals by selecting (through differential rates of reproduction) those who are best adapted to their environment. Moreover competition for resources ensures that only the best adapted will survive. Darwin's model of nature was greatly influenced by contemporary political economy's description of a competitive market. It led him to see that the struggle for existence took placed between *individuals* rather than between groups or species, and this in turn permitted him to break from Lyell's essentialist notion that species were fixed. As a consequence, however, nature became a hostile, ruthless environment, rather than a benign and ordered one – that 'best possible world' of natural theology. Even more controversially man's place in nature was no longer privileged, and nature could no longer be said to be created 'for' man. Furthermore, in the constant struggle for survival, there was no direction or purpose to natural selection; there could be no line of development (no progress) because the constantly changing environment meant that every process of selection was (as it were) a 'new beginning' – an adaptation to those circumstances only.

Although *On the Origin of Species* had an immediate impact, much of the detail of Darwin's thesis was imperfectly understood at the time of its original publication. Moreover, many of those who called themselves Darwinists did not agree with every aspect of Darwin's argument. Thomas Huxley, for example, while accepting common descent and gradualism (principles dramatically expounded in his deliberately provocative *Evidence as to Man's Place in Nature*), rejected geographical speciation and natural selection. Other figures, such as Herbert Spencer, misappropriated the principle of natural selection to underwrite a form of social engineering. Social Darwinism (as it later became known) asserted that the sufferings of the poor or weak were an inevitable consequence of the 'survival of the fittest' (a phrase actually coined by Spencer); hence any attempt by the state to intervene in order to alleviate such suffering had the negative impact of hindering the 'progress' of society as a whole.

It has been argued that despite the rediscovery of genetics in 1900, it was not in fact until the late 1930s that natural selection was properly understood and finally accepted. (It is indisputable that the most systematic attempts to use eugenics to engineer society took place in the 1930s and 1940s.) Hence when we talk about Darwinism or the impact of Darwin's views about evolution, we need to exercise some caution. Most importantly, perhaps, Darwinism in the nineteenth century meant different things to different people. These caveats aside, though, it is none the less true that his impact on the culture of his time was immediate and far-reaching. It is worth stressing that Darwin's view of nature and of man's origins was directly opposed both to traditional creationist arguments and to attempted accommodations between creationism and science. In short, after the publication of *On the Origin of Species* it was increasingly difficult to see a compatibility between science and religion. Darwin's scrupulous empiricism was important here, for in many of the controversies over his work it was the overwhelming detail of the evidence which he had marshalled which proved decisive. In other words, *On the Origin of Species* represented not only the vindication of a particular scientific theory, but also a triumph of the intellectual coherence of the scientific method itself. Thereafter science no longer had to prove itself in the court of religion; rather religion had to justify itself in the face of a scientifically based scepticism. One way in which this process can be seen is in the application of the scientific method to the Bible itself.

In the second half of the nineteenth century, influenced by German biblical criticism, a number of Anglican theologians argued that it was no longer possible to dismiss the results of recent scientific inquiry and scholarship, and that the status of theology (and the Bible) would be better served by actively employing such methods rather than ignoring them. In broad terms this programme amounted to substituting a historicised reading of the Bible for the more usual literal reading. As Benjamin Jowett argued, the Bible should be treated as any other book – not, that is, as the product of direct divine inspiration, but as a historically determined document expressive of the individual characteristics of its various authors. In 1860 a group of seven liberal Anglicans published a collection of pieces broadly in this vein, although they had no editorial policy and no overall plan for their volume. Entitled *Essays and Reviews*, the book caused a furore and was republished several times within the next few years.[3] However, far from reconciling science with religion (as its authors had hoped), *Essays and Reviews* was widely interpreted as an attack on faith, and one to be regretted all the more because it came from clergymen. It was condemned by the Church of England in 1864, and an attempt was made to prosecute two of the essayists, Roland Williams and H. B. Wilson, in an ecclesiastical court. Williams and Wilson were found guilty, but the decision was eventually reversed on appeal by the Judicial Committee of the Privy Council. In all the whole procedure took nearly three years. Meanwhile in 1862 another controversy arose over the publication of the first part of *The Pentateuch and Book of Joshua Critically Examined* by the Bishop of Natal, William John Colenso. Again the work sold well, reaching its fifth edition the following year. Colenso (like Jowett) questioned literal and inspirational interpretations of the Bible, arguing that they could not account for historical inaccuracies and inconsistencies. Colenso was brought to trial on a charge of heresy and was eventually forced to relinquish his bishop's office.

Neither of these incidents had an immediately disruptive consequence for everyday church-going, or for theology, or for the authority of the Church. But they do represent significant and symbolic moments in the decline of the intellectual prestige and political and social influence of the Christian Church in Britain. They are also symbolic moments in the growth of the secular and sceptical mentality which late nineteenth-century science in part employed and in part promoted, and which is so much a feature of early twentieth-century literature.

# 4

# GOD AND NATURE
Evolutionary theory

**CHARLES LYELL, *PRINCIPLES OF GEOLOGY. VOLUME I***
**(1830)**

The influence of Charles Lyell (1797–1875) on nineteenth-century debates about science and nature is widely acknowledged. Yet today most of his works, including *Principles of Geology,* are virtually unread – a situation which belies the popularity and prestige he enjoyed among Victorian readers. Lyell's career began conventionally enough; after Oxford, he entered Lincoln's Inn and qualified as a barrister. However, eye trouble made professional work difficult, and he decided to pursue a career as a writer. His chosen subject was geology – an interest which had first been aroused at Oxford when Lyell had attended an extracurricular lecture course by the celebrated naturalist, William Buckland. In 1823 Lyell was elected Secretary of the Geological Society; he later held posts as its Foreign Secretary and President. In 1823 Lyell also visited Paris and made contact with some leading French geologists. In 1826 he was elected to the Royal Society, membership of which consolidated his position at the centre of the London scientific community. Lyell's earliest writing on geology, in which he began to raise questions about the methodology of the subject, appeared in the *Quarterly Review*. However, it was not until the publication of his *Principles of Geology* (1830–3) that the full extent of Lyell's theoretical heterodoxy became clear. Established geological opinion, including the work of Buckland, argued that the earth's history was broadly developmental or directional. By contrast, Lyell claimed that the geological landscape had been formed through uniform action during vast geological periods – that is, that it was 'steady-state' rather than progressive. His thesis was illustrated by a store of empirical evidence gathered on a long field trip through France and Italy undertaken in 1828–9. Initially Lyell's views found little sympathy, but they provoked a lively debate – not only about geology, but also about scientific methodology. In 1838 Lyell published *Elements of Geology* – a recasting of the third volume of the *Principles*. In the 1840s and 1850s he made several visits to America, and his experiences formed the subject of two books: *Travels in North America* (1845) and *A Second Visit to the United States of North America* (1849). In 1863 he published *The Geological Evidences of the Antiquity of Man*, and in 1864 was elected President of the British Association. In 1866 further honours came with the award of the Wollaston medal of the Geological Society. One of Lyell's last works was *The Student's Elements of Geology* (1871).

### From Charles Lyell, *Principles of Geology. Volume I* (London: John Murray, 1830)[1]

#### Chapter V

Review of the causes which have retarded the progress of Geology – Effects of prepossessions in regard to the duration of past time – Of prejudices arising from our peculiar position as inhabitants of the land – Of those occasioned by our not seeing subterranean changes now in progress – All these causes combine to make the former course of Nature appear different from the present – Several objections to the assumption, that existing causes have produced the former changes of the earth's surface, removed by modern discoveries.

We have seen that, during the progress of geology, there have been great fluctuations of opinion respecting the nature of the causes to which all former changes of the earth's surface are referrible.[2] The first observers conceived that the monuments which the geologist endeavours to decipher, relate to a period when the physical constitution of the earth differed entirely from the present, and that, even after the creation of living beings, there have been causes in action distinct in kind or degree from those now forming part of the economy of nature. These views have been gradually modified, and some of them entirely abandoned in proportion as observations have been multiplied, and the signs of former mutations more skilfully interpreted. Many appearances, which for a long time were regarded as indicating mysterious and extraordinary agency, are finally recognized as the necessary result of the laws now governing the material world; and the discovery of this unlooked for conformity has induced some geologists to infer that there has never been any interruption to the same uniform order of physical events. The same assemblage of general causes, they conceive, may have been sufficient to produce, by their various combinations, the endless diver-

undertaken in 1828–9. Initially Lyell's views found little sympathy, but they provoked a lively debate – not only about geology, but also about scientific methodology. In 1838 Lyell published *Elements of Geology* – a recasting of the third volume of the *Principles*. In the 1840s and 1850s he made several visits to America, and his experiences formed the subject of two books: *Travels in North America* (1845) and *A Second Visit to the United States of North America* (1849). In 1863 he published *The Geological Evidences of the Antiquity of Man*, and in 1864 was elected President of the British Association. In 1866 further honours came with the award of the Wollaston medal of the Geological Society. One of Lyell's last works was *The Student's Elements of Geology* (1871).

### From Charles Lyell, *Principles of Geology. Volume I* (London: John Murray, 1830)[1]

#### Chapter V

Review of the causes which have retarded the progress of Geology – Effects of prepossessions in regard to the duration of past time – Of prejudices arising from our peculiar position as inhabitants of the land – Of those occasioned by our not seeing subterranean changes now in progress – All these causes combine to make the former course of Nature appear different from the present – Several objections to the assumption, that existing causes have produced the former changes of the earth's surface, removed by modern discoveries.

We have seen that, during the progress of geology, there have been great fluctuations of opinion respecting the nature of the causes to which all former changes of the earth's surface are referrible.[2] The first observers conceived that the monuments which the geologist endeavours to decipher, relate to a period when the physical constitution of the earth differed entirely from the present, and that, even after the creation of living beings, there have been causes in action distinct in kind or degree from those now forming part of the economy of nature. These views have been gradually modified, and some of them entirely abandoned in proportion as observations have been multiplied, and the signs of former mutations more skilfully interpreted. Many appearances, which for a long time were regarded as indicating mysterious and extraordinary agency, are finally recognized as the necessary result of the laws now governing the material world; and the discovery of this unlooked for conformity has induced some geologists to infer that there has never been any interruption to the same uniform order of physical events. The same assemblage of general causes, they conceive, may have been sufficient to produce, by their various combinations, the endless diversity of effects, of which the shell of the earth has preserved the memorials, and, consistently with these principles, the recurrence of analogous changes is expected by them in time to come.

Whether we coincide or not in this doctrine, we must admit that the gradual progress of opinion concerning the succession of phenomena in remote eras, resembles in a singular manner that which accompanies the growing intelligence of every people, in regard to the economy of nature in modern times. In an early stage of advancement, when a great number of natural appearances are unintelligible, an eclipse, an earthquake, a flood, or the approach of a comet, with many other occurrences afterwards found to belong to the regular course of events, are regarded as prodigies. The same delusion prevails as to moral phenomena, and many of these are ascribed to the intervention of demons, ghosts, witches, and other immaterial and supernatural agents. By degrees, many of the enigmas of the moral and physical world are explained, and, instead of being due to extrinsic and irregular causes, they are found to depend on fixed and invariable laws. The philosopher at last becomes convinced of the undeviating uniformity of secondary causes,[3] and, guided by his faith in this principle, he determines the probability of accounts transmitted to him of former occurrences, and often rejects the fabulous tales of former ages, on the ground of their being irreconcilable with the experience of more enlightened ages.

As a belief in want of conformity in the physical constitution of the earth, in ancient and modern times, was for a long time universally prevalent, and that too amongst men who were convinced that the order of nature is *now* uniform, and has continued so for several thousand years; every circumstance which could have influenced their minds and given an undue bias to their opinions deserves particular attention. Now the reader may easily satisfy himself, that, however undeviating the course of nature may have been from the earliest epochs, it was impossible for the first cultivators of geology to come to such a conclusion, so long as they were under a delusion as to the age of the world, and the date of the first creation of animate beings. However fantastical some theories of the sixteenth century may now appear to us, – however unworthy of men of great talent and sound judgment, we may rest assured that, if the same misconceptions now prevailed in regard to the memorials of human transactions, it would give rise to a similar train of absurdities. Let us imagine, for example, that Champollion,[4] and the French and Tuscan literati now engaged in exploring the antiquities of Egypt, had visited that country with a firm belief that the banks of the Nile were never peopled by the human race before the beginning of the nineteenth century, and that their faith in this dogma was as difficult to shake as the opinion of our ancestors, that the earth was never the abode of living beings until the creation of the present continents, and of the species now existing, – it is easy to perceive what extravagant systems they would frame, while under the influence of this delusion, to account for the monuments discovered in Egypt. The sight of the pyramids, obelisks, colossal statues, and ruined temples, would fill them with such astonishment, that for a time they would be as men spellbound – wholly incapacitated to reason with sobriety. They might incline at first to refer the construction of such stupendous works to some superhuman powers of a primeval world. A system might be invented resembling that so gravely advanced by Manetho, who relates that a dynasty of gods originally ruled in Egypt, of whom Vulcan, the first monarch, reigned nine thousand years. After them came Hercules and other demi-gods,[5] who were at last succeeded by human kings. When some fanciful speculations of this kind had amused the imagination for a time, some vast repository of mummies would be discovered and would immediately undeceive those antiquaries who enjoyed an opportunity of personally examining them, but the prejudices of others at a distance, who were not eye-witnesses of the whole phenomena, would not be so easily overcome. The concurrent report of many travellers would indeed render it necessary for them to accommodate ancient theories to some of the new facts, and much wit and ingenuity would be required to modify and defend their old positions. Each new invention would violate a greater number of known analogies; for if a theory be required to embrace some false principle, it becomes more visionary in proportion as facts are multiplied, as would be the case if geometers were now required to form an astronomical system on the assumption of the immobility of the earth. [ . . . ][6]

These speculations, if advocated by eloquent writers, would not fail to attract many zealous votaries, for they would relieve men from the painful necessity of renouncing preconceived opinions. Incredible as such scepticism may appear, it would be rivalled by many systems of the sixteenth and seventeenth centuries, and among others by that of the learned Falloppio,[7] who regarded the tusks of fossil elephants as earthy concretions, and the vases of Monte Testaceo, near Rome, as works of nature, and not of art. But when one generation had passed away, and another not compromised to the support of antiquated dogmas had succeeded, they would review the evidence afforded by mummies more impartially, and would no longer controvert the preliminary question, that human beings had lived in Egypt before the nineteenth century: so that when a hundred years perhaps had been lost, the industry and talents of the philosopher would be at last directed to the elucidation of points of real historical importance.

But we have adverted to one only of many prejudices with which the earlier geologists had to contend. Even when they conceded that the earth had been peopled with animate beings at an earlier period than was at first supposed, they had no conception that the quantity of time bore so great a proportion to the historical era as is now generally conceded. How fatal every error as to the quantity of time must prove to the introduction of rational views concerning the state of things in former ages, may be conceived by supposing that the annals of the civil and military transactions of a great nation were perused under the impression that they occurred in a period of one hundred instead of two thousand years. Such a portion of history would immediately assume the air of a romance; the events would seem devoid of credibility, and inconsistent with the present course of human affairs. A crowd of incidents would follow each other

216

in thick succession. Armies and fleets would appear to be assembled only to be destroyed, and cities built merely to fall in ruins. There would be the most violent transitions from foreign or intestine war to periods of profound peace, and the works effected during the years of disorder or tranquillity would be alike super-human in magnitude.

He who should study the monuments of the natural world under the influ-ence of a similar infatuation, must draw a no less exaggerated picture of the energy and violence of causes, and must experience the same insurmountable difficulty in reconciling the former and present state of nature. If we could behold in one view all the volcanic cones thrown up in Iceland, Italy, Sicily, and other parts of Europe, during the last five thousand years, and could see the lavas which have flowed during the same period; the dislocations, subsidences and elevations caused by earthquakes; the lands added to various deltas, or devoured by the sea, together with the effects of devastation by floods, and imagine that all these events had happened in one year, we must form most exalted ideas of the activity of the agents, and the suddenness of the revolutions. Were an equal amount of change to pass before our eyes in the next year, could we avoid the conclusion that some great crisis of nature was at hand? If geolo-gists, therefore, have misinterpreted the signs of a succession of events, so as to conclude that centuries were implied where the characters imported thousands of years, and thousands of years where the language of nature signified millions, they could not, if they reasoned logically from such false premises, come to any other conclusion, than that the system of the natural world had undergone a complete revolution.

We should be warranted in ascribing the erection of the great pyramid to superhuman power, if we were convinced that it was raised in one day; and if we imagine, in the same manner, a mountain chain to have been elevated, during an equally small fraction of the time which was really occupied in upheaving it, we might then be justified in inferring, that the subterranean movements were once far more energetic than in our own times. We know that one earthquake may raise the coast of Chili[8] for a hundred miles to the average height of about five feet. A repetition of two thousand shocks of equal violence might produce a mountain chain one hundred miles long, and ten thousand feet high. Now, should one only of these convulsions happen in a century, it would be consistent with the order of events experienced by the Chilians from the earliest times; but if the whole of them were to occur in the next hundred years, the entire district must be depopulated, scarcely any animals or plants could survive, and the surface would be one confused heap of ruin and desolation.

One consequence of undervaluing greatly the quantity of past time is the apparent coincidence which it occasions of events necessarily disconnected, or which are so unusual, that it would be inconsistent with all calculation of chances to suppose them to happen at one and the same time. When the unlooked for association of such rare phenomena is witnessed in the present course of nature, it scarcely ever fails to excite a suspicion of the preternatural in those minds which are not firmly convinced of the uniform agency of secondary causes; – as if the death of some individual in whose fate they are interested, happens to be accompanied by the appearance of a luminous meteor, or a comet, or the shock of an earthquake. It would be only necessary to multiply such coincidences indefinitely, and the mind of every philosopher would be disturbed. Now it would be difficult to exaggerate the number of physical events, many of them most rare and unconnected in their nature, which were imagined by the Woodwardian hypothesis[9] to have happened in the course of a few months; and numerous other examples might be found of popular geological theories, which require us to imagine that a long succession of events happened in a brief and almost momentary period.

The sources of prejudice hitherto considered may be deemed as in a great degree peculiar to the infancy of the science, but others are common to the first cultivators of geology and to ourselves, and are all singularly calculated to produce the same deception, and to strengthen our belief that the course of nature in the earlier ages differed widely from that now established. Although we cannot fully explain all these circumstances, without assuming some things as proved, which it will be the object of another part of this work to demonstrate, we must briefly allude to them in this place.

The first and greatest difficulty, then, consists in our habitual unconsciousness that our position as observers is essentially unfavourable, when we endeavour to estimate the magnitude of the changes now in progress. In consequence of our inattention to this subject, we are liable to the greatest mistakes in contrasting the present with former states of the globe. We inhabit about a fourth part of the surface; and that portion is almost exclusively the theatre of decay and not of reproduction. We know, indeed, that new deposits are annually formed in seas and lakes, and that every year some new igneous rocks are produced in the bowels of the earth, but we cannot watch the progress of their formation; and, as they are only present to our minds by the aid of reflection, it requires an effort both of the reason and the imagination to appreciate duly their importance. It is, therefore, not surprising that we imperfectly estimate the result of operations invisible to us; and that, when analogous results of some former epoch are presented to our inspection, we cannot recognise the analogy. He who has observed the quarrying of stone from a rock, and has seen it shipped for some distant port, and then endeavours to conceive what kind of edifice will be raised by the materials, is in the same predicament as a geologist, who, while he is confined to the land, sees the decomposition of rocks, and the transportation of matter by rivers to the sea, and then endeavours to picture to himself the new strata which Nature is building beneath the waters. Nor is his position less unfavourable when, beholding a volcanic eruption, he tries to conceive what changes the column of lava has produced, in its passage upwards, on the inter-sected strata; or what form the melted matter may assume at great depths on cooling down; or what may be the extent of the subterranean rivers and reser-voirs of liquid matter far beneath the surface. It should, therefore, be remembered, that the task imposed on those who study the earth's history requires no ordinary share of discretion, for we are precluded from collating the corresponding parts of a system existing at two different periods. If we were inhabitants of another element – if the great ocean were our domain, instead of the narrow limits of the land, our difficulties would be considerably lessened; while, on the other hand, there can be little doubt, although the reader may, perhaps, smile at the bare suggestion of such an idea, that an amphibious being, who should possess our faculties, would still more easily arrive at sound theoretical opinions in geology, since he might behold, on the one hand, the decomposition of rocks in the atmosphere, and the transportation of matter by running water; and, on the other, examine the deposition of sediment in the sea, and the imbedding of animal remains in new strata. He might ascertain, by direct observation, the action of a mountain torrent, as well as of a marine current; might compare the products of volcanoes on the land with those poured out beneath the waters; and might mark, on the one hand, the growth of the forest, and on the other that of the coral reef. Yet, even with these advantages, he would be liable to fall into the greatest errors when endeavouring to reason on rocks of subterranean origin. He would seek in vain, within the sphere of his observation, for any direct analogy to the process of their formation, and would therefore be in danger of attributing them, wherever they are upraised to view, to some 'primeval state of nature.' But if we may be allowed so far to indulge the imagination, as to suppose a being, entirely confined to the nether world – some 'dusky melancholy sprite,' like Umbriel, who could 'flit on sooty pinions to the central earth,' but who was never permitted to 'sully the fair face of light,'[10] and emerge into the regions of water and of air; and if this being should busy himself in investigating the structure of the globe, he might frame theories the exact converse of those usually adopted by human philosophers. He might infer that the stratified rocks, containing shells and other organic remains, were the oldest of created things, belonging to some original and nascent state of the planet. 'Of these masses,' he might say, 'whether they consist of loose incoherent sand, soft clay, or solid rock, none have been formed in modern times. Every year some part of them are broken and shattered by earthquakes, or melted up by volcanic fire; and, when they cool down slowly from a state of fusion, they assume a crystalline form, perfectly distinct from those inexplicable rocks which are so regularly bedded, and contain stones full of curious impressions and fantastic markings. This process cannot have been carried on for an indefinite time, for in that case all the stratified rocks would long ere this have been fused and crystallized. It is therefore probable that the whole planet once consisted of these curiously-bedded formations, at a time when the volcanic fire had not yet been brought into activity. Since that period there seems to have been a gradual development of heat, and this augmentation we may expect to continue till the whole globe shall be in a state of fluidity and incandescence.'

Such might be the system of the Gnome[11] at the very same time that the followers of Leibniz,[12] reasoning on what they saw on the outer surface, would be teaching the doctrine of gradual refrigeration, and averring that the earth had begun its career as a fiery comet, and would hereafter become a frozen icy mass. The tenets of the schools of the nether and of the upper world would be directly opposed to each other, for both would partake of the prejudices inevitably resulting from the continual contemplation of one class of phenomena to the exclusion of another. Man observes the annual decomposition of crystalline and igneous rocks, and may sometimes see their conversion into stratified deposits; but he cannot witness the reconversion of the sedimentary into the crystalline by subterranean fire. He is in the habit of regarding all the sedimentary rocks as more recent than the unstratified, for the same reason that we may suppose him to fall into the opposite error if he saw the origin of the igneous class only.

It is only by becoming sensible of our natural disadvantages that we shall be roused to exertion, and prompted to seek out opportunities of discovering the operations now in progress, such as do not present themselves readily to view. We are called upon, in our researches into the state of the earth, as in our endeavours to comprehend the mechanism of the heavens, to invent means for overcoming the limited range of our vision. We are perpetually required to bring, as far as possible, within the sphere of observation, things to which the eye, unassisted by art, could never obtain access. It was not an impossible contingency that astronomers might have been placed, at some period, in a situation much resembling that in which the geologist seems to stand at present. If the Italians, for example, in the early part of the twelfth century, had discovered at Amalphi, instead of the pandects of Justinian,[13] some ancient manuscripts filled with astronomical observations relating to a period of three thousand years, and made by some ancient geometers who possessed optical instruments as perfect as any in modern Europe, they would probably, on consulting these memorials, have come to a conclusion that there had been a great revolution in the solar and sidereal systems. 'Many primary and secondary planets,' they might say, 'are enumerated in these tables, which exist no longer. Their positions are assigned with such precision, that we may assure ourselves that there is nothing in their place at present but the blue ether. Where one star is visible to us, these documents represent several thousands. Some of those which are now single, consisted then of two separate bodies, often distinguished by different colours, and revolving periodically round a common centre of gravity. There is no analogy to them in the universe at present, for they were neither fixed stars nor planets, but stood in the mutual relation of sun and planet to each other. We must conclude, therefore, that there has occurred, at no distant period, a tremendous catastrophe, whereby thousands of worlds have been annihilated at once, and some heavenly bodies absorbed into the substance of others.' When such doctrines had prevailed for ages, the discovery of one of the worlds, supposed to have been lost, by aid of the first rude telescope, would not dissipate the delusion, for the whole burden of proof would now be thrown on those who insisted on the stability of the system from the beginning of time, and these philosophers would be required to demonstrate the existence of *all* the worlds said to have been annihilated. Such popular prejudices would be most unfavourable to the advancement of astronomy; for, instead of persevering in the attempt to improve their instruments, and laboriously to make and record observations, the greater number would despair of verifying the continued existence of the heavenly bodies not visible to the naked eye. Instead of confessing the extent of their ignorance, and striving to remove it by bringing to light new facts, they would be engaged in the indolent employment of framing imaginary theories concerning catastrophes and mighty revolutions in the system of the universe.

For more than two centuries the shelly strata of the Subapennine hills afforded matter of speculation to the early geologists of Italy, and few of them had any suspicion that similar deposits were then forming in the neighbouring sea. They were as unconscious of the continued action of causes still producing similar effects, as the astronomers, in the case supposed by us, of the existence of certain heavenly bodies still giving and reflecting light, and performing their movements as in the olden time. Some imagined that the strata, so rich in organic remains, instead of being due to secondary agents, had been so created in the beginning of things by the fiat of the Almighty; and others ascribed the imbedded fossil bodies to some plastic power which resided in the earth in the early ages of the world. At length Donati explored the bed of the Adriatic,[14] and found the closest resemblance between the new deposits there forming, and those which constituted hills above a thousand feet high in various parts of the peninsula. He ascertained that certain genera of living testacea[15] were grouped together at the bottom of the sea in precisely the same manner as were their fossil analogues in the strata of the hills, and that some species were common to the recent and fossil world. Beds of shells, moreover, in the Adriatic, were becoming incrusted with calcareous rock; and others were recently enclosed in deposits of sand and clay, precisely as fossil shells were found in the hills. This splendid discovery of the identity of modern and ancient submarine operations was not made without the aid of artificial instruments, which, like the telescope, brought phenomena into view not otherwise within the sphere of human observation.

In like manner, in the Vicentin, a great series of volcanic and marine sedimentary rocks were examined in the early part of the last century; but no geologist suspected, before the time of Arduino,[16] that these were partly composed of ancient submarine lavas. If, when these enquiries were first made, geologists had been told that the mode of formation of such rocks might be fully elucidated by the study of processes then going on in certain parts of the Mediterranean, they would have been as incredulous as geometers would have been before the time of Newton, if any one had informed them that, by making experiments on the motion of bodies on the earth, they might discover the laws which regulated the movements of distant planets.

The establishment, from time to time, of numerous points of identification, drew at length from geologists a reluctant admission, that there was more correspondence between the physical constitution of the globe, and more uniformity in the laws regulating the changes in its surface, from the most remote eras to the present, than they at first imagined. If, in this state of the science, they still despaired of reconciling every class of geological phenomena to the operations of ordinary causes, even by straining analogy to the utmost limits of credibility, we might have expected, that the balance of probability at least would now have been presumed to incline towards the identity of the causes. But, after repeated experience of the failure of attempts to speculate on different classes of geological phenomena, as belonging to a distinct order of things, each new sect persevered systematically in the principles adopted by their predecessors. They invariably began, as each new problem presented itself, whether relating to the animate or inanimate world, to assume in their theories, that the economy of nature was formerly governed by rules quite independent of those now established. Whether they endeavoured to account for the origin of certain igneous rocks, or to explain the forces which elevated hills or excavated valleys, or the causes which led to the extinction of certain races of animals, they first presupposed an original and dissimilar order of nature; and when at length they approximated, or entirely came round to an opposite opinion, it was always with the feeling, that they conceded what they were justified *à priori* in deeming improbable. In a word, the same men who, as natural philosophers, would have been greatly surprised to find any deviation from the usual course of Nature *in their own time*, were equally surprised, as geologists, not to find such deviations at every period of the past.

The Huttonians[17] were conscious that no check could be given to the utmost licence of conjecture in speculating on the causes of geological phenomena, unless we can assume invariable constancy in the order of Nature. But when they asserted this uniformity without any limitation as to time, they were considered, by the majority of their contemporaries, to have been carried too far, especially as they applied the same principle to the laws of the organic, as well as of the inanimate world.[a]

We shall first advert briefly to many difficulties which formerly appeared insurmountable, but which, in the last forty years, have been partially or entirely removed by the progress of science; and shall afterwards consider the objections that still remain to the doctrine of absolute uniformity.

---

a   Playfair, after admitting the extinction of some species, says, 'The inhabitants of the globe, then, like all other parts of it, are subject to change. It is not only the individual that perishes, but whole *species*, and even perhaps *genera*, are extinguished.' – 'A change in the animal kingdom seems to be a *part of the order of nature*, and is visible in instances to which human power cannot have extended.' – Illustrations of the Huttonian Theory, §413. [John Playfair (1748–1819), Scottish mathematician, physicist and geologist, and Professor of Mathematics at the University of Edinburgh. On the death of James Hutton (see note 17) Playfair took on the responsibility of expanding and popularising his friend's work and the resulting *Illustrations of the Huttonian Theory* (1802) became a landmark in the development of modern geological concepts.]

In the first place, it was necessary for the supporters of this doctrine to take for granted incalculable periods of time, in order to explain the formation of sedimentary strata by causes now in diurnal action. The time which they required theoretically, is now granted, as it were, or has become absolutely requisite, to account for another class of phenomena brought to light by more recent investigations. It must always have been evident to unbiassed minds, that successive strata, containing, in regular order of superposition, distinct beds of shells and corals, arranged in families as they grow at the bottom of the sea, could only have been formed by slow and insensible degrees in a great lapse of ages; yet, until organic remains were minutely examined and specifically determined, it was rarely possible to prove that the series of deposits met with in one country was not formed simultaneously with that found in another. But we are now able to determine, in numerous instances, the relative dates of sedimentary rocks in distant regions, and to show, by their organic remains, that they were not of contemporary origin, but formed in succession. We often find, that where an interruption in the consecutive formation in one district is indicated by a sudden transition from one assemblage of fossil species to another, the chasm is filled up, in some other district, by other important groups of strata. The more attentively we study the European continent, the greater we find the extension of the whole series of geological formations. No sooner does the calendar appear to be completed, and the signs of a succession of physical events arranged in chronological order, than we are called upon to intercalate, as it were, some new periods of vast duration. A geologist, whose observations have been confined to England, is accustomed to consider the superior and newer groups of marine strata in our island as modern, and such they are, comparatively speaking; but when he has travelled through the Italian peninsula and in Sicily,[18] and has seen strata of more recent origin forming mountains several thousand feet high, and has marked a long series both of volcanic and submarine operations, all newer than any of the regular strata which enter largely into the physical structure of Great Britain, he returns with more exalted conceptions of the antiquity of some of those modern deposits, than he before entertained of the oldest of the British series. We cannot reflect on the concessions thus extorted from us, in regard to the duration of past time, without foreseeing that the period may arrive when part of the Huttonian theory will be combated on the ground of its departing too far from the assumption of uniformity in the order of nature. On a closer investigation of extinct volcanoes, we find proofs that they broke out at successive eras, and that the eruptions of one group were often concluded long before others had commenced their activity. Some were burning when one class of organic beings were in existence, others came into action when different races of animals and plants existed, – it follows, therefore, that the convulsions caused by subterranean movements, which are merely another portion of the volcanic phenomena, occurred also in succession, and their effects must be divided into separate sums, and assigned to separate periods of time; and this is not all: – when we examine the volcanic products, whether they be lavas which flowed out under water or upon dry land, we find that intervals of time, often of great length, intervened between their formation, and that the effects of one eruption were not greater in amount than that which now results during ordinary volcanic convulsions. The accompanying or preceding earthquakes, therefore, may be considered to have been also successive, and to have been in like manner interrupted by intervals of time, and not to have exceeded in violence those now experienced in the ordinary course of nature. Already, therefore, we may regard the doctrine of the sudden elevation of whole continents by paroxysmal eruptions as invalidated; and there was the greatest inconsistency in the adoption of such a tenet by the Huttonians, who were anxious to reconcile former changes to the present economy of the world. It was contrary to analogy to suppose, that Nature had been at any former epoch parsimonious of time and prodigal of violence – to imagine that one district was not at rest while another was convulsed – that the disturbing forces were not kept under subjection, so as never to carry simultaneous havoc and desolation over the whole earth, or even over one great region. If it could have been shown, that a certain combination of circumstances would at some future period produce a crisis in the subterranean action, we should certainly have had no right to oppose our experience for the last three thousand years as an argument against the probability of such occurrences in past ages; but it is not pretended that such a combination can be foreseen. In speculating on catastrophes by water, we may certainly anticipate great floods in future, and we may therefore presume that they have happened again and again in past time. The existence of enormous seas of fresh-water, such as the North American lakes, the largest of which is elevated more than six hundred feet above the level of the ocean, and is in parts twelve hundred feet deep, is alone sufficient to assure us, that the time will come, however distant, when a deluge will lay waste a considerable part of the American continent. No hypothetical agency is required to cause the sudden escape of the confined waters. Such changes of level, and opening of fissures, as have accompanied earthquakes since the commencement of the present century, or such excavations of ravines as the receding cataract of Niagara is now effecting, might breach the barriers. Notwithstanding, therefore, that we have not witnessed within the last three thousand years the devastation by deluge of a large continent, yet, as we may predict the future occurrence of such catastrophes, we are authorized to regard them as part of the present order of Nature, and they may be introduced into geological speculations respecting the past, provided we do not imagine them to have been more frequent or general than we expect them to be in time to come.

The great contrast in the aspect of the older and newer rocks, in their texture, structure, and in the derangement of the strata, appeared formerly one of the strongest grounds for presuming that the causes to which they owed their origin were perfectly dissimilar from those now in operation. But this incongruity may now be regarded as the natural result of subsequent modifications, since the difference of relative age is demonstrated to have been so immense, that, however slow and insensible the change, it must have become important in the course of so many ages. In addition to volcanic heat, to which the Vulcanists[19] formerly attributed too much influence, we must allow for the effect of mechanical pressure, of chemical affinity, of percolation by mineral waters, of permeation by elastic fluids, and the action, perhaps, of many other forces less understood, such as electricity and magnetism. In regard to the signs of upraising and sinking, of fracture and contortion in rocks, it is evident that newer strata cannot be shaken by earthquakes, unless the subjacent rocks are also affected; so that the contrast in the relative degree of disturbance in the more ancient and the newer strata, is one of many proofs that the convulsions have happened in different eras, and the fact confirms the uniformity of the action of subterranean forces, instead of their greater violence in the primeval ages.

The popular doctrine of universal formations, or the unlimited geographical extent of strata, distinguished by similar mineral characters, appeared for a long time to present insurmountable objections to the supposition, that the earth's crust had been formed by causes now acting. If it had merely been assumed, that rocks originating from fusion by subterranean fire presented in all parts of the globe a perfect correspondence in their mineral composition, the assumption would not have been extravagant; for, as the elementary substances that enter largely into the composition of rocks are few in number, they may be expected to arrange themselves invariably in the same forms, whenever the elementary particles are freely exposed to the actions of chemical affinities. But when it was imagined that sedimentary mixtures, including animal and vegetable remains, and evidently formed in the beds of ancient seas, were of homogeneous nature throughout a whole hemisphere, or even farther, the dogma precluded at once all hope of recognizing the slightest analogy between the ancient and modern causes of decay and reproduction. For we know that existing rivers carry down from different mountain-chains sediment of distinct colours and composition; where the chains are near the sea, coarse sand and gravel is swept in; where they are distant, the finest mud. We know, also, that the matter introduced by springs into lakes and seas is very diversified in mineral composition; in short, contemporaneous strata now in the progress of formation are greatly varied in their composition, and could never afford formations of homogeneous mineral ingredients co-extensive with the greater part of the earth's surface. This theory, however, is as inapplicable to the effects of those operations to which the formation of the earth's crust is due, as to the effects of existing causes. The first investigators of sedimentary rocks had never reflected on the great areas occupied by modern deltas of large rivers; still less on the much greater areas over which marine currents, preying alike on river-deltas, and continuous lines of sea-coast, might be diffusing homogeneous mixtures. They were ignorant of the vast spaces over which calcareous and other mineral springs abound upon the land and in the sea, especially in and near volcanic regions, and of the quantity of matter discharged by them. When, therefore, they ascertained the extent of the geographical distribution of certain groups of ancient strata – when they traced them continuously from one extremity of Europe to the other, and found them flanking, throughout their entire range, great mountain-chains, they were astonished at so unexpected a discovery; and, considering themselves at liberty to disregard all modern analogy, they indulged in the sweeping generalization, that the law of continuity prevailed throughout strata of contemporaneous origin over the whole planet. The difficulty of dissipating this delusion was extreme, because some rocks, formed under similar circumstances at different epochs, present the same external characters, and often the same internal composition; and all these were assumed to be contemporaneous until the contrary could be shown, which, in the absence of evidence derived from direct superposition,[20] and in the scarcity of organic remains, was often impossible.

Innumerable other false generalizations have been derived from the same source; such, for instance, as the former universality of the ocean, now disproved by the discovery of the remains of terrestrial vegetation, contemporary with every successive race of marine animal; but we shall dwell no longer on exploded errors, but proceed at once to contend against weightier objections, which will require more attentive consideration.

## CHARLES DARWIN, *ON THE ORIGIN OF SPECIES BY MEANS OF NATURAL SELECTION* (1859)

In contrast to many Victorian intellectuals, the reputation of Charles Darwin (1809–82) is much greater today than it was among his contemporaries. Indeed *On The Origin of Species* can claim to be one of the most influential books ever written. For the Victorians, however, Darwin was always a highly controversial figure, and his burial at Westminster Abbey disguises the fact that acceptance among established intellectual circles of the time was hard won. From his early youth Darwin showed a passionate interest in the natural world, but his first choice of career was medicine. However, his distaste for anatomy and his dislike of pure science led him to abandon his studies at Edinburgh University after only two years. He then decided on a career in the Church and entered Cambridge University to study theology. Once there his attention became increasingly taken up with botany and geology, and influenced by the Professor of Botany, J. S. Henslow, Darwin decided to pursue these subjects. In 1831 Henslow arranged for Darwin to join HMS *Beagle* for a world voyage which lasted five years and which provided Darwin with the data for his subsequent writings on evolution. On his return in 1836 Darwin sent his collections to various specialists to be classified, and it was with the aid of the ornithologist John Gould, who identified distinct species of birds among Darwin's findings in the Galapagos Islands, that Darwin developed the radical concept of speciation. In 1837 he jotted down his ideas in a notebook, but did not publish them until twenty years later. In the meantime, from 1838 until 1841, he was Secretary of the Geological Society; at this time he also struck up a lasting friendship with the geologist Charles Lyell. In 1842–6 he published a three-volume study of the geological findings of his voyage on the *Beagle*, and from the mid-1840s until the early 1850s he spent most of his energy on a specialist study of barnacles, published in 1854 under the title, *A Monograph on the Fossil Balanidae and Verrucidae of Great Britain*. In June 1858 Darwin received a paper from Alfred Russel Wallace. Wallace's work appeared to anticipate Darwin's own views on speciation on which he had been working intermittently since the 1840s. On the advice of colleagues, Darwin wrote a short paper outlining his argument which was read, together with that of Wallace, to the Linnean Society of London in July; both papers were simultaneously published by the Society. It was now necessary for Darwin to publish a more substantial piece, and the result was his most famous work, *On the Origin of Species*, which appeared in November 1859. The book was oversubscribed and sold out on the first day; it continued to sell well throughout Darwin's lifetime. The publication in 1871 of *The Descent of Man* and in 1872 of the *Expression of the Emotions in Man and Animals* completed the trilogy of works which made Darwin famous. Throughout this period, however, Darwin continued to publish specialist monographs, mainly on botany and entomology. This work was as important to him as his more popular titles. Indeed his last project, like his ten-year study of barnacles, was characteristically modest – a monograph published in 1881 and entitled *The Formation of Vegetable Mould, through the Action of Worms*.

### *From* Charles Darwin, *On the Origin of Species by Means of Natural Selection, or the Preservation of Favoured Races in the Struggle for Life* (London: John Murray, 1859)[1]

From *Chapter IV: Natural Selection*

Natural Selection – its power compared with man's selection – its power on characters of trifling importance – its power at all ages and on both sexes – Sexual Selection – On the generality of intercrosses between individuals of the same species – Circumstances favourable and unfavourable to Natural Selection, namely, intercrossing, isolation, number of individuals – Slow action – Extinction caused by Natural Selection – Divergence of Character, related to the diversity of inhabitants of any small area, and to naturalisation – Action of Natural Selection, through Divergence of Character and Extinction, on the descendants from a common parent – Explains the Grouping of all organic beings.

How will the struggle for existence, discussed too briefly in the last chapter, act in regard to variation? Can the principle of selection, which we have seen is so potent in the hands of man, apply in nature? I think we shall see that it can act more effectually. Let it be borne in mind in what an endless number of strange peculiarities our domestic productions, and, in a lesser degree, those under nature, vary; and how strong the hereditary tendency is. Under domestication, it may be truly said that the whole organisation becomes in some degree plastic. Let it be borne in mind how infinitely complex and close-fitting are the mutual relations of all organic beings to each other and to their physical conditions of life. Can it, then, be thought improbable, seeing that variations useful to man have undoubtedly occurred, that other variations useful in some way to each being in the great and complex battle of life, should sometimes occur in the course of thousands of generations? If such do occur, can we doubt (remembering that many more individuals are born than can possibly survive) that individuals having any advantage, however slight, over others, would have the best chance of surviving and of procreating their kind? On the other hand, we may feel sure that any variation in the least degree injurious would be rigidly destroyed. This preservation of favourable variations and the rejection of injurious variations, I call Natural Selection. Variations neither useful nor injurious would not be affected by natural selection, and would be left a fluctuating element, as perhaps we see in the species called polymorphic.

We shall best understand the probable course of natural selection by taking the case of a country undergoing some physical change, for instance, of climate. The proportional numbers of its inhabitants would almost immediately undergo a change, and some species might become extinct. We may conclude, from what we have seen of the intimate and complex manner in which the inhabitants of each country are bound together, that any change in the numerical proportions of some of the inhabitants, independently of the change of climate itself, would most seriously affect many of the others. If the country were open on its borders, new forms would certainly immigrate, and this also would seriously disturb the relations of some of the former inhabitants. Let it be remembered how powerful the influence of a single introduced tree or mammal has been shown to be. But in the case of an island, or of a country partly surrounded by barriers, into which new and better adapted forms could not freely enter, we should then have places in the economy of nature which would assuredly be better filled up, if some of the original inhabitants were in some manner modified; for, had the area been open to immigration, these same places would have been seized on by intruders. In such case, every slight modification, which in the course of ages chanced to arise, and which in any way favoured the individuals of any of the species, by better adapting them to their altered conditions, would tend to be preserved; and natural selection would thus have free scope for the work of improvement.

We have reason to believe, as stated in the first chapter, that a change in the conditions of life, by specially acting on the reproductive system, causes or increases variability; and in the foregoing case the conditions of life are supposed to have undergone a change, and this would manifestly be favourable to natural selection, by giving a better chance of profitable variations occurring; and unless profitable variations do occur, natural selection can do nothing. Not that, as I believe, any extreme amount of variability is necessary; as man can certainly produce great results by adding up in any given direction mere individual differences, so could Nature, but far more easily, from having incomparably longer time at her disposal. Nor do I believe that any great physical change, as of climate, or any unusual degree of isolation to check immigration, is actually necessary to produce new and unoccupied places for natural selection to fill up by modifying and improving some of the varying inhabitants. For as all the inhabitants of each country are struggling together with nicely balanced forces, extremely slight modifications in the structure or habits of one inhabitant would often give it an advantage over others; and still further modifications of the same kind would often still further increase the advantage. No country can be named in which all the native inhabitants are now so perfectly adapted to each other and to the physical conditions under which they live, that none of them could anyhow be improved; for in all countries, the natives have been so far conquered by naturalised productions, that they have allowed foreigners to take firm possession of the land. And as foreigners have thus everywhere beaten some of the natives, we may safely conclude that the natives might have been modified with advantage, so as to have better resisted such intruders.

As man can produce and certainly has produced a great result by his methodical and unconscious means of selection, what may not nature effect? Man can act only on external and visible characters: nature cares nothing for appearances, except in so far as they may be useful to any being. She can act on every internal organ, on every shade of constitutional difference, on the whole machinery of life. Man selects only for his own good; Nature only for that of the being which she tends. Every selected character is fully exercised by her; and the being is placed under well-suited conditions of life. Man keeps the natives of many climates in the same country; he seldom exercises each selected character in some peculiar and fitting manner; he feeds a long and a short beaked pigeon on the same food; he does not exercise a long-backed or long-legged quadruped in any peculiar manner; he exposes sheep with long and short wool to the same climate. He does not allow the most vigorous males to struggle for the females. He does not rigidly destroy all inferior animals, but protects during each varying season, as far as lies in his power, all his productions. He often begins his selection by some half-monstrous form; or at least by some modification prominent enough to catch his eye, or to be plainly useful to him. Under nature, the slightest difference of structure or constitution may well turn the nicely-balanced scale in the struggle for life, and so be preserved. How fleeting are the wishes and efforts of man! how short his time! and consequently how poor will his products be, compared with those accumulated by nature during whole geological periods. Can we wonder, then, that nature's productions should be far 'truer' in character than man's productions; that they should be infinitely better adapted to the most complex conditions of life, and should plainly bear the stamp of far higher workmanship?

It may be said that natural selection is daily and hourly scrutinising, throughout the world, every variation, even the slightest; rejecting that which is bad, preserving and adding up all that is good; silently and insensibly working, whenever and wherever opportunity offers, at the improvement of each organic being in relation to its organic and inorganic conditions of life. We see nothing of these slow changes in progress, until the hand of time has marked the long lapse of ages, and then so imperfect is our view into long past geological ages, that we only see that the forms of life are now different from what they formerly were.

Although natural selection can act only through and for the good of each being, yet characters and structures, which we are apt to consider as of very trifling importance, may thus be acted on. When we see leaf-eating insects green, and bark-feeders mottled-grey; the alpine ptarmigan white in winter, the red-grouse the colour of heather, and the black-grouse that of peaty earth, we must believe that these tints are of service to these birds and insects in preserving them from danger. Grouse, if not destroyed at some period of their lives, would increase in countless numbers; they are known to suffer largely from birds of prey; and hawks are guided by eyesight to their prey, – so much so, that on parts of the Continent persons are warned not to keep white pigeons, as being the most liable to destruction. Hence I can see no reason to doubt that natural selection might be most effective in giving the proper colour to each kind of grouse, and in keeping that colour, when once acquired, true and constant. Nor ought we to think that the occasional destruction of an animal of any particular colour would produce little effect: we should remember how essential it is in a flock of white sheep to destroy every lamb with the faintest trace of black. In plants the down on the fruit and the colour of the flesh are considered by botanists as char-acters of the most trifling importance: yet we hear from an excellent horticulturist, Downing,[2] that in the United States smooth-skinned fruits suffer far more from a beetle, a curculio, than those with down; that purple plums suffer far more from a certain disease than yellow plums; whereas another disease attacks yellow-fleshed peaches far more than those with other coloured flesh. If, with all the aids of art, these slight differences make a great difference in cultivating the several varieties, assuredly, in a state of nature, where the trees would have to struggle with other trees and with a host of enemies, such differ-ences would effectually settle which variety, whether a smooth or downy, a yellow or purple fleshed fruit, should succeed.

In looking at many small points of difference between species, which, as far as our ignorance permits us to judge, seem to be quite unimportant, we must not forget that climate, food, &c., probably produce some slight and direct effect. It is, however, far more necessary to bear in mind that there are many unknown laws of correlation of growth, which, when one part of the organisation is modi-fied through variation, and the modifications are accumulated by natural selection for the good of the being, will cause other modifications, often of the most unexpected nature.

As we see that those variations which under domestication appear at any particular period of life, tend to reappear in the offspring at the same period; – for instance, in the seeds of the many varieties of our culinary and agricultural plants; in the caterpillar and cocoon stages of the varieties of the silkworm; in the eggs of poultry, and in the colour of the down of their chickens; in the horns of our sheep and cattle when nearly adult; – so in a state of nature, natural selec-tion will be enabled to act on and modify organic beings at any age, by the accumulation of profitable variations at that age, and by their inheritance at a corresponding age. If it profit a plant to have its seeds more and more widely disseminated by the wind, I can see no greater difficulty in this being effected through natural selection, than in the cotton-planter increasing and improving by selection the down in the pods of his cotton-trees. Natural selection may modify and adapt the larva of an insect to a score of contingencies, wholly different from those which concern the mature insect. These modifications will no doubt affect, through the laws of correlation, the structure of the adult; and probably in the case of those insects which live only for a few hours, and which never feed, a large part of their structure is merely the correlated result of successive changes in the structure of their larvae. So, conversely, modifications in the adult will probably often affect the structure of the larva; but in all cases natural selection will ensure that modifications consequent on other modifications at a different period of life, shall not be in the least degree injurious: for if they became so, they would cause the extinction of the species.

Natural selection will modify the structure of the young in relation to the parent, and of the parent in relation to the young. In social animals it will adapt the structure of each individual for the benefit of the community; if each in consequence profits by the selected change. What natural selection cannot do, is to modify the structure of one species, without giving it any advantage, for the good of another species; and though statements to this effect may be found in works of natural history, I cannot find one case which will bear investigation. A structure used only once in an animal's whole life, if of high importance to it, might be modified to any extent by natural selection; for instance, the great jaws possessed by certain insects, and used exclusively for opening the cocoon – or the hard tip to the beak of nestling birds, used for breaking the egg. It has been asserted, that of the best short-beaked tumbler-pigeons more perish in the egg than are able to get out of it; so that fanciers assist in the act of hatching. Now, if nature had to make the beak of a full-grown pigeon very short for the bird's own advantage, the process of modification would be very slow, and there would be simultaneously the most rigorous selection of the young birds within the egg, which had the most powerful and hardest beaks, for all with weak beaks would inevitably perish: or, more delicate and more easily broken shells might be selected, the thickness of the shell being known to vary like every other structure.

### Sexual Selection

Inasmuch as peculiarities often appear under domestication in one sex and become hereditarily attached to that sex, the same fact probably occurs under nature, and if so, natural selection will be able to modify one sex in its functional relations to the other sex, or in relation to wholly different habits of life in the two sexes, as is sometimes the case with insects. And this leads me to say a few words on what I call Sexual Selection. This depends, not on a struggle for existence, but on a struggle between the males for possession of the females; the result is not death to the unsuccessful competitor, but few or no offspring. Sexual selection is, therefore, less rigorous than natural selection. Generally, the most vigorous males, those which are best fitted for their places in nature, will leave most progeny. But in many cases, victory will depend not on general vigour, but on having special weapons, confined to the male sex. A hornless stag or spurless cock would have a poor chance of leaving offspring. Sexual selection by always allowing the victor to breed might surely give indomitable courage, length to the spur, and strength to the wing to strike in the spurred leg, as well as the brutal cock-fighter, who knows well that he can improve his breed by careful selection of the best cocks. How low in the scale of nature this law of battle descends, I know not; male alligators have been described as fighting, bellowing, and whirling round, like Indians in a war-dance, for the possession of the females; male salmons have been seen fighting all day long; male stag-beetles sometimes bear wounds from the huge mandibles of other males. The war is, perhaps, severest between the males of polygamous animals, and these seem oftenest provided with special weapons. The males of carnivorous animals are already well armed; though to them and to others, special means of defence may be given through means of sexual selection, as the mane to the lion, the shoulder-pad to the boar, and the hooked jaw to the male salmon; for the shield may be as important for victory, as the sword or spear.

Amongst birds, the contest is often of a more peaceful character. All those who have attended to the subject, believe that there is the severest rivalry between the males of many species to attract by singing the females. The rock-thrush of Guiana, birds of Paradise, and some others, congregate; and successive males display their gorgeous plumage and perform strange antics before the females, which standing by as spectators, at last choose the most attractive partner. Those who have closely attended to birds in confinement well know that they often take individual preferences and dislikes: thus Sir R. Heron[3] has described how one pied peacock was eminently attractive to all his hen birds. It may appear childish to attribute any effect to such apparently weak means: I cannot here enter on the details necessary to support this view; but if man can in a short time give elegant carriage and beauty to his bantams, according to his standard of beauty, I can see no good reason to doubt that female birds, by selecting, during thousands of generations, the most melodious or beautiful males, according to their standard of beauty, might produce a marked effect. I strongly suspect that some well-known laws with respect to the plumage of male and female birds, in comparison with the plumage of the young, can be explained on the view of plumage having been chiefly modified by sexual selection, acting when the birds have come to the breeding age or during the breeding season; the modifications thus produced being inherited at corresponding ages or seasons, either by the males alone, or by the males and females; but I have not space here to enter on this subject.

Thus it is, as I believe, that when the males and females of any animal have the same general habits of life, but differ in structure, colour, or ornament, such differences have been mainly caused by sexual selection; that is, individual males have had, in successive generations, some slight advantage over other males, in their weapons, means of defence, or charms; and have transmitted these advantages to their male offspring. Yet, I would not wish to attribute all such sexual differences to this agency: for we see peculiarities arising and becoming attached to the male sex in our domestic animals (as the wattle in male carriers, horn-like protuberances in the cocks of certain fowls, &c.), which we cannot believe to be either useful to the males in battle, or attractive to the females. We see analogous cases under nature, for instance, the tuft of hair on the breast of the turkey-cock, which can hardly be either useful or ornamental to this bird; – indeed, had the tuft appeared under domestication, it would have been called a monstrosity.

### Illustrations of the action of Natural Selection

In order to make it clear how, as I believe, natural selection acts, I must beg permission to give one or two imaginary illustrations. Let us take the case of a wolf, which preys on various animals, securing some by craft, some by strength, and some by fleetness; and let us suppose that the fleetest prey, a deer for instance, had from any change in the country increased in numbers, or that other prey had decreased in numbers, during that season of the year when the wolf is hardest pressed for food. I can under such circumstances see no reason to doubt that the swiftest and slimmest wolves would have the best chance of surviving, and so be preserved or selected, – provided always that they retained strength to master their prey at this or some other period of the year, when they might be compelled to prey on other animals. I can see no more reason to doubt this, than that man can improve the fleetness of his greyhounds by careful and methodical selection, or by that unconscious selection which results from each man trying to keep the best dogs without any thought of modifying the breed.

Even without any change in the proportional numbers of the animals on which our wolf preyed, a cub might be born with an innate tendency to pursue certain kinds of prey. Nor can this be thought very improbable; for we often observe great differences in the natural tendencies of our domestic animals; one cat, for instance, taking to catch rats, another mice; one cat, according to Mr St John,[4] bringing home winged game, another hares or rabbits, and another hunting on marshy ground and almost nightly catching woodcocks or snipes. The tendency to catch rats rather than mice is known to be inherited. Now, if any slight innate change of habit or of structure benefited an individual wolf, it would have the best chance of surviving and of leaving offspring. Some of its young would probably inherit the same habits or structure, and by the repetition of this process, a new variety might be formed which would either supplant or co-exist with the parent-form of wolf. Or, again, the wolves inhabiting a mountainous district, and those frequenting the lowlands, would naturally be forced to hunt different prey; and from the continued preservation of the individuals best fitted for the two sites, two varieties might slowly be formed. These varieties would cross and blend where they met; but to this subject of intercrossing we shall soon have to return. I may add, that, according to Mr Pierce,[5] there are two varieties of the wolf inhabiting the Catskill Mountains in the United States, one with a light greyhound-like form, which pursues deer, and the other more bulky, with shorter legs, which more frequently attacks the shepherd's flocks.

Let us now take a more complex case. Certain plants excrete a sweet juice, apparently for the sake of eliminating something injurious from their sap: this is effected by glands at the base of the stipules in some Leguminosae,[6] and at the back of the leaf of the common laurel. This juice, though small in quantity, is greedily sought by insects. Let us now suppose a little sweet juice or nectar to be excreted by the inner bases of the petals of a flower. In this case insects in seeking the nectar would get dusted with pollen, and would certainly often transport the pollen from one flower to the stigma of another flower. The flowers of two distinct individuals of the same species would thus get crossed; and the act of crossing, we have good reason to believe (as will hereafter be more fully alluded to), would produce very vigorous seedlings, which consequently would have the best chance of flourishing and surviving. Some of these seedlings would probably inherit the nectar-excreting power. Those individual flowers which had the largest glands or nectaries, and which excreted most nectar, would be oftenest visited by insects, and would be oftenest crossed; and so in the long-run would gain the upper hand. Those flowers, also, which had their stamens and pistils placed, in relation to the size and habits of the particular insects which visited them, so as to favour in any degree the transportal of their pollen from flower to flower, would likewise be favoured or selected. We might have taken the case of insects visiting flowers for the sake of collecting pollen instead of nectar; and as pollen is formed for the sole object of fertilisation, its destruction appears a simple loss to the plant; yet if a little pollen were carried, at first occasionally and then habitually, by the pollen-devouring insects from flower to flower, and a cross thus effected, although nine-tenths of the pollen were destroyed, it might still be a great gain to the plant; and those individuals which produced more and more pollen, and had larger and larger anthers, would be selected.

When our plant, by this process of the continued preservation or natural selection of more and more attractive flowers, had been rendered highly attractive to insects, they would, unintentionally on their part, regularly carry pollen from flower to flower; and that they can most effectually do this, I could easily show by many striking instances. I will give only one – not as a very striking case, but as likewise illustrating one step in the separation of the sexes of plants, presently to be alluded to. Some holly-trees bear only male flowers, which have four stamens producing rather a small quantity of pollen, and a rudimentary pistil; other holly-trees bear only female flowers; these have a full-sized pistil, and four stamens with shrivelled anthers, in which not a grain of pollen can be detected. Having found a female tree exactly sixty yards from a male tree, I put the stigmas of twenty flowers, taken from different branches, under the microscope, and on all, without exception, there were pollen-grains, and on some a profusion of pollen. As the wind had set for several days from the female to the male tree, the pollen could not thus have been carried. The weather had been cold and boisterous, and therefore not favourable to bees, nevertheless every female flower which I examined had been effectually fertilised by the bees, accidentally dusted with pollen, having flown from tree to tree in search of nectar. But to return to our imaginary case: as soon as the plant had been rendered so highly attractive to insects that pollen was regularly carried from flower to flower, another process might commence. No naturalist doubts the advantage of what has been called the 'physiological division of labour;'[7] hence we may believe that it would he advantageous to a plant to produce stamens alone in one flower or on one whole plant, and pistils alone in another flower or on another plant. In plants under culture and placed under new conditions of life, sometimes the male organs and sometimes the female organs become more or less impotent; now if we suppose this to occur in ever so slight a degree under nature, then as pollen is already carried regularly from flower to flower, and as a more complete separation of the sexes of our plant would be advantageous on the principle of the division of labour, individuals with this tendency more and more increased, would be continually favoured or selected, until at last a complete separation of the sexes would be effected.

Let us now turn to the nectar-feeding insects in our imaginary case: we may suppose the plant of which we have been slowly increasing the nectar by continued selection, to be a common plant; and that certain insects depended in main part on its nectar for food. I could give many facts, showing how anxious bees are to save time; for instance, their habit of cutting holes and sucking the nectar at the bases of certain flowers, which they can, with a very little more trouble, enter by the mouth. Bearing such facts in mind, I can see no reason to doubt that an accidental deviation in the size and form of the body, or in the curvature and length of the proboscis, &c., far too slight to be appreciated by us, might profit a bee or other insect, so that an individual so characterised would be able to obtain its food more quickly, and so have a better chance of living and leaving descendants. Its descendants would probably inherit a tendency to a similar slight deviation of structure. The tubes of the corollas of the common red and incarnate clovers (Trifolium pratense and incarnatum) do not on a hasty glance appear to differ in length; yet the hive-bee can easily suck the nectar out of the incarnate clover, but not out of the common red clover, which is visited by humble-bees alone; so that whole fields of the red clover offer in vain an abundant supply of precious nectar to the hive-bee. Thus it might be a great advantage to the hive-bee to have a slightly longer or differently constructed proboscis. On the other hand, I have found by experiment that the fertility of clover greatly depends on bees visiting and moving parts of the corolla, so as to push the pollen on to the stigmatic surface. Hence, again, if humble-bees were to become rare in any country, it might be a great advantage to the red clover to have a shorter or more deeply divided tube to its corolla, so that the hive-bee could visit its flowers. Thus I can understand how a flower and a bee might slowly become, either simultaneously or one after the other, modified and adapted in the most perfect manner to each other, by the continued preservation of individuals presenting mutual and slightly favourable deviations of structure.

I am well aware that this doctrine of natural selection, exemplified in the above imaginary instances, is open to the same objections which were at first urged against Sir Charles Lyell's[8] noble views on 'the modern changes of the earth, as illustrative of geology;' but we now very seldom hear the action, for instance, of the coast-waves, called a trifling and insignificant cause, when applied to the excavation of gigantic valleys or to the formation of the longest lines of inland cliffs. Natural selection can act only by the preservation and accumulation of infinitesimally small inherited modifications, each profitable to the preserved being; and as modern geology has almost banished such views as the excavation of a great valley by a single diluvial wave, so will natural selection, if it be a true principle, banish the belief of the continued creation of new organic beings, or of any great and sudden modification in their structure. [ . . . ][9]

## Circumstances favourable to Natural Selection

This is an extremely intricate subject. A large amount of inheritable and diversified variability is favourable, but I believe mere individual differences suffice for the work. A large number of individuals, by giving a better chance for the appearance within any given period of profitable variations, will compensate for a lesser amount of variability in each individual, and is, I believe, an extremely important element of success. Though nature grants vast periods of time for the work of natural selection, she does not grant an indefinite period; for as all organic beings are striving, it may be said, to seize on each place in the economy of nature, if any one species does not become modified and improved in a corresponding degree with its competitors, it will soon be exterminated.

In man's methodical selection, a breeder selects for some definite object, and free intercrossing will wholly stop his work. But when many men, without intending to alter the breed, have a nearly common standard of perfection, and all try to get and breed from the best animals, much improvement and modification surely but slowly follow from this unconscious process of selection, notwithstanding a large amount of crossing with inferior animals. Thus it will be in nature; for within a confined area, with some place in its polity not so perfectly occupied as might be, natural selection will always tend to preserve all the individuals varying in the right direction, though in different degrees, so as better to fill up the unoccupied place. But if the area be large, its several districts will almost certainly present different conditions of life; and then if natural selection be modifying and improving a species in the several districts, there will be intercrossing with the other individuals of the same species on the confines of each. And in this case the effects of intercrosses can hardly be counterbalanced by natural selection always tending to modify all the individuals in each district in exactly the same manner to the conditions of each; for in a continuous area, the conditions will generally graduate away insensibly from one district to another. The intercrossing will most affect those animals which unite for each birth, which wander much, and which do not breed at a very quick rate. Hence in animals of this nature, for instance in birds, varieties will generally be confined to separated countries; and this I believe to be the case. In hermaphrodite organisms which cross only occasionally, and likewise in animals which unite for each birth, but which wander little and which can increase at a very rapid rate, a new and improved variety might be quickly formed on any one spot, and might there maintain itself in a body, so that whatever intercrossing took place would be chiefly between the individuals of the same new variety. A local variety when once thus formed might subsequently slowly spread to other districts. On the above principle, nurserymen always prefer getting seed from a large body of plants of the same variety, as the chance of intercrossing with other varieties is thus lessened.

Even in the case of slow-breeding animals, which unite for each birth, we must not overrate the effects of intercrosses in retarding natural selection; for I can bring a considerable catalogue of facts, showing that within the same area, varieties of the same animal can long remain distinct, from haunting different stations, from breeding at slightly different seasons, or from varieties of the same kind preferring to pair together.

Intercrossing plays a very important part in nature in keeping the individuals of the same species, or of the same variety, true and uniform in character. It will obviously thus act far more efficiently with those animals which unite for each birth; but I have already attempted to show that we have reason to believe that occasional intercrosses take place with all animals and with all plants. Even if these take place only at long intervals, I am convinced that the young thus produced will gain so much in vigour and fertility over the offspring from long-continued self-fertilisation, that they will have a better chance of surviving and propagating their kind; and thus, in the long run, the influence of intercrosses, even at rare intervals, will be great. If there exist organic beings which never intercross, uniformity of character can be retained among them, as long as their conditions of life remain the same, only through the principle of inheritance, and through natural selection destroying any which depart from the proper type; but if their conditions of life change and they undergo modification, uniformity of character can be given to their modified offspring, solely by natural selection preserving the same favourable variations.

Isolation, also, is an important element in the process of natural selection. In a confined or isolated area, if not very large, the organic and inorganic conditions of life will generally be in a great degree uniform; so that natural selection will tend to modify all the individuals of a varying species throughout the area in the same manner in relation to the same conditions. Intercrosses, also, with the individuals of the same species, which otherwise would have inhabited the surrounding and differently circumstanced districts, will be prevented. But isolation probably acts more efficiently in checking the immigration of better adapted organisms, after any physical change, such as of climate or elevation of the land, &c.; and thus new places in the natural economy of the country are left open for the old inhabitants to struggle for, and become adapted to, through modifications in their structure and constitution. Lastly, isolation, by checking immigration and consequently competition, will give time for any new variety to be slowly improved; and this may sometimes be of importance in the production of new species. If, however, an isolated area be very small, either from being surrounded by barriers, or from having very peculiar physical conditions, the total number of the individuals supported on it will necessarily be very small; and fewness of individuals will greatly retard the production of new species through natural selection, by decreasing the chance of the appearance of favourable variations.

If we turn to nature to test the truth of these remarks, and look at any small isolated area, such as an oceanic island, although the total number of the species inhabiting it, will be found to be small, as we shall see in our chapter on geographical distribution; yet of these species a very large proportion are endemic, – that is, have been produced there, and nowhere else. Hence an oceanic island at first sight seems to have been highly favourable for the production of new species. But we may thus greatly deceive ourselves, for to ascertain whether a small isolated area, or a large open area like a continent, has been most favourable for the production of new organic forms, we ought to make the comparison within equal times; and this we are incapable of doing.

Although I do not doubt that isolation is of considerable importance in the production of new species, on the whole I am inclined to believe that largeness of area is of more importance, more especially in the production of species, which will prove capable of enduring for a long period, and of spreading widely. Throughout a great and open area, not only will there be a better chance of favourable variations arising from the large number of individuals of the same species there supported, but the conditions of life are infinitely complex from the large number of already existing species; and if some of these many species become modified and improved, others will have to be improved in a corresponding degree or they will be exterminated. Each new form, also, as soon as it has been much improved, will be able to spread over the open and continuous area, and will thus come into competition with many others. Hence more new places will be formed, and the competition to fill them will be more severe, on a large than on a small and isolated area. Moreover, great areas, though now continuous, owing to oscillations of level, will often have recently existed in a broken condition, so that the good effects of isolation will generally, to a certain extent, have concurred. Finally, I conclude that, although small isolated areas probably have been in some respects highly favourable for the production of new species, yet that the course of modification will generally have been more rapid on large areas; and what is more important, that the new forms produced on large areas, which already have been victorious over many competitors, will be those that will spread most widely, will give rise to most new varieties and species, and will thus play an important part in the changing history of the organic world.

We can, perhaps, on these views, understand some facts which will be again alluded to in our chapter on geographical distribution; for instance, that the productions of the smaller continent of Australia have formerly yielded, and apparently are now yielding, before those of the larger Europaeo-Asiatic area. Thus, also, it is that continental productions have everywhere become so largely naturalised on islands. On a small island, the race for life will have been less severe, and there will have been less modification and less extermination. Hence, perhaps, it comes that the flora of Madeira, according to Oswald Heer,[10] resembles the extinct tertiary flora of Europe. All fresh-water basins, taken together, make a small area compared with that of the sea or of the land; and, consequently, the competition between fresh-water productions will have been less severe than elsewhere; new forms will have been more slowly formed, and old forms more slowly exterminated. And it is in fresh water that we find seven genera of Ganoid fishes,[11] remnants of a once preponderant order: and in fresh water we find some of the most anomalous forms now known in the world, as the Ornithorhynchus and Lepidosiren,[12] which, like fossils, connect to a certain extent orders now widely separated in the natural scale. These anomalous forms may almost be called living fossils; they have endured to the present day, from having inhabited a confined area, and from having thus been exposed to less severe competition.

To sum up the circumstances favourable and unfavourable to natural selection, as far as the extreme intricacy of the subject permits. I conclude, looking to the future, that for terrestrial productions a large continental area, which will probably undergo many oscillations of level, and which consequently will exist for long periods in a broken condition, will be the most favourable for the production of many new forms of life, likely to endure long and to spread widely. For the area will first have existed as a continent, and the inhabitants, at this period numerous in individuals and kinds, will have been subjected to very severe competition. When converted by subsidence into large separate islands, there will still exist many individuals of the same species on each island: intercrossing on the confines of the range of each species will thus be checked: after physical changes of any kind, immigration will be prevented, so that new places in the polity of each island will have to be filled up by modifications of the old inhabitants; and time will be allowed for the varieties in each to become well modified and perfected. When, by renewed elevation, the islands shall be reconverted into a continental area, there will again be severe competition: the most favoured or improved varieties will be enabled to spread: there will be much extinction of the less improved forms, and the relative proportional numbers of the various inhabitants of the renewed continent will again be changed; and again there will be a fair field for natural selection to improve still further the inhabitants, and thus produce a new species.

That natural selection will always act with extreme slowness, I fully admit. Its action depends on there being places in the polity of nature, which can be better occupied by some of the inhabitants of the country undergoing modification of some kind. The existence of such places will often depend on physical changes, which are generally very slow, and on the immigration of better adapted forms having been checked. But the action of natural selection will probably still oftener depend on some of the inhabitants becoming slowly modified; the mutual relations of many of the other inhabitants being thus disturbed. Nothing can be effected, unless favourable variations occur, and variation itself is apparently always a very slow process. The process will often be greatly retarded by free intercrossing. Many will exclaim that these several causes are amply sufficient wholly to stop the action of natural selection. I do not believe so. On the other hand, I do believe that natural selection will always act very slowly, often only at long intervals of time, and generally on only a very few of the inhabitants of the same region at the same time. I further believe, that this very slow, intermittent action of natural selection accords perfectly well with what geology tells us of the rate and manner at which the inhabitants of this world have changed.

Slow though the process of selection may be, if feeble man can do much by his powers of artificial selection, I can see no limit to the amount of change, to the beauty and infinite complexity of the coadaptations between all organic beings, one with another and with their physical conditions of life, which may be effected in the long course of time by nature's power of selection.

### Extinction

This subject will be more fully discussed in our chapter on Geology; but it must here be alluded to from being intimately connected with natural selection. Natural selection acts solely through the preservation of variations in some way advantageous, which consequently endure. But as from the high geometrical powers of increase of all organic beings, each area is already fully stocked with inhabitants, it follows that as each selected and favoured form increases in number, so will the less favoured forms decrease and become rare. Rarity, as geology tells us, is the precursor to extinction. We can, also, see that any form represented by few individuals will, during fluctuations in the seasons or in the number of its enemies, run a good chance of utter extinction. But we may go further than this; for as new forms are continually and slowly being produced, unless we believe that the number of specific forms goes on perpetually and almost indefinitely increasing, numbers inevitably must become extinct. That the number of specific forms has not indefinitely increased, geology shows us plainly; and indeed we can see reason why they should not have thus increased, for the number of places in the polity of nature is not indefinitely great, – not that we have any means of knowing that any one region has as yet got its maximum of species. Probably no region is as yet fully stocked, for at the Cape of Good Hope, where more species of plants are crowded together than in any other quarter of the world, some foreign plants having become naturalised without causing, as far as we know, the extinction of any natives.

Furthermore, the species which are most numerous in individuals will have the best chance of producing within any given period favourable variations. We have evidence of this, in the facts given in the second chapter, showing that it is the common species which afford the greatest number of recorded varieties, or incipient species. Hence, rare species will be less quickly modified or improved within any given period, and they will consequently be beaten in the race for life by the modified descendants of the commoner species.

From these several considerations I think it inevitably follows, that as new species in the course of time are formed through natural selection, others will become rarer and rarer, and finally extinct. The forms which stand in closest competition with those undergoing modification and improvement, will naturally suffer most. And we have seen in the chapter on the Struggle for Existence that it is the most closely allied forms, – varieties of the same species, and species of the same genus or of related genera, – which, from having nearly the same structure, constitution, and habits, generally come into the severest competition with each other. Consequently, each new variety or species, during the progress of its formation, will generally press hardest on its nearest kindred, and tend to exterminate them. We see the same process of extermination amongst our domesticated productions, through the selection of improved forms by man. Many curious instances could be given showing how quickly new breeds of cattle, sheep, and other animals, and varieties of flowers, take the place of older and inferior kinds. In Yorkshire, it is historically known that the ancient black cattle were displaced by the long-horns, and that these 'were swept away by the short-horns' (I quote the words of an agricultural writer) 'as if by some murderous pestilence.'

### Divergence of character

The principle, which I have designated by this term, is of high importance on my theory, and explains, as I believe, several important facts. In the first place, varieties, even strongly-marked ones, though having somewhat of the character of species – as is shown by the hopeless doubts in many cases how to rank them – yet certainly differ from each other far less than do good and distinct species. Nevertheless, according to my view, varieties are species in the process of formation, or are, as I have called them, incipient species. How, then, does the lesser difference between varieties become augmented into the greater difference between species? That this does habitually happen, we must infer from most of the innumerable species throughout nature presenting well-marked differences; whereas varieties, the supposed prototypes and parents of future well-marked species, present slight and ill-defined differences. Mere chance, as we may call it, might cause one variety to differ in some character from its parents, and the offspring of this variety again to differ from its parent in the very same character and in a greater degree; but this alone would never account for so habitual and large an amount of difference as that between varieties of the same species and species of the same genus.

As has always been my practice, let us seek light on this head from our domestic productions. We shall here find something analogous. A fancier is struck by a pigeon having a slightly shorter beak; another fancier is struck by a pigeon having a rather longer beak; and on the acknowledged principle that 'fanciers do not and will not admire a medium standard, but like extremes,' they both go on (as has actually occurred with tumbler-pigeons) choosing and breeding from birds with longer and longer beaks, or with shorter and shorter beaks. Again, we may suppose that at an early period one man preferred swifter horses; another stronger and more bulky horses. The early differences would be very slight; in the course of time, from the continued selection of swifter horses by some breeders, and of stronger ones by others, the differences would become greater, and would be noted as forming two sub-breeds; finally, after the lapse of centuries, the sub-breeds would become converted into two well-established and distinct breeds. As the differences slowly become greater, the inferior animals with intermediate characters, being neither very swift nor very strong, will have been neglected, and will have tended to disappear. Here, then, we see in man's productions the action of what may be called the principle of divergence, causing differences, at first barely appreciable, steadily to increase, and the breeds to diverge in character both from each other and from their common parent.

But how, it may be asked, can any analogous principle apply in nature? I believe it can and does apply most efficiently, from the simple circumstance that the more diversified the descendants from any one species become in structure, constitution, and habits, by so much will they be better enabled to seize on many and widely diversified places in the polity of nature, and so be enabled to increase in numbers.

We can clearly see this in the case of animals with simple habits. Take the case of a carnivorous quadruped, of which the number that can be supported in any country has long ago arrived at its full average. If its natural powers of increase be allowed to act, it can succeed in increasing (the country not undergoing any change in its conditions) only by its varying descendants seizing on places at present occupied by other animals: some of them, for instance, being enabled to feed on new kinds of prey, either dead or alive; some inhabiting new stations, climbing trees, frequenting water, and some perhaps becoming less carnivorous. The more diversified in habits and structure the descendants of our carnivorous animals became, the more places they would be enabled to occupy. What applies to one animal will apply throughout all time to all animals – that is, if they vary – for otherwise natural selection can do nothing. So it will be with plants. It has been experimentally proved, that if a plot of ground be sown with one species of grass, and a similar plot be sown with several distinct genera of grasses, a greater number of plants and a greater weight of dry herbage can thus be raised. The same has been found to hold good when first one variety and then several mixed varieties of wheat have been sown on equal spaces of ground. Hence, if any one species of grass were to go on varying, and those varieties were continually selected which differed from each other in at all the same manner as distinct species and genera of grasses differ from each other, a greater number of individual plants of this species of grass, including its modified descendants, would succeed in living on the same piece of ground. And we well know that each species and each variety of grass is annually sowing almost countless seeds; and thus, as it may be said, is striving its utmost to increase its numbers. Consequently, I cannot doubt that in the course of many thousands of generations, the most distinct varieties of any one species of grass would always have the best chance of succeeding and of increasing in numbers, and thus of supplanting the less distinct varieties; and varieties, when rendered very distinct from each other, take the rank of species.

The truth of the principle, that the greatest amount of life can be supported by great diversification of structure, is seen under many natural circumstances. In an extremely small area, especially if freely open to immigration, and where the contest between individual and individual must be severe, we always find great diversity in its inhabitants. For instance, I found that a piece of turf, three feet by four in size, which had been exposed for many years to exactly the same conditions, supported twenty species of plants, and these belonged to eighteen genera and to eight orders, which shows how much these plants differed from each other. So it is with the plants and insects on small and uniform islets; and so in small ponds of fresh water. Farmers find that they can raise most food by a rotation of plants belonging to the most different orders: nature follows what may be called a simultaneous rotation. Most of the animals and plants which live close round any small piece of ground, could live on it (supposing its not to be in any way peculiar in its nature), and may be said to be striving to the utmost to live there; but, it is seen, that where they come into the closest competition with each other, the advantages of diversification of structure, with the accompanying differences of habit and constitution, determine that the inhabitants, which thus jostle each other most closely, shall, as a general rule, belong to what we call different genera and orders.

The same principle is seen in the naturalisation of plants through man's agency in foreign lands. It might have been expected that the plants which have succeeded in becoming naturalised in any land would generally have been closely allied to the indigenes; for these are commonly looked at as specially created and adapted for their own country. It might, also, perhaps, have been expected that naturalised plants would have belonged to a few groups more especially adapted to certain stations in their new homes. But the cause is very different; and Alph. De Candolle[13] has well remarked in his great and admirable work, that floras gain by naturalisation, proportionally with the number of the native genera and species, far more in new genera than in new species. To give a single instance: in the last edition of Dr Asa Gray's 'Manual of the Flora of the Northern United States,'[14] 260 naturalised plants are enumerated, and these belong to 162 genera. We thus see that these naturalised plants are of a highly diversified nature. They differ, moreover, to a large extent, from the indigenes, for out of the 162 genera, no less than 100 genera are not there indigenous and thus a large proportional addition is made to the genera of these States.

By considering the nature of the plants or animals which have struggled successfully with the indigenes of any country, and have there become naturalised, we can gain some crude idea in what manner some of the natives would have had to be modified, in order to have gained an advantage over the other natives; and we may, I think, at least safely infer that diversification of structure, amounting to new generic differences, would have been profitable to them.

The advantage of diversification in the inhabitants of the same region is, in fact, the same as that of the physiological division of labour in the organs of the same individual body – a subject so well elucidated by Milne Edwards.[15] No physiologist doubts that a stomach by being adapted to digest vegetable matter alone, or flesh alone, draws most nutriment from these substances. So in the general economy of any land, the more widely and perfectly the animals and plants are diversified for different habits of life, so will a greater number of individuals be capable of there supporting themselves. A set of animals, with their organisation but little diversified, could hardly compete with a set more perfectly diversified in structure. It may be doubted, for instance, whether the Australian marsupials, which are divided into groups differing but little from each other, and feebly representing, as Mr Waterhouse[16] and others have remarked, our carnivorous, ruminant, and rodent animals, could successfully compete with these well-pronounced orders. In the Australian mammals, we see the process of diversification in an early and incomplete state of development.

After the foregoing discussion, which ought to have been much amplified, we may, I think, assume that the modified descendants of any one species will succeed by so much the better as they become more diversified in structure, and are thus enabled to encroach on places occupied by other beings. Now let us see how this principle of great benefit being derived from divergence of character, combined with the principles of natural selection and of extinction, will tend to act.

The accompanying diagram [see Figure 1] will aid us in understanding this rather perplexing subject. Let A to L represent the species of a genus large in its own country; these species are supposed to resemble each other in unequal degrees, as is so generally the case in nature, and as is represented in the diagram by the letters standing at unequal distances. I have said a large genus, because we have seen in the second chapter, that on an average more of the species of large genera vary than of small genera; and the varying species of the large genera present a greater number of varieties. We have, also, seen that the species, which are the commonest and the most widely-diffused, vary more than rare species with restricted ranges. Let (A) be a common, widely-diffused, and varying species, belonging to a genus large in its own country. The little fan of diverging dotted lines of unequal lengths proceeding from (A), may represent its varying offspring. The variations are supposed to be extremely slight, but of the most diversified nature; they are not supposed all to appear simultaneously, but often after long intervals of time; nor are they all supposed to endure for equal periods. Only those

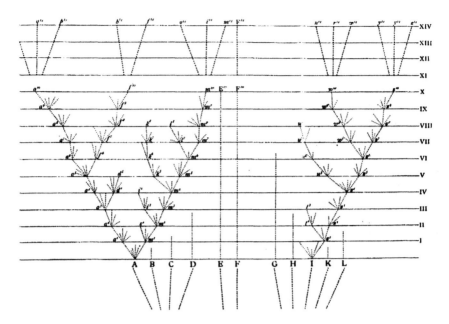

[Figure 1]

variations which are in some way profitable will be preserved or naturally selected. And here the importance of the principle of benefit being derived from divergence of character comes in; for this will generally lead to the most different or divergent variations (represented by the outer dotted lines) being preserved and accumulated by natural selection. When a dotted line reaches one of the horizontal lines, and is there marked by a small numbered letter, a sufficient amount of variation is supposed to have been accumulated to have formed a fairly well-marked variety, such as would be thought worthy of record in a systematic work.

The intervals between the horizontal lines in the diagram, may represent each a thousand generations; but it would have been better if each had represented ten thousand generations. After a thousand generations, species (A) is supposed to have produced two fairly well-marked varieties, namely $a^1$ and $m^1$. These two varieties will generally continue to be exposed to the same conditions which made their parents variable, and the tendency to variability is in itself hereditary, consequently they will tend to vary, and generally to vary in nearly the same manner as their parents varied. Moreover, these two varieties, being only slightly modified forms, will tend to inherit those advantages which made their common parent (A) more numerous than most of the other inhabitants of the same country; they will likewise partake of those more general advantages which made the genus to which the parent-species belonged, a large genus in its own country. And these circumstances we know to be favourable to the production of new varieties.

246

If, then, these two varieties be variable, the most divergent of their variations will generally be preserved during the next thousand generations. And after this interval, variety $a^1$ is supposed in the diagram to have produced variety $a^2$, which will, owing to the principle of divergence, differ more from (A) than did variety $a^1$. Variety $m^1$ is supposed to have produced two varieties, namely $m^2$ and $s^2$, differing from each other, and more considerably from their common parent (A). We may continue the process by similar steps for any length of time; some of the varieties, after each thousand generations, producing only a single variety, but in a more and more modified condition, some producing two or three varieties, and some failing to produce any. Thus the varieties or modified descendants, proceeding from the common parent (A), will generally go on increasing in number and diverging in character. In the diagram the process is represented up to the ten-thousandth generation, and under a condensed and simplified form up to the fourteen-thousandth generation.

But I must here remark that I do not suppose that the process ever goes on so regularly as is represented in the diagram, though in itself made somewhat irregular. I am far from thinking that the most divergent varieties will invariably prevail and multiply: a medium form may often long endure, and may or may not produce more than one modified descendant; for natural selection will always act according to the nature of the places which are either unoccupied or not perfectly occupied by other beings; and this will depend on infinitely complex relations. But as a general rule, the more diversified in structure the descendants from any one species can be rendered, the more places they will be enabled to seize on, and the more their modified progeny will be increased. In our diagram the line of succession is broken at regular intervals by small numbered letters marking the successive forms which have become sufficiently distinct to be recorded as varieties. But these breaks are imaginary, and might have been inserted anywhere, after intervals long enough to allow the accumulation of a considerable amount of divergent variation.

As all the modified descendants from a common and widely-diffused species, belonging to a large genus, will tend to partake of the same advantages which made their parent successful in life, they will generally go on multiplying in number as well as diverging in character: this is represented in the diagram by the several divergent branches proceeding from (A). The modified offspring from the later and more highly improved branches in the lines of descent, will, it is probable, often take the place of, and so destroy, the earlier and less improved branches: this is represented in the diagram by some of the lower branches not reaching to the upper horizontal lines. In some cases I do not doubt that the process of modification will be confined to a single line of descent, and the number of the descendants will not be increased; although the amount of divergent modification may have been increased in the successive generations. This case would be represented in the diagram, if all the lines proceeding from (A) were removed, excepting that from $a^1$ to $a^{10}$. In the same way, for instance, the English race-horse and English pointer have apparently both gone on slowly diverging in character from their original stocks, without either having given off any fresh branches or races.

After ten thousand generations, species (A) is supposed to have produced three forms, $a^{10}$, $f^{10}$, and $m^{10}$, which, from having diverged in character during the successive generations, will have come to differ largely, but perhaps unequally, from each other and from their common parent. If we suppose the amount of change between each horizontal line in our diagram to be excessively small, these three forms may still be only well-marked varieties; or they may have arrived at the doubtful category of sub-species; but we have only to suppose the steps in the process of modification to be more numerous or greater in amount, to convert these three forms into well-defined species: thus the diagram illustrates the steps by which the small differences distinguishing varieties are increased into the larger differences distinguishing species. By continuing the same process for a greater number of generations (as shown in the diagram in a condensed and simplified manner), we get eight species, marked by the letters between $a^{14}$ and $m^{14}$, all descended from (A). Thus, as I believe, species are multiplied and genera are formed.

In a large genus it is probable that more than one species would vary. In the diagram I have assumed that a second species (I) has produced, by analogous steps, after ten thousand generations, either two well-marked varieties ($w^{10}$ and $z^{10}$) or two species, according to the amount of change supposed to be represented between the horizontal lines. After fourteen thousand generations, six new species, marked by the letters $n^{14}$ to $z^{14}$, are supposed to have been produced. In each genus, the species, which are already very different in character, will generally tend to produce the greatest number of modified descendants; for these will have the best chance of filling new and widely different places in the polity of nature: hence in the diagram I have chosen the extreme species (A), and the nearly extreme species (I), as those which have largely varied, and have given rise to new varieties and species. The other nine species (marked by capital letters) of our original genus, may for a long period continue transmitting unaltered descendants; and this is shown in the diagram by the dotted lines not prolonged far upwards from want of space.

But during the process of modification, represented in the diagram, another of our principles, namely that of extinction, will have played an important part. As in each fully stocked country natural selection necessarily acts by the selected form having some advantage in the struggle for life over other forms, there will be a constant tendency in the improved descendants of any one species to supplant and exterminate in each stage of descent their predecessors and their original parent. For it should be remembered that the competition will generally be most severe between those forms which are most nearly related to each other in habits, constitution, and structure. Hence all the intermediate forms between the earlier and later states, that is between the less and more improved state of a species, as well as the original parent-species itself, will generally tend to become extinct. So it probably will be with many whole collateral lines of descent, which will be conquered by later and improved lines of descent. If, however, the modified offspring of a species get into some distinct country, or become quickly adapted to some quite new station, in which child and parent do not come into competition, both may continue to exist.

If then our diagram be assumed to represent a considerable amount of modification, species (A) and all the earlier varieties will have become extinct, having been replaced by eight new species ($a^{14}$ to $m^{14}$); and (I) will have been replaced by six ($n^{14}$ to $z^{14}$) new species.

But we may go further than this. The original species of our genus were supposed to resemble each other in unequal degrees, as is so generally the case in nature; species (A) being more nearly related to B, C, and D, than to the other species; and species (I) more to G, H, K, L, than to the others. These two species, (A) and (I), were also supposed to be very common and widely diffused species, so that they must originally have had some advantage over most of the other species of the genus. Their modified descendants, fourteen in number at the fourteenth-thousandth generation, will probably have inherited some of the same advantages: they have also been modified and improved in a diversified manner at each stage of descent, so as to have become adapted to many related places in the natural economy of their country. It seems, therefore, to be extremely probable that they will have taken the places of, and thus exterminated, not only their parents (A) and (I), but likewise some of the original species which were most nearly related to their parents. Hence very few of the original species will have transmitted offspring to the fourteen-thousandth generation. We may suppose that only one (F), of the two species which were least closely related to the other nine original species, has transmitted descendants to this late stage of descent.

The new species in our diagram descended from the original eleven species, will now be fifteen in number. Owing to the divergent tendency of natural selection, the extreme amount of difference in character between species $a^{14}$ and $z^{14}$ will be much greater than that between the most different of the original eleven species. The new species, moreover, will be allied to each other in a widely different manner. Of the eight descendants from (A) the three marked $a^{14}$, $q^{14}$, $p^{14}$, will be nearly related from having recently branched off from $a^{10}$; $b^{14}$ and $f^{14}$, from having diverged at an earlier period from $a^5$, will be in some degree distinct from the three first-named species; and lastly, $o^{14}$, $e^{14}$, and $m^{14}$, will be nearly related one to the other, but from having diverged at the first commencement of the process of modification, will be widely different from the other five species, and may constitute a sub-genus or even a distinct genus.

The six descendants from (I) will form two sub-genera or even genera. But as the original species (I) differed largely from (A), standing nearly at the extreme points of the original genus, the six descendants from (I) will, owing to inheritance, differ considerably from the eight descendants from (A); the two groups, moreover, are supposed to have gone on diverging in different directions. The intermediate species, also (and this is a very important consideration), which connected the original species (A) and (I), have all become, excepting (F), extinct, and have left no descendants. Hence the six new species descended from (I), and the eight descended from (A), will have to be ranked as very distinct genera, or even as distinct sub-families.

Thus it is, as I believe, that two or more genera are produced by descent, with modification, from two or more species of the same genus. And the two or more parent-species are supposed to have descended from some one species of an earlier genus. In our diagram, this is indicated by the broken lines, beneath the capital letters, converging in sub-branches downwards towards a single point; this point representing a single species, the supposed single parent of our several new sub-genera and genera.

It is worth while to reflect for a moment on the character of the new species $F^{14}$, which is supposed not to have diverged much in character, but to have retained the form of (F), either unaltered or altered only in a slight degree. In this case, its affinities to the other fourteen new species will be of a curious and circuitous nature. Having descended from a form which stood between the parent-species (A) and (I), now supposed to be extinct and unknown, it will be in some degree intermediate in character between the two groups descended from these species. But as these two groups have gone on diverging in character from the type of their parents, the new species ($F^{14}$) will not be directly intermediate between them, but rather between types of the two groups, and every naturalist will be able to bring some such case before his mind.

In the diagram, each horizontal line has hitherto been supposed to represent a thousand generations, but each may represent a million or hundred million generations, and likewise a section of the successive strata of the earth's crust including extinct remains. We shall, when we come to our chapter on Geology, have to refer again to this subject, and I think we shall then see that the diagram throws light on the affinities of extinct beings, which, though generally belonging to the same orders, families, or genera, with those now living, yet are often, in some degree, intermediate in character between existing groups; and we can understand this fact, for the extinct species lived at very ancient epochs when the branching lines of descent had diverged less.

I see no reason to limit the process of modification, as now explained, to the formation of genera alone. If, in our diagram, we suppose the amount of change represented by each successive group of diverging dotted lines to be very great, the forms marked $a^{14}$ to $p^{14}$, those marked $b^{14}$ and $f^{14}$, and those marked $o^{14}$ to $m^{14}$, will form three very distinct genera. We shall also have two very distinct genera descended from (I); and as these latter two genera, both from continued divergence of character and from inheritance from a different parent, will differ widely from the three genera descended from (A), the two little groups of genera will form two distinct families, or even orders, according to the amount of divergent modification supposed to be represented in the diagram. And the two new families, or orders, will have descended from two species of the original genus; and these two species are supposed to have descended from one species of a still more ancient and unknown genus.

250

We have seen that in each country it is the species of the larger genera which oftenest present varieties or incipient species. This, indeed, might have been expected; for as natural selection acts through one form having some advantage over other forms in the struggle for existence, it will chiefly act on those which already have some advantage; and the largeness of any group shows that its species have inherited from a common ancestor some advantage in common. Hence, the struggle for the production of new and modified descendants, will mainly lie between the larger groups, which are all trying to increase in number. One large group will slowly conquer another large group, reduce its numbers, and thus lessen its chance of further variation and improvement. Within the same large group, the later and more highly perfected sub-groups, from branching out and seizing on many new places in the polity of Nature, will constantly tend to supplant and destroy the earlier and less improved sub-groups. Small and broken groups and sub-groups will finally tend to disappear. Looking to the future, we can predict that the groups of organic beings which are now large and triumphant, and which are least broken up, that is, which as yet have suffered least extinction, will for a long period continue to increase. But which groups will ultimately prevail, no man can predict; for we well know that many groups, formerly most extensively developed, have now become extinct. Looking still more remotely to the future, we may predict that, owing to the continued and steady increase of the larger groups, a multitude of smaller groups will become utterly extinct, and leave no modified descendants; and consequently that of the species living at any one period, extremely few will transmit descendants to a remote futurity. I shall have to return to this subject in the chapter on Classification, but I may add that on this view of extremely few of the more ancient species having transmitted descendants, and on the view of all the descendants of the same species making a class, we can understand how it is that there exist but very few classes in each main division of the animal and vegetable kingdoms. Although extremely few of the most ancient species may now have living and modified descendants, yet at the most remote geological period, the earth may have been as well peopled with many species of many genera, families, orders, and classes, as at the present day.

## Summary of chapter

If during the long course of ages and under varying conditions of life, organic beings vary at all in the several parts of their organisation, and I think this cannot be disputed; if there be, owing to the high geometrical powers of increase of each species, at some age, season, or year, a severe struggle for life, and this certainly cannot be disputed; then, considering the infinite complexity of the relations of all organic beings to each other and to their conditions of existence, causing an infinite diversity in structure, constitution, and habits, to be advantageous to them, I think it would be a most extraordinary fact if no variation ever had occurred useful to each being's own welfare, in the same way as so

251

many variations have occurred useful to man. But if variations useful to any organic being do occur, assuredly individuals thus characterised will have the best chance of being preserved in the struggle for life; and from the strong principle of inheritance they will tend to produce offspring similarly characterised. This principle of preservation, I have called, for the sake of brevity, Natural Selection. Natural selection, on the principle of qualities being inherited at corresponding ages, can modify the egg, seed, or young, as easily as the adult. Among many animals, sexual selection will give its aid to ordinary selection, by assuring to the most vigorous and best adapted males the greatest number of offspring. Sexual selection will also give characters useful to the males alone, in their struggles with other males.

Whether natural selection has really thus acted in nature, in modifying and adapting the various forms of life to their several conditions and stations, must be judged of by the general tenor and balance of evidence given in the following chapters. But we already see how it entails extinction; and how largely extinction has acted in the world's history, geology plainly declares. Natural selection, also, leads to divergence of character; for more living beings can be supported on the same area the more they diverge in structure, habits, and constitution, of which we see proof by looking at the inhabitants of any small spot or at naturalised productions. Therefore, during the modification of the descendants of any one species, and during the incessant struggle of all species to increase in numbers, the more diversified these descendants become, the better will be their chance of succeeding in the battle of life. Thus the small differences distinguishing varieties of the same species, will steadily tend to increase till they come to equal the greater differences between species of the same genus, or even of distinct genera.

We have seen that it is the common, the widely-diffused, and widely-ranging species, belonging to the larger genera, which vary most; and these will tend to transmit to their modified offspring that superiority which now makes them dominant in their own countries. Natural selection, as has just been remarked, leads to divergence of character and to much distinction of the less improved and intermediate forms of life. On these principles, I believe, the nature of the affinities of all organic beings may be explained. It is a truly wonderful fact – the wonder of which we are apt to overlook from familiarity – that all animals and all plants throughout all time and space should be related to each other in group subordinate to group, in the manner which we everywhere behold – namely, varieties of the same species most closely related together, species of the same genus less closely and unequally related together, forming sections and sub-genera, species of distinct genera much less closely related, and genera related in different degrees, forming sub-families, families, orders, sub-classes, and classes. The several subordinate groups in any class cannot be ranked in a single file, but seem rather to be clustered round points, and these round other points, and so on in almost endless cycles. On the view that each species has been independently created, I can see no explanation of this great fact in the classification of all organic beings; but, to the best of my judgement, it is explained through inheritance and the complex action of natural selection, entailing extinction and divergence of character, as we have seen illustrated in the diagram.

The affinities of all the beings of the same class have sometimes been represented by a great tree. I believe this simile largely speaks the truth. The green and budding twigs may represent existing species; and those produced during each former year may represent the long succession of extinct species. At each period of growth all the growing twigs have tried to branch out on all sides, and to overtop and kill the surrounding twigs and branches, in the same manner as species and groups of species have tried to overmaster other species in the great battle for life. The limbs divided into great branches, and these into lesser and lesser branches, were themselves once, when the tree was small, budding twigs; and this connexion of the former and present buds by ramifying branches may well represent the classification of all extinct and living species in groups subordinate to groups. Of the many twigs which flourished when the tree was a mere bush, only two or three, now grown into great branches, yet survive and bear all the other branches; so with the species which lived during long-past geological periods, very few now have living and modified descendants. From the first growth of the tree, many a limb and branch has decayed and dropped off; and these lost branches of various sizes may represent those whole orders, families, and genera which have now no living representatives, and which are known to us only from having been found in a fossil state. As we here and there see a thin straggling branch springing from a fork low down in a tree, and which by some chance has been favoured and is still alive on its summit, so we occasionally see an animal like the Ornithorhynchus or Lepidosiren, which in some small degree connects by its affinities two large branches of life, and which has apparently been saved from fatal competition by having inhabited a protected station. As buds give rise by growth to fresh buds, and these, if vigorous, branch out and overtop on all sides many a feebler branch, so by generation I believe it has been with the great Tree of Life, which fills with its dead and broken branches the crust of the earth, and covers the surface with its ever branching and beautiful ramifications.

# THOMAS HENRY HUXLEY, *EVIDENCE AS TO MAN'S PLACE IN NATURE* (1863)

Thomas Henry Huxley (1825–95) is probably best remembered as Charles Darwin's 'bull-dog'. It was Huxley – young, energetic and combative – who defended Darwin in the famous exchange with the Bishop of Oxford, Samuel Wilberforce, in the meeting in 1860 of the British Association for the Advancement of Science; Darwin, by contrast, had kept firmly in the background. It was also Huxley who, in the frontispiece to his first main work, *Evidence as to Man's Place in Nature* (1863), provided one of the most memorable and dramatic images of evolutionary theory – a line of skeletons 'advancing' from gibbon, to orang, to chimpanzee, to gorilla and finally to man. Huxley's career began with a scholarship to study medicine at Charing Cross Medical School. He left before qualifying at the age of 21 and took up a position as assistant ship's surgeon on HMS *Rattlesnake*. He subsequently embarked on a four-year exploration of the South Seas from where he regularly sent home essays and observations which were published in the journals of the Royal Society and Royal Institution. By the time he returned to England in 1850 Huxley had already made something of a name for himself. Within a year he was elected a fellow of the Royal Society. In the 1850s he began to write papers on a variety of botanical and entomological subjects, as well as on science and scientific education. In 1854 he secured a post at the School of Mines in London, where he remained for his whole academic career, becoming honorary dean of what later became (in 1885) the Normal School of Science. Throughout the 1860s Huxley wrote extensively on palaeontology, taxonomy and ethology. As well as *Evidence* (or as Darwin called it, the 'Monkey book'), Huxley published *Lessons on Elementary Physiology* (1866), *An Introduction to the Classification of Animals* (1869) and *Protoplasm: The Physical Basis of Life* (1869). During this period he also held an impressive number of public positions at the Geological Society, the Royal College of Surgeons, the Ethnological Society and the London Working Men's College; later he became Secretary (and then President) of the Royal Society. In the 1870s Huxley was the dominant member of the first London School Board and he played a major role in the reorganisation of British education. He contributed scholarly articles to the *Encyclopaedia Britannica* and published two influential scientific text-books: *A Manual of the Anatomy of Vertebrated Animals* (1871) and *A Manual of the Anatomy of Invertebrated Animals* (1877).

He also produced books on Darwin and Hume as well as several collections of essays and addresses. In his late years Huxley developed an interest in philosophy and theology, publishing *Science and Culture* (1881), *Essays Upon Some Controverted Questions* (1892) and *Evolution and Ethics* (1893). He died from bronchitis in 1895.

*From* **Thomas Henry Huxley,** *Evidence as to Man's Place in Nature* **(London: Williams and Norgate, 1863)**[1]

From *II. – On the Relations of Man to the Lower Animals*[2]

The question of questions for mankind – the problem which underlies all others, and is more deeply interesting than any other – is the ascertainment of the place which Man occupies in nature and of his relations to the universe of things. Whence our race has come; what are the limits of our power over nature, and of nature's power over us; to what goal we are tending; are the problems which present themselves anew and with undiminished interest to every man born into the world. Most of us, shrinking from the difficulties and dangers which beset the seeker after original answers to these riddles, are contented to ignore them altogether, or to smother the investigating spirit under the featherbed of respected and respectable tradition. But, in every age, one or two restless spirits, blessed

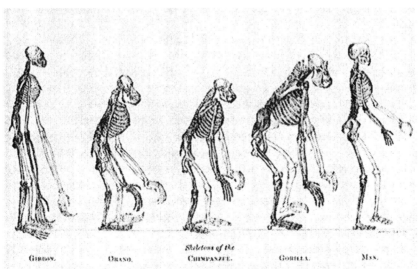

Skeletons of the
GIBBON.    ORANG.    CHIMPANZEE.    GORILLA.    MAN.

*Photographically reduced from Diagrams of the natural size (except that of the Gibbon, which was twice as large as nature), drawn by Mr. Waterhouse Hawkins, from specimens in the Museum of the Royal College of Surgeons.*

*[Frontispiece]*

255

with that constructive genius, which can only build on a secure foundation, or cursed with the spirit of mere scepticism, are unable to follow in the well-worn and comfortable track of their forefathers and contemporaries, and unmindful of thorns and stumbling-blocks, strike out into paths of their own. The sceptics end in the infidelity which asserts the problem to be insoluble, or in the atheism which denies the existence of any orderly progress and governance of things: The men of genius propound solutions which grow into systems of Theology or of Philosophy, or veiled in musical language which suggest more than it asserts, take the shape of the Poetry of an epoch.

Each such answer to the great question, invariably asserted by the followers of its propounder, if not by himself, to be complete and final, remains in high authority and esteem, it may be for one century, or it may be for twenty: but, as invariably, Time proves each reply to have been a mere approximation to the truth – tolerable chiefly on account of the ignorance of those by whom it was accepted, and wholly intolerable when tested by the larger knowledge of their successors.

In a well-worn metaphor, a parallel is drawn between the life of man and the metamorphosis of the caterpillar into the butterfly; but the comparison may be more just as well as more novel, if for its former term we take the mental progress of the race. History shows that the human mind, fed by constant accessions of knowledge, periodically grows too large for its theoretical coverings, and bursts them asunder to appear in new habiliments, as the feeding and growing grub, at intervals, casts its too narrow skin and assumes another, itself but temporary. Truly the imago[3] state of Man seems to be terribly distant, but every moult is a step gained, and of such there have been many.

Since the revival of learning, whereby the Western races of Europe were enabled to enter upon that progress towards true knowledge, which was commenced by the philosophers of Greece, but was almost arrested in subsequent long ages of intellectual stagnation, or, at most, gyration, the human larva has been feeding vigorously, and moulting in proportion. A skin of some dimension was cast in the 16th century, and another towards the end of the 18th, while, within the last fifty years, the extraordinary growth of every department of physical science has spread among us mental food of so nutritious and stimulating a character that a new ecdysis[4] seems imminent. But this is a process not unusually accompanied by many throes and some sickness and debility, or, it may be, by graver disturbances; so that every good citizen must feel bound to facilitate the process, and even if he have nothing but a scalpel to work withal, to ease the cracking integument[5] to the best of his ability.

In this duty lies my excuse for the publication of these essays. For it will be admitted that some knowledge of man's position in the animate world is an indispensable preliminary to the proper understanding of his relations to the universe – and this again resolves itself, in the long run, into an inquiry into the

nature and the closeness of the ties which connect him with those singular creatures whose history[a] has been sketched in the preceding pages.

The importance of such an inquiry is indeed intuitively manifest. Brought
face to face with these blurred copies of himself, the least thoughtful of men is
conscious of a certain shock, due perhaps, not so much to disgust at the aspect of
what looks like an insulting caricature, as to the awakening of a sudden and
profound mistrust of time-honoured theories and strongly-rooted prejudices
regarding his own position in nature, and his relations to the under-world of life;
while that which remains a dim suspicion for the unthinking, becomes a vast
argument, fraught with the deepest consequences, for all who are acquainted
with the recent progress of the anatomical and physiological sciences.

I now propose briefly to unfold that argument, and to set forth, in a form
intelligible to those who possess no special acquaintance with anatomical science,
the chief facts upon which all conclusions respecting the nature and the extent of
the bonds which connect man with the brute world must be based: I shall then
indicate the one immediate conclusion which, in my judgement, is justified by
those facts, and I shall finally discuss the bearing of that conclusion upon the
hypotheses which have been entertained respecting the Origin of Man.

The facts to which I would first direct the reader's attention, though ignored
by many of the professed instructors of the public mind, are easy of demonstration and are universally agreed to by men of science; while their significance is
so great, that whoso has duly pondered over them will, I think, find little to
startle him in the other revelations of Biology. I refer to those facts which have
been made known by the study of Development.

It is a truth of very wide, if not of universal, application, that every living
creature commences its existence under a form different from, and simpler than,
that which it eventually attains.

The oak is a more complex thing than the little rudimentary plant contained
in the acorn; the caterpillar is more complex than the egg; the butterfly than the
caterpillar; and each of these beings, in passing from its rudimentary to its
perfect condition, runs through a series of changes, the sum of which is called its
Development. In the higher animals these changes are extremely complicated;
but, within the last half century, the labours of such men as Von Baer, Rathke,
Reichert, Bischoff, and Remak,[6] have almost completely unravelled them, so that
the successive stages of development which are exhibited by a Dog, for example,
are now as well known to the embryologist as are the steps of the metamorphosis
of the silk-worm moth to the school-boy. It will be useful to consider with attention the nature and the order of the stages of canine development, as an
example of the process in the higher animals generally.

---

a    It will be understood that, in the preceding Essay, I have selected for notice from the vast mass of
papers which have been written upon the man-like Apes, only those which seem to me to be of
special moment.

The Dog, like all animals, save the very lowest (and further inquiries may not improbably remove the apparent exception), commences its existence as an egg: as a body which is, in every sense, as much an egg as that of a hen, but is devoid of that accumulation of nutritive matter which confers upon the bird's egg its exceptional size and domestic utility; and wants the shell, which would not only be useless to an animal incubated within the body of its parent, but would cut it off from access to the source of that nutriment which the young creature requires, but which the minute egg of the mammal does not contain within itself.

The Dog's egg is, in fact, a little spheroidal bag (Fig. 13), formed of a delicate transparent membrane called the *vitelline membrane*, and about $\frac{1}{130}$ to $\frac{1}{120}$th of an inch in diameter. It contains a mass of viscid[7] nutritive matter – the '*yelk*' – within which is inclosed a second much more delicate spheroidal bag, called the '*germinal vesicle*' (*a*). In this, lastly, lies a more solid rounded body, termed the '*germinal spot*' (*b*).

The egg, or 'Ovum,' is originally formed within a gland, from which, in due season, it becomes detached, and passes into the living chamber fitted for its protection and maintenance during the protracted process of gestation. Here, when subjected to the required conditions, this minute and apparently insignificant particle of living matter, becomes animated by a new and mysterious activity. The germinal vesicle and spot cease to be discernible (their precise fate being one of the yet unsolved problems of embryology), but the yelk becomes circumferentially indented, as if an invisible knife had been drawn round it, and thus appears divided into two hemispheres (Fig. 13, C).

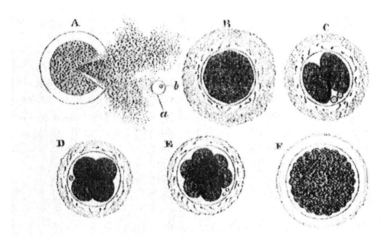

Figure 13. – A. Egg of the Dog, with the vitelline membrane burst, so as to give exit to the yelk, the germinal vesicle (*a*), and its included spot (*b*). B. C. D. E. F. Successive changes of the yelk indicated in the text. After Bischoff.

By the repetition of this process in various planes, these hemispheres become subdivided, so that four segments are produced (D); and these, in like manner, divide and subdivide again, until the whole yelk is converted into a mass of granules, each of which consists of a minute spheroid of yelk-substance, inclosing a central particle, the so-called '*nucleus*' (F). Nature, by this process, has attained much the same result as that at which a human artificer arrives by his operations in a brick field. She takes the rough plastic material of the yelk and breaks it up into well-shaped tolerably even-sized masses – handy for building up into any part of the living edifice.

Next, the mass of organic bricks, or '*cells*' as they are technically called, thus formed, acquires an orderly arrangement, becoming converted into a hollow spheroid with double walls. Then, upon one side of this spheroid, appears a thickening, and, by and by, in the centre of the area of thickening, a straight shallow groove (Fig. 14, A) marks the central line of the edifice which is to be raised, or, in other words, indicates the position of the middle line of the body of the future dog. The substance bounding the groove on each side next rises up into a fold, the rudiment of the side wall of that long cavity, which will eventually lodge the spinal marrow and the brain; and in the floor of this chamber appears a solid cellular cord, the so-called '*notochord.*' One end of the inclosed cavity dilates to form the head (Fig. 14, B), the other remains narrow, and eventually becomes the tail; the side walls of the body are fashioned out of the downward continuation of the walls of the groove; and from them, by and by, grow out little buds which, by degrees, assume the shape of limbs. Watching the fashioning process stage by stage, one is forcibly reminded of the modeller in

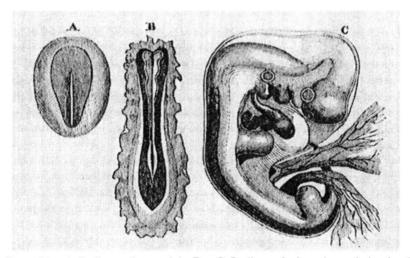

Figure 14. – A. Earliest rudiment of the Dog. B. Rudiment further advanced, showing the foundations of the head, tail, and vertebral column. C. The very young puppy, with attached ends of the yelk-sac and allantois, and invested in the amnion.

clay. Every part, every organ, is at first, as it were, pinched up rudely, and sketched out in the rough; then shaped more accurately; and only, at last, receives the touches which stamp its final character.

Thus, at length, the young puppy assumes such a form as is shewn in Fig. 14, C. In this condition it has a disproportionately large head, as dissimilar to that of a dog as the bud-like limbs are unlike his legs.

The remains of the yelk, which have not yet been applied to the nutrition and growth of the young animal, are contained in a sac attached to the rudimentary intestine, and termed the yelk sac, or 'umbilical vesicle.' Two membranous bags, intended to subserve respectively the protection and nutrition of the young creature, have been developed from the skin and from the under and hinder surface of the body; the former, the so-called 'amnion,' is a sac filled with fluid, which invests the whole body of the embryo, and plays the part of a sort of water bed for it; the other, termed the 'allantois,' grows out, loaded with blood-vessels, from the ventral region, and eventually applying itself to the walls of the cavity, in which the developing organism is contained, enables these vessels to become the channel by which the stream of nutriment, required to supply the wants of the offspring, is furnished to it by the parent.

The structure which is developed by the interlacement of the vessels of the offspring with those of the parent, and by means of which the former is enabled to receive nourishment and to get rid of effete matters, is termed the 'Placenta.'

It would be tedious, and it is unnecessary for my present purpose, to trace the process of development further; suffice it to say, that, by a long and gradual series of changes, the rudiment here depicted and described, becomes a puppy, is born, and then, by still slower and less perceptible steps, passes into the adult Dog.

There is not much apparent resemblance between a barn-door Fowl and the Dog who protects the farm-yard. Nevertheless the student of development finds, not only that the chick commences its existence as an egg, primarily identical, in all essential respects, with that of the Dog, but that the yelk of this egg undergoes division – that the primitive groove arises, and that the contiguous parts of the germ are fashioned, by precisely similar methods, into a young chick, which, at one stage of its existence, is so like the nascent Dog, that ordinary inspection would hardly distinguish the two.

The history of the development of any other vertebrate animal, Lizard, Snake, Frog, or Fish, tells the same story. There is always, to begin with, an egg having the same essential structure as that of the Dog: – the yelk of that egg always undergoes division, or 'segmentation' as it is often called: the ultimate products of that segmentation constitute the building materials for the body of the young animal; and this is built up round a primitive groove, in the floor of which a notochord is developed. Furthermore, there is a period in which the young of all these animals resemble one another, not merely in outward form, but in all essentials of structure, so closely, that the differences between them are inconsiderable, while, in their subsequent course, they diverge more and more widely from one another. And it is a general law, that, the more closely any animals resemble one another in adult structure, the longer and the more intimately do their embryos resemble one another: so that, for example, the embryos of a Snake and of a Lizard remain like one another longer than do those of a Snake and of a Bird; and the embryo of a Dog and of a Cat remain like one another for a far longer period than do those of a Dog and a Bird; or of a Dog and an Opossum; or even than those of a Dog and a Monkey.

Thus the study of development affords a clear test of closeness of structural affinity, and one turns with impatience to inquire what results are yielded by the study of the development of Man. Is he something apart? Does he originate in a totally different way from Dog, Bird, Frog, and Fish, thus justifying those who assert him to have no place in nature and no real affinity with the lower world of animal life? Or does he originate in a similar germ, pass through the same slow and gradually progressive modifications, – depend on the same contrivances for protection and nutrition, and finally enter the world by the help of the same mechanism? The reply is not doubtful for a moment, and has not been doubtful any time these thirty years. Without question, the mode of origin and the early stages of the development of Man are identical with those of the animals immediately below him in the scale: – without a doubt, in these respects, he is far nearer the Apes, than the Apes are to the Dog.

The Human ovum is about $\frac{1}{125}$ of an inch in diameter, and might be described in the same terms as that of the Dog, so that I need only refer to the figure illustrative (15, A) of its structure. It leaves the organ in which it is formed in a similar fashion and enters the organic chamber prepared for its reception in the same way, the conditions of its development being in all respects the same. It has not yet been possible (and only by some rare chance can it ever be possible) to study the human ovum in so early a developmental stage as that of yelk division, but there is every reason to conclude that the changes it undergoes are identical with those exhibited by the ova of other vertebrated animals; for the formative materials of which the rudimentary human body is composed, in the earliest conditions in which it has been observed, are the same as those of other animals. Some of these earliest stages are figured below and, as will be seen, they are strictly comparable to the very early stages of the Dog; the marvellous correspondence between the two which is kept up, even for some time, as development advances, becoming apparent by the simple comparison of the figures with those on page [259].

Indeed, it is very long before the body of the young human being can be readily discriminated from that of the young puppy; but, at a tolerably early period, the two become distinguishable by the different form of their adjuncts, the yelk-sac and the allantois. The former, in the Dog, becomes long and spindle-shaped, while in Man it remains spherical: the latter, in the Dog, attains an extremely large size, and the vascular processes which are developed from it and eventually give rise to the formation of the placenta (taking root, as it

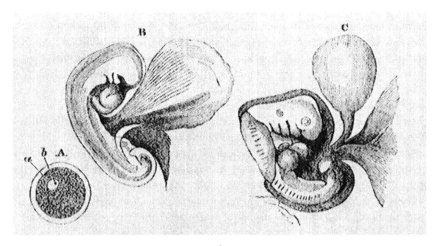

Figure 15 – A. Human ovum (after Kölliker).[8] *a.* germinal vesicle. *b.* germinal spot. B. A very early condition of Man, with yelk-sac, allantois and amnion (original). C. A more advanced stage (after Kölliker), compare fig. 14, C.

were, in the parental organism, so as to draw nourishment therefrom, as the root of a tree extracts it from the soil) are arranged in an encircling zone, while in Man, the allantois remains comparatively small, and its vascular rootlets are eventually restricted to one disk-like spot. Hence, while the placenta of the Dog is like a girdle, that of Man has the cake-like form, indicated by the name of the organ.

But, exactly in those respects in which the developing Man differs from the Dog, he resembles the ape, which, like man, has a spheroidal yelk-sac and a discoidal[9] – sometimes partially-lobed – placenta.

So that it is only quite in the later stages of development that the young human being presents marked differences from the young ape, while the latter departs as much from the dog in its development, as the man does.

Startling as the last assertion may appear to be, it is demonstrably true, and it alone appears to me sufficient to place beyond all doubt the structural unity of man with the rest of the animal world, and more particularly and closely with the apes.

Thus, identical in the physical processes by which he originates – identical in the early stages of his formation – identical in the mode of his nutrition before and after birth, with the animals which lie immediately below him in the scale – Man, if his adult and perfect structure be compared with theirs, exhibits, as might be expected, a marvellous likeness of organization. He resembles them as they resemble one another – he differs from them as they differ from one another. – And, though these differences and resemblances cannot be weighed and measured, their value may be readily estimated; the scale or standard of judgment, touching that value, being afforded and expressed by the system of classification of animals now current among zoologists.

A careful study of the resemblances and differences presented by animals has, in fact, led naturalists to arrange them into groups, or assemblages, all the members of each group presenting a certain amount of definable resemblance, and the number of points of similarity being smaller as the group is larger and *vicê versâ*. Thus, all creatures which agree only in presenting the few distinctive marks of animality form the 'Kingdom' ANIMALIA. The numerous animals which agree only in possessing the special characters of Vertebrates form one 'Sub-kingdom' of this Kingdom. Then the Sub-Kingdom VERTEBRATA is subdivided into the five 'Classes,' Fishes, Amphibians, Reptiles, Birds, and Mammals, and these into smaller groups called 'Orders;' these into 'Families' and 'Genera;' while the last are finally broken up into the smallest assemblages, which are distinguished by the possession of constant, non-sexual, characters. These ultimate groups are Species.

Every year tends to bring about a greater uniformity of opinion throughout the zoological world as to the limits and characters of these groups, great and small. At present, for example, no one has the least doubt regarding the characters of the classes Mammalia, Aves'[10] or Reptilia; nor does the question arise whether any thoroughly well-known animal should be placed in one class or the other. Again, there is a very general agreement respecting the characters and limits of the orders of Mammals, and as to the animals which are structurally necessitated to take a place in one or another order.

No one doubts, for example, that the Sloth and the Anteater, the Kangaroo and the Opossum, the Tiger and the Badger, the Tapir and the Rhinoceros, are respectively members of the same orders. These successive pairs of animals may, and some do, differ from one another immensely, in such matters as the proportions and structure of their limbs; the number of their dorsal and lumbar vertebrae; the adaptation of their frames to climbing, leaping, or running; the number and form of their teeth; and the characters of their skulls and of the contained brain. But, with all these differences, they are so closely connected in all the more important and fundamental characters of their organization, and so distinctly separated by these same characters from other animals, that zoologists find it necessary to group them together as members of one order. And if any new animal were discovered, and were found to present no greater difference from the Kangaroo or from the Opossum, for example, than these animals do from one another, the zoologist would not only be logically compelled to rank it in the same order with these, but he would not think of doing otherwise.

Bearing this obvious course of zoological reasoning in mind, let us endeavour for a moment to disconnect our thinking selves from the mask of humanity; let us imagine ourselves scientific Saturnians,[11] if you will, fairly acquainted with such animals as now inhabit the Earth, and employed in discussing the relations they bear to a new and singular 'erect and featherless biped,' which some enterprising traveller, overcoming the difficulties of space and gravitation, has brought from that distant planet for our inspection, well preserved, may be, in a cask of rum. We should all, at once, agree upon placing him among the mammalian vertebrates; and his lower jaw, his molars, and his brain, would leave no room for doubting this systematic position of the new genus among those mammals, whose young are nourished during gestation by means of a placenta, or what are called the 'placental mammals.'

Further, the most superficial study would at once convince us that, among the orders of placental mammals, neither the Whales, nor the hoofed creatures, nor the Sloths and Anteaters, nor the carnivorous Cats, Dogs, and Bears, still less the Rodent Rats and Rabbits, or the Insectivorous Moles and Hedgehogs, or the Bats, could claim our '*Homo*' as one of themselves.

There would remain then, but one order for comparison, that of the Apes (using that word in its broadest sense), and the question for discussion would narrow itself to this – is Man so different from any of these Apes that he must form an order by himself? Or does he differ less from them than they differ from one another, and hence must take his place in the same order with them?

Being happily free from all real, or imaginary, personal interest in the results of the inquiry thus set afoot, we should proceed to weigh the arguments on one side and on the other, with as much judicial calmness as if the question related to a new Opossum. We should endeavour to ascertain, without seeking either to magnify or diminish them, all the characters by which our new Mammal differed from the Apes; and if we found that these were of less structural value, than those which distinguish certain members of the Ape order from others univer- sally admitted to be of the same order, we should undoubtedly place the newly discovered tellurian[12] genus with them.

I now proceed to detail the facts which seem to me to leave us no choice but to adopt the last mentioned course.

It is quite certain that the Ape which most nearly approaches man, in the totality of its organization, is either the Chimpanzee or the Gorilla; and as it makes no practical difference, for the purposes of my present argument, which is selected for comparison, on the one hand, with Man, and on the other hand, with the rest of the Primates,[b] I shall select the latter (so far as its organization is known) – as a brute now so celebrated in prose and verse, that all must have heard of him, and have formed some conception of his appearance. I shall take up as many of the most important points of difference between man and this remarkable creature, as the space at my disposal will allow me to discuss, and the necessities of the argument demand; and I shall inquire into the value and magnitude of these differences, when placed side by side with those which sepa- rate the Gorilla from other animals of the same order.

---

b   We are not at present thoroughly acquainted with the brain of the Gorilla, and therefore, in discussing cerebral characters, I shall take that of the Chimpanzee as my highest term among the Apes.

In the general proportions of the body and limbs there is a remarkable difference between the Gorilla and Man, which at once strikes the eye. The Gorilla's
brain-case is smaller, its trunk larger, its lower limbs shorter, its upper limbs
longer in proportion than those of Man.

I find that the vertebral column of a full grown Gorilla, in the Museum of the
Royal College of Surgeons, measures 27 inches along its anterior curvature, from
the upper edge of the atlas, or first vertebra of the neck, to the lower extremity
of the sacrum; that the arm, without the hand is 31½ inches long; that the leg,
without the foot, is 26½ inches long; that the hand is 9¾ inches long; the foot
11¼ inches long.

In other words, taking the length of the spinal column as 100, the arm equals
115, the leg 96, the hand 36, and the foot 41.

In the skeleton of a male Bosjesman,[13] in the same collection, the proportions,
by the same measurement, to the spinal column, taken as 100, are – the arm 78,
the leg 110, the hand 26, and the foot 32. In a woman of the same race the arm is
83, and the leg 120, the hand and foot remaining the same. In a European
skeleton I find the arm to be 80, the leg 117, the hand 26, and the foot 35.

Thus the leg is not so different as it looks at first sight, in its proportion to the
spine in the Gorilla and in the Man – being very slightly shorter than the spine
in the former, and between ⅒ and ⅕ longer than the spine in the latter. The foot
is longer and the hand much longer in the Gorilla; but the great difference is
caused by the arms, which are very much longer than the spine in the Gorilla,
very much shorter than the spine in the Man.

The question now arises how are the other Apes related to the Gorilla in
these respects – taking the length of the spine, measured in the same way, at 100.
In an adult Chimpanzee, the arm is only 96, the leg 90, the hand 43, the foot 39
– so that the hand and the leg depart more from the human proportion and the
arm less, while the foot is about the same as in the Gorilla.

In the Orang, the arms are very much longer than in the Gorilla (122), while
the legs are shorter (88); the foot is longer than the hand (52 and 48), and both
are much longer in proportion to the spine.

In the other man-like Apes again, the Gibbons, these proportions are still
further altered; the length of the arms being to that of the spinal column as 19
to 11; while the legs are also a third longer than the spinal column, so as to be
longer than in Man, instead of shorter. The hand is half as long as the spinal
column, and the foot, shorter than the hand, is about ⁵⁄₁₁ths of the length of the
spinal column.

Thus *Hylobates*[14] is as much longer in the arms than the Gorilla, as the Gorilla
is longer in the arms than Man; while, on the other hand, it is as much longer in
the legs than the Man, as the Man is longer in the legs than the Gorilla, so that it
contains within itself the extremest deviations from the average length of both
pairs of limbs (see the Frontispiece).

The Mandrill[15] presents a middle condition, the arms and legs being nearly
equal in length, and both being shorter than the spinal column; while hand

and foot have nearly the same proportions to one another and to the spine, as in Man.

In the Spider monkey (*Ateles*) the leg is longer than the spine, and the arm than the leg; and, finally, in that remarkable Lemurine form, the Indri,[16] (*Lichanotus*) the leg is about as long as the spinal column, while the arm is not more than ¹¹/₁₈ of its length; the hand having rather less and the foot rather more, than one third the length of the spinal column.

These examples might be greatly multiplied, but they suffice to show that, in whatever proportion of its limbs the Gorilla differs from Man, the other Apes depart still more widely from the Gorilla, and that, consequently, such differences of proportion can have no ordinal value. [ ... ][17]

But in enunciating this important truth I must guard myself against a form of misunderstanding, which is very prevalent. I find, in fact, that those who endeavour to teach what nature so clearly shows us in this matter, are liable to have their opinions misrepresented and their phraseology garbled, until they seem to say that the structural differences between man and even the highest apes are small and insignificant. Let me take this opportunity then of distinctly asserting, on the contrary, that they are great and significant; that every bone of a Gorilla bears marks by which it might be distinguished from the corresponding bone of a Man; and that, in the present creation, at any rate, no intermediate link bridges over the gap between *Homo* and *Troglodytes*.[18]

It would be no less wrong than absurd to deny the existence of this chasm; but it is at least equally wrong and absurd to exaggerate its magnitude, and, resting on the admitted fact of its existence, to refuse to inquire whether it is wide or narrow. Remember, if you will, that there is no existing link between Man and the Gorilla, but do not forget that there is a no less sharp line of demarcation, a no less complete absence of any transitional form, between the Gorilla and the Orang, or the Orang and the Gibbon. I say, not less sharp, though it is somewhat narrower. The structural differences between Man and the Man-like apes certainly justify our regarding him as constituting a family apart from them; though, inasmuch as he differs less from them than they do from other families of the same order, there can be no justification for placing him in a distinct order.

And thus the sagacious foresight of the great lawgiver of systematic zoology, Linnaeus,[19] becomes justified, and a century of anatomical research brings us back to his conclusion, that man is a member of the same order (for which the Linnean term PRIMATES ought to be retained) as the Apes and Lemurs. This order is now divisible into seven families, of about equal systematic value: the first, the ANTHROPINI, contains Man alone; the second, the CATARHINI, embraces the old world apes; the third, the PLATYRHINI, all new world apes, except the Marmosets; the fourth, the ARCTOPITHECINI, contains the Marmosets; the fifth, the LEMURINI, the Lemurs – from which *Cheiromys* should probably be excluded to form a sixth distinct family, the CHEIROMYINI; while the seventh, the GALEOPITHECINI, contains only the flying Lemur *Galeopithecus*, –

strange form which almost touches on the Bats, as the *Cheiromys* puts on a Rodent clothing, and the Lemurs simulate Insectivora.

Perhaps no order of mammals presents us with so extraordinary a series of gradations as this – leading us insensibly from the crown and summit of the animal creation down to creatures, from which there is but a step, as it seems, to the lowest, smallest, and least intelligent of the placental Mammalia. It is as if nature herself had foreseen the arrogance of man, and with Roman severity had provided that his intellect, by its very triumphs, should call into prominence the slaves, admonishing the conqueror that he is but dust.[20]

These are the chief facts, this the immediate conclusion from them to which I adverted in the commencement of this Essay. The facts, I believe, cannot be disputed; and if so, the conclusion appears to me to be inevitable.

But if Man be separated by no greater structural barrier from the brutes than they are from one another – then it seems to follow that if any process of physical causation can be discovered by which the genera and families of ordinary animals have been produced, that process of causation is amply sufficient to account for the origin of Man. In other words, if it could be shown that the Marmosets, for example, have arisen by gradual modification of the ordinary Platyrhini,[21] or that both Marmosets and Platyrhini are modified ramifications of a primitive stock – then, there would be no rational ground for doubting that man might have originated, in the one case, by the gradual modification of a man-like ape; or, in the other case, as a ramification of the same primitive stock as those apes.

At the present moment, but one such process of physical causation has any evidence in its favour; or, in other words, there is but one hypothesis regarding the origin of species of animals in general which has any scientific existence – that propounded by Mr Darwin. For Lamarck,[22] sagacious as many of his views were, mingled them with so much that was crude and even absurd, as to neutralize the benefit which his originality might have effected, had he been a more sober and cautious thinker; and though I have heard of the announcement of a formula touching 'the ordained continuous becoming of organic forms,'[23] it is obvious that it is the first duty of a hypothesis to be intelligible, and that a qua-quâ-versal proposition of this kind, which may be read backwards, or forwards, or sideways, with exactly the same amount of signification, does not really exist, though it may seem to do so.

At the present moment, therefore, the question of the relation of man to the lower animals resolves itself, in the end, into the larger question of the tenability or untenability of Mr Darwin's views. But here we enter upon difficult ground, and it behoves us to define our exact position with the greatest care.

It cannot be doubted, I think, that Mr Darwin has satisfactorily proved that what he terms selection, or selective modification, must occur, and does occur, in nature; and he has also proved to superfluity that such selection is competent to produce forms as distinct, structurally, as some genera even are. If the animated world presented us with none but structural differences, I should have no hesitation in saying that Mr Darwin had demonstrated the existence of a true physical cause, amply competent to account for the origin of living species, and of man among the rest.

But, in addition to their structural distinctions, the species of animals and plants, or at least a great number of them, exhibit physiological characters – what are known as distinct species, structurally, being for the most part either altogether incompetent to breed one with another; or if they breed, the resulting mule, or hybrid, is unable to perpetuate its race with another hybrid of the same kind.

A true physical cause is, however, admitted to be such only on one condition – that it shall account for all the phenomena which come within the range of its operation. If it is inconsistent with any one phenomenon, it must be rejected; if it fails to explain any one phenomenon, it is so far weak, so far to be suspected; though it may have a perfect right to claim provisional acceptance.

Now, Mr Darwin's hypothesis is not, so far as I am aware, inconsistent with any known biological fact; on the contrary, if admitted, the facts of Development, of Comparative Anatomy, of Geographical Distribution, and of Palaeontology, become connected together, and exhibit a meaning such as they never possessed before; and I, for one, am fully convinced, that if not precisely true, that hypothesis is as near an approximation to the truth as, for example, the Copernican hypothesis[24] was to the true theory of the planetary motions.

But, for all this, our acceptance of the Darwinian hypothesis must be provisional so long as one link in the chain of evidence is wanting; and so long as all the animals and plants certainly produced by selective breeding from a common stock are fertile, and their progeny are fertile with one another, that link will be wanting. For, so long, selective breeding will not be proved to be competent to do all that is required of it to produce natural species.

I have put this conclusion as strongly as possible before the reader, because the last position in which I wish to find myself is that of an advocate for Mr Darwin's, or any other views – if by an advocate is meant one whose business it is to smooth over real difficulties, and to persuade where he cannot convince.

In justice to Mr Darwin, however, it must be admitted that the conditions of fertility and sterility are very ill understood, and that every day's advance in knowledge leads us to regard the hiatus in his evidence as of less and less importance, when set against the multitude of facts which harmonize with, or receive an explanation from, his doctrines.

I adopt Mr Darwin's hypothesis, therefore, subject to the production of proof that physiological species may be produced by selective breeding; just as a physical philosopher may accept the undulatory theory of light, subject to the proof of the existence of the hypothetical ether;[25] or as the chemist adopts the atomic theory,[26] subject to the proof of the existence of atoms; and for exactly the same reasons, namely, that it has an immense amount of primâ facie probability; that it is the only means at present within reach of reducing the chaos of observed facts to order; and lastly, that it is the most powerful instrument of investigation which had been presented to naturalists since the invention of the natural system of classification, and the commencement of the systematic study of embryology.[27]

But even leaving Mr Darwin's views aside, the whole analogy of natural operations furnishes so complete and crushing an argument against the intervention of any but what are termed secondary causes,[28] in the production of all the phenomena of the universe; that, in view of the intimate relations between Man and the rest of the living world; and between the forces exerted by the latter and all other forces, I can see no excuse for doubting that all are co-ordinated terms of Nature's great progression, from the formless to the formed – from the inorganic to the organic – from blind force to conscious intellect and will.

Science has fulfilled her function when she has ascertained and enunciated truth; and were these pages addressed to men of science only, I should now close this essay, knowing that my colleagues have learned to respect nothing but evidence, and to believe that their highest duty lies in submitting to it, however it may jar against their inclinations.

But desiring, as I do, to reach the wider circle of the intelligent public, it would be unworthy cowardice were I to ignore the repugnance with which the majority of my readers are likely to meet the conclusions to which the most careful and conscientious study I have been able to give to this matter, has led me.

On all sides I shall hear the cry – 'We are men and women, not a mere better sort of apes, a little longer in the leg, more compact in the foot, and bigger in brain than your brutal Chimpanzees and Gorillas. The power of knowledge – the conscience of good and evil – the pitiful tenderness of human affections, raise us out of all real fellowship with the brutes, however closely they may seem to approximate us.'

To this I can only reply that the exclamation would be most just and would have my own entire sympathy, if it were only relevant. But, it is not I who seek to base Man's dignity upon his great toe, or insinuate that we are lost if an Ape has a hippocampus minor.[29] On the contrary, I have done my best to sweep away this vanity. I have endeavoured to show that no absolute structural line of demarcation, wider than that between the animals which immediately succeed us in the scale, can be drawn between the animal world and ourselves; and I may add the expression of my belief that the attempt to draw a psychical distinction is equally futile, and that even the highest faculties of feeling and intellect begin to germinate in lower forms of life.[c] At the same time, no one is more strongly convinced

---

c   It is so rare a pleasure for me to find Professor Owen's opinions in entire accordance with my own, that I cannot forbear from quoting a paragraph which appeared in his Essay 'On the Characters, &c. of the Class Mammalia,' in the 'Journal of the Proceedings of the Linnean Society of London' for 1857, but is unaccountably omitted in the 'Reade Lecture' delivered

[continued]

than I am of the vastness of the gulf between civilized man and the brutes; or is more certain that whether *from* them or not, he is assuredly not *of* them. No one is less disposed to think lightly of the present dignity, or despairingly of the future hopes, of the only consciously intelligent denizen of this world.

We are indeed told by those who assume authority in these matters, that the two sets of opinions are incompatible, and that the belief in the unity of origin of man and brutes involves the brutalization and degradation of the former. But is this really so? Could not a sensible child confute, by obvious arguments, the shallow rhetoricians who would force this conclusion upon us? Is it, indeed, true, that the Poet, or the Philosopher, or the Artist whose genius is the glory of his age, is degraded from his high estate by the undoubted historical probability, not to say certainty, that he is the direct descendant of some naked and bestial savage, whose intelligence was just sufficient to make him a little more cunning that the Fox, and by so much more dangerous than the Tiger? Or is he bound to howl and grovel on all fours because of the wholly unquestionable fact, that he was once an egg, which no ordinary power of discrimination could distinguish from that of a Dog? Or is the philanthropist or the saint to give up his endeavours to lead a noble life, because the simplest study of man's nature reveals, at its foundations, all the selfish passions and fierce appetites of the merest quadruped? Is mother-love vile because a hen shows it, or fidelity base because dogs possess it?

The common sense of the mass of mankind will answer these questions without a moment's hesitation. Healthy humanity, finding itself hard pressed to escape from real sin and degradation, will leave the brooding over speculative pollution to the cynics and the 'righteous overmuch' who, disagreeing in everything else, unite in blind insensibility to the nobleness of the visible world, and in inability to appreciate the grandeur of the place Man occupies therein.

Nay more, thoughtful men, once escaped from the blinding influences of

---

before the University of Cambridge two years later, which is otherwise nearly a reprint of the paper in question. Prof. Owen writes:

> 'Not being able to appreciate or conceive of the distinction between the psychical phenomena of a Chimpanzee and of a Boschisman or of an Aztec, with arrested brain growth, as being of a nature so essential as to preclude a comparison between them, or as being other than a difference of degree, I cannot shut my eyes to the significance of that all-pervading similitude of structure – every tooth, every bone, strictly homologous – which makes the determination of the difference between *Homo* and *Pithecus* the anatomist's difficulty.'

Surely it is a little singular, that the 'anatomist' who finds it 'difficult' to 'determine the difference' between *Homo* and *Pithecus*, should yet range them on anatomical grounds, in distinct sub-classes! [For Owen, see note 29, page 580; the paper Huxley refers to was written in 1857 but was not published in the *Journal of the Proceedings of the Linnean Society* until 1858. The term 'pithecus' refers to the higher or anthropoid apes.]

traditional prejudice, will find in the lowly stock whence man has sprung, the best evidence of the splendour of his capacities; and will discern in his long progress through the Past, a reasonable ground of faith in his attainment of a nobler Future.

They will remember that in comparing civilized man with the animal world, one is as the Alpine traveller, who sees the mountains soaring into the sky and can hardly discern where the deep shadowed crags and roseate peaks end, and where the clouds of heaven begin. Surely the awe-struck voyager may be excused if, at first, he refuses to believe the geologist, who tells him that these glorious masses are, after all, the hardened mud of primeval seas, or the cooled slag of subterranean furnaces – of one substance with the dullest clay, but raised by inward forces to that place of proud and seemingly inaccessible glory.

But the geologist is right; and due reflection on his teachings, instead of diminishing our reverence and our wonder, adds all the force of intellectual sublimity, to the mere aesthetic intuition of the uninstructed beholder.

And after passion and prejudice have died away, the same result will attend the teachings of the naturalist respecting that great Alps and Andes of the living world – Man. Our reverence for the nobility of manhood will not be lessened by the knowledge, that Man is, in substance and in structure, one with the brutes; for he alone possesses the marvellous endowment of intelligible and rational speech, whereby, in the secular period of his existence, he has slowly accumulated and organized the experience which is almost wholly lost with the cessation of every individual life in other animals; so that now he stands raised upon it as on a mountain top, far above the level of his humble fellows, and transfigured from his grosser nature by reflecting, here and there, a ray from the infinite source of truth.

# SAMUEL WILBERFORCE, 'ART VII. – *ON THE ORIGIN OF SPECIES* . . . ' (1860)

Samuel Wilberforce (1805–73), third son of the anti-slavery philan-thropist, William Wilberforce, was the very embodiment of Victorian orthodoxy. He played a central role in two of the most famous intellec-tual controversies of his time: the 'evolutionary' debate at the British Association for the Advancement of Science (BAAS) and the theological arguments following the publication of *Essays and Reviews* – both of which took place in 1860. Wilberforce was ordained as an Anglican priest in 1829, but it was not until the early 1840s, during his ministry at Alverstoke in Hampshire, that he came to public attention. It was at this time that Wilberforce became involved with the Oxford Movement – an attempt led by Edward Pusey, John Keble and John Henry Newman to reintroduce seventeenth-century High Church ideals into the Church of England. Although Wilberforce was not a wholehearted supporter of the Movement, he nevertheless exerted his influence to prevent its disinte-gration when Newman converted to Roman Catholicism. In so doing, Wilberforce marked himself out as a conservative in religious matters – a position which was reinforced by his subsequent attacks on liberal bishops, Dissenters and biblical scholars. In 1843 Wilberforce became sub-almoner to the Queen, and from 1847–69 he served as lord high almoner. In 1845 Wilberforce was promoted to Dean of Westminster. In a matter of months he was offered the Bishopric of Oxford where he remained for the next twenty-five years, founding in 1854 one of the first Anglican theological colleges at Cuddesdon. It was also at Oxford that Wilberforce was drawn into debate with the Darwinists, and although there is no reliable record of the events at the BAAS meeting in 1860, it is generally agreed that in the exchange with T. H. Huxley, Wilberforce was the loser. Wilberforce published the substance of his attack in a long review of *Origin of Species* in the Tory *Quarterly Review* – a period-ical for which he wrote regularly. He also used its pages to condemn the authors of *Essays and Reviews*, arguing that their attacks on the doctrines of atonement, of original sin and of justification by faith were inconsistent with clergymen of the Established Church. Wilberforce's essays for the *Quarterly* are among his best remembered work; they were collected in two volumes in 1874. He also published numerous speeches, addresses, sermons and prayer-books. In 1869 he was promoted to Bishop of Winchester. One of his last projects before he died was the modernisation of the King James Bible – a project which resulted in the publication of the *Revised Version* (1881–95).

From [Samuel Wilberforce] 'Art VII. – *On the Origin of Species, by means of Natural Selection; or the Preservation of Favoured Races in the Struggle for Life*. By Charles Darwin, M.A., F.R.S. London, 1860.', *Quarterly Review*, CVIII (July 1860), pp. 225–64[1]

[ . . . ] Few things have more deeply injured the cause of religion than the busy fussy energy with which men, narrow and feeble alike in faith and in science, have bustled forth to reconcile all new discoveries in physics with the word of inspiration. For it continually happens that some larger collection of facts, or some wider view of the phenomena of nature, alter the whole philosophic scheme; whilst Revelation has been committed to declare an absolute agreement with what turns out after all to have been a misconception or an error. We cannot, therefore, consent to test the truth of natural science by the Word of Revelation. But this does not make it the less important to point out on scientific grounds scientific errors, when those errors tend to limit God's glory in creation, or to gainsay the revealed relations of that creation to Himself. To both these classes of error, though, we doubt not, quite unintentionally on his part, we think that Mr Darwin's speculations directly tend.

Mr Darwin writes as a Christian, and we doubt not that he is one. We do not for a moment believe him to be one of those who retain in some corner of their hearts a secret unbelief which they dare not vent; and we therefore pray him to consider well the grounds on which we brand his speculations with the charge of such a tendency. First, then, he not obscurely declares that he applies his scheme of the action of the principle of natural selection to MAN himself, as well as to the animals around him. Now, we must say at once, and openly, that such a notion is absolutely incompatible not only with single expressions in the word of God on that subject of natural science with which it is not immediately concerned, but, which in our judgment is of far more importance, with the whole representation of that moral and spiritual condition of man which is its proper subject-matter. Man's derived supremacy over the earth; man's power of articulate speech; man's gift of reason; man's free-will and responsibility; man's fall and man's redemption; the incarnation of the Eternal Son; the indwelling of the Eternal Spirit, – all are equally and utterly irreconcilable with the degrading notion of the brute origin of him who was created in the image of God, and redeemed by the Eternal Son assuming to himself his nature. Equally inconsistent, too, not with any passing expressions, but with the whole scheme of God's dealings with man as recorded in His word, is Mr Darwin's daring notion of man's further development into some unknown extent of powers, and shape, and size, through natural selection acting through that long vista of ages which he casts mistily over the earth upon the most favoured individuals of his species. We care not in these pages to push the argument further. We have done enough for our purpose in thus succinctly intimating its course. If any of our readers doubt what must be the result of such speculations carried to their logical and legitimate conclusion, let them turn to the pages of Oken,[2] and see for themselves the end of that path the opening of which is decked out in these pages with the bright hues and seemingly innocent deductions of the transmutation-theory.

Nor can we doubt, secondly, that this view, which thus contradicts the revealed relation of creation to its Creator, is equally inconsistent with the fulness of His glory. It is, in truth, an ingenious theory for diffusing throughout creation the working and so the personality of the Creator. And thus, however unconsciously to him who holds them, such views really tend inevitably to banish from the mind most of the peculiar attributes of the Almighty.

How, asks Mr Darwin, can we possibly account for the manifest plan, order, and arrangement which pervade creation, except we allow to it this self-developing power through modified descent?

> 'As Milne-Edwards[3] has well expressed it, Nature is prodigal in variety, but niggard in innovation. Why, on the theory of creation, should this be so? Why should all the parts and organs of many independent beings, each supposed to have been separately created for its proper place in nature, be so commonly linked together by graduated steps? Why should not Nature have taken a leap from structure to structure?' – p. 194.[4]

And again: –

> 'It is a truly wonderful fact – the wonder of which we are apt to overlook from familiarity – that all animals and plants throughout all time and space should be related to each other in group subordinate to group, in the manner which we everywhere behold, namely, varieties of the same species most closely related together, species of the same genus less closely and unequally related together, forming sections and sub-genera, species of distinct genera much less closely related, and genera related in different degrees, forming sub-families, families, orders, sub-classes, and classes.' – pp. 128–9.

How can we account for all this? By the simplest and yet the most comprehensive answer. By declaring the stupendous fact that all creation is the transcript in matter of ideas eternally existing in the mind of the Most High – that order in the utmost perfectness of its relation pervades His works, because it exists as in its centre and highest fountain-head in Him the Lord of all. Here is the true account of the fact which has so utterly misled shallow observers, that Man himself, the Prince and Head of this creation, passes in the earlier stages of his being through phases of existence closely analogous, so far as his earthly tabernacle is concerned, to those in which the lower animals ever remain. At that point of being the development of the protozoa[5] is arrested. Through it the embryo of their chief passes to the perfection of his earthly frame. But the types of those lower forms of being must be found in the animals which never advance beyond them – not in man for whom they are but the foundation for an after-development; whilst he too, Creation's crown and perfection, thus bears witness in his own frame to the law of order which pervades the universe.

In like manner could we answer every other question as to which Mr Darwin thinks all oracles are dumb unless they speak his speculation. He is, for instance, more than once troubled by what he considers imperfections in Nature's work. 'If,' he says, 'our reason leads us to admire with enthusiasm a multitude of inimitable contrivances in Nature, this same reason tells us that some other contrivances are less perfect.'

> 'Nor ought we to marvel if all the contrivances in nature be not, as far as we can judge, absolutely perfect; and if some of them be abhorrent to our idea of fitness. We need not marvel at the sting of the bee causing the bee's own death; at drones being produced in such vast numbers for one single act, with the great majority slaughtered by their sterile sisters; at the astonishing waste of pollen by our fir-trees; at the instinctive hatred of the queen-bee for her own fertile daughters; at ichneumonidae[6] feeding with the live bodies of caterpillars; and at other such cases. The wonder indeed is, on the theory of natural selection, that more cases of the want of absolute perfection have not been observed.' – p. 472.

We think that the real temper of this whole speculation as to nature itself may be read in these few lines. It is a dishonouring view of nature.

That reverence for the work of God's hands with which a true belief in the All-wise Worker fills the believer's heart is at the root of all great physical discovery; it is the basis of philosophy. He who would see the venerable features of Nature must not seek with the rudeness of a licensed roysterer violently to unmask her countenance; but must wait as a learner for her willing unveiling. There was more of the true temper of philosophy in the poetic fiction of the Pan-ic shriek,[7] than in the aetheistic speculations of Lucretius.[8] But this temper must beset those who do in effect banish God from nature. And so Mr Darwin not only finds in it these bungling contrivances which his own greater skill could amend, but he stands aghast before its mightier phenomena. The presence of death and famine seems to him inconceivable on the ordinary idea of creation; and he looks almost aghast at them until reconciled to their presence by his own theory that 'a ratio of increase so high as to lead to a struggle for life, and as a consequence to natural selection entailing divergence of character and the extinction of less improved forms, is decidedly followed by the most exalted object which we are capable of conceiving, namely, the production of the higher animals' (p. 490). But we can give him a simpler solution still for the presence of these strange forms of imperfection and suffering amongst the works of God.

We can tell him of the strong shudder which ran through all this world when its head and ruler fell. When he asks concerning the infinite variety of these multi-plied works which are set in such an orderly unity, and run up into man as their reasonable head, we can tell him of the exuberance of God's goodness and remind him of the deep philosophy which lies in those simple words – 'All thy works praise Thee, O God, and thy saints give thanks unto Thee.' For it is one office of redeemed man to collect the inarticulate praises of the material creation, and pay them with conscious homage into the treasury of the supreme Lord. [ . . . ][9]

It is by our deep conviction of the truth and importance of this view for the scientific mind of England that we have been led to treat at so much length Mr Darwin's speculation. The contrast between the sober, patient, philosophical courage of our home philosophy, and the writings of Lamarck[10] and his followers and predecessors, of MM Demaillet, Bory de Saint Vincent, Virey,[11] and Oken,[a] is indeed most wonderful; and it is greatly owing to the noble tone which has been given by those great men whose words we have quoted[12] to the school of British science. That Mr Darwin should have wandered from this broad highway of nature's works into the jungle of fanciful assumption is no small evil. We trust that he is mistaken in believing that he may count Sir C. Lyell[13] as one of his converts. We know indeed the strength of the temptations which he can bring to bear upon his geological brother. The Lyellian hypothesis, itself not free from some of Mr Darwin's faults, stands eminently in need for its own support of some such new scheme of physical life as that propounded here. Yet no man has been more distinct and more logical in the denial of the trans-mutation of species than Sir C. Lyell, and that not in the infancy of his scientific life, but in its full vigour and maturity.[14]

Sir C. Lyell devotes the 33rd to the 36th chapter of his 'Principles of Geology' to an examination of this question. He gives a clear account of the mode in which Lamarck supported his belief of the transmutation of species; he 'interrupts the author's argument to observe that no positive fact is cited to exemplify the substitution of some *entirely new* sense, faculty, or organ – because no examples were to be found; and remarks that when Lamarck talks' of 'the effects of internal sentiment' &c., as causes whereby animals and plants may

a    It may be worth while to exhibit to our readers a few of Dr Oken's postulates or arguments as specimens of his views: -

      'I wrote the first edition of 1810 in a kind of inspiration.
      '4. Spirit is the motion of mathematical ideas.
      '10. Physio-philosophy has to . . . portray the first period of the world's development from nothing; how the elements and heavenly bodies originated; in what method by self-evolution into higher and manifold forms they separated into minerals, became finally organic, and in man attained self-consciousness.
      '42. The mathematical monad is eternal.
      '43. The eternal is one and the same with the zero of mathematics.'

    [The reference appears to be to an English translation of Oken's work by Alfred Tuck, entitled *Elements of physio-philosophy* (1854).]

acquire *new organs*, he substitutes names for things, and with a disregard to the strict rules of induction resorts to fictions.

He shows the fallacy of Lamarck's reasoning, and by anticipation confutes the whole theory of Mr Darwin, when gathering clearly up into a few heads the recapitulation of the whole argument in favour of the reality of species in nature. He urges: -

1.   That there is a capacity in all species to accommodate themselves to a certain extent to a change of external circumstances.
4.   The entire variation from the original type . . . may usually be effected in a brief period of time, after which no further deviation can be obtained.
5.   The intermixing [of] distinct species is guarded against by the sterility of the mule offspring.
6.   It appears that species have a real existence in nature, and that each was endowed at the time of its creation with the attributes and organization by which it is now distinguished.[b]

We trust that Sir C. Lyell abides still by these truly philosophical principles; and that with his help and with that of his brethren this flimsy speculation may be as completely put down as was what in spite of all denials we must venture to call its twin though less-instructed brother, the 'Vestiges of Creation.'[15] In so doing they will assuredly provide for the strength and continually growing progress of British science.

Indeed, not only do all laws for the study of nature vanish when the great principle of order pervading and regulating all her processes is given up, but all that imparts the deepest interest in the investigation of her wonders will have departed too. Under such influences a man soon goes back to the marvelling stare of childhood at the centaurs and hippogriffs[16] of fancy, or if he is of a philosophic turn, he comes like Oken to write a scheme of creation under 'a sort of inspiration;' but it is the frenzied inspiration of the inhaler of mephitic gas.[17] The whole world of nature is laid for such a man under a fantastic law of glamour, and he becomes capable of believing anything: to him it is just as prob-able that Dr Livingstone[18] will find the next tribe of negroes with their heads growing under their arms as fixed on the summit of the cervical vertebrae; and he is able, with a continually growing neglect of all the facts around him, with equal confidence and equal delusion, to look back to any past and to look on to any future.

b    'Principles of Geology,' edit. 1853.

# HERBERT SPENCER, 'THE STUDY OF SOCIOLOGY. XIV. – PREPARATION IN BIOLOGY' (1873)

*From* Herbert Spencer, 'The Study of Sociology. XIV. – Preparation in Biology', *Contemporary Review*, XXII (August 1873), pp. 325–46[1]

*The Study of Sociology. XIV. – Preparation in Biology.*[2]

[ . . . ] Turn we now from the indirect influence which Biology exerts on Sociology, by supplying it with rational conceptions of social development and organization, to the direct influence it exerts by furnishing an adequate theory of the social unit – Man. For while Biology is mediately connected with Sociology by a certain parallelism between the groups of phenomena they deal with, it is immediately connected with Sociology by having within its limits this creature whose properties originate social evolution. The human being is at once the terminal problem of Biology and the initial factor of Sociology.

If Man were uniform and unchangeable, so that those attributes of him which lead to social phenomena could be learnt and dealt with as constant, it would not much concern the sociologist to make himself master of other biological truths than those cardinal ones above dwelt upon. But since, in common with every other creature, Man is modifiable – since his modifications, like those of every other creature, are ultimately determined by surrounding conditions – and since surrounding conditions are in part constituted by social arrangements; it becomes requisite that the sociologist should acquaint himself with the laws of modification to which organized beings in general conform. Unless he does this he must continually err, both in thought and deed. As thinker, he will fail to understand the unceasing action and reaction of institutions and character, each slowly modifying the other through successive generations. As actor, his further-ance of this or that public policy, being unguided by a true theory of the effects wrought on citizens, will probably be mischievous rather than beneficial; since there are more ways of going wrong than of going right. How needful is enlight-enment on this point, will be seen on remembering that scarcely anywhere is attention given to the modifications which a new agency, political or other, will produce in men's natures. Immediate influence on actions is alone contemplated; and the immeasurably more important influence on the bodies and minds of future generations, is wholly ignored.

Yet the biological truths which should check this random political speculation and rash political action, are conspicuous; and might, one would have thought, have been recognized by everyone, even without special preparation in Biology. That faculties and powers of all orders, while they grow by exercise dwindle when not used; and that alterations of nature descend to posterity; are facts continually thrust on men's attention, and more or less admitted by all. Though the evidence of heredity, when looked at in detail, seems obscure, because of the multitudinous differences of parents and of ancestors, which all take their varying shares in each new product; yet, when looked at in the mass, the evidence is overwhelming. Not to dwell on the countless proofs furnished by domesticated animals of many kinds, as modified by breeders, the proofs furnished by the human races themselves are amply sufficient. That each variety of man goes on so reproducing itself that adjacent generations are nearly alike, however appreciable may sometimes be the divergence in a long series of generations, is undeniable. Chinese are recognizable as Chinese in whatever part of the globe we see them; every one assumes a black ancestry for any Negro he meets; and no one doubts that the less-marked racial varieties have great degrees of persistence. On the other hand, it is unquestionable that the likeness which the members of one human stock preserve, generation after generation, where the conditions of life remain constant, give place to unlikenesses that slowly increase in the course of centuries and thousands of years, if members of that stock, spreading into different habitats, fall under different sets of conditions. If we assume the original unity of the human race, we have no alternative but to admit such divergences consequent on such causes; and even if we do not assume this original unity, we have still, among the races classed by the community of their languages as Aryan,[3] abundant proofs that subjection to different modes of life, produces in course of ages permanent bodily and mental differences: the Hindu and the Englishman, the Greek and the Dutchman, have acquired undeniable contrasts of nature, physical and psychical, which can be ascribed to nothing but the continuous effects of circumstances, material, moral, social, on the activities and therefore on the constitution. So that, as above said, one might have expected that biological training would scarcely be needed to impress men with these cardinal truths, all-important as elements in sociological conclusions.

As it is, however, we see that a deliberate study of Biology cannot be dispensed with. It is requisite that these scattered evidences which but few citizens put together and think about, should be set before them in an orderly way; and that they should recognize in them the universal truths which living things at large exhibit. There requires a multiplicity of illustrations, many in their kinds, often repeated and dwelt upon. Only thus can there be produced an adequately-strong conviction that all organic beings are modifiable, that modifications are inheritable, and that therefore the remote issues of any new influence brought to bear on the members of a community must be serious.

To give a more definite and effective shape to this general inference, let me here comment on certain courses pursued by philanthropists and legislators eager for immediate good results, but pursued without regard of biological truths which, if borne in mind, would make them hesitate if not desist.

Every species of creature goes on multiplying till it reaches the limit at which its mortality from all causes balances its fertility. Diminish its mortality by removing or mitigating any one of these causes, and inevitably its numbers increase until mortality and fertility are again in equilibrium. However many injurious influences are taken away, the same thing holds, for the reason that the remaining injurious influences grow more intense. Either the pressure on the means of subsistence becomes greater; or some enemy of the species, multiplying in proportion to the abundance of its prey, becomes more destructive; or some disease, encouraged by greater proximity, becomes more prevalent. This general truth, everywhere exemplified among inferior races of beings, holds of the human race. True, it is in this case variously traversed and obscured. By emigration, the limits against which population continually presses are partially evaded; by improvements in production, they are continually removed further away; and along with increase of knowledge there comes an avoidance of detrimental agencies. Still, these are but qualifications of an inevitable action and reaction.

Let us here glance at the relation between this general truth and the legislative measures adopted to ward off certain causes of death. Every individual eventually dies from inability to withstand some environing action. It may be a mechanical force that cannot be resisted by the strengths of his bodily structures; it may be a deleterious gas which, absorbed into his blood, so deranges the processes throughout his body as finally to overthrow their balance; or it may be, and most frequently is, an absorption of his bodily heat by surrounding things that is too great for his enfeebled functions to meet. In all cases, however, it is one, or some, of the many forces to which he is exposed, and in presence of which his vital activities have to be carried on. He may succumb early or late, according to the goodness of his structure and the incidents of his career. But in the natural working of things, those having imperfect structures succumb before they have offspring: leaving those with fitter structures to produce the next generation. And obviously, the working of this process is such that as many will continue to live and to reproduce as can do so under the conditions then existing: if the assemblage of influences becomes more difficult to withstand, a larger number of the feebler disappear early; if the assemblage of influences is made more favourable by the removal of, or mitigation of, some unfavourable influence, there is an increase in the number of the feebler who survive and leave posterity. Hence two proximate results,[4] conspiring to the same ultimate result. First, population increases at a greater rate than it would otherwise have done: so subjecting all persons to certain other destroying agencies in more-intense forms. Second, by intermarriage of the feebler who now survive, with the stronger who would otherwise have alone survived, the general constitution is brought down to the level of strength required to meet these more-favourable conditions. That is to say, there by and by arises a state of things under which a general decrease in the power of withstanding this mitigated destroying cause, and a general increase in the activity of other destroying causes, consequent on greater numbers, bring mortality and fertility into the same relation as before – there is a somewhat larger number of a somewhat weaker race.

There are further ways in which this process necessarily works a like general effect, however far it is carried. For as fast as more and more detrimental agencies are removed or mitigated, and as fast as there goes on an increasing survival and propagation of those having delicately-balanced constitutions, there arise new destructive agencies. Let the average vitality be diminished by more effectually guarding the weak against adverse conditions, and inevitably there come fresh diseases. A general constitution previously able to bear without derangement certain variations in atmospheric conditions and certain degrees of other unfavourable actions, if lowered in tone, will become subject to new kinds of perturbation and new causes of death. In illustration, I need but refer to the many diseases from which civilized races suffer, but which were not known to the uncivilized. Nor is it only by such new causes of death that the rate of mortality, when decreased in one direction increases in another. The very precautions against death are themselves in some measure new causes of death. Every further appliance for meeting an evil, every additional expenditure of effort, every extra tax to meet the cost of supervision, becomes a fresh obstacle to living. For always in a society where population is pressing on the means of subsistence, and where the efforts required to fulfil the vital needs are so great that they here and there cause premature death, the powers of producers cannot be further strained by calling on them to support a new class of non-producers, without, in some cases, increasing the wear and tear to a fatal extent. And in proportion as this policy is carried further – in proportion as the enfeeblement of constitution is made greater, the required precautions multiplied, and the cost of maintaining these precautions augmented; it must happen that the increasing physiological expenditure thrown on these enfeebled constitutions, must make them succumb so much the earlier: the mortality evaded in one shape must come round in another.

The clearest conception of the state brought about, will be gained by supposing the society thus produced to consist of old people. Age differs from maturity and youth in being less able to withstand influences that tend to derange the functions, as well as less able to bear the efforts needed to get the food, clothing, and shelter, by which resistance to these influences may be carried on; and where no aid is received from the younger, this decreased strength and increased liability to derangement by incident forces, make the life of age difficult and wearisome. Those who, though young, have weak constitutions, are much in the same position: their liabilities to derangement are similarly multiplied, and where they have to support themselves, they are similarly over-taxed by the effort, relatively great to them and made greater by the maintaining of precaution. A society of enfeebled people, then, must lead a life like that led by a society of people who had outlived the vigour of maturity, and yet had none to help them; and their life must also be like in lacking that overflowing energy which, while it makes labours easy, makes enjoyments keen. In proportion as vigour declines, not only do the causes of pain multiply, while the tax on the energies becomes more trying, but the possibilities of pleasure decrease: many delights demanding, or accompanying, exertion are shut out; and others fail to raise the flagging spirits. So that, to sum up, lowering the average type of constitution to a level of strength *below that which meets without difficulty the ordinary strains and perturbations and dangers*, while it fails eventually to diminish the rate of mortality, makes life more a burden and less a gratification.

I am aware that this reasoning may be met by the criticism that, carried out rigorously, it would [have] negative social ameliorations in general. Some, perhaps, will say that even those measures by which order is maintained, might be opposed for the reason that there results from them a kind of men less capable of self-protection that would otherwise exist. And there will doubtless be suggested the corollary that no influences detrimental to health ought to be removed. I am not concerned to meet such criticisms, for the reason that I do not mean the conclusions above indicated to be taken without qualification. It is obvious enough that up to a certain point the removal of destructive causes leaves a balance of benefit. The simple fact that with a largely-augmented population, longevity is greater now that heretofore, goes far towards showing that up to the time lived through by those who die in our day, there had been a decrease of the causes of mortality in some directions, greater than their increase in other directions. Though a considerable drawback may be suspected – though, on observing how few thoroughly-strong people we meet, and how prevalent are chronic ailments notwithstanding the care taken of health, it may be inferred that bodily life now is lower in quality than it was, though greater in quantity; yet there has probably been gained a surplus of advantage. All I wish to show is, that there are limits to the good gained by such a policy. It is supposed in the Legislature, and by the public at large, that if, by measures taken, a certain number of deaths by disease have been prevented, so much pure benefit has been secured. But it is not so. In any case, there is a set-off from the benefit; and if such measures are greatly multiplied, the deductions may eat up the benefit entirely, and leave an injury in its place. Where such measures ought to stop, is a question that may be left open. Here my purpose is simply to point out the way in which a far-reaching biological truth underlies rational conclusions in Sociology; and also to point out that formidable evils may arise from ignoring it.

Other evils, no less serious, are entailed by legislative actions and by actions of individuals, single and combined, which overlook or disregard a kindred biological truth. Besides an habitual neglect of the fact that the quality of a society is physically lowered by the artificial preservation of its feeblest members, there is an habitual neglect of the fact that the quality of a society is lowered morally and intellectually, by the artificial preservation of those who are least able to take care of themselves.

If anyone denies that children bear likeness to their progenitors in character and capacity – if he holds that men whose parents and grandparents were habitual criminals, have tendencies as good as those of men whose parents and grandparents were industrious and upright, he may consistently hold that it matters not from what families in a society the successive generations descend. He may think it just as well if the most active, and capable, and prudent, and conscientious people die without issues; while many children are left by the reckless and dishonest. But whoever does not espouse so insane a proposition, must admit that social arrangements which retard the multiplication of the mentally-best, and facilitate the multiplication of the mentally-worst, must be extremely injurious.

For if the unworthy are helped to increase by shielding them from that mortality which their unworthiness would naturally entail, the effect is to produce, generation after generation, a greater unworthiness. From decreased use of self-conserving faculties already deficient, there must result, in posterity, still smaller amounts of self-conserving faculties. The general law which we traced above in its bodily applications, may be traced here in its mental applications. Removal of certain difficulties and dangers which have to be met by intelligence and activity, is followed by a diminished ability to meet difficulties and dangers. Among children born to the more capable who marry with the less capable, thus artificially preserved, there is not simply a lower average power of self-preservation than would else have existed, but the incapacity reaches in some cases a greater extreme. Smaller difficulties and dangers become fatal in proportion as greater ones are warded off. Nor is this the whole mischief. For such members of a population as do not take care of themselves, but are taken care of by the rest, inevitably bring on the rest extra exertion; either in supplying them with the necessaries of life, or in maintaining over them the required supervision, or in both. That is to say, in addition to self-conservation and the conservation of their own offspring, the best, having to undertake the conservation of the worst, and of their offspring, are subject to an overdraw upon their energies. In some cases this stops them from marrying; in other cases it diminishes the numbers of their children; in other cases it causes inadequate feeding of their children; in other cases it brings their children to orphanhood – in every way tending to arrest the increase of the best, to deteriorate their constitutions, and to pull them down towards the level of the worst.

Fostering the good-for-nothing at the expense of the good, is an extreme cruelty. It is a deliberate storing-up of miseries for future generations. There is no greater curse to posterity than that of bequeathing them an increasing population of imbeciles and idlers and criminals. To aid the bad in multiplying, is, in effect, the same as maliciously providing for our descendants a multitude of enemies. It may be doubted whether the maudlin philanthropy which, looking only at immediate mitigations, persistently ignores remote results, does not inflict a greater total of misery than the extremest selfishness inflicts. Refusing to consider the remote influences of his incontinent generosity, the thoughtless giver stands but a degree above the drunkard who thinks only of to-day's pleasure and ignores to-morrow's pain, or the spendthrift who seeks immediate delights at the cost of ultimate poverty. In one respect, indeed, he is worse; since, while getting the present pleasure produced in giving pleasure, he leaves the future miseries to be borne by others – escaping them himself. And calling for still stronger reprobation is that scattering of money prompted by misinterpretation of the saying that 'charity covers a multitude of sins.' For in the many whom this misinterpretation leads to believe that by large donations they can compound for evil deeds, we may trace an element of positive baseness – an effort to get a good place in another world, no matter at what injury to fellow-creatures.

How far the mentally-superior may, with a balance of benefit to society, shield the mentally-inferior from the evil results of their inferiority, is a question too involved to be here discussed at length. Doubtless it is in the order of things that parental affection, the regard of relatives, and the spontaneous sympathy of friends and even of strangers, should mitigate the pains which incapacity has to bear, and the penalties which unfit impulses bring round. Doubtless, in many cases the reactive influences of this sympathetic care which the better take of the worse, is morally beneficial, and in a degree compensates by good in one direction for evil in another. It may be fully admitted that individual altruism, left to itself, will work advantageously – wherever, at least, it does not go to the extent of helping the unworthy to multiply. But an unquestionable mischief is done by agencies which undertake in a wholesale way the preservation of good-for-nothings: putting a stop to that natural process of elimination by which otherwise society continually purifies itself. For not only by such agencies is this conservation of the worst and destruction of the best carried further than it would else be, but there is scarcely any of that compensating advantage which individual altruism implies. A mechanically-working State-apparatus, distributing money drawn from grumbling ratepayers, produces little or no moralizing effect on the capables to make up for multiplication of the incapables. Here, however, it is needless to dwell on the perplexing questions hence arising. My purpose is simply to show that a rational policy must recognize certain general truths of Biology; and to insist that only when study of these general truths, as illustrated throughout the living world, has woven them into the conceptions of things, is there gained an adequately-strong conviction that enormous mischief must result from ignoring them.[a]

Biological truths and their corollaries, presented under these special forms as bases for sociological conclusions, are introductory to a more general biological truth including them – a general biological truth which underlies all rational legislation. I refer to the truth that every species of organism, including the human, is always adapting itself, both directly and indirectly, to its conditions of existence.

The actions which have produced every variety of man, – the actions which have established in the Negro and the Hindu constitutions that thrive in climates fatal to Europeans, and in the Fuegian[5] a constitution enabling him to bear

---

a    Probably most readers will conclude that in this, and in the preceding Section, I am simply carrying out the views of Mr Darwin in their applications to the human race. Under the circumstances, perhaps, I shall be excused for pointing out that the same beliefs, otherwise expressed, are contained in Chapters XXV. and XXVIII. of *Social Statics*, published in December, 1850.

without clothing an inclemency almost too great for other races well clothed – the actions which have developed in the Tartar-races[6] nomadic habits that are almost insurmountable, while they have given to North American Indians desires and aptitudes which, fitting them for a hunting life, make a civilized life intolerable – the actions doing this, are also ever at work moulding citizens into correspondence with their circumstances. While the bodily nature of citizens are being fitted to the physical influences and industrial activities of their locality, their mental natures are being fitted to the structure of the society they live in. Though, as we have seen, there is always an approximate fitness of the social unit to its social aggregate, yet the fitness can never be more than approximate, and re-adjustment is always going on. Could a society remain unchanged, something like a permanent equilibrium between the nature of the individual and the nature of the society would presently be reached. But the type of each society is continually being modified by two causes – by growth, and by the actions, warlike or other, of adjacent societies. Increase in the bulk of a society inevitably leads to change of structure; as also does any alteration in the ratio of the predatory to the industrial activities. Hence continual social metamorphosis, involving continual alteration of the conditions under which the citizen lives, produces in him an adaptation of character which, tending towards completeness, is ever made incomplete by further social metamorphosis.

While, however, each society, and each successive phase of each society, presents conditions more or less special, to which the natures of citizens adapt themselves, there are certain general conditions which, in every society, must be fulfilled to a considerable extent before it can hold together, and which must be fulfilled completely before social life can be complete. Each citizen has to carry on his activities in such ways as not to impede other citizens in the carrying-on of their activities more than he is impeded by them. That any citizen may so behave as not to deduct from the aggregate welfare, it is needful that he shall perform such function, or share of function, as is of value equivalent at least to what he consumes and it is further needful that, both in discharging his function and in pursuing his pleasure, he shall leave others similarly free to discharge their functions and to pursue their pleasures. Obviously a society formed of units who cannot live without mutual hindrance, is one in which the happiness is of smaller amount than it is in a society formed of units who can live without mutual hindrance – numbers and physical conditions being supposed equal. And obviously the sum of happiness in such a society is still less than that in a society of which the units voluntarily aid one another.

Now, under one of its chief aspects, civilization is a process of developing in citizens a nature capable of fulfilling these all-essential conditions; and, neglecting their superfluities, laws and the appliances for enforcing them, are expressions and embodiments of these all-essential conditions. On the one hand, those severe systems of slavery, and serfdom, and punishment for vagabondage, which characterized the less-developed social types, stand for the necessity that the social unit shall be self-supporting. On the other hand, the punishments for murder, assault, theft, etc., and the penalties on breach of contract, stand for the necessity that, in the course of the activities by which he supports himself, the citizen shall neither directly injure other citizens, nor shall injure them indirectly, by taking or intercepting the returns their activities bring. And it needs no detail to show that a fundamental trait in social progress is an increase of industrial energy, leading citizens to support themselves without being coerced in the harsh ways once general; that another fundamental trait is the progressive establishment of such a nature in citizens that, while pursuing their respective ends, they injure and impede one another in smaller degrees; and that a concomitant trait is the growth of governmental restraints which more effectually check the remaining aggressiveness. That is to say, while the course of civilization shows us a clearer recognition and better enforcement of these essential conditions, it also shows us a gradual moulding of humanity into correspondence with them.

Along with the proofs thus furnished that the biological law of adaptation, holding of all other species, holds of the human species, and that the change of nature undergone by the human species since societies began to develop, has been an adaptation of it to the conditions implied by harmonious social life, we receive the lesson, that the one thing needful is a rigorous maintenance of these conditions. While all see that the immediate function of our chief social institutions is the securing of an orderly social life by maintaining these conditions, very few see that their further function, and in one sense more important function, is that of fitting men to fulfil these conditions spontaneously. The two functions are inseparable. From the biological laws we have been contemplating, it is, on the one hand, an inevitable corollary that if these conditions are maintained, human nature will gradually adapt itself to them; while, on the other hand, it is an inevitable corollary that by no other discipline than subjection to these conditions, can fitness to the social state be produced. Enforce these conditions, and adaptation to them will continue. Relax these conditions, and by so much there will be a cessation of the adaptive changes. Abolish these conditions, and, after the consequent social dissolution, there will commence (unless they are re-established) an adaptation to the conditions then resulting – those of savage life. These are conclusions from which there is no escape, if man is subject to the laws of life in common with living things in general.

It may, indeed, be rightly contended that if those who are but little fitted to the social state are rigorously subjected to these conditions, evil will result: intolerable restraint, it if does not deform or destroy life, will be followed by violent reaction. We are taught by analogy, that greatly-changed conditions from which there is no escape, fail to produce adaptation because they produce death. Men having constitutions fitted for one climate, cannot be fitted to an extremely-different climate by persistently living in it, because they do not survive, generation after generation. Such changes can be brought about only by slow spreadings of the race through intermediate regions having intermediate climates, to which successive generations are accustomed little by little. And doubtless the like holds mentally. The intellectual and emotional natures

286

required for high civilization, are not to be obtained by forcing on the completely-uncivilized, the needful activities and restraints in unqualified forms: gradual decay and death, rather than adaptation, would result. But so long as a society's institutions are indigenous, no danger is to be apprehended from a too-strict maintenance of the conditions to the ideally-best social life; since there can exist neither the required appreciation of them nor the required appliances for enforcing them. Only in those abnormal cases where a race of one type is subject to a race of much-superior type, is this qualification pertinent. In our own case, as in the cases of all societies having populations approximately homogeneous in character, and having institutions evolved by that character, there may rightly be aimed at the greatest rigour possible. The merciful policy, no less that the just policy, is that of insisting that these all-essential requirements of self-support and non-aggression, shall be conformed to – the just policy, because failing to insist is failing to protect the better or more-adapted natures against the worse or less-adapted; the merciful policy, because the pains accompanying the process of adaptation to the social state *must* be gone through, and it is better that they should be gone through once than gone though twice, as they have to be when any relaxation of these conditions permits retrogression.

Thus, that which sundry precepts of the current religion embody – that which ethical systems, intuitive or utilitarian, equally urge, is also that which Biology, generalizing the laws of life at large, dictates. All further requirements are unimportant compared with this primary requirement, that each shall so live as neither to burden others nor to injure others. And all further appliances for influencing the actions and natures of men, are unimportant compared with those serving to maintain and increase the conformity to this primary requirement. But unhappily, legislators and philanthropists, busy with schemes which, instead of aiding adaptation, indirectly hinder it, give little attention to the enforcing and improving of those arrangements by which adaptation is effected. [ ... ][7]

Neither the limits of this chapter, nor its purpose, permit exposition of the various other truths which Biology yields as data for Sociology. Enough has been said in proof of that which was to be shown – the need for biological study as a preparation for grasping sociological truths.

The effect to be looked for from it, is that of giving strength and clearness to convictions otherwise feeble and vague. Sundry of the doctrines I have presented under their biological aspects, are doctrines admitted in considerable degrees. Such acquaintance with the laws of life as they have gathered incidently, lead many to suspect that appliances for preserving the physically-feeble, bring results that are not wholly good. Others there are who occasionally get glimpses of evils caused by fostering the reckless and the stupid. But their suspicions and qualms fail to determine their conduct, because the *inevitableness* of the bad consequences has not been made adequately clear by the study of Biology at large. When countless illustrations have shown them that all strength, all faculty, all fitness, presented by every living thing, has arisen partly by a growth of each power

287

consequent on exercise of it, and partly by the more frequent survival and greater multiplication of the better-endowed individuals, entailing gradual disappearance of the worse-endowed – when it is seen that all perfection, bodily and mental, has been achieved through this process, and that suspension of it must cause cessation of progress, while reversal of it would bring universal decay – when it is seen that the mischiefs entailed by disregard of these truths, though they may be slow, are certain; there comes a conviction that social policy must be conformed to them, and that to ignore them is madness.

Did not experience prepare one to find everywhere a degree of irrationality remarkable in beings who distinguish themselves as rational, one might have assumed that, before devising modes of dealing with citizens in their corporate relations, special attention would be given to the natures of these citizens individually considered, and by implication to the natures of living things at large. Put a carpenter into a blacksmith's shop, and set him to forge, to weld, to harden, to anneal, etc., and he will not need the blacksmith's jeers to show him how foolish is the attempt to make and mend tools before he has learnt the properties of iron. Let the carpenter challenge the blacksmith, who knows little about wood in general and nothing about particular kinds of wood, to do his work, and unless the blacksmith declines to make himself a laughing-stock, he is pretty certain to saw askew, to choke up his plane, and presently to break his tools or cut his fingers. But while everyone sees the folly of supposing that wood or iron can be shaped and fitted, without an apprenticeship during which their ways of behaving are made familiar; no one sees any folly in undertaking to devise institutions, and to shape human nature in this way or that way, without a preliminary study of Man, and of Life in general as explaining Man's life. For simple functions we insist on elaborate special preparations extending through years; while for the most complex function, to be adequately discharged not even by the wisest, we require no preparation!

How absurd are the prevailing conceptions about these matters, we shall see still more clearly on turning to consider that more special discipline which should precede the study of Sociology; namely, the study of Mental Science.

# GOD AND REASON

## Biblical scholarship

### BENJAMIN JOWETT, 'ON THE INTERPRETATION OF SCRIPTURE' (1860)

Benjamin Jowett (1817–93) is chiefly remembered today for his classical scholarship – particularly his translations of Plato – and for his influence on university teaching during his Mastership at Balliol College, Oxford. His contribution in 1860 to *Essays and Reviews* occurred relatively early in his career, before he had achieved public recognition and before he had gained any real institutional power. Jowett had been made a fellow of Balliol in 1838 and a tutor in 1842 – the same year in which he was made an Anglican deacon. He was ordained as a priest in 1845. His first brush with controversy occurred in 1855 with the publication of *The Epistles of St Paul* which was an unorthodox examination of the Christian doctrine of Atonement. Jowett's views were bitterly attacked, but they did not debar him from being appointed as Regius Professor of Greek at Oxford. That opposition was revived, however, a few years later by Jowett's involvement in *Essays and Reviews*, and this time Jowett's opponents went before the Vice-Chancellor's Court to accuse him of heresy. Jowett's main concern in his essay was with the new 'Biblical Criticism' which substituted a historical reading of the Bible for a literal reading. Jowett claimed that the 'meaning' of the Bible had been obscured by a series of culturally specific interpretations; historical scholarship avoided such anachronism by recovering the Bible's 'original' meaning, defined by Jowett as 'the meaning which it has to the mind of the prophet or evangelist who first uttered or wrote, to the hearers or readers who first received it'. This amounted to treating the Bible (in Jowett's own words) as 'any other book'. It also involved acknowledging the Bible's inconsistencies and thus denying the idea of Scriptural inspiration. The proceedings against Jowett were eventually dropped, but attempts to supplement his salary were consistently opposed until 1865. During the late 1860s Jowett began to attract less controversial attention with his lectures on Plato. In 1870 he was elected Master of Balliol; the following year saw the publication of a four-volume translation of the *Dialogues* of Plato. In 1881 Jowett published a translation of Thucydides' *History*. From 1882–6 he was Vice-Chancellor of Oxford University. During this period he completed a translation of Aristotle's *Politics*, published in 1885. A final edition of Plato's *Republic*, on which he had been working for thirty years, was published posthumously in 1894.

### *From* Benjamin Jowett, 'On the Interpretation of Scripture' in *Essays and Reviews* (London: John Parker and Son, 1860), pp. 330–433[1]

*On the Interpretation of Scripture*[2]

It is a strange, though familiar fact, that great differences of opinion exist respecting the Interpretation of Scripture. All Christians receive the Old and New Testament as sacred writings, but they are not agreed about the meaning which they attribute to them. The book itself remains as at the first; the commentators seem rather to reflect the changing atmosphere of the world or of the Church. Different individuals or bodies of Christians have a different point of view, to which their interpretation is narrowed or made to conform. It is assumed, as natural and necessary, that the same words will present one idea to the mind of the Protestant, another to the Roman Catholic; one meaning to the German, another to the English interpreter. The Ultramontane[3] or Anglican divine is not supposed to be impartial in his treatment of passages which afford an apparent foundation for the doctrine of purgatory or the primacy of St Peter on the one hand, or the three orders of clergy and the divine origin of episcopacy on the other. It is a received view with many, that the meaning of the Bible is to be defined by that of the prayer-book; while there are others who interpret 'the Bible and the Bible only' with a silent reference to the traditions of the Reformation. Philosophical differences are in the background, into which the differences about Scripture also resolve themselves. They seem to run up at last into a difference of opinion respecting Revelation itself – whether given beside the human faculties or through them, whether an interruption of the laws of nature or their perfection and fulfilment.

This effort to pull the authority of Scripture in different directions is not peculiar to our own day; the same phenomenon appears in the past history of the Church. At the Reformation, in the Nicene or Pelagian[4] times, the New Testament was the ground over which men fought; it might also be compared to the armoury which furnished them with weapons. Opposite aspects of the truth which it contains were appropriated by different sides. 'Justified by faith without works' and 'justified by faith as well as works' are equally Scriptural expressions; the one has become the formula of Protestants, the other of Roman Catholics. The fifth and ninth chapters of the Romans, single verse such as I Corinthians iii. 15, John iii. 3, still bear traces of many a life-long strife on the pages of commentators. The difference of interpretation which prevails among ourselves is partly traditional, that is to say, inherited from the controversies of former ages. The use made of Scripture by Fathers of the Church, as well as by Luther and Calvin,[5] affects our idea of its meaning at the present hour.

Another cause of the multitude of interpretations is the growth or progress of the human mind itself. Modes of interpreting vary as time goes on; they partake of the general state of literature or knowledge. It has not been easily or at once that mankind have learned to realize the character of sacred writings – they seem almost necessarily to veil themselves from human eyes as circumstances change; it is the old age of the world only that has at length understood its child-hood. (Or rather perhaps is beginning to understand it, and learning to make allowance for its own deficiency of knowledge; for the infancy of the human race, as of the individual, affords but few indications of the workings of the mind within.) More often than we suppose the great sayings and doings upon the earth, 'thoughts that breathe and words that burn,'[6] are lost in a sort of chaos to the apprehension of those that come after. Much of past history is dimly seen and receives only a conventional interpretation, even when the memorials of it remain. There is a time at which the freshness of early literature is lost; mankind have turned rhetoricians, and no longer write or feel in the spirit which created it. In this unimaginative period in which sacred or ancient writings are partially unintelligible, many methods have been taken at different times to adapt the ideas of the past to the wants of the present. One age has wandered into the flowery paths of allegory,

'In pious meditation fancy fed.'[7]

Another has straitened the liberty of the Gospel by a rigid application of logic, the former being a method which was at first more naturally applied to the Old Testament, the latter to the New. Both methods of interpretation, the mystical and logical, as they may be termed, have been practised on the Vedas[8] and the Koran, as well as on the Jewish and Christian Scriptures, the true glory and note of divinity in these latter being not that they have hidden mysterious or double meanings, but a simple and universal one, which is beyond them and will survive them. Since the revival of literature, interpreters have not unfrequently fallen into error of another kind from a pedantic and misplaced use of classical learning; the minute examination of words often withdrawing the mind from more important matters. A tendency may be observed within the last century to clothe systems of philosophy in the phraseology of Scripture. But new wine cannot thus be put 'into old bottles.' Though roughly distinguishable by different ages, these modes or tendencies also exist together; the remains of all of them may be remarked in some of the popular commentaries of our own day.

More common than any of these methods, and not peculiar to any age, is that which may be called by way of distinction the rhetorical one. The tendency to exaggerate or amplify the meaning of simple words for the sake of edification may indeed have a practical use in sermons, the object of which is to awaken not so much the intellect as the heart and conscience. Spiritual food, like natural, may require to be of a certain bulk to nourish the human mind. But this 'tendency to edification' has had an unfortunate influence on the interpretation of Scripture. For the preacher almost necessarily oversteps the limits of actual knowledge, his feelings overflow with the subject; even if he have the power, he has seldom the time for accurate thought or inquiry. And in the course of years spent in writing, perhaps, without study, he is apt to persuade himself, if not others, of the truth of his own repetitions. The trivial consideration of making a discourse of sufficient length is often a reason why he overlays the words of Christ and his Apostles with commonplaces. The meaning of the text is not always the object which he has in view, but some moral or religious lesson which he has found it necessary to append to it; some cause which he is pleading, some error of the day which he has to combat. And while in some passages he hardly dares to trust himself with the full force of Scripture (Matthew v. 34; ix. 13; xix. 21; Acts v. 29), in others he extracts more from words than they really imply (Matthew xxii. 21; xxviii. 20; Romans xiii. 1; &c.),[9] being more eager to guard against the abuse of some precept than to enforce it, attenuating or adapting the utterance of prophecy to the requirements or to the measure of modern times. Any one who has ever written sermons is aware how hard it is to apply Scripture to the wants of his hearers and at the same time to preserve its meaning.

The phenomenon which has been described in the preceding pages is so familiar, and yet so extraordinary, that it requires an effort of thought to appreciate its true nature. We do not at once see the absurdity of the same words having many senses, or free our minds from the illusion that the Apostle or Evangelist must have written with a reference to the creeds or controversies or circumstances of other times. Let it be considered, then, that this extreme variety of interpretation is found to exist in the case of no other book, but of the Scriptures only. Other writings are preserved to us in dead languages – Greek, Latin, Oriental, some of them in fragments, all of them originally in manuscript. It is true that difficulties arise in the explanation of these writings, especially in the most ancient, from our imperfect acquaintance with the meaning of words, or the defectiveness of copies, or the want of some historical or geographical information which is required to present an event or character in its true bearing. In comparison with the wealth and light of modern literature, our knowledge of Greek classical authors, for example, may be called imperfect and shadowy. Some of them have another sort of difficulty arising from subtlety or abruptness in the use of language; in lyric poetry especially, and some of the earlier prose, the greatness of the thought struggles with the stammering lips. It may be observed that all these difficulties occur also in Scripture; they are found equally in sacred and profane literature. But the meaning of classical authors is known with comparative certainty; and the interpretation of them seems to rest on a scientific basis. It is not, therefore, to philological or historical difficulties that the greater past of the uncertainty in the interpretation of Scripture is to be attributed. No ignorance of Hebrew or Greek is sufficient to account for it. Even the Vedas and the Zendavesta,[10] though beset by obscurities of language probably greater than are found in any portion of the Bible, are interpreted, at least by European scholars, according to fixed rules, and beginning to be clearly understood.

To bring the parallel home, let us imagine the remains of some well-known Greek author, as Plato or Sophocles, receiving the same treatment at the hands of the world which the Scriptures have experienced. The text of such an author, when first printed by Aldus or Stephens,[11] would be gathered from the imperfect or miswritten copies which fell in the way of the editors; after awhile older and better manuscripts come to light, and the power of using and estimating the value of manuscripts is greatly improved. We may suppose, further, that the readings of these older copies do not always conform to some received canons of criticism. Up to the year 1550, or 1624, alterations, often preceding on no principle, have been introduced into the text; but now a stand is made – an edition which appeared at the latter of the two dates just mentioned is invested with authority; this authorized texts is a *pièce de resistance* against innovation. Many reasons are given why it is better to have bad readings to which the world is accustomed than good ones which are novel and strange – why the later manuscripts of Plato or Sophocles are often to be preferred to earlier ones – why it is useless to remove imperfections where perfect accuracy is not to be attained. A fear of disturbing the critical canons which have come down from former ages is, however, suspected to be one reason for the opposition. And custom and prejudice, and the nicety of the subject, and all the arguments which are intelligible to the many against the truth, which is intelligible only to the few, are thrown into the scale to preserve the works of Plato or Sophocles as nearly as possible in the received text.

Leaving the text we precede to interpret and translate. The meaning of Greek words is known with tolerable certainty; and the grammar of the Greek language has been minutely analysed both in ancient and modern times. Yet the interpretation of Sophocles is tentative and uncertain; it seems to vary from age to age: to some the great tragedian has appeared to embody in his choruses certain theological or moral ideas of his own age or country; there are others who find there an allegory of the Christian religion or of the history of modern Europe. Several schools of critics have commented on his works; to the Englishman he has presented one meaning, to the Frenchman another, to the German a third; the interpretations have also differed with the philosophical systems which the interpreters espoused. To one the same words have appeared to bear a moral, to another a symbolical meaning; a third is determined wholly by the authority of old commentators; while there is a disposition to condemn the scholar who seeks to interpret Sophocles from himself only and with reference to the ideas and beliefs of the age in which he lived. And the error of such an one is attributed not only to some intellectual but even to a moral obliquity which prevents his seeing the true meaning.

It would be tedious to follow into details the absurdity which has been supposed. By such methods it would be truly said that Sophocles or Plato may be made to mean anything. It would seem as if some *Novum Organum*[12] were needed to lay down rules of interpretation for ancient literature. Still one other supposition has to be introduced which will appear, perhaps, more extravagant than any which have preceded. Conceive then that these modes of interpreting Sophocles had existed for ages; that great institutions and interests had become interwoven with them, and in some degree even the honour of nations and churches – is it too much to say that in such a case they would be changed with difficulty, and that they would continue to be maintained long after critics and philosophers had seen that they were indefensible?

No one who has a Christian feeling would place classical on a level with sacred literature; and there are other particulars in which the preceding comparison fails, as, for example, the style and subject. But, however different the subject, although the interpretation of Scripture requires 'a vision and faculty divine,' or at least a moral and religious interest which is not needed in the study of a Greek poet or philosopher, yet in what may be termed the externals of interpretation, that is to say, the meaning of words, the connexion of sentences, the settlement of the text, the evidence of facts, the same rules apply to the Old and New Testaments as to other books. And the figure is no exaggeration of the erring fancy of men in the use of Scripture, or of the tenacity with which they cling to the interpretations of other times, or of the arguments by which they maintain them. All the resources of knowledge may be turned into a means not of discovering the true rendering, but of upholding a received one. Grammar appears to start from an independent point of view, yet inquiries into the use of the article of the preposition have been observed to wind round into a defence of some doctrine. Rhetoric often magnifies its own want of taste into the design of inspiration. Logic (that other mode of rhetoric) is apt to lend itself to the illusion, by stating erroneous explanations with a clearness which is mistaken for truth. 'Metaphysical aid' carries away the common understanding into a region where it must blindly follow. Learning obscures as well as illustrates; it heaps up chaff when there is no more wheat. These are some of the ways in which the sense of Scripture has become confused, by the help of tradition, in the course of ages, under a load of commentators.

The book itself remains as at the first unchanged amid the changing interpretations of it. The office of the interpreter is not to add another, but to recover the original one; the meaning, that is, of the words as they first struck on the ears or flashed before the eyes of these who heard and read them. He has to transfer himself to another age; to imagine that he is a disciple of Christ or Paul; to disengage himself from all that follows. The history of Christendom is nothing to him; but only the scene at Galilee or Jerusalem, the handful of believers who gathered themselves together at Ephesus, or Corinth, or Rome. His eye is fixed on the form of one like the Son of man, or of the prophet who was girded with a garment of camel's hair, or of the Apostle who had a thorn in the flesh. The greatness of the Roman Empire is nothing to him; it is an inner not an outer world that he is striving to restore. All the after-thoughts of theology are nothing to him; they are not the true lights which light him in difficult places. His concern is with a book in which as in other ancient writings are some things of which we are ignorant; which defect of our knowledge cannot however be supplied by the conjectures of fathers or divines. The simple words of that book he tries to preserve absolutely pure from the refinements or distinctions of later times. He acknowledges that they are fragmentary, and would suspect himself, if out of fragments he were able to create a well-rounded system or a continuous history. The greater part of his learning is a knowledge of the text itself; he has no delight in the voluminous literature which has overgrown it. He has no theory of interpretation; a few rules guarding against common errors are enough for him. His object is to read Scripture like any other book, with a real interest and not merely a conventional one. He wants to be able to open his eyes and see or imagine things as they truly are.

Nothing would be more likely to restore a natural feeling on this subject than a history of Interpretation of Scripture. It would take us back to the beginning; it would prevent in one view the causes which have darkened the meaning of words in the course of ages; it would clear away the remains of dogmas, systems, controversies, which are encrusted upon them. It would show us the 'erring fancy' of interpreters assuming sometimes to have the Spirit of God Himself, yet unable to pass beyond the limits of their own age, and with a judgement often biassed by party. Great names there have been among them, names of men who may be reckoned also among the benefactors of the human race, yet comparatively few who have understood the thoughts of other times, or who have bent their minds to 'interrogate' the meaning of words. Such a work would enable us to separate the elements of doctrines and tradition with which the meaning of Scripture is encumbered in our own day. It would mark the different epochs of interpretation from the time when the living word was in process of becoming a book to Origen and Tertullian, from Origen to Jerome and Augustine, from Jerome and Augustine to Abelard and Aquinas;[13] again making a new beginning with the revival of literature, from Erasmus, the father of Biblical criticism in more recent times, with Calvin and Beza for his immediate successors, through Grotius and Hammond, down to De Wette and Meier, our own contemporaries.[14] We should see how the mystical interpretations of Scripture originated in the Alexandrine age; how it blended with the logical and rhetorical; how both received weight and currency from their use in support of the claims and teaching of the Church. We should notice how the 'new learning' of the fifteenth and sixteenth centuries gradually awakened the critical faculty in the study of the sacred writings; how Biblical criticism has slowly but surely followed in the track of philological and historical (not without a remoter influence exercised upon it also by natural science); how, too, the form of the scholastic literature,[15] and even of notes on the classics, insensibly communicated itself to commentaries on Scripture. We should see how the word inspiration, from being used in a general way to express what may be called the prophetic spirit of Scripture, has passed, within the last two centuries, into a sort of technical term; how, in other instances, the practice or feeling of earlier ages has been hollowed out into the theory or system of later ones. We should observe how the popular explanations of prophecy as in heathen (Thucyd. ii. 54),[16] so also in Christian times, had adapted themselves to the circumstances of mankind. We might remark that in our country, and in the present generation especially, the interpretation of Scripture had assumed an apologetic character, as though making an effort to defend itself against some supposed inroad of science and criticism; while among German commentators there is, for the first time in the history of the world, an approach to agreement and certainty. For example, the diversity among German writers on prophecy is far less than among English ones. That is a new phenomenon which has to be acknowledged. More than any other subject of human knowledge, Biblical criticism has hung to the past; it has been hitherto found truer to the traditions of the Church than to the words of Christ. It has made, however, two great steps onward – at the time of the Reformation and in our day. The diffusion of a critical spirit in history and literature is affecting the criticism of the Bible in our own day in a manner not unlike the burst of intellectual life in the fifteenth or sixteenth centuries. Educated persons are beginning to ask, not what Scripture may be made to mean, but what it does. And it is no exaggeration to say that he who in the present state of knowledge will confine himself to the plain meaning of words and the study of their context may know more of the original spirit and intention of the authors of the New Testament than all the controversial writers of former ages put together.

Such a history would be of great value to philosophy as well as to theology. It would be the history of the human mind in one of its most remarkable manifestations. For ages which are not original show their character in the interpretation of ancient writings. Creating nothing, and incapable of that effort of imagination which is required in a true criticism of the past, they read and explain the thoughts of former times by the conventional modes of their own. Such a history would form a kind of preface or prolegomena to the study of Scripture. Like the history of science, it would save many a useless toil; it would indicate the uncertainties on which it is not worth while to speculate further; the bypaths or labyrinths in which men lose themselves; the mines that are already worked out. He who reflects on the multitude of explanations which already exist of the 'number of the beast,' 'the two witnesses,' 'the little horn,' 'the man of sin,' who observes the manner in which these explanation have varied with the political movements of our own time, will be unwilling to devote himself to a method of inquiry in which there is so little appearance of certainty or progress. These interpretations would destroy one another if they were all placed side by side in a tabular analysis. It is an instructive fact, which may be mentioned in passing, that Joseph Mede,[17] the greatest authority on this subject, twice fixed the end of the world in the last century and once during his own lifetime. In like manner, he who notices the circumstance that the explanations of the first chapter of Genesis have slowly changed, and, as it were, retreated before the advance of geology, will be unwilling to add another to the spurious reconcilements of science and revelation. Or to take an example of another kind, the Protestant divine who perceives that the types and figures of the Old Testament are employed by Roman Catholics in support of the tenets of their church, will be careful not to use weapons which it is impossible to guide, and which may with equal force be turned against himself. Those who have handled them on the Protestant side have before now fallen victims to them, not observing as they fell that it was by their own hand.

Much of the uncertainty which prevails in the interpretation of Scripture arises out of party efforts to wrest its meaning to different sides. There are, however, deeper reasons which have hindered the natural meaning of the text from immediately and universally prevailing. One of these is the unsettlement of many questions which have an important but indirect bearing on this subject. Some of these questions veil themselves in ambiguous terms; and no one likes to draw them out of their hiding-place into the light of day. In natural science it is felt to be useless to build on assumptions; in history we look with suspicion on *a priori* ideas of what ought to have been; in mathematics, when a step is wrong, we pull the house down until we reach the point at which the error is discovered. But in theology it is otherwise; there the tendency has been to conceal the unsoundness of the foundation under the fairness and loftiness of the superstructure. It has been thought safer to allow arguments to stand which, although fallacious, have been on the right side, than to point out their defect. And thus many principles have imperceptibly grown up which have overridden facts. No one would interpret Scripture, as many do, but for certain previous suppositions with which we come to the perusal of it. 'There can be no error in the Word of God,' therefore the discrepancies in the books of Kings and Chronicles are only apparent, or may be attributed to differences in the copies. 'It is a thousand times more likely that the interpreter should err than the inspired writer.' For a like reason the failure of a prophecy is never admitted, in spite of Scripture and of history (Jer. xxxvi. 30; Isai. xxiii.; Amos vii. 10–17); the mention of a name later than the supposed age of the prophet is not allowed, as in other writings, to be taken in evidence of the date (Isiah xlv. 1).[18] The accuracy of the Old Testament is measured not by the standard of primeval history, but of a modern critical one, which, contrary to all probability, is supposed to be attained; this arbitrary standard once assumed, it becomes a point of honour or of faith to defend every name, date, place, which occurs. Or to take another class of questions, it is said that 'the various theories of the origin of the three first Gospels are all equally unknown to the Holy Catholic Church,' or as another writer of a different school expresses himself, 'they tend to sap the inspiration of the New Testament.' Again, the language in which our Saviour speaks of his own union with the Father is interpreted by the language of the creeds. Those who remonstrate against double senses, allegorical interpretations, forced reconcilements, find themselves met by a sort of presupposition that 'God speaks not as man speaks.' The limitation of the human faculties is confusedly appealed to as a reason for abstaining from investigations which are quite within their limits. The suspicion of Deism,[19] or perhaps of Atheism, awaits inquiry. By such fears a good man refuses to be influenced, a philosophical mind is apt to cast them aside with too much bitterness. It is better to close the book than to read it under conditions of thought which are imposed from without. Whether those conditions of thought are the traditions of the Church, or the opinions of the religious world – Catholic or Protestant – makes no difference. They are inconsistent with the freedom of the truth and the moral character of the Gospel. It becomes necessary, therefore, to examine briefly some of these prior questions which lie in the way of a reasonable criticism.

## JOHN WILLIAM COLENSO, *THE PENTATEUCH AND BOOK OF JOSHUA CRITICALLY EXAMINED* (1862)

The career of John William Colenso (1814–83) began unremarkably: after a successful undergraduate career at Cambridge, he took up a post as mathematics tutor at Harrow School. His time there was dogged by a series of misfortunes, and he returned to Cambridge as a tutor at St John's where he produced the first of a number of text-books on mathematics: *Arithmetic Designed for the Use of Schools* (1843) and *The Elements of Algebra* (1841). In 1846 Colenso was made Rector of Forncett St Mary's Church in Norfolk. He continued his interest in mathematics, publishing in 1849–50 *A Key to Algebra*. In 1853 Colenso became Bishop of Natal – an appointment which was to change his life completely. In 1855 he published *Ten Weeks in Natal*, an account of his first experiences in his new country, and *Remarks on the Proper Treatment of Cases of Polygamy* – a controversial work which appeared to advocate a tolerance of the practice. In 1861 Colenso continued to court controversy with his 'Commentary on St Paul's Epistle to the Romans' which opposed the doctrine of eternal punishment. It in turn was followed in 1862 by the first volume of the seven-part *The Pentateuch and Book of Joshua Critically Examined* (1862–79) – a work which all but ruined Colenso's career. In the late 1850s, Colenso's experiences with Zulu converts had led him to question the authority of his beliefs – particularly those derived from the *Pentateuch*. After undertaking a rigorous examination of its sources, Colenso argued that the *Pentateuch* could not be taken as literally true – as a faithful record of Jewish life – because it was in fact written considerably later than events described as contemporary. The first volume caused a storm of protest and provoked a host of written replies. Colenso was summoned by his superior, Bishop Robert Gray of Cape Town, to appear before him on a charge of heresy, and he was convicted the following year. Colenso claimed that the charge was null and void because Gray's 'Cape Town' court had no legal jurisdiction – a position which was confirmed in 1865 by the judicial committee of the Church Privy Council in England, and in 1866 Colenso's right to his episcopal income was affirmed. Also in 1866 his *Natal Sermons* were published; they were followed by a second series in 1868. Colenso's victory, however, proved to be shortlived, for as soon as the Church of South Africa gained its autonomy (a few years later), Colenso was promptly deposed (in 1869). Nevertheless he remained stubbornly at his post, working alongside the new Bishop and (initially at least) attracting considerable support. During this period he continued with his work on the *Pentateuch*. In 1871 he published *First Steps in Zulu* – a continuation of an interest begun much earlier with the publication of *An Elementary Grammar of the Zulu-Kafir Language* (1855). In fact during his time in Natal Colenso produced a whole series of educational works for a Zulu readership – not only on language, but also on science, history, geography and astronomy. The notoriety of Colenso's religious writings make it easy to forget this body of work.

**From John William Colenso (Bishop of Natal),** *The Pentateuch and Book of Joshua Critically Examined* **(London: Longman, 1862)**[1]

*Chapter I: Introductory Remarks*

1. The first five books of the Bible, – commonly called the Pentateuch (ἡ πεντάτευχος Βίβλος, Pentateuchus, sc. liber), or Book of Five Volumes, – are supposed by most English readers of the Bible to have been written by Moses, except the last chapter of Deuteronomy, which records the death of Moses, and which, of course, it is generally allowed, must have been added by another hand, perhaps that of Joshua. It is believed that Moses wrote under such special guidance and teaching of the Holy Spirit, that he was preserved from making any error in recording those matters, which came within his own cognisance, and was instructed also in respect of events, which took place before he was born – before, indeed, there was a human being on the earth to take note of what was passing. He was in this way, it is supposed, enabled to write a true account of the Creation. And, though the accounts of the Fall and of the Flood, as well as of later events, which happened in the time of Abraham, Isaac, and Jacob, may have been handed down by tradition from one generation to another, and even, some of them, perhaps, written down in words, or represented in hieroglyphics, and Moses may, probably, have derived assistance from these sources also in the composition of his narrative, yet in all his statements, it is believed, he was under such constant control and superintendence of the Spirit of God, that he was kept from making any serious error, and certainly from writing anything altogether untrue. We may rely with undoubting confidence – such is the statement usually made – on the historical veracity, and infallible accuracy, of the Mosaic narrative in all its main particulars. Thus Archdeacon PRATT[2] writes, *Science and Scripture not at Variance, p.* 102: –

By the inspiration of Holy Scripture I understand, that the Scriptures were written under the guidance of the Holy Spirit, who communicated to the writers facts before unknown, directed them in the selection of other facts already known, and *preserved them from error of every kind in the records they made.*

2. But, among the many results of that remarkable activity in scientific enquiry of every kind, which, by God's own gift, distinguishes the present age, this also must be reckoned, that attention and labour are now being bestowed, more closely and earnestly than ever before, to search into the real foundations for such a belief as this. As the Rev. A. W. HADDAN[3] has well said, (*Replies to Essays and Reviews, p.* 349,) –

It is a time when religious questions are being sifted with an apparatus of knowledge, and with faculties and a temper of mind, seldom, if ever, before brought to bear upon them. The entire creation of new departments of knowledge, such as philology, – the discovery, as of things before absolutely unknown, of the physical history of the globe, – the rising from the grave, as it were, of whole periods of history contemporary with the Bible, through newly found or newly interpreted monuments, – the science of manuscripts and of settling texts, – all these, and many more that might be named, embrace in themselves a whole universe of knowledge bearing upon religion, and specially upon the Bible, to which our fathers were utter strangers. And beyond all these is the change in the very spirit of thought itself, equally great, and equally appropriate to the conditions of the present conflict, – the transformation of history by the critical weighing of evidence, by the separation from it of the subjective and the mythical, by the treatment of it in a living and real way, – *the advance in Biblical Criticism, which has undoubtedly arisen from the more thorough application to the Bible of the laws of human criticism.*

3. This must, in fact, be deemed, undoubtedly, *the* question of the present day, upon the reply to which depend vast and momentous interests. The time is come, as I believe, in the Providence of God, when this question can no longer be put by, – when it must be resolutely faced, and the whole matter fully and freely examined, if we would be faithful servants of the God of Truth. Whatever the result may be, it is our bounded duty to 'buy the truth' at any cost, even at the sacrifice, if need be, of much, which we have hitherto held to be most dear and precious. We are certain that He, who has given us our reasoning powers, intends and requires us to use them, reverently and devoutly, but faithfully and diligently, in His service. We must 'try the spirits, whether they are of God'; we must 'prove all things, and hold fast that which is good.' We must do this in watchfulness and prayer, as those who desire only to know the Will of God and do it. For, as Dr. DAVIDSON[4] has truly said, *Introd. to the O.T.* i, 151, –

Piety, humility, and prayer are much needed here, by the side of acuteness and learning.

4. For myself, I have become engaged in this enquiry, from no wish or purpose of my own, but from the plain necessities of my position as a Missionary Bishop. I feel, however, that I am only drawn in with the stream, which in this our age is setting steadily in this direction, and swelling visibly from day to day. What the end may be, God only, the God of Truth, can foresee. Meanwhile, believing and trusting in His guidance, I have launched my bark upon the flood, and am carried along by the waters. Most gladly would I have turned away from all such investigations as these, if I *could* have done so, – as, in fact, I did, until I could do so no longer. It is true that my very office as a Clergyman, and much more as a Bishop, required me 'faithfully to exercise myself in the Holy Scriptures.' But the study of the practical and devotional parts of Scripture for a long time occupied me sufficiently, to satisfy my conscience in respect of this vow. And though, of course, aware – as every thinking person must be – of some serious difficulties, which present themselves in reading the earlier portions of the Bible, I have been content to rest satisfied that the belief, in which so many thousands of pious and able minds, of all ages and countries, have acquiesced, must be, – in its main particulars, at least, – correct.

5. There was a time, indeed, in my life, before my attention had been drawn to the facts, which make such a view impossible for most reflecting and enquiring minds, when I could have heartily assented to such language as the following, which BURGON,[5] *Inspiration and Interpretation, p.* 89, asserts to be the creed of orthodox believers, and which, probably, expresses the belief of many English Christians at the present day: –

The BIBLE is none other than *the Voice of Him that sitteth upon the Throne!* Every book of it – every chapter of it – every verse of it – every word of it – every syllable of it – (where are we to stop?) every *letter* of it – is the direct utterance of the Most High! The Bible is none other than the Word of God – not some part of it, some part of it less, but all alike, the utterance of Him who sitteth upon the Throne – absolute – faultless – unerring – supreme.

Such was the creed of the School in which I was educated. God is my witness! what hours of wretchedness have I spent at times, while reading the Bible devoutly from day to day, and reverencing every word of it as the Word of God, when petty contradictions met me, which seemed to my reason to conflict with the notion of the absolute historical veracity of every part of Scripture, and which, as I felt, *in the study of any other book*, we should honestly treat as errors or misstatements, without in the least detracting from the real value of the book! But, in those days, I was taught that it was my duty to fling the suggestion from me at once, 'as if it were a loaded shell, shot into the fortress of my soul,' or to stamp out desperately, as with an iron heel, each spark of honest doubt, which God's own gift, the love of Truth, had kindled in my bosom. And by many a painful effort I succeeded in doing so for a season; though, while thus dealing with my own doubts, I never certainly presumed to think – with one who 'thanks God' that 'the cold shade of unbelief has never for an instant darkened his own spirit' – that each 'solitary doubter was paying the bitter penalty, doubtless, of his sin (!),' BURGON, *p.* ccix.

6. I thank God that I was not able long to throw dust in the eyes of my own mind, and do violence to the love of truth in this way. With increase of mental power and general knowledge, it was, I felt, impossible to maintain the extreme view above stated. And, without allowing that there actually *were* any real contra-dictions, – without, in fact, caring to examine too closely and curiously into the question, – yet, when feeling the pressure of such difficulties, I have taken refuge, as I imagine very many educated persons do in the present day, in some such thoughts as those, which Prof. HAROLD BROWNE[6] recommends as a stay and support to the mind under such perplexities, *Aids to Faith, p.* 317, 318, –

> If we believe that God has in different ages authorised certain persons to communicate objective truth to mankind, – if, in the Old Testament history and the books of the Prophets, we find manifest indications of the Creator, – it is then a secondary consideration, and a question in which we may safely agree to differ, whether or not every book of the Old Testament was written so completely under the dictation of God's Holy Spirit, that every word, not only doctrinal, but also *historical* or *scientific*, must be infallibly correct and true ... Whatever conclusion may be arrived at, as to the infallibility of the writers on matters of *science* or of *history*, still the whole collection of the books will be really the oracles of God, the Scriptures of God, the record and depository of God's supernatural revelations in early times to men ... With all the pains and ingenuity, which have been bestowed upon the subject, no charge of error, even in matters of human knowledge, has ever yet been substantiated against any of the writers of Scripture. But, even if it had been otherwise, is it not conceivable that there might have been infal-lible Divine teachings in all things *spiritual* and *heavenly*, whilst, on mere matters of *history* or of *daily life*, Prophets and Evangelists might have been suffered to write as men? Even if this were true, we need not be perplexed or disquieted, so we can be agreed that the divine element was ever such as to secure the infallible truth of Scripture *in all things divine.*

7. But my labours, as a translator of the Bible, and a teacher of intelligent catechumens,[7] have brought me face to face with questions, from which I had hitherto shrunk, but from which, under the circumstances, I felt it would be

sinful abandonment of duty any longer to turn away. I have, therefore, as in the sight of God Most High, set myself deliberately to find the answer to such questions, with, I trust and believe, a sincere desire to know the Truth, as God wills us to know it, and with a humble dependence on that Divine Teacher, who alone can guide us into that knowledge, and help us to use the light of our minds aright. The result of my enquiry is this, that I have arrived at the conviction, – as painful to myself at first, as it may be to my reader, though painful now no longer under the clear shining Light of Truth, – that the Pentateuch, as a whole, cannot possibly have been written by Moses, or by any one acquainted personally with the facts which it professes to describe, and, further, that the (so-called) Mosaic narrative, by whomsoever written, and though imparting to us, as I fully believe it does, revelations of the Divine Will and Character, cannot be regarded as *historically true*.

8. Let it be observed that I am not here speaking of a number of petty variations and contradictions, such as, on closer examination, are found to exist throughout the books, but which may be in many cases sufficiently explained, by alleging our ignorance of all the circumstances of the case, or by supposing some misplacement, or loss, or corruption, of the original manuscript, or by suggesting that a later writer has inserted his own gloss here and there, or even whole passages, which may contain facts or expressions at variance with the true Mosaic Books, and throwing an unmerited suspicion upon them. However perplexing such contradictions are, when found in a book which is believed to be divinely infallible, yet a humble and pious faith will gladly welcome the aid of a friendly criticism, to relieve it in this way of its doubts. I can truly say that I would do so heartily myself. Nor are the difficulties, to which I am now referring, of the same kind as those, which arise from considering the accounts of the Creation and the Deluge, (though these of themselves are very formidable,) or the stupendous character of certain miracles, as that of the sun and moon standing still, – or the waters of the river Jordan standing in heaps as solid walls, while the stream, we must suppose, was still running, – or the ass speaking with human voice, – or the miracles wrought by the magicians of Egypt, such as the conversion of a rod into a snake, and the latter being endowed with life. They are not such, even, as are raised, when we regard the trivial nature of a vast number of conversations and commands, ascribed directly to Jehovah, especially the multiplied ceremonial minutiae, laid down in the Levitical Law.[8] They are not such, even, as must be started at once in most pious minds, when such words as these are read, professedly coming from the Holy and Blessed One, the Father and 'Faithful Creator' of all mankind: –

'If the master (of a Hebrew servant) have given him a wife, and she have borne him sons or daughters, *the wife and her children shall be her master's*, and he shall go out free by himself,' E. xxi. 4:

the wife and the children in such a case being placed under the protection of such other words as these, –

'If a man smite his servant, or his maid, with a rod, and he die under his hand, he shall be surely punished. *Notwithstanding*, if he continue a day or two, he shall not be punished: for *he is his money.*' E. xxi. 20, 21.

9. I shall never forget the revulsion of feeling, with which a very intelligent Christian nature, with whose help I was translating these words into the Zulu tongue, first heard them as words said to be uttered by the same great and gracious Being, whom I was teaching him to trust in and adore. His whole soul revolted against the notion, that the Great and Blessed God, the Merciful Father of all mankind, would speak of a servant or maid as mere 'money,' and allow a horrible crime to go unpunished, because the victim of the brutal usage had survived a few hours. My own heart and conscience at the time fully sympathised with his. But I then clung to the notion, that the main substance of the narrative was historically true. And I relieved his difficulty and my own for the present by telling him, that I supposed that such words as these were written down by Moses, and believed by him to have been divinely given to him, because the thought of them arose in his heart, as he conceived, by the inspiration of God, and that hence to all such Laws he prefixed the formula, 'Jehovah said unto Moses,' without it being on that account necessary for us to suppose that they were actually spoken by the Almighty. This was, however, a very great strain upon the cord, which bound me to the ordinary belief in the historical veracity of the Pentateuch; and since then that cord has snapped in twain altogether.

10. But I wish to repeat here most distinctly that my reason, for no longer receiving the Pentateuch as historically true, is not that I find insuperable difficulties with regard to the *miracles*, or supernatural *revelations* of Almighty God, recorded in it, but solely that I cannot, as a true man, consent any longer to shut my eyes to the absolute, palpable, self-contradictions of the narrative. The notion of miraculous or supernatural interferences does not present to my own mind the difficulties which it seems to present to some. I could believe and receive the miracles of Scripture heartily, if only they were authenticated by a veracious history; though, if this is not the case with the Pentateuch, any miracles, which rest on such an unstable support, must necessarily fall to the ground with it. The language, therefore, of Prof. MANSEL,[9] *Aids to Faith, p.* 9, is wholly inapplicable to the present case: –

The real question at issue, between the believer and the unbeliever in the Scripture miracles, is not whether they are established by sufficient testimony, but whether they can be established by any testimony at all.

And I must equally demur to that of Prof. BROWNE, *Aids to Faith, p.* 296, who, in his Essay, admirable as it is for its general candour and fairness, yet implies that doubts of the Divine Authority of any portion of the Scriptures *must*, in all or most cases, arise from 'unbelieving opinions,' while 'criticism comes afterwards.' Of course, a *thorough searching* criticism *must*, from the nature of the case, 'come afterwards.' But the 'unbelieving opinions' in my own case, and, I doubt not, in the case of many others, have been the necessary consequence of my having been led, in the plain course of my duty, to shake off the incubus of a dogmatic education, and steadily look one or two facts in the face. In my case, critical enquiry to some extent has preceded the formation of these opinions; but the one has continually reacted on the other.

11. For the conviction of the unhistorical character of the (so-called) Mosaic narrative seems to be forced upon us, by the consideration of the many absolute *impossibilities* involved in it, when treated as relating simple matters of fact, and without taking account of any argument, which throws discredit on the story merely by reason of the miracles, or supernatural appearances, recorded in it, or particular laws, speeches, and actions, ascribed in it to the Divine Being. We need only consider well the statements made in the books themselves, by whomsoever written, about matters which they profess to narrate as facts of common history, – statements, which every Clergyman, at all events, and every Sunday-School Teacher, not to say, every Christian, is surely bound to examine thoroughly, and try to understand rightly, comparing one passage with another, until he comprehends their actual meaning, and is able to explain that meaning to others. If we do this, we shall find them to contain a series of manifest contradictions and inconsistencies, which leave us, it would seem, no alternative but to conclude that main portions of the story of the Exodus, though based, probably, on some real historical foundation, yet are certainly not to be regarded as historically true.

12. The proofs, which seem to me to be conclusive on this point, I feel it to be my duty, in the service of God and the Truth, to lay before my fellow-men, not without a solemn sense of the responsibility which I am thus incurring, and not without a painful foreboding of the serious consequences which, in many cases, may ensue from such a publication. There will be some now, as in the time of the first preaching of Christianity, or in the days of the Reformation, who will seek to turn their liberty into a 'cloke of lasciviousness.' 'The unrighteous will be unrighteous still; the filthy will be filthy still.' The heart, that is unclean and impure, will not fail to find excuse for indulging its lusts, from the notion that somehow the very principle of a living faith in GOD is shaken, because belief in the Pentateuch is shaken. But it is not so. Our belief in the Living GOD remains as sure as ever, though not the Pentateuch only, but the whole Bible, were removed. It is written on our hearts by GOD's own Finger, as surely as by the hand of the Apostle in the Bible, that 'GOD IS, and is a rewarder of them that diligently seek Him.' It is written there also, as plainly as in the Bible, that 'GOD is not mocked,' – that, 'whatsoever a man soweth, that shall he also reap,' – and that 'he that soweth to the flesh, shall of the flesh reap corruption.'

13. But there will be others of a different stamp, – meek, lowly, loving souls,

who are walking daily with God, and have been taught to consider a belief in the historical veracity of the story of the Exodus an essential part of their religion, upon which, indeed, as it seems to them, the whole fabric of their faith and hope in God is based. It is not really so: the Light of God's Love did not shine less truly on pious minds, when Enoch 'walked with God' of old, though there was then no Bible in existence, than it does now. And it is, perhaps, God's Will that we shall be taught in this our day, among other precious lessons, not to build up our faith upon a Book, though it be the Bible itself, but to realise more truly the blessedness of knowing that He Himself, the Living God, our Father and Friend, is nearer and closer to us than any book can be, – that His Voice within the heart may be heard continually by the obedient child that listens for it, and *that* shall be our Teacher and Guide, in the path of duty, which is the path of life, when all other helpers – even the words of the Best of Books – may fail us.

14. In discharging, however, my present duty to God and to the Church, I trust that I shall be preserved from saying a single word that may cause *unnecessary* pain to those who now embrace with all their hearts, as a primary article of faith, the ordinary view of Scripture Inspiration. *Pain*, I know, I must cause to some. But I feel very deeply that it behoves every one, who would write on such a subject as this, to remember how closely the belief in the historical truth of every portion of the Bible is interwoven, at the present time, in England, with the faith of many, whose piety and charity may far surpass his own. He must beware lest, even by rudeness or carelessness of speech, he 'offend one of these little ones;' while yet he may feel it to be his duty, as I do now, to tell out plainly the truth, as God, he believes, has enabled him to see it. And that truth in the present instance, as I have said, is this, that the Pentateuch, as a whole, was not written by Moses, and that, with respect to some, at least, of the chief portions of the story, it cannot be regarded as historically true. It does not, therefore, cease to 'contain the true Word of God,' with 'all things necessary for salvation,' to be 'profitable for doctrine, reproof, correction, instruction in righteousness.' It still remains an integral portion of that Book, which, whatever intermixture it may show of human elements, – of error, infirmity, passion, and ignorance, – has yet, through God's Providence, and the special working of His Spirit on the minds of its writers, been the means of revealing to us His True Name, the Name of the only Living and True God, and has all along been, and, as far as we know, will never cease to be, the mightiest instrument in the hand of the Divine Teacher, for awakening in our minds just conceptions of His Character, and of His gracious and merciful dealings with the children of men. Only we must not attempt to put into the Bible what we think *ought* to be there: we must not indulge that 'forward delusive faculty,' as Bishop BUTLER[10] styles the 'imagination,' and lay it down for certain beforehand that God could only reveal Himself to us by means of an infallible Book. We must be content to take the Bible as it is, and draw from it those Lessons which it really contains. Accordingly, that which I have done, or endeavoured to do, in this book, is to make out from the Bible – at least, from the first part of it – what account it gives of itself, what it

really is, what, if we love the truth, we must understand and believe it to be, what, if we will speak the truth, we must represent it to be.

15. I shall omit for the present a number of plain, but less obvious, indications of the main point which I have asserted; because it may be possible, in some, at least, of such cases, to explain the meaning of the Scripture words in some way, so as to make them agree with known facts, or with statements seemingly contradictory, which are made elsewhere. My object will first be to satisfy the reader's mind as soon as possible that the case is certainly as I have stated it, that so he may go on with the less hesitation, and pursue with me the much more difficult enquiry into the real origin and meaning of these books. I shall endeavour to relieve him at once, in the very outset of our investigations, from that painful sense of fear and misgiving, which now, I imagine, deters so many, as it has so long deterred me, from looking resolutely and deliberately into the matter, and applying to these books the same honest, though respectful, criticism, which they would apply to other writings, however highly esteemed. So long as the spirit is oppressed with this sense of dread, it is impossible to come to the consideration of the matter before us with the calmness, and composure of mind, which the case requires. In this way, also, we shall best be able to disentangle the subject from the mass of sophistical arguments, which, as will appear abundantly in the course of this work, have been adduced by various writers in support of the ordinary view, and which will never cease to be adduced by well-meaning writers, and be eagerly acquiesced in by pious minds, so long as it is assumed *à priori*, as an Article of Faith, that the Pentateuch, as God's Word, is, therefore, also as an historical record, in all its parts, infallibly true, and that, consequently, *some* account *must* be given, however far-fetched and unsatisfactory, of the strange phenomena, which it presents to a thoughtful and enquiring reader.

16. It may not be easy, nor even possible, to determine with absolute certainty, when, and by whom, and under what peculiar circumstances, the different portions of the Pentateuch were written; though I shall hope to show, as we proceed, that much light may be thrown upon this point. But, in order to elucidate it more fully, we need the cooperation of many minds of different quality, who shall engage themselves vigorously in the enquiry, with the different talents which God has vouchsafed to them, and with the help of all the aids of modern science. At present there are but few, comparatively, – in England, at all events, – who have devoted themselves in a pious and reverent spirit to these studies. The number, indeed, of such students, is increasing, and will, I am sure, increase daily. But still there are not a few, who are unwilling to disturb, it may be, the repose of their souls, by examining into the fundamental truth of matters, which are believed, or, at least, acquiesced in, by the great mass of Christendom. And there are others, who dread lest, in making such enquiries, they shall, perhaps, be going 'beyond what is written,' and who shrink, as from an act of sacrilege, from the very though of submitting, what they deem to be, in the most literal sense, the very Word of God, to human criticism.

17. Nevertheless, I believe, as I have said, that the time is come, in the

ordering of God's Providence and in the history of the world, when such a work as this must be taken in hand, not in a light and scoffing spirit, but in that of a devout and living faith, which seeks only Truth, and follows fearlessly its footsteps, – when such questions as these must be asked, – be asked reverently, as by those who feel that they are treading on holy ground, – but be asked firmly, as by those who would be able to give an account of the hope which is in them, and to know that the grounds are sure, on which they rest their trust for time and for Eternity. The spirit, indeed, in which such a work should be carried on, cannot be better described than in the words of BURGON, who says, *p.* cxli: –

> Approach the volume of Holy Scripture with the same candour, and in the same unprejudiced spirit, with which you would approach any other famous book of high antiquity. Study it with, at least, the same attention. Give, at least, equal heed to *all* its statements. Acquaint yourself at least as industriously with its method and principle, employing and applying either with at least equal fidelity in its interpretation. *Above all, beware of playing tricks with its plain language.* Beware of suppressing any part of the evidence which it supplies to its own meaning. Be truthful, and unprejudiced, and honest, and consistent, and logical, and exact throughout, in your work of interpretation.

And again he writes, commending a closer attention to Biblical studies to the younger members of the University of Oxford, *p.* 12, –

> I contemplate the continued exercise of a most curious and prying, as well as a most vigilant and observing, eye. *No* difficulty is to be neglected; *no* peculiarity of expression is to be disregarded; *no* minute detail is to be overlooked. The hint, let fall in an earlier chapter, is to be compared with a hint let fall in the later place. *Do they tally or not? And what follows?*

Bishop BUTLER also truly observes, *Analogy of Religion,*[11] Part II, chap. viii, i, 1, –

> The Scripture-history in general is to be admitted as an authentic genuine history, till somewhat positive be alleged sufficient to invalidate it.

But he adds –

> *General incredibility in the things related, or inconsistencies in the general turn of the history, would prove it to be of no authority.*

# Part III

# ART AND CULTURE

## CONTENTS

INTRODUCTION                                                          313

6 ART AS MORALITY                                                     325
   *From* John Ruskin, *The Stones of Venice. Volume II* (1853)  *325*
   *From* Matthew Arnold, 'Art VIII – The Functions of Criticism at the
      Present Time' (1864)  *351*

7 ART FOR ART'S SAKE                                                  369
   *From* Algernon Swinburne, *Notes on Poems and Reviews* (1866)  *369*
   *From* Walter Pater, *Studies in the History of the Renaissance* (1873)  *383*
   *From* Oscar Wilde, 'The Decay of Lying: A Dialogue' (1889)  *390*
   *From* Arthur Symons, *The Symbolist Movement in Literature* (1899)  *410*

8 ART AS PATHOLOGY                                                    415
   *From* Max Nordau, *Degeneration* (1895)  *415*

9 ART AND THE STATE                                                   433
   *From* William Morris, 'Art Under Plutocracy' (1884)  *433*
   *From* William John Courthope, *Life in Poetry: Law in Taste* (1901)  *446*

# INTRODUCTION

The period between 1830 and 1901 saw an intense interest in the fine and applied arts. The extent of that interest is to be seen in any number of areas: for example, in the founding of national art institutions (including the National Gallery, the National Portrait Gallery and the Victoria and Albert Museum), in the explosion in popular publishing and the founding of many public libraries (which together brought about the association of reading and leisure), in the formal introduction of the study of literature and art into university curricula, and in the success of events such as the 1851 Great Exhibition at the Crystal Palace. In addition new travel opportunities and colonial expansion brought about an increased interest in the art of foreign countries and ancient civilisations. Tastes ranged from an enthusiasm for the art of the Italian Renaissance to the obsession in the 1890s with 'Japonisme' (particularly the collecting of Japanese prints and blue china). The nature and range of all these interests are, even to a modern eye, quite startling. Together they can be seen as evidence for the enfranchising of middle- and lower middle-class taste.

In one way, the enormously enlarged public participation in art is easy to explain. As I have suggested in Part I, the British economy expanded quickly (if not in a particularly steady way) throughout the nineteenth century. The increasing availability of what economists call 'surplus value' permitted new markets for art to develop – especially among the middle classes. These markets in turn gave rise to an art industry which set the pattern for the variety of art institutions which are still in existence today. An exception to this rule, however, was the influence in Victorian Britain of literary and art critics, figures who collectively possessed much more social prestige than their modern counterparts do. For example, John Ruskin's *Modern Painters*, with its vivid 'word-painting', its emphasis on pictorial art as a moral narrative, and its attention to the experience of the individual 'beholder', helped to mediate to a much larger audience the fine art which was being assembled in national galleries and museums and reproduced by new printing technologies. Art became part of domestic life. In the process, and like so many other areas of private activity in Victorian Britain, art also came under increased public scrutiny. Indeed one effect of the growth of this art industry in the nineteenth century was to bring the issue of aesthetic value – of what constitute acceptable canons of taste – into the public arena, and therefore open to debate and contention.

Broadly speaking, these debates centred on two main topics. First there was the question of the *nature* of aesthetic value – basically, that is, what were the criteria which defined a good novel or painting. Today we tend to think of this problem as the most intractable in philo-sophical aesthetics, for we recognise that questions of taste are inextricably intertwined with the wider interests of particular social groups: in other words we tend to acknowledge that within a culture there may be many (and often competing) definitions of aesthetic value. By contrast, the Victorians were much more confident about the possibility of a consensus on matters of taste. This certainty was due in part to the fact that the voices in such debates were confined to a fairly narrow interest group (as I indicated in the Introduction to this book, they were mainly male, middle- or upper-middle class, and exclusively white). But the confidence of the Victorians was also related to the second main topic in Victorian debates about aesthetics – the attention given to the *social* function of art.

Generally speaking, the nineteenth century emphasised the ideal popularised by Sir Philip Sidney, that art should teach by delighting. To a Victorian mind, in matters of art the term 'teaching' meant moral teaching. In other words, for the Victorians, the primary function of art was to socialise individual readers or spectators into the moral values of their culture. Such an ambition clearly demanded that art should be accessible – that it should communicate its moral message clearly and unequivocally to as wide an audience as possible. It should therefore come as no surprise that in defining their criteria of aesthetic value, the Victorians tended to judge a novel or a painting primarily in terms of its representational qualities – that is, in terms of its verisimilitude or its ability to embody 'real life'. It followed from such a view that realism was the mode of writing or pictorial art which the Victorians valued most, and that the novel and narrative painting were their most popular art-forms. Moreover, in the case of Victorian poetry, this emphasis on the communicative function of literature produced prescriptions about poetic language – that it should be clear, simple and direct, and that deliberate obfuscation (verbal complexity for its own sake) should be avoided.

To the modern reader, alert to arguments about cultural relativism and to the acknowledgement that the art of interest groups or sub-cultures may express different but not necessarily inferior or less important values, the Victorian emphasis on art as a form of moral instruction will inevitably be seen as normative. Whose definition of morals, we might wish to ask, determines acceptability? More precisely, what kind of reader did reviewers have in mind when they decided whether a work was clear or obscure, instructive or shocking? In practice, most consumers of art were middle-class – for example, readers of fiction were principally middle-class women and, as George Moore bitterly complained in 1885, it was *their* sense of probity (or rather, the views of their fathers or husbands about what was suitable reading-matter for women) which determined literary taste.[1] In short, we (like George Moore and several other late Victorian writers) will certainly detect a politics lurking behind the social and moral role which the Victorians predicated of culture. For many other Victorians, however, certainly in the early and middle decades of the century, such conflicts of interest were not nearly so apparent. This was largely because the Victorians typically viewed art as a realm of absolute, rather than relative, value: that is, the status of the moral knowledge which art was held to embody was simply taken for granted. For critics such as Ruskin, for example, the authority of art was ultimately sanctioned by faith: great art was simply incompatible with 'any viciousness of soul, with any mean anxiety, any gnawing lust, any wretchedness of spite or remorse, any consciousness of rebellion against the law of God.'[2] Importantly, it was precisely such a quality which guaranteed art its special function in society, for it was seen as providing the ground upon which factional differences of particular interest groups could be dissolved. Matthew Arnold, for example, could see culture uniting the best elements in all groups, thus providing the basis of social cohesion – it constituted what he called a society's 'best self'. For Arnold art or culture could be seen as a kind of social glue. To the modern eye, however, there is the making of a paradox here: the assumption that the moral value which defines art is absolute and self-evident (in John Stuart Mill's succinct formula, 'poetry . . . is truth')[3] in practice became a rationale for policing it – for, that is, the establishing of art-institutions (with a range of explicitly coercive functions) to shape and control public taste. Theatre, fiction-writing, and to some extent pictorial art were all subject to various forms of public or self-censorship. That such agencies existed is testimony to the seriousness with which the Victorians viewed art; but it also hints at a deep anxiety about the strength of the social consensus upon which this moral definition of aesthetic and artistic value clearly depended.

Of course the main motivation behind works such as *Culture and Anarchy* in the 1860s was a perception (and a fear) that the existing consensus was in the process of breaking up, if indeed it had ever really existed. The reasons were various. Most obviously (as I have described in Part I) debates about political representation and agitation over the extension of the franchise had revealed profound resentments and fundamental conflicts of interest between different groups in society – matters which were exacerbated by the unevenness of economic growth and recurring economic slumps (which tended to be much deeper than their modern equivalents). A further source of unease was the frequent violent social unrest and political agitation on the Continent, and particularly in France. The French Revolution and its aftershocks in 1848 and 1870 haunted nineteenth-century British political life. More generally (as I have indicated in Part II) the traditional ground for shared interests and values – religion – was being gradually eroded, and in three ways: by dissent within the established (Anglican) church, by the increasing influence of dissenting religions (such as Methodism and Unitarianism) and by the growing hegemony of science. In the second half of the century the issue of social cohesion increasingly came to be seen not only as a political but also as a theoretical problem. The result, as Part I has demonstrated, was a flowering of British social theory in which a variety of commentators tried to rethink the relationship between the individual and the social. Not surprisingly, the erosion of old certainties about 'community' and the concepts which had underwritten it had profound consequences for practising artists and writers and the art institutions which tried to control them. The moment when arguments for the centripetal functions of art became most strident is ironically also the moment when the condition for their success – that is, a consensus about social life itself – had all but disappeared.

316

One distinct kind of response to this problematising of the concept of consensus is represented by the English Aesthetic Movement in the late 1860s to early 1880s. Traditionally literary historians have located Aestheticism's origins in French models, typically in the work of Théophile Gautier in the 1830s and 1840s and Charles Baudelaire in the 1850s and 1860s.[4] While there are clear similarities between Gautier's celebration of 'l'art pour l'art' and his English counterparts' valorisation of 'Art for Art's Sake', they should not be overstressed.[5] In an English context, the contentiousness of 'Art for Art's Sake' resided in its opposition to a normative view of art as the embodiment and distillation of a culture's moral values. The advocates of English Aestheticism interpreted the phrase 'Art for Art's Sake' as an appeal to free art from moral concerns, and therefore from any social responsibility – as Oscar Wilde famously protested in the preface to his novel, The Picture of Dorian Gray, 'All art is quite useless'. Rather than stressing the social function of art, the Aesthetes asserted its value only in terms of the individual: that is, they defined the experience of art as purely private, one which was moreover vouchsafed only to special kinds of individuals, and which was in its very essence ephemeral. In this view the experience of art was characteristically one of reverie or contemplation, an escape from life rather than an engagement with it. In the words of Walter Pater, Aestheticism's earliest and most able proponent, 'Art comes to you proposing frankly to give nothing but the highest quality to your moments as they pass, and simply for those moments' sake'.

The theoretical basis of this emphasis on the experience of art or beauty for its own sake derived in part from a revival and reinterpretation of Romantic ideologies of creativity. This reinterpretation was in turn confirmed by contemporary developments in philosophy and particularly in psychology – the latter body of knowledge providing the Aesthetes with a specialised (and in part a 'scientific') vocabulary to describe the nature of aesthetic experience.[6] Like their English Romantic predecessors, the Aesthetes stressed the importance of the uniqueness of the individual creative mind; however, they rejected the Wordsworthian notion that the creative act was a participation in (and revelation of) a principle of divine order. Instead they emphasised the artist's fidelity to personally felt experience; good writing, as Pater argued apropos of Rossetti, was finding the 'just transcript of that peculiar phase of soul which he alone knew, precisely as he knew it' – it meant finding a language appropriate to inner experience. Such an argument was tantamount to suggesting that the language of art, far from being public, social and communal (as Arnold and indeed the Romantics had argued), was private, individual and esoteric. In other words the language of art was by definition non-normative in the sense that any attempt to impose norms or prescriptions would do violence to the very notion of expressive authenticity which determined its aesthetic value. One of the conundrums of Aestheticism, then, was that although it emphasised both form and content (that is, it was concerned with the relationship between the medium and the message, rather than the message itself), at the same time it did not possess – and could not possibly have possessed – any common critical vocabulary or communally agreed standards which would have allowed stylistic success to be determined. Both the experience of art, *and* its creation, then, were completely private processes.

As I have suggested, the Aesthetes came to public attention at precisely the moment when the normative view of art as a socially cohesive realm of value was itself being placed under threat. The result was that Aestheticism was given much more serious attention than might otherwise have been expected from a theory of aesthetic experience which attempted to separate art from social life. To its critics, the relativist implications of Aestheticism appeared as a form of social anarchy: that is, its stress on the importance of *individual* judgement – on the individual as the sole arbiter of the quality of an aesthetic experience – appeared to license what they considered to be undesirable and possibly transgressive experiences. Or, more precisely, Aestheticism denied the grounds upon which it would be possible to discriminate authoritatively between normative and non-normative values. The suspicion that Aestheticism was deeply (and theoretically) 'anti-social' was fuelled by the personal lives of its most prominent advocates: Swinburne, Pater and (most infamously) Wilde to a greater or lesser degree all scandalised their audiences; all were the subject of allegations of sexual impropriety – allegations which in fact were broadly true. To its detractors, then, Aestheticism could all too easily be seen as a self-serving apology for an amoral, selfish hedonism – for an attitude to life (and a lifestyle) which threatened the very basis of civil society.

In the last decade of the century these kinds of suspicions – which were often referred to as the 'morbid' tendencies of Aestheticism – seemed to be publicly played out in a literary movement known today as the English Decadence. The movement centred on a group of poets for whom life and art seemed to be inextricably linked in the sense that they attempted to live their lives *as art*. And art for them included the celebration of illicit experiences, particularly what were then seen as morbid sexual fantasies. These experiences included the affiliation of sexual desire with children, with death and with what were then euphemistically called 'light loves'. We now refer to these themes by altogether less pleasant names: child abuse, necrophilia and prostitution. For the Decadents, though, such experiences could be romanticised because they stood for the gratification of desire without any hint of an accompanying social responsibility. Interestingly, the Decadents also developed a theory of literary expressivity which seemed to their contemporaries to embody a parallel irresponsibility towards language. In the Decadent theory of the symbol, as it was expounded by the poet and critic Arthur Symons, symbolic utterance was celebrated for its ability to represent the difficulty or impossibility of knowledge. Such a view was in direct opposition to Romantic symbolism and its Victorian counterpart, typology, which had been popularised in the middle of the century by Ruskin and the Pre-Raphaelites. In these instances the function of the symbol or 'type' was to fix or 'authorise' knowledge by establishing a connection with the divine. For the Decadents, however, symbols were by their very nature polyvalent; open to multiple interpretations, they revealed not epistemological certainty, but its exact opposite – a sense that all knowledge was mysterious and ineffable. In other words, the relativisation of language which was implicit in Aestheticism's emphasis on the uniqueness of individual expression had become, in the poetry of the Decadents, an overt cultivation of the esoteric and obscure – qualities which in turn undermined any claim that literature might have a social utility.

As we might expect, the attempt by the Decadents and Aesthetes to divorce art from social life was met with a vehement reassertion of the social and cultural centrality of literary and artistic expression. However, the crucial difference between articulating such a position in the 1880s and 1890s rather than in the earlier half of the century lay in the fact that the moral certainties which had underwritten the polemic of Ruskin or Arnold could no longer be assumed. One consequence was that in the late decades of the century the normative role of culture simply could not be ignored, and arguments about aesthetic value, or the social role of art, became explicit disagreements about political values and the nature of civil society.

The changed nature of late nineteenth-century debates about the social function of art can be glimpsed in the development of a new critical vocabulary – of terms such as 'degeneration', 'morbidity', 'perversity', 'inversion' – which began to emerge in the late 1870s, and which had become commonplace in literary and art discourses by the 1890s. In general terms, that vocabulary associated artistic dissidence with a much more fundamental social, spiritual and physiological decline. It drew upon a variety of sources. Primarily there was the impact of Social Darwinism, with its proposition that society was an organism with functionally interdependent parts and that if one element was 'diseased', then all of society was threatened. This view provided traditional arguments about the 'health' of a nation or the 'health' of a culture with a compelling new and scientific rationale. More particularly, contemporary developments in psychology and the scientific study of human sexuality had hinted at a pathology of artistic creativity, a line of argument popularised by the translation of Max Nordau's *Degeneration* in 1895. Examining late nineteenth-century society, Nordau pointed to a growing 'contempt in traditional views of custom and morality' which he identified with what he termed a *'fin-de-siècle* disposition'. Particularly visible in 'the tendencies of contemporary art and poetry' (including the work of the Aesthetes and Decadents), this disposition, according to Nordau, had its basis in organic (and generally hereditary) disease. This notion of cultural decay also drew upon classical scholarship, particularly analogies between late nineteenth-century Britain and the fall of the Roman Empire. It is worth remembering that the Aesthetes and Decadents had claimed to find in classical culture an acceptance and celebration of precisely those non-normative desires anathematised in the nineteenth century.

Further evidence for the changed nature of debates about the social function of art in the late decades of the century exists in the variety of arguments which were articulated within this general position. So although many (indeed the majority of) critics were in agreement about the need to reassert the social nature of art and literature, they nevertheless differed profoundly on the kind of social role it should possess, and the kinds of common values it should embody. We can see the dimensions of those disagreements in the contrast between the work of the conservative critic and Professor of Poetry at Oxford, William Courthope and the socialist polemic of William Morris. Both Courthope and Morris were critical of Aestheticism, and of what they saw as the divisive élitism of its rarefied view of aesthetic experience. Both sought to reintegrate art with life; and both saw in art a repository of moral value. Courthope drew freely upon the rhetoric of degeneration and decay to argue that art could only regain its 'health' and 'manliness' (favourite terms in the lexicon of conservatives), and therefore its cultural and social centrality, by a renewed regard for the rules of artistic expression authorised by literary tradition. In this respect he was at one with Matthew Arnold's notion of 'touchstones' of aesthetic or literary value. Where Courthope differed, however, was in his explicit acknowledgement that tradition – what we would now refer to as the canon – was defined in *national*, rather than absolute terms: culture, that is, embodied 'interested' (as opposed to Arnold's insistence on 'disinterested') values. It was thus, for example, that John Campbell Shairp, Courthope's predecessor at Oxford, could talk in 1881 of 'the noble English style' and of 'the poetry of England' as 'the bloom of her national life'.[7] Courthope's and Shairp's academic status adds a further dimension to this line of argument. In the late nineteenth century there was a fierce controversy about whether the study of literature should be an autonomous university discipline. The arguments were complex and involved several different issues, one of which concerned the social utility of academic literary study. It is worth noting that some enthusiasts for the academic study of literature pointed out that such a condition could be usefully met by the argument that literature embodied (and preserved) a national identity.

William Morris's concern with the social role of art could not have been more different. Like Courthope, Morris equated contemporary artistic practices with the preservation of certain aspects of contemporary social life, particularly class divisions. Unlike Courthope, however, in Morris's eyes this 'stabilising' function of art was a symptom of the fundamental corruption of his society – it was a cause of, rather than cure for, social discontents. Morris thus argued for a wholesale change in the ways in which art was defined, valued and practised. As Part II has indicated, these changes in turn were conceived as part of a much more radical revolution in the structural basis of society. There were two aspects of current art institutions which Morris particularly deplored. One was a reverence for tradition. Morris was as sensitive as Courthope to the national significance of the art of the past; indeed he campaigned vigorously for the preservation of ancient buildings, and throughout his life retained a youthful fascination with medievalism. Where Morris differed from conservatives, however, was in his insistence that the art of the past could *not* provide the present with models or precedents (as had been the practice, for example, in Victorian imitations of Gothic architecture popularised by the writing and embodied in the work of Augustus Pugin). Drawing on aspects of Ruskin's work, Morris emphasised the importance of art as expressive of a society's unique historical situation, a circumstance which, by definition, rendered imitation itself wholly inauthentic. Another of Morris's complaints concerned the relationship between what he termed art and 'commerce' – that is, the dominance of the competitive values of the free market. In Morris's view, it had led to a situation where art had become a luxury – the preserve of a wealthy élite. More importantly, the removal of art from everyday life had reduced the work of the 'ordinary' man or woman to mere mechanical drudgery. Morris saw in the revival of traditional handicrafts (with their emphasis on art as work and on co-operative methods of production) the possibility for the full reintegration of art and life – for, that is, a truly popular art which was (in his terms) 'by the people and for the people'.

In practice, of course, Morris's hand-crafted artefacts turned out to be anything but 'popular' art; ironically they proved so expensive to produce that only the wealthiest could afford to possess them. This discrepancy is more important than it might seem, for it points to the vexed nature of the relationship between theories of art and the actual art market. There is evidence that as the market for art expanded in the nineteenth century so it also diversified: for example, along with the development of popular publishing forms, such as railway fiction, or 'penny-dreadfuls', there was also an increase in coterie publishing – the production of elaborate, expensive and very limited editions, such as the works produced by Morris's own Kelmscott Press (established in 1890). For some critics, these developments have been interpreted as heralding the beginnings of the division between mass culture and élite culture: that is, actual changes documented in the economy of art are claimed to correspond to (and in part explain) changes in the way art was defined and valued. More recently, other critics have stressed the complexity of those new markets, and the acuity which artists and writers needed to exploit them fully. Certainly, the late nineteenth century saw a much greater awareness of the commercial element of literary and artistic production. For Morris this was a source of regret and anger; for other figures (such as Wilde) it was a situation to be exploited. Indeed the literary success of Wilde and some of his contemporaries in the early 1890s has been explained in terms of a very modern appreciation of consumerism – a willingness, that is, to market themselves and their work self-consciously and systematically, and to appeal not to the absolute court of a Ruskin or Arnold, but simply to fashion. The extent of this alleged 'commodification' of aesthetic value in the late nineteenth century is a rather contentious issue.[8] However, the general drift of its argument echoes a theme which has persisted in any number of histories of Victorian culture: that late nineteenth-century art and literature is distinguished from work produced earlier in the century by a certain 'modernity'. In other words, the rejection of 'high' Victorian values which we find in movements such as Aestheticism and the Decadence anticipates (and helps provide the conditions for) the much more thoroughgoing formal and ideological iconoclasm associated with the modernist movement in particular, and with the diversity of twentieth-century art-forms in general. It is clearly beyond the scope of the present anthology to explore such relationships, but it is worth noting in passing how little the terms of discussion about art and aesthetics have changed since the Victorian period. So today the issue of the social function of the arts and their relationship to national life – in debates over whether public resources should fund opera or, say, community drama – are still pressing and are still matters of some dispute.

# 6

# ART AS MORALITY

## JOHN RUSKIN, *THE STONES OF VENICE. VOLUME II* (1853)

At the height of his fame in the middle decades of the nineteenth century, John Ruskin (1819–1900) was the most influential art critic in England. His writing career began in the late 1830s with contributions to several magazines. His first main work was the first volume of the five-volume *Modern Painters* (1843–60). Inspired by his admiration for the late work of the landscape artist, J. M. W. Turner, the book established Ruskin's reputation virtually overnight. His vivid style, described as 'word-painting', combined with his interpretations of individual works in terms of a moral narrative, made art accessible to a new kind of public. The emphasis on art as the embodiment of moral knowledge also informed his next major works – *The Seven Lamps of Architecture* (1849) and *The Stones of Venice* (3 vols., 1851–3) – in which Ruskin connected artistic achievement with the moral health of the nation. The latter work became an influence on the Gothic Revival in architecture in the early and middle decades of the nineteenth century, and had a lasting influence on English architecture. In 1848 Ruskin married Effie Gray; in 1851 he befriended Dante Gabriel Rossetti and began his association with the Pre-Raphaelite Brotherhood. Effie, meanwhile, fell in love with one of the brotherhood's members, John Everett Millais whom she married in 1854 following the annulment of her marriage to Ruskin on the grounds of non-consummation. In 1857 Ruskin published *The Elements of Drawing*, and gave some lectures in Manchester published that same year as *The Political Economy of Art*. The following year he met and 'fell in love' with the ten year-old Rose la Touche; he proposed marriage to her (unsuccessfully) in 1866. 1858 was also the year of what Ruskin termed his 'unconversion'. This loss of faith in the strict Evangelical Anglicanism of his youth marked a turning away from art towards more social and political concerns. *Unto This Last*, an attack on political economy, appeared in book form in 1862 (it was partially serialised in the *Cornhill Magazine* in 1860). In 1865 he published *Sesame and Lilies* which contained his controversial lecture on gender roles – 'Of Queens' Gardens'. This interest in social issues was continued with *The Ethics of the Dust* and *The Crown of Wild Olive*, both published in 1866. In 1867 *Time and Tide* appeared, a book of letters on the 'Laws of Work' addressed to Thomas Dixon, a cork-cutter in Sunderland. In 1869 Ruskin was made first Slade Professor of Fine Art at Oxford; his inaugural series of lectures were published in 1870. With the exception of *Fors Clavigera*, a second series of letters to working men issued monthly from 1871 to 1884, Ruskin's publications in the 1870s and 1880s marked a return to artistic subjects and a new interest in natural history and botany. With the death of Rose la Touche in 1875, Ruskin became increasingly frail and unstable, suffering a series of mental breakdowns. One of his last works, before his complete breakdown in 1889, was the autobiographical *Praeterita*. The last ten years of Ruskin's life were spent in silence and incapacity. Ironically the death in seclusion of this archetypal Victorian intellectual coincided almost exactly with the end of the Victorian age.

### From John Ruskin, *The Stones of Venice. Volume II: The Sea-Stories* (London: Smith, Elder and Co., 1853)[1]

From *Chapter VI: The Nature Of Gothic*[2]

§I. If the reader will look back to the division of our subject which was made in the first chapter of the first volume,[3] he will find that we are now about to enter upon the examination of that school of Venetian architecture which forms an intermediate step between the Byzantine and Gothic forms; but which I find may be conveniently considered in its connexion with the latter style. In order that we may discern the tendency of each step of this change, it will be wise in the outset to endeavour to form some general idea of its final result. We know already what the Byzantine architecture is from which the transition was made, but we ought to know something of the Gothic architecture into which it led. I shall endeavour therefore to give the reader in this chapter an idea, at once broad and definite, of the true nature of *Gothic* architecture, properly so called; not of that of Venice only, but of universal Gothic: for it will be one of the most interesting parts of our subsequent inquiry to find out how far Venetian architecture reached the universal or perfect type of

Gothic, and how far it either fell short of it, or assumed foreign and independent forms.

§II. The principal difficulty in doing this arises from the fact that every building of the Gothic period differs in some important respect from every other; and many include features which, if they occurred in other buildings, would not be considered Gothic at all; so that all we have to reason upon is merely, if I may be allowed so to express it, a greater or less degree of *Gothicness* in each building we examine. And it is this Gothicness, – the character which, according as it is found more or less in a building, makes it more or less Gothic, – of which I want to define the nature; and I feel the same kind of difficulty in doing so which would be encountered by any one who undertook to explain, for instance, the nature of Redness, without any actually red thing to point to, but only orange and purple things. Suppose he had only a piece of heather and a dead oak-leaf to do it with. He might say, the colour which is mixed with the yellow in this oak-leaf, and with the blue in this heather, would be red, if you had it separate; but it would be difficult, nevertheless, to make the abstraction perfectly intelligible: and it is so in a far greater degree to make the abstraction of the Gothic character intelligible, because that character itself is made up of many mingled ideas, and can consist only in their union. That is to say, pointed arches do not constitute Gothic, nor vaulted roofs, nor flying buttresses,[4] nor grotesque sculptures; but all or some of these things, and many other things with them, when they come together so as to have life.

§III. Observe also, that, in the definition proposed, I shall only endeavour to analyze the idea which I suppose already to exist in the reader's mind. We all have some notion, most of us a very determined one, of the meaning of the term Gothic, but I know that many persons have this idea in their minds without being able to define it: that is to say, understanding generally that Westminster Abbey is Gothic, and St Paul's is not, that Strasburg Cathedral is Gothic, and St Peter's is not, they have, nevertheless, no clear notion of what it is that they recognize in the one or miss in the other, such as would enable them to say how far the work at Westminster or Strasburg is good and pure of its kind; still less to say of any nondescript building, like St James's Palace or Windsor Castle, how much right Gothic element there is in it, and how much wanting. And I believe this inquiry to be a pleasant and profitable one; and that there will be found something more than usually interesting in tracing out this grey, shadowy, many-pinnacled image of the Gothic spirit within us; and discerning what fellowship there is between it and our Northern hearts. And if, at any point of the inquiry, I should interfere with any of the reader's previously formed conceptions, and use the term Gothic in any sense which he would not willingly attach to it, I do not ask him to accept, but only to examine and understand, my interpretation, as necessary to the intelligibility of what follows in the rest of the work.

§IV. We have, then, the Gothic character submitted to our analysis, just as the rough mineral is submitted to that of the chemist, entangled with many other foreign substances, itself perhaps in no place pure, or ever to be obtained or seen in purity for more than an instant; but nevertheless a thing of definite and separate nature, however inextricable or confused in appearance. Now observe: the chemist defines his mineral by two separate kinds of character; one external, its crystalline form, hardness, lustre, etc.; the other internal, the proportions and nature of its constituent atoms. Exactly in the same manner, we shall find that Gothic architecture has external forms and internal elements. Its elements are certain mental tendencies of the builders, legibly expressed in it; as fancifulness, love of variety, love of richness, and such others. Its external forms are pointed arches, vaulted roofs, etc. And unless both the elements and the forms are there, we have no right to call the style Gothic. It is not enough that it has the Form, if it have not also the power and life. It is not enough that it has the Power, if it have not the form. We must therefore inquire into each of these characters successively; and determine first, what is the Mental Expression, and secondly, what the Material Form of Gothic architecture, properly so called.

1st. Mental Power or Expression. What characters, we have to discover, did the Gothic builders love, or instinctively express in their work, as distinguished from all other builders?

§V. Let us go back for a moment to our chemistry, and note that, in defining a mineral by its constituent parts, it is not one nor another of them, that can make up the mineral, but the union of all: for instance, it is neither in charcoal, nor in oxygen, nor in lime, that there is the making of chalk, but in the combination of all three in certain measures; they are all found in very different things from chalk, and there is nothing like chalk either in charcoal or in oxygen, but they are nevertheless necessary to its existence.

So in the various mental characters which make up the soul of Gothic. It is not one nor another that produces it; but their union in certain measures. Each one of them is found in many other architectures beside Gothic; but Gothic cannot exist where they are not found, or, at least, where their place is not in some way supplied. Only there is this great difference between the composition of the mineral and of the architectural style, that if we draw one of its elements from the stone, its form is utterly changed, and its existence as such and such a mineral is destroyed; but if we withdraw one of its mental elements from the Gothic style, it is only a little less Gothic than it was before, and the union of two or three of its elements is enough already to bestow a certain Gothicness of character, which gains in intensity as we add the others, and loses as we again withdraw them.

§VI. I believe, then, that the characteristic or moral elements of Gothic are the following, placed in the order of their importance:

1. Savageness.
2. Changefulness.
3. Naturalism.
4. Grotesqueness.
5. Rigidity.
6. Redundance.

These characters are here expressed as belonging to the building; as belonging to the builder, they would be expressed thus: – 1. Savageness or Rudeness. 2. Love of Change. 3. Love of Nature. 4. Disturbed Imagination. 5. Obstinacy. 6. Generosity. And I repeat, that the withdrawal of any one, or any two, will not at once destroy the Gothic character of a building, but the removal of a majority of them will. I shall proceed to examine them in their order.

§VII. (1.) SAVAGENESS. I am not sure when the word 'Gothic' was first generically applied to the architecture of the North;[5] but I presume that, whatever the date of its original usage, it was intended to imply reproach, and express the barbaric character of the nations among whom that architecture arose. It never implied that they were literally of Gothic lineage, far less that their architecture had been originally invented by the Goths[6] themselves; but it did imply that they and their buildings together exhibited a degree of sternness and rudeness, which, in contradistinction to the character of Southern and Eastern nations, appeared like a perpetual reflexion of the contrast between the Goth and the Roman in their first encounter. And when that fallen Roman, in the utmost impotence of his luxury, and insolence of his guilt, became the model for the imitation of civilized Europe, at the close of the so-called Dark ages, the word Gothic became a term of unmitigated contempt, not unmixed with aversion. From that contempt, by the exertion of the antiquaries and architects of this century, Gothic architecture has been sufficiently vindicated; and perhaps some among us, in our admiration of the magnificent science of its structure, and sacredness of its expression, might desire that the term of ancient reproach should be withdrawn, and some other, of more apparent honourableness, adopted in its place. There is no chance, as there is no need, of such a substitution. As far as the epithet was used scornfully, it was used falsely; but there is no reproach in the word, rightly understood; on the contrary, there is a profound truth, which the instinct of mankind almost unconsciously recognizes. It is true, greatly and deeply true, that the architecture of the North is rude and wild; but it is not true, that, for this reason, we are to condemn it, or despise. Far otherwise: I believe it is in this very character that it deserves our profoundest reverence.

§VIII. The charts of the world which have been drawn up by modern science have thrown into a narrow space the expression of a vast amount of knowledge, but I have never yet seen any one pictorial enough to enable the spectator to imagine the kind of contrast in physical character which exists between Northern and Southern countries. We know the differences in detail, but we have not that broad glance and grasp which would enable us to feel them in their fulness. We know that gentians grow in the Alps, and olives in the Apennines; but we do not enough conceive for ourselves that variegated mosaic of the world's surface which a bird sees in its migration, that difference between the district of the gentian and of the olive which the stork and the swallow see far off, as they lean upon the sirocco wind.[7] Let us, for a moment, try to raise ourselves even above the level of their flight, and imagine the Mediterranean lying beneath us like an irregular lake, and all its ancient promontories sleeping in the sun: here and there an angry spot of thunder, a grey stain of storm, moving upon the burning field; and here and there a fixed wreath of white volcano smoke, surrounded by its circle of ashes; but for the most part a great peacefulness of light, Syria and Greece, Italy and Spain, laid like pieces of a golden pavement into the sea-blue, chased, as we stoop nearer to them, with bossy[8] beaten work of mountain chains, and glowing softly with terraced gardens, and flowers heavy with frankincense, mixed among masses of laurel, and orange, and plumy palm, that abate with their grey-green shadows the burning of the marble rocks, and of the ledges of porphyry[9] sloping under lucent sand. Then let us pass farther towards the north, until we see the orient colours change gradually into a vast belt of rainy green, where the pastures of Switzerland, and poplar valleys of France, and dark forests of the Danube and Carpathians stretch from the mouths of the Loire to those of the Volga, seen through clefts in grey swirls of raincloud and flaky veils of the mist of the brooks, spreading low along the pasture lands: and then, farther north still, to see the earth heave into mighty masses of leaden rock and heathy moor, bordering with a broad waste of gloomy purple that belt of field and wood, and splintering into irregular and grisly islands amidst the northern seas, beaten by storm, and chilled by ice-drift, and tormented by furious pulses of contending tide, until the roots of the last forests fail from among the hill ravines, and the hunger of the north wind bites their peaks into barrenness; and, at last, the wall of ice, durable like iron, sets, deathlike, its white teeth against us out of the polar twilight. And, having once traversed in thought this gradation of the zoned iris of the earth in all its material vastness, let us go down nearer to it, and watch the parallel change in the belt of animal life; the multitudes of swift and brilliant creatures that glance in the air and sea, or tread the sands of the southern zone; striped zebras and spotted leopards, glistening serpents, and birds arrayed in purple and scarlet. Let us contrast their delicacy and brilliancy of colour, and swiftness of motion, with the frost-cramped strength, and shaggy covering, and dusky plumage of the northern tribes; contrast the Arabian horse with the Shetland, the tiger and leopard with the wolf and bear, the antelope with the elk, the bird of paradise with the osprey; and then, submissively acknowledging the great laws by which the earth and all that it bears are ruled throughout their being, let us not condemn, but rejoice in the expression by man of his own rest in the statues of the lands that gave him birth. Let us watch him with reverence as he sets side by side the burning gems, and smooths with soft sculpture the jasper pillars, that are to reflect a ceaseless sunshine, and rise into a cloudless sky: but not with less reverence let us stand by him, when, with rough strength and hurried stroke, he smites an uncouth animation out of the rocks which he has torn from among the moss of the moorland, and heaves into the darkened air the pile of iron buttress and rugged wall, instinct with work of an imagination as wild and wayward as the northern sea; creations of ungainly shape and rigid

330

limb, but full of wolfish life; fierce as the winds that beat, and changeful as the clouds that shade them.

There is, I repeat, no degradation, no reproach in this, but all dignity and honourableness: and we should err grievously in refusing either to recognize as an essential character of the existing architecture of the North, or to admit as a desirable character in that which it yet may be, this wildness of thought, and roughness of work; this look of mountain brotherhood between the cathedral and the Alp; this magnificence of sturdy power, put forth only the more energetically because the fine finger-touch was chilled away by the frosty wind, and the eye dimmed by the moor-mist, or blinded by the hail; this out-speaking of the strong spirit of men who may not gather redundant fruitage from the earth, nor bask in dreamy benignity of sunshine, but must break the rock for bread, and cleave the forest for life, and show, even in what they did for their delight, some of the hard habits of the arm and heart that grew on them as they swung the axe or pressed the plough.

§IX. If, however, the savageness of Gothic architecture, merely as an expression of its origin among Northern nations, may be considered, in some sort, a noble character, it possesses a higher nobility still, when considered as an index, not of climate, but of religious principle.

In the 13th and 14th paragraphs of Chapter XXI. of the first volume of this work, it was noticed that the systems of architectural ornament, properly so called, might be divided into three: – 1. Servile ornament, in which the execution or power of the inferior workman is entirely subjected to the intellect of the higher; – 2. Constitutional ornament, in which the executive inferior power is, to a certain point, emancipated and independent, having a will of its own, yet confessing its inferiority and rendering obedience to higher powers; – 3. Revolutionary ornament, in which no executive inferiority is admitted at all. I must here explain the nature of these divisions at somewhat greater length.

Of Servile ornament, the principal schools are the Greek, Ninevite,[10] and Egyptian; but their servility is of different kinds. The Greek master-workman was far advanced in knowledge and power above the Assyrian or Egyptian. Neither he nor those for whom he worked could endure the appearance of imperfection in anything; and, therefore, what ornament he appointed to be done by those beneath him was composed of mere geometrical forms, – balls, ridges, and perfectly symmetrical foliage, – which could be executed with absolute precision by line and rule, and were as perfect in their way, when completed, as his own figure sculpture. The Assyrian and Egyptian, on the contrary, less cognisant of accurate form in anything, were content to allow their figure sculpture to be executed by inferior workmen, but lowered the method of its treatment to a standard which every workman could reach, and then trained him by discipline so rigid, that there was no chance of his falling beneath the standard appointed. The Greek gave to the lower workman no subject which he could not perfectly execute. The Assyrian gave him subjects which he could only execute imperfectly, but fixed a legal standard for his imperfection. The workman was, in both systems, a slave.[a]

§X. But in the mediaeval, or especially Christian, system of ornament,[11] this slavery is done away with altogether; Christianity having recognized, in small things as well as great, the individual value of every soul. But it not only recognizes its value; it confesses its imperfection, in only bestowing dignity upon the acknowledgement of unworthiness. That admission of lost power and fallen nature, which the Greek or Ninevite felt to be intensely painful, and, as far as might be, altogether refused, the Christian makes daily and hourly, contemplating the fact of it without fear, as tending, in the end, to God's greater glory. Therefore, to every spirit which Christianity summons to her service, her exhortation is: Do what you can, and confess frankly what you are unable to do; neither let your effort be shortened for fear of failure, nor your confession silenced for fear of shame. And it is, perhaps, the principal admirableness of the Gothic schools of architecture, that they thus receive the results of the labour of inferior minds; and out of fragments full of imperfection, and betraying that imperfection in every touch, indulgently raise up a stately and unaccusable whole.

§XI. But the modern English mind has this much in common with that of the Greek, that it intensely desires, in all things, the utmost completion or perfection compatible with their nature. This is a noble character in the abstract, but becomes ignoble when it causes us to forget the relative dignities of that nature itself, and to prefer the perfectness of the lower nature to the imperfection of the higher; not considering that as, judged by such a rule, all the brute animals would be preferable to man, because more perfect in their functions and kind, and yet are always held inferior to him, so also in the works of man, those which are more perfect in their kind are always inferior to those which are, in their nature, liable to more faults and shortcomings. For the finer the nature, the more flaws it will show through the clearness of it; and it is a law of this universe, that the best things shall be seldomest seen in their best form. The wild grass grows well and strongly, one year with another; but the wheat is, according to the greater nobleness of its nature, liable to the bitterer blight. And therefore, while in all things that we see or do, we are to desire perfection, and strive for it, we are nevertheless not to set the meaner thing, in its narrow accomplishment, above the nobler thing, in its mighty progress; not to esteem smooth minuteness above shattered majesty; not to prefer mean victory to honourable defeat; not to lower the level of our aim, that we may the more surely enjoy the complacency of success.[12] But, above all, in our dealings with the souls of other men, we are to

---

a    The third kind of ornament, the Renaissance, is that in which the inferior detail becomes principal, the executor of every minor portion being required to exhibit skill and possess knowledge as great as that which is possessed by the master of the design; and in the endeavour to endow him with this skill and knowledge, his own original power is overwhelmed, and the whole building becomes a wearisome exhibition of well-educated imbecility. We must fully inquire into the nature of this form of error, when we arrive at the examination of the Renaissance schools.

take care how we check, by severe requirement or narrow caution, efforts which might otherwise lead to a noble issue; and, still more, how we withhold our admiration from great excellencies, because they are mingled with rough faults. Now, in the make and nature of every man, however rude or simple, whom we employ in manual labour, there are some powers for better things; some tardy imagination, torpid capacity of emotion, tottering steps of thought, there are, even at the worst; and in most cases it is all our own fault that they *are* tardy or torpid. But they cannot be strengthened, unless we are content to take them in their feebleness, and unless we prize and honour them in their imperfection above the best and most perfect manual skill. And this is what we have to do with all our labourers; to look for the *thoughtful* part of them, and get that out of them, whatever we lose for it, whatever faults and errors we are obliged to take with it. For the best that is in them cannot manifest itself, but in company with much error. Understand this clearly: You can teach a man to draw a straight line, and to cut one; to strike a curved line, and to carve it; and to copy and carve any number of given lines and forms, with admirable speed and perfect precision; and you find his work perfect of its kind: but if you ask him to think about any of those forms, to consider if he cannot find any better in his own head, he stops; his execution becomes hesitating; he thinks, and ten to one he thinks wrong; ten to one he makes a mistake in the first touch he gives to his work as a thinking being. But you have made a man of him for all that. He was only a machine before, an animated tool.

§XII. And observe, you are put to stern choice in this matter. You must either make a tool of the creature, or a man of him. You cannot make both. Men were not intended to work with the accuracy of tools, to be precise and perfect in all their actions. If you will have that precision out of them, and make their fingers measure degrees like cog-wheels, and their arms strike curves like compasses, you must unhumanize them. All the energy of their spirits must be given to make cogs and compasses of themselves. All their attention and strength must go to the accomplishment of the mean act. The eye of the soul must be bent upon the finger-point, and the soul's force must fill all the invisible nerves that guide it, ten hours a day, that it may not err from its steely precision, and so soul and sight be worn away, and the whole human being be lost at last – a heap of sawdust, so far as its intellectual work in this world is concerned: saved only by its Heart, which cannot go into the form of cogs and compasses, but expands, after the ten hours are over, into fireside humanity. On the other hand, if you will make a man of the working creature, you cannot make a tool. Let him but begin to imagine, to think, to try to do anything worth doing; and the engine-tuned precision is lost at once. Out come all his roughness, all his dullness, all his incapability; shame upon shame, failure upon failure, pause after pause: but out comes the whole majesty of him also; and we know the height of it only when we see the clouds settling upon him. And, whether the clouds be bright or dark, there will be transfiguration behind and within them.

§XIII. And now, reader, look round this English room of yours, about which you have been proud so often, because the work of it was so good and strong, and the ornaments of it so finished. Examine again all those accurate mouldings, and perfect polishings, and unerring adjustments of the seasoned wood and tempered steel. Many a time you have exulted over them, and thought how great England was, because her slightest work was done so thoroughly. Alas! if read rightly, these perfectnesses are signs of a slavery in our England a thousand times more bitter and more degrading than that of the scourged African, or helot[13] Greek. Men may be beaten, chained, tormented, yoked like cattle, slaughtered like summer flies, and yet remain in one sense, and the best sense, free. But to smother their souls with them, to blight and hew into rotting pollards the suckling branches of their human intelligence, to make the flesh and skin which, after the worm's work on it, is to see God, into leathern thongs to yoke machinery with, – this is to be slave-masters indeed; and there might be more freedom in England, though her feudal lords' lightest words were worth men's lives, and though the blood of the vexed husbandman dropped in the furrows of her fields, than there is while the animation of her multitudes is sent like fuel to feed the factory smoke, and the strength of them is given daily to be wasted into the fineness of a web, or racked into the exactness of a line.

§XIV. And, on the other hand, go forth again to gaze upon the old cathedral front, where you have smiled so often at the fantastic ignorance of the old sculptures: examine once more those ugly goblins, and formless monsters, and stern statues, anatomiless[14] and rigid; but do not mock at them, for they are signs of the life and liberty of every workman who struck the stone; a freedom of thought, and rank in scale of being, such as no laws, no charters, no charities can secure; but which it must be the first aim of all Europe at this day to regain for her children.

§XV. Let me not be thought to speak wildly or extravagantly. It is verily this degradation of the operative into a machine, which, more than any other evil of the times, is leading the mass of the nations everywhere into vain, incoherent, destructive struggling for a freedom of which they cannot explain the nature to themselves. Their universal outcry against wealth, and against nobility, is not forced from them either by the pressure of famine, or the sting of mortified pride. These do much, and have done much in all ages; but the foundations of society were never yet shaken as they are at this day. It is not that men are ill fed, but that they have no pleasure in the work by which they make their bread, and therefore look to wealth as the only means of pleasure. It is not that men are pained by the scorn of the upper classes, but they cannot endure their own; for they feel that the kind of labour to which they are condemned is verily a degrading one, and makes them less than men. Never had the upper classes so much sympathy with the lower, or charity for them, as they have at this day, and yet never were they so much hated by them: for, of old, the separation between the noble and the poor was merely a wall built by law; now it is a veritable difference in level of standing, a precipice between upper and lower grounds in the field of humanity, and there is pestilential air at the bottom of it. I know not if a day is ever to come when the nature of right freedom will be understood, and when men will see that to obey another man, to labour for him, yield reverence to him or to his place, is not slavery. It is often the best kind of liberty, – liberty from care. The man who says to one, Go, and he goeth, and to another, Come, and he cometh,[15] has, in most cases, more sense of restraint and difficulty than the man who obeys him. The movements of the one are hindered by the burden on his shoulder; of the other by the bridle on his lips: there is no way by which the burden may be lightened; but we need not suffer from the bridle if we do not champ at it. To yield reverence to another, to hold ourselves and our likes at his disposal, is not slavery; often it is the noblest state in which a man can live in this world. There is, indeed, a reverence which is servile, that is to say, irrational or selfish: but there is also noble reverence, that is to say, reasonable and loving; and a man is never so noble as when he is reverent in this kind; nay, even if the feeling pass the bounds of mere reason, so that it be loving, a man is raised by it. Which had, in reality, most of the serf nature in him, – the Irish peasant who was lying in wait yesterday for his landlord, with his musket muzzle thrust through the ragged hedge;[16] or that old mountain servant, who 200 years ago, at Inverkeithing,[17] gave up his own life and the lives of his seven sons for his chief? – as each fell, calling forth his brother to the death, 'Another for Hector!'.[b] And therefore, in all ages and all countries, reverence has been paid and sacrifice made by men to each other, not only without complaint, but rejoicingly; and famine, and peril, and sword, and all evil, and all shame, have been borne willingly in the causes of masters and kings; for all these gifts of the heart ennobled the men who gave, not less than the men who received them, and nature prompted, and God rewarded the sacrifice. But to feel their souls withering within them, unthanked, to find their whole being sunk into an unrecognized abyss, to be counted off into a heap of mechanism numbered with its wheels, and weighed with its hammer strokes – this, nature bade not, – this, God blesses not, – this, humanity for no long time is able to endure.

§XVI. We have much studied and much perfected, of late, the great civilized invention of the division of labour,[18] only we give it a false name. It is not, truly speaking, the labour that is divided; but the men: – Divided into mere segments of men – broken into small fragments and crumbs of life; so that all the little piece of intelligence that is left in a man is not enough to make a pin, or a nail, but exhausts itself in making the point of a pin or the head of a nail. Now it is a good and desirable thing, truly, to make many pins in a day; but if we could only see with what crystal sand their points were polished, – sand of human soul, much to be magnified before it can be discerned for what it is – we should think there might be some loss in it also. And the great cry that rises from all our manufacturing cities, louder than their furnace blast, is all in very deed for this, – that we manufacture everything there except men; we blanch cotton, and strengthen steel, and refine sugar,

b  Vide Preface to *Fair Maid of Perth*. [See note 17.]

and shape pottery; but to brighten, to strengthen, to refine, or to form a single living spirit, never enters into our estimate of advantages. And all the evil to which that cry is urging our myriads can be met only in one way: not by teaching nor preaching, for to teach them is but to show them their misery, and to preach to them, if we do nothing more than preach, is to mock at it. It can be met only by a right understanding, on the part of all classes, of what kinds of labour are good for men, raising them, and making them happy; by a determined sacrifice of such convenience, or beauty, or cheapness as is to be got only by the degradation of the workman; and by equally determined demand for the products and results of healthy and ennobling labour.

§XVII. And how, it will be asked, are these products to be recognized, and this demand to be regulated? Easily: by the observance of three broad and simple rules:

1.  Never encourage the manufacture of any article not absolutely necessary, in the production of which *Invention* has no share.
2.  Never demand an exact finish for its own sake, but only for some practical or noble end.
3.  Never encourage imitation or copying of any kind, except for the sake of preserving records of great works.

The second of these principles is the only one which directly rises out of the consideration of our immediate subject; but I shall briefly explain the meaning and extent of the first also, reserving the enforcement of the third for another place.

1. Never encourage the manufacture of anything not necessary, in the production of which invention has no share.

For instance. Glass beads are utterly unnecessary, and there is no design or thought employed in their manufacture. They are formed by first drawing out the glass into rods; these rods are chopped up into fragments of the size of beads by the human hand, and the fragments are then rounded in the furnace. The men who chop up the rods sit at their work all day, their hands vibrating with a perpetual and exquisitely timed palsy, and the beads dropping beneath their vibration like hail.[19] Neither they, nor the men who draw out the rods or fuse the fragments, have the smallest occasion for the use of any single human faculty; and every young lady, therefore, who buys glass beads is engaged in the slave-trade, and in a much more cruel one than that which we have so long been endeavouring to put down.[20]

But glass cups and vessels may become the subjects of exquisite invention; and if in buying these we pay for the invention, that is to say, for the beautiful form, or colour, or engraving, and not for mere finish of execution, we are doing good to humanity.

§XVIII. So, again, the cutting of precious stones, in all ordinary cases, requires little exertion of any mental faculty; some tact and judgment in avoiding flaws, and so on, but nothing to bring out the whole mind. Every person who wears cut jewels merely for the sake of their value is, therefore, a slave-driver.

But the working of the goldsmith, and the various designing of grouped jewellery and enamel-work, may become the subject of the most noble human intelligence. Therefore, money spent in the purchase of well-designed plate, of precious engraved vases, cameos, or enamels, does good to humanity; and, in work of this kind, jewels may be employed to heighten its splendour; and their cutting is then a price paid for the attainment of a noble end, and thus perfectly allowable.

§XIX. I shall perhaps press this law farther elsewhere, but our immediate concern is chiefly with the second, namely, never to demand an exact finish, when it does not lead to a noble end. For observe, I have only dwelt upon the rudeness of Gothic, or any other kind of imperfectness, as admirable, where it was impossible to get design or thought without it. If you are to have the thought of a rough and untaught man, you must have it in a rough and untaught way; but from an educated man, who can without effort express his thoughts in an educated way, take the graceful expression, and be thankful. Only *get* the thought, and do not silence the peasant because he cannot speak good grammar, or until you have taught him his grammar. Grammar and refinement are good things, both, only be sure of the better thing first. And thus in art, delicate finish is desirable from the greatest masters, and is always given by them. In some places Michael Angelo, Leonardo, Phidias, Perugino,[21] Turner, all finished with the most exquisite care; and the finish they give always leads to the fuller accomplishment of their noble purposes. But lower men than these cannot finish, for it requires consummate knowledge to finish consummately, and then we must take their thoughts as they are able to give them. So the rule is simple: Always look for invention first, and after that, for such execution as will help the invention, and as the inventor is capable of without painful effort, and *no more*. Above all, demand no refinement of execution where there is no thought, for that is slaves' work, unredeemed. Rather choose rough work than smooth work, so only that the practical purpose be answered, and never imagine there is reason to be proud of anything that may be accomplished by patience and sand-paper.

§XX. I shall only give one example, which however will show the reader what I mean, from the manufacture already alluded to, that of glass. Our modern glass is exquisitely clear in substance, true in its form, accurate in its cutting. We are proud of this. We ought to be ashamed of it. The old Venice glass was muddy, inaccurate in all its forms, and clumsily cut, if at all. And the old Venetian was justly proud of it. For there is this difference between the English and Venetian workman, that the former thinks only of accurately matching his patterns, and getting his curves perfectly true and his edges perfectly sharp, and becomes a mere machine for rounding curves and sharpening edges; while the old Venetian cared not a whit whether his edges were sharp or not, but he invented a new design for every glass that he made, and never moulded a handle or a lip without a new fancy in it. And therefore, though some Venetian glass is

337

ugly and clumsy enough when made by clumsy and uninventive workmen, other Venetian glass is so lovely in its forms that no price is too great for it; and we never see the same form in it twice. Now you cannot have the finish and the varied form too. If the workman is thinking about his edges, he cannot be thinking of his design; if of his design, he cannot think of his edges. Choose whether you will pay for the lovely form or the perfect finish, and choose at the same moment whether you will make the worker a man or a grindstone.

§XXI. Nay, but the reader interrupts me, – 'If the workman can design beautifully, I would not have him kept at the furnace. Let him be taken away and made a gentleman, and have a studio, and design his glass there, and I will have it blown and cut by common workmen, and so I will have my design and my finish too.'

All ideas of this kind are founded upon two mistaken suppositions: the first, that one man's thoughts can be, or ought to be, executed by another man's hands; the second, that manual labour is a degradation, when it is governed by intellect.

On a large scale, and in work determinable by line and rule, it is indeed both possible and necessary that the thoughts of one man should be carried out by the labour of others; in this sense I have already defined the best architecture to be the expression of the mind of manhood by the hands of childhood. But on a smaller scale, and in a design which cannot be mathematically defined, one man's thoughts can never be expressed by another: and the difference between the spirit of touch of the man who is inventing, and of the man who is obeying directions, is often all the difference between a great and a common work of art. How wide the separation is between original and second-hand execution, I shall endeavour to show elsewhere; it is not so much to our purpose here as to mark the other and more fatal error of despising manual labour when governed by intellect; for it is no less fatal an error to despise it when thus regulated by intellect, than to value it for its own sake. We are always in these days endeavouring to separate the two; we want one man to be always thinking, and another to be always working, and we call one a gentleman, and the other an operative; whereas the workman ought often to be thinking, and the thinker often to be working, and both should be gentlemen, in the best sense. As it is, we make both ungentle, the one envying, the other despising, his brother; and the mass of society is made up of morbid thinkers and miserable workers. Now it is only by labour that thought can be made healthy, and only by thought that labour can be made happy, and the two cannot be separated with impunity. It would be well if all of us were good handicraftsmen in some kind, and the dishonour of manual labour done away with altogether; so that though there should still be a trenchant distinction of race between nobles and commoners, there should not, among the latter, be a trenchant distinction of employment, as between idle and working men, or between men of liberal and illiberal professions. All professions should be liberal, and there should be less pride felt in peculiarity of employment, and more in excellence of achievement. And yet more, in each several profession, no master should be too proud to do its hardest work. The painter should grind his own colours; the architect work in the mason's yard with his men; the master-manufacturer be himself a more skilful operative than any man in his mills; and the distinction between one man and another be only in experience and skill, and the authority and wealth which these must naturally and justly obtain.

§XXII. I should be led far from the matter in hand, if I were to pursue this interesting subject. Enough, I trust, has been said to show the reader that the rudeness or imperfection which at first rendered the term 'Gothic' one of reproach is indeed, when rightly understood, one of the most noble characters of Christian architecture, and not only a noble but an *essential* one. It seems a fantastic paradox, but it is nevertheless a most important truth, that no architecture can be truly noble which is *not* imperfect. And this is easily demonstrable. For since the architect, whom we will suppose capable of doing all in perfection, cannot execute the whole with his own hands, he must either make slaves of his workmen in the old Greek, and present English fashion, and level his work to a slave's capacities, which is to degrade it; or else he must take his workmen as he finds them, and let them show their weaknesses together with their strength, which will involve the Gothic imperfection, but render the whole work as noble as the intellect of the age can make it.

§XXIII. But the principle may be stated more broadly still. I have confined the illustration of it to architecture, but I must not leave it as if true of architecture only. Hitherto I have used the words imperfect and perfect merely to distinguish between work grossly unskilful, and work executed with average precision and science; and I have been pleading that any degree of unskilfulness should be admitted, so only that the labourer's mind had room for expression. But, accurately speaking, no good work whatever can be perfect, and *the demand for perfection is always a sign of a misunderstanding of the ends of art.*

§XXIV. This for two reasons, both based on everlasting laws. The first, that no great man ever stops working till he has reached his point of failure: that is to say, his mind is always far in advance of his powers of execution, and the latter will now and then give way in trying to follow it; besides that he will always give to the inferior portions of his work only such inferior attention as they require; and according to his greatness he becomes so accustomed to the feeling of dissatisfaction with the best he can do, that in moments of lassitude or anger with himself he will not care though the beholder be dissatisfied also. I believe there has only been one man who would not acknowledge this necessity, and strove always to reach perfection, Leonardo; the end of his vain effort being merely that he would take ten years to a picture and leave it unfinished. And therefore, if we are to have great men working at all, or less men doing their best, the work will be imperfect, however beautiful. Of human work none but what is bad can be perfect, in its own bad way.[c]

c    The Elgin marbles are supposed by many persons to be 'perfect.' In the most important portions

[continued]

§XXV. The second reason is, that imperfection is in some sort essential to all that we know of life. It is the sign of life in a mortal body, that is to say, of a state of progress and change. Nothing that lives is, or can be, rigidly perfect; part of it is decaying, part nascent. The foxglove blossom, – a third part bud, a third part past, a third part in full bloom, – is a type of the life of this world. And in all things that live there are certain irregularities and deficiencies which are not only signs of life, but sources of beauty. No human face is exactly the same in its lines on each side, no leaf perfect in its lobes, no branch in its symmetry. All admit irregularity as they imply change; and to banish imperfection is to destroy expression, to check exertion, to paralyze vitality. All things are literally better, lovelier, and more beloved for the imperfections which have been divinely appointed, that the law of human life may be Effort, and the law of human judgement, Mercy.

Accept this then for a universal law, that neither architecture nor any other noble work of man can be good unless it be imperfect; and let us be prepared for the otherwise strange fact, which we shall discern clearly as we approach the period of the Renaissance, that the first cause of the fall of the arts of Europe was a relentless requirement of perfection, incapable alike either of being silenced by veneration for greatness, or softened into forgiveness of simplicity.

Thus far then of the Rudeness or Savageness, which is the first mental element of Gothic architecture. It is an element in many other healthy architectures also, as the Byzantine and Romanesque; but true Gothic cannot exist without it.

§XXVI. The second mental element above named was CHANGEFULNESS, or Variety.

I have already enforced the allowing independent operation to the inferior workman, simply as a duty *to him*, and as ennobling the architecture by rendering it more Christian. We have now to consider what reward we obtain for the performance of this duty, namely, the perpetual variety of every feature of the building.

Wherever the workman is utterly enslaved, the parts of the building must of course be absolutely like each other; for the perfection of his execution can only he reached by exercising him in doing one thing, and giving him nothing else to do. The degree in which the workman is degraded may be thus known at a glance, by observing whether the several parts of the building are similar or not; and if, as in Greek work, all the capitals are alike, and all the mouldings unvaried, then the degradation is complete; if, as in Egyptian or Ninevite work, though the manner of executing certain figures is always the same, the order of

---

they indeed approach perfection, but only there. The draperies are unfinished, the hair and wool of the animals are unfinished, and the entire bas-reliefs of the frieze are roughly cut. [The Elgin Marbles refer to a collection of Greek sculptures and architectural details which were removed from the Parthenon and other ancient buildings by Thomas Bruce, Lord Elgin; they were brought to England in a series of shipments from 1802 to 1812, and were purchased by the crown in 1816. Their ownership is still a matter of dispute today.]

design is perpetually varied, the degradation is less total; if, as in Gothic work, there is perpetual change both in design and execution, the workman must have been altogether set free.

§XXVII. How much the beholder gains from the liberty of the labourer may perhaps be questioned in England, where one of the strongest instincts in nearly every mind is that Love of Order which makes us desire that our house windows should pair like our carriage horses, and allows us to yield our faith unhesitatingly to architectural theories which fix a form for everything, and forbid variation on it. I would not impeach love of order: it is one of the most useful elements of the English mind; it helps us in our commerce and in all purely practical matters; and it is in many cases one of the foundation stones of morality. Only do not let us suppose that love of order is love of art. It is true that order, in its highest sense, is one of the necessities of art, just as time is a necessity of music; but love of order has no more to do with our right enjoyment of architecture or painting, than love of punctuality with the appreciation of an opera. Experience, I fear, teaches us that accurate and methodical habits in daily life are seldom characteristic of those who either quickly perceive, or richly possess, the creative powers of art; there is, however, nothing inconsistent between the two instincts, and nothing to hinder us from retaining our business habits, and yet fully allowing and enjoying the noblest gifts of Invention. We already do so, in every other branch of art except architecture, and we only do *not* so there because we have been taught that it would be wrong. Our architects gravely inform us that, as there are four rules of arithmetic, there are five orders of architecture; we, in our simplicity, think that this sounds consistent, and believe them. They inform us also that there is one proper form for Corinthian capitals, another for Doric, and another for Ionic.[22] We, considering that there is also a proper form for the letters A, B, and C, think that this also sounds consistent, and accept the proposition. Understanding, therefore, that one form of the said capitals is proper, and no other, and having a conscientious horror of all impropriety, we allow the architect to provide us with the said capitals, of the proper form, in such and such a quantity, and in all other points to take care that the legal forms are observed; which having done, we rest in forced confidence that we are well housed.

§XXVIII. But our higher instincts are not deceived. We take no pleasure in the building provided for us, resembling that which we take in a new book or a new picture. We may be proud of its size, complacent in its correctness, and happy in its convenience. We may take the same pleasure in its symmetry and workmanship as in a well-ordered room, or a skilful piece of manufacture. And this we suppose to be all the pleasure that architecture was ever intended to give us. The idea of reading a building as we would read Milton or Dante, and getting the same kind of delight out of the stones as out of the stanzas, never enters our mind for a moment. And for good reason; – There is indeed rhythm in the verses, quite as strict as the symmetries or rhythm of the architecture, and a thousand times more beautiful, but there is something else than rhythm. The

341

verses were neither made to order, nor to match, as the capitals were; and we have therefore a kind of pleasure in them other than a sense of propriety. But it requires a strong effort of common sense to shake ourselves quit of all that we have been taught for the last two centuries, and wake to the perception of a truth just as simple and certain as it is new: that great art, whether expressing itself in words, colours, or stones, does *not* say the same thing over and over again; that the merit of architectural, as of every other art, consists in its saying new and different things; that to repeat itself is no more a characteristic of genius in marble than it is of genius in print; and that we may, without offending any laws of good taste, require of an architect, as we do of a novelist, that he should be not only correct, but entertaining.

Yet all this is true, and self-evident; only hidden from us, as many other self-evident things are, by false teaching. Nothing is a great work of art, for the production of which either rules or models can be given. Exactly so far as architecture works on known rules, and from given models, it is not an art, but a manufacture; and it is, of the two procedures, rather less rational (because more easy) to copy capitals or mouldings for Phidias, and call ourselves architects, than to copy heads and hands from Titian,[23] and call ourselves painters.

§XXIX. Let us then understand at once that change or variety is as much a necessity to the human heart and brain in buildings as in books; that there is no merit, though there is some occasional use, in monotony; and that we must no more expect to derive either pleasure or profit from an architecture whose ornaments are of one pattern, and whose pillars are of one proportion, than we should out of a universe in which the clouds were all of one shape, and the trees all of one size.

§XXX. And this we confess in deeds, though not in words. All the pleasure which the people of the nineteenth century take in art, is in pictures, sculpture, minor objects of virtù, or medieval architecture, which we enjoy under the term picturesque:[24] no pleasure is taken anywhere in modern buildings, and we find all men of true feeling delighting to escape out of modern cities into natural scenery: hence, as I shall hereafter show, that peculiar love of landscape, which is characteristic of the age. It would be well, if in all other matters, we were as ready to put up with what we dislike, for the sake of compliance with established law, as we are in architecture.

§XXXI. How so debased a law ever came to be established, we shall see when we come to describe the Renaissance schools; here we have only to note, as a second most essential element of the Gothic spirit, that it broke through that law wherever it found it in existence; it not only dared, but delighted in, the infringement of every servile principle; and invented a series of forms of which the merit was, not merely that they were new, but that they were *capable of perpetual novelty*. The pointed arch was not merely a bold variation from the round, but it admitted of millions of variations in itself; for the proportions of a pointed arch are changeable to infinity, while a circular arch is always the same. The grouped shaft[25] was not merely a bold variation from the single one, but it admitted of millions of variations in its grouping, and in the proportions resultant from its grouping. The introduction of tracery[26] was not only a startling change in the treatment of window lights, but admitted endless changes in the interlacement of the tracery bars themselves. So that, while in all living Christian architecture the love of variety exists, the Gothic schools exhibited that love in culminating energy; and their influence, wherever it extended itself, may be sooner and farther traced by this character than by any other; the tendency to the adoption of Gothic types being always first shown by greater irregularity, and richer variation in the forms of architecture it is about to supersede, long before the appearance of the pointed arch or of any other recognizable *outward* sign of the Gothic mind. [ . . . ][27]

§XL. I must now refer for a moment, before we quit the consideration of this, the second mental element of Gothic, to the opening of the third chapter of the *Seven Lamps of Architecture*, in which the distinction was drawn (§II) between man gathering and man governing; between his acceptance of the sources of delight from nature, and his development of authoritative or imaginative power in their arrangement: for the two mental elements, not only of Gothic, but of all good architecture, which we have just been examining, belong to it, and are admirable in it, chiefly as it is, more than any other subject of art, the work of man, and the expression of the average power of man. A picture or poem is often little more than a feeble utterance of man's admiration of something out of himself; but architecture approaches more to a creation of his own, born of his necessities, and expressive of his nature. It is also, in some sort, the work of the whole race, while the picture or statue is the work of one only, in most cases more highly gifted than his fellows. And therefore we may expect that the first two elements of good architecture should be expressive of some great truths commonly belonging to the whole race, and necessary to be understood or felt by them in all their work that they do under the sun. And observe what they are: the confession of Imperfection, and the confession of Desire of Change. The building of the bird and the bee needs not express anything like this. It is perfect and unchanging. But just because we are something better than birds or bees, our building must confess that we have not reached the perfection we can imagine, and cannot rest in the condition we have attained. If we pretend to have reached either perfection or satisfaction, we have degraded ourselves and our work. God's work only may express that; but ours may never have that sentence written upon it, – 'And behold, it was very good.'[28] And, observe again, it is not merely as it renders the edifice a book of various knowledge, or a mine of precious thought, that variety is essential to its nobleness. The vital principle is not the love of *Knowledge*, but the love of *Change*. It is that strange *disquietude* of the Gothic spirit that is its greatness; that restlessness of the dreaming mind, that wanders hither and thither among the niches, and flickers feverishly around the pinnacles, and frets and fades in labyrinthine knots and shadows along wall and roof, and yet is not satisfied, nor shall be satisfied. The Greek could stay in his triglyph furrow,[29] and be at peace; but the work of the Gothic heart is fretwork still, and it can neither rest in, nor from, its labour, but must pass on, sleeplessly, until its love of change shall be pacified for ever in the change that must come alike on them that wake and them that sleep.[30]

§XLI. The third constituent element of the Gothic mind was stated to be NATURALISM; that is to say, the love of natural objects for their own sake, and the effort to represent them frankly, unconstrained by artistical laws.

This characteristic of the style partly follows in necessary connection with those named above. For, so soon as the workman is left free to represent what subjects he chooses, he must look to the nature that is round him for material, and will endeavour to represent it as he sees it, with more or less accuracy according to the skill he possesses, and with much play of fancy, but with small respect for law. There is, however, a marked distinction between the imaginations of the Western and Eastern races, even when both are left free; the Western, or Gothic, delighting most in the representation of facts, and the Eastern (Arabian, Persian, and Chinese) in the harmony of colours and forms. Each of these intellectual dispositions has its particular forms of error and abuse, which, though I have often before stated, I must here again briefly explain; and this the rather, because the word Naturalism is, in one of its senses, justly used as a term of reproach, and the questions respecting the real relations of art and nature are so many and so confused throughout all the schools of Europe at this day, that I cannot clearly enunciate any single truth without appearing to admit, in fellowship with it, some kind of error, unless the reader will bear with me in entering into such an analysis of the subject as will serve us for general guidance. [ . . . ][31]

§LXIII. [ . . . ] [T]he reader may already be somewhat wearied with a statement which has led us apparently so far from our immediate subject. But the digression was necessary, in order that I might clearly define the sense in which I use the word Naturalism when I state it to be the third most essential characteristic of Gothic architecture. I mean that the Gothic builders belong to the central or greatest rank in *both* the classifications of artists which we have just made; that considering all artists as either men of design, men of facts, or men of both, the Gothic builders were men of both; and that again, considering all artists as either Purists, Naturalists or Sensualists, the Gothic builders were Naturalists.[32]

§LXIV. I say first, that the Gothic builders were of that central class which unites fact with design; but that the part of the work which was more especially their own was the truthfulness. Their power of artistical invention or arrangement was not greater than that of Romanesque and Byzantine workmen: by those workmen they were taught the principles, and from them received their models, of design; but to the ornamental feeling and rich fancy of the Byzantine the Gothic builder added a love of *fact* which is never found in the South. Both Greek and Roman used conventional foliage in their ornament, passing into something that was not foliage at all, knotting itself into strange cup-like buds or clusters, and growing out of lifeless rods instead of stems; the Gothic sculptor received these types, at first, as things that ought to be, just as we have a second time received them; but he could not rest in them. He saw there was no veracity in them, no knowledge, no vitality. Do what he would, he could not help liking the true leaves better; and cautiously, a little at a time, he put more of nature into his work, until at last it was all true, retaining, nevertheless, every valuable character of the original well-disciplined and designed arrangement.[33]

§LXV. Nor is it only in external and visible subject that the Gothic workman wrought for truth: he is as firm in his rendering of imaginative as of actual truth; that is to say, when an idea would have been by a Roman, or Byzantine, symbolically represented, the Gothic mind realizes it to the utmost. For instance, the purgatorial fire is represented in the mosaic of Torcello[34] (Romanesque) as a red stream, longitudinally striped like a riband, descending out of the throne of Christ, and gradually extending itself to envelope the wicked. When we are once informed what this means, it is enough for its purpose; but the Gothic inventor does not leave the sign in need of interpretation. He makes the fire as like real fire as he can; and in the porch of St Maclou at Rouen[35] the sculptured flames burst out of the Hades gate,[36] and flicker up, in writhing tongues of stone, through the interstices[37] of the niches, as if the church itself were on fire. This is an extreme instance, but it is all the more illustrative of the entire difference in temper and thought between the two schools of art, and of the intense love of veracity which influenced the Gothic design.

§LXVI. I do not say that this love of veracity is always healthy in its operation. I have above noticed the errors into which it falls from despising design; and there is another kind of error noticeable in the instance just given, in which the love of truth is too hasty, and seizes on a surface truth instead of an inner one. For in representing the Hades fire, it is not the mere *form* of the flame which needs most to be told, but its unquenchableness, its Divine ordainment and limitation, and its inner fierceness, not physical and material, but in being the expression of the wrath of God. And these things are not to be told by imitating the fire that flashes out of a bundle of sticks. If we think over the symbol a little, we shall perhaps find that the Romanesque builder told more truth in that likeness of a blood-red stream, flowing between definite shores, and out of God's throne, and expanding, as if fed by a perpetual current, into the lake wherein the wicked are cast,[38] than the Gothic builder in those torch-flickerings about his niches. But this is not to our immediate purpose; I am not at present to insist upon the faults into which the love of truth was led in the later Gothic times, but on the feeling itself, as a glorious and peculiar characteristic of the Northern builders. For, observe, it is not, even in the above instance, love of truth, but want of thought, which *causes* the fault. The love of truth, as such, is good, but when it is misdirected by thoughtlessness or over-excited by vanity, and either seizes on facts of small value, or gathers them chiefly that it may boast of its grasp and apprehension, its work may well become dull or offensive. Yet let us not, therefore, blame the inherent love of facts, but the incautiousness of their selection, and impertinence of their statement.

§LXVII. I said, in the second place, that Gothic work, when referred to the arrangement of all art, as purist, naturalist, or sensualist, was naturalist. This character follows necessarily on its extreme love of truth, prevailing over the sense of beauty, and causing it to take delight in portraiture of every kind, and to express the various characters of the human countenance and form, as it did the varieties of leaves and the ruggedness of branches. And this tendency is both increased and ennobled by the same Christian humility which we saw expressed in the first character of Gothic work, its rudeness. For as that resulted from a humility which confessed the imperfection of the *workman*, so this naturalist portraiture is rendered more faithful by the humility which confesses the imperfection of the *subject*. The Greek sculptor could neither bear to confess his own feebleness, nor to tell the faults of the forms that he portrayed. But the Christian workman, believing that all is finally to work together for good, freely confesses both, and neither seeks to disguise his own roughness of work, nor his subject's roughness of make. Yet this frankness being joined, for the most part, with depth of religious feeling in other directions, and especially with charity, there is sometimes a tendency to Purism[39] in the best Gothic sculpture; so that it frequently reaches great dignity of form and tenderness of expression, yet never so as to lose the veracity of portraiture wherever portraiture is possible: not exalting its kings into demi-gods, nor its saints into archangels, but giving what kingliness and sanctity was in them, to the full, mixed with due record of their faults; and this in the most part with a great indifference like that of Scripture history, which sets down, with unmoved and unexcusing resoluteness, the virtues and errors of all men of whom it speaks, often leaving the reader to form his own estimate of them, without an indication of the judgment of the historian. And this veracity is carried out by the Gothic sculptors in the minuteness and generality, as well as the equity, of their delineation: for they do not limit their art to the portraiture of saints and kings, but introduce the most familiar scenes and most simple subjects: filling up the backgrounds of Scripture histories with vivid and curious representations of the commonest incidents of daily life, and availing themselves of every occasion in which, either as a symbol, or an explanation of a scene or time, the things familiar to the eye of the workman could be introduced and made of account. Hence Gothic sculpture and painting are not only full of valuable portraiture of the greatest men, but copious records of all the domestic customs and inferior arts of the ages in which it flourished.[d] [ . . . ][40]

§LXXII. The fourth essential element of the Gothic mind was above stated in the sense of the GROTESQUE; but I shall defer the endeavour to define this most curious and subtle character until we have occasion to examine one of the divisions of the Renaissance schools, which was morbidly influenced by it (Vol. III. Chap. III.). It is the less necessary to insist upon it here, because every reader

---

d    The best art either represents the facts of its own day, or, if facts of the past, expresses them with accessories of the time in which the work was done. All good art, representing past events, is therefore full of the most frank anachronism, and always *ought* to be. No painter has any business to be an antiquarian. We do not want his impressions or suppositions respecting things that are past. We want his clear assertions respecting things present.

familiar with Gothic architecture must understand what I mean, and will, I believe, have no hesitation in admitting, that the tendency to delight in fantastic and ludicrous, as well as in sublime, images, is a universal instinct of the Gothic imagination.

§LXXIII. The fifth element above named was RIGIDITY; and this character I must endeavour carefully to define, for neither the word I have used, nor any other that I can think of, will express it accurately. For I mean, not merely stable, but *active* rigidity; the peculiar energy which gives tension to movement, and stiffness to resistance, which makes the fiercest lightning forked rather than curved, and the stoutest oak-branch angular rather than bending, and is as much seen in the quivering of the lance as in the glittering of the icicle.

§LXXIV. I have before had occasion (Vol. I. Chap. XIII. §VII.) to note some manifestations of this energy or fixedness; but it must be still more attentively considered here, as it shows itself throughout the whole structure and decoration of Gothic work. Egyptian and Greek buildings stand, for the most part, by their own weight and mass, one stone passively incumbent on another; but in the Gothic vaults and traceries there is a stiffness analogous to that of the bones of a limb, or fibres of a tree; an elastic tension and communication of force from part to part, and also a studious expression of this throughout every visible line of the building. And, in like manner, the Greek and Egyptian ornament is either mere surface engraving, as if the face of the wall had been stamped with a seal, or its lines were flowing, lithe, and luxuriant; in either case, there is no expression of energy in the framework of the ornament itself. But the Gothic ornament stands out in prickly independence, and frosty fortitude, jutting into crockets,[41] and freezing into pinnacles;[42] here starting up into a monster, there germinating into a blossom, anon knitting itself into a branch, alternately thorny, bossy, and bristly, or writhed into every form of nervous entanglement; but, even when most graceful, never for an instant languid, always quickset: erring, if at all, ever on the side of brusquerie.

§LXXV. The feelings or habits in the workman which give rise to this character in the work, are more complicated and various than those indicated by any other sculptural expression hitherto named. There is, first, the habit of hard and rapid working; the industry of the tribes of the North, quickened by the coldness of the climate, and giving an expression of sharp energy to all they do (as above noted, Vol. I. Chap. XIII. §VII.), as opposed to the languor of the Southern tribes, however much of fire there may be in the heart of that languor, for lava itself may flow languidly. There is also the habit of finding enjoyment in the signs of cold, which is never found, I believe, in the inhabitants of countries south of the Alps. Cold is to them an unredeemed evil, to be suffered and forgotten as soon as may be; but the long winter of the North forces the Goth (I mean the Englishman, Frenchman, Dane, or German), if he would lead a happy life at all, to find sources of happiness in foul weather as well as fair, and to rejoice in the leafless as well as in the shady forest. And this we do with all our hearts; finding perhaps nearly as much contentment by the Christmas fire as in the summer sunshine, and gaining health and strength on the ice-fields of winter, as well as among the meadows of spring. So that there is nothing adverse or painful to our feelings in the cramped and stiffened structure of vegetation checked by cold; and instead of seeking, like the Southern sculpture, to express only the softness of leafage nourished in all tenderness, and tempted into all luxuriance by warm winds and glowing rays, we find pleasure in dwelling upon the crabbed, perverse, and morose animation of plants that have known little kindness from earth or heaven, but, season after season, have had their best efforts palsied by frost, their brightest buds buried under snow, and their goodliest limbs lopped by tempest.

§LXXVI. There are many subtle sympathies and affections which join to confirm the Gothic mind in this peculiar choice of subject; and when we add to the influence of these, the necessities consequent upon the employment of a rougher material, compelling the workman to seek for vigour of effect, rather than refinement of texture or accuracy of form, we have direct and manifest causes for much of the difference between the Northern and Southern cast of conception: but there are indirect causes holding a far more important place in the Gothic heart, though less immediate in their influence on design. Strength of will, independence of character, resoluteness of purpose, impatience of undue control, and that general tendency to set the individual reason against authority, and the individual deed against destiny, which, in the Northern tribes, has opposed itself throughout all ages, to the languid submission, in the Southern, of thought to tradition, and purpose to fatality, are all more or less traceable in the rigid lines, vigorous and various masses, and daringly projecting and independent structure of the Northern Gothic ornament: while the opposite feelings are in like manner legible in the graceful and softly guided waves and wreathed bands, in which Southern decoration is constantly disposed; in its tendency to lose its independence, and fuse itself into the surface of the masses upon which it is traced; and in the expression seen so often, in the arrangement of those masses themselves, of an abandonment of their strength to an inevitable necessity, or a listless repose.

§LXXVII. There is virtue in the measure, and error in the excess, of both these characters of mind, and in both of the styles which they have created; the best architecture, and the best temper, are those which unite them both; and this fifth impulse of the Gothic heart is therefore that which needs most caution in its indulgence. It is more definitely Gothic than any other, but the best Gothic building is not that which is *most* Gothic: it can hardly be too frank in its confession of rudeness, hardly too rich in its changefulness, hardly too faithful in its

---

e   See the account of the meeting at Talla Linns, in 1682, given in the fourth chapter of the *Heart of Midlothian*. At length they arrived at the conclusion that 'they who owned (or allowed) such names as Monday, Tuesday, January, February, and so forth, served themselves heirs to the same if not greater punishment that had been denounced against the idolaters of old.' [The reference is to Walter Scott's novel, *The Heart of Midlothian* (1818).]

naturalism; but it may go too far in its rigidity, and, like the great Puritan spirit in its extreme, lose itself either in frivolity of division, or perversity of purpose.[e] It actually did so in its later times; but it is gladdening to remember that in its utmost nobleness, the very temper which has been thought most adverse to it, the Protestant spirit of self-dependence and inquiry, was expressed in its every line. Faith and aspiration there were, in every Christian ecclesiastical building, from the first century to the fifteenth; but the moral habits to which England in this age owes the kind of greatness that she has, – the habits of philosophical investigation, of accurate thought, of domestic seclusion and independence, of stern self-reliance and sincere upright searching into religious truth, – were only traceable in the features which were the distinctive creation of the Gothic schools, in the veined foliage, and thorny fretwork, and shadowy niche, and buttressed pillar, and fearless height of subtle pinnacle and crested tower, sent like an 'unperplexed question up to Heaven.'[f]

§LXXVIII. Last, because the least essential, of the constituent elements of this noble school, was placed that of REDUNDANCE, – the uncalculating bestowal of the wealth of its labour. There is, indeed, much Gothic, and that of the best period, in which this element is hardly traceable, and which depends for its effect almost exclusively on loveliness of simple design and grace of uninvolved proportion; still, in the most characteristic buildings, a certain portion of their effect depends upon accumulation of ornament; and many of those which have most influence on the minds of men, have attained it by means of this attribute alone. And although, by careful study of the school, it is possible to arrive at a condition of taste which shall be better contented by a few perfect lines than by a whole facade covered with fretwork, the building which only satisfies such a taste is not to be considered the best. For the very first requirement of Gothic architecture being, as we saw above, that it shall both admit the aid, and appeal to the admiration, of the rudest as well as the most refined minds, the richness of the work is, paradoxical as the statement may appear, a part of its humility. No architecture is so haughty as that which is simple; which refuses to address the eye, except in a few clear and forceful lines; which implies, in offering so little to our regards, that all it has offered is perfect; and disdains, either by the complexities or the attractiveness of its features, to embarrass our investigation, or betray us into delight. That humility, which is the very life of the Gothic school, is shown not only in the imperfection, but in the accumulation, of ornament. The inferior rank of the workman is often shown as much in the richness, as the roughness, of his work; and if the co-operation of every hand, and the sympathy of every heart, are to be received, we must be content to allow the redundance

f    See the beautiful description of Florence in Elizabeth Browning's *Casa Guidi Windows*, which is
     not only a noble poem, but the only book I have seen which, favouring the Liberal cause in Italy,
     gives a just account of the incapacities of the modern Italian. [*Casa Guidi Windows*, published in
     1851, was seen as an explicit attempt to win sympathy for the Florentine cause.]

which disguises the failure of the feeble, and wins the regard of the inattentive. There are, however, far nobler interests mingling, in the Gothic heart, with the rude love of decorative accumulation: magnificent enthusiasm, which feels as if it never could do enough to reach the fulness of its ideal; an unselfishness of sacrifice, which would rather cast fruitless labour before the altar than stand idle in the market;[43] and, finally, a profound sympathy with the fulness and wealth of the material universe, rising out of that Naturalism whose operation we have already endeavoured to define. The sculptor who sought for his models among the forest leaves, could not but quickly and deeply feel that complexity need not involve the loss of grace, nor richness that of repose; and every hour which he spent in the study of the minute and various work of Nature, made him feel more forcibly the barrenness of what was best in that of man: nor is it to be wondered at, that, seeing her perfect and exquisite creations poured forth in a profusion which conception could not grasp nor calculation sum, he should think that it ill became him to be niggardly of his own rude craftsmanship; and where he saw throughout the universe a faultless beauty lavished on measureless spaces of broidered field and blooming mountain, to grudge his poor and imperfect labour to the few stones that he had raised one upon the another, for habitation or memorial. The years of his life passed away before his task was accomplished; but generation succeeded generation with unwearied enthusiasm, and the cathedral front was at last lost in the tapestry of its traceries, like a rock among the thickets and herbage of spring.

§LXXIX. We have now, I believe, obtained a view approaching to completeness of the various moral or imaginative elements which composed the inner spirit of Gothic architecture.

# MATTHEW ARNOLD, 'ART VIII. – THE FUNCTIONS OF CRITICISM AT THE PRESENT TIME' (1864)

## Matthew Arnold, 'Art VIII. – The Functions of Criticism at the Present Time', *National Review*, I n.s. (November 1864), pp. 230–51[1]

*Art VII. – The Functions of Criticism at the Present Time*

Many objections have been made to a proposition which, in some remarks of mine on translating Homer,[2] I ventured to put forth; a proposition about criticism, and its importance at the present day. I said that 'of the literature of France and Germany, as of the intellect of Europe in general, the main effort, for now many years, had been a critical effort; the endeavour, in all branches of knowledge, theology, philosophy, history, art, science, to see the object as in itself it really is.' I added, that owing to the operation in English literature of certain causes, 'almost the last thing for which one would come to English literature was just that very thing which now Europe most desires – criticism;' and that the power and value of English literature was thereby impaired. More than one rejoinder declared that the importance I here assigned to criticism was excessive, and asserted the inherent superiority of the creative effort of the human spirit over its critical effort. And the other day, having been led by an excellent notice of Wordsworth published in the *North British Review*, to turn again to his biography,[3] I found, in the words of this great man, whom I, for one, must always listen to with the profoundest respect, a sentence passed on the critic's business, which seems to justify every possible disparagement of it. Wordsworth says in one of his letters:

'The writers in these publications' (the Reviews), 'while they prosecute their glorious employment, cannot be supposed to be in a state of mind very favourable for being affected by the finer influences of a thing so pure as genuine poetry.'[4]

And a trustworthy reporter[5] of his conversation quotes a more elaborate judgement to the same effect:

'Wordsworth holds the critical power very low, infinitely lower than the inventive; and he said to-day that if the quantity of time consumed in writing critiques on the works of others were given to original composition, of whatever kind it might be, it would be much better employed; it would make a man find out sooner his own level, and it would do indefinitely less mischief. A false or malicious criticism may do much injury to the minds of others; a stupid invention, either in prose or verse, is quite harmless.'

351

It is almost too much to expect of poor human nature, that a man capable of producing some effect in one line of literature, should, for the greater good of society, voluntarily doom himself to impotence and obscurity in another. Still less is this to be expected from men addicted to the composition of the 'false or malicious criticism,' of which Wordsworth speaks. However, everybody would admit that a false or malicious criticism had better never have been written. Everybody, too, would be willing to admit, as a general proposition, that the critical faculty is lower than the inventive. But is it true that criticism is really, in itself, a baneful and injurious employment; is it true that all time given to writing critiques on the works of others would be much better employed if it were given to original composition, of whatever kind this may be? Is it true that Johnson had better have gone on producing more *Irenes* instead of writing his *Lives of the Poets*; nay, is it certain that Wordsworth himself was better employed in making his Ecclesiastical Sonnets than when he made his celebrated Preface, so full of criticism, and criticism of the works of others? Wordsworth was himself a great critic, and it is to be sincerely regretted that he has not left us more criticism; Goethe was one of the greatest of critics, and we may sincerely congratulate ourselves that he has left us so much criticism.[6] Without wasting time over the exaggeration which Wordsworth's judgment on criticism clearly contains, or over an attempt to trace the causes – not difficult I think to be traced – which may have led Wordsworth to this exaggeration, a critic may with advantage seize an occasion for trying his own conscience, and for asking himself of what real service, at any given moment, the practice of criticism either is, or may be made, to his own mind and spirit, and to the minds and spirits of others.

The critical power is of lower rank than the creative. True; but in assenting to this proposition, one or two things are to be kept in mind. It is undeniable that the exercise of a creative power, that a free creative activity, is the true function of man; it is proved to be so by his finding in it his true happiness. But it is undeniable, also, that men may have the sense of exercising this free creative activity in other ways than in producing great works of literature or art; if it were not so, all but a very few men would be shut out from the true happiness of all men; they may have it in well-doing, they may have it in learning, they may have it even in criticising. This is one thing to be kept in mind. Another is, that the exercise of the creative power in the production of great works of literature or art, however high this exercise of it may rank, is not at all epochs and under all conditions possible; and that therefore labour may be vainly spent in attempting it, and may with more fruit be used in preparing for it, in rendering it possible. This creative power works with elements, with materials; what if it has not those materials, those elements, ready for its use? In that case it must surely wait till they are ready. Now in literature – I will limit myself to literature, for it is about literature that the question arises – the elements with which the creative power works are ideas; the best ideas, on every matter which literature touches, current at the time; at any rate we may lay it down as certain that in modern literature no manifestation of the creative power not working with these can be very important or fruitful. And I say current at the time, not merely accessible at the time; for creative literary genius does not principally show itself in discovering new ideas; that is rather the business of the philosopher; the grand work of literary genius is a work of synthesis and exposition, not of analysis and discovery; its gift lies in the faculty of being happily inspired by a certain intellectual and spiritual atmosphere, by a certain order of ideas, when it finds itself in them; of dealing divinely with these ideas, presenting them in the most effective and attractive combinations, making beautiful works with them, in short. But it must have the atmosphere, it must find itself amidst the order of ideas, in order to work freely; and these it is not so easy to command. This is why great creative epochs in literature are so rare; this is why there is so much that is unsatisfactory in the productions of many men of real genius; because for the creation of a master-work of literature two powers must concur, the power of the man and the power of the moment, and the man is not enough without the moment; the creative power has, for its happy exercise, appointed elements, and those elements are not in its own control.

Nay, they are more within the control of the critical power. It is the business of the critical power, as I said in the words already quoted, 'in all branches of knowledge, theology, philosophy, history, art, science, to see the object as in itself it really is.' Thus it tends, at last, to make an intellectual situation of which the creative power can profitably avail itself. It tends to establish an order of ideas, if not absolutely true, yet true by comparison with that which it displaces; to make the best ideas prevail. Presently these new ideas reach society, the touch of truth is the touch of life, and there is a stir and growth everywhere; out of this stir and growth come the creative epochs of literature.

Or, to narrow our range and quit these considerations of the general march of genius and of society, considerations which are apt to become too abstract and impalpable, – every one can see that a poet, for instance, ought to know life and the world before dealing with them in poetry; and life and the world being, in modern times, very complex things, the creation of a modern poet, to be worth much, implies a great critical effort behind it; else it would be a comparatively poor, barren, and short-lived affair. This is why Byron's poetry had so little endurance in it, and Goethe's so much; both had a great productive power, but Goethe's was nourished by a great critical effort providing the true materials for it, and Byron's was not; Goethe knew life and the world, the poet's necessary subjects, much more comprehensively and thoroughly than Byron. He knew a great deal more of them, and he knew them much more as they really are.

It has long seemed to me that the burst of creative activity in our literature, through the first quarter of this century, had about it, in fact, something premature; and that from this cause its productions are doomed, most of them, in spite of the sanguine hopes which accompanied and do still accompany them, to prove hardly more lasting than the productions of far less splendid epochs. And this prematureness comes from its having proceeded without having its proper data, without sufficient materials to work with.[7] In other words, the English poetry of the first quarter of this century, with plenty of energy, plenty of creative force, did not know enough. This makes Byron so one-toned, Shelley so incoherent, Wordsworth even, profound as he is, yet so wanting in completeness and variety. Wordsworth cared little for books, and disparaged Goethe. I admire Wordsworth, as he is, so much that I cannot wish him different; and it is vain, no doubt, to imagine such a man different from what he is, to suppose that he could have been different; but surely the one thing wanting to make Wordsworth an even greater poet than he is, – his thought richer, and his influence of wider application, – was that he should have read more books, among them, no doubt, those of that Goethe whom he disparaged without reading him. But to speak of books and reading may easily lead to a misunderstanding here. It was not really books and reading that lacked to our poetry, at this epoch; Shelley had plenty of reading, Coleridge had immense reading. Pindar and Sophocles[8] – as we all say so glibly, and often with so little discernment of the real import of what we are saying – had not many books; Shakespeare was no deep reader. True; but in the Greece of Pindar and Sophocles, in the England of Shakespeare, the poet lived in a current of ideas in the highest degree animating and nourishing to the creative power; society was, in the fullest measure, permeated by fresh thought, intelligent and alive; and this state of things is the true basis for the creative power's exercise, in this it finds its data, its materials, truly ready for its hand; all the books and reading in the world are only valuable as they are helps to this. Even when this does not actually exist, books and reading may enable a man to construct a kind of semblance of it in his own mind; a world of knowledge and intelligence in which he may live and work; this is by no means an equivalent, to the artist, for the nationally diffused life and thought of the epochs of Sophocles or Shakespeare, but, besides that it may be a means of preparation for such epochs, it does really constitute, if many share in it, a quickening and sustaining atmosphere of great value. Such an atmosphere that many-sided learning and the long and widely-combined critical effort of Germany formed for Goethe, when he lived and worked. There was no national glow of life and thought there, as in the Athens of Pericles,[9] or the England of Elizabeth. That was the poet's weakness. But there was a sort of equivalent for it in the complete culture and unfettered thinking of a large body of Germans. That was his strength. In the England of the first quarter of this century there was neither a national glow of life and thought, such as we had in the age of Elizabeth, nor yet a culture and a force of learning and criticism such as were to be found in Germany. Therefore the creative power of poetry wanted for success in the highest sense, materials and a basis; a thorough interpretation of the world was necessarily denied to it.

At first sight it seems strange that out of the immense stir of the French Revolution and its age should not have come a crop of works of genius equal to that which came out of the stir of the great productive time of Greece, or out of that of the Renaissance, with its powerful episode the Reformation. But the truth is that the stir of the French Revolution took a character which essentially distinguished it from such movements as these. These were, in the main, disinterestedly intellectual and spiritual movements; movements in which the human spirit looked for its satisfaction in itself and in the increased play of its own activity: the French Revolution took a political, practical character. This Revolution – the object of so much blind love and so much blind hatred – found, indeed, its motive-power in the intelligence of men and not in their practical sense; – this is what distinguishes it from the English Revolution of Charles I's time; this is what makes it a more spiritual event that our Revolution, an event of much more powerful and world-wide interest, though practically less successful; – it appeals to an order of ideas which are universal, certain, permanent. 1789 asked of a thing, Is it rational? 1642 asked of a thing, Is it legal? or, when it went furthest, Is it according to conscience? This is the English fashion, a fashion to be treated, within its own sphere, with the highest respect; for its success, within its own sphere, has been prodigious. But what is law in one place, is not law in another; what is law here to-day, is not law even here tomorrow; and as for conscience, what is binding on one man's conscience is not binding on another's; the old woman who threw her stool at the head of the surpliced clergyman in the Tron Church at Edinburgh obeyed an impulse to which millions of the human race may be permitted to remain strangers.[10] But the prescriptions of reason are absolute, unchanging, of universal validity; *to count by tens is the simplest way of counting,* – that is a proposition of which every one, from here to the Antipodes, feels the force; at least, I should say so, if we did not live in a country where it is not impossible that any morning we may find a letter in the *Times* declaring that a decimal coinage is an absurdity.[11] That a whole nation should have been penetrated with an enthusiasm for pure reason and with an ardent zeal for making its descriptions triumph, is a very remarkable thing when we consider how little of mind or anything so worthy and quickening as mind comes into the motives which alone, in general, *impel* great masses of men. In spite of the extravagant direction given to this enthusiasm, in spite of the crimes and follies in which it lost itself, the French Revolution derives, from the force, truth, and universality of the ideas which it took for its law, and from the passion with which it could inspire a multitude for these ideas, a unique and still living power; it is, – it will probably long remain, – the greatest, the most animating event in history. And as no sincere passion for the things of the mind, even though it turn out in many respects an unfortunate passion, is ever quite thrown away and quite barren of good, France has reaped from hers one fruit, the natural and legitimate fruit, though not precisely the grand fruit she expected; she is the country in Europe where *the people* is most alive.

But the mania for giving an immediate political and practical application to all these fine ideas of the reason was fatal. Here an Englishman is in his element: on this theme we can all go on for hours. And all we are in the habit of saying on it has undoubtedly a great deal of truth. Ideas cannot be too much prized in and for themselves, cannot be too much lived with; but to transport them abruptly into the world of politics and practice, violently to revolutionise this world to their bidding, that is quite another thing. There is the world of ideas and there is the world of practice; the French are often for suppressing one and the English the other; but neither is to be suppressed. A member of the House of Commons said to me the other day:[12] 'That a thing is an anomaly, I consider to be no objection to it whatever.' I venture to think he was wrong; that a thing is an anomaly *is* an objection to it, but absolutely and in the sphere of ideas: it is not necessarily, under such and such circumstances, or at such and such a moment, an objection to it in the sphere of politics and practice. Joubert has said beautifully: 'C'est la force et le droit qui règlent toutes choses dans le monde; la force en attendant le droit.'[13] Force and right are the governors of this world; force till right is ready. *Force till right is ready*; and till right is ready, force, the existing order of things, is justified, is the legitimate ruler. But right is something moral, and implies inward recognition, free assent of the will; we are not ready for right – right, so far as we are concerned, is not ready – until we have attained this sense of seeing it and willing it. The way in which for us it may change and transform force, the existing order of things, and become, in its turn, the legitimate ruler of the world, will depend on the way in which, when our time comes, we see it and will it. Therefore for other people enamoured of their own newly discerned right, to attempt to impose it upon us as ours, and violently to substitute their right for our force, is an act of tyranny, and to be resisted. It sets at nought the second great half of our maxim, *force till right is ready*. This was the grand error of the French Revolution, and its movement of ideas, by quitting the intellectual sphere and rushing furiously into the political sphere, ran, indeed, a prodigious and memorable course, but produced no such intellectual fruit as the movement of ideas of the Renaissance, and created, in opposition to itself, what I may call an *epoch of concentration*. The great force of that epoch of concentration was England: and the great voice of that epoch of concentration was Burke.[14] It is the fashion to treat Burke's writings on the French Revolution as superannuated and conquered by the event; as the eloquent but unphilosophical tirades of bigotry and prejudice. I will not deny that they are often disfigured by the violence and passion of the moment, and that in some directions Burke's view was bounded, and his observation therefore at fault; but on the whole, and for those who can make the needful corrections, what distinguished these writings is their profound, permanent, fruitful, philosophical truth; they contain the true philosophy of an epoch of concentration, dissipate the heavy atmosphere which its own nature is apt to engender round it, and make its resistance rational instead of mechanical.

But Burke is so great because, almost alone in England, he brings thought to bear upon politics, he saturates politics with thought; it is his accident that his ideas were at the service of an epoch of concentration, not an epoch of expansion; it is his characteristic that he so lived by ideas, and had such a source of them welling up within him, that he could float even an epoch of concentration and English Tory politics with them. It does not hurt him that Dr Price[15] and the Liberals were displeased with him; it does not even hurt him that George III and the Tories were enchanted with him. His greatness is that he lived in a world which neither English Liberalism nor English Toryism is apt to enter – the world of ideas, not the world of catchwords and party habits. So far is it from being really true of him that he 'to party gave up what was meant for mankind,'[16] that at the very end of his fierce struggle with the French Revolution, after all his invectives against its false pretensions, hollowness, and madness, with his sincere conviction of its mischievousness, he can close a memorandum on the best means of combating it – some of the last pages he ever wrote – the *Thoughts on French Affairs*,[17] in 1791, – with these striking words: –

> 'The evil is stated, in my opinion, as it exists. The remedy must be where power, wisdom, and information, I hope, are more united with good intentions than they can be with me. I have done with this subject, I believe, for ever. It has given me many anxious moments for the last two years. *If a great change is to be made in human affairs, the minds of men will be fitted to it; the general opinions and feelings will draw that way. Every fear, every hope will forward it; and then they who persist in opposing this mighty current in human affairs, will appear rather to resist the decrees of Providence itself, than the mere designs of men. They will not be resolute and firm, but perverse and obstinate.*'

That return of Burke upon himself has always seemed to me one of the finest things in English literature, or indeed, in any literature. That is what I call living by ideas; when one side of a question has long had your earnest support, when all your feelings are engaged, when you hear round you no language but one, when your party talks this like a steam-engine and can imagine no other, – still to be able to think, still to be irresistibly carried, if so it be, by the current of thought to the opposite side of the question, and, like Balaam,[18] to be unable to speak anything *but what the Lord has put in your mouth*. I know nothing more striking, and I must add that I know nothing more un-English.

For the Englishman in general is like my friend the Member of Parliament, and believes, point-blank, that for a thing to be an anomaly is absolutely no objection to it whatever. He is like the Lord Auckland[19] of Burke's day, who, in a memorandum on the French Revolution, talks of 'certain miscreants, assuming the name of philosophers, who have presumed themselves capable of establishing a new system of society.' The Englishman has been called a political animal,[20] and he values what is political and practical so much that ideas easily become objects of dislike in his eyes, and thinkers 'miscreants,' because ideas and thinkers have rashly meddled with politics and practice. This would be all very well if the dislike and neglect confined themselves to ideas transported out of their own sphere, and meddling rashly with practice; but they are inevitably extended to ideas as such, and to the whole life of intelligence; practice is everything, a free play of the mind is nothing. The notion of the free play of the mind upon all subjects being a pleasure in itself, being an object of desire, being an essential provider of elements without which a nation's spirit, whatever compensations it may have for them, must, in the long run, die of inanition, hardly enters into an Englishman's thoughts. It is noticeable that the word *curiosity*, which in other languages is used in a good sense, to mean, as a high and fine quality of man's nature, just this disinterested love of a free play of the mind on all its subjects, for its own sake – it is noticeable, I say, that this word has in our language no sense of the kind, no sense but a rather bad and disparaging one. But criticism, real criticism, is essentially the exercise of this very quality; it obeys an instinct prompting it to try to know the best that is known and thought in the world, irrespectively of practice, politics, and everything of the kind; and to value knowledge and thought as they approach this best, without the intrusion of any other considerations whatever. This is an instinct for which there is, I think, little original sympathy in the practical English nature, and what there was of it has undergone a long benumbing period of check and suppression in the epoch of concentration which followed the French Revolution.

But epochs of concentration cannot well endure for ever; epochs of expansion, in the due course of things, follow them. Such an epoch of expansion seems to be opening in this country. In the first place all danger of a hostile forcible pressure of foreign ideas upon our practice has long disappeared; like the traveller in the fable, therefore, we begin to wear our cloak a little more loosely.[21] Then, with a long peace, the ideas of Europe steal gradually and amicably in, and mingle, though in infinitesimally small quantities at a time, with our own notions. Then, too, in spite of all that is said about the absorbing and brutalising influence of our passionate material progress, it seems to me indisputable that this progress is likely, though not certain, to lead in the end to an apparition of intellectual life, and that man, after he has made himself perfectly comfortable and has now to determine what to do with himself next, may begin to remember that he has a mind, and that the mind may be made the source of great pleasure. I grant it is mainly the privilege of faith, at present, to discern this end to our railways, our business, and our fortune-making; but we shall see if, here as elsewhere, faith is not in the end the true prophet. Our ease, our travelling, and our unbounded liberty to hold just as hard and securely as we please to the practice to which our notions have given birth, all tend to beget an inclination to deal a little more freely with these notions themselves, to canvas them a little, to penetrate a little into their real nature. Flutterings of curiosity, in the foreign sense of the word, appear amongst us; and it is in these that criticism must look to find its account. Criticism first; a time of true creative activity, perhaps – which, as I have said, must inevitably be preceded amongst us by a time of criticism – hereafter, when criticism has done its work.

It is of the last importance that English criticism should clearly discern what rules for its course, in order to avail itself of the field now opening to it, and to produce fruit for the future, it ought to take. The rules may be given in one word; by being *disinterested*.[22] And how is it to be disinterested? By keeping aloof from practice; by resolutely following the law of its own nature, which is to be a free play of the mind on all subjects which it touches; by steadily refusing to lend itself to any of those ulterior, political, practical considerations about ideas which plenty of people will be sure to attach to them, which perhaps ought often to be attached to them, which in this country at any rate are certain to be attached to them quite sufficiently, but which criticism has really nothing to do with. Its business is, as I have said, simply to know the best that is known and thought in the world, and, by in its turn making this known, to create a current of true and fresh ideas. Its business is to do this with inflexible honesty, with due ability; but its business is to do no more, and to leave alone all questions of practical consequences and applications, questions which will never fail to have due prominence given to them. Else criticism, besides being really false to its own nature, merely continues in the old rut which it has hitherto followed in this country, and will certainly miss the chance now given to it. For what is at present the bane of criticism in this country? It is that practical considerations cling to it and stifle it; it subserves interest not its own; our organs of criticism are organs of men and parties having practical ends to serve, and with them those practical ends are the first thing and the play of the mind the second; so much play of mind as is compatible with the prosecution of those practical ends is all that is wanted. An organ like the *Revue des Deux Mondes*,[23] having for its main function to understand and utter the best that is known and thought in the world, existing, it may be said, as just an organ for a free play of the mind, we have not; but we have the *Edinburgh Review*, existing as an organ of the old Whigs, and for as much play of mind as may suit its being that; we have the *Quarterly Review*, existing as an organ of the Tories, and for as much play of mind as may suit its being that; we have the *British Quarterly Review*, existing as an organ of the political Dissenters,[24] and for as much play of mind as may suit its being that; we have the *Times*, existing as an organ of the common, satisfied, well-to-do Englishman, and for as much play of mind as may suit its being that. And so on through all the various fractions, political and religious, of our society; every fraction has, as such, its organ of criticism, but the notion of combining all fractions in the common pleasure of a free disinterested play of mind meets with no favour. Directly this play of mind wants to have more scope, and to forget the pressure of practical considerations a little, it is checked, it is made to feel its chain; we saw this the other day in the extinction, so much to be regretted, of the *Home and Foreign Review*;[25] perhaps in no organ of criticism in this country was there so much knowledge, so much play of mind; but these could not save it; the *Dublin Review* subordinates play of mind to the practical business of Roman Catholicism, and lives. It must needs be that men should act in sects and parties, that each of these sects and parties should have its organ, and should make this organ subserve the interests of its action; but it would be well, too, that there should be a criticism, not the minister of these interests, not their enemy, but absolutely and entirely independent of them. No other criticism will ever attain any real authority or make any real way towards its end – the creating a current of true and fresh ideas.

It is because criticism has so little kept in the pure intellectual sphere, has so little detached itself from practice, has been so directly polemical and controversial, that it has so ill accomplished, in this country, its true spiritual work; which is to keep man from a self-satisfaction which is retarding and vulgarising, to lead him towards perfection, by making his mind dwell upon what is excellent in itself, and the absolute beauty and fitness of things. A polemical practical criticism makes men blind even to the ideal imperfection of their practice, makes them willingly assert its ideal perfection, in order the better to secure it against attack; and clearly this is narrowing and baneful for them. If they were reassured on the practical side, speculative considerations of ideal perfection they might be brought to entertain, and their spiritual horizon would thus gradually widen. Mr Adderley[26] says to the Warwickshire farmers:

> 'Talk of the improvement of breed! Why, the race we ourselves represent, the men and women, the old Anglo-Saxon race, are the best breed in the whole world . . . The absence of a too enervating climate, too unclouded skies, and a too luxurious nature, has produced so vigorous a race of people, and has rendered us so superior to all the world.'

Mr Roebuck[27] says to the Sheffield cutlers:

> 'I look around me and ask what is the state of England? Is not property safe? Is not every man able to say what he likes? Can you not walk from one end of England to the other in perfect security? I ask you whether, the world over or in past history, there is anything like it? Nothing. I pray that out unrivalled happiness may last.'

Now obviously there is a peril for poor human nature in words and thoughts of such exuberant self-satisfaction, until we find ourselves safe in the streets of the Celestial City.

> Das wenige verschwindet leicht dem Blicke
> Der vorwärts sieht wie viel noch übrig bleibt—[28]

says Goethe; the little that is done seems nothing, when we look forward and see how much we have yet to do. Clearly this is a better line of reflection for weak humanity, so long as it remains on this earthly field of labour and effort. But neither Mr Adderley nor Mr Roebuck are by nature inaccessible to considerations of this sort. They only lose sight of them owing to the controversial life we all lead, and the practical form which all speculation takes with us. They have in view opponents whose aim is not ideal, but practical, and in their zeal to uphold their own practice against these innovators, they go so far as even to attribute to this practice an ideal perfection. Somebody has been wanting to introduce a six-pound franchise, or to abolish church-rates, or to collect agricultural statistics by force, or to diminish local self-government.[29] How natural, in reply to such proposals, very likely improper or ill-timed, to go a little beyond the mark, and to say stoutly: 'Such a race of people as we stand, so superior to all the world! The old Anglo-Saxon race, the best breed in the whole world! I pray that our unrivalled happiness may last. I ask you whether, the world over or in past history, there is anything like it?' And so long as criticism answers this dithyramb[30] by insisting that the old Anglo-Saxon race would be still more superior to all others if it had no church-rates, or that our unrivalled happiness would last yet longer with a six-pound franchise, so long will the strain, 'The best breed in the whole world!' swell louder and louder, everything ideal and refining will be lost out of sight, and both the assailed and their critics will remain in a sphere, to say the truth, perfectly unintelligent, a sphere in which spiritual progression is impossible. But let criticism leave church-rates and the franchise alone, and in the most candid spirit, without a single lurking thought of practical innovation, confront with our dithyramb this paragraph on which I stumbled in a newspaper soon after reading Mr Roebuck: –

> 'A shocking child murder has just been committed at Nottingham. A girl named Wragg left the Workhouse there on Saturday morning with her young illegitimate child. The child was soon afterwards found dead on Mapperly Hills, having been strangled. Wragg is in custody.'[31]

Nothing but that; but, in juxtaposition with the absolute eulogies of Mr Adderley and Mr Roebuck, how eloquent, how suggestive are those few lines! 'Our old Anglo-Saxon breed, the best in the whole world!' – how much that is harsh and ill-favoured there is in this best. Wragg! If we are to talk of ideal perfection, of 'the best in the whole world,' has anyone reflected what a touch of grossness in our race, what an original shortcoming in the most delicate spiritual perceptions, is shown by the natural growth amongst us of such hideous names – Higginbottom, Stiggins, Bugg! In Ionia and Attica they were luckier in this respect than 'the best race in the world;' by the Ilissus there was no Wragg, poor thing![32] And 'our unrivalled happiness' – what an element of grimness, bareness, and hideousness mixes with it and blurs it; the workhouse, the dismal Mapperly Hills, – how dismal those who have seen them will remember; – the gloom, the smoke, the cold, the strangled illegitimate child! 'I ask you whether the world over, or in past history, there is anything like it?' It may be so, one is inclined to answer; but at any rate, in that case, the world is very much to be pitied. And the final touch – short, bleak, and inhuman: *Wragg is in custody*. The sex lost in the confusion of our unrivalled happiness; or, shall I say, the superfluous Christian name lopped off by the straightforward vigour of our old Anglo-Saxon breed? There is profit for the spirit in such contrasts as this; criticism serves the cause of perfection by establishing them. By eluding sterile conflict, by refusing to remain in the sphere where alone narrow and relative conceptions have any worth and validity, criticism may diminish its momentary importance, but only in this way has it a chance of gaining admittance for those wider and more perfect conceptions to which all its duty is really owed. Mr Roebuck will have a poor opinion of an adversary who replies to his defiant songs of triumph only by murmuring under his breath, *Wragg is in custody*; but in no other way will these songs of triumph be induced gradually to moderate themselves, to get rid of what in them is excessive and offensive, and to fall into a softer and truer key.

It will be said that it is a very subtle and indirect action which I am thus prescribing for criticism, and that by embracing in this manner the Indian virtue of detachment and abandoning the sphere of practical life, it condemns itself to a slow and obscure work. Slow and obscure it may be, but it is the only proper work of criticism. The mass of mankind will never have any ardent zeal for seeing things as they are; very inadequate ideas will always satisfy them. On these inadequate ideas reposes, and must repose, the general practice of the world. That is as much as saying that whoever sets himself to see things as they are will find himself one of a very small circle; but it is only by the small circle resolutely doing its own work that adequate ideas will ever get current at all. The rush and roar of practical life will always have a dizzying and attracting effect upon the most collected spectator, and tend to draw him into its vortex; most of all will this be the case where that life is so powerful as it is in England. But it is only by remaining collected, and refusing to lend himself to the point of view of the practical man, that the critic can do the practical man any service; and it is only by the greatest sincerity in pursuing his own course, and by at last convincing even the practical man of his sincerity, that he can escape misunderstandings which perpetually threaten him.

For the practical man is not apt for fine distinctions, and yet in these distinctions truth and the highest culture greatly find their account. But it is not easy to lead a practical man, – unless you reassure him as to your practical intentions you have no chance of leading him – to see that a thing which he has always been used to look at from one side only, which he greatly values, and which, looked at from that side more than deserves, perhaps, all the prizing and admiring which he bestows upon it – that this thing looked at from another side may appear much less beneficent and beautiful, and yet retain all its claims to our practical allegiance. Where shall we find language innocent enough, how shall we make the spotless purity of our intentions evident enough, to enable us to say to the political Englishman that the British constitution itself, which seen from the practical side, looks such a magnificent organ of progress and virtue, seen from the speculative side, – with its compromises, its love of facts, its horror of theory, its studied avoidance of clear thoughts, – that seen from this side, our august constitution sometimes looks – forgive me, shade of Lord Somers![33] – a colossal machine for the manufacture of Philistines.[34] How is Cobbett[35] to say this and not be misunderstood, blackened as he is with the smoke of a lifelong conflict in the field of political practice? how is Mr Carlyle to say it and not be misunderstood, after his furious raid into this field with his *Latter-Day Pamphlets*? how is Mr Ruskin, after his pugnacious political economy?[36] I say the critic must keep out of the region of immediate practice in the political, social, humanitarian sphere, if he wants to make a beginning for that more free speculative treatment of things, which may perhaps one day make its benefits felt even in this sphere, but in a natural and thence irresistible manner.

Do what he will, however, the critic will still remain exposed to frequent misunderstandings, and nowhere more than in this country. For here people are particularly indisposed even to comprehend that without this free disinterested treatment of things truth and the highest culture are out of the question. So immersed are they in practical life, so accustomed to take all their notions from this life and its processes, that they are apt to think that truth and culture themselves can be reached by the processes of this life, and that it is an impertinent singularity to think of reaching them in any other. 'We are all *terrae filii*,'[37] cries their eloquent advocate; 'all Philistines together. Away with the notion of proceeding by any other way than the way dear to the Philistines; let us have a social movement, let us organise and combine a party to pursue truth and new thought, let us call it *the liberal party*, and let us all stick to each other and back each other up. Let us have no nonsense about independent criticism, and intellectual delicacy, and the few and the many; don't let us trouble ourselves about foreign thought; we shall invent the whole thing for ourselves as we go along; if one of us speaks well, applaud him; if one of us speaks ill, applaud him too; we are all in the same movement, we are all liberals, we are all in pursuit of truth.' In this way the pursuit of truth becomes really a social, practical, pleasurable affair, almost requiring a chairman, a secretary, and advertisements; with the excitement of a little resistance, an occasional scandal to give the happy sense of difficulty overcome; but, in general, plenty of bustle and very little thought. To act is so easy, as Goethe says;[38] to think is so hard! It is true that the critic has many temptations to go with the stream, to make one of the party of movement, one of these *terrae filii*; it seems ungracious to refuse to be a *terrae filius*, when so many excellent people are; but the critic's duty is to refuse, or, if resistance is vain, at least to cry with Obermann: *Périssons en résistant.*[39]

How serious a matter it is to try and resist, I had ample opportunity of experiencing when I ventured some time ago to criticise the celebrated first volume of Bishop Colenso.[40] The echoes of the storm which was then raised I still, from time to time, hear grumbling round me. That storm arose out of a misunderstanding almost inevitable. It is a result of no little culture to attain to a clear perception that science and religion are two wholly different things; the multitude will for ever confound them, but happily that is of no great real importance, for while it imagines itself to live by its false science it does really live by its true religion. Dr Colenso, however, in his first volume did all he could to strengthen the confusion, and to make it dangerous. He did this with the best intentions, I freely admit, and with the most candid ignorance that this was the natural effect of what he was doing; but, says Joubert, 'Ignorance, which in matters of morals extenuates the crime, is itself, in intellectual matters, a crime of the first order.'[41] I criticised Bishop Colenso's speculative confusion. Immediately there was a cry raised: 'What is this? here is a liberal attacking a liberal. Do not you belong to the movement? are not you a friend of truth. Is not Bishop Colenso in pursuit of truth? then speak with proper respect of his book. Dr Stanley[42] is another friend of truth, and you speak with proper respect of his book; why make these invidious differences? both books are excellent, admirable, liberal; Bishop Colenso's perhaps the most, because it is the boldest, and will have the best practical consequences for the liberal cause. Do you want to encourage to the attack of a fellow liberal his, and your, and our implacable enemies, the *Church and State Review* or the *Record* – the High Church rhinoceros and the Evangelical hyaena?[43] Be silent, therefore; or rather speak, speak as loud as ever you can, and go into ecstasies over the 800 and odd pigeons.' But criticism cannot follow this coarse and indiscriminate method. It is unfortunately possible for a man in pursuit of truth to write a book which reposes upon a false conception. Even the practical consequences of a book are to genuine criticism no recommendation of it, if the book is, in the highest sense, blundering. I see that a lady who herself, too, is in pursuit of truth, and who writes with great ability, but a little too much perhaps, under the influence of the practical spirit of the English liberal movement, classes Bishop Colenso's book and M Renan's[44] together, in her survey of the religious state of Europe, as facts of the same order, works, both of them of 'great importance;' 'great ability, power, and skill;' Bishop Colenso's, perhaps, the most powerful; at least, Miss Cobbe[45] gives special expression to her gratitude that to Bishop Colenso 'has been given the strength to grasp, and the courage to teach truths of such deep import.' In the same way, more than one popular writer has compared him to Luther.[46] Now it is just this kind of false estimate which the critical spirit is, it seems to me, bound to resist. It is really the strongest possible proof of the low ebb at which, in England, the critical spirit is, that while the critical hit in the religious literature of Germany is Dr Strauss's book,[47] in that of France M Renan's book; the book of Bishop Colenso is the critical hit in the religious literature of England. Bishop Colenso's book reposes on a total misconception of the essential elements of the religious problem, as that problem is now presented for solution. To criticism, therefore, which seeks to have the best that is known and thought on this problem, it is, however well meant, of no importance whatever. M Renan's book attempts a new synthesis of the elements furnished to us by the Four Gospels. It attempts, in my opinion, a synthesis perhaps premature, perhaps impossible, certainly not successful. Perhaps we shall always have to acquiesce in Fleury's sentence on such recastings of the Gospel story; *Quiconque s'imagine la pouvoir mieux écrire, ne l'entende pas.*[48] M Renan had himself passed by anticipation a like sentence on his own work, when he said: 'If a new presentation of the character of Jesus were offered to me, I would not have it; its very clearness would be, in my opinion, the best proof of its insufficiency.'[49] His friends may with perfect truth rejoin that at the sight of the Holy Land, and of the actual scene of the Gospel-story, all the current of M Renan's thoughts may have naturally changed, and a new casting of that story irresistibly suggested itself to him, and that this is just a case for applying Cicero's maxim: Change of mind is not inconsistency – *nemo unquam voluit muta-*

*tionem consilii inconstantiam esse habendam.*[50] Nevertheless, for criticism, M Renan's first thought must still be the truer one, as long as his new casting so fails, more fully to commend itself, more fully (to use Coleridge's happy phrase about the Bible)[51] to *find* us. Still M Renan's attempt is for criticism of the most real interest and importance, since, with all its difficulty, a new synthesis of the New Testament *data* is the very essence of the religious problem, as now presented; and only by efforts in this direction can it receive a solution.

Again, in the same spirit in which she judges Bishop Colenso, Miss Cobbe, like so many earnest liberals of our practical race, both here and in America, herself sets vigorously about a positive reconstruction of religion, about making a religion of the future out of hand, or at least setting about making it; we must not rest, she and they are always thinking and saying, in negative criticism, we must be creative and constructive; hence, we have such works as her recent *Religious Duty*,[52] and works still more considerable, perhaps, by others, which will be in every one's mind. These works often have much ability; they often spring out of sincere convictions, and a sincere wish to do good; and they sometimes, perhaps, do good. Their fault is (if I may be permitted to say so) one which they have in common with the British College of Health, in the New Road.[53] Every one knows the British College of Health; it is that building with the lion and the statue of the Goddess Hygeia before it; at least I am sure about the lion, though I am not absolutely certain about the Goddess Hygeia. This building does credit, perhaps, to the resources of Dr Morrison and his disciples; but it falls a good deal short of one's idea of what a British College of Health should be. In England, where we hate public interference, and love individual enterprise, we have a whole crop of places like the British College of Health; the grand name without the grand thing. Unluckily, creditable to individual enterprise as they are, they tend to impair our taste by making us forget what a more grandiose, noble, or beautiful character properly belongs to a public institution. The same may be said of the religions of the future of Miss Cobbe and others. Creditable, like the British College of Health, to the resources of their authors, they yet tend to make us forget what more grandiose, noble, or beautiful character properly belongs to religious constructions. The historic religions, with all their faults, have had this; it certainly belongs to the religious sentiment, when it truly flowers, to have this; and we impoverish our spirit if we allow a religion of the future without it. What then is the duty of criticism here? To take the practical point of view, to applaud the liberal movement and all its works, its New Road religions of the future into the bargain, for their general utility's sake? By no means; but to be perpetually dissatisfied with these works, while they perpetually fall short of a high and noble ideal.

In criticism these are elementary laws; but they never can be popular, and in this country they have been very little followed, and one meets immense obstacles in following them. That is a reason for asserting them again and again. Criticism must maintain its independence of the practical spirit and its aims. Even with well-meant efforts of the practical spirit it must express dissatisfaction if in the sphere of the ideal they seem impoverishing and limiting. It must not hurry on to the goal because of its practical importance. It must be patient, and know how to wait; and flexible, and know how to attach itself to things and how to withdraw from them. It must be apt to study and praise elements that for the fulness of spiritual perfection are wanted, even though they belong to a power which in the practical sphere may be maleficent. It must be apt to discern the spiritual shortcomings or illusions of powers that in the practical sphere may be beneficent. And this without any notion of favouring or injuring, in the practical sphere, one power or the other; without any notion of playing off, in this sphere, one power against the other. When one looks, for instance, at the English Divorce Court[54] – an institution which no doubt has its practical conveniences, but which in the ideal sphere is so hideous; an institution which neither makes separation impossible nor makes it decent, which allows a man to get rid of his wife, or a wife of her husband, but makes them drag one another first, for the public edification, through a mire of unutterable infamy – when one looks at this charming institution, I say, with its crowded benches, its newspaper-reports, and its money-compensations, this institution in which the gross unregenerate British Philistine has indeed stamped an image of himself – one may be permitted to find the marriage-theory of Catholicism refreshing and elevating. Or when Protestantism, in virtue of its supposed rational and intellectual origin, gives the law to criticism too magisterially, criticism may and must remind it that its pretensions, in this respect, are illusive and do it harm; that the Reformation was a moral rather than an intellectual event; that Luther's theory of grace[55] no more exactly reflects the mind of the spirit than Bossuet's philosophy of history reflects it,[56] and that there is no more antecedent probability of the Bishop of Durham's stock of ideas being agreeable to perfect reason than of Pope Pius the Ninth's.[57] But criticism will not on that account forget the achievements of Protestantism in the practical and moral sphere; nor that, even in the intellectual sphere, Protestantism, though in a blind and stumbling manner, continued the Renaissance, while Catholicism threw itself violently across its path.

I lately heard a man of thought and energy contrasting the want of ardour and movement which he now found amongst young men in this country with what he remembered in his own youth, twenty years ago. 'What reformers we were then,' he exclaimed, 'what a zeal we had! how we canvassed every institution in Church and State, and were prepared to remodel them all on first principles.' He was inclined to regret, as a spiritual flagging, the lull which he saw. I am disposed rather to regard it as a pause in which the turn to a new mode of spiritual progress is being accomplished. Everything was long seen, by the young and ardent amongst us, in inseparable connection with politics and practical life; we have pretty well exhausted the benefits of seeing them in this connection, we have got all that can be got by so seeing them. Let us try a more disinterested mode of seeing them; let us betake ourselves more to the serener life of the mind and spirit. This life, too, may have its excesses and dangers; but they are not for us at present. Let us think of quietly enlarging our stock of true and fresh ideas, and not, as soon as we get an idea or half an idea, be running out with it into the street, and trying to make it rule there. Our ideas will, in the end, shape the world all the better for maturing a little. Perhaps in fifty years' time it will in the English House of Commons be an objection to an institution that it is an anomaly, and my friend, the Member of Parliament, will shudder in his grave. But let us in the meanwhile rather endeavour that in twenty years' time it may, in English literature, be an objection to a proposition that it is absurd. That will be a change so vast, that the imagination almost fails to grasp it. *Ab integro saeclorum nascitur ordo.*[58]

If I have insisted so much on the course which criticism must take where politics and religion are concerned, it is because, where these burning matters are in question, it is most likely to go astray. In general its course is determined for it by the idea which is the law of its being; the idea of a disinterested endeavour to learn and propagate the best that is known and thought in the world, and thus to establish a current of fresh and true ideas. By the very nature of things, as England is not all the world, much of the best that is known and thought in the world cannot be of English growth, must be foreign; by the nature of things again, it is just this that we are least likely to know, while English thought is streaming upon us from all sides and takes excellent care that we shall not be ignorant of its existence; the English critic, therefore, must dwell much on foreign thought, and with particular heed on any part of it, which, while significant and fruitful in itself, is for any reason likely to escape him. Judging is often spoken of as the critic's one business; and so in some sense it is; but the judgment which almost insensibly forms itself in a fair and clear mind, along with fresh knowledge, is the valuable one; and thus knowledge, and ever fresh knowledge, must be his great concern for himself, and it is by communicating fresh knowledge, and letting his own judgment pass along with it, – but insensibly, and in the second place not the first, as a sort of companion and clue, not as an abstract law-giver, – that he will generally do most good to his readers. Sometimes, no doubt, for the sake of establishing an author's place in literature, and his relation to a central standard, (and if this is not done how are we to get at our *best in the world*) criticism may have to deal with a subject-matter so familiar that fresh knowledge is out of the question, and then it must be all judgment; an enunciation and detailed application of principles. Here the great safeguard is never to let oneself become abstract, always to retain an intimate and lively consciousness of what one is saying, and, the moment this fails us, to be sure that something is wrong. But under all circumstances this mere judgment and application of principles is, in itself, not the most satisfactory work to the critic; like Mathematics it is tautological, and cannot well give us, like fresh learning, the sense of creative activity. To have this sense, is as I said at the beginning, the great happiness and the great proof of being alive, and it is not denied to criticism to have it; but then criticism must be sincere, simple, flexible, ardent, ever widening its knowledge. Then it may have in no contemptible measure, a joyful sense of creative activity: a sense which a man of insight and conscience will prefer to what he might derive from a poor, starved, fragmentary, inadequate creation. And at some epochs no other creation is possible.

Still, in full measure, the sense of creative activity belongs only to genuine creation; in literature we must never forget that. But what true men of letters ever can forget it? It is no such common matter for a gifted nature to come into possession of a current of true and living ideas, and to produce amidst the inspiration of them, that we are likely to underrate it. The epochs of Aeschylus[59] and Shakespeare make us feel their pre-eminence. In an epoch like those, is, no doubt the true life of a literature; there is the promised land towards which criticism can only beckon. That promised land it will not be ours to enter, and we shall die in the wilderness: but to have desired to enter it, to have saluted it from afar, is already, perhaps, the best distinction among contemporaries; it will certainly be the best title to esteem with posterity.

# 7

# ART FOR ART'S SAKE

## ALGERNON SWINBURNE, *NOTES ON POEMS AND REVIEWS* (1866)

The career of Algernon Charles Swinburne (1837–1909) was punctuated by a series of gestures specifically designed to shock a conservative Victorian public. Born into a distinguished family, Swinburne entered Balliol College, Oxford in 1856 with Benjamin Jowett as his tutor. His interest in writing began almost immediately with contributions of poems and essays to *Undergraduate Papers*, a publication which had been recently taken over by the Old Mortality Society – an Oxford discussion group of which Swinburne was a founder and which was later to number Walter Pater as a member. At this time Swinburne also became friendly with the Pre-Raphaelite painters, Edward Burne Jones and Dante Gabriel Rossetti who (along with William Morris) took part in the ill-fated decoration of the Oxford Union's new hall. In 1860 Swinburne left Oxford without a degree and in dubious circumstances. He in part compensated for this failure, though, with the publication that same year of the dramas, *The Queen-Mother* and *Rosamond*. In 1861 he travelled to Italy, and later in the year was granted an annual pension of £200 by his father which allowed him to settle in London. In 1862 Swinburne produced notable reviews of the French writers, Victor Hugo and Charles Baudelaire; he also moved into Tudor House, the home of Dante Gabriel Rossetti in Cheyne Walk. In 1863 he began work on a classical drama, *Atalanta in Calydon*, which was published with some success in 1865. In the meantime Swinburne's relationship with Rossetti had cooled, and he moved out of Tudor House. The year 1865 also saw the publication of a third drama, *Chastelard*. It received some hostile notices – an anticipation of the much greater outrage which greeted the publication of his next work, *Poems and Ballads* (1866). Swinburne was attacked with unusual venom; accused of paganism, blasphemy, sensuality and immorality, he was dubbed by John Morley as 'the libidinous laureate of a pack of satyrs'. The volume was withdrawn by Moxon & Co. and its publication taken over by John Camden Hotten, a less prominent publisher who urged Swinburne to reply. The result was his pamphlet, *Notes on Poems and Reviews*, a short, caustic and by no means conciliatory defence of his work which predictably provoked yet further hostility: *Punch*, for example, renamed him 'Swine-born'. Matters were further exacerbated with the publication in 1871 of a second volume of poetry, *Songs before Sunrise*; it was attacked (along with Rossetti's verse) by the conservative critic Robert Buchanan in an anonymous article in the *Contemporary Review* entitled 'The Fleshly School of Poetry'. This time Swinburne's reply – *Under the Microscope* (1872) – was longer and more wide ranging in its targets; his critics, though, largely ignored it. In 1874 Swinburne changed publishers and brought out another drama, *Bothwell*; it was followed in 1875 by two critical works, *Essays and Studies* and *George Chapman*. In 1876 Swinburne was once more embroiled in controversy; on this occasion he was the subject of a successful libel suit brought against him by Buchanan because of some defamatory pieces in the *Examiner*. In 1877 his father died and Swinburne inherited considerable wealth which he proceeded to squander on satisfying his varied and extravagant tastes. Perhaps because of this over-indulgence two years later he suffered a complete physical collapse. Swinburne, however, was fortunate to be 'rescued' by the literary critic, Theodore Watts Dunton who restored him to health and continued to look after him for the next thirty years. During this period, Swinburne, now a more sober, respectable, and in some respects a reactionary figure, wrote prolifically, producing several further dramas, a number of volumes of poetry, as well as critical works. He died from pneumonia in 1909.

## Algernon Swinburne, *Notes on Poems and Reviews* (London: John Camden Hotten, 1866)[1]

It is by no wish of my own that I accept the task now proposed to me. To vindicate or defend myself from the assault or the charge of men whom, but for their attacks, I might never have heard of, is an office which I, or any writer who respects his work, cannot without reluctance stoop to undertake. As long as the attacks on my book – I have seen a few, I am told there are many – were confined within the usual limits of the anonymous press,[2] I let them pass without

370

the notice to which they appeared to aspire. Sincere or insincere, insolent or respectful, I let my assailants say out their say unheeded.

I have now undertaken to write a few words on this affair, not by way of apology or vindication, of answer or appeal. I have none such to offer. Much of the criticism I have seen is as usual, in the words of Shakspeare's greatest follower,

> 'As if a man should spit against the wind;
> The filth returns in's face.'[3]

In recognition of his fair dealing with me in this matter, I am bound by my own sense of right to accede to the wish of my present publisher, and to the wishes of friends whose advice I value, that on his account, if not on mine, I should make some reply to the charges brought against me – as far as I understand them. The work is not fruitful of pleasure, of honour, or of profit; but, like other such tasks, it may be none the less useful and necessary. I am aware that it cannot be accomplished without some show of egotism; and I am perforce prepared to incur the consequent charge of arrogance. The office of commentator on my own works has been forced upon me by circumstances connected with the issue and re-issue of my last book. I am compelled to look sharply into it, and inquire what passage, what allusion, or what phrase can have drawn down such sudden thunder from the serene heavens of public virtue. A mere libeller I have no wish to encounter; I leave it to saints to fight with beasts at Ephesus or nearer.[4] 'For in these strifes, and on such persons, it were as wretched to affect a victory, as it is unhappy to be committed with them.'[5]

Certain poems of mine, it appears, have been impugned by judges, with or without a name, as indecent or as blasphemous. To me, as I have intimated, their verdict is a matter of infinite indifference: it is of equally small moment to me whether in such eyes as theirs I appear moral or immoral, Christian or pagan. But, remembering that science must not scorn to investigate animalcules and infusoria,[6] I am ready for once to play the anatomist.

With regard to any opinion implied or expressed throughout my book, I desire that one thing should be remembered: the book is dramatic, many-faced, multifarious; and no utterance of enjoyment or despair, belief or unbelief, can properly be assumed as the assertion of its author's personal feeling or faith. Were each poem to be accepted as the deliberate outcome and result of the writer's conviction, not mine alone but most other men's verses would leave nothing behind them but a sense of cloudy chaos and suicidal contradiction. Byron and Shelley, speaking in their own persons, and with what sublime effect we know, openly and insultingly mocked and reviled what the English of their day held most sacred. I have not done this. I do not say that, if I chose, I would not do so to the best of my power; I do say that hitherto I have seen fit to do nothing of the kind.

It remains then to inquire what in that book can be reasonably offensive to the English reader. In order to resolve this problem, I will not fish up any of the ephemeral scurrilities born only to sting if they can, and sink as they must. I will take the one article that lies before me; the work (I admit) of an enemy, but the work (I acknowledge) of a gentleman. I cannot accept it as accurate; but I readily and gladly allow that it neither contains nor suggests anything false or filthy. To him therefore, rather than to another, I address my reclamation. Two among my poems, it appears, are in his opinion 'especially horrible.'[7] Good. Though the phrase be somewhat 'inexpressive,' I am content to meet him on this ground. It is something – nay, it is much – to find an antagonist who has a sufficient sense of honesty and honour to mark out the lists in which he, the challenger, is desirous to encounter the challenged.

The first, it appears, of these especially horrible poems is *Anactoria*. I am informed, and have not cared to verify the assertion, that this poem has excited, among the chaste and candid critics of the day or hour or minute, a more vehement reprobation, a more virtuous horror, a more passionate appeal, than any other of my writing. Proud and glad as I must be of this distinction, I must yet, however reluctantly, inquire what merit or demerit has incurred such unexpected honour. I was not ambitious of it; I am not ashamed of it; but I am overcome by it. I have never lusted after the praise of reviewers; I have never feared their abuse; but I would fain know why the vultures should gather here of all places; what congenial carrion they smell, who can discern such (it is alleged) in any rose-bed. And after a little reflection I do know, or conjecture. Virtue, as she appears incarnate in British journalism and voluble through that unsavoury organ, is something of a compound creature–

'A lump neither alive nor dead,
Dog-headed, bosom-eyed, and bird-footed;'[8]

nor have any dragon's jaws been known to emit on occasion stronger and stranger sounds and odours. But having, not without astonishment and disgust, inhaled these odours, I find myself at last able to analyse their component parts. What my poem means, if any reader should want that explained, I am ready to explain, though perplexed by the hint that explanation may be required. What certain reviewers have imagined it to imply, I am incompetent to explain, and unwilling to imagine. I am evidently not virtuous enough to understand them. I thank Heaven that I am not. *Ma corruption rougirait de leur pudeur.*[9] I have not studied in those schools whence that full-fledged phoenix, the 'virtue' of professional pressmen, rises chuckling and crowing from the dunghill, its birthplace and its deathbed. But there are birds of alien feather, if not of higher flight; and these I would now recall into no hencoop or preserve of mine, but into the open and general field where all may find pasture and sunshine and fresh air: into places whither the prurient prudery and the virulent virtue of pressmen and prostitutes cannot follow; into an atmosphere where calumny cannot speak, and fatuity cannot breathe; in a word, where backbiters and imbeciles become impossible. I neither hope nor wish to change the unchangeable, to purify the impure. To conciliate them, to vindicate myself in their eyes, is a task which I should not condescend to attempt, even were I sure to accomplish.

In this poem I have simply expressed, or tried to express, that violence of affection between one and another which hardens into rage and deepens into despair. The key-note which I have here touched was struck long since by Sappho.[10] We in England are taught, are compelled under penalties to learn, to construe, and to repeat, as schoolboys, the imperishable and incomparable verses of that supreme poet; and I at least am grateful for the training. I have wished, and I have even ventured to hope, that I might be in time competent to translate into a baser and later language the divine words which even when a boy I could not but recognise as divine. That hope, if indeed I dared ever entertain such a hope, I soon found fallacious. To translate the two odes and the remaining fragments of Sappho is the one impossible task; and as witness of this I will call up one of the greatest among poets. Catullus[11] 'translated' – or as his countrymen would now say 'traduced' – the Ode to Anactoria – Εἰς Ἐρωμέναν: a more beautiful translation there never was and will never be; but compared with the Greek, it is colourless and bloodless, puffed out by additions and enfeebled by alterations. Let any one set against each other the two first stanzas, Latin and Greek, and pronounce. (This would be too much to ask of all of my critics; but some among the journalists of England may be capable of achieving the not exorbitant task.) Where Catullus failed I could not hope to succeed; I tried instead to reproduce in a diluted and dilated form the spirit of a poem which could not be reproduced in the body.

Now, the ode Εἰς Ἐρωμέναν – the 'Ode to Anactoria' (as it is named by tradition) – the poem which English boys have to get by heart – the poem (and this is more important) which has in the whole world of verse no companion and no rival but the Ode to Aphrodite,[12] has been twice at least translated or 'traduced.' I am not aware that Mr Ambrose Phillips, or M Nicolas Boileau-Despréaux[13] was ever impeached before any jury of moralists for his sufficiently grievous offence. By any jury of poets both would assuredly have been convicted. Now, what they did I have not done. To the best (and bad is the best) of their ability, they have 'done into' bad French and bad English the very words of Sappho. Feeling that although I might do it better I could not do it well, I abandoned the idea of translation – ἔχων ἀέχοντί γε Θυμῷ.[14] I tried, then, to write some paraphrase of the fragment which the Fates[15] and the Christians have spared us. I have not said, as Boileau and Phillips have, that the speaker sweats and swoons at sight of her favourite by the side of a man. I have abstained from touching on such details, for this reason: that I felt myself incompetent to give adequate expression in English to the literal and absolute words of Sappho; and would not debase and degrade them into a viler form. No one can feel more deeply than I do the inadequacy of my work. 'That is not Sappho,' a friend said once to me. I could only reply, 'It is as near as I can come; and no man can come close to her.' Her remaining verses are the supreme success, the final achievement, of the poetic art.

But this, it may be, is not to the point. I will try to draw thither; though the descent is immeasurable from Sappho's verse to mine, or to any man's. I have striven to cast my spirit into the mould of hers, to express and represent not the poem but the poet. I did not think it requisite to disfigure the page with a foot-note wherever I had fallen back upon the original text. Here and there, I need not say, I have rendered into English the very words of Sappho. I have tried also to work into words of my own some expression of their effect: to bear witness how, more than any other's, her verses strike and sting the memory in lonely places, or at sea, among all loftier sights and sounds – how they seem akin to fire and air, being themselves 'all air and fire;'[16] other element there is none in them. As to the angry appeal against the supreme mystery of oppressive heaven, which I have ventured to put into her mouth at that point only where pleasure culmi-nates in pain, affection in anger, and desire in despair – as to the 'blasphemies'[a] against God or Gods of which here and elsewhere I stand accused, – they are to be taken as the first outcome or outburst of foiled and fruitless passion recoiling on itself. After this, the spirit finds time to breathe and repose above all vexed senses of the weary body, all bitter labours of the revolted soul; the poet's pride of place is resumed, the lofty conscience of invincible immortality in the memo-ries and the mouths of men.

What is there now of horrible in this? the expressions of fierce fondness, the ardours of passionate despair? Are these so unnatural as to affright or disgust? Where is there an unclean detail? where an obscene allusion? A writer as impure as my critics might of course have written, on this or on any subject, an impure poem; I have not. And if to translate or paraphrase Sappho be an offence, indict the heavier offenders who have handled and rehandled this matter in their wretched versions of the ode. Is my poem more passionate in detail, more unmistakable in subject? I affirm that it is less; and what I affirm I have proved.

Next on the list of accusation stands the poem of *Dolores*. The gist and

---

a    As I shall not return to this charge of 'blasphemy,' I will here cite a notable instance of what does seem permissible in that line to the English reader. (I need not say that I do not question the right, which hypocrisy and servility would deny, of author and publisher to express and produce what they please. I do not deprecate, but demand for all men freedom to speak and freedom to hear. It is the line of demarcation which admits, if offence there be, the greater offender and rejects the less – it is this that I do not understand.) After many alternate curses and denials of God, a great poet talks of Christ 'veiling his horrible Godhead,' of his 'malignant soul,' his 'godlike malice.' Shelley outlived all this and much more; but Shelley wrote all this and much more. Will no Society for the Suppression of Common Sense – no Committee for the Propagation of Cant – see to it a little? or have they not already tried their hands at it and broken down? For the poem which contains the words above quoted continues at this day to bring credit and profit to its publishers – Messrs Moxon and Co. [The quotations are from Shelley's *Queen Mab* (1813), vii. ll. 164, 172, 180.]

bearing of this I should have thought evident enough, viewed by the light of others which precede and follow it. I have striven here to express that transient state of spirit through which a man may be supposed to pass, foiled in love and weary of loving, but not yet in sight of rest; seeking refuge in those 'violent delights' which 'have violent ends,'[17] in fierce and frank sensualities which at least profess to be no more than they are. This poem, like *Faustine*, is so distinctly symbolic and fanciful that it cannot justly be amenable to judgement as a study in the school of realism. The spirit, bowed and discoloured by suffering and by passion (which are indeed the same thing and the same word), plays for awhile with its pleasures and its pains, mixes and distorts them with a sense half-humorous and half-mournful, exults in bitter and doubtful emotions –

'Moods of fantastic sadness, nothing worth.'[18]

It sports with sorrow, and jests against itself; cries out for freedom and confesses the chain; decorates with the name of goddess, crowns anew as the mystical Cotytto,[19] some woman, real or ideal, in whom the pride of life with its companion lusts is incarnate. In her lover's half-shut eyes, her fierce unchaste beauty is transfigured, her cruel sensual eyes have a meaning and a message; there are memories and secrets in the kisses of her lips. She is the darker Venus, fed with burnt-offering and blood-sacrifice; the veiled image of that pleasure which men impelled by satiety and perverted by power have sought through ways as strange as Nero's[20] before and since his time; the daughter of lust and death, and holding of both her parents; Our Lady of Pain,[21] antagonist alike of trivial sins and virtues; no Virgin, and unblessed of men; no mother of the Gods or God; no Cybele, served by sexless priests or monks, adored of Origen or of Atys; no likeness of her in Dindymus or Loreto.[22]

The next act in this lyrical monodrame of passion represents a new stage and scene. The worship of desire has ceased; the mad commotion of sense has stormed itself out; the spirit, clear of the old regret that drove it upon such violent ways for a respite, healed of the fever that wasted it in the search for relief among fierce fancies and tempestuous pleasures, dreams now of truth discovered and repose attained. Not the martyr's ardour of selfless love, an unprofitable flame that burnt out and did no service – not the rapid rage of pleasure that seemed for a little to make the flesh divine, to clothe the naked senses with the fiery raiment of faith; but a stingless love, an innocuous desire. 'Hesperia,' the tenderest type of woman or of dream, born in the westward 'islands of the blest,'[23] where the shadows of all happy and holy things live beyond the sunset a sacred and a sleepless life, dawns upon his eyes a western dawn, risen as the fiery day of passion goes down, and risen where it sank. Here, between moonrise and sunset, lives the love that is gentle and faithful, neither giving too much nor asking – a bride rather than a mistress, a sister rather than a bride. But not at once, or not for ever, can the past be killed and buried; hither also the huntress follows her flying prey, wounded and weakened, still fresh from the pangs of passion; the cruel hands, the amorous eyes, still glitter and allure. *Qui a bu boira*:[24] the feet are drawn back towards the ancient ways. Only by lifelong flight, side by side with the goddess that redeems, shall her slave of old escape from the goddess that consumes: if even thus one may be saved, even thus distance the bloodhounds.

This is the myth or fable of my poem; and it is not without design that I have slipped in, between the first and the second part, the verses called *The Garden of Proserpine*, expressive, as I meant they should be, of that brief total pause of passion and of thought, when the spirit, without fear or hope of good things or evil, hungers and thirsts only after the perfect sleep. Now, what there is in all this unfit to be written – what there is here indecent in manner or repulsive in matter – I at least do not yet see; and before I can see it, my eyes must be purged with the euphrasy and rue[25] which keep clear the purer eyes of professional virtue. The insight into evil of chaste and critical pressmen, their sharp scent for possible or impossible impurities, their delicate ear for a sound or a whisper of wrong – all this knowledge 'is too wonderful and excellent for me; I cannot attain unto it.'[26] In one thing, indeed, it seems I have erred: I have forgotten to prefix to my work the timely warning of a great poet and humorist:–

'J'en préviens les mères des familles,
Ce que j'écris n'est pas pour les petites filles
Dont on coupe le pain en tartines; mes vers
Sont des vers de jeune homme.'[27]

I have overlooked the evidence which every day makes clearer, that our time has room only for such as are content to write for children and girls. But this oversight is the sum of my offence.

It would seem indeed as though to publish a book were equivalent to thrusting it with violence into the hands of every mother and nurse in the kingdom as fit and necessary food for female infancy. Happily there is no fear that the supply of milk for babes will fall short of the demand for some time yet. There are moral milkmen enough, in all conscience, crying their ware about the streets and by-ways; fresh or stale, sour or sweet, the requisite fluid runs from a sufficiently copious issue. In due time, perhaps, the critical doctors may prescribe a stronger diet for their hypochondriac patient, the reading world; or that gigantic *malade imaginaire* called the public may rebel against the weekly draught or the daily drug of MM Purgon and Diafoirus.[28] We, meanwhile, who profess to deal neither in poison nor in pap, may not unwillingly stand aside. Let those read who will, and let those who will abstain from reading. *Caveat emptor*.[29] No one wishes to force men's food down the throats of babes and sucklings. The verses last analysed were assuredly written with no moral or immoral design; but the upshot seems to me moral rather than immoral, if it must needs be one or the other, and if (which I cannot be sure of) I construe aright those somewhat misty and changeable terms.

These poems thus disposed of are (I am told) those which have given most offence and scandal to the venal virtue of journalism. As I have not to review my reviewers, I need not be at pains to refute at length every wilful error or unconscious lie which a workman that way inclined might drag into light. To me, as to all others who may read what I write, the whole matter must continue to seem too pitiable and trivial to waste a word or thought on it which we can help wasting. But having begun this task, I will add yet a word or two of annotation. I have heard that even the little poem of *Faustine* has been to some readers a thing to make the scalp creep and the blood freeze. It was issued with no such intent. Nor do I remember that any man's voice or heel was lifted against it when it first appeared, a new-born and virgin poem, in the *Spectator* newspaper for 1862.[30] Virtue, it would seem, has shot up surprisingly in the space of four years or less – a rank and rapid growth, barren of blossom and rotten at root. *Faustine* is the reverie of a man gazing on the bitter and vicious loveliness of a face as common and as cheap as the morality of reviewers, and dreaming of past lives in which this fair face may have held a nobler or fitter station; the imperial profile may have been Faustina's, the thirsty lips a Maenad's,[31] when first she learnt to drink blood or wine, to waste the loves and ruin the lives of men; through Greece and again through Rome she may have passed with the same face which now comes before us dishonoured and discrowned. Whatever of merit or demerit there may be in the verses, the idea that gives them such life as they have is simple enough; the transmigration of a single soul, doomed as though by accident from the first to all evil and no good, through many ages and forms, but clad always in the same type of fleshly beauty. The chance which suggested to me this poem was one which may happen any day to any man – the sudden sight of a living face which recalled the well-known likeness of another dead for centuries: in this instance, the noble and faultless type of the elder Faustina, as seen in coin and bust. Out of that casual glimpse and sudden recollection these verses sprang and grew.

Of the poem in which I have attempted once more to embody the legend of Venus and her knight,[32] I need say only that my first aim was to rehandle the old story in a new fashion. To me it seemed that the tragedy began with the knight's return to Venus – began at the point where hitherto it had seemed to leave off. The immortal agony of a man lost after all repentance – cast down from fearful hope into fearless despair – believing in Christ and bound to Venus – desirous of penitential pain, and damned to joyless pleasure – this, in my eyes, was the kernel and nucleus of a myth comparable only to that of the foolish virgins,[33] and bearing the same burden. The tragic touch of the story is this: that the knight who has renounced Christ believes in him; the lover who has embraced Venus disbelieves in her. Vainly and in despair would he make the best of that which is the worst – vainly remonstrate with God, and argue on the side he would fain desert. Once accept or admit the least admixture of pagan worship, or of modern thought, and the whole story collapses into froth and smoke. It was not till my poem was completed that I received from the hands of its author the admirable pamphlet of Charles Baudelaire on Wagner's *Tannhäuser*.[34] If any one desires to see, expressed in better words than I can command, the conception of the mediaeval Venus which it was my aim to put into verse, let him turn to the magnificent passage in which M Baudelaire describes the fallen goddess, grown diabolic among ages that would not accept her as divine. In another point, as I then found, I concur with the great musician and his great panegyrist. I have made Venus the one love of her knight's whole life, as Mary Stuart of Chastelard's;[35] I have sent him, poet and soldier, fresh to her fierce embrace. Thus only both legend and symbol appear to me noble and significant. Light loves and harmless errors must not touch the elect of heaven or of hell. The queen of evil, the lady of lust, will endure no rival but God; and when the vicar of God rejects him, to her only can he return to abide the day of his judgment in weariness and sorrow and fear.

These poems do not seem to me condemnable, unless it be on the ground of bad verse; and to any charge of that kind I should of course be as unable as reluctant to reply. But I certainly was even less prepared to hear the batteries of virtue open fire in another quarter. Sculpture I knew was a dead art; buried centuries deep out of sight, with no angel keeping watch over the sepulchre; its very grave-clothes divided by wrangling and impotent sectaries,[36] and no chance anywhere visible of a resurrection. I knew that belief in the body was the secret of sculpture, and that a past age of ascetics could no more attempt or attain it than the present age of hypocrites; I knew that modern moralities and recent religions were, if possible, more averse and alien to this purely physical and pagan art than to the others; but how far averse I did not know. There is nothing lovelier, as there is nothing more famous, in later Hellenic art, than the statue of Hermaphroditus.[37] No one would compare it with the greatest works of Greek sculpture. No one would lift Keats on a level with Shakespeare. But the Fates have allowed us to possess at once Othello and Hyperion, Theseus[38] and Hermaphroditus. At Paris, at Florence, at Naples, the delicate divinity of this

b    Witness Shelley's version: –

> 'A sexless thing it was, and in its growth
> It seemed to have developed no defect
> Of either sex, yet all the grace of both;
> In gentleness and strength its limbs were decked;
> The bosom lightly swelled with its full youth,
> The countenance was such as might select
> Some artist, that his skill should never die,
> Imaging forth such perfect purity.'

*Witch of Atlas*, st. xxxvi

But Shelley had not studied purity in the school of reviewers. It is well for us that we have teachers able to enlighten our darkness, or Heaven knows into what error such as he, or such as I, might not fall. We might even, in time, come to think it possible to enjoy the naked beauty of a statue or a picture without any virtuous vision behind it of a filthy fancy; which would be immoral.

work has always drawn towards it the eyes of artists and poets.[b] A creature at once foul and dull enough to extract from a sight so lovely, from a thing so noble, the faintest, the most fleeting idea of impurity, must be, and must remain, below comprehension and below remark. It is incredible that the meanest of men should derive from it any other than the sense of high and grateful pleasure. Odour and colour and music are not more tender or more pure. How favourite and frequent a vision among the Greeks was this of the union of sexes in one body of perfect beauty, none need be told. In Plato the legend has fallen into a form coarse, hard, and absurd.[39] The theory of God splitting in two the double archetype of man and woman, the original hermaphrodite which had to get itself bisected into female and male, is repulsive and ridiculous enough. But the idea thus incarnate, literal or symbolic, is merely beautiful. I am not the first who has translated into written verse this sculptured poem: another before me, as he says, has more that once 'caressed it with a sculptor's love.'[40] It is, indeed, among statues as a lyric among tragedies; it stands below the Niobe as Simonides below Aeschylus, as Correggio beneath Titian.[41] The sad and subtle moral of this myth, which I have desired to indicate in verse, is that perfection once attained on all sides is a thing thenceforward barren of use or fruit; whereas the divine beauty of separate woman and man – a thing inferior and imperfect – can serve all turns of life. Ideal beauty, like ideal genius, dwells apart, as though by compulsion; supremacy is solitude. But leaving this symbolic side of the matter, I cannot see why this statue should not be the text for yet another poem. Treated in the grave and chaste manner as a serious 'thing of beauty,'[42] to be for ever applauded and enjoyed, it can give no offence but to the purblind and the prurient. For neither of these classes have I ever written or will I ever write. 'Loathsome and abominable' and full of 'unspeakable foulnesses' must be that man's mind who could here discern evil;[43] unclean and inhuman the animal which could suck from this mystical rose of ancient loveliness the foul and rancid juices of an obscene fancy. It were a scavenger's office to descend with torch or spade into such depths of mental sewerage, to plunge or peer into subterranean sloughs of mind impossible alike to enlighten or to cleanse.

I have now gone over the poems which, as I hear, have incurred most blame; whether deservedly or not, I have shown. For the terms in which certain critics have clothed their sentiments I bear them no ill-will: they are welcome for me to write unmolested, as long as they keep to simple ribaldry. I hope it gives them amusement; I presume it brings them profit; I know it does not affect me. Absolute falsehood may, if it be worth while, draw down contradiction and disproof; but the mere calling of bad names is a child's trick, for which the small fry of the press should have a child's correction at the hands of able editors; standing as these gentlemen ought to do in a parental or pedagogic relation to their tender charges. They have, by all I see and hear, been sufficiently scurrilous – one or two in particular.

'However, from one crime they are exempt;

379

They do not strike a brother, striking *me*.'[44]

I will only throw them one crumb of advice in return; I fear the alms will be of no avail, but it shall not be withheld: –

'Why grudge them lotus-leaf and laurel,
 O toothless mouth or swinish maw,
Who never grudged you bells and coral,
 Who never grudged you troughs and straw?

Lie still in kennel, sleek in stable,
 Good creatures of the stall or sty;
Shove snouts for crumbs below the table;
 Lie still; and rise not up to lie.'[45]

To all this, however, there is a grave side. The question at issue is wider than any between a single writer and his critics, or it might well be allowed to drop. It is this: whether or not the first and last requisite of art is to give no offence; whether or not all that cannot be lisped in the nursery or fingered in the school-room is therefore to be cast out of the library; whether or not the domestic circle is to be for all men and writers the outer limit and extreme horizon of their world of work. For to this we have come; and all students of art must face the matter as it stands. Who has not heard it asked, in a final and triumphant tone, whether this book or that can be read aloud by her mother to a young girl? whether such and such a picture can properly be exposed to the eyes of young persons? If you reply that this is nothing to the point, you fall at once into the ranks of the immoral. Never till now, and nowhere but in England, could so monstrous an absurdity rear for one moment its deformed and eyeless head. In no past century were artists ever bidden to work on these terms; nor are they now, except among us. The disease, of course, afflicts the meanest members of the body with most virulence. Nowhere is cant at once so foul-mouthed and so tight-laced as in the penny, twopenny, threepenny, or sixpenny press. Nothing is so favourable to the undergrowth of real indecency as this overshadowing foliage of fictions, this artificial network of proprieties. *L'Arioste rit au soleil, l'Arétin ricane à l'ombre.*[46] The whiter the sepulchre without, the ranker the rottenness within. Every touch of plaster is a sign of advancing decay. The virtue of our critical journals is a dowager of somewhat dubious antecedents: every day that thins and shrivels her cheek thickens and hardens the paint on it; she consumes more chalk and ceruse[47] than would serve a whole courtful of crones. 'It is to be presumed,' certainly, that in her case 'all is not sweet, all is not sound.'[48] The taint on her fly-blown reputation is hard to overcome by patches and perfumery. Literature, to be worthy of men, must be large, liberal, sincere; and cannot be chaste if it be prudish. Purity and prudery cannot keep house together. Where free speech and fair play are interdicted, foul hints and evil suggestions are hatched into fetid life.

And if literature indeed is not to deal with the full life of man and the whole nature of things, let it be cast aside with the rods and rattles of childhood. Whether it affect to teach or to amuse, it is equally trivial and contemptible to us; only less so than the charge of immorality. Against how few really great names has not this small and dirt-encrusted pebble been thrown! A reputation seems imperfect without this tribute also: one jewel is wanting to the crown. It is good to be praised by those whom all men should praise; it is better to be reviled by those whom all men should scorn.

Various chances and causes must have combined to produce a state of faith or feeling which would turn all art and literature 'into the line of children.' One among others may be this: where the heaven of invention holds many stars at once, there is no fear that the highest and largest will either efface or draw aside into its orbit all lesser lights. Each of these takes its own way and sheds its proper lustre. But where one alone is dominant in heaven, it is encircled by a pale procession of satellite moons, filled with shallow and stolen radiance. Thus, with English versifiers now, the idyllic form is alone in fashion. The one great and prosperous poet of the time has given out the tune, and the hoarser choir takes it up. His highest lyrical work remains unimitated, being in the main inimitable. But the trick of tone which suits an idyl is easier to assume; and the note has been struck so often that the shrillest songsters can affect to catch it up. We have idyls good and bad, ugly and pretty; idyls of the farm and the mill; idyls of the dining-room and the deanery; idyls of the gutter and the gibbet.[49] If the Muse of the minute will not feast with 'gig-men' and their wives, she must mourn with costermongers and their trulls.[50] I fear the most ancient Muses are guests at neither house of mourning nor house of feasting.

For myself, I begrudge no man his taste or his success; I can enjoy and applaud all good work, and would always, when possible, have the workman paid in full. There is much excellent and some admirable verse among the poems of the day: to none has it given more pleasure than to me, and from none, had I been a man of letters to whom the ways were open, would it have won heartier applause. I have never been able to see what should attract men to the profession of criticism but the noble pleasure of praising. But I have no right to claim a place in the silver flock of idyllic swans. I have never worked for praise or pay, but simply by impulse, and to please myself; I must therefore, it is to be feared, remain where I am, shut out from the communion of these. At all events, I shall not be hounded into emulation of other men's work by the baying of unleashed beagles. There are those with whom I do not wish to share the praise of their praisers. I am content to abide a far different judgment: –

> 'I write as others wrote
> On Sunium's height.'[51]

I need not be over-careful to justify my ways in other men's eyes; it is enough for me that they also work after their kind, and earn the suffrage, as they labour after the law, of their own people. The idyllic form is best for domestic and pastoral poetry. It is naturally on a lower level than that of tragic or lyric verse. Its gentle and maidenly lips are somewhat narrow for the stream and somewhat cold for the fire of song. It is very fit for the sole diet of girls; not very fit for the sole sustenance of men.

When England has again such a school of poetry, so headed and so followed, as she has had at least twice before, or as France has now; when all higher forms of the various art are included within the larger limits of a stronger race; then, if such a day should ever rise or return upon us, it will be once more remembered that the office of adult art is neither puerile nor feminine, but virile; that its purity is not that of the cloister or the harem; that all things are good in its sight, out of which good work may be produced. Then the press will be as impotent as the pulpit to dictate the laws and remove the landmarks of art; and those will be laughed at who demand from one thing the qualities of another – who seek for sermons in sonnets and morality in music. Then all accepted work will be noble and chaste in the wider masculine sense, not truncated and curtailed, but out-spoken and full-grown; art will be pure by instinct and fruitful by nature, no clipped and forced growth of unhealthy heat and unnatural air; all baseness and all triviality will fall off from it, and be forgotten; and no one will then need to assert, in defence of work done for the work's sake, the simple laws of his art which no one will then be permitted to impugn.

## WALTER PATER, *STUDIES IN THE HISTORY OF THE RENAISSANCE* (1873)

With the exception of a short period during in the early 1870s, the life of Walter Pater (1839–94) was remarkably quiet. A scholarship from King's School, Canterbury took him to Oxford where he graduated in 1862 with second-class honours. For the next two years he earned a living by coaching private pupils (who included Gerard Manley Hopkins), and in 1864 he was elected on probation to a classical fellowship at Brasenose College, where he took up residence as its first non-clerical fellow. Given a permanent post in 1865, Pater remained at Brasenose for his whole career. This was also the year of Pater's first travels in Italy. In 1866 he produced his first published essay, 'Coleridge's Writings', for the *Westminster Review*; it was followed by further pieces for the *Fortnightly Review*. His first main work, *Studies in the History of the Renaissance*, was published in 1873. Over the next three or four years it became the focus of considerable hostility towards Pater; principally reviewers objected to its amoral hedonism. Moreover, Pater was the subject of a cruel satire in W. H. Mallock's *The New Republic* which was published in *Belgravia* in 1876–7 and in book form in 1877. He appeared there as 'Mr Rose' – an effete, impotent, sensualist with a penchant for erotic literature and beautiful young men. In the second edition of *The Renaissance* the 'Conclusion' was removed, partly in response to the public ridicule, but mainly because of pressure brought to bear on Pater within Oxford by figures such as Benjamin Jowett. In particular, the discovery of his 'relationship' with William Money Hardinge, a Balliol undergraduate, threatened Pater with a sexual scandal; Pater's act of self-censorship seems to have been designed to protect both his reputation and that of his Oxford college. In 1883 Pater began work on his novel, *Marius the Epicurean*. Later that year he resigned his tutorship to work full-time at his writing, but he remained a college fellow. He also gave up his Oxford house, living at Brasenose during term time and in London at the home of his two sisters during the vacations. *Marius the Epicurean* was published in 1885 and was followed in 1887 by *Imaginary Portraits*, a series of studies of mythico-historical figures from classical Greece to eighteenth-century Germany. In 1888 a second novel, *Gaston de Latour*, began serialisation in *Macmillan's Magazine*, only to be abandoned by Pater after a few months. This year also saw the publication of a third edition of *The Renaissance* with the 'Conclusion' restored. In 1889 Pater published *Appreciations*, a collection of critical essays which had appeared previously in the periodical press. His last main work, *Plato and Platonism*, a version of lectures given at Oxford over a number of years, appeared in 1893. The following year Pater died of a heart attack. The unfinished *Gaston de Latour* was published posthumously in 1896 by his literary executor Charles Shadwell; other posthumous works included: *Greek Studies* (1895), *Miscellaneous Essays* (1895) and *Essays from 'The Guardian'* (1896).

## *From* Walter Pater, *Studies in the History of the Renaissance* (London: Macmillan and Co., 1873)[1]

### *Preface*

Many attempts have been made by writers on art and poetry to define beauty in the abstract, to express it in the most general terms, to find a universal formula for it.[2] The value of such attempts has most often been in the suggestive and penetrating things said by the way. Such discussions help us very little to enjoy what has been well done in art or poetry, to discriminate between what is more and what is less excellent in them, or to use words like beauty, excellence, art, poetry, with more meaning than they would otherwise have. Beauty, like all other qualities presented to human experience, is relative; and the definition of it becomes unmeaning and useless in proportion to its abstractness. To define beauty not in the most abstract, but in the most concrete terms possible, not to find a universal formula for it, but the formula which expresses most adequately this or that special manifestation of it, is the aim of the true student of aesthetics.

'To see the object as in itself it really is,'[3] has been justly said to be the aim of all true criticism whatever; and in aesthetic criticism the first step towards seeing one's object as it really is, is to know one's own impression as it really is, to discriminate it, to realise it distinctly. The objects with which aesthetic criticism deals, music, poetry, artistic and accomplished forms of human life, are indeed receptacles of so many powers or forces; they possess, like natural elements, so many virtues or qualities. What is this song or picture, this engaging personality presented in life or in a book, to *me*? What effect does it really produce on me? Does it give me pleasure? and if so, what sort or degree of pleasure? How is my nature modified by its presence and under its influence? The answers to these questions are the original facts with which the aesthetic critic has to do; and, as in the study of light, of morals, of number, one must realise such primary data for oneself or not at all. And he who experiences these impressions strongly, and drives directly at the analysis and discrimination of them, need not trouble himself with the abstract question what beauty is in itself, or its exact relation to truth or experience, – metaphysical questions, as unprofitable as metaphysical questions elsewhere. He may pass them all by as being, answerable or not, of no interest to him.

The aesthetic critic, then, regards all the objects with which he has to do, all works of art and the fairer forms of nature and human life, as powers or forces, producing pleasurable sensations, each of a more or less peculiar and unique kind. This influence he feels and wishes to explain, analysing it, and reducing it to its elements. To him, the picture, the landscape, the engaging personality in life or in a book, La Gioconda, the hills of Carrara, Pico of Mirandula,[4] are valuable for their virtues, as we say in speaking of a herb, a wine, a gem; for the property each has of affecting one with a special, unique impression of pleasure. Education grows in proportion as one's susceptibility to these impressions increases in depth and variety. And the function of the aesthetic critic is to distinguish, analyse, and separate from its adjuncts, the virtue by which a picture, a landscape, a fair personality in life or in a book, produces this special impression of beauty or pleasure, to indicate what the source of that impression is, and under what conditions it is experienced. His end is reached when he has disengaged that virtue, and noted it, as a chemist notes some natural element, for himself and others; and the rule for those who would reach this end is stated with great exactness in the words of a recent critic of Sainte-Beuve: 'De se borner à connaître de près les belles choses, et à s'en nourrir en exquis amateurs, en humanistes accomplis.'[5]

What is important, then, is not that the critic should possess a correct abstract definition of beauty for the intellect, but a certain kind of temperament, the power of being deeply moved by the presence of beautiful objects. He will remember always beauty exists in many forms. To him all periods, types, schools of taste, are in themselves equal. In all ages there have been some excellent workmen and some excellent work done. The question he asks is always, In whom did the stir, the genius, the sentiment of the period find itself? who was the receptacle of its refinement, its elevation, its taste? 'The ages are all equal,' says William Blake, 'but genius is always above its age.'[6]

Often it will require great nicety to disengage this virtue from the commoner elements with which it may be found in combination. Few artists, not Goethe[7] or Byron even, work quite cleanly, casting off all debris, and leaving us only what the heat of their imagination has wholly fused and transformed. Take for instance the writings of Wordsworth. The heat of his genius, entering into the substance of his work, has crystallised a part, but only a part, of it; and in that great mass of verse there is much which might well be forgotten. But scattered up and down it, sometimes fusing and transforming entire compositions, like the Stanzas on 'Resolution and Independence' and the Ode on the 'Recollections of Childhood,'[8] sometimes, as if at random, turning a fine crystal here and there, in a matter it does not wholly search through and transform, we trace the action of his unique incommunicable faculty, that strange mystical sense of a life in natural things, and of man's life as a part of nature, drawing strength and colour and character from local influences, from the hills and streams and natural sights and sounds. Well! that is the *virtue*, the active principle in Wordsworth's poetry; and then the function of the critic of Wordsworth is to trace that active principle, to disengage it, to mark the degree in which it penetrates his verse.

The subjects of the following studies are taken from the history of the Renaissance, and touch what I think the chief points in that complex, many-sided movement. I have explained in the first of them what I understand by the word, giving it a much wider scope than was intended by those who originally used it to denote only that revival of classical antiquity in the fifteenth century which was but one of many results of a general stimulus and enlightening of the human mind, and of which the great aim and achievements of what, as Christian art,[9] is often falsely opposed to the Renaissance, were another result. This outbreak of the human spirit may be traced far into the middle age itself, with its qualities already clearly pronounced, the care for physical beauty, the worship of the body, the breaking down of those limits which the religious system of the middle age imposed on the heart and the imagination.[10] I have taken as an example of this movement, this earlier Renaissance within the middle age itself, and as an expression of its qualities, a little composition in early French; not because it is the best possible expression of them, but because it helps the unity of my series, inasmuch as the Renaissance ends also in France, in French poetry, in a phase of which the writings of Joachim du Bellay[11] are in many ways the most perfect illustration; the Renaissance thus putting forth in France an aftermath, a wonderful later growth, the products of which have to the full the subtle and delicate sweetness which belong to a refined and comely decadence; just as its earliest phases have the freshness which belongs to all periods of growth in art, the charm of *ascêsis*,[12] of the austere and serious girding of the loins in youth.

But it is in Italy, in the fifteenth century, that the interest of the Renaissance mainly lies, in that solemn fifteenth century which can hardly be studied too much, not merely for its positive results in the things of the intellect and the imagination, its concrete works of art, its special and prominent personalities, with their profound aesthetic charm, but for its general spirit and character, for the ethical qualities of which it is a consummate type.

The various forms of intellectual activity which together make up the culture of an age, move for the most part from different starting points and by unconnected roads. As products of the same generation they partake indeed of a common character and unconsciously illustrate each other; but of the producers themselves, each group is solitary, gaining what advantage or disadvantage there may be in intellectual isolation. Art and poetry, philosophy and the religious life, and that other life of refined pleasure and action in the open places of the world, are each of them confined to its own circle of ideas, and those who prosecute either of them are generally little curious of the thoughts of others. There come however from time to time eras of more favourable conditions, in which the thoughts of men draw nearer together than is their wont, and the many interests of the intellectual world combine in one complete type of general culture. The fifteenth century in Italy is one of these happier eras; and what is sometimes said of the age of Pericles is true of that of Lorenzo[13] – it is an age productive in personalities, many-sided, centralised, complete. Here, artists and philosophers and those whom the action of the world has elevated and made keen, do not live in isolation, but breathe a common air and catch light and heat from each other's thoughts. There is a spirit of general elevation and enlightenment in which all alike communicate. It is the unity of this spirit which gives unity to all the various products of the Renaissance, and it is to this intimate alliance with mind, this participation in the best thoughts which that age produced, that the art of Italy in the fifteenth century owes much of its grave dignity and influence.

I have added an essay on Winckelmann,[14] as not incongruous with the studies which precede it, because Winckelmann, coming in the eighteenth century, really belongs in spirit to an earlier age. By his enthusiasm for the things of the intellect and the imagination for their own sake, by his Hellenism, his life-long struggle to attain to the Greek spirit, he is in sympathy with the humanists of an earlier century. He is the last fruit of the Renaissance, and explains in a striking way its motive and tendencies.

### Conclusion

Δέγει που Ἡράκλειτος ὅτι πάντα χωρεῖ καὶ οὐδὲν μένει.[15]

To regard all things and principles of things as inconstant modes or fashions has more and more become the tendency of modern thought. Let us begin with that which is without – our physical life. Fix upon it in one of its more exquisite intervals, the moment, for instance, of delicious recoil from the flood of water in summer heat. What is the whole physical life in that moment but a combination of natural elements to which science gives their names? But these elements, phosphorus and lime and delicate fibres, are present not in the human body alone: we detect them in places most remote from it. Our physical life is a perpetual motion of them – the passage of the blood, the wasting and repairing of the lenses of the eye, the modification of the tissues of the brain by every ray of light and sound – processes which science reduces to simpler and more elementary forces. Like the elements of which we are composed, the action of these forces extends beyond us; it rusts iron and ripens corn. Far out on every side of us these elements are broadcast, driven by many forces; and birth and gesture and death and the springing of violets from the grave[16] are but a few out of ten thousand resulting combinations. That clear perpetual outline of face and limb is but an image of ours under which we group them – a design in a web, the actual threads of which pass out beyond it. This at least of flame-like our life has, that it is but the concurrence, renewed from moment to moment, of forces parting sooner or later on their ways.

Or if we begin with the inward world of thought and feeling, the whirlpool is still more rapid, the flame more eager and devouring. There it is no longer the gradual darkening of the eye and fading of colour from the wall, – the move-ment of the shore side, where the water flows down indeed, though in apparent rest, – but the race of the midstream, a drift of momentary acts of sight and passion and thought. At first sight experience seems to bury us under a flood of external objects, pressing upon us with a sharp importunate reality, calling us out of ourselves in a thousand forms of action. But when reflection begins to act upon those objects they are dissipated under its influence; the cohesive force is suspended like a trick of magic; each object is loosed into a group of impres-sions, – colour, odour, texture, – in the mind of the observer. And if we continue to dwell on this world, not of objects in the solidity with which language invests them, but of impressions unstable, flickering, inconsistent, which burn and are extinguished with our consciousness of them, it contracts still further; the whole scope of observation is dwarfed to the narrow chamber of the individual mind. Experience, already reduced to a swarm of impressions, is ringed round for each one of us by that thick wall of personality through which no real voice has ever pierced on its way to us, or from us to that which we can only conjecture to be without. Every one of those impressions is the impression of the individual in his isolation, each mind keeping as a solitary prisoner its own dream of a world.

Analysis goes a step further still, and tells us that those impressions of the individual to which, for each one of us, experience dwindles down, are in perpetual flight; that each of them is limited by time, and that as time is infinitely divisible, each of them is infinitely divisible also; all that is actual in it being a single moment, gone while we try to apprehend it, of which it may ever be more truly said that it has ceased to be than that it is. To such a tremulous wisp constantly reforming itself on the stream, to a single sharp impression, with a sense in it, a relic more or less fleeting, of such moments gone by, what is *real* in our life fines itself down. It is with the movement, the passage and dissolution of impressions, images, sensations, that analysis leaves off, – that continual vanishing away, that strange perpetual weaving and unweaving of ourselves.

*Philosophiren*, says Novalis, *ist dephlegmatisiren, vivificiren.*[17] The service of philos-ophy, and of religion and culture as well, to the human spirit, is to startle it into a sharp and eager observation. Every moment some form grows perfect in hand or face; some tone on the hills or sea is choicer than the rest; some mood of passion or insight or intellectual excitement is irresistibly real and attractive for us, – for that moment only. Not the fruit of experience, but experience itself is the end. A counted number of pulses only is given to us of a variegated, dramatic life. How may we see in them all that is to be seen in them by the finest senses? How can we pass most swiftly from point to point, and be present always at the focus where the greatest number of vital forces unite in their purest energy?

To burn always with this hard gem-like flame, to maintain this ecstasy, is success in life. Failure is to form habits; for habit is relative to a stereotyped world; meantime it is only the roughness of the eye that makes any two persons, things, situations, seem alike. While all melts under our feet, we may well catch at any exquisite passion, or any contribution to knowledge that seems, by a lifted horizon, to set the spirit free for a moment, or any stirring of the senses, strange dyes, strange flowers, and curious odours, or work of the artist's hands, or the face of one's friend. Not to discriminate every moment some passionate attitude in those about us, and in the brilliance of their gifts some tragic dividing of forces on their ways is, on this short day of frost and sun, to sleep before evening. With this sense of the splendour of our experience and of its awful brevity, gathering all we are into one desperate effort to see and touch, we shall hardly have time to make theories about the things we see and touch. What we have to do is to be for ever curiously testing new opinions and courting new impressions, never acquiescing in a facile orthodoxy of Comte or of Hegel,[18] or of our own. Theories, religious or philosophical ideas, as points of view, instruments of criticism, may help us to gather up what might otherwise pass unregarded by us. *La philosophie, c'est la microscope de la pensée.*[19] The theory, or idea, or system, which requires of us the sacrifice of any part of this experience, in consideration of some interest into which we cannot enter, or some abstract morality we have not identified with ourselves, or what is only conventional, has no real claim upon us.

One of the most beautiful places in the writings of Rousseau is that in the sixth book of the 'Confessions,'[20] where he describes the awakening in him of the literary sense. An indefinable taint of death had always clung about him, and now in early manhood he believed himself stricken by mortal disease. He asked himself how he might make as much as possible of the interval that remained; and he was not biassed by anything in his previous life when he decided that it must be by intellectual excitement, which he found in the clear, fresh writings of Voltaire.[21] Well, we are all *condamnés*, as Victor Hugo says: *les hommes sont tous condamnés à mort avec des sursis indéfinis:*[22] we have an interval, and then our place knows us no more. Some spend this interval in listlessness, some in high passions, the wisest in art and song. For our one chance is in expanding that interval, in getting as many pulsations as possible into the given time. High passions give one this quickened sense of life, ecstasy and sorrow of love, political or religious enthusiasm, or the 'enthusiasm of humanity.' Only, be sure it is passion, that it does yield you this fruit of a quickened, multiplied consciousness. Of this wisdom, the poetic passion, the desire of beauty, the love of art for art's sake has most; for art comes to you professing frankly to give nothing but the highest quality to your moments as they pass, and simply for those moments' sake.

## OSCAR WILDE, 'THE DECAY OF LYING: A DIALOGUE'
### (1889)

Oscar Wilde (1854–1900) is one of the best-known figures in literary history. In practice, though, Wilde's moment of literary and social celebrity was relatively short-lived, lasting from the first production of *Lady Windermere's Fan* in 1892 until his imprisonment in 1895 for gross indecency. The years before this period were those of a hard-working writer struggling to make his mark, and the years after were spent in a self-imposed exile and poverty on the Continent. Wilde was educated at Trinity College, Dublin; in 1874 he won a scholarship to Magdalen College, Oxford where his academic success continued with a first-class degree and the Newdigate prize for poetry. Nevertheless Wilde failed to gain a college fellowship, and turned to lecturing to fund a writing career. His first main publication, *Poems* (1881), was not particularly successful. At this time Wilde began to fashion the first (and most enduring) of his 'personalities' – that of the 'aesthete' – which he subsequently exploited during a lecture tour of America and Canada in 1882 made in order to publicise W. S. Gilbert's and Arthur Sullivan's comic operetta, *Patience*. In 1883 Wilde's first play, *Vera; or, the Nihilists*, was produced unsuccessfully in New York. In 1884 he married Constance Lloyd, moved to Chelsea, and settled into more regular journalistic work in order to support his growing family – two sons were born in 1885 and 1886. In 1887 Wilde took over the editorship of a lady's magazine which he transformed and renamed *Woman's World*. Despite these efforts, the magazine failed and Wilde resigned his editorship in 1889. In the meantime he had begun to develop his skills in fiction-writing, publishing his first collection of stories, *The Happy Prince and Other Tales*, in 1888 and his enigmatic tale of the origins of Shakespeare's sonnets, 'The Portrait of Mr W. H.', in *Blackwood's Magazine* in 1889. 1890 saw the first version of Wilde's only novel, *The Picture of Dorian Gray*, published in the American *Lippincott's Monthly Magazine*; attempts to find a publisher in Britain were unsuccessful until finally Ward, Lock and Co. (the British distributor of *Lippincott's*) agreed to bring out a substantially revised version in 1891. That year also saw an American production of his second play, *The Duchess of Padua* (a verse-drama based on Renaissance models), and the publication of two further volumes of stories, *Lord Arthur Savile's Crime and Other Stories* and *A House of Pomegranates*, *Intentions* (a collection of four critical essays) and, in the *Fortnightly Review*, his essay 'The Soul of Man Under Socialism'.

But 1891 was to prove a memorable year in other ways too, for it marked his first meeting with Lord Alfred Douglas who soon became Wilde's lover. In the period from 1892 to 1895 success followed upon success: after *Lady Windermere's Fan*, there were West End productions of *A Woman of No Importance*, *An Ideal Husband* and *The Importance of Being Earnest* – indeed the last two plays ran simultaneously. In 1894 *The Sphinx* was published. The only 'failure' of this period was Wilde's symbolist drama, *Salomé*, which was refused a licence by the Lord Chamberlain's Office. In 1895 this charmed life came to an abrupt end when Wilde failed in an action for criminal libel which he brought against Douglas's father, the Marquess of Queensberry. Wilde was himself arrested, and two trials later was convicted of 'acts of gross indecency with other male persons'. He was sentenced to two years' imprisonment with hard labour; shortly afterwards he was also declared bankrupt. From prison Wilde wrote a long letter of recrimination to Douglas, later entitled *De Profundis*. On his release he immediately went to France. He wrote two further letters about prison conditions which were published in the *Daily Chronicle* in 1897 and 1898; his poem, *The Ballad of Reading Gaol*, was also published in 1898. He died in Paris in 1900, alone and in poverty.

### From Oscar Wilde, 'The Decay of Lying: A Dialogue', *The Nineteenth Century*, CXLIII (January 1889), pp. 35–56[1]

*The Decay Of Lying: A Dialogue*

Scene. – The Library of a Country House in England.
Persons. – Cyril and Vivian.[2]

*Cyril (coming in through the open window from the terrace).* My dear Vivian, don't coop yourself up all day in the library. It is a perfectly lovely afternoon. Let us go and lie on the grass and smoke cigarettes and enjoy nature.

*Vivian.* Enjoy nature! I am glad to say that I have entirely lost that faculty. People tell us that art makes us love nature more than we loved her before; that it reveals her secrets to us; and that after a careful study of Corot and Constable[3] we see things in her that had escaped us. My own experience is that the more we study art, the less we care for nature. What art really reveals to us is nature's lack of design, her curious crudities, her extraordinary monotony, her absolutely unfinished condition. When I look at a landscape I cannot help seeing all its defects. It is fortunate for us, however, that nature is so imperfect, as otherwise we should have had no art at all. Art is our spirited protest, our gallant attempt to teach Nature her proper place. As for the infinite variety of Nature, that is a pure myth. It is not to be found in Nature herself, but in the imagination, or fancy, or cultivated blindness, of the man who looks at her.

*C.* Well, you need not look at the landscape. You can lie on the grass and smoke and talk.

*V.* But nature is so uncomfortable. Grass is hard and lumpy and damp, and full of horrid little black insects. Why, even Maple[4] can make you a more comfortable seat than nature can. Nature pales before the Tottenham Court Road. I don't complain. If nature had been comfortable, mankind would never have invented architecture, and I prefer houses to the open air. In a house we all feel of the proper proportions. Everything is subordinated to us, fashioned for our use and our pleasure. Egotism itself, which is so necessary to a proper sense of human dignity, is absolutely the result of indoor life. Out of doors one becomes abstract and impersonal. One's individuality absolutely leaves one. And then nature is so indifferent, so unappreciative. Whenever I am walking in the park here, I always feel that I am no more to nature than the cattle that browse on the slope, or the burdock that blooms in the ditch. Nothing is clearer than that Nature hates Mind. Thinking is the most unhealthy thing in the world, and people die of it just as of any other disease. Fortunately, in England at least, it is not catching. Our splendid physique as a people is entirely due to our national stupidity. I only hope that we shall be able to keep this great historic bulwark of our happiness for many years to come; but I am afraid that we are beginning to be over-educated; at least everybody who is incapable of learning has taken to teaching – that is really what our enthusiasm for education has come to. In the meantime you had better go back to your wearisome uncomfortable Nature, and leave me to correct my proofs.

*C.* Writing an article! That is not very consistent after what you have just said.

*V.* Who wants to be consistent? The dullard and the doctrinaire, the tedious people who carry out their principles to the bitter end of action, to the *reductio ad absurdum* of practice? Not I. Like Emerson, I write over the door of my library the word 'Whim.'[5] Besides, my article is really a most salutary and valuable warning. If it is attended to, there may be a new Renaissance of Art.[6]

*C.* What is the subject?

*V.* I intend to call it 'The Decay of Lying: A Protest.'

*C.* Lying! I should have thought our politicians kept up that habit.

*V.* I assure you they do not. They never rise beyond the level of misrepresentation, and actually condescend to prove, to discuss, to argue. How different from the temper of the true liar, with his frank, fearless statements, his superb irresponsibility, his healthy, natural disdain of proof of any kind! After all, what is a fine lie? Simply that which is its own evidence. If a man is sufficiently unimaginative to produce evidence in support of a lie, he might just as well speak the truth at once. No, the politicians won't do, and besides, what I am pleading for is lying in art. Shall I read you what I have written? It might do you a great deal of good.

*C.* Certainly, if you give me a cigarette. Thanks. By the way, what magazine do you intend it for?

*V.* For the *Retrospective Review*.[7] I think I told you that we had revived it.

*C.* Whom do you mean by 'we'?

*V.* Oh, the Tired Hedonists of course. It is a club to which I belong. We are supposed to wear faded roses in our button-holes when we meet, and to have a sort of cult for Domitian.[8] I am afraid you are not eligible. You are too fond of simple pleasures.

*C.* I should be black-balled[9] on the ground of animal spirits, I suppose?

*V.* Probably. Besides, you are a little too old. We don't admit anyone who is of the usual age.

*C.* Well, I should fancy you are all a good deal bored with each other.

*V.* We are. That is one of the objects of the club. Now, if you promise not to interrupt too often, I will read you my article.

*C. (flinging himself down on the sofa).* All right.

*V. (reading in a very clear, musical voice).* 'THE DECAY OF LYING: A PROTEST. – One of the chief causes of the curiously commonplace character of most of the literature of our age is undoubtedly the decay of lying as an art, a science, and a social pleasure. The ancient historians gave us delightful fiction in the form of fact; the modern novelist presents us with dull facts under the guise of fiction. The blue-book[10] is rapidly becoming his ideal both for method and manner. He has his tedious *"document humain,"* his miserable little *"coin de la création,"*[11] into which he peers with his microscope. He is to be found at the Librairie Nationale, or at the British Museum, shamelessly reading up his subject. He has not even the courage of other people's ideas,[12] but insists on going directly to life for everything, and ultimately, between encyclopaedias and personal experience, he comes to the ground, having drawn his types from the family circle or from the weekly washer-woman, and having acquired an amount of useful information from which he never, even in his most thoughtful moments, can thoroughly free himself.

'The loss that results to literature in general from this false ideal of our time can hardly be overestimated. People have a careless way of talking about a "born liar," just as they talk about a "born poet." But in both cases they are wrong. Lying and poetry are arts – arts, as Plato saw, not unconnected with each other[13] – and they require the most careful study, the most disinterested devotion. Indeed, they have their technique, just as the more material arts of painting and sculpture have, their subtle secrets of form and colour, their craft-mysteries, their deliberate artistic methods. As one knows the poet by his fine music, so one can recognise the liar by his rich rhythmic utterance, and in neither case will the causal inspiration of the moment suffice. Here, as elsewhere, practice must precede perfection. But in modern days while the fashion of writing poetry has become far too common, and should, if possible, be discouraged, the fashion of lying has almost fallen into disrepute. Many a young man starts in life with a natural gift for exaggeration which, if nurtured in congenial and sympathetic surroundings, or by the imitation of the best models, might grow into something really great and wonderful. But, as a rule, he comes to nothing. He either falls into careless habits of accuracy – '

393

*C.* My dear Vivian!

*V.* Please don't interrupt in the middle of a sentence. 'He either falls into careless habits of accuracy, or takes to frequenting the society of the aged and the well-informed. Both things are equally fatal to his imagination, as indeed they would be fatal to the imagination of anybody, and in a short time he develops a morbid and unhealthy faculty of truth-telling, begins to verify all statements made in his presence, has no hesitation in contradicting people who are younger than himself, and often ends by writing novels which are so like life that no one can possibly believe in them. This is no isolated instance that we are giving. It is simply one example out of many; and if something cannot be done to check, or at least to modify, our monstrous worship of facts, art will become sterile, and beauty will pass away from the land.

'Even Mr Robert Louis Stevenson, that delightful master of delicate and fanciful prose, is tainted with this modern vice, for we positively know no other name for it. There is such a thing as robbing a story of its reality by trying to make it too true, and *The Black Arrow* is so inartistic that it does not contain a single anachronism to boast of, while the transformation of Dr Jekyll reads dangerously like an experiment out of the *Lancet*.[14] As for Mr Rider Haggard,[15] who really has, or had once, the makings of a perfectly magnificent liar, he is now so afraid of being suspected of genius that when he does tell us anything marvellous, he feels bound to invent a personal reminiscence, and to put it into a footnote as a kind of cowardly corroboration. Nor are our other novelists much better. Mr Henry James writes fiction as if it was a painful duty, and wastes upon mean motives and imperceptible "points of view" his neat literary style, his felicitous phrases, his swift and caustic satire.[16] Mrs Oliphant[17] prattles pleasantly about curates, lawn-tennis parties, domesticity, and other wearisome things. Mr Marion Crawford has immolated himself upon the alter of local colour. He is like the lady in the French comedy who keeps talking about "le beau ciel d'Italie."[18] Besides, he has fallen into a bad habit of uttering moral platitudes. At times he is almost edifying. *Robert Elsmere* is of course a masterpiece – a masterpiece of the "genre ennuyeux,"[19] the one form of literature that the English people seem to thoroughly enjoy. Indeed it is only in England that such a novel could be possible. As for that great and daily increasing school of novelists for whom the sun always rises in the East-End,[20] the only thing that can be said about them is that they find life crude, and leave it raw.

'In France, though nothing so deliberately tedious as *Robert Elsmere* has been produced, things are not much better. M Guy de Maupassant,[21] with his keen mordant irony and his hard vivid style, strips life of the few poor rags that still cover her, and shows us foul sore and festering wound. He writes lurid little tragedies in which everybody is ridiculous; bitter comedies at which one cannot laugh for very tears. M Zola, true to the lofty principle that he lays down in one of his pronunciamientos on literature, "L'homme de génie n'a jamais de l'esprit," is determined to show that, if he has not got genius, he can at least be dull. And how well he succeeds! He is not without power. Indeed at times, as in

*Germinal*, there is something almost epic in his work.[22] But his work is entirely wrong from beginning to end, and wrong not on the ground of morals, but on the ground of art. From any ethical standpoint his work is just what it should be. He is perfectly truthful, and describes things exactly as they happen. What more can any moralist desire? I have no sympathy at all with the moral indignation of our time against M Zola. It is simply the rage of Caliban on seeing his own face in a glass.[23] But from the standpoint of art, what can be said in favour of the author of *L'Assommoir*, *Nana* and *Pot-Bouille*?[24] Nothing. Mr Ruskin once described the characters in George Eliot's novels as being like the sweepings of a Pentonville omnibus,[25] but M Zola's characters are much worse. They have their dreary vices, and their drearier virtues. The record of their lives is absolutely without interest. Who cares what happens to them? In literature we require distinction, charm, beauty, and imaginative power. We don't want to be harrowed and disgusted with an account of the doings of the lower orders. M Daudet is better. He has *esprit*, a light touch, and an amusing style. But he has lately committed literary suicide. Nobody can possibly care for Delobelle with his "Il faut lutter pour l'art," or for Valmajour with his eternal refrain about the nightingale, or for the poet in *Jack* with his "mots cruels," now that we have learned from *Vingt Ans de ma Vie littéraire* that these characters were taken directly from life.[26] To me they seem to have suddenly lost all their vitality, all the few qualities they ever possessed. The only real people are the people who never existed, and if a novelist is base enough to go to life for his personages he should at least pretend that they are creations and not boast of them as copies. As for M Paul Bourget, the master of the *romain psychologique*,[27] he commits the error of imagining that the men and woman of modern life are capable of being infinitely analysed for an innumerable series of chapters. In point of fact what is interesting about people in good society – and M Bourget never moves out of the Faubourg,[28] – is the mask that each one of them wears, not the reality that lies behind the mask. It is a humiliating confession, but we are all of us made out of the same stuff. In Falstaff there is something of Hamlet, in Hamlet there is not a little of Falstaff.[29] The fat knight has his moods of melancholy, and the young prince his moments of coarse humour. Where we differ from each other is purely in accidentals: in dress, in manner, tone of voice, personal appearance, tricks of habit and the like. The more one analyses people, the more all reasons for analysis disappear. Sooner or later one comes to that dreadful universal thing called human nature. Indeed, as any one who has ever worked among the poor knows only too well, the brotherhood of man is no mere poet's dream, it is a terrible reality; and if a writer insists upon analysing the upper classes he might just as well write of match-girls and costermongers at once.' However, my dear Cyril, I will not detain you any further on this point. I quite admit that modern novels have many good points. All I say is that, as a class, they are quite unreadable.

*C.* That is certainly a very grave qualification, but I must say that I think you are rather unfair in some of your strictures. I like *Robert Elsmere* for instance. Not that I can look upon it as a serious work. As a statement of the problems that confront the earnest Christian it is ridiculous and antiquated. It is simply Arnold's *Literature and Dogma* with the literature left out. It is as much behind the age as Paley's *Evidences*, or Colenso's method of Biblical exegesis.[30] Nor could anything be less impressive than the unfortunate hero gravely heralding a dawn that rose long ago, and so completely missing its true significance that he proposes to carry on the business of the old firm under the new name. On the other hand, it contains several clever caricatures, and a heap of delightful quotations, and Green's philosophy[31] very pleasantly sugars the somewhat bitter pill of the author's fiction. I also cannot help expressing my surprise that you have said nothing about the two novelists whom you are always reading, Balzac and George Meredith.[32] Surely they are realists, both of them?

*V.* Ah! Meredith! Who can define him? His style is chaos illuminated by flashes of lightening. As a writer he has mastered everything, except language: as a novelist he can do everything, except tell a story: as an artist he is everything except articulate. Somebody in Shakespeare – Touchstone, I think[33] – talks about a man who is always breaking his shins over his own wit, and it seems to me that this might serve as the basis of a criticism of Meredith's method. But whatever he is, he is not a realist. Or rather I would say that he is a child of realism who is not on speaking terms with his father. By deliberate choice he has made himself a romanticist. He has refused to bow the knee to Baal,[34] and after all, even if the man's fine spirit did not revolt against the noisy assertions of realism, his style would be quite sufficient of itself to keep life at a respectful distance. By its means he has planted round his garden a hedge full of thorns, and with some wonderful roses. As for Balzac, he was a most remarkable combination of the artistic temperament with the scientific spirit. The latter he bequeathed to his disciples: the former was entirely his own. The difference between such a book as M Zola's *L'Assommoir* and Balzac's *Illusions Perdues* is the difference between unimaginative realism and imaginative reality. 'All Balzac's characters,' said Baudelaire, 'are gifted with the same ardour of life that animated himself. All his fictions are as deeply coloured as dreams. Each mind is a weapon loaded to the muzzle with will. The very scullions have genius.'[35] A steady course of Balzac reduces our living friends to shadows, and our acquaintances to the shadows of shades. His characters have a kind of fervent fiery-coloured existence. They dominate us and defy scepticism. One of the greatest tragedies of my life is the death of Lucien Rubempré.[36] It is a grief from which I have never been able to completely rid myself. But Balzac is no more a realist that Holbein[37] was. He created life, he did not copy it. I admit, however, that he set far too high a value on modernity of form, and that, consequently, there is no book of his that, as an artistic masterpiece, can rank with *Salammbô*, or *Esmond*, or *The Cloister and the Hearth*, or the *Vicomte de Bragelonne*.[38]

*C.* Do you object to modernity of form then?

*V.* Yes. It is a huge price to pay for a very poor result. Pure modernity of form is always somewhat vulgarising. It cannot help being so. The public imagine that, because they are interested in their immediate surroundings, art should be interested in them also, and should take them as her subject-matter. But the mere fact that they are interested in these things makes them unsuitable subjects for art. The only beautiful things, as somebody once said, are the things that do not concern us. As long as a thing is useful or necessary to us, or affects us in any way, either for pain or for pleasure, or appeals strongly to our sympathies, or is a vital part of the environment in which we live, it is outside the proper sphere of art. To art's subject-matter we should be more or less indifferent. We should, at any rate, have no preferences, no prejudices, no partisan feeling of any kind. It is exactly because Hecuba is nothing to us that her sorrows are such an admirable motive for tragedy.[39] I do not know anything in the whole history of literature sadder than the artistic career of Charles Reade. He wrote one beautiful book, *The Cloister and the Hearth*, a book as much above *Romola* as *Romola* is above *Daniel Deronda*,[40] and wasted the rest of his life in a foolish attempt to be modern, to draw public attention to the state of our convict prisons and the management of our private lunatic asylums.[41] Charles Dickens was depressing enough in all conscience when he tried to arouse our sympathy for the victims of the poor-law administration;[42] but Charles Reade, an artist, a scholar, a man with a true sense of beauty, raging and roaring over the abuses of modern life like a common pamphleteer or a sensational journalist, is really a sight for the angels to weep over. Believe me, my dear Cyril, modernity of form and modernity of subject-matter are entirely and absolutely wrong. We have mistaken the common livery of the age for the vesture of the Muses, and spend our days in the sordid streets and hideous suburbs of our vile cities when we should be out on the hillside with Apollo.[43] Certainly we are a degraded race, and have sold our birthright for a mess of facts.

*C.* There is something in what you say, and there is no doubt that whatever amusement we may find in reading an absolutely modern novel, we have rarely any artistic pleasure in re-reading it. And this is perhaps the best rough test of what is literature and what is not. If one cannot enjoy reading a book over and over again, there is no good reading it at all. But what do you say about the return to Life and Nature? This is the panacea that is always being recommended to us.

*V. (taking up his proofs).* I will read you what I say on that subject. The passage comes later on in the article, but I may as well read it now: –

'The popular cry of our time is "Let us return to Life and Nature; they will recreate Art for us, and send the red blood coursing through her veins; they will give her feet swiftness and make her hand strong." But, alas! we are mistaken in our amiable and well-meaning efforts. Nature is always behind the age; and as for Life, she is the solvent that breaks up Art, the enemy that lays waste her house.'

*C.* What do you mean by saying that nature is always behind the age?

*V.* Well, perhaps that is rather obscure. What I mean is this. If we take nature to mean natural simple instinct as opposed to self-conscious culture, the work produced under this influence is always old-fashioned, antiquated, and out of date. If, on the other hand, we regard nature as the collection of phenomena external to man, people only discover in her what they bring to her. She has no suggestions of her own. Wordsworth went to the lakes, but he was never a lake poet. He found in stones the sermons he had already hidden there.[44] He went moralising about the district, but his good work was produced when he returned, not to nature but to poetry. Poetry gave him 'Laodamia,' and the fine sonnets, and the great 'Ode to Immortality,' and nature gave him 'Martha Ray' and 'Peter Bell.'[45]

*C.* I think that view might be questioned. I am rather inclined to believe in 'the impulse from a vernal wood,'[46] though of course the artistic value of such an impulse depends entirely on the kind of temperament that receives it. However, proceed with your article.

*V. (reading).* 'Art begins with abstract decoration, with purely imaginative and pleasurable work dealing with what is unreal and non-existent. This is the first stage. Then Life becomes fascinated with this new wonder, and asks to be admitted into the charmed circle. Art takes Life as part of her rough material, recreates it, and refashions it in fresh forms, is absolutely indifferent to fact, invents, imagines, dreams, and keeps between herself and reality the impenetrable barrier of beautiful style, of decorative or ideal treatment. The third stage is when Life gets the upper hand, and drives Art out into the wilderness. This is the decadence, and it is a from this that we are now suffering.

'Take the case of the English drama. At first in the hands of the monks dramatic art was abstract, decorative, and mythological. Then she enlisted life in her service, and using some of life's external forms, she created an entirely new race of beings, whose sorrows were more terrible than any sorrow man has ever felt, whose joys were keener than lover's joys, who had the rage of the Titans[47] and the calm of the gods, who had monstrous and marvellous sins, monstrous and marvellous virtues. To them she gave a language different from that of actual life, a language full of resonant music and sweet rhythm, made stately by solemn cadence, or made delicate by fanciful rhyme, jewelled with wonderful words, and enriched with lofty diction. She clothed her children in strange raiment and gave them masks, and at her bidding the antique world rose from its marble tomb. A new Caesar stalked through the streets of risen Rome, and with purple sail and flute-led oars another Cleopatra passed up the river to Antioch.[48] Old myth and legend and dream took form and substance. History was entirely rewritten, and there was hardly one of the dramatists who did not recognise that *the object of art is not simple truth but complex beauty.* In this they were perfectly right. Art herself is simply a form of exaggeration; and selection, which is the very spirit of art, is nothing more than an intensified mode of over-emphasis.

'But life soon shattered the perfection of the form. Even in Shakespeare we can see the beginning of the end. It shows itself by the gradual breaking up of the blank verse in the later plays, by the predominance given to prose, and by the over-importance assigned to characterisation. The passages in Shakespeare – and there are many – where the language is uncouth, vulgar, exaggerated, fantastic, obscene even, are due entirely to life calling for an echo of its own voice, and rejecting the intervention of beautiful style, through which alone it should be allowed to find expression. Shakespeare is not by any means a flawless artist. He is too fond of going directly to life, and borrowing life's natural utterance. He forgets that when *art surrenders her imaginative medium she surrenders everything.* Goethe says somewhere –

In der Beschränkung zeigt sich erst der Meister,[49]

"It is in working within limits that the master reveals himself," and the limitation, the very condition, of any art is style. However, we will not linger any longer over Shakespeare's realism. The *Tempest* is the best of palinodes.[50] All that we desired to point out was, that the magnificent work of the Elizabethan and Jacobean artists contained within itself the seeds of its own dissolution, and that if it drew some of its strength from using life as rough material, it drew all its weakness from using life as an artistic method. As the inevitable result of this substitution of an imitative for a creative medium, this surrender of an imaginative form, we have the modern English melodrama. The characters in these plays talk on the stage exactly as they would talk off it; they are taken directly from life and reproduce its vulgarity down to the smallest detail; they have the gait, manner, costume, and accent of real people; they would pass unnoticed in a third-class railway carriage. And yet how wearisome the plays are! They do not succeed in producing even that impression of reality at which they aim, and which is their only reason for existing. As a method realism is a complete failure.

'What is true about the drama and the novel is no less true about those arts that we call the decorative arts. The whole history of decorative art in Europe is the record of the struggle between Orientalism, with its frank rejection of imitation, its love of artistic convention, its dislike to the actual representation of any object in nature, and our own imitative spirit. Wherever the former has been paramount, as in Byzantium, Sicily, and Spain, by actual contact, or in the rest of Europe by the influence of the Crusades, we have had beautiful and imaginative work in which the visible things of life are transmuted into artistic conventions, and the things that life has not are invented and fashioned for her. But wherever we have returned to life and nature, our work has always become vulgar, common, and uninteresting. Modern tapestry, with its aerial effects, its elaborate perspective, its broad expanses of waste sky, its faithful and laborious realism, has no beauty whatsoever. The pictorial glass of Germany is absolutely detestable. We are beginning to weave possible carpets in England, but only because we have returned to the method and spirit of the East. Our rugs and carpets of twenty years ago, with their healthy national feeling, their inane worship of nature, their sordid reproductions of visible objects, have become, even to the Philistine,[51] a source of laughter. A cultured Mahomedan[52] once remarked to me, "You Christians are so occupied in misinterpreting the fourth commandment that you have never thought of making an artistic application of the second." He was perfectly right, and the whole truth of the matter is this: *the proper school to learn art in is not Life but Art.*'

And now let me read you a passage which deals with the commonplace character of our literature: –

'It was not always thus. We need not say anything about the poets, for they, with the unfortunate exception of Mr Wordsworth, have always been faithful to their high mission, and are universally recognised as being absolutely unreliable. But in the works of Herodotus, who, in spite of the shallow and ungenerous attempts of modern sciolists to verify his history, may be justly called the "Father of Lies;" in the published speeches of Cicero and the biographies of Suetonius; in Tacitus at his best; in Pliny's *Natural History*; in Hanno's *Periplus*; in all the early chronicles; in the Lives of the Saints; in Froissart and Sir Thomas Mallory; in the travels of Marco Polo; in Olaus Magnus, and Aldrovandus, and Conrad Lycosthenes, with his magnificent *Prodigiorum et Ostentorum Chronicon*; in the autobiography of Benvenuto Cellini; in the memoirs of Casanuova; in Defoe's *History of the Plague*; in Boswell's *Life of Johnson*; in Napoleon's despatches, and in the works of our own Carlyle, whose *French Revolution* is one of the most fascinating historical romances ever written, facts are either kept in their proper subordinate position, or else entirely excluded on the general ground of dulness.[53] Now everything is changed. Facts are not merely finding a footing in history, but they are usurping the domain of Fancy, and have invaded the kingdom of Romance. Their chilling touch is over everything. They are vulgarising mankind. The crude commercialism of America, its materialising spirit, its indifference to the poetical side of things, and its lack of imagination and of high, unattainable ideals, are entirely due to that country having adopted for its national hero, a man, who according to his own confession, was incapable of telling a lie, and it is not too much to say that the story of George Washington and the cherry-tree[54] has done more harm, and in a shorter space of time, than any other moral tale in the whole of literature.'

*C.* My dear boy!

*V.* I assure you it is quite true, and the amusing part of the whole thing is that the story of the cherry-tree is an absolute myth. However, you must not think that I am too despondent about the artistic future of America or of our own country. Listen to this: –

'That some change will take place before this century has drawn to its close, we have no doubt whatsoever. Bored by the tedious and improving conversation of those who have neither the wit to exaggerate nor the genius to romance, tired of the intelligent person whose reminiscences are always based upon memory, whose statements are invariably limited by probability, and who is at any time liable to be corroborated by the merest Philistine who happens to be present, society sooner or later must return to its lost leader, the cultured and fascinating liar. Who he was who first, without ever having gone out to the rude chase, told the wandering cave-men at sunset how he had dragged the Megatherium[55] from the purple darkness of its jasper cave, or slain the Mammoth in single combat

400

and brought back its gilded tusks, we cannot tell, and not one of our modern anthropologists, with all their much-boasted science, has had the ordinary courage to tell us. Whatever his name or race, he was certainly the true founder of social intercourse. For the aim of the liar is simply to charm, to delight, to give pleasure. He is the very basis of civilised society, and without him a dinner party, even at the mansions of the great, is as dull as a lecture at the Royal Society or a debate at the Incorporated Authors.[56]

'Nor will he be welcomed merely by society. Art, breaking from the prison-house of realism, will run to greet him and will kiss his false, beautiful lips, knowing that he alone is in possession of the great secret of all her manifestations, the secret that truth is entirely and absolutely a matter of style. While Life – poor, probable, uninteresting human life – tired of repeating herself for the benefit of Mr Herbert Spencer,[57] scientific historians, and the compilers of statistics in general, will follow meekly after him, and try to reproduce, in her own simple and untutored way, some of the marvels of which he talks.

'No doubt there will always be critics who, like a recent writer in the *Saturday Review*, will gravely censure the teller of fairy tales for his defective knowledge of natural history,[58] who will measure imaginative work by their own lack of any imaginative faculty, and will hold up their inkstained hands in horror if some honest gentleman, who has never been farther than the yew trees of his own garden, pens a fascinating book of travels like Sir John Mandeville, or, like great Raleigh, writes a whole history of the world, in prison, without knowing anything about the past.[59] To excuse themselves they will try and shelter under the shield of him who made Prospero the magician, and gave him Caliban and Ariel as his servants, who heard the Tritons blowing their horns round the coral reefs of the Enchanted Isle and the fairies singing to each other in a wood near Athens, who led the phantom kings in dim procession across the misty Scottish Heath, and hid Hecate in a cave with the weird sisters.[60] They will call upon Shakespeare – they always do – and will quote that hackneyed passage about Art holding up the mirror to Nature, forgetting that his unfortunate aphorism is deliberately said by Hamlet in order to convince the bystanders of his absolute insanity in art-matters.'[61]

*C.* Ahem! Ahem! Another cigarette, please.

*V.* My dear fellow, whatever you may say, it is merely a dramatic utterance, and no more represents Shakespeare's real views upon art than the speeches of Iago[62] represent his real views upon morals. But let me get to the end of the passage: –

'Art finds her own perfection within, and not outside, herself. She is not to be judged by any external standard of resemblance. She is a veil, rather than a mirror. She has flowers that no botanist knows of, birds that no museum possesses. She makes and unmakes many worlds, and can draw the moon from heaven with a scarlet thread. Hers are the "forms more real than living man,"[63] and hers the great archetypes of which things that have existence are but unfinished copies. Nature has, in her eyes, no laws, no uniformity. She can work

401

miracles at her will, and when she calls monsters from the deep they come. She can bid the almond tree blossom in winter, and send the snow upon the ripe cornfield. At her word the frost lays its silver finger on the burning mouth of June, and the winged lions creep out from the hollows of the Lydian hills. The dryads peer from the thicket as she passes by, and the brown fauns smile strangely at her when she comes near them. She has hawk-faced gods that worship her, and the centaurs gallop at her side.'[64]

*C.* Is that the end of this dangerous article?

*V.* No. There is one more passage, but it is purely practical. It simply suggests some methods by which we could revive this lost art of lying.

*C.* Well, before you read me that, I should like to ask you a question. What do you mean by saying that life, 'poor, probable, uninteresting human life,' will try to reproduce the marvels of art? I can quite understand your objection to art being treated as a mirror. You think it would reduce genius to the position of a cracked looking-glass. But you don't mean to say that you seriously believe that life imitates art, that life in fact is the mirror, and art the reality?

*V.* Certainly I do. Paradox though it may seem – and paradoxes are always dangerous things – it is none the less true that *life imitates art far more than art imitates life*. We have all seen in our own day in England how a certain curious and fascinating type of beauty, invented and emphasised by two imaginative painters, has so influenced life that whenever one goes to a private view or to an artistic salon one sees here the mystic eyes of Rossetti's dream, the long ivory throat, the strange square-cut jaw, the loosened shadowy hair that he so ardently loved,[65] there the sweet maidenhood of 'The Golden Stair,' the blossom-like mouth and weary loveliness of the 'Laus Amoris,' the passion-pale face of Andromeda, the thin hands and lithe beauty of the Vivien in 'Merlin's Dream.'[66] And it has always been so. A great artist invents a type, and Life tries to copy it, to reproduce it in a popular form, like an enterprising publisher. Neither Holbein nor Vandyck[67] found in England what they have given us. They brought their types with them, and Life with her keen imitative faculty set herself to supply the master with models. The Greeks, with their quick artistic instinct, understood this, and set in the bride's chamber the statue of Hermes or of Apollo,[68] that she might bear children like the works of art that she looked at. They knew that life gains from art not merely spirituality, depth of thought and passion, soul-turmoil or soul-peace, but that she can form herself on the very lines and colours of art, and can reproduce the dignity of Pheidias as well as the grace of Praxiteles.[69] Hence came their objection to realism. They disliked it on purely social grounds. They felt that it inevitably makes people ugly, and they were perfectly right. We try to improve the conditions of the race by means of good air, sunlight, wholesome water, and hideous bare buildings for the better housing of the people. But these things merely produce health, they do not produce beauty. For this art is required, and the true disciples of the great artist are not his studio-imitators, but those who become like his works of art, be they plastic as in Greek days, or pictorial as in modern times: in fact, Life is Art's best, Art's only pupil.

As it is with the visible arts, so it is with literature. The most obvious and the vulgarest form in which this is shown is in the case of the silly boys who, after reading the adventures of Jack Sheppard or Dick Turpin,[70] pillage stalls of unfortunate apple-women, break into sweet-shops at night, and alarm old gentlemen who are returning from the city by leaping out on them, with black masks and unloaded revolvers. This interesting phenomenon, which always occurs after the appearance of a new edition of either of the books I have named, is usually attributed to the influence of literature on the imagination. But this is a mistake. The imagination is essentially creative and always seeks for a new form. The boy-burglar is simply the inevitable result of life's imitative instinct. He is Fact, occupied, as Fact usually is, with trying to reproduce Fiction, and what we see in him is repeated on an extended scale through the whole of life. Schopenhauer[71] has analysed the pessimism that characterises modern thought, but Hamlet invented it. The world has become sad because a puppet was once melancholy. The Nihilist, that strange martyr who has no faith, who goes to the stake without enthusiasm, and dies for what he does not believe in, is a purely literary product. He was invented by Tourguénieff, and completed by Dostoieffski.[72] Robespierre came out of the pages of Rousseau, as surely as the People's Palace rose out of the *débris* of a novel.[73] Literature always anticipates life. It does not copy it, but moulds it to its purpose. The nineteenth century, as we know it, is largely an invention of Balzac. Our Luciens de Rubempré, our Rastignacs, and De Marsays made their first appearance in the stage of the *Comédie Humaine*.[74] We are merely carrying out, with footnotes and unnecessary additions, the whim or fancy of a great novelist. I once asked a lady, who knew Thackeray intimately, whether he had had any model for Becky Sharp. She told me that Becky was an invention, but that the idea of the character had been partly suggested by a governess who lived in the neighbourhood of Kensington Square, and was the companion of a very selfish and rich old woman. I inquired what became of the governess, and she replied that, oddly enough, some years after the appearance of *Vanity Fair*, the governess ran away with the nephew of the lady with whom she was living, and for a short time made a great splash in society, quite in Mrs Rawdon Crawley's style, and entirely by Mrs Rawdon Crawley's methods. Ultimately she came to grief, disappeared to the Continent, and used to be occasionally seen at Monte Carlo and other gambling places. The noble gentleman from whom the same great sentimentalist drew Colonel Newcome died, a few months after *The Newcomes* had reached a fourth edition, with the word 'Adsum' on his lips.[75] Shortly after Mr Stevenson published his curious psychological story of transformation, a friend of mine, called Mr Hyde, was in the north of London, and being anxious to get to a railway station, he took what he thought was a short cut, lost his way, and found himself in a network of mean, evil-looking streets. Feeling rather nervous he was walking extremely fast, when suddenly out of an archway ran a child right between his legs. The child fell on the pavement, he tripped over it, and trampled upon it. Being of course very much frightened and not a little hurt, it began to scream, and in a few seconds the whole street was full of rough people who kept pouring out of the houses like ants. They surrounded him, and asked him his name. He was just about to give it when he suddenly remembered the opening incident in Mr Stevenson's story. He was so filled with horror at having realised in his own person that terrible scene, and at having done accidentally what the Mr Hyde of fiction had done with deliberate intent, that he ran away as hard as he could go. He was, however, very closely followed, and he finally took refuge in a surgery, the door of which happened to be open, where he explained to a young man, apparently an assistant, who happened to be there, exactly what had occurred. The crowd was induced to go away on his giving them a small sum of money, and as soon as the coast was clear he left. As he passed out, the name on the brass door-plate of the surgery caught his eye. It was 'Jekyll.'

Here the imitation was of course accidental. In the following case the imitation was self-conscious. In the year 1879, just after I had left Oxford, I met at a reception at the house of one of the Foreign Ministers a lady who interested me very much, not merely in appearance, but in nature. What interested me most in her was her strange vagueness of character. She seemed to have no personality at all, but simply the possibility of many types. Sometimes she would give herself up entirely to art, turn her drawing-room into a studio, and spend two or three days a week at picture-galleries or museums. Then she would take to attending race-meetings, would wear the most horsey clothes, and talk about nothing but betting. She was a kind of Proteus, and as much a failure in all her transformations as the sea-god when Odysseus laid hold of him.[76] One day a serial began in one of the French magazines. At that time I used to read serial stories, and I well remember the shock of surprise I felt when I came to the description of the heroine. She was so like my friend that I brought her the magazine, and she recognised herself in it immediately, and seemed fascinated by the resemblance. I should tell you, by the way, that the story was translated from the Russian, so that the author had not taken his type from my friend. Well, to put the matter briefly, some months afterwards I was in Venice, and finding the magazine in the reading-room of the hotel, I took it up to see what had become of the heroine. It was a most piteous tale, as the heroine had ended by running away with a man inferior to her, not merely in social station, but in nature and in intellect also. I wrote to my friend that evening, and added a postscript to the effect that her double had behaved in a very silly manner. I don't know why I wrote, but I remember I had a sort of dread over me that she might do the same thing. Before my letter had reached her, she had run away with a man who deserted her in six months. I saw her in 1884 in Paris, where she was living with her mother, and I asked her whether the story had had anything to do with her action. She told me that she had felt an absolutely irresistible impulse to follow the heroine step by step in her strange and fatal progress, and that it was with a feeling of real terror that she had looked forward to the last few chapters of the story. When they appeared it seemed to her that she was compelled to reproduce them in life, and she did so. It was a most clear example of this imitative instinct of which I was speaking, and an extremely tragic one.

However, I do not wish to dwell any further upon individual instances. Personal experience is a most vicious and limited circle. All that I desire to point out is the general principle that life imitates art far more than art imitates life, and I feel sure that if you think seriously about it you will find that it is true. Life holds the mirror up to art, and either reproduces some strange type imagined by a painter or a sculptor, or realises in fact what has been dreamed in fiction. Scientifically speaking, the basis of life – the energy of life, as Aristotle would call it – is simply the desire for expression, and art is always presenting various forms through which this expression can be attained. Life seizes on them and uses them, even if they be to her own hurt. Young men have committed suicide because Rolla did so, have died by their own hand because by his own hand Werther died.[77] Think of what we owe to the imitation of Christ, of what we owe to the imitation of Caesar.

C. The theory is certainly a very curious one. But even admitting this strange imitative instinct in life, surely you would acknowledge that art expresses the temper of its age, the spirit of its time, the moral and social conditions that surround it, and under whose influence it is produced.

V. Certainly not! *Art never expresses anything but itself.* This is the principle of my new aesthetics; and it is this, and not any vital connection between form and substance, as Mr Pater fancies, that makes music the true type of all the arts.[78] Of course, nations and individuals, with that healthy natural vanity which is the secret of life, are always under the impression that it is of them that the Muses are talking, always trying to find in the calm dignity of the imaginative art some mirror of their own turbid passions, always forgetting that the singer of life is not Apollo but Marsyas.[79] Remote from reality and with her eyes turned away from the shadows of the cave,[80] Art reveals her own perfection, and the wondering crowd that watches the opening of the marvellous, many-petalled rose fancies that it is its own history that is being told to it, its own spirit that is finding expression in a new form. But it is not so. The highest art rejects the burden of the human spirit, and gains more from a new medium or of a fresh material than she does from any enthusiasm for art, or from any lofty passion, or from any great awakening of the human consciousness. She develops purely on her own lines. She is not symbolic of any age. It is the ages that are her symbols, her reflections, her echoes.

Even those who hold that Art is representative of time and place and people, cannot help admitting that the more imitative an art is, the less it represents to us the spirit of its age. The evil faces of the Roman emperors look out at us from the foul porphyry and spotted jasper[81] in which the realistic artists of the day delighted to work, and we fancy that in those cruel lips and heavy sensual jaws we can find the secret of the ruin of the Empire. But it was not so. The vices of Tiberius could not destroy that great civilisation, any more than the virtues of the Antonines could save it.[82] It fell for other, for greater reasons. The Sibyls and

405

prophets of the Sistine[83] may indeed serve to interpret for some that new birth of the emancipated spirit that we call the Renaissance; but what do the drunken boors and bawling peasants of Dutch art tell us about the great soul of Holland?[84] The more abstract, the more ideal an art is, the more it reveals to us the temper of its age. If we wish to understand a nation by means of its art, let us look at its architecture or its music.

*C.* I do not quite agree with you there. The spirit of an age may be best expressed in the abstract ideal arts, for the spirit itself is abstract and ideal; but for the visible aspect of an age, for its look, as the phrase goes, we must surely go to the arts of imitation.

*V.* I don't think so. After all, what the imitative arts really give us are merely the various styles of particular artists, or of particular schools of artists. Surely you don't imagine that the people of the Middle Ages bore any resemblance at all to the figures on mediaeval stained glass, or in mediaeval stone and wood carving, or on mediaeval metal-work, or tapestries, or illuminated MSS. They were probably very ordinary-looking people, with nothing grotesque, or remarkable, or fantastic about them. The Middle Ages, as we know them in art, are simply a form of style, and there is no reason at all why an artist with this style should not be produced in the nineteenth century. No great artist ever sees things as they really are. If he did, he would cease to be an artist. Take an example from our own day. I know that you are fond of Japanese art. Now, do you really imagine that the Japanese people, as they are presented to us in art, have any existence? If you do, you have never understood Japanese art at all. The Japanese people are the deliberate creation of certain individual artists. If you set a picture by Hokusai, or Hokkei,[85] or any of the great native painters, beside a real Japanese gentleman or lady, or beside a photograph of a Japanese gentleman or lady, you will see that there is not the slightest resemblance between them. The actual people who live in Japan are not unlike the general run of English people; that is to say, they are extremely commonplace, and have nothing curious or extraordinary about them. In fact the whole of Japan is a pure invention. There is no such country, there are no such people. One of our most charming painters, whose tiny full-length portraits of children are so beautiful and so powerful that he should be named the Velasquez to the Court of Lilliput, went recently to Japan in the foolish hope of seeing the Japanese. All he saw, all he had the chance of painting, were a few lanterns and some fans. He was unable to discover the inhabitants, as [his] delightful exhibition at Messrs Dowdeswell's Gallery showed only too well.[86] He did not know that the Japanese people are, as I have said, simply a mode of style, a whimsical fancy of art. Take the Greeks. Do you think that Greek art ever tells us what the Greek people were like? Do you believe that the Athenian women were like the stately dignified figures of the Parthenon frieze, or like those marvellous goddesses who sat in the triangular pediments of the same building? If you judge from the art, they certainly were so. But read an authority, like Aristophanes[87] for instance. You will find that the Athenian ladies laced tightly, wore high-heeled shoes, dyed their hair yellow, painted and rouged their faces, and were exactly like any silly fashionable or fallen creature of our own day. We look back on the ages entirely through the medium of Art, and Art very fortunately has never once told us the truth.

*C.* But modern portraits by English painters, what of them? Surely they are like the people they pretend to represent?

*V.* Quite so. They are so like them that a hundred years from now no one will believe in them. The only portraits that one believes in are portraits where there is very little of the sitter and a great deal of the artist. Holbein's portraits of the men and women of his time impress us with a sense of their absolute reality. But this is simply because Holbein compelled life to accept his conditions, to restrain itself within his limitations, to reproduce his type, and to appear as he wished it to appear. It is style that makes us believe in a thing – nothing but style. Most of our modern portrait painters never paint what they see. *They paint what the public sees, and the public never sees anything.*

*C.* Well, after that I think I should like to hear the end of your article.

*V.* With pleasure. Whether it will do any good I really cannot say. Ours is certainly the dullest and most prosaic century possible. Why, even Sleep has played us false, and has closed up the gates of ivory, and opened the gates of horn.[88] The dreams of the great middle classes of this country, as recorded in Mr Myers's two bulky volumes on the subject and in the Transactions of the Psychical Society,[89] are the most depressing things I have ever read. There is not even a fine nightmare among them. They are commonplace, sordid, and probable. As for the Church, I cannot conceive anything better for the culture of a country than the presence in it of a body of men whose duty it is to believe in the supernatural, to perform daily miracles, and to keep alive that mythopoeic faculty which is so essential for the imagination. But in the English Church a man succeeds, not through his capacity for belief, but through his capacity for disbelief. Ours is the only Church where the sceptic stands at the altar, and where St Thomas[90] is regarded as the ideal apostle. Many a worthy clergyman, who passes his life in good works of kindly charity, lives and dies unnoticed and unknown; but it is sufficient for some shallow and uneducated passman out of either University[91] to get up in his pulpit and express his doubts about Noah's ark, or Balaam's ass,[92] or Jonah and the whale, for half of London to flock to his church and to sit open-mouthed in rapt admiration at his superb intellect. The growth of common sense in the English Church is a thing very much to be regretted. It is really a degrading concession to a low form of realism. However, I must read the end of my article: –

'What we have to do, what at any rate it is our duty to do, is to revive this old art of lying. Much of course may be done, in the way of educating the public, by amateurs in the domestic circle, at literary lunches, and at afternoon teas. But this is merely the light and graceful side of lying, such as was probably heard at Cretan dinner parties. There are many other forms. Lying for the sake of gaining some immediate personal advantage, for instance – lying for a moral purpose, as it is usually called – though of late it has been rather looked down upon, was extremely popular with the antique world. Athena laughs when Odysseus tells her what a Cambridge professor once eloquently termed a "whopper,"[93] and the glory of mendacity illumines the pale brow of the stainless hero of Euripidean tragedy, and sets amongst the noble women of the world the young bride of one of Horace's most exquisite odes.[94] Later on what at first had been merely a natural instinct was elevated into a self-conscious science. Elaborate rules were laid down for the guidance of mankind, and an important school of literature grew up round the subject. Indeed, when one remembers the excellent philosophical treatise of Sanchez[95] on the whole question, one cannot help regretting that no one has ever thought of publishing a cheap and condensed edition of the works of that great casuist. A short primer, "When to Lie and how," if brought out in an attractive and not too expensive form, would no doubt command a large sale, and would prove of real practical service to many earnest and deep-thinking people. Lying for the sake of the improvement of the young, which is the basis of home education, still lingers amongst us, and its advantages are so admirably set forth in the early books of the *Republic* that it is unnecessary to dwell upon them here. It is a form of lying for which all good mothers have peculiar capabilities, but it is capable of still further development, and has been sadly overlooked by the School Board.[96] Lying for the sake of a monthly salary is of course well known in Fleet Street, and the profession of a political leader-writer is not without its advantages. But it is said to be a some-what dull occupation, and it certainly does not lead to much beyond a kind of ostentatious obscurity. The only form of lying that is absolutely beyond reproach is lying for its own sake, and the highest development of this is, as we have already pointed out, lying in Art. Just as those who do not love Plato more than truth cannot pass beyond the threshold of the Academe,[97] so those who do not love beauty more than truth never know the inmost shrine of Art. The solid stolid British intellect lies in the desert sands like the Sphinx in Flaubert's marvel-lous tale, and fantasy, *La Chimère*,[98] dances round it, and calls to it with her false, flute-toned voice. It may not hear her now, but surely some day, when we are all bored to death with the commonplace character of modern fiction, it will hearken to her and try to borrow her wings.

'And when that day dawns, or sunset reddens, how joyous we shall be! Facts will be regarded as discreditable, Truth will be found mourning over her fetters, and Romance, with her temper of wonder, will return to the land. The very aspect of the world will change to our startled eyes. Out of the sea will rise Behemoth and Leviathan,[99] and sail round the high-pooped galleys, as they do on the delightful maps of those ages when books on geography were actually readable. Dragons will wander about the waste places, and the phoenix will soar from her nest of fire into the air. We shall lay our hands upon the basilisk, and see the jewel in the toad's head. The hippogriff will stand in our stalls, champing his gilded oats, and over our heads will float the Blue Bird singing of beautiful and impossible things, of things that are lovely and that never happen, of things

that are not and that should be.[100] But before this comes to pass we must cultivate the lost art of lying.'

*C.* Then we must certainly cultivate it at once. But in order to avoid making
any error I want you to briefly tell me the doctrines of the new aesthetics.

*V.* Briefly, then, they are these. Art never expresses anything but itself. It has
an independent life, just as Thought has, and develops purely on its own lines. It
is not necessarily realistic in an age of realism, nor spiritual in an age of faith. So
far from being the creation of its time, it is usually in direct opposition to it, and
the only history that it preserves for us is the history of its own progress.
Sometimes it returns on its own footsteps, and revives some old form, as
happened in the archaistic movement of late Greek art, and in the pre-
Raphaelite movement of our own day. At other times it entirely anticipates its
age, and produces in one century work that it takes another century to understand, to appreciate, and to enjoy. In no case does it reproduce its age. To pass
from the art of a time to the time itself is the great fallacy of all historians.

The second doctrine is this. All bad art comes from returning to life and
nature, and elevating them into ideals. Life and nature may sometimes be used
as part of art's rough material, but before they are of any real service to art they
must be translated into artistic conventions. The moment art surrenders its imaginative medium it surrenders everything. As a method Realism is a complete
failure, and the two things that every artist should avoid are modernity of form
and modernity of subject-matter. To us, who live in the nineteenth century, any
century is a suitable subject for art except our own. The only beautiful things are
things that do not concern us. It is, to have the pleasure of quoting myself,
exactly because Hecuba is nothing to us that her sorrows are so suitable a motive
for tragedy.

The third doctrine is that Life imitates Art far more than Art imitates Life.
This results not merely from Life's imitative instinct, but from the fact that the
desire of Life is simply to find expression, and that Art offers it certain beautiful
forms through which it may realise that energy. It is a theory that has never been
formularised before, but it is extremely fruitful, and throws an entirely new light
on the history of Art.

The last doctrine is that Lying, the telling of beautiful untrue things, is the
proper aim of Art. But of this I think I have spoken at sufficient length. And now
let us go out on the terrace, where 'the milk-white peacock glimmers like a
ghost,' while the evening star 'washes the dusk with silver.'[101] At twilight nature
becomes a wonderfully suggestive effect and is not without loveliness, though
perhaps its chief use is to illustrate quotations from the poets. Come! We have
talked long enough.

## ARTHUR SYMONS, *THE SYMBOLIST MOVEMENT IN LITERATURE* (1899)

Although his career extended considerably beyond the 1890s, Arthur Symons (1865–1945) is largely remembered as a member and chronicler of the English Decadent movement. He first came to attention in the late 1880s with critical writings such as *An Introduction to the Study of Browning* (1886) and his facsimile editions of *Venus and Adonis* (1886), *Titus Andronicus* (1886) and *Henry V* (1886) for the New Shakespeare Society. In 1888 he met Walter Pater (two years after they had first corresponded), and in 1889 made the first of many trips to the Continent, meeting French writers such as Stéphane Mallarmé, J.-K. Huysmans and Remy de Gourmont. 1889 also saw the publication of Symons' first volume of poems, *Days and Nights*, which was dedicated to Pater. In 1890 he met the French poet, Paul Verlaine, who profoundly influenced his next and typically Decadent volume of poems, *Silhouettes* (1892). In the meantime, in 1891 he had joined the Rhymers' Club, striking up what was to become a close friendship with the Irish poet W. B. Yeats. In November 1893 Symons published an essay entitled 'The Decadent Movement in Literature' in *Harper's Monthly Magazine*, thereby declaring himself as the foremost propagandist for the new literary movement; the essay remains one of the most important discussions of Decadence. In 1896, following a traumatic break with 'Lydia', a dancer with whom he had become fascinated in 1894, he visited Ireland in the company of Yeats. In the same year he also met Aubrey Beardsley with whom he co-edited *The Savoy*. In 1898 Symons met his future wife, Rhoda Bowser; their marriage (which took place in 1901) brought certain financial pressures which led Symons to spend more time on journalism rather than poetry in order to provide for his new wife. One fruit of this activity was his most significant work (much influenced by Yeats), *The Symbolist Movement in Literature* (1899). In the early 1900s Symons published several further critical works before suffering a mental breakdown in 1908 while travelling in Italy. Partly recovered, he retired in 1910 to a cottage in Kent where he lived for the next thirty-five years. Although Symons continued writing, the quality of his later work was marred by the effects of his earlier illness. He died in 1945.

## From Arthur Symons, *The Symbolist Movement in Literature* (London: Heinemann, 1899)[1]

### *Introduction*

'It is in and through Symbols that man, consciously or unconsciously, lives, works, and has his being: those ages, moreover, are accounted the noblest which can the best recognise symbolical worth, and prize it highest.' – CARLYLE[2]

Without symbolism there can be no literature; indeed, not even language. What are words themselves but symbols, almost as arbitrary as the letters which compose them, mere sounds of the voice to which we have agreed to give certain significations, as we have agreed to translate these sounds by those combinations of letters? Symbolism began with the first words uttered by the first man, as he named every living thing; or before them, in heaven, when God named the world into being. And we see, in these beginnings, precisely what Symbolism in literature really is: a form of expression, at the best but approximate, essentially but arbitrary, until it has obtained the force of a convention, for an unseen reality apprehended by the consciousness. It is sometimes permitted to us to hope that our convention is indeed the reflection rather than merely the sign of that unseen reality. We have done much if we have found a recognisable sign.

'A symbol,' says Comte Goblet d'Alviella,[3] in his book on *The Migration of Symbols*, 'might be defined as a representation which does not aim at being a reproduction.' Originally, as he points out, used by the Greeks to denote 'the two halves of the tablet they divided between themselves as a pledge of hospitality,' it came to be used of every sign, formula, or rite by which those initiated in any mystery made themselves secretly known to one another. Gradually the word extended its meaning, until it came to denote every conventional representation of idea by form, of the unseen by the visible. 'In a Symbol,' says Carlyle, 'there is concealment and yet revelation: hence therefore, by Silence and by Speech acting together, comes a double significance.' And, in that fine chapter of *Sartor Resartus*, he goes further, vindicating for the word its full value: 'In the Symbol proper, what we can call a Symbol, there is ever, more or less distinctly and directly, some embodiment and revelation of the Infinite; the Infinite is made to blend itself with the Finite, to stand visible, and as were, attainable there.'

It is in such a sense as this that the word Symbolism has been used to describe a movement which, during the last generation, has profoundly influenced the course of French literature. All such words, used of anything so living, variable, and irresponsible as literature, are, as symbols themselves must so often be, mere compromises, mere indications. Symbolism, as seen in the writers of our day, would have no value if it were not seen also, under one disguise or another, in every great imaginative writer. What distinguishes the Symbolism of our day

411

from that Symbolism of the past is that it has now become conscious of itself, in a sense in which it was unconscious even in Gérard de Nerval,[4] to whom I trace the particular origin of the literature which I call Symbolist. The forces which mould the thought of men change, or men's resistance to them slackens; with the change of men's thought comes a change of literature, alike in its inmost essence and in its outward form: after the world has starved its soul long enough in the contemplation and the re-arrangement of material things, comes the turn of the soul; and with it comes the literature of which I write in this volume, a literature in which the visible world is no longer a reality, and the unseen world no longer a dream.

The great epoch in French literature which preceded this epoch was that of the offshoot of Romanticism which produced Baudelaire, Flaubert, the Goncourts, Taine, Zola, Leconte de Lisle.[5] Taine was the philosopher both of what had gone before him and of what came immediately after; so that he seems to explain at once Flaubert and Zola. It was the age of Science, the age of material things; and words, with that facile elasticity which there is in them, did miracles in the exact representation of everything that visibly existed, exactly as it existed. Even Baudelaire, in whom the spirit is always an uneasy guest at the orgy of life, had a certain theory of Realism which tortures many of his poems into strange, metallic shapes, and fills them with imitative odours, and disturbs them with a too deliberate rhetoric of the flesh. Flaubert, the one impeccable novelist who has ever lived, was resolute to be the novelist of a world in which art, formal art, was the only escape from the burden of reality, and in which the soul was of use mainly as the agent of fine literature. The Goncourts caught at Impressionism[6] to render the fugitive aspects of a world which existed only as a thing of flat spaces, and angles, and coloured movement, in which sun and shadow were the artists; as moods, no less flitting, were the artists of the merely receptive consciousness of men and women. Zola has tried to build in brick and mortar inside the covers of a book; he is quite sure that the soul is a nervous fluid, which he is quite sure some man of science is about to catch for us, as a man of science has bottled the air, a pretty, blue liquid. Leconte de Lisle turned the world to stone, but saw, beyond the world, only a pause from misery in a Nirvana[7] never subtilised to the Eastern ecstasy. And, with all these writers, form aimed above all things at being precise, at saying rather than suggesting, at saying what they had to say so completely that nothing remained over, which it might be the business of the reader to divine. And so they have expressed, finally, a certain aspect of the world; and some of them have carried style to a point beyond which the style that says, rather than suggests, cannot go. The whole of that movement comes to a splendid funeral in Heredia's sonnets,[8] in which the literature of form says its last word, and dies.

Meanwhile, something which is vaguely called Decadence had come into being. That name, rarely used with any precise meaning, was usually either hurled as a reproach or hurled back as a defiance. It pleased some young men in various countries to call themselves Decadents, with all the thrill of unsatisfied virtue masquerading as uncomprehended vice. As a matter of fact, the term is in its place only when applied to style; to that ingenious deformation of the language, in Mallarmé,[9] for instance, which can be compared with what we are accustomed to call the Greek and Latin of the Decadence. No doubt perversity of form and perversity of matter are often found together, and, among the lesser men especially, experiment was carried far, not only in the direction of style. But a movement which in this sense might be called Decadent could but have been a straying aside from the main road of literature. Nothing, not even conventional virtue, is so provincial as conventional vice; and the desire to 'bewilder the middle-classes'[10] is itself middle-class. The interlude, half a mock-interlude, of Decadence, diverted the attention of the critics while something more serious was in preparation. That something more serious has crystallised, for the time, under the form of Symbolism, in which art returns to the one pathway, leading through beautiful things to the eternal beauty.

In most of the writers whom I have dealt with as summing up in themselves all that is best in Symbolism, it will be noticed that the form is very carefully elaborated, and seems to count for at least as much as in those writers of whose over-possession by form I have complained. Here, however, all this elaboration comes from a very different motive, and leads to other ends. There is such a thing as perfecting form that form may be annihilated. All the art of Verlaine[11] is in bringing verse to a bird's song, the art of Mallarmé in bringing verse to a song of an orchestra. In Villiers de l'Isle-Adam drama becomes the embodiment of spiritual forces, in Maeterlinck not even their embodiment, but the remote sound of their voices.[12] It is all an attempt to spiritualise literature, to evade the old bondage of rhetoric, the old bondage of exteriority. Description is banished that beautiful things may be evoked, magically; the regular beat of verse is broken in order that words may fly, upon subtler wings. Mystery is no longer feared, as the great mystery in whose midst we are islanded was feared by those to whom that unknown sea was only a great void. We are coming closer to nature, as we seem to shrink from it with something of horror, disdaining to catalogue the trees of the forest. And as we brush aside the accidents of daily life, in which men and women imagine that they are alone touching reality, we come closer to humanity, to everything in humanity that may have begun before the world and may outlast it.

Here, then, in this revolt against exteriority, against rhetoric, against a materialistic tradition; in this endeavour to disengage the ultimate essence, the soul, of whatever exists and can be realised by the consciousness; in this dutiful waiting upon every symbol by which the soul of things can be made visible; literature, bowed down by so many burdens, may at last attain liberty, and its authentic speech. In attaining this liberty, it accepts a heavier burden; for in speaking to us so intimately, so solemnly, as only religion had hitherto spoken to us, it becomes itself a kind of religion, with all the duties and responsibilities of the sacred ritual.

8

# ART AS PATHOLOGY

## MAX NORDAU, *DEGENERATION* (1895)

Max Nordau (1849–1923) was born into a Hungarian Jewish family. He began his career by changing his surname (from Südfeld to Nordau) and by travelling widely in Europe in connection with his work as a newspaper correspondent. In 1880 he arrived in Paris. The city became his new home and he stayed there for most of the remainder of his life. Dissatisfied with journalism as his only means of support, Nordau had taken a medical degree, and with formidable energy he established a successful medical practice in Paris while at the same time pursuing a prolific writing career. In all he produced nine volumes of novels and short stories, seven plays and fifteen works of cultural criticism. He also wrote the annual political review for the *Neue Freie Presse*, the most influential newspaper in Central Europe, and was foreign correspondent for the Berlin *Vossische Zeitung*. During his lifetime, his most popular work was *Die Conventionellen Lügen der Kultermenschheit* (1884); it ran to over seventy editions. Translated as *Conventional Lies of Our Civilisation*, the book was a bitter attack on the inadequacies of nineteenth-century institutions, including the Church. Today, however, Nordau is probably better remembered (certainly among literary historians) for *Entartung* (1892), which was translated into English as *Degeneration* in 1895. It was dedicated to the Italian criminologist, Cesare Lombroso, whose work greatly influenced Nordau. In particular Lombroso had claimed in *Genio e Follia* (1863) that individuals' personalities and ways of living were determined by their physical constitution. In *Entartung* Nordau identified in the literary and artistic tendencies of the time a type of modern individual which he named the degenerate. Distinguished by a lack of mental discipline and a contempt for conventional custom and morality, the degenerate, according to Nordau, also exhibited a number of mental and physical 'stigmata' which were in turn symptoms of a diseased and exhausted brain. Nordau's pathology of creativity was underwritten by a Darwinian fear that the degenerate's lack of 'fitness' threatened the survival of the species. The book was immediately controversial and provoked several replies, including the anonymous *Regeneration: A Reply to Max Nordau* (1895) (written by Alfred Egmont Hake) and a few years later George Bernard Shaw's *The Sanity of Art: An Exposure of the Current Nonsense about Artists Being Degenerate* (1908). In 1892 Nordau's meeting with the Jewish nationalist leader, Theodor Herzel, led him to become a prominent, if controversial, member of the Zionist movement. In the early 1900s, however, following Herzel's death, Nordau's influence began to wane, and by 1914 it was insignificant. With the outbreak of war, Nordau, as an Austrian subject, was forced to leave France for exile in Spain. This period also saw a rapid decline in his literary reputation; no new editions of his work were brought out, and by the time of his death in 1923, he had been virtually forgotten.

### *From* Max Nordau, *Degeneration* (London: W. Heinemann, 1895)[1]

From *Chapter III: Diagnosis*

[ . . . ][2] The physician, especially if he have devoted himself to the special study of nervous and mental maladies, recognises at a glance, in the *fin-de-siècle* disposition, in the tendencies of contemporary art and poetry, in the life and conduct of the men who write mystic, symbolic and 'decadent' works, and the attitude taken by their admirers in the tastes and aesthetic instincts of fashionable society, the confluence of two well-defined conditions of disease, with which he is quite familiar, viz. degeneration (degeneracy) and hysteria, of which the minor stages are designated as neurasthenia. These two conditions of the organism differ from each other, yet have many features in common, and frequently occur together; so that it is easier to observe them in their composite forms, than each in isolation.

The conception of degeneracy, which, at this time, obtains throughout the science of mental disease, was first clearly grasped and formulated by Morel.[3] In his principal work – often quoted, but, unfortunately, not sufficiently read[a] – the following definition of what he wishes to be understood by 'degeneracy' is given

---

a   *Traité des Dégénérescences physiques, intellectuelles et morales de l'Espèce humaines et des Causes qui produisent ces Variétés maladives.* Par le Dr B. A. Morel. Paris, 1857, p. 5.

by this distinguished expert in mental pathology, who was, for a short time, famous in Germany, even outside professional circles.[b]

> 'The clearest notion we can form of degeneracy is to regard it as *a morbid deviation from an original type*. This deviation, even if, at the outset, it was ever so slight, contained transmissible elements of such a nature that anyone bearing in him the germs becomes more and more incapable of fulfilling his functions in the world; and mental progress, already checked in his own person, finds itself menaced also in his descendants.'

When under any kind of noxious influences an organism becomes debilitated, its successors will not resemble the healthy, normal type of the species, with capacities for development, but will form a new sub-species, which, like all others, possesses the capacity of transmitting to its offspring, in a continuously increasing degree, its peculiarities, these being morbid deviations from the normal form – gaps in development, malformations and infirmities. That which distinguishes degeneracy from the formation of new species (phylogeny) is, that the morbid variation does not continuously subsist and propagate itself, like one that is healthy, but, fortunately, is soon rendered sterile, and after a few generations often dies out before it reaches the lowest grade of organic degradation.[c]

Degeneracy betrays itself among men in certain physical characteristics, which are denominated 'stigmata,' or brand-marks – an unfortunate term derived from a false idea, as if degeneracy were necessarily the consequence of a fault, and the indication of it a punishment. Such stigmata consist of deformities, multiple and stunted growths in the first line of asymmetry, the unequal development of the two halves of the face and cranium; then imperfection in the development of the external ear, which is conspicuous for its enormous size, or protrudes from the head, like a handle, and the lobe of which is either lacking or adhering to the head, and the helix of which is not involuted; further, squint-eyes, hare-lips, irregularities in the form and position of the teeth; pointed or flat palates, webbed or supernumerary figures (syn- and poly-dactylia), etc. In the

b    At the instigation of his mistress Ebergenyi, Count Chorinsky had poisoned his wife, previously an actress. The murderer was an epileptic, and a 'degenerate,' in the Morelian sense. His family summoned Morel from Normandy to Munich, for the purpose of proving to the jury, before whom the case (1868) was tried, that the accused was irresponsible. The latter was singularly indignant at this; and the Attorney-General also contradicted, in the most emphatic manner, the evidence of the French alienist [i.e. someone who studies mental illness], and supported himself by the approbation of the most prominent alienists in Munich. Chorinsky was pronounced guilty. Nevertheless, only a short time after his conviction, insanity developed itself in him, and a few months later he died, in the deepest mental darkness, thus justifying all the previous assertions of the French physician, who had, in the German tongue, demonstrated to a German jury the incompetence of his professional confrères in Munich.

c    Morel, *op. cit.*, p. 683.

book from which I have quoted, Morel gives a list of the anatomical phenomena of degeneracy, which later observers have largely extended. In particular, Lombroso[d] has conspicuously broadened our knowledge of stigmata, but he apportions them merely to his 'born criminals' – a limitation which from the very scientific standpoint of Lombroso himself cannot be justified, his 'born criminals' being nothing but a subdivision of degenerates. Féré[e] expresses this very emphatically then he says, 'Vice, crime and madness are only distinguished from each other by social prejudices.'[4]

There might be a sure means of proving that the application of the term 'degenerates' to the originators of all the *fin-de-siècle* movements in art and literature is not arbitrary, that it is no baseless conceit, but a fact; and that would be a careful physical examination of the persons concerned, and an inquiry into their pedigree. In almost all cases, relatives would be met with who were undoubtedly degenerate, and one or more stigmata discovered which would indisputably establish the diagnosis of 'Degeneration.' Of course, from human consideration, the result of such an inquiry could often not be made public; and he alone would be convinced who should be able to undertake it himself.

Science, however, has found, together with these physical stigmata, others of a mental order, which betoken degeneracy quite as clearly as the former; and they allow of an easy demonstration from all the vital manifestations, and, in particular, from all the works of degenerates, so that it is not necessary to measure the cranium of an author, or to see the lobe of a painter's ear, in order to recognise the fact that he belongs to the class of degenerates.

Quite a number of different designations have been found for these persons. Maudsley and Ball[5] call them 'Borderland dwellers' – that is to say, dwellers on the borderland between reason and pronounced madness. Magnan[6] gives to them the name of 'higher degenerates' (*dégénérés supérieurs*), and Lombroso speaks of 'mattoids' (from *matto*, the Italian for insane), and 'graphomaniacs,' under which he classifies those semi-insane persons who feel a strong impulse to write. In spite, however, of this variety of nomenclature, it is a question simply of one single species of individuals, who betray their fellowship by the similarity of their mental physiognomy.

In the mental development of degenerates, we meet with the same irregularity that we have observed in their physical growth. The asymmetry of face and cranium finds, as it were, its counterpart in their mental faculties. Some of the latter are completely stunted, others morbidly exaggerated. That which nearly all degenerates lack is the sense of morality and of right and wrong. For them there exists no law, no decency, no modesty. In order to satisfy any momen-

---

d    *L'Uomo delinquente in rapporto all'Antropologia, Giurisprudenza e alle Discipline carcerarie.* 3ª edizione. Torino, 1884, p. 147 *et seq.* See also Dr Ch. Féré, 'La famille nevropathique.' Paris, 1894, pp. 176–212.

e    'La Famille nevropathique,' *Archives de Nevrologie*, 1884, *Nos.* 19 *et* 20.

tary impulse, or inclination, or caprice, they commit crimes and trespasses with the greatest calmness and self-complacency, and do not comprehend that other persons take offence thereat. When this phenomenon is present in a high degree, we speak of 'moral insanity' with Maudsley;[f] there are, nevertheless, lower stages in which the degenerate does not, perhaps, himself commit any act which will bring him into conflict with the criminal code, but at least asserts the theoretical legitimacy of crime; seeks, with philosophically sounding fustian,[7] to prove that 'good' and 'evil,' virtue and vice, are arbitrary distinctions; goes into raptures over evildoers and their deeds; professes to discover beauties in the lowest and most repulsive things; and tries to awaken interest in, and so-called 'comprehension' of, every bestiality. The two psychological roots of moral insanity, in all its degrees of development, are, firstly, unbounded egoism,[g] and, secondly, impulsiveness[h] – i.e., inability to resist a sudden impulse to any deed; and these characteristics also constitute the chief intellectual stigmata of degenerates. In the following sections of this work, I shall find occasion to show on what organic grounds, and in consequence of what peculiarities of their brain and nervous system, degenerates are necessarily egoistical and impulsive. In these introductory remarks I would wish only to point out the stigma itself.

Another mental stigma of degenerates is their emotionalism. Morel[i] has even wished to make this peculiarity their chief characteristic – erroneously, it seems to me, for it is present in the same degree among hysterics, and, indeed, is to be found in perfectly healthy persons, who, from any transient cause, such as illness, exhaustion, or any mental shock, have been temporarily weakened. Nevertheless it is a phenomenon rarely absent in a degenerate. He laughs until he sheds tears, or weeps copiously without adequate occasion; a commonplace line of poetry or of prose sends a shudder down his back; he falls into raptures before indifferent pictures or statues; and music especially,[j] even the most insipid and least commendable, arouses in him the most vehement emotions. He is quite proud of

f   See, on this subject, in particular, [Richard Freiherr von] Krafft Ebing, *Die Lehre vom moralischen Wahnsinn*, 1871; H. Maudsley, *Responsibility in Mental Disease*, International Scientific Series; and Ch. Féré, *Dégénérescence et Criminalité*, Paris, 1888.

g   J[acques] Roubinovitch, *Hystérie mâle et Dégénérescence*, Paris, 1890, p. 62: 'The society which surrounds him (the degenerate) always remains strange to him. He knows nothing, and takes interest in nothing but himself.'
     [Paul Maurice] Legrain, *Du Délire chez les Dégénérés*, Paris, 1886, p. 10: 'The patient is . . . the plaything of his passions; he is carried away by his impulses, and has only one care – to satisfy his appetites.' P. 27: 'They are egotistical, arrogant, conceited, self-infatuated,' etc.

h   Henry [i.e. Henri] Colin, *Essai sur l'Etat mental des Hystériques*, Paris, 1890, p. 59: 'Two great facts control the being of the hereditary degenerate: obsession {the tyrannical domination of one thought from which a man cannot free himself; [Carl Friedrich Otto] Westphal has created for this the good term 'Zwangs-Vorstellung,' i.e., coercive idea} and impulsion – both irresistible.'

i   Morel, 'Du Délire émotif,' *Archives générales*, 6 série, vol. vii., pp. 385 and 530. See also Roubinovitch, *op. cit.*, p. 53.

j   J. Roubinovitch, *op. cit.*, p. 68: 'Music excites him keenly.'

being so vibrant a musical instrument, and boasts that where the Philistine[8] remains completely cold, he feels his inner self confounded, the depths of his being broken up, and the bliss of the Beautiful possessing him to the tips of his fingers. His excitability appears to him a mark of superiority; he believes himself to be possessed by a peculiar insight lacking in other mortals, and he is fain to despise the vulgar herd for the dulness and narrowness of their minds. The unhappy creature does not suspect that he is conceited about a disease and boasting of a derangement of the mind; and certain silly critics, when, through fear of being pronounced deficient in comprehension, they make desperate efforts to share the emotions of a degenerate in regard to some insipid or ridiculous production, or when they praise in exaggerated expressions the beauties which the degenerate asserts he finds therein, are unconsciously simulating one of the stigmata of semi-insanity.

Besides moral insanity and emotionalism, there is to be observed in the degenerate a condition of mental weakness and despondency, which, according to the circumstances of his life, assumes the form of pessimism, a vague fear of all men, and of the entire phenomenon of the universe, or self-abhorrence. 'These patients,' says Morel,[k] 'feel perpetually compelled . . . to commiserate themselves, to sob, to repeat with the most desperate monotony the same questions and words. They have delirious presentations of ruin and damnation, and all sorts of imaginary fears.' 'Ennui never quits me,' said a patient of this kind, whose case Roubinovitch[l] describes, 'ennui of myself.' 'Among moral stigmata,' says the same author,[m] 'there are also to be specified those undefinable apprehensions manifested by degenerates when they see, smell, or touch any object.' And he further[n] calls to notice 'their unconscious fear of everything and everyone.' In this picture of the sufferer from melancholia; downcast, sombre, despairing of himself and the world, tortured by fear of the Unknown, menaced by undefined but dreadful dangers, we recognise in every detail the man of the Dusk of the Nations and the *fin-de-siècle* frame of mind, described in the first chapter.

With this characteristic dejectedness of the degenerate, there is combined, as a rule, a disinclination to action of any kind, attaining possibly to abhorrence of activity and powerlessness to will (*aboulia*). Now, it is a peculiarity of the human mind, known to every psychologist, that, inasmuch as the law of causality governs a man's whole thought, he imputes a rational basis to all his own decisions. This was prettily expressed by Spinoza when he said: 'If a stone flung by a human hand could think, it would certainly imagine that it flew because it wished to fly.'[9] Many mental conditions and operations of which we become conscious are the result of causes which do not reach our consciousness. In this

k   Morel, 'Du Délire panophobique des Aliénés gémisseurs,' *Annales médico-psychologiques*, 1871.
l   Roubinovitch, *op. cit.*, p. 28.
m   *Ibid.*, p. 37.
n   *Ibid.*, p. 66.

case we fabricate causes *a posteriori* for them, satisfying our mental need of distinct causality, and we have no trouble in persuading ourselves that we have now truly explained them. The degenerate who shuns action, and is without will-power, has no suspicion that his incapacity for action is a consequence of his inherited deficiency of brain. He deceives himself into believing that he despises action from free determination, and takes pleasure in inactivity; and, in order to justify himself in his own eyes, he constructs a philosophy of renunciation and of contempt for the world and men, asserts that he has convinced himself of the excellence of Quietism, calls himself with consummate self-consciousness a Buddhist, and praises Nirvana in poetically eloquent phrases as the highest and worthiest ideal of the human mind. The degenerate and insane are the predes-tined disciples of Schopenhauer and Hartmann,[10] and need only to acquire a knowledge of Buddhism to become converts to it.

With the incapacity for action there is connected the predilection for inane reverie. The degenerate is not in a condition to fix his attention long, or indeed at all, on any subject, and is equally incapable of correctly grasping, ordering, or elaborating into ideas and judgements the impressions of the external world conveyed to his distracted consciousness by his defectively operating senses. It is easier and more convenient for him to allow his brain-centres to produce semi-lucid, nebulously blurred ideas and inchoate embryonic thoughts, and to surrender himself to the perpetual obfuscation of a boundless, aimless, and shoreless stream of fugitive ideas; and he rarely rouses himself to the painful attempt to check or counteract the capricious, and, as a rule, purely mechanical associations of ideas and succession of images, and bring under discipline the disorderly tumult of his fluid presentations. On the contrary, he rejoices in his faculty of imagination, which he contrasts with the insipidity of the Philistine, and devotes himself with predilection to all sorts of unlicensed pursuits permitted by the unshackled vagabondage of his mind; while he cannot endure well-ordered civil occupations, requiring attention and constant heed to reality. He calls this 'having an idealist temperament,' ascribes to himself irresistible aesthetic propinquities, and proudly styles himself an artist.[o]

We will briefly mention some peculiarities frequently manifested by a degen-erate. He is tormented by doubts, seeks for the basis of all phenomena, especially those whose first causes are completely inaccessible to us, and is unhappy when his inquiries and ruminations lead, as is natural, to no result.[p] He is ever supplying new recruits to the army of system-inventing metaphysicians, profound expositors of the riddle of the universe, seekers for the philosopher's

o   [Jean-Martin] Charcot, 'Leçons du Mardi à la Salpêtrière,' *Policlinique*, Paris, 1890, 2ᵉ partie, p. 392: 'This person {the invalid mentioned} is a performer at fairs; he calls himself "artist." The truth is that his art consists in personating a "wild man" in fair-booths.'

p   Legrain, *op. cit.*, p. 73: 'The patients are perpetually tormented by a multitude of questions which invade their minds, and to which they can give no answer; inexpressible moral sufferings result from this incapacity. Doubt envelops every possible subject: – metaphysics, theology, etc.'

stone, the squaring of the circle and perpetual motion.[q] These last three subjects have such a special attraction for him, that the Patent Office at Washington is forced to keep on hand printed replies to the numberless memorials in which patents are constantly demanded for the solution of these chimerical problems. In view of Lombroso's researches,[r] it can scarcely be doubted that the writings and acts of revolutionists and anarchists are also attributable to degeneracy. The degenerate is incapable of adapting himself to existing circumstances. This incapacity, indeed, is an indication of morbid variation in every species, and probably a primary cause of their sudden extinction. He therefore rebels against conditions and views of things which he necessarily feels to be painful, chiefly because they impose upon him the duty of self-control, of which he is incapable on account of his organic weakness of will. Thus he becomes an improver of the world, and devises plans for making mankind happy, which, without exception, are conspicuous quite as much by their fervent philanthropy, and often pathetic sincerity, as by their absurdity and monstrous ignorance of all real relations.

Finally, a cardinal mark of degeneration which I have reserved to the last, is mysticism. Colin says:[s] 'Of all the delirious manifestations peculiar to the hereditarily-afflicted, none indicates the condition more clearly, we think, than mystical delirium, or, when the malady has not reached this point, the being constantly occupied with mystical and religious questions, an exaggerated piety, etc.' I will not here multiply evidence and quotations. In the following books, where the art and poetry of the times are treated of, I shall find occasion to show the reader that no difference exists between these tendencies and the religious manias observed in nearly all degenerates and sufferers from hereditary mental taint.

I have enumerated the most important features characterizing the mental condition of the degenerate. The reader can now judge for himself whether or not the diagnosis 'degeneration' is applicable to the originators of the new aesthetic tendencies. It must not for that matter be supposed that degeneration is synonymous with absence of talent. Nearly all the inquirers who have had degenerates under their observation expressly establish the contrary. 'The degenerate,' says Legrain,[t] 'may be a genius. A badly balanced mind is susceptible of the highest conceptions, while, on the other hand, one meets in the same mind with traits of meanness and pettiness all the more striking from the fact that they co-exist with the most brilliant qualities.' We shall find this reservation in all

q  Magnan, 'Considérations sur la Folie des Héréditaires ou Dégénerés,' *Progrès médical*, 1886, p. 1110 (in the report of a medical case): 'He also thought of seeking for the philosopher's stone, and of making gold.'
r  Lombroso, 'La Physionomie des Anarchistes,' *Nouvelle Revue*, May 15, 1891, p. 227: 'They {the anarchists} frequently have those characteristics of degeneracy which are common to criminals and lunatics, for they are anomalies, and bear hereditary taints.' See also the same author's *Pazzi ed Anomali.* Turin, 1884.
s  Colin, *op. cit.*, p. 154.
t  Legrain, *op. cit.*, p. 11.

authors who have contributed to the natural history of the degenerate. 'As regards their intellect, they can,' says Roubinovitch,[u] 'attain to a high degree of development, but from a moral point of view their existence is completely deranged. . . . A degenerate will employ his brilliant faculties quite as well in the service of some grand object as in the satisfaction of the basest propensities.' Lombroso[v] has cited a large number of undoubted geniuses who were equally undoubted mattoids, graphomaniacs, or pronounced lunatics; and the utterance of a French savant, Guérinsen, 'Genius is a disease of the nerves,' has become a 'winged word.'[11] This expression was imprudent, for it gave ignorant blabbers a pretext, and apparently a right, to talk of exaggeration, and to contemn experts in nervous and mental diseases, because they professedly saw a lunatic in everyone who ventured to be something more than the most ordinary, character-less, average being. Science does not assert that every genius is a lunatic; there are some geniuses of super-abundant power whose high privilege consists in the possession of one or other extraordinarily developed faculty, without the rest of their faculties falling short of the average standard. Just as little, naturally, is every lunatic a genius; most of them, even if we disregard idiots of different degrees, are much rather pitiably stupid and incapable; but in many, nay, in abundant cases, the 'higher degenerate' of Magnan, just as he occasionally exhibits gigantic bodily stature or the disproportionate growth of particular parts, has some mental gift exceptionally developed at the cost, it is true, of the remaining faculties, which are wholly or partially atrophied.[w] It is this which enables the well-informed to distinguish at the first glance between the sane genius, and the highly, or even the most highly, gifted degenerate. Take from the former the special capacity through which he becomes a genius, and there still remains a capable, often conspicuously intelligent, clever, moral, and judicious man, who will hold his ground with propriety in our social mechanism. Let the same be tried in the case of a degenerate, and there remains only a criminal or madman, for whom healthy humanity can find no use. If Goethe[12] had never written a line of verse, he would, all the same, have still remained a man of the world, of good principles, a fine art connoisseur, a judicious collector, a keen observer of nature. Let us, on the contrary, imagine a Schopenhauer who had written no astounding books, and we should have before us only a repulsive *lusus*

---

u    Roubinovitch, *op. cit.*, p. 33

v    Lombroso, *Genie und Irrsinn*; German translation by A. Courth. Reclam's *Universal Bibliothek*, Bde. 2313–16. See also in particular, J[ohn] F[erguson] Nisbet, *The Insanity of Genius*. London, 1891.

w    [Jules Philippe] Falret, *Annales médico-psychologiques*, 1867, p. 76: 'From their childhood they usually display a very unequal development of their mental faculties, which, weak in their entirety, are remarkable for certain special aptitudes; they have shown an extraordinary gift for drawing, arithmetic, music, sculpture, or mechanics . . . and, together with those specially developed aptitudes, obtaining for them the fame of "infant phenomena," they for the most part give evidence of very great deficiencies in their intelligence, and of a radical debility in the remaining faculties.'

*naturae*,[13] whose morals would necessarily exclude him from all respectable society, and whose fixed idea that he was a victim of persecution would point him out as a subject for a madhouse. The lack of harmony, the absence of balance, the singular incapacity of usefully applying, or deriving satisfaction from, their own special faculty among highly-gifted degenerates, strikes every healthy censor who does not allow himself to be prejudiced by the noisy admiration of critics, themselves degenerates: and will always prevent his mistaking the mattoid for the same exceptional man who opens out new paths for humanity and leads it to higher developments. I do not share Lombroso's opinion[x] that highly-gifted degenerates are an active force in the progress of mankind. They corrupt and delude; they do, alas! frequently exercise a deep influence, but this is always a baneful one. It may not be at once remarked, but it will reveal itself subsequently. If contemporaries do not recognise it, the historian of morals will point it out *a posteriori*. They, likewise, are leading men along the paths they themselves have found to new goals; but these goals are abysses or waste places. They are guides to swamps like will-o'-the-wisps, or to ruin like the ratcatcher of Hammelin. Observers lay stress on their unnatural sterility. 'They are,' says Tarabaud,[y] 'cranks; wrongheaded, unbalanced, incapable creatures; they belong to the class of whom it may not be said that they have no mind, but whose mind produces nothing.' 'A common type,' writes Legrain,[z] 'unites them: – weakness of judgement and unequal development of mental powers. . . . Their conceptions are never of a high order. They are incapable of great thoughts and prolific ideas. This fact forms a peculiar contrast to the frequently excessive development of their powers of imagination.' 'If they are painters,' we read in Lombroso,[aa] 'then their predominant attribute will be the colour-sense; they will be decorative. If they are poets, they will be rich in rhyme, brilliant in style, but barren of thought; sometimes they will be "decadents".'

Such are the qualities of the most gifted of those who are discovering new paths, and are proclaimed by enthusiastic followers as the guides to the promised land of the future. Among them degenerates and mattoids predominate. The second of the above-mentioned diagnosis, on the contrary, applies for the most part to the multitude who admire these individuals and swear by them, who imitate the fashions they design, and take delight in the extravagances described in the previous chapter. In their case we have to deal chiefly with hysteria, or neurasthenia.

For reasons which will be elucidated in the next chapter, hysteria has hitherto been less studied in Germany than in France, where, more than elsewhere, it has formed a subject of earnest inquiry. We owe what we know of it almost exclusively to French investigators. The copious treatises of Axenfeld,[bb] Richter,[cc] and

x   *Nouvelle Revue,* July 15, 1891.
y   Tarabaud, *Des Rapports de la Dégénérescence mentale et de l'Hystérie.* Paris, 1888, p. 12.
z   Legrain, *op. cit.,* pp. 24 and 26.
aa  Lombroso, *Nouvelles recherches de Psychiatrie et d'Anthropologie criminelle.* Paris, 1892, p. 74.

in particular Gilles de la Tourette,[dd] adequately comprise our present knowledge of this malady; and I shall refer to these works when I enumerate the symptoms chiefly indicative of hysteria.

Among the hysterical – and it must not be thought that these are met with exclusively, or even preponderantly, among females, for they are quite as often, perhaps oftener, found among males[ee] – among the hysterical, as among the degenerate, the first thing which strikes us is an extraordinary emotionalism. 'The leading characteristic of the hysterical,' says Colin,[ff] 'is the disproportionate impressionability of their psychic centres. . . . They are, above all things, impressionable.' From this primary peculiarity proceeds a second quite as remarkable and important – the exceeding ease with which they can be made to yield to suggestion.[gg] The earlier observers always mentioned the boundless mendacity of the hysterical; growing, indeed, quite indignant at it, and making it the most prominent mark of the mental condition of such patients. They were mistaken. The hysterical subject does not consciously lie. He believes in the truth of his craziest inventions. The morbid mobility of his mind, the excessive excitability of his imagination, conveys to his consciousness all sorts of queer and senseless ideas. He suggests to himself that these ideas are founded on true perceptions, and believes in the truth of his foolish inventions until a new suggestion – perhaps his own, perhaps that of another person – has ejected the earlier one. A result of the susceptibility of the hysterical subject to suggestion is his irresistible passion for imitation,[hh] and the eagerness with which he yields to all the suggestions of writers and artists.[ii] When he sees a picture, he wants to become like it in attitude and dress; when he reads a book, he adopts its views blindly. He takes as a pattern the heroes of the novels which he has in his hand at the moment, and infuses himself into the characters moving before him on the stage.

Added to this emotionalism and susceptibility to suggestion is a love of self never met with in a sane person in anything like the same degree. The hysterical person's own 'I' towers up before his inner vision, and so completely fills his mental horizon that it conceals the whole of the remaining universe. He cannot endure that others should ignore him. He desires to be as important to his fellow-men as he is to himself. 'An incessant need pursues and governs the hysterical – to busy those about them with themselves.'[jj] A means of satisfying this

bb  [Alexandre] Axenfeld, *Des Névroses*. 2 vols., 2ᵉ édition, revue et complétée par le Dr Huchard. Paris, 1879.
cc  Paul Richer, *Etudes cliniques sur l'Hystéro-épilepsie ou Grande Hystérie*. Paris, 1891.
dd  Gilles de la Tourette, *Traité clinique et thérapeutique de l'Hystérie*. Paris, 1891.
ee  Paul Michaut, *Contribution à l'Etude des Manifestations de l'Hystérie chez l'Homme*. Paris 1890.
ff  Colin, *op. cit.*, p. 14.
gg  Gilles de la Tourette, *op. cit.*, p. 548 *et passim*.
hh  Colin, *op. cit.*, pp. 15 and 16.
ii  Gilles de la Tourette, *op. cit.*, p. 493.
jj  *Ibid.*, p. 303.

need is the fabrication of stories by which they become interesting. Hence come the adventurous occurrences which often enough occupy the police and the reports of the daily press. In the busiest thoroughfare the hysterical person is set upon, robbed, maltreated and wounded, dragged to a distant place, and left to die. He picks himself up painfully, and informs the police. He can show the wounds on his body. He gives all the details. And there is not a single word of truth in the whole story; it is all dreamt and imagined. He has himself inflicted his wounds in order for a short time to become the centre of public attention. In the lower stages of hysteria this need of making a sensation assumes more harmless forms. It displays itself in eccentricities of dress and behaviour. 'Other hysterical subjects are passionately fond of glaring colours and extravagant forms; they wish to attract attention and make themselves talked about.'[kk]

It is certainly unnecessary to draw the reader's attention in a special manner to the complete coincidence of this clinical picture of hysteria with the description of the peculiarities of the *fin-de-siècle* public, and to the fact that in the former we meet with all the features made familiar to us by the consideration of contemporary phenomena; in particular with the passion for imitating in externals – in dress, attitude, fashion of the hair and beard – the figures in old and modern pictures, and the feverish effort, through any sort of singularity, to make themselves talked about. The observation of pronounced cases of degeneration and hysteria, whose condition makes them necessary subjects for medical treatment, gives us also the key to the comprehension of subordinate details in the fashions of the day. The present rage for collecting, the piling up, in dwellings, of aimless bric-à-brac, which does not become any more useful or beautiful by being fondly called *bibelots*,[14] appear to us in a completely new light when we know that Magnan has established the existence of an irresistible desire among the degenerate to accumulate useless trifles. It is so firmly imprinted and so peculiar that Magnan declares it to be a stigma of degeneration, and has invented for it the name 'oniomania,' or 'buying craze.' This is not be confounded with the desire for buying, which possesses those who are in the first stage of general paralysis. The purchases of these persons are due to their delusion as to their own greatness. They lay in great supplies because they fancy themselves millionaires. The oniomaniac, on the contrary, neither buys enormous quantities of one and the same thing, nor is the price a matter of indifference to him as with the paralytic. He is simply unable to pass by any lumber without feeling an impulse to acquire it.

The curious style of certain recent painters – 'impressionists,' 'stipplers,' or 'mosaists,' 'papilloteurs' or 'quiverers,' 'roaring' colourists, dyers in gray and faded tints – becomes at once intelligible to us if we keep in view the researches of the Charcot school into the visual derangements in degeneration and hysteria.[15] The painters who assure us that they are sincere, and reproduce

kk  Legrain, *op. cit.*, p. 39.

nature as they see it, speak the truth. The degenerate artist who suffers from *nystagmus*, or trembling of the eyeball, will, in fact, perceive the phenomena of nature trembling, restless, devoid of firm outline, and, if he is a conscientious painter, will give us pictures reminding us of the mode practised by the draftsmen of the *Fliegende Blätter*[16] when they represent a wet dog shaking himself vigorously. If his pictures fail to produce a comic effect, it is only because the attentive beholder reads in them the desperate effort to reproduce fully an impression incapable of reproduction by the expedients of the painter's art as devised by men of normal vision.

There is hardly a hysterical subject whose retina is not partly insensitive.[ll] As a rule the insensitive parts are connected, and include the outer half of the retina. In these cases the field of vision is more or less contracted, and appears to him not as it does to the normal man – as a circle – but as a picture bordered by whimsically zigzag lines. Often, however, the insensitive parts are not connected, but are scattered in isolated spots over the entire retina. Then the sufferer will have all sorts of gaps in his field of vision, producing strange effects, and if he paints what he sees, he will be inclined to place in juxtaposition larger or smaller points or spots which are completely or partially dissociated. The insensitiveness need not be complete, and may exist only in the case of single colours, or of all. If the sensitiveness is completely lost ('achromatopsy') he then sees everything in a uniform grey, but perceives differences in the degree of lustre. Hence the picture of nature presents itself to him as a copper-plate or a pencil drawing, where the effect of the absent colours is replaced by differences in the intensity of light, by greater or less depth and power of the white and black portions. Painters who are insensitive to colour will naturally have a predilection for neutral-toned painting; and a public suffering from the same malady will find nothing objectionable in falsely-coloured pictures. But if, besides the whitewash of a Puvis de Chavannes, obliterating all colours equally, fanatics are found for the screaming yellow, blue, and red of a Besnard, this also has a cause, revealed to us by clinical science.[17] 'Yellow and blue,' Gilles de la Tourette[mm] teaches us, 'are peripheral colours' (*i.e.*, they are seen with the outermost parts of the retina); 'they are, therefore, the last to be perceived' (if the sensitiveness for the remaining colours is destroyed). 'These are ... the very two colours the sensations of which in hysterical amblyopia {dulness of vision} endure the longest. In many cases, however, it is the red, and not the blue, which vanishes last.'

Red has also another peculiarity explanatory of the predilection shown for it by the hysterical. The experiments of Binet[nn] have established that the impres-

ll   Dr Emile Berger, *Les Maladies des Yeux dans leurs rapports avec la Pathologie général.* Paris, 1892, p. 129 *et seq.*
mm  *Traité clinique et thérapeutique de l'Hystérie,* p. 339. See also Drs A. Marie et J. Bonnet, *La Vision chez Idiots et les Imbéciles.* Paris, 1892.
nn  Alfred Binet, 'Recherches sur les Altérations de la Conscience chez les Hystériques,' *Revue philosophique,* 1889, vol xxvii.

sions conveyed to the brain by the sensory nerves exercise an important influence on the species and strength of the excitation distributed by the brain to the motor nerves. Many sense-impressions operate enervatingly and inhibitively on the movements; others, on the contrary, make these more powerful, rapid and active; they are 'dynamogenous,' or 'force-producing.' As a feeling of pleasure is always connected with dynamogeny, or the production of force, every living thing, therefore, instinctively seeks for dynamogenous sense-impressions, and avoids enervating and inhibitive ones. Now, red is especially dynamogenous. 'When,' says Binet,[oo] in a report of an experiment on a female hysterical subject who was paralyzed in one half of her body, 'we place a dynamometer in the anaesthestically insensible right hand of Amélie Cle . . . . . . the pressure of the hand amounts to 12 kilogrammes. If at the same time she is made to look at a red disc, the number indicating the pressure in kilogrammes is at once doubled.' Hence it is intelligible that hysterical painters revel in red, and that hysterical beholders take special pleasure in pictures operating dynamogenously, and producing feelings of pleasure.

If red is dynamogenous, violet is conversely enervating and inhibitive.[pp] It was not by accident that violet was chosen by many nations as the exclusive colour for mourning, and by us also for half-mourning. The sight of this colour has a depressing effect, and the unpleasant feeling awakened by it induces dejection in a sorrowfully-disposed mind. This suggests that painters suffering from hysteria and neurasthenia will be inclined to cover their pictures uniformly with the colour most in accordance with their condition of lassitude and exhaustion. Thus originate the violet pictures of Manet and his school,[18] which spring from no actually observable aspect of nature, but from a subjective view due to the condition of the nerves. When the entire surface of walls in salons and art exhibitions of the day appears veiled in uniform half-mourning, this predilection for violet is simply an expression of the nervous debility of the painter.

There is yet another phenomenon highly characteristic in some cases of degeneracy, in others of hysteria. This is the formation of close groups or schools uncompromisingly exclusive to outsiders, observable to-day in literature and art. Healthy artists or authors, in possession of minds in a condition of well-regulated equilibrium, will never think of grouping themselves into an association, which may at pleasure be termed a sect or band; of devising a catechism, of binding themselves to definite aesthetic dogmas, and of entering the lists for these with the fanatical intolerance of Spanish inquisitors. If any human activity is individualistic, it is that of the artist. True talent is always personal. In its creations it reproduces itself, its own views and feelings, and not the articles of

oo  *Op. cit.*, p. 150.
pp  Ch. Féré, 'Sensation et Mouvement,' *Revue philosophique*, 1886. See also the same author's *Sensation et Mouvement*, Paris, 1887; *Dégénérescence et criminalité*, Paris 1888; and 'L'Energie et la Vitesse des Mouvements volontaires,' *Revue philosophique*, 1889.

faith learnt from any aesthetic apostle; it follows its creative impulses, not a theo-retical formula preached by the founder of a new artistic or literary church; it constructs its work in the form organically necessary to it, not in that proclaimed by a leader as demanded by the fashion of the day. The mere fact that an artist or author allows himself to be sworn in to the party cry of any 'ism,' that he perambulates with jubilations behind a banner and Turkish music, is complete evidence of his lack of individuality – that is, of talent. If the mental movements of a period – even those which are healthy and prolific – range themselves, as a rule, under certain main tendencies, which receive each its distinguishing name, this is the work of historians of civilization or literature, who subsequently survey the combined picture of an epoch, and for their own convenience undertake divisions and classifications, in order that they may more correctly find their way among the multifariousness of the phenomena. These are, however, almost always arbitrary and artificial. Independent minds (we are not here speaking of mere imitators), united by a good critic into a group, may, it is true, have a certain resemblance to each other, but, as a rule, this resemblance will be the consequence, not of actual internal affinity, but of external influences. No one is able completely to withdraw himself from the influences of his time, and under the impression of events which affect all contemporaries alike, as well as of the scientific views prevailing at a given time, certain features develop themselves in all the works of an epoch, which stamp them as of the same date. But the same men who subsequently appear so naturally in each other's company, in historical works, that they seem to form a family, went when they lived their separate ways far asunder, little suspecting that at one time they would be united under one common designation. Quite otherwise it is when authors or artists consciously and intentionally meet together and found an aesthetic school, as a joint-stock bank is founded, with a title for which, if possible, the protection of the law is claimed, with by-laws, joint capital, etc. This may be ordinary speculation, but as a rule it is disease. The predilection for forming societies met with among all the degenerate and hysterical may assume different forms. Criminals unite in bands, as Lombroso expressly establishes.[qq] Among pronounced lunatics it is the *folie à deux*, in which a deranged person completely forces his insane ideas on a companion; among the hysterical it assumes the form of close friendships, causing Charcot to repeat at every opportunity: 'Persons of highly-strung nerves attract each other;'[rr] and finally authors found schools.

The common organic basis of these different forms of one and the same phenomenon – of the *folie à deux*, the association of neuropaths, the founding of aesthetic schools, the banding of criminals – is, with the active part, viz., those who lead and inspire, the predominance of obsessions: with the associates, the disciples, the submissive part, weakness of will and morbid susceptibility to

qq  Lombroso, *L'Uomo délinquente*, p. 524.
rr  'Les Nerveux se recherchent,' Charcot, *Leçons du Mardi, passim.*

suggestion.[ss] The possessor of an obsession is an incomparable apostle. There is no rational conviction arrived at by sound labour of intellect, which so completely takes possession of the mind, subjugates so tyrannically its entire activity, and so irresistibly impels it to words and deeds, as delirium. Every proof of the senselessness of his ideas rebounds from the deliriously insane or half-crazy person. No contradiction, no ridicule, no contempt, affects him; the opinion of the majority is to him a matter of indifference; facts which do not please him he does not notice, or so interprets that they seem to support his delirium; obstacles do not discourage him, because even his instinct of self-preservation is unable to cope with the power of his delirium, and for the same reason he is often enough ready, without further ado, to suffer martyrdom. Weak-minded or mentally-unbalanced persons, coming into contact with a man possessed by delirium, are at once conquered by the strength of his diseased ideas, and are converted to them. By separating them from the source of inspiration, it is often possible to cure them of their transmitted delirium, but frequently their acquired derangement outlasts this separation.

This is the natural history of the aesthetic schools. Under the influence of an obsession, a degenerate mind promulgates some doctrine or other – realism, pornography, mysticism, symbolism, diabolism. He does this with vehement penetrating eloquence, with eagerness and fiery heedlessness. Other degenerate, hysterical, neurasthenical minds flock around him, receive from his lips the new doctrine, and live thenceforth only to propagate it.

In this case all the participants are sincere – the founder as well as the disciples. They act as, in consequence of the diseased constitution of their brain and nervous system, they are compelled to act. The picture, however, which from a clinical standpoint is perfectly clear, gets dimmed if the apostle of a craze and his followers succeed in attracting to themselves the attention of wider circles. He then receives a concourse of unbelievers, who are very well able to recognise the insanity of the new doctrine, but who nevertheless accept it, because they hope, as associates of the new sect, to acquire fame and money. In every civilized nation which has a developed art and literature there are numerous intellectual eunuchs, incapable of producing with their own powers a living mental work, but quite able to imitate the process of production. These cripples form, unfortunately, the majority of professional authors and artists, and their many noxious followers often enough stifle true and original talent. Now it is these who hasten to act as camp-followers for every new tendency which seems to come into fashion. They are naturally the most modern of moderns, for no precept of individuality, no artistic knowledge, hinders them from bunglingly imitating the newest model with all the assiduity of an artisan. Clever in discerning externals,

ss   Legrain, *op. cit.*, p. 173: 'The true explanation of the occurrence of *folie à deux* must be sought for, on the one hand, in the predisposition to insanity, and, on the other hand, in the accompanying weakness of mind.' See also [Emmanuel] Régis, *La Folie à Deux*. Paris, 1880.

unscrupulous copyists and plagiarists, they crowd round every original phenomenon, be it healthy or unhealthy, and without loss of time set about disseminating counterfeit copies of it. To-day they are symbolists, as yesterday they were realists or pornographists. If they can promise themselves fame and a good sale, they write of mysteries with the same fluency as if they were spinning romances of knights and robbers, tales of adventure, Roman tragedies, and village stories at a time when newspaper critics and the public seemed to demand these things in preference to others. Now these practitioners, who, let it be again asserted, constitute the great majority of the mental workers of the fashionable sects in art and literature, and therefore of the associates of these sects also, are intellectually quite sane, even if they stand at a very low level of development, and were anyone to examine them, he might easily doubt the accuracy of the diagnosis 'Degeneration' as regards the confessors of the new doctrines. Hence some caution must be exercised in the inquiry, and the sincere originators be always distinguished from the aping intriguers, – the founder of the religion and his apostles from the rabble to whom the Sermon on the Mount is of less concern than the miraculous draught of fishes and the multiplication of loaves.

It has now been shown how schools originate. They arise from the degeneration of their founders and of the imitators they have convinced. That they come into fashion, and for a short time attain a noisy success, is due to the peculiarities of the recipient public, namely, to hysteria. We have seen that hypersusceptibility to suggestion is the distinguishing characteristic of hysteria. The same power of obsession with which the degenerate in mind wins imitators, gathers round him adherents. When a hysterical person is loudly and unceasingly assured that a work is beautiful, deep, pregnant with the future, he believes in it. He believes in everything suggested to him with sufficient impressiveness. When the little cowgirl, Bernadette, saw the vision of the Holy Virgin in the grotto of Lourdes,[19] the women devotees and hysterical males of the surrounding country who flocked thither did not merely believe that the hallucinate maiden had herself seen the vision, but all of them saw the Holy Virgin with their own eyes. M E. de Goncourt[tt] relates that in 1870, during the Franco-Prussian War, a multitude of men, numbering tens of thousands, in and before the Bourse[20] in Paris, were convinced that they had themselves seen – indeed, a part of them had read – a telegram announcing French victories fastened to a pillar inside the Exchange, and at which people were pointing with their finger; but as a matter of fact it never existed. It would be possible to cite examples by the dozen, of illusions of the senses suggested to excited crowds. Thus the hysterical allow themselves without more ado to be convinced of the magnificence of a work, and even find in it beauties of the highest kind, unthought of by the authors themselves and the appointed trumpeters of their fame. If the sect is so completely established

tt  *Journal des Goncourts*. Dernière série, premier volume, 1870–71. Paris, 1890, p. 17.

that, in addition to the founders, the priests of the temple, the paid sacristans and choir-boys, it has a congregation, processions, and far-sounding bells, it then attaches to itself other converts besides the hysterical who have accepted the new belief by way of suggestion. Young persons without judgement, still seeking their way, go whither they see the multitude streaming, and unhesitatingly follow the procession, because they believe it to be marching on the right road. Superficial persons, fearing nothing so much as to be thought behind the times, attach themselves to the procession, shouting 'Hurrah!' and 'All hail!' so as to convince themselves that they also are really dancing along before the latest conqueror and newest celebrity. Decrepit greybeards, filled with a ridiculous dread of betraying their real age, eagerly visit the new temple and mingle their quavering voices in the song of the devout, because they hope to be thought young when seen in an assembly in which young persons predominate.

Thus a regular concourse is established about a victim of degeneration. The fashionable coxcomb, the aesthetic 'gigerl,'[uu] peeps over the shoulder of the hysterical whose admiration has been suggested to him; the intriguer marches at the heel of the dotard, simulating youth; and between all these comes pushing the inquisitive young street-loafer, who must always be in every place where 'something is going on.' And this crowd, because it is driven by disease, self-interest and vanity, makes very much more noise and bustle than a far larger number of sane men, who, without self-seeking after-thought, take quiet enjoyment in works of sane talent, and do not feel obliged to shout out their appreciation in the streets, and to threaten with death harmless passers-by who do not join in their jubilations.

uu  Viennese for 'fop.' – TRANSLATOR.

# 9

# ART AND THE STATE

**WILLIAM MORRIS, 'ART UNDER PLUTOCRACY' (1884)**

The life of William Morris (1834–96) was exceptional both in terms of its diversity and productivity. After his education at Exeter College, Oxford, Morris's literary career began with contributions of poems and romantic stories to the *Oxford and Cambridge Magazine* (founded in 1856). In 1858 Morris's first main work, *The Defence of Guenevere and Other Poems*, was published. In 1859 he married Jane Burden and began to build 'The Red House' (designed by Philip Webb) at Upton. His decision to design its furniture and furnishings led to the founding in 1861 of a company of decorators – Morris, Marshall, Faulkner & Co. – which specialised in producing high quality furniture, textiles, wallpapers and carpets. In 1865 the Red House was sold and Morris moved to Bloomsbury. The year 1867 saw the publication of his next major poetical work, *The Life and Death of Jason*, followed in 1868–70 by *The Earthly Paradise* which established his reputation as one of the period's most popular poets. In 1869 Morris produced the 'Gretta Saga' – the first of several Icelandic translations which later included *The Story of Sigurd the Volsung* (1876). In 1871 Morris moved for the third time – to Kelmscott Manor in Oxfordshire. That year he also visited Iceland. In 1873 *Love is Enough* was published, and in 1875 Morris reorganised and took control of the decorating company; in addition he produced a translation of Virgil's *Aeneid*. The 1870s was also notable for Morris's increasing involvement in public life: for example, in 1877 he founded and led a pressure group, the 'Society for the Protection of Ancient Buildings' (popularly known as 'Anti-scrape'), and he also became involved in politics – first as a liberal, campaigning in 1876 against Britain's attempt to preserve Turkish rule in the Balkans, and then, disillusioned with Gladstone's party, as a socialist. Much of Morris's energy for the next twenty years was devoted to propagandising socialism through his activities in organisations such as the Socialist League (founded in 1884 and dissolved in 1892) and through his writing and his lecturing. Indeed in this role Morris travelled all over the country speaking to many thousands of working people. From 1885–9 he edited and contributed to *The Commonweal* (the journal of the Socialist League) which printed his narrative poem, *The Pilgrims of Hope* (1886), and his socialist allegory, *News from Nowhere* (1891). The 1880s and 1890s also saw the publication of translations of Homer's *Odyssey* (1887) and, with A. J. Wyatt, *Beowulf* (1895); several stories and long prose romances – including *A Dream of John Ball and A King's Lesson* (1888), *The House of the Wolfings* (1889), *Roots of the Mountains* (1890), *The Story of the Glittering Plain* (1891), *The Wood Beyond the World* (1894) and *The Sundering Flood* (1897); *Poems by the Way* (1891); and two political works – with H. M. Hyndman, *A Summary of the Principles of Socialism* (1884) and with E. Bax, *Socialism: Its Growth and Outcome* (1893). In 1891 Morris founded the Kelmscott Press; he also suffered a serious illness and died in 1896, never having fully recovered his health.

### *From* William Morris, 'Art Under Plutocracy', *To-Day*, (February and March 1884)[1]

#### Art Under Plutocracy

You may well think I am not here to criticize any special school of art or artist, or to plead for any special style, or to give you any instructions, however general, as to the practice of the arts. Rather I want to take counsel with you as to what hindrances may lie in the way towards making art what it should be, a help and solace to the daily life of all men. Some of you here may think that the hindrances in the way are none, or few, and easy to be swept aside. You will say that there is on many sides much knowledge of the history of art, and plenty of taste for it, at least among the cultivated classes; that many men of talent, and some few of genius, practise it with no mean success; that within the last fifty years there has been something almost like a fresh renaissance of art, even in directions where such a change was least to be hoped for. All this is true as far as it goes; and I can well understand this state of things being a cause of gratulation amongst those who do not know what the scope of art really is, and how closely it is bound up with the general condition of society, and especially with the lives of those who live by manual labour and whom we call the working classes. For my part, I cannot help noting that under the apparent satisfaction with the progress of art of late years there lies in the minds of most thinking people a feeling of mere despair as to the prospects of art in the future; a despair which seems to me fully justified if we look at the present condition of art without considering the causes which have led to it, or the hopes which may exist for a change in those causes. For, without beating about the bush, let us consider what the real state of art is. And first I must ask you to extend the word art beyond those matters which are consciously works of art, to take in not only painting and sculpture, and architecture, but the shapes and colours of all household goods, nay, even the arrangement of the fields for tillage and pasture, the management of towns and of our highways of all kinds; in a word, to extend it to the aspect of all the externals of our life. For I must ask you to believe that every one of the things that goes to make up the surroundings among which we live must be either beautiful or ugly, either elevating or degrading to us, either a torment and burden to the maker of it to make, or a pleasure and a solace to him. How does it fare therefore with our external surroundings in these days? What kind of an account shall we be able to give to those who come after us of our dealings with the earth, which our forefathers handed down to us still beautiful, in spite of all the thousands of years of strife and carelessness and selfishness?

Surely this is no light question to ask ourselves; nor am I afraid that you will think it a mere rhetorical flourish if I say that it is a question that may well seem a solemn one when it is asked here in Oxford, amidst sights and memories which we older men at least regard with nothing short of love. He must be indeed a man of narrow incomplete mind, who, amidst the buildings raised by the hopes of our forefathers, amidst the country which they made so lovely, would venture to say that the beauty of the earth was a matter of little moment. And yet, I say, how have we of these latter days treated the beauty of the earth, or that which we call art?

Perhaps I had best begin by stating what will scarcely be new to you, that art must be broadly divided into two kinds, of which we may call the first Intellectual, and the second Decorative Art, using the words as mere forms of convenience. The first kind addresses itself wholly to our mental needs; the things made by it serve no other purpose but to feed the mind, and, as far as material needs go, might be done without altogether. The second, though so much of it as is art does also appeal to the mind, is always but a part of things which are intended primarily for the service of the body. I must further say that there have been nations and periods which lacked the purely Intellectual art but positively none which lacked the Decorative (or at least some pretence of it); and furthermore, that in all times when the arts were in a healthy condition there was an intimate connexion between the two kinds of art; a connexion so close, that in the times when art flourished most, the higher and lower kinds were divided by no hard and fast lines. The highest intellectual art was meant to please the eye, as the phrase goes, as well as to excite the emotions and train the intellect. It appealed to all men, and to all the faculties of a man. On the other hand, the

435

humblest of the ornamental art shared in the meaning and emotion of the intellectual; one melted into the other by scarce perceptible gradations; in short, the best artist was a workman still, the humblest workman was an artist. This is not the case now, nor has been for two or three centuries in civilized countries. Intellectual art is separated from Decorative by the sharpest lines of demarcation, not only as to the kind of work produced under those names, but even in the social position of the producers; those who follow the Intellectual arts being all professional men or gentlemen by virtue of their calling, while those who follow the Decorative are workmen earning weekly wages, non-gentlemen in short.

Now, as I have already said, many men of talent and some few of genius are engaged at present in producing works of Intellectual art, paintings and sculpture chiefly. It is nowise my business here or elsewhere to criticize their works; but my subject compels me to say that those who follow the Intellectual arts must be divided into two sections, the first composed of men who would in any age of the world have held a high place in their craft; the second of men who hold their position of gentleman-artist either by the accident of their birth, or by their possessing industry, business habits, or such-like qualities, out of all proportion to their artistic gifts. The work which these latter produce seems to me of little value to the world, though there is a thriving market for it, and their position is neither dignified nor wholesome; yet they are mostly not to be blamed for it personally, since often they have gifts for art, though not great ones, and would probably not have succeeded in any other career. They are, in fact, good decorative workmen spoiled by a system which compels them to ambitious individualist effort, by cutting off from them any opportunity for co-operation with others of greater or less capacity for the production of popular art.

As to the first section of artists, who worthily fill their places and make the world wealthier by their work, it must be said of them that they are very few. These men have won their mastery over their craft by dint of incredible toil, pains, and anxiety, by qualities of mind and strength of will which are bound to produce something of value. Nevertheless they are injured also by the system which insists on individualism and forbids co-operation. For first, they are cut off from tradition, that wonderful, almost miraculous accumulation of the skill of ages, which men find themselves partakers in without effort on their part. The knowledge of the past and the sympathy with it which the artists of to-day have, they have acquired, on the contrary, by their own most strenuous individual effort; and as that tradition no longer exists to help them in their practice of the art, and they are heavily weighted in the race by having to learn everything from the beginning, each man for himself, so also, and that is worse, the lack of it deprives them of a sympathetic and appreciative audience.

Apart from the artists themselves and a few persons who would be also artists but for want of opportunity and for insufficient gifts of hand and eye, there is in the public of to-day no real knowledge of art, and little love for it. Nothing, save at the best certain vague prepossessions, which are but the phantom of that tradition which once bound artist and public together. Therefore the artists are obliged to express themselves, as it were, in a language not understanded of the people. Nor is this their fault. If they were to try, as some think they should, to meet the public half-way and work in such a manner as to satisfy at any cost those vague prepossessions of men ignorant of art, they would be casting aside their special gifts, they would be traitors to the cause of art, which it is their duty and glory to serve. They have no choice save to do their own personal individual work unhelped by the present, stimulated by the past, but shamed by it, and even in a way hampered by it; they must stand apart as possessors of some sacred mystery which, whatever happens, they must at least do their best to guard. It is not to be doubted that both their own lives and their works are injured by this isolation. But the loss of the people; how are we to measure that? That they should have great men living and working amongst them, and be ignorant of the very existence of their work, and incapable of knowing what it means if they could see it!

In the times when art was abundant and healthy, all men were more or less artists; that is to say, the instinct for beauty which is inborn in every complete man had such force that the whole body of craftsmen habitually and without conscious effort made beautiful things, and the audience for the authors of intellectual art was nothing short of the whole people. And so they had each an assured hope of gaining that genuine praise and sympathy which all men who exercise their imagination in expression most certainly and naturally crave, and the lack of which does certainly injure them in some way; makes them shy, over-sensitive, and narrow, or else cynical and mocking, and in that case well-nigh useless. But in these days, I have said and repeat, the whole people is careless and ignorant of art; the inborn instinct for beauty is checked and thwarted at every turn; and the result on the less intellectual or decorative art is that as a spontaneous and popular expression of the instinct for beauty it does not exist at all.

It is a matter of course that everything made by man's hand is now obviously ugly, unless it is made beautiful by conscious effort; nor does it mend the matter that men have not lost the habit deduced from the times of art, of professing to ornament household goods and the like; for this sham ornament, which has no least intention of giving anyone pleasure, is so base and foolish that the words upholstery and upholsterer have come to have a kind of secondary meaning indicative of the profound contempt which all sensible men have for such twaddle.

This, so far, is what decorative art has come to, and I must break off a while here and ask you to consider what it once was, lest you think over hastily that its degradation is a matter of little moment. Think, I beg you, to go no further back in history, of the stately and careful beauty of S. Sophia at Constantinople, of the golden twilight of S. Mark's at Venice, of the sculptured cliffs of the great French cathedrals,[2] of the quaint and familiar beauty of our own minsters; nay, go through Oxford streets and ponder on what is left us there unscathed by the fury of the thriving shop and the progressive college; or wander some day through some of the out-of-the-way villages and little towns that lie scattered about the country-side within twenty miles of Oxford; and you will surely see that the loss of decorative art is a grievous loss to the world.

Thus then in considering the state of art among us I have been driven to the conclusion that in its co-operative form it is extinct, and only exists in the conscious efforts of men of genius and talent, who themselves are injured, and thwarted, and deprived of due sympathy by the lack of co-operative art.

But furthermore, the repression of the instinct for beauty which has destroyed the Decorative and injured the Intellectual arts has not stopped there in the injury it has done us. I can myself sympathize with a feeling which I suppose is still not rare, a craving to escape sometimes to mere Nature, not only from ugliness and squalor, not only from a condition of superabundance of art, but even from a condition of art severe and well ordered, even, say, from such surroundings as the lovely simplicity of Periclean Athens.[3] I can deeply sympathize with a weary man finding his account in interest in mere life and communion with external nature, the face of the country, the wind and weather, and the course of the day, and the lives of animals, wild and domestic; and man's daily dealings with all this for his daily bread, and rest, and innocent beast-like pleasure. But the interest in the mere animal life of man has become impossible to be indulged in in its fulness by most civilized people. Yet civilization, it seems to me, owes us some compensation for the loss of this romance, which now only hangs like a dream about the country life of busy lands. To keep the air pure and the rivers clean, to take some pains to keep the meadows and tillage as pleasant as reasonable use will allow them to be; to allow peaceable citizens freedom to wander where they will, so they do no hurt to garden or cornfield; nay, even to leave here and there some piece of waste or mountain sacredly free from fence or tillage as a memory of man's ruder struggles with nature in his earlier days: is it too much to ask civilization to be so far thoughtful of man's pleasure and rest, and to help so far as this her children to whom she has most often set such heavy tasks of grinding labour? Surely not an unreasonable asking. But not a whit of it shall we get under the present system of society. That loss of the instinct for beauty which has involved us in the loss of popular art is also busy in depriving us of the only compensation possible for that loss, by surely and not slowly destroying the beauty of the very face of the earth. Not only are London and our other great commercial cities mere masses of sordidness, filth, and squalor, embroidered with patches of pompous and vulgar hideousness, no less revolting to the eye and the mind when one knows what it means: not only have whole counties of England, and the heavens that hang over them, disappeared beneath a crust of unutterable grime, but the disease, which, to a visitor coming from the times of art, reason, and order, would seem to be a love of dirt and ugliness for its own sake, spreads all over the country, and every little market-town seizes the opportunity to imitate, as far as it can, the majesty of the hell of London and Manchester. Need I speak to you of the wretched suburbs that sprawl all round our fairest and most ancient cities? Must I speak to you of the degradation that has so speedily befallen this city, still the most beautiful of them all; a city which, with its surroundings, would, if we had had a grain of common sense, have been treated like a most precious jewel, whose beauty was to be preserved at any cost? I say at any cost, for it was a possession which did not belong to us, but which we were trustees of for all posterity. I am old enough to know how we have treated that jewel; as if it were any common stone kicking about on the highway, good enough to throw at a dog. When I remember the contrast between the Oxford of to-day and the Oxford which I first saw thirty years ago, I wonder I can face the misery (there is no other word for it) of visiting it, even to have the honour of addressing you to-night. But furthermore, not only are the cities a disgrace to us, and the smaller towns a laughing-stock; not only are the dwellings of man grown inexpressibly base and ugly, but the very cowsheds and cart-stables, nay, the merest piece of necessary farm-engineering, are tarred with the same brush. Even if a tree is cut down or blown down, a worse one, if any, is planted in its stead, and, in short, our civilization is passing like a blight, daily growing heavier and more poisonous, over the whole face of the country, so that every change is sure to be a change for the worse in its outward aspect. So then it comes to this, that not only are the minds of great artists narrowed and their sympathies frozen by their isolation, not only has co-operative art come to a standstill, but the very food on which both the greater and the lesser art subsists is being destroyed; the well of art is poisoned at its spring.

Now I do not wonder that those who think that these evils are from hence-forth for ever necessary to the progress of civilization should try to make the best of things, should shut their eyes to all they can, and praise the galvanized life of the art of the present day; but, for my part, I believe that they are not necessary to civilization, but only accompaniments to one phase of it, which will change and pass into something else, like all prior phases have done. I believe also that the essential characteristic of the present state of society is that which has so ruined art, or the pleasure of life; and that this having died out, the inborn love of man for beauty and the desire for expressing it will no longer be repressed, and art will be free. At the same time I not only admit, but declare, and think it most important to declare, that so long as the system of competition in the production and exchange of the means of life goes on, the degradation of the arts will go on; and if that system is to last for ever, then art is doomed, and will surely die; that is to say, civilization will die. I know it is at present the received opinion that the competitive or 'Devil take the hindmost' system is the last system of economy which the world will see; that it is perfection, and therefore finality has been reached in it; and it is doubtless a bold thing to fly in the face of this opinion, which I am told is held even by the most learned men. But though I am not learned, I have been taught that the patriarchal system died out into that of the citizen and chattel slave, which in its turn gave place to that of the feudal lord and the serf, which, passing through a modified form, in which the burgher, the gild-craftsman and his journeyman played their parts, was supplanted by the system of so-called free contract now existing. That all things since the beginning

439

of the world have been tending to the development of this system I willingly admit, since it exists; that all the events of history have taken place for the purpose of making it eternal, the very evolution of those events forbids me to believe.

For I am 'one of the people called Socialists;' therefore I am certain that evolution in the economical conditions of life will go on, whatever shadowy barriers may be drawn across its path by men whose apparent self-interest binds them, consciously or unconsciously, to the present, and who are therefore hopeless for the future. I hold that the condition of competition between man and man is bestial only, and that of associations human; I think that the change from the undeveloped competition of the Middle Ages, trammelled as it was by the personal relations of feudality, and the attempts at associations of the gild-craftsmen into the full-blown *laissez-faire*[4] competition of the nineteenth century, is bringing to birth out of its own anarchy, and by the very means by which it seeks to perpetuate that anarchy, a spirit of association founded on that antagonism which has produced all former changes in the condition of men, and which will one day abolish all classes and take definite and practical form, and substitute association for competition in all that relates to the production and exchange of the means of life. I further believe that as that change will be beneficent in many ways, so especially will it give an opportunity for the new birth of art, which is now being crushed to death by the money-bags of competitive commerce.

My reason for this hope for art is founded on what I feel quite sure is a truth, and an important one, namely that all art, even the highest, is influenced by the conditions of labour of the mass of mankind, and that any pretensions which may be made for even the highest intellectual art to be independent of these general conditions are futile and vain; that is to say, that any art which professes to be founded on the special education or refinement of a limited body or class must of necessity be unreal and short-lived. Art is man's expression of his joy in labour. If those are not Professor Ruskin's[5] words they embody at least his teaching on this subject. Nor has any truth more important ever been stated; for if pleasure in labour be generally possible, what a strange folly it must be for men to consent to labour without pleasure; and what a hideous injustice it must be for society to compel most men to labour without pleasure! For since all men not dishonest must labour, it becomes a question either of forcing them to lead unhappy lives or allowing them to live unhappily. Now the chief accusation I have to bring against the modern state of society is that it is founded on the art-lacking or unhappy labour of the greater part of men; and all that external degradation of the face of the country of which I have spoken is hateful to me not only because it is a cause of unhappiness to some few of us who still love art, but also and chiefly because it is a token of the unhappy life forced on the great mass of the population by a system of competitive commerce.

The pleasure which ought to go with the making of every piece of handicraft has for its basis the keen interest which every healthy man takes in healthy life, and is compounded, it seems to me, chiefly of three elements: variety, hope of creation, and the self-respect which comes of a sense of usefulness; to which must be added that mysterious bodily pleasure which goes with the deft exercise of the bodily powers. I do not think I need spend many words in trying to prove that these things, if they really and fully accompanied labour, would do much to make it pleasant. As to the pleasures of variety, any of you who have ever made anything, I don't care what, will well remember the pleasure that went with the turning out of the first specimen. What would have become of that pleasure if you had been compelled to go on making it exactly the same for ever? As to the hope of creation, the hope of producing some worthy or even excellent work which without you, the craftsman, would not have existed at all, a thing which needs you and can have no substitute for you in the making of it – can we any of us fail to understand the pleasure of this? No less easy, surely, is it to see how much the self-respect born of the consciousness of usefulness must sweeten labour. To feel that you have to do a thing not to satisfy the whim of a fool or a set of fools, but because it is really good in itself, that is useful, would surely be a good help to getting through the day's work. As to the unreasoning, sensuous pleasure in handiwork, I believe in good sooth that it has more power of getting rough and strenuous work out of men, even as things go, than most people imagine. At any rate it lies at the bottom of the production of all art, which cannot exist without it even in its feeblest and rudest form.

Now this compound pleasure in handiwork I claim as the birthright of all workmen. I say that if they lack any part of it they will be so far degraded, but that if they lack it altogether they are, so far as their work goes, I will not say slaves, the word would not be strong enough, but machines more or less conscious of their own unhappiness.

I have appealed already to history in aid of my hopes for a change in the system of the conditions of labour. I wish to bring forward now the witness of history that this claim of labour for pleasure rests on a foundation stronger than a mere fantastic dream; what is left of the art of all kinds produced in all periods and countries where hope of progress was alive before the development of the commercial system shows plainly enough to those who have eyes and understanding that pleasure did always in some degree accompany its production. This fact, however difficult it may be to demonstrate in a pedantic way, is abundantly admitted by those who have studied the arts widely; the very phrases so common in criticism that such and such a piece of would-be art is done mechanically, or done without feeling, express accurately enough the general sense of artists of a standard deduced from times of healthy art; for this mechanical and feelingless handiwork did not exist till days comparatively near our own, and it is the condition of labour under plutocratic rule which has allowed it any place at all.

The craftsman of the Middle Ages no doubt often suffered grievous material oppression, yet in spite of the rigid line of separation drawn by the hierarchical system under which he lived between him and his feudal superior, the difference between them was arbitrary rather than real; there was no such gulf in language, manners, and ideas as divides a cultivated middle-class person of to-day, a 'gentleman,' from even a respectable lower-class man; the mental qualities necessary to an artist, intelligence, fancy, imagination, had not then to go through the mill of the competitive market, nor had the rich (or successful competitors) made good their claim to be the sole possessors of mental refinement.

As to the conditions of handiwork in those days, the crafts were drawn together into gilds which indeed divided the occupations of men rigidly enough, and guarded the door to those occupations jealously; but as outside among the gilds there was little competition in the markets, wares being made in the first instance for domestic consumption, and only the overplus of what was wanted at home close to the place of production ever coming into the market or requiring anyone to come and go between the producer and consumer, so inside the gilds there was but little division of labour; a man or youth once accepted as an apprentice to a craft learned it from end to end, and became as a matter of course the master of it; and in the earlier days of the gilds, when the masters were scarcely small capitalists, there was no grade in the craft save this temporary one. Later on, when the masters became capitalists in a sort, and the apprentices were, like the masters, privileged, the class of journeymen-craftsmen came into existence; but it does not seem that the difference between them and the aristocracy of the gild was anything more than an arbitrary one. In short, during all this period the unit of labour was an intelligent man. Under this system of handiwork no great pressure of speed was put on a man's work, but he was allowed to carry it through leisurely and thoughtfully; it used the whole of a man for the production of a piece of goods, and not small portions of many men; it developed the workman's whole intelligence according to his capacity, instead of concentrating his energy on one-sided dealing with a trifling piece of work; in short, it did not submit the hand and soul of the workman to the necessities of the competitive market, but allowed them freedom for due human development. It was this system, which had not learned the lesson that man was made for commerce, but supposed in its simplicity that commerce was made for man, which produced the art of the Middle Ages, wherein the harmonious co-operation of free intelligence was carried to the furthest point which has yet been attained, and which alone of all art can claim to be called Free. The effect of this freedom, and the widespread or rather universal sense of beauty to which it gave birth, became obvious enough in the outburst of the expression of splendid and copious genius which marks the Italian Renaissance. Nor can it be doubted that this glorious art was the fruit of the five centuries of free popular art which preceded it, and not of the rise of commercialism which was contemporaneous with it; for the glory of the Renaissance faded out with strange rapidity as commercial competition developed, so that about the end of the seventeenth century, both in the intellectual and the decorative arts, the commonplace or body still existed, but the romance or soul of them was gone. Step by step they had faded and sickened before the advance of commercialism, now speedily gathering force throughout civilization. The domestic or architectural arts were becoming (or become) mere toys for the competitive market through which all material wares used by civilized men now had to pass. Commercialism had by this time well-nigh destroyed the craft-system of labour, in which, as aforesaid, the unit of labour is a fully instructed craftsman, and had supplanted it by what I will ask leave to call the workshop-system, wherein, when complete, division of labour[6] in handiwork is carried to the highest point possible, and the unit of manufacture is no longer a man, but a group of men, each member of which is dependent on his fellows, and is utterly useless by himself. This system of the workshop division of labour was perfected during the eighteenth century by the efforts of the manufacturing classes, stimulated by the demands of the ever-widening markets; it is still the system in some of the smaller and more domestic kinds of manufacture, holding much the same place amongst us as the remains of the craft-system did in the days when that of the workshop was still young. Under this system, as I have said, all the romance of the arts died out, but the commonplace of them flourished still; for the idea that the essential aim of manufacture is the making of goods still struggled with a newer idea which has since obtained complete victory, namely, that it is carried on for the sake of making a profit for the manufacturer on the one hand, and on the other for the employment of the working classes.

This idea of commerce being an end in itself and not a means merely, being but half developed in the eighteenth century, the special period of the workshop-system, some interest could still be taken in those days in the making of wares. The capitalist-manufacturer of the period had some pride in turning out goods which would do him credit, as the phrase went; he was not willing wholly to sacrifice his pleasure in this kind to the imperious demands of commerce; even his workman, though no longer an artist, that is a free workman, was bound to have skill in his craft, limited though it was to the small fragment of it which he had to toil at day by day for his whole life.

But commerce went on growing, stimulated still more by the opening up of new markets, and pushed on the invention of men, till their ingenuity produced the machines which we have now got to look upon as necessities of manufacture, and which have brought about a system the very opposite to the ancient craft-system; that system was fixed and conservative of methods; there was no real difference in the method of making a piece of goods between the time of Pliny and the time of Sir Thomas More;[7] the method of manufacture, on the contrary, in the present time, alters not merely from decade to decade, but from year to year; this fact has naturally helped the victory of this machine-system, the system of the Factory, where the machine-like workmen of the workshop period are supplanted by actual machines, of which the operatives (as they are now called) are but a portion, and a portion gradually diminishing both in importance and numbers. This system is still short of its full development, there-fore to a certain extent the workshop-system is being carried on side by side with it, but it is being speedily and steadily crushed out by it; and when the process is complete, the skilled workman will no longer exist, and his place will be filled by machines directed by a few highly trained and very intelligent experts, and tended by a multitude of people, men, women, and children, of whom neither skill nor intelligence is required.

This system, I repeat, is as near as may be the opposite of that which produced the popular art which led up to that splendid outburst of art in the days of the Italian Renaissance which even cultivated men will sometimes deign to notice nowadays; it has therefore produced the opposite of what the old craft-system produced, the death of art and not its birth; in other words the degradation of the external surroundings of life, or simply and plainly unhappiness. Through all society spreads that curse of unhappiness: from the poor wretches, the news of whom we middle-class people are just now receiving with such naif wonder and horror: from those poor people whom nature forces to strive against hope, and to expend all the divine energy of man in competing for something less than a dog's lodging and a dog's food, from them up to the cultivated and refined person, well lodged, well fed, well clothed, expensively educated, but lacking all interest in life except, it may be, the cultivation of unhappiness as a fine art.

Something must be wrong then in art, or the happiness of life is sickening in the house of civilization. What has caused the sickness? Machine-labour will you say? Well, I have seen quoted a passage from one of the ancient Sicilian poets rejoicing in the fashioning of a water-mill, and exulting in labour being set free from the toil of the hand-quern in consequence;[8] and that surely would be a type of a man's natural hope when foreseeing the invention of labour-saving machinery as 'tis called; natural surely, since though I have said that the labour of which art can form a part should be accompanied by pleasure, no one could deny that there is some necessary labour even which is not pleasant in itself, and plenty of unnecessary labour which is merely painful. If machinery had been used for minimizing such labour, the utmost ingenuity would scarcely have been wasted on it; but is that the case in any way? Look round the world, and you must agree with John Stuart Mill[9] in his doubt whether all the machinery of modern times has lightened the daily work of one labourer. And why have our natural hopes been so disappointed? Surely because in these latter days, in which as a matter of fact machinery has been invented, it was by no means invented with the aim of saving the pain of labour. The phrase labour-saving machinery is elliptical, and means machinery which saves the cost of labour, not the labour itself, which will be expended when saved on tending other machines. For a doctrine which, as I have said, began to be accepted under the workshop-system, is now universally received, even though we are yet short of the complete development of the system of the Factory. Briefly, the doctrine is this, that the essential aim of manufacture is making a profit; that it is frivolous to consider whether the wares when made will be of more or less use to the world so long as any one can be found to buy them at a price which, when the workman engaged in making them has received of necessaries and comforts as little as he can be got to take, will leave something over as a reward to the capitalist who has employed him. This doctrine of the sole aim of manufacture (or indeed of life) being the profit of the capitalist and the occupation of the workman, is held, I say, by almost everyone; its corollary is, that labour is necessarily unlimited, and that to attempt to limit it is not so much foolish as wicked, whatever misery may be caused to the community by the manufacture and sale of the wares made.

It is this superstition of commerce being an end in itself, of man made for commerce, not commerce for man, of which art has sickened; not of the accidental appliances which that superstition when put in practice has brought to its aid; machines and railways and the like, which do now verily control us all, might have been controlled by us, if we had not been resolute to seek profit and occupation at the cost of establishing for a time that corrupt and degrading anarchy which has usurped the name of Society. It is my business here to-night and everywhere to foster your discontent with that anarchy and its visible results; for indeed I think it would be an insult to you to suppose that you are contented with the state of things as they are; contented to see all beauty vanish from our beautiful city, for instance; contented with the squalor of the black country, with the hideousness of London, the wen of all wens, as Cobbett called it;[10] contented with the ugliness and baseness which everywhere surround the life of civilized man; contented, lastly, to be living above that unutterable and sickened misery of which a few details are once again reaching us as if from some distant unhappy country, of which we could scarcely expect to hear, but which I tell you is the necessary foundation on which our society, our anarchy, rests.[11]

# WILLIAM JOHN COURTHOPE, *LIFE IN POETRY: LAW IN TASTE* (1901)

William John Courthope (1842–1917) enjoyed two parallel careers: that of a man of letters and that of a civil servant. He took a first at Oxford, won the Newdigate Prize for Poetry in 1864 and the Vice Chancellor's prize with his essay, *On the Genius of Spenser*, in 1868. An academic career, however, was ruled out by an only modest patrimony which made a university fellowship out of the question. Consequently in 1869 he entered the Education Office as an examiner. In 1887 he became a Civil Service commissioner, and as a senior commissioner (1892–1907) he was responsible for reforming the examinations to higher appointments. In 1895 Courthope was elected to the Professorship of Poetry at Oxford and the following year he was made an honorary fellow of New College. Courthope's writing career centred on two large undertakings: the editorship of the works of Alexander Pope which he took over from Whitwell Elwin in the early 1880s and which he concluded in 1889 with his *Life of Alexander Pope*; and his six-volume *History of English Poetry* (1895–1910). Courthope's other main editorial work concerned his appointment from 1883–7 as joint editor (with Alfred Austin) of the newly-founded conservative periodical, the *National Review*. For the first number he contributed an article on 'Conservatism and Art' and over the next few years published further contributions in this vein. Courthope's *oeuvre* also included critical works, such as a monograph on *Addison* (1884) for the 'English Men of Letters' series, *The Liberal Movement in English Literature* (1885) and in 1901 *Life in Poetry: Law in Taste* (his Oxford lectures); *Ludibria Lunae* (1869), an allegorical burlesque on the 'woman question'; together with several volumes of poetry – *The Paradise of Birds* (1870), *The Longest Reign* (1897), *Selections from the Epigrams of M. Valerius Martialis* (1914) and *The Country Town and Other Poems* (1920).

### From William John Courthope, *Life in Poetry: Law in Taste* (London: Macmillan and Co., 1901)[1]

#### X. Conclusion

Now that I have come to the close of this series of lectures, it only remains for me to look back over the ground that has been covered, and to sum up the results of the argument that I have endeavoured to develop. But before doing so it is perhaps not unnatural for me on this, the last occasion on which I shall have the honour of addressing you, to review for a moment the general circumstances

446

of the period, during which I have held the Chair of Poetry – circumstances which have doubtless exercised an unconscious influence in directing me to the choice of my subject, and I suppose also in shaping to some extent the tendency of my thought. By a curious coincidence I was chosen Professor of Poetry just after a general election had decided an issue of the gravest importance to the fortunes of the United Kingdom; I lay down my office after another general election had given the verdict of the people on a policy which, for good or ill, must be regarded as a turning-point in the destinies of the British Empire.[2] Unless we are to look on art as an abstract almost inhuman region, remote from the actions and emotions of the living world, it is impossible not to feel that great events like these must reverberate in the spiritual sphere, and perhaps awake fresh movements of taste and imagination.

By another coincidence, not less noteworthy, I bring my term of office to an end with the close of a century. It may be the effect of fancy or superstition, but we are certainly moved by a common instinct to look on each cycle of a hundred years as marking by itself a definite stage in the course of human affairs. Successive centuries present themselves under separate and distinctive aspects, and seem to carry forward the stages of the world's history like the connected acts of a drama. If we turn our imagination back to the time when the distinctively modern era begins, we see in the sixteenth century the great movements of the Renaissance, and the Reformation at work to undermine the Catholic fabric of the Papacy and the Empire, which constituted the order of mediaeval Europe, and to lay the foundations of the Balance of Power,[3] which holds together the society of our own times. Here we have the opening of the drama – the δέσις as Aristotle would have called it,[4] or the evolution of the situation. A second act seems to begin with the seventeenth century, as we watch the progress of the disintegrating movement in the heart of each nation, and the struggle of rival monarchies, representing separate national interests, to obtain the preponderance of power within the newly balanced European system. The eighteenth century is the third act, in which the structural interest of the drama reaches its climax: from the dawn of the century to its last decade the solvent of Philosophy continues to loosen the exterior framework of Feudal Absolutism, raised up by the joint labours of the Renaissance and the Reformation, till it is on the point of toppling to its fall in the French Revolution.

The fourth act brings us to the close of our own century. And as we look back on its long scene of change and transformation, we recognise that the master passion of the dying era has been Liberty. Liberty, in the first place, for peoples. From the carnivals of the first Revolution, in the streets of Paris, down to the last earthquake shocks of 1848, races and nationalities start into infant life, and strive after ideals as yet but dimly understood amid the chaotic struggle for existence. Liberty is aimed at, in the second place, for the individual. In one way or another the tendency of the century, at any rate the first half of it, has been to seek to confine the functions of the State within the narrowest possible limits, so as to allow the individual the fullest play in developing his capacities as he chooses. Each individual must have complete freedom of action. Every house-holder must have his individual share in the government of the country. The workman must be freed from all restraints upon his right to sell his labour to whom, at the place where, and at the time when, he chooses. The merchant, freed from the trammels of Navigation Laws and protective duties, has to think simply and solely of buying in the cheapest market, and selling in the dearest.

Again, the individual must enjoy the largest liberty of thought; the religious sectarian is not only to be permitted the freedom of worshipping undisturbed in his own way, but of attacking, if he wishes, the foundation of the corporate Religion of the State; the advanced thinker must be free to push his intellectual theories in public up to that dim and doubtful point, at which the expression of obscenity or blasphemy may seem to imperil the well-being of society. And this because Liberty is regarded – and in a sense rightly regarded – as being an end in itself; so that the aim of philosophy in England, at least up to the middle of the nineteenth century, might be summed up in the phrase *laisser faire*,[5] 'let be,' and has consisted rather in preventing the State from interfering with the liberty of the individual than in directing its energies to a constructive social end.

Those who can carry back their thoughts as far as I can will remember the enthusiasm with which young University men, in the sixth and seventh decades of the century, embraced the doctrines of the most influential teacher of this school, John Stuart Mill, especially as expounded in his book *On Liberty*.[6] Their thoughts and feelings were those described by Wordsworth – pre-eminently the poet of Individualism – as prevailing at the opening of the Revolutionary era:

> O pleasant exercise of hope and joy,
> For mighty were the auxiliars which then stood
> Upon our side, us who were strong in love.
> Bliss was in it in that dawn to be alive;
> But to be young was very heaven.[7]

And the ideals of young Oxford were those of which the same poet speaks after-wards in a passage less well known:

> What delight,
> How glorious, in self-knowledge and self-rule,
> To look through all the frailties of the world,
> And with a resolute mastery, shaking off
> Infirmities of nature, time, and place,
> Build social upon personal Liberty,
> Which to the blind restraints of general laws
> Superior, magisterially adopts
> One guide, the light of circumstances, flashed
> Upon an independent intellect!
> Thus expectation rose again: thus hope,

From her first ground expelled, grew proud once more.
Oft as my thoughts were turned to human kind,
I scorned indifference, but inflamed with thirst
Of a secure intelligence, and, sick
Of other longing, I pursued what seemed
A more exalted Nature; wished that Man
Should start out of his earthy worm-like state,
And spread abroad the wings of Liberty,
Lord of himself and undisturbed delights.[8]

Such were the aspirations of that individual self-consciousness, generated by the atmosphere of Revolutionary liberty, which prevailed till about the year 1870. Then came the necessary reaction. From the exaggerated hopes of human progress men passed into a fit of revolutionary pessimism, and the world of Culture began to exchange the somewhat bourgeois Liberalism of Mill for the gloomy disdain of Schopenhauer.[9] Nevertheless, throughout the remainder of the century individual liberty has still asserted itself as the end and goal of existence, individual consciousness as the standard of all intellectual measurement; only instead of looking forward with Wordsworth to political Liberty as the aim of human society, the Decadents, the Symbolists, the votaries of the *Fin du Siècle*, and other philosophical sects which have sprung out of the study of Schopenhauer, now aspire to the freedom of Art and Imagination, as a kind of heaven of self-culture, in which each man can, if he thinks fit, find a refuge and solace from the evils of existence. From the enthusiastic dreams of Revolutionary progress we have turned to the opiates of intellectual Buddhism.

Men of sense and manliness will not allow themselves to be infected with the despair of fantastic sects; pessimism is merely the unbalanced recoil from an exaggerated optimism, not warranted by facts and experience. One of the greatest benefits of increased individual liberty has been that it has stimulated the conscience of society; and the vast development of a free press, while it perplexes us with the multiformity of facts and opinions converging on all sides upon our consciousness, enables us to face these in a spirit free from prejudice. No right-thinking man has given up his belief in the advantages of rational and constitutional liberty; but, on the other hand, every sound reasoner is much more ready than he was to acknowledge that Liberty itself is not the solution of human ills; that much more is to be said than was supposed for such old authoritative methods of dealing with men and things as were not long ago accounted relics of benighted barbarism; that, in fact, the remedy of *laisser faire*, of letting things go, of leaving each man as a separate unit to think, speak, and do as he likes, however simple and attractive it seemed in the outset, has itself been the cause of a thousand difficulties, which require to be dealt with on quite another principle.

It is well to look at concrete examples of these truths, in order to realise exactly wherein lies the fallacy of the doctrine of *laisser faire*. Take the philosophy of the Manchester School – why has not Cobden's prophecy been fulfilled, that, if the principle of Free Trade were once proclaimed, it would be universally adopted?[10] Is it not plain that Cobden, regarding the world as if it consisted only of a number of money-making units, left out of his calculation most important factors? On the external side he omitted national organisation and the European Balance of Power, and, on the spiritual side, the passion of envy and the mutual antagonism of class interests; he formed therefore quite a wrong estimate of the strength of the forces which have resulted in the ideals of Protection and Socialism.

Look again at the principle of *laisser faire* in its operation within the sphere of Religion. How has it worked in France, the classic land of Revolution, where the doctrine of Liberty, Equality, Fraternity, when first proclaimed, was understood to mean, in spiritual matters, that each individual was free to think as he chose? At the present moment the Waldeck-Rousseau Ministry, which is supposed to reflect in its composition all shades of Republicanism,[11] has proclaimed that, though the doctrine still applies to everybody who choses to restrict his active energies within the sphere of private life, it must be so interpreted as to exclude from the service of the State every man whose character and opinions have been formed in a place of religious education. I am not so presumptuous as to cast obloquy on the legislation of a foreign state, with the inner concerns of which no Englishman has a right to interfere; I merely wish to show how the doctrine of *laisser faire* has been qualified in practice, and to call your attention to the practical rejection by French Liberals of their old ideal: 'A public career open to all the talents.'

In the sphere of imagination we find a phrase exactly analogous to the phrase of *laisser faire* in commerce and politics: *De gustibus non est disputandum.*[12] The soundness of this maxim was some months ago asserted by a leader of English thought and action, justly exercising great influence over the opinions of his countrymen, and I doubt not that he arrived at his conclusion from his observation of the multiplicity and self-contradiction of modern tastes, and the complete absence of any recognised standard of judgement in contemporary literature. But in the first place, it is to be remembered that this state of anarchy did not always exist; it is, in fact, itself the result of a reaction against the absolute and anthoritative method of criticism, which used to be applied to works of art by men of taste in almost all European countries in the eighteenth century. The revolt, in the name of Liberty, against the classical conventions accepted as a starting-point by the critics of that age, has ended in a demand for the emancipation of the artist from all rules whatever. But as to this we have to observe that the violent assertion of individual liberty is one of the inconsistencies of human nature: men are not content to differ. Look at the antagonism between the Classicists and the Romantics in the early part of the century, between the Naturalists and the Impressionists in the latter half;[13] how ideal is it to say that there should be no disputing about taste, when men dispute, and will continue to dispute, about it every hour of their lives! If they reject the technical standard imposed on them by authority, they erect a metaphysical authority for themselves, and seek to impose this on as large a circle of true believers as they can rally to the worship of their particular Cult.

We have then to recognise the existing condition of things: there is now a general consciousness – we may almost call it a consciousness of the State – that the problems with which we are obliged to deal must be considered, with a view, not so much to enlarging the liberty of the individual, as to promoting the welfare of society. Granted that the development of all the faculties of the human intellect is good in itself, the result will not be good, unless these energies are directed to the promotion of some social end. It is perceived that the task of the new century will be to discover what St James in his Epistle calls 'the perfect law of liberty,'[14] the discernment of design in the constitution and tendency of things, which is always being more or less defeated by the corruption of human nature. And hence, just as in religion and politics so in the sphere of taste, we are bound to examine whether there be not an eternal law, above and beyond the aesthetic perceptions of the individual, binding the poet and painter to direct their conceptions towards some social end, which must be understood alike by artist and critic before either can produce or judge a work of Fine Art. To search for and define this law has been my object in the series of lectures I am bringing to a close, and my last words shall be devoted to reminding you of the course we have taken.

I pointed out, in the first place, the existence of that general law, or prevailing instinct, in human nature, on which Aristotle bases his reasoning about Fine Art, the motion of the spirit, that is to say, which, on the one hand, impels the artist to put the idea of his own mind into his imitation of Nature, and, on the other, justifies the critic in requiring that the artistic imitation shall express the general sense of what ought to be. This is Aristotle's Law of the Universal;[15] it is founded on the consideration that all human beings, however great their individual varieties, are constituted fundamentally in the same way, and therefore that it is the duty of the artist to be acquainted, not only with the workings of his own imagination, but with the imaginative expectations of men as such. The validity of this law is proved equally by its theoretical certainty, and by the fact that it has been obeyed by all the greatest artists of the world; so that the kind of pleasure which is felt *semper, ubique, ab omnibus*,[16] becomes necessarily the standard to which every work, claiming to be one of Fine Art, is brought for the determination of its value.

The definition of the Law of the Universal, however, only carries us to a point at which our minds are steadied with a belief that, amid the infinity of tastes and opinions, there is a stable foundation of judgement. We are immediately confronted with the further fact that each great master-work of genius has a life of its own, distinguishing it from every other work of genius that the world possesses. Are we to conclude from this that genius is a law unto itself, and not to be made subject to any discoverable law of art? By no means: for that would destroy the validity of the Law of the Universal. The fact is explained when we

451

consider that, though the Universal is something absolutely existing in itself, it can only be reflected through the medium of minds differing in constitution and character. Besides the Law of the Universal noted by Aristotle, we have to recognise the existence of another law, the operation of which Aristotle himself did not observe, and indeed had no opportunity of observing, the Law of National Character. By this I mean the social instinct which compels the artist unconsciously to individualise his idea of the Universal in the light of the race tendencies, the methods of education, and the political history and character of the nation to which he belongs. In so far as his view of the Universal represents faithfully the sum of the national life, the man is a great painter or poet, and his work becomes a monumental standard by reference to which the quality of other artistic work produced in his nation can be judged. But in order that the critic may be able to declare and apply this Law of National Character, he must, by means of conscious analysis, investigate the nature of the spiritual forces by which the artist has been unconsciously inspired, observe the modes in which these operate at different periods and in different nations, and finally judge in what respect each work of Fine Art is a faithful reflection of the life of the society out of which it springs.

I have endeavoured in several successive lectures to illustrate the actual existence and operation of the Law of National Character. I have shown the permanence of the four great forces – Catholicism, Feudalism, Humanism, and Protestantism – by which the course of life in European nations has been determined, and the different way in which they have operated in each nation according to the character of the people; and further, how the bent of the national character and history has been in each country reflected in the course of the national poetry. We have seen, for example, how the French character seems to have given a definite direction to French history in striking contrast with that of Germany, and how the English character, as manifested in history, differs from them both: we have noted with what rare representative fidelity poets like Dante, Chaucer, Milton, Molière, La Fontaine, Goethe, and Heine,[17] reflect the character of their countrymen, and how their works may be taken as the abstract and brief chronicles of their time.

Phenomena so regular, so invariable, as those which I have illustrated in my lectures ought, I think, to furnish sufficient proof of, at least, the unconscious operation of the two great Laws of Taste. But it may be asked: Granting their existence, can these laws be consciously applied? Can we, when we are judging of a newly-created picture or poem, submit it to the practical test of law so as to decide with any confidence as to its possession of permanent qualities? I think we can, on certain conditions. The first, and the most indispensable, is the acknowledgement of the principle of Authority. We must allow the existence of law in an external form – that is to say, in the work of the greatest artists, not because these have in an arbitrary manner created the law, but because the universal and enduring pleasure which their work affords is a sufficient proof that they have obeyed it. Their work is therefore to be studied in a liberal and intelligent spirit, in order that we may discover the reason of their method and procedure, which the method of all genuine artists is bound to resemble, though not slavishly to reproduce.

When the source of authority has been recognised in principle, it should be practically used in education. Besides collecting the law of art from the practice of the greatest artists, we must also study it in the treatises of those who have most scientifically declared it – that is to say, of the most philosophical critics. The head and source of this study is to be sought in the *Poetics* of Aristotle, not for the reason that made the scholars of the Italian Renaissance turn to the authority of Aristotle, as being an absolute Dictator in the sphere of taste, but because he was the first to investigate by analysis the imaginative principles underlying the creation of the most artistically constituted of all races, so that the elementary conditions of fine art are more clearly defined in his treatise than anywhere else. The long and persistent misinterpretation of Aristotle's meaning was, it is true, the cause of much artistic aberration in the sixteenth, seventeenth, and eighteenth centuries; but the patient labours of modern scholars have removed the old stumbling-blocks, and any English reader, who studies the *Poetics* with the aid afforded him by the admirable essays of Professor Butcher,[18] may now make himself acquainted with all that is essential in the Theory of Fine Art.

Though the Law of the Universal can be most thoroughly studied in the *Poetics* of Aristotle, the student of taste ought not to let this treatise monopolise his attention. The Law of National Character has to be collected from other critical sources. No doubt almost all Aristotle's critical successors into quite modern times have looked at the Universal more or less through his reasoning; but most of them, in so far as they have been men of original thought, have made some contribution of value to Criticism, derived from the peculiar character and complexion of the society to which they have belonged. Roman, Florentine, French, German, and English – Quintilian, Dante, Boileau, Lessing, Johnson, and many others – have formed their own characteristic idea of the Law of the Universal;[19] and if any one desires to satisfy himself of the identity and permanence of the problems of taste from the dawn of Greek civilisation downwards, he will find the subject exhaustively treated in the excellent *History of Criticism*, of which the first volume has recently been published by Professor Saintsbury.[20] It is certain that a critic who comes to the judgement of a modern work of imagination equipped with the knowledge of the varied operations of the Universal Law of Rhetoric[21] need not be doubtful of his right to decide with authority.

You will see that the authority in taste for which I am pleading is something quite different from the authority of an Academy. The Italian Academies of the sixteenth century and the French Academy were simply assemblies of representative men who discussed points of taste among themselves, and laid down rules in an arbitrary manner which carried with them just so much conventional authority as was due to the collective agreement of able and learned scholars. But almost all of them regarding the reasoning of Aristotle as axiomatic, and their misinterpretation of the text of the *Poetics* being frequent, the rules and regulations which they endeavoured to impose upon the taste of the world were devoid of a really rational basis. There is nothing *a priori* or abstract in the critical method I have suggested. The two Laws we have been considering are founded on the constitution of the human mind; their operation is discovered by inductions from observation and experience. The only surrender of liberty demanded from the individual taste is, in the first place, the suspension of judgement till the aesthetic perception has been justly trained, and, in the second place, a submission of the intellect, in the early stages of its schooling, to the judgement of the world on the works of art deemed most worthy of admiration. When the judging faculty has been disciplined to view things in all their bearings, and has become robust and mature, the mind resumes its native liberty, and is free to revise its early decisions. Such is the course of what has been well called Humanism in Education.

I am well aware that the recognition of lawful authority in the sphere of imagination is not likely to be attained without a painful effort. The passion for novelty in the human breast; the instinct of democracy which makes the majority of the moment the supreme Court of appeal; commercial interest which finds its account in following the law of demand and supply; all these influences favour the assertion of unrestricted liberty of taste. But the dangers to civilisation and refinement, arising out of the present anarchical conditions of things, ought to show the lovers of true liberty the necessity of rallying round an authoritative standard of taste. 'I do not think,' says Sir Richard Jebb, in his lecture on Humanism in Education,[22]

'there is any exaggeration in what Mr Froude[23] said thirteen years ago, that if we ever lose those studies our national taste and the tone of our national intellect will suffer a serious decline. Classical studies help to preserve sound standards in literature. It is not difficult to lose such standards, even for a nation with the highest material civilisation, with abounding mental activity, and with a great literature of its own. It is peculiarly easy to do so in days when the lighter and more ephemeral kinds of writing form for many people the staple of daily reading. The fashions of the hour may start a movement not in the best direction, which may go on until the path is difficult to retrace. The humanities, if they cannot prevent such a movement, can do something to temper and counteract it; because they appeal to permanent things, to the instinct for beauty in human nature, and to the emotions, and in any one who is at all susceptible to their influence, they develop a literary conscience.'

Nothing can be added to the force of these admirable words. My only regret is that, in placing before us the advantage, nay the necessity, of recognising a definite standard of taste for the purposes of education, Sir Richard Jebb did not at the same time insist on the duty of promoting this aim by organised endeavour. He seems to rely on the permeating influence of our old established system of Humanism in Education, and on the inspiring example of individual scholars – that is to say, he is content to trust to the principle of *laisser faire*. Great and beneficial as the indirect effect of the labours of eminent scholars may be on the thought of society, it is impossible that the ideal they represent should stand against the overwhelming pressure of the forces of materialism around us, unless it is proclaimed, defined, and systematically defended. For this end we need the concerted efforts of all who desire to maintain the Humanist tradition; above all, we need a deliberate and sustained assertion of the principle on the part of the Universities.

I venture to think that, at the present moment, the English Universities are hardly acting up to their traditions in the amount of attention that they bestow on the training of taste. From very early days, Oxford and Cambridge assimilated with their system of mediaeval education all the ideas that flowed in upon them with the rise of the New Learning. But they did not, like the later Italian Humanists, regard art and learning as something to be pursued for its own sake, and without reference to the active life of the State. On the contrary, as the College system expanded, the ideal of civic education grew always stronger; the Universities shared to the full in the sympathies and interest which were moving the mind of the nation at large, and instead of developing into monasteries devoted to the purposes of knowledge and research, they became rather schools for preparing the minds of youth for the discharge of public affairs. Oxford and Cambridge, having participated to the full in the internal struggle caused by the Reformation and the Civil Wars, continued to send from their seminaries the men who presided over the business of the country as judges and statesmen; poets and essayists went forth from the seclusion of their colleges to apply the stores of knowledge, there derived from the study of antiquity, to the problems of living thought. This bracing political atmosphere helped to invigorate the studies of the Universities themselves, making the scholar sympathise with the civic spirit of the great classical authors, and vivify the literatures of Greece and Rome with analogies drawn from the society about him.

While my own official duties permit me to observe with satisfaction how largely the public service is still recruited from the Universities, I am doubtful whether Oxford, at all events, derives as much nourishment as was formerly the case from the outer world. There seems within the last fifty years to have been some diminution in the intercourse between the life of this University and that of the State. Perhaps the tendency arises from a natural antipathy to the utilitarian forces in society, generated in the atmosphere of democratic politics, a reaction which has driven the scholar to seek his own ideal of liberty in Self-Culture. At any rate no one, I think, can read the books of my eminent predecessor, Matthew Arnold, without perceiving that a certain exclusive instinct of self-esteem has been for a long time impelling Academic society to exalt itself at the expense of the Gentile world, classified as Barbarians, Philistines, and Populace.[24] The University man has his own aesthetic aim, his own ideal of Self-

Culture, to pursue, apart from the main impulse of social action in the State. And the result of this Academic monasticism has been, if I may dare to say so before such an audience as this, a decline in the robustness of Oxford taste. I seem to find evidence of a falling off in the prize exercises I have been called on to judge as Professor of Poetry. I note in the Essays, for example, a failure of power to treat a subject as a whole, a tendency to cultivate style as a thing desirable in itself apart from the subject-matter, and, on the other hand, a passion for making points and epigrams without any regard to perspective and proportion.

This is one of the mischiefs that arise out of separating the interests of Art and Taste from the movement of life and action; Taste tends to become effeminate. There is a danger of an opposite kind, also encouraged by the prevalent tendency of *laisser faire* and the principle of *De gustibus non est disputandum*. I mean the excess of scientific curiosity which prompts the inquirer to study all tastes alike in a spirit of Epicurean indifference. In the enjoyment we derive from watching the operations of the human mind, we are inclined to leave out of account the moral bearing of taste, and to content ourselves with a mere analysis of artistic motives, without determining whether these are good or bad, right or wrong. Such a habit of thought is readily engendered by the study of history; and I venture to think that Professor Saintsbury, the value of whose *History of Criticism* can hardly be overestimated, comes perilously near the encouragement of dilettante trifling when he says: 'The point on which I am content to be called a critical Pangloss[25] is this: that I have hardly the slightest desire to alter – if I could do so by the greatest of all miracles, that of retroactive change – the literary course of the world. No doubt things might have been better still: but one may also be perfectly contented with the actual result.'

If it be the case that Aristotle – as Professor Saintsbury says, and Mr Bosanquet, in his *History of Aesthetic*,[26] seems to be of the same opinion – 'oversteps the genus a little in his generalisation, and merges Poetics in Ethics,' then I am well content to err with Aristotle. But, in truth, I do not think that he does err. I have said, in my lecture on Aristotle, that all his philosophy about human affairs regards man, not from the mere metaphysical standpoint of Kant and modern philosophers, as an isolated individual, but as πολιτικὸν ζῷον, a social being.[27] It would therefore have been impossible for him to eliminate moral considerations from the theory of Fine Art, and in all his reasoning about Pleasure as the end of Art, there is the underlying assumption that the pleasure produced by Art must be such as is to promote the health and well-being of the State. Those who think that his reasoning in this respect is sound will conclude that, beyond the Law of the Universal, there is no absolute law in Aesthetics, and that the only law binding on the artist is the Law of National Character, as interpreted by the educated conscience of society, which necessarily includes those religious and moral considerations that determine our conduct as individuals.

By pursuing, or seeming to pursue, too exclusively the aim of Self-culture, by failing to direct liberal or Humanist Education to a moral, a practical, a social end, I think we have brought ourselves within measurable distance of a great danger. This may be seen dimly approaching in the light of the address recently delivered by Lord Rosebery as Rector of Glasgow University.[28] I read with sympathy Lord Rosebery's saying that the affairs of the British Empire ought to be conducted on business principles; but when I ask how this ideal is to be translated into action, I find that, in his view, the tradition of education in the Universities should be altered so as to make them into schools of technical training in the business of commercial and professional life. Hence the old foundation of the Humanities is to be abandoned. 'The protest,' says Lord Rosebery, 'against the educational bondage of the dead languages is being raised in Edinburgh again to-day, but this time by the voice of the mercantile community. The leading bodies of that calling appointed a Committee to consider the subject of Commercial Education. Their Report is well worth reading. They speak of the ancient tongues with courtesy and respect, but they demand something more practical, useful, less divorced from everyday life. . . . There is required, they say, on the part of the educational authorities an admission that a man may be educated, and even a cultured gentleman, although he has not studied Latin or Greek; and they further point out that both France and Germany possess invaluable literatures, with the advantage that they are in languages which are living and are not dead.'

The fallacy underlying this reasoning is as transparent as it is time-honoured. The *raison d'être* of our Universities is to promote liberal education, and the aim of liberal education is not to impart knowledge for utilitarian purposes, but so to cultivate the moral and intellectual faculties of the scholar as to fit him, on his entrance into life, for the duties of a citizen. Such has been the fundamental idea of the English University course from the days of the Renaissance; such is still the effect on the mind of our great Oxford school of *Literae Humaniores*.[29] To depart from this ideal, to do away with this foundation, to attempt to build up a fabric of culture on the study of modern languages and literatures, without reference to the art and literatures of antiquity, would be to reduce the system of liberal education to anarchy. Men of independent minds no doubt make their way by native force of character; but education in itself must be organised, and how is it possible for a man to be comprehensively instructed in the history of human society, in the meaning of law and government, in the various relations of thought, in the useful and beautiful arts of expression, unless he begins at the beginning?

At the same time, the demand that liberal education shall be practical in the high and imperial sense of the term is a just one. The Universities should be prepared to show that their schools are animated with the public spirit of the πολιτικὴ παιδεία,[30] the civic training, that was given in the city states of Greece in the days of their greatness and liberty. Our educational aims ought to be brought into conformity with the law of our social being as disclosed in the course of our national history, and they will then be seen to be equally remote from a narrow utilitarianism and from the pursuit of art and science as ends in themselves.

Let us recognise the principle that the tendency of our time towards the consolidation of the Empire carries with it a corresponding ideal of imperial Culture. The Universities are the natural guardians of the traditions of Humanism. It is for us to show our scholars that, in submitting themselves to a course of education founded on the study of the 'ancient tongues,' they are not 'divorcing themselves from everyday life,' not dissecting a dead body, not learning Greek and Latin in a mere spirit of archaeology, but are familiarising themselves with a science that can reveal to them the genius of their own ancient customs and Christian institutions, inseparably associated as these are with the civic spirit of free Pagan antiquity. From the vantage ground of historic science it is the privilege, and should be the aim, of the Universities to maintain the standard of purity in the English language. In our school of English Language and Literature – at least as it might be – the student may learn to trace from age to age the development of our tongue, and to observe the flexibility with which its character has adapted itself to the gradual changes in our national life and society. Nor ought we to study our own language and literature in a mere insular temper, but, by comparing it with the genius of the languages and literatures of the Continent, to teach the scholar how to appreciate justly the relative character of English Art and Poetry, as the vehicle of ideas common to all the Christian nations of Europe.

Such was, in principle, the method of English University education that called forth the ever memorable tribute from the illustrious Döllinger,[31] cited in my Inaugural Lecture: 'The colleges of Oxford and Cambridge have many a time, as I observed their working on the spot, awakened in me feelings of envy, and led me to long for the time when we might again have something of the kind; for I could plainly perceive that their effect was to make instruction take root in the mind, and become a part of it, and that their influence extended beyond the mere communication of knowledge, to the ennobling elevation of the life and character.' *Nolumus leges Angliae mutari*: we will do nothing to weaken the groundwork of the national character; for, as was asked of old, 'if the foundations be destroyed, what can the righteous do?' If, on the other hand, these ethical foundations are kept sacred and untouched, the most ample opportunity is given for expanding the principle of individual liberty, according to the ever-changing needs of our imperial society:

> Nought shall make us rue,
> If England to itself do rest but true.[32]

Do we ask for some practical guide in the exercise of rational freedom in taste and politics, I know not what more majestic monument of Law we can find than the continuous growth of our institutions as reflected in our language and literature. In that ideal mirror, illuminated by history, may be seen an image of the life of the people which will enable the statesman to proceed safely on his path of necessary reconstruction, stimulate the invention of the painter and the poet, and prove to the philosopher that the perfecting of the law of liberty consists in maintaining the standard of duty imposed on us alike by the actions and by the art of our fathers.

# Part IV

# SEX AND GENDER

## CONTENTS

INTRODUCTION 463

10 DEFINING THE NORM 473
*From* William Acton, *The Functions and Disorders of the*
    *Reproductive Organs* (1857) *473*
*From* Henry Havelock Ellis, *Man and Woman: A Study of*
    *Human Secondary Sexual Characters* (1894) *486*

11 DEFINING WOMEN 495
*From* Sarah Stickney Ellis, *The Women of England:*
    *Their Social Duties, and Domestic Habits* (n.d. 1843?) *495*
*From* John Ruskin, *Sesame and Lilies* (1865) *505*
*From* John Stuart Mill, *The Subjection of Women* (1869) *520*

12 DEFINING MEN 535
*From* Edward Carpenter, *Homogenic Love and its Place in a*
    *Free Society* (1894) *535*
*From* John Addington Symonds, *A Problem in Modern Ethics* (1896) *549*

# INTRODUCTION

Sex and gender roles have become one of the main focuses of contemporary interest in the culture of the Victorian period. One of the dangers which this interest has brought with it, however, is that of over-familiarity. As Roy Porter and Lesley Hall have recently observed, 'the Victorians and sex have been exhaustingly, if not exhaustively, written about.'[1] As a consequence, the history of Victorian sexual relations can all too easily become a series of clichés. Some of the most familiar of those clichés include the following: women represented as either angels or whores; the double standard in sexual morals which at one and the same time exonerated male promiscuity and condemned female sexual appetites, celebrated monogamy and tolerated wide-scale prostitution; the idealisation of romantic love and the accompanying repression of sex itself; a refusal to acknowledge the existence of unconventional sexualities except in terms of their pathology – the list could be extended considerably. Not surprisingly, then, the history of Victorian gender relations has also become stereotyped: the division between public and private domains whereby women were confined to the home and men were sent into the world; gender discrimination in education, property laws, the franchise, marriage and the workplace; the valorisation of maternity above intellectual pursuits. The paradigms which all these examples draw upon are once again familiar: those of inequality, repression and oppression. Of course in one sense all clichés will have some basis in truth or practice, but we need to be cautious before uncritically accepting this binary view of Victorian sex and gender.

In the first place, in the nineteenth century – as in our own age – evidence for sexual attitudes and practices is not always to be taken at face value. Moreover, in the Victorian period we need to be alert to the discrepancies between personal statements (often to be found in completely private documents such as diaries and letters, or in privately printed pamphlets intended for a very restricted circulation) and those assembled by government officials or self-appointed experts who were often forced to take their evidence from non-representative samples of the population (such as the criminally insane or prostitutes). We further need to realise the simple fact that the opinions of many Britons about sexual matters were never canvassed, and that they were constrained by having to speak in an idiom inappropriate to describing their experiences. For example, as John Stuart Mill tartly pointed out in *The Subjection of Women*, much of the prescriptive literature on female sexuality and feminine natures was in fact written by men whose main experience of women was limited to a knowledge of their wives and perhaps their sisters.

Secondly, we need to be alert to the possibility of considerable differences between ideology and practice. Here we should first simply note the extent of the Victorians' obsession with sexual behaviour – evidenced in phenomena such as the profusion of manuals dealing with sexual conduct and practice, the thriving trade in pornography, the prurient interest in anatomical wax museums with their displays of sexual freaks and sexual diseases, the numbers of prostitutes on the streets of all Victorian cities, and so on. But we should also be alert to the fact that such sheer abundance of evidence makes it difficult to take the stereotype of sexual repression and ignorance at its face value. Certainly Victorian sexual ideologies were an attempt to police sexuality; but they did not necessarily define it in practice. Indeed measures such as the 1857 Divorce Act and the Contagious Diseases Acts of 1864, 1866 and 1869, the proliferation of quack literature on venereal disease and the burgeoning interest of the medical profession in sexual behaviour are all suggestive of an increase in both the level and visibility of illicit sexual activity. In other words the Victorian obsession with policing sexuality is not necessarily evidence of a triumph of control and repression, as the French cultural historian Michel Foucault tended to argue.[2] Rather, it can also be seen as an expression of fear – a defensive rear-guard action waged against a proliferation of activities which had passed beyond the ability of convention alone to restrain. Perhaps the most obvious expression of that fear was the association between desire and disease. So what was considered illicit or unconventional sexual activity – masturbation and homosexuality, prostitution, or simply what some Victorians coyly termed 'over-indulgence' – was not only to be avoided on moral grounds, but also for its allegedly debilitating effects on the body. As Ibsen's *Ghosts* was to point out at the end of the century, venereal diseases (and in particular syphilis) were all too easily seen as a punishment for immoral behaviour: the sins of the fathers were seen to be literally visited on their children – a 'morbidity' or a 'degeneration' (to use the favourite moralising terms of the *fin-de-siècle*) which threatened the 'fitness of the nation' and therefore also threatened that cherished Victorian nostrum of progress. Most importantly, this association of unconventional sexuality with national decline made sexual behaviour a public rather than a private matter.

Thirdly, it is also worth emphasising that sex and gender ideologies were neither monolithic nor hegemonic in the sense that considerable disagreement existed over quite fundamental issues – such as, for example, the nature of female desire. So while a surgeon such as William Acton could blithely claim that most 'modest' women seldom desired sexual pleasure, the controversy over the clitoridectomies performed by Isaac Baker Brown in the mid-1860s suggested a rather different understanding of female desire (albeit one still driven by male sexual anxiety).[3] In a similar way the popularity of George Drysdale's *Elements of Social Science* (in print constantly from 1845 until the early decades of the twentieth century) challenged conventional views on sexual continence by claiming that it was repression (particularly in adolescence and in women as well as men) rather than indulgence which was the origin of most sexual problems – a diagnosis which, Drysdale argued, called for early marriage and the widespread use of contraception, itself an extremely contentious topic throughout the century. On the one hand, then, while it is certainly the case (as Michel Foucault again argued) that in the nineteenth century there is an increase in the number and variety of discourses on sexuality and gender, it is equally true (as Foucault perhaps failed fully to appreciate) that those discourses tend to reveal complex and often contradictory attitudes. For example, the trend for producing manuals of sexual conduct and etiquette books ranged from the conservative prescriptions of writers such as Sarah Stickney Ellis in her series of works addressed to the 'Women', 'Wives' and 'Daughters' of England, to the controversial *Wife's Handbook* (1886) by H. A. Allbutt which was the subject of a prosecution through the courts for its advice to women on methods of contraception. Moreover, even for those who agreed on the pre-eminence of women's domestic roles, there was nevertheless room for debate about the precise nature of that domesticity and the kind of education appropriate to it. So works such as Edwin Lee's *The Education of Women* (1843), a translation of *Sur l'éducation des mères* by the French writer Aimé Martin,[4] advocated a more rigorous and intellectually challenging form of education than the emphasis on 'sympathy' and 'feeling' proposed by John Ruskin in his lecture 'Of Queens' Gardens'. Moreover, Lee recognised that female education was important for its own sake, for the woman herself, rather than (as Ruskin implied) simply in order to make her a better companion for her husband.

These contradictions and inconsistencies in the evidence for sexual and gender norms are further complicated by difficulties involved in ascertaining the status or authority of particular documents, and hence the nature of their social influence. For example, on the one hand, there were semi-official or professional publications, such as Acton's *The Functions and Disorders of the Reproductive Organs*; on the other, there were cheap populist publications by less reputable figures, such as Samuel La'mert's *Self-Preservation: A Medical Treatise on Nervous and Physical Debility, Spermatorrhoea, Impotence and Sterility*. The title of the latter work seems equally authoritative, but in fact La'mert possessed no medical degree. The late nineteenth century also saw the emergence of polemical literature propagandising illicit or unconventional sexual practices; however, as I have suggested, the fact that this literature was usually printed privately and circulated among very small interest groups makes its impact at the time extremely difficult to assess. It was generally the case that price (rather than content alone) was a key factor in whether or not works were tolerated. The result was that the most radical or subversive thinking often appeared in very expensive publications and was therefore available to only a limited readership. What all this means is that before we address the question of *how* sexual knowledge influenced sexual practice, there are some much more basic problems about what exactly counted as 'knowledge' and – more importantly perhaps – to which groups in the population it was directed.

Middle-class sexual and gender ideology almost certainly did not represent universal sexual practices or gender roles. This suggestion that Victorian debates about sex and gender were class-based is in fact more important than it might seem. For example, the 'woman question' (as it was then known) was largely a concern of middle-class women: the activists were mainly middle class and the issues which interested them – the right to work, to vote, to higher education and to own property – these were also more relevant to middle-class rather than working-class lives. During the nineteenth century most working-class women were just that: they had no choice about combining maternity with work. Moreover, for the majority of the female population, and certainly for all working-class women, careers (as they were understood by the professional classes) were simply not an issue, and neither was higher education. In his radical novel of the 1890s, *The Odd Women*, George Gissing has one of his characters, Winifred Haven, state the dilemma quite bluntly: 'I really don't think . . . that there can be any solidarity of ladies with servant girls.' One obvious reason for this division was that the sexual morality and experience of working-class women was widely assumed (at least by middle-class writers and intellectuals) to be of a fundamentally different character from that of their middle-class sisters. William Acton again makes this discrepancy clear (but not perhaps in the way he intended) when he assumed that in any extra-marital sexual activity – or 'casual relations', as he termed it – the woman involved would automatically be 'beneath [the man] in station and education'. Much of the pornographic literature of the period, from *My Secret Life* to *Teleny*, takes as its subject a gentleman's encounters with a variety of working-class women or servants. Even the serious literature and drama of the time, such as Thomas Hardy's *Jude the Obscure*, Elizabeth Gaskell's *Mary Barton* or Arthur Wing Pinero's *The Second Mrs Tanqueray*, reinforce the prejudice that sexual and class issues were for the Victorians inextricably linked. Class was also an issue in the attempt to prohibit other forms of unconventional sexual behaviour. So at the centre of many of the homosexual scandals in the late nineteenth century, including the trials of Oscar Wilde in 1895, was the issue of the involvement of public figures or aristocrats with 'renters' or working-class male prostitutes. Indeed many gay apologists have claimed that Wilde was on trial not simply for his homosexuality, but also for his familiarity with men from a different class – as his testimony at his trials disclosed, for allowing his working-class lovers, a 'valet' and a 'groom', to drink champagne with him at the Savoy Hotel, and to call him by his first name.[5] In this instance we see a particularly pernicious example of the sexual double-standard: illicit sexual behaviour was tolerated (but not necessarily condoned) so long as it was private and restricted to one class.

What emerges from all this is a picture rather different from those simple stereotypes of oppression and repression through which Victorian society is popularly understood today. As recent social histories are beginning to show, Victorian sex and gender relations are an extremely subtle and complex topic; to quote once again the words of Roy Porter and Lesley Hall, it is a picture where 'all rules had many exceptions [and] any generalization was readily contradictable'.[6] Nevertheless it is still useful to identify some general trends or patterns in order to distinguish Victorian debates from those of earlier centuries. Here there are two interrelated issues of particular importance: the role of science (particularly of biology) and the role of law.

In a general sense Victorian prescriptions about appropriate male and female behaviour were based upon assumptions about the givenness of male and female 'natures'. Historically these had been drawn from the Bible and from what modern critics have identified as a Judaeo-Christian tradition of misogyny. In the early nineteenth century, such stereotypes were given particular emphasis by the strength of evangelical religion among the middle classes. This evangelical zeal can be detected in writers such as Sarah Stickney Ellis and John Ruskin, both of whom subscribed to the idealised virtues of the 'Angel in the House' as qualities natural to women. However in the general shift from religious to secular and scientific authority (described in Part II), the concept of nature itself, and therefore of what was to be understood as 'naturally' masculine and feminine, came under a new and intense scrutiny. The result was a variety of opinions which served to problematise any simple conjunction of the moral and the natural, and therefore of sex with gender roles.

Most obviously there were developments in biological knowledge and these led to new ways of understanding the physiology of sex. Some medical practitioners (such as Acton) used these developments simply to endorse traditional moral judgements. So Acton's painstaking documentation of the physiology of sexual practices and disorders (drawn from a variety of scientific 'experts') was interpreted through a familiar Christian opposition of continence and indulgence, normality and abnormality. On the other hand, however, science also produced the more enlightened views of figures such as Sir James Paget who, though disliking masturbation as a 'nasty practice', refused to condemn it on physiological grounds, claiming (almost regretfully) that it did no more harm to the body that any other kind of over-indulgence. It has been argued in general terms that the scientific (and particularly the medical) establishments' attempted 'colonisation' of sexuality in the nineteenth century – the definition of it as a 'problem' which required investigation and treatment – was in itself an exercise in control and oppression. In some senses this observation is clearly true. But against such arguments we need to set the example of gay proselytisers such as John Addington Symonds and Edward Carpenter for whom the authority of science – particularly the new 'sexology' being imported into Britain from France and Germany – could be positively liberating. In their view, the conclusion that homosexuality was instinctive and congenital (the result, according to the German writer, Karl Ulrichs, of changes in the embryo) made the case for tolerating rather than repressing unconventional desires: it was evidence, Carpenter claimed, that to the homosexual 'homogenic love appears healthy and natural, and indeed necessary to the concretation of his individuality'. In other words, although science neither resolved debates about sex and gender, nor produced agreed definitions of what could be considered to be natural behaviour, it permitted such topics to be discussed in new, more open, more informed and certainly much less complacent ways. As Symonds suggested apropos of homosexuality, by giving such desires a 'neutral nomenclature' – that of 'sexual inversion' – science allowed for an 'unprejudiced' investigation of it. Of course today we would almost certainly want to qualify both Symonds' faith in the objectivity of science and the accuracy of Victorian medical knowledge. Moreover, as I have suggested, historians have tended to identify in Victorian science's pathologising of sexuality an inherently repressive and discriminatory attitude. Furthermore (and again as I have already hinted) we also need to recognise that there were several different kinds of science being practised, and that a different authority attached to each of them. The existence of such a hierarchy explains why nineteenth-century sexologists' reliance on individual case-studies and personal testimony could be treated dismissively by a medical establishment more at home with biological or anatomical evidence. These caveats and complexities aside, though, Symonds' argument is nevertheless understandable. When seen in the context of the prurience and reticence of the early Victorian period, his belief that science (of whatever kind) could offer the best prospect of a dispassionate debate about human sexuality was logical enough. Indeed even some feminists found that science could be an ally rather than an enemy. So in the late nineteenth century we also find examples of feminist journals using science to investigate traditional stereotypes about female chastity and sexual appetites.

Medical men and sexologists were not the only kind of scientists who were interested in sex and gender. Towards the end of the nine-teenth century there were also a number of what we can usefully call sexual anthropologists. The most notorious was the explorer and writer, Sir Richard Burton, whose surveys of the sexual practices of other cultures (particularly Arabian countries) so challenged British orthodoxies that they came to be seen as pornography. Less obvi-ously controversial was the early work of Havelock Ellis, whose exhaustive cross-cultural study of sexual characters in *Man and Woman* revealed a variability which challenged any simple normative categorisation. In particular Ellis argued that knowledge of 'the radical and essential characters of men and women uninfluenced by external modifying circumstances' was still very imperfect – a circumstance which in turn, he argued, should arouse deep suspicion of any attempt to ground 'social laws' in simple biological or anatomical 'facts'. At least at this stage in his career Ellis was enough of a Victorian to trust that male and female capacities were ultimately determined (and limited) by 'natural law', and that maleness and femaleness were fundamentally different. Nevertheless, his Darwinian suggestion that it was 'experience' rather than social prescription which should deter-mine 'the fitness of men and women for any kind of work or any kind of privilege' pointed to a more tolerant and judicious attitude towards sexual difference and gender roles – a position which later informed his much more controversial (and today more widely read) *Studies in the Psychology of Sex* (1897–1928).

Perhaps prompted by these anthropological studies of sexual behaviour, the late decades of the nineteenth century also saw an interest in the historical study of sexuality. The most systematic attempt to justify unconventional sexualities – homosexuality, pederasty and lesbianism – in terms of their continued presence in history was via the study of classical cultures, particularly that of ancient Greece.[7] Many apologists for homosexuality frequently drew upon historical precedents, and the alleged tolerance and celebration of male–male desire in the past, as evidence of its naturalness. Carpenter, for example, went so far as to use history to revalue homo-sexuality, seeing it as an inherently positive force in society. The general drift of this polemic is perhaps best seen in Oscar Wilde's famous apologia for 'the love that dare not speak its name' which he made from the dock in the Old Bailey: it was that 'great affection of an elder for a younger man as there was between David and Jonathan, such as Plato made the very basis of his philosophy, and such as you find in the sonnets of Michelangelo and Shakespeare'.[8] None the less it is important to note that this appeal to historical precedent was no less problematic than the use of scientific authority, because exactly the same classical tradition had been interpreted earlier in the century as a byword for debauchery and excess, responsible (in the words of the eighteenth-century historian Edward Gibbon) for the classical world's 'decline and fall'. In other words it is interesting to witness how both sexual radicals and conservatives often felt themselves obliged to use the self-same language and traditions.

The extent of the disagreements in the scientific and medical establishments led some writers on sex and gender, most notably John Stuart Mill, to eschew these arguments altogether in favour of those drawn from legal and political spheres. In *The Subjection of Women*, Mill argued (in a manner not dissimilar to Havelock Ellis) that the inadequacy of contemporary knowledge of male or female natures stood in the way of any attempt to ground behavioural norms in biology or sex. Moreover, what had historically been taken to be 'natural' behaviour, Mill claimed, was merely the result of custom and practice. So for Mill historical precedent was ultimately just as unreliable a source of evidence as that of science or medicine (although when the occasion demanded, Mill was quite prepared to use as evidence examples drawn from both history and current practice). Unlike many polemicists, Mill did not attempt to make a conclusive case for the givenness of any particular gender roles; instead, he concentrated on redefining what would count as evidence in such an argument. So for Mill (again like Ellis) it was only experience which would demonstrate whether or not women and men were capable of the same kinds of activities; moreover, for such experience to be properly assessed, he argued that it was necessary for women to be given the same opportunities as men – a circumstance which required a principled assumption of sexual equality which in turn would be guaranteed by the sanction of law. Mill's argument amounted to the proposition that gender roles should be determined by free competition with the law acting as an umpire. As he bluntly put it, unless women were given the right to vote and the opportunity to be elected to public office, it was impossible to know whether or not they were capable or suited to such occupations. In such an argument, one of the key issues (as it had been in *On*

*Liberty*) was defining when and under what circumstances the law should intervene to ensure equality of treatment. Mill identified three areas which particularly constrained women solely because of their sex – property rights, divorce and the suffrage – although *The Subjection of Women* only discussed the first and last of these in any detail.

Mill's attempt to separate questions of gender roles from prescriptive definitions of 'natural' or 'normal' behaviour gives his writing a distinctly modern note. However, in its naive appeal to human reasonableness, it remains quintessentially Victorian. Mill gave no compelling reasons why his male contemporaries would in practice be persuaded by argument alone to give up their power over women, any more than (to use his analogy) American slave-owners had proved themselves amenable to reason over emancipation. As the history of the women's movement demonstrates, the political rights which Mill sees as self-evidently desirable were only won after long and sometimes violent struggle – that is, through force rather than through a liberal appeal to reason. More importantly, perhaps, neither did Mill adequately explain the grounds and the conditions for free competition between the sexes. Modern experience has shown that the ability of the law to guarantee equality of opportunity (irrespective of whether or not women participate in the legislative process) is limited. Here it is worth noting that the history of actual nineteenth-century gender-related legal reforms is a rather a chequered one. So legislation such as the Married Women's Property Acts has to be balanced against the institutional discrimination enshrined in the 1857 marriage reforms. The Married Women's Property Acts entitled women to become legal agents controlling money and possessing property, but the divorce reforms (which created civil divorce procedures) were so one-sided that women were, to all intents and purposes, still trapped by marriage. Similarly, in the 1885 Criminal Law Amendment Act legislation originally designed to protect girls from sexual exploitation by men resulted in one of the most draconian measures against any social group: Labouchère's Amendment, introduced at a late stage in the Bill's passage through Parliament, criminalised any expression of male–male desire, either in public or private. In all these senses, the relationship between ideology, law and actual practice was as complex in Victorian Britain as it is in our own age.

# 10

# DEFINING THE NORM

## WILLIAM ACTON, *THE FUNCTIONS AND DISORDERS OF THE REPRODUCTIVE ORGANS* (1857)

William Acton (1813–75) was the second son of a clergyman. He began his medical career by enrolling in 1831 as an apprentice to the resident apothecary at Bartholomew's Hospital in London. In 1836, having developed an interest in diseases of the urinary and generative organs, Acton travelled to Paris to work under Philippe Ricord, a well-known specialist in genito-urinary surgery. During this period, he also spent time at the Female Venereal Hospital in Paris – an experience which later informed his work on the connection between prostitution and venereal diseases in Britain. In 1840 Acton returned to England where he was admitted to the Royal College of Surgeons; in 1842 he became a fellow of the Royal Medical and Chirurgical Society of London. These positions allowed him to set up a successful medical practice; he also worked for some time as surgeon to the Islington Dispensary. His main interest, however, was in writing and in 1841 he produced his first and principal work: *A Complete Practical Treatise on Venereal Diseases* (in later editions entitled *A Practical Treatise on Diseases of the Urinary and Generative Organs in Both Sexes*); by the time of his death, it had reached its fourth edition. In 1857 part of that work was published separately as *The Functions and Disorders of the Reproductive Organs*. Again the book was a considerable success: in 1863 it was translated into French and by 1875 it was in its sixth edition. In it Acton rehearses what have now become the clichés of Victorian sexual knowledge: that desire is a dangerous force, that sex is therefore a problem, that sexual maladies have physiological (rather than psychological) causes and that control and abstinence are the most appropriate remedies for them. Acton's book focused almost wholly on men – an exclusiveness which is not particularly surprising, although his insistence on male responsibility for exercising sexual restraint sheds an interesting light on the supposed condoning of the double standard. There has been considerable debate among historians as to how representative Acton's views were; some have argued that he was an eccentric, others that his views were normative. At the very least the sales of his books suggest that they enjoyed a substantial readership. Acton was also known for his involvement in the Contagious Diseases Acts of 1864, 1866 and 1869 which attempted to control venereal diseases among the armed forces by subjecting female prostitutes to compulsory examination and treatment. Although the Contagious Diseases Acts have now become a byword for Victorian hypocrisy, at the time Acton's humanising treatment of prostitutes, advocated in his *Prostitution Considered in its Moral, Social, and Sanitary Aspects in London and Other Large Cities* (1857), was relatively enlightened.

### *From* William Acton, *The Functions and Disorders of the Reproductive Organs in Youth, in Adult Age, and in Advanced Life. Considered in Their Physiological, Social, and Psychological Relations* (London: John Churchill, 1857)[1]

From *Chapter II: Normal Functions in Adult Age*[2]

[ . . . ] If, then, we admit, with those who have written on the subject, the full force of the 'sex-passion,' let us at the same time take care that we ourselves are not carried away by the subject, and under pretence of showing its importance, advocate a line of conduct in consonance, as some think, with it, but opposed to all principles of religion, morality, and social rights. This I believe an anonymous writer[3] has done who maintains –

'To have offspring is not to be regarded as a luxury, but as a great primary necessary of health and happiness, of which every man and woman should have a fair share.'
'The ignorance of the necessity of sexual intercourse to the health and virtue of both man and woman, is the most fundamental error in medical and moral philosophy.'
'The hopes of man lie in a nutshell: they are all comprehended in this question of questions – Is it possible to have both food and love? Is it possible that each individual among us can have a due share of food, love, and leisure?'

'Rather than resign love, rather than practise increased sexual abstinence, and so check population, they (mankind) have been willing to
submit to the smallest proportion of food and leisure which the human
frame could for a season endure. The want of love is so miserable a
state of constraint, and, moreover, so destructive to the health of body
and mind, that people who have a choice in the matter, will rather put
up with any evils than endure it.'

Now, had the writer of these paragraphs been speaking of the animal
creation, we might have been able to agree with him; but notwithstanding all the
force of the 'sexual instinct,' Man, we must not forget, is furnished with
reasoning powers; a knowledge of good and evil has been given him; he knows,
or ought to learn, that he must keep his feelings within bounds: in this he differs
from the beasts that perish.

As physiologists, we do not wish to shut our eyes to the force of the sex-
passion in Man: we admit that it is as strong as has been described; but we join
issue with a declaration made by this same author, who says – 'It may be
mentioned as curious, that a young man entering on puberty indulges the exercise of all his organs, all his feelings, except that of the most violent – namely,
love.'

We maintain that a young man[a] at puberty does not, and should not, indulge
all his instinct; for if he did, much mischief would happen to him. But with
respect to the sex-passion particularly, let me say a few words. It is not well that
he should (even if he had the opportunity) indulge his passions. Sexual indulgence at this early part of his life is attended, as we shall presently see, with the
worst consequences to the individual; the produce of such youths are in general
weakly, sickly children that can be with difficulty reared. All breeders of cattle
have long since ceased to raise their stock from either young males or females.
The frame of the sire or dam must be perfected before their owners can call on
the procreative functions to be discharged. Parise[4] has said, very truly, to 'diffuse
the species, the species ought to be perfect and in perfection.' Puberty must not
be just dawning; it must be in full vigour: hence the necessity of man's controlling his sexual feelings at an early age. Observation on a large class of men has
convinced me that this precocious sexual feeling betokens an unsatisfactory state
of mind, and augurs ill for the future.

The same anonymous writer (whose work I should not further allude to, were
he not the mouthpiece of a large class of young men who pretend that fornication is necessary, together with its attendant evils) is obliged, for consistency's

---

a   Even in animals, time is allowed for the perfection of the species by a wise dispensation, and
    vigour in the male is the quality sought and obtained. Neither is it even given to most animals to
    so indulge their instincts. Thus we find that the young bucks are driven away by the older and
    stronger ones. In a farm-yard, the cock must show his prowess, and *win his spurs*, before he is
    allowed by the more powerful birds to tread the hens.

sake, to admit, that what he calls *unmarried intimacy*, should be sanctioned, precautions being taken to prevent the females having children; and he proposes that the frail sisterhood be received into society, because both they and their paramours but follow Nature's laws, and indulge sexual desires which Nature has given them for their own gratification.

I mention these things here, not with any intention of refuting them, but to show my young readers the consequences such an argument must lead to, if carried out; and I leave it to their imagination to depict the state of society which would ensue if such things could be. But, fortunately for the world, the sex-passion, strong as it is, can be, and ought to be, kept within bounds. This abstinence and self-denial is better for the individual, as will be presently shown; it is absolutely necessary for the well-being of society, and is in conformity with the laws of natural and revealed religion.

The advice given by Carpenter[5] in the last edition of his work, p. 779, is as follows: –

'The author would say to those of his younger readers, who urge the wants of nature as an excuse for the illicit gratification of the sexual passion, "try the effects of close mental application to some of those ennobling pursuits to which your profession introduces you, in combination with vigorous bodily exercise, before you assert that the appetite is unrestrainable, and act upon that assertion." Nothing tends so much to increase the desire, as the continual direction of the mind towards the objects of its gratification, especially under the favouring influence of sedentary habits; whilst nothing so effectually represses it as the determinate exercise of the mental faculties upon other objects, and the expenditure of nervous energy in other channels.'

Dr Carter,[6] in his 'Treatise on Hysteria,' makes some striking remarks on the effect of continual direction of the mind in producing emotional congestion of organs, which illustrate this view of the subject. He says (p. 13),

'The glands liable to emotional congestion are those which, by forming their products in larger quantity, subserve to the gratification of the excited feeling. Thus, blood is directed to the mammae[7] by the maternal emotions, to the testes by the sexual, and to the salivary glands by the influence of appetizing odours; while in either case the sudden demand may produce an exsanguine condition of other organs, and may check some function which was being actively performed – as, for instance, the digestive.'

He also relates a very remarkable example of the intensity of the emotional influence.

476

'A lady, who was watching her little child at play, saw a heavy window-sash fall upon its hand, cutting off three of the fingers; and she was so much overcome by fright and distress, as to be unable to render it any assistance. A surgeon was speedily obtained, who, having dressed the wounds, turned himself to the mother, whom he found seated, moaning and complaining of pain in her hand. On examination, three fingers corresponding to those injured in the child, were discovered to be swollen and inflamed, although they had ailed nothing prior to the accident. In four-and-twenty hours, incisions were made into them and pus was evacuated; sloughs were afterwards discharged, and the wounds ultimately healed.

'Now in this case there can be no doubt that the mother's emotion was directed, by observation of the parts injured, upon the corresponding parts of her own system, there working a change in the circulation or nutrition, sufficient to excite acute inflammatory action.'

In treating of this subject further on, we shall find many instances in which there is good reason to believe in such emotional influences, and that a long-directed attention to the organs in hypochondriacs and others, have set up a deranged state of the nervous and circulating powers.

I am inclined to believe that many of the penances which ascetics in former times set themselves – such as starvation, scourging, and exposure, – were the most potent means then known of restraining the animal passions, and teaching the suffering to control their feelings; with the same object we may believe that many a hermit shut himself out from the world in order to escape the effect of female society. In the present day I am acquainted with individuals who in former times would have become such misdirected enthusiasts; – for human nature is little changed, although the fashion of self-chastisement has gone out. There are self-made martyrs in this the nineteenth century, as there were in the sixteenth.

To show the importance of the fluid semen, which young men would thus lavishly expend, let my young readers turn to [ . . . ][8] where they will read what Parise says of it. The same author observes elsewhere that

'The venereal act is the act of the strong, let *him* be cautious who does not comprehend this great truth! And yet, nevertheless, in general, men exaggerate the necessity of this generative function, urged on by passion, by luxury, by a polluted imagination, by fatal habits, they mistake often for an irresistible necessity the effect of excitement, which is foreign to them, and which is little in consonance with their constitutions. Is it not strange to demand of desire the most acute, yea, the most capricious, that which the organic and physiological condition of man refuses, and will always refuse? Many a spendthrift will continue his excesses, and yet have more than enough: and we may say that he will only learn to economise his funds when he has become a bankrupt.'

A striking example of what resolution can do was related to me lately by a patient.

'You may be somewhat surprised, Mr Acton,' said he, 'by the statement I am about to make to you, that before my marriage I lived a perfectly continent life. During my university career my passions were very strong, sometimes almost uncontrollable, but I have the satisfaction of thinking that I mastered them; but it was, however, by great efforts. I obliged myself to take violent physical exertion; I was the best oar of my year, and when I felt particularly strong sexual desire, I sallied out to take more exercise. I was victorious always; and I never committed fornication; you see in what robust health I am, it was exercise that alone saved me.'

I may mention that this gentleman took a most excellent degree, and has reached the highest point of his profession. This is another instance of what energy of character, indomitable perseverance, and good health will effect. I shall presently be obliged to present the reverse of this picture, where men give themselves up to their uncontrolled appetites.

I believe I have already alluded to the fact that the intellectual qualities are usually in an inverse ratio to the sexual appetites. It would almost seem as if the two were incompatible; the exercise of the one annihilating the other. Thus we meet with so many unmarried men among the intellectual, and some of the ablest works have been written by bachelors. Newton and Pitt were single, Kant disliked women; and the ancients allegorically alluded to this in giving to Minerva, the goddess of science, the surname of a woman without breasts. Apollo and the Muses are represented as single.[9] I observe every day that men who are, or have recently been, reading hard at the universities come to me with complaints of impotency, which I am happy enough to prove to them is for the time being only, and to be accounted for as above.

Having thus dwelt upon the strength of the sex-passion, and shown how necessary it is to keep it in abeyance, I cannot quit the subject without alluding to the time when the gratification of love may be allowed. My advice to all young men above twenty-five, who are in good health, is, to marry as soon as circumstances permit them to maintain a wife. Everything tends to prove that the moderate gratification of the sex-passion in married life is doubtless followed by the happiest consequences to the individual. Carpenter expresses himself very happily on this subject. He says (p. 793),

'The instinct, when once aroused, even though very obscurely felt, acts upon the mental faculties and moral feelings, and thus becomes the source, though almost unconsciously so to the individual, of the tendency to form that kind of attachment towards one of the opposite sex which is known as *love*. This tendency cannot be regarded as a simple passion or emotion, since it is the result of the combined operations of the reason, the imagination, and the moral feelings; and it is in this engraftment (so as to speak) of the psychical attachment upon the mere corporeal instinct, that a difference exists between the sexual relations of Man and those of the lower animals. In proportion as the human being makes the temporary gratification of the mere sexual appetite his chief object, and overlooks the happiness arising from spiritual communion which is not only purer but more permanent, and of which a renewal may be anticipated in another world – does he degrade himself to a level with the brutes that perish: yet how lamentably frequent is this degradation.'

The effect on the individual is well put by Lallemand,[10] who says:

'When connexion is followed by a joyous feeling, a *bien être général*,[11] as well as fresh vigour; when the head feels more free and easy, the body more elastic and lighter; when a greater disposition to exercise or intellectual labour arises, and the genital organs evince an increase of vigour and activity, we may infer than an imperious want has been satisfied within the limits necessary for health. The happy influence which all the organs experience is similar to that which follows the accomplishment of every function necessary to the economy.'

Parise remarks, 'we must admit, if the pleasurable moments, as well as the torments, which attend love lasted, there would be no human force capable of supporting them, unless our actual condition were changed.'

I should be ill discharging the duties I owe the profession and those who have consulted me, did I pass by in silence the scenes of *sexual suffering* which I have witnessed. I have [ . . . ][12] described one who has by great strength of mind overcome the tempter; but it must be candidly observed that a state of celibacy in many persons is one of infinite suffering. Mr Farr, in his report on the late census,[13] thus speaks of celibacy, and it is in this way that the subject is usually treated: –

'Certain duties of the most exalted, as well as of the humblest kind in the world, are most efficiently performed by these classes (the unmarried); and although the proposition, "that the best works, and of the greatest merit for the public, have proceeded from the unmarried or childless men," may not be absolutely true as it is put by Bacon,[14] they have unquestionably contributed their full share to public works, which often absorb the powers of mind to an extent that might embarrass him that in "wife and children has given hostages to fortune." '

It is the fashion in this statistical way thus to settle the social values of bachelors; and it is customary among the happily settled class to allot to them little else than misery and discomfort; but let the man who has married early, pause, hear a voice seldom heard, and when heard, seldom listened to. Let him learn that his felicity and his bodily ease may be imperilled even now, while he smiles in fancied security.

My friend Dr— is constantly attending for serious diseases of the womb the wives of clergymen, as well as of dissenting ministers, in whose cases, for months together, marital intercourse is necessarily forbidden. He tells me that he has often been surprised at the amount of sexual suffering – the result of their compulsory celibacy – endured by the husbands of some of his patients – men in every other relation of life most determined and energetic. Consider for a moment the position of such men, who for years may have indulged, with moderation, the sex-passion as we have described it, untrained to mortification in the shape of food or exercise, or marital intercourse, the secretion of perfect semen going on in obedience to the healthy *régime* of a married man's existence, – conceive them reined up suddenly, as it were, and bidden to do battle with their instincts. Religion and morality prevent them, more than others, from having sexual intercourse with strange women; intense ignorance on the subject of the sex-passion in general, as well as misapprehension of the effects of disuse of the generative organs, only aggravate their suffering: conceive all this, and need you strain your imagination to believe that affections of the brain may supervene? Here is one phase of sexual suffering.

Let me recapitulate what Pittard says on this subject, in the 'Cyclop. of Anatomy'[15] (article, Vesiculae Seminales), as I prefer the testimony of a disinterested physiologist before the mere reiteration of my own opinions.

> 'During the period of excitement, spermatozoa are becoming rapidly adult, the testicles and the ducts are full of semen, the individual is in the condition of a fish with a full milt, or a bird or stag with enlarged testes. He now instinctively seeks the society of women. These things are not so much matters of chance as is generally imagined, and the testicles may be blameable for much of what is usually ascribed to the heart. Lascivious dalliance increases his excitement, and all is ready for the copulative act.'

If this, then, is the plain description of the physiological state of the generative organs among adult males in health, is there no compassion to be shown to the continent bachelor? Does he not, think you, often fall a victim to sexual misery? Reader, take my word for it, this sexual feeling has caused many a suicide, it has made many a misanthrope; many are the cells now peopled by single men who, unable to control their feelings, have sought the monastery as an alleviation of their sufferings, and there found it in fasting, penance, and prayer. The Catholic Church must know much of sexual misery, and doubtless by recognising it, has greatly benefited mankind, as well as filled its convents.

The Protestant Church offers no such refuge, and I fear many a lunatic asylum now contains inmates who would, under proper direction, have become useful members of well-organized lay societies. Our Church replies to applicants – practise resignation, have patience, marry if you are able, read religious books; but does not, like the Catholic, enjoin fasting, or demand imperious, never-ceasing duty, under the superintendence of one who knows himself, perhaps, what it is to have laboured under sexual suffering in its acutest form.

I have daily cause to regret that in the present civilized age, pecuniary considerations render the marriage tie so frequently beyond the reach of our patients. This is another difficulty which attends the subject of the sexual feelings; and as it is often hopeless to expect that our patients can 'afford to marry;' one of the means of alleviation we have at our disposal is thus cut from under us. I unequivocally state that I never can or will take upon myself the responsibility of recommending illicit sexual intercourse. Setting aside moral considerations, I feel fully convinced that no physiological or other motives can justify a medical man in suggesting the promiscuous or systematic breach of the seventh commandment.

The occasional indulgence of the sexual feelings is not, in the first place, medically desirable, as stimulating without satisfying the appetite. And each casual intercourse, again, is attended with this danger: – that it may but initiate a more permanent *liaison*, often fraught with painful consequences. If it once assume regularity, a man may form ties most difficult to break. The class of persons who accept his attentions on these terms without marriage, is beneath him in station and education. He finds himself presently in a false position. If the female is true to him alone, there is often great inducement to make her what in common parlance is called, 'an honest woman.' Should a real marriage ensue, the ill-fated youth finds he has learnt too late a bitter lesson for the rest of his life. The requirements of society are such that men only can, or do virtually, visit at his house, even if his social position is good. His family may try to make the best of matters, but the well-educated female declines to look over the new-promoted wife's antecedent. The latter may sometimes merit much compassion, when, with every disposition to act well, she finds the entrance into good society closed against her. Her imperfect education unfits her for her new position; she pines away, becomes cross-tempered; and those who have seen the interiors of such domestic establishments, know that marriages of this sort rarely turn out well, and that the husband is often the first to see the error of his ways.

And when the sensual young man is fortunate or shrewd enough to avoid the 'permanent *liaison*,' and wise, no doubt, in his own conceit, indulges his passions by promiscuous illicit intercourse, the day is not far off when he will contract disease – particularly in England, where the complaints of women are shamefully uncared for. The late Father Mathew[16] knew his countrymen well when he enjoined, not moderate indulgence, but total abstinence from spirituous liquors. So it is with the sexual passion. I feel convinced that it is easier to abstain altogether, than to be occasionally incontinent and then continent for a period. And the youth is a dreamer who would open the floodgates of an ocean, and then attempt to prescribe at will a limit to the inundation. The half-continent man will soon find the truth of the description given by Pittard [ . . . ];[17] and that however great has been the previous difficulty of self-restraint, it is doubled after the gratification of the sexual passion. Before quitting the subject, I must answer one objection to continence which I find often urged, and I believe with sincerity, by my patients: – If we do not exercise our organs they will become atrophied, and when we marry we shall be impotent: this is the reason why we commit fornication. There is not a greater error than this. As well say that it is necessary to eat or walk all day, lest the muscles become absorbed. There is no physiological truth in this want of exercise of the sexual organs. In the first place, I may state that I have never seen a single instance of atrophy of the generative organs from this cause. I have witnessed, it is true, the complaint alluded to – but under what circumstances does it occur? If arises in all instances from the exactly opposite cause – abuse: then the organ ceases to act, and hence atrophy. Physiologically considered, it is impossible, as I have stated above, that the sex-passion should be annihilated in well-formed adults. The function goes on in the organ always, from puberty to old age. Semen is secreted sometimes slowly, sometimes quickly; and very frequently under the influence of the will [ . . . ].[18] We shall presently see that when the seminal vessels are full, emission at night is not unfrequent. This will tend to show the novice that the testes are fully equal to their work when called upon. Let the continent man, then, be not deterred by this apocryphal fear of atrophy of the testes from living a chaste life. Let him take my word, – it is a device of the unchaste, – a lame excuse for their own incontinence, unfounded on any physiological law, – a nameless bugbear which the youth will do well to discharge from his calculations, reserving his moral energies for the running fight I have proposed to him with the grosser instincts of his nature. The testes will take care that their action is not interfered with. I have already hinted at emissions acting as a safety-valve in man, and that continence is not followed by impotence, is shown most forcibly in animals. Mr Varnell,[19] Assistant-Professor at the Veterinary College, tells me of an instance in the case of an entire horse, kept by a friend of his for hunting. This animal was never allowed to have mares, yet was quiet in their presence, and hunted regularly. When twenty years old, he was allowed to mount mares for the first time, and became a sure foal-getter.

Among the arguments for incontinence not unfrequently urged on my attention by patients, are –

'that a state of continence after a certain time produces a most irritable condition of the nervous system, that the individual is unable to settle his mind to anything: study becomes impossible; the student cannot sit still; sedentary occupations are unbearable; and sexual ideas intrude perpetually on the patient's thoughts. That in such cases the self-prescribed remedy has been most effective, and sexual intercourse enabled the student at once to recommence his labours, the poet his verses, and the faded imagination of the painter to resume its fervour and its brilliancy; while the writer who for days has not been able to construct two phrases that he considered readable, has found himself, after relief of the seminal vessels, in a condition to dictate his best performances.'

I have heard such statements from so many single men, that I am obliged to believe that continence induces this state of irritability. But had the deponents been further examined, I should doubtless have found that the last remedy they would entertain, would be that first recommended by a professional man, viz., attention to diet – and in fact, *régime*. The concurrence of testimony in favour of the remedy considered agreeable, and the absence of any as to that involving constraint or inconvenience, certainly induce me to suppose that the witnesses who so boldly come forward have no experience of both systems. It is better to live a continent life. The strictly continent suffer from no such irritability; but the incontinent, as soon as seminal plethora occurs, suffer in one or other of the ways above spoken of; but if effective, as such persons allege, their nostrum requires repetition as often as the inconvenience returns. I, however, on the contrary, affirm that low diet, aperient medicine,[20] gymnastic exercise, and self-control, will relieve the symptoms; and precautions mentioned elsewhere will prevent a repetition of the seminal plethora which is the cause of the irritability. Such treatment is, however, not palatable to the Young England school.[21]

If, then, I have shown that incontinence, immature and secret states of cohabitation, are to be reprehended, what shall I say of early marriages in the sphere of life compatible with the circumstances of the wedded parties? That I think them very advisable. The marriage state is the best and most natural cure for sexual suffering of many a human being; but to marry with the chance of happiness,[b] many things are necessary. Let the youngster green to the ways of the

---

b     Listen to what Parise says on *Marriage*: 'Amidst the abundant statistics which have been collected lately, it has been demonstrated that bachelors live a shorter time than the Benedicks [i.e. nineteenth-century slang for newly married men, especially apparently confirmed bachelors who marry]. This assertion is only true provided the married couples live happily together; otherwise bachelors must have the advantage. In a happy marriage, everything conduces to enjoyment, to well-being, health, and longevity, for life is passed without shocks and agitation; there is a kernel of felicity, around which is superimposed all the other pleasures which can arise, and which must soften the misfortunes to which human nature is inevitably doomed. In an unhappy marriage, when each person is a perpetual cross for the other, everything is anguish, torment, trouble, and

*[continued]*

483

world pause, otherwise he may run from one misery into another. The light literature of the day furnishes ample materials showing the folly that besets the boy in love; here it is that the sex-passion again, uncontrolled, may, by inducing him to marry the first pretty doll that smiles on him and welcomes his attentions, plunge him into irretrievable ruin. But of what avail is advice – how is it possible to control some men who have not common sense? I fear they must sink – nothing can help them – they will not be guided, so great is their belief in their own superior attainments. If they escape the intriguing mother, they may fall into the hands of the bill discounter; if unplucked by him, they become the prey of some other harpy,[22] particularly if they possess a little money. They fall out of the ranks of society and decay, – its very rubbish, – beside the onward path of those whose career is happier, because conformable to physical and moral laws.

Early marriages, however, rest not with the medical man; the laws of supply and demand will regulate this, as seen in the following statistics. [ . . . ][23]

These figures – although, being based upon examination of the entire population, they may be no safe guide to conclusions as to the marriage statistics of the higher classes – tell the actual state of the marriageable people of the community. Think, reader, of the numbers here set down; realize to yourself that each individual may represent a living picture of what I have attempted to describe as the force of the 'sex-passion;' how many are subject to the 'sexual misery' I have shown to exist, can be known only to the individuals. Can man hope to remedy it? I think much may be done. Of one thing I am quite certain – if alleviation can be sought, it must be by well-directed attempts at education. By education I do not mean reading and writing, but training, drilling, directing, and, in fact, educating our sexual instincts, and the passions they govern. I feel confident the giving way to sexual indulgences will not correct the evils; they can only aggravate them. Self-control taught early in life, a knowledge of common things, common sense, and sterling religious views – not cant, or words alone, but true Christian charity, and perchance lessons on Christianity – together with greater attention to the physical education of the frame, may do much to induce the young to follow, not break through, nature's laws. In the over-crowded state of society early marriages are impossible. Not only must continence then be enjoined, but I think individuals, as well as the masses, must be taught how to practise it.

---

disquietude; to-day, to-morrow, and always, at each moment the bitter cup, full to overflowing, approaches and touches the lips. Is there a constitution sufficiently strong, or health sufficiently robust, a soul sufficiently firm to flatter itself that it can resist such cruel attacks?'

But I fear that, after all, however advisable on medical grounds, early marriage in the upper classes of life must form the exception, not the rule, being governed mainly by the imperious laws of society, and considerations of finance.

Spinsters, derived from the custom prevalent before the introduction of machinery, that a maiden should have spun a certain tale or task of woollen yarn before she was considered a qualified housewife.

Before quitting this subject of marriage, I should allude to the sexual duties which man is called upon to fulfil. The greatest ignorance prevails on these matters, and hence the excesses which are committed. I would refer my readers [ ... ]24 to the extent to which a man may illustrate his ignorance of nature's laws, and the consequences. As a general rule, great sexual excesses are committed; and I may be asked what should be the rule? what is excess? I reply, that I wish to lay down no general law in a case where so much must depend upon temperament, age, climate, and other circumstances, as well as the health and strength of both parties. I maintain that the continuance of a high degree of bodily vigour is inconsistent with more than a very moderate indulgence on sexual intercourse, and the still higher principle holds good, that man was not alone created to indulge his sexual appetites, and that their indulgence should not be encouraged. Sexual congress ought not to take place more frequently than once in seven or ten days. Mottray states, in his Travels, vol. i. p. 250,25 that the Turkish law obliges husbands to cohabit with their wives once a week, and that if they neglect to do so, the wife can lodge a complaint before a magistrate.

I may here take the opportunity of remarking, that when my opinion is asked by patients whose natural desires are strong, I advise those wishing to control their passions to indulge in intercourse twice on the same night. I have noticed that in many persons a single intercourse does not effectually empty the vasa deferentia,26 and that within the next twenty-four hours strong sexual feelings again arise; whereas, if sexual intercourse is repeated on the same night, the patient is able to so restrain his feelings, that ten days or a fortnight may elapse without having recourse to sexual congress. The further advantage of a second emission taking place is [ ... ]27 that one vas deferens is only emptied at each emission. I believe the non-observance of some such rule as this is a very frequent cause of sterility in the female, as the spermatozoa are not fully formed.

## HAVELOCK ELLIS, *MAN AND WOMAN: A STUDY OF HUMAN SECONDARY SEXUAL CHARACTERS* (1894)

Throughout his career Henry Havelock Ellis (1859–1939) enjoyed two very different reputations: to a select group of friends and medical specialists he was the distinguished author of a number of ground-breaking works on human sexuality, including the seven-volume *Studies in the Psychology of Sex* (1897–1928). For the larger reading public, however, he was simply a purveyor of pornography. After studying medicine at St Thomas' Hospital in London, Ellis moved initially in literary circles. He became friendly with figures such as John Addington Symonds and George Bernard Shaw and in 1887 he was made editor of the 'Mermaid Series of Old Dramatists' (designed to bring seventeenth-century dramatists to a wider public). Around this time he also proposed and edited the 'Contemporary Scientific Series' which was again directed towards the general rather than specialist reader. In 1890 in this series he published his first main scientific work, *The Criminal*, which was followed in 1892 by *The Nationalisation of Health* (published by Fisher Unwin). In 1894 *Man and Woman* appeared, again under the aegis of the Contemporary Scientific Series. It proved to be one of Ellis' most popular works and established his interest in sexology. Using data which he had begun collecting over twelve years earlier, Ellis examined whether attributes such as intelligence, hysteria, emotional capacity and artistic ability had their origins in sexual difference. By grounding the study of gender in biology *Man and Woman* was very much of its time; equally familiar was Ellis' suggestion of a perfect equipoise between male and female difference. The body of research behind the book also prompted the more ambitious (and much more controversial) *Studies in the Psychology of Sex*. The first volume of the series, entitled *Sexual Inversion*, was initially planned as a collaboration with J. A. Symonds. While living in Switzerland, Symonds had assembled a series of homo-sexual case histories which were to form the basis of the volume's documentary evidence, and Symonds' own experiences, recounted in *A Problem in Greek Ethics*, was to be included as an appendix. The work was published in 1897, four years after Symonds' death. However, Symonds' literary executor, Horatio F. Brown, was horrified and immediately suppressed the volume by buying up all the copies (with the exception of a small number which had already been distributed). Later in the same year, Ellis brought out a revised version of the work from which Symonds' name and contributions had been removed. However the police confiscated the edition and the book-seller, George Bedborough, was arrested. An attempt to forestall a trial by defending the work's scientific merits was rejected by the judge and the 'Bedborough trial' – as it was known – went ahead. However, to incur a light sentence Bedborough pleaded guilty and a disappointed Ellis later published his thoughts on the matter in a privately printed pamphlet, *A Note on the Bedborough Trial* (1898). *Sexual Inversion* (renumbered as Volume II of *Studies in the Psychology of Sex*) was finally published in 1901 in America where for a number of years it was legally available only to a specialist medical readership. For the remainder of his career Ellis continued to write prolifically and – with titles such as *The Erotic Rights of Women* (1918) and *The Play-Function of Sex* (1921) – controversially.

### From Havelock Ellis, *Man and Woman: A Study of Human Secondary Sexual Characters* (London: Walter Scott Ltd, 1894)[1]

*Chapter XVIII: Conclusion*

The knowledge we have gained does not enable us definitely to settle special problems – what it does enable us to do – women are nearer to children than are men – but woman is not undeveloped man – the child represents a higher degree of evolution than the adult – the progress of the race had been a progress in youthfulness – in some respects it has been a progress in feminisation – absurdity of speaking of the superiority of one sex over another – the sexes perfectly poised – but social readjustments may still be necessary – we may face all such readjustments with equanimity.

We have examined Man and Woman, as precisely as may be, from various points of view. It is time to pause, as we do so bringing together a few general observations suggested by the multifarious facts we have encountered.

It is abundantly evident that we have not reached the end proposed at the outset. We have not succeeded in determining the radical and essential characters of men and women uninfluenced by external modifying conditions. Sometimes a sufficiently wide induction of facts (as in the question of the alleged sexual differences in respiration) suffices to show us what is artificial and what is real; at other times (as in the question of differences in tactile sensibility) the wider our induction of facts the more complex and mobile become our results. We have to recognise that our present knowledge of men and women cannot tell us what they might be or what they ought to be, but what they actually are, under the conditions of civilisation. By showing us that under varying conditions men and women are, within certain limits, indefinitely modifiable, a precise knowledge of the actual facts of the life of men and women forbids us to dogmatise rigidly concerning the respective spheres of men and women. It is a matter which experience alone can demonstrate in detail. If this is not exactly the result which we set out to attain, it is still a result of very considerable importance. It lays the axe at the root of many pseudo-scientific superstitions. It clears the ground of much unnecessary verbiage and fruitless discussion, and enables us to see more clearly the really essential points at issue. The small group of women who wish to prove the absolute inferiority of the male sex, the larger group of men who wish to circumscribe rigidly the sphere of women, must alike be ruled out of court. Nor may we listen to those would-be scientific dogmatists who on *a priori* grounds, on the strength of some single and often doubtful anatomical fact, lay down social laws for mankind at large. The ludicrous errors of arrogant and over-hasty brain anatomists in the past should alone suffice to teach us this caution. The facts are far too complex to enable us to rush hastily to a conclusion as to their significance. The facts, moreover, are so numerous that even when we have ascertained the precise significance of some one fact, we cannot be sure that it is not contradicted by other facts. And so many of the facts are modifiable under a changing environment that in the absence of experience we cannot pronounce definitely regarding the behaviour of either the male or female organism under different conditions. There is but one tribunal whose sentence is final and without appeal. Only Nature can pronounce concerning the legitimacy of social modifications. The sentence may be sterility or death, but no other tribunal, no appeal to common-sense, will serve instead.

Yet there are certain general conclusions which have again and again presented themselves, even when we have been occupied in considering very diverse aspects of the physical and psychic phenomena of human life. One of these is the greater variability of the male; this is true for almost the whole of the field we have covered, and it has social and practical consequences of the widest significance. The whole of our human civilisation would have been a different thing if in early zoological epochs the male had not acquired a greater variational tendency than the female. Another general conclusion of an equally far-reaching character is the precocity of women, involving greater rapidity of growth and its earlier arrest than in men. The result of this precocity is that women, taken altogether, present the characters of short men, and to some extent of children. The whole organism of the average woman, physical and psychic, is fundamentally unlike that of the average man, on account of this fact alone. The differences may often be of a slight or subtle character, but they are none the less real, and they extend to the smallest details of organic constitution. We have found over and over again that when women differ from men, it is the latter who have diverged, leaving women nearer to the child-type. The earlier arrest of development in women is thus connected with the variational tendency of men. And all these sexual differences probably have their origin in the more intimate connection of women with offspring.

Further evidence regarding the infantile diathesis of women, as we may call it, is found in pathological statistics. It is difficult to find diseases that are common in children and men and rare in women, and still more difficult to find diseases that are rare in children and men and common in women. On the other hand, it is very easy to find diseases which are common in children and women and rare in men, and diseases which are rare in children and women and common in men. [ . . . ][2]

This general character of women's organic development has long been recognised.[a] Its significance has by no means been so clearly recognised. To assume, as Herbert Spencer[3] and many others have assumed, that on this account woman is 'undeveloped man,' is to state the matter in an altogether misleading manner. That the adult man diverges to a greater extent from the child-type than the adult woman is on the whole certainly true – though even this is not entirely true of the more primary sexual organs and functions – and, so far as it is true, it is a fact not merely of human life, but of animal life generally. To add, however, that woman is undeveloped man is only true in the same sense as it is to state that man is undeveloped woman; in each sex there are undeveloped organs and functions which in the other sex are developed. In order to appraise rightly the significance of the fact that women remain somewhat nearer to children than do men, we must have a clear idea of the position occupied by the child in the human and allied species. In Chapter II, I alluded to the curious fact that among the anthropoids the infant ape is very much nearer to Man than the adult ape. This means that the infant ape is higher in the line of evolution than the adult, and the female ape, by approximating to the infant type, is somewhat higher than the male. Man, in carrying on the line of evolution, started not from some adult male simian, but from the infant ape, and in a less degree from the female ape. The human infant bears precisely the same relation to his species as the simian infant bears to his, and we are bound to conclude that his relation to the future evolution of the race is similar.[b] The human infant presents in an exaggerated form the chief distinctive characters of humanity – the large head and brain, the small face, the hairlessness, the delicate bony system. By some strange confusion of thought we usually ignore this fact, and assume that the adult form is more highly developed than the infantile form.[c] From the point of view of

---

a  Thus [Paul] Topinard points out that, structurally, woman is intermediate between the child and the adult man. [The reference is probably to Topinard's *De l'Evolution des races humaines* (1877).] Dr H. Campbell (*Nervous Organisation of Man and Woman*, chaps. viii., ix.) has an interesting discussion of this question.

b  It may be argued, in explanation of the phenomena, that the ape has descended from a more human ancestor, but there is no ground for such an assumption.

c  The confusion has, however, often been pointed out. 'It is a gross error,' remarked [Karl Friedrich] Burdach, whose intuitions were rarely wrong, 'to suppose that increase in age is increase in the scale of perfection.' (*Phys.* i. p. 383.) [The reference is to Burdach's *Die Physiologie als Erfahrungs Wissenschaft* (1853).]

adaptation to the environment it is undoubtedly true that the coarse, hairy, large-boned, and small-brained gorilla is better fitted to make his way in the world than his delicate offspring, but from a zoological point of view we witness anything but progress. In Man, from about the third year onwards, further growth – though an absolutely necessary adaptation to the environment – is to some extent growth in degeneration and senility. It is not carried to so low a degree as in the apes, although by it Man is to some extent brought nearer to the apes, and among the higher human races the progress towards senility is less marked than among the lower human races. The child of many African races is scarcely if at all less intelligent than the European child, but while the African as he grows up becomes stupid and obtuse, and his whole social life falls into a state of hide-bound routine, the European retains much of his childlike vivacity. And if we turn to what we are accustomed to regard as the highest human types, as represented in men of genius, we shall find a striking approximation to the child-type. The average man of genius is short and large-brained – the two chief characteristics of the child – and his general facial expression, as well as his temperament, recall the child.[d] 'You Greeks are always children;' such was the impression given by the ancient people whom we are taught to regard as the highest type the world has reached. According to the formula of an old mystic, the reign of the Father gave place to the reign of the Son, which must be succeeded by the reign of the Holy Ghost. It might be said that this formula corresponds to a zoological verity. The progress of our race has been a progress in youthfulness.[e]

When we have realised the position of the child in relation to evolution we can take a clearer view as to the natural position of woman. She bears the special characteristics of humanity in a higher degree than man (as Burdach pointed out), and led evolution in the matter of hairiness (as Darwin, following Burdach, pointed out), simply because she is nearer to the child. Her conservatism is thus compensated and justified by the fact that she represents more nearly than man the human type to which man is approximating. This is true of physical characters: the large-headed, delicate-faced, small-boned man of urban civilisation is much nearer to the typical woman than is the savage. Not only by his large brain, but by his large pelvis, the modern man is following a path first marked out by woman: the skull of the modern woman is more markedly feminine than that of the savage woman, while that of the modern man has approximated to it; the pelvis of the modern woman is much more feminine in character than that of the primitive woman, and the modern man's pelvis is also slowly becoming more feminine.

---

d   I do not here insist further on the infantile characters of genius, as I hope to deal elsewhere with the man of genius, so far as it is at present possible to study him from the anthropological standpoint.

e   The facts encountered in our consideration of the cephalic index in Chapter V., for example, are interesting from this point of view.

We may note also that, as many investigators have found, the student (to whose type the modern man has approximated) occupies, both physically and mentally, a position intermediate between that of women and ordinary men. Throughout the whole course of human civilisation we see men following women and taking up their avocations, with more energy, more thoroughness, often more eccentricity. Savagery and barbarism have more usually than not been predominantly militant, that is to say masculine, in character, while modern civilisation is becoming industrial, that is to say feminine, in character, for the industries belonged primitively to women, and they tend to make men like women. Even in quite recent times, and in reference to many of the details of life, it is possible to see the workings of this feminisation; although, it is scarcely necessary to caution the reader, this is but one tendency in our complex modern civilisation. I have pointed out [ . . . ][4] how, even during very recent years, there appears to have been a movement amongst men in favour of adopting feminine methods of committing suicide. We have, again, but to compare the various conveniences of our streets, and of locomotion to-day, with the condition of the streets of a large city a century ago, or even in many respects ten years ago, to realise the progress that has been made in affording equal facilities for women with men, and in so doing to make life easier for men as well as for women. St Clement of Alexandria[5] was of the opinion that women should be allowed to wear shoes; it was not, he said, suitable for their feet to be shown naked; 'besides woman is a tender thing, easily hurt. But for a man bare feet are quite in keeping.'[f] To-day a man also is a 'tender thing,' and there is less and less inclination to recognise any distinctions of this kind. It would not be difficult, had it been part of my task, to multiply examples of the ways in which women are leading evolution. In the saying with which Goethe closed his *Faust*[6] lies a biological verity not usually suspected by those who quote it.

Any reader who has turned to this book for facts or arguments bearing on the everlasting discussion regarding the 'alleged inferiority of women,' and who has followed me so far, will already have gathered the natural conclusion we reach on this point. We may regard all such discussion as absolutely futile and foolish. If it is a question of determining the existence and significance of some particular physical or psychic sexual difference a conclusion may not be impossible. To make any broad statement of the phenomena is to recognise that no general conclusion is possible. Now and again we come across facts which group themselves with a certain degree of uniformity, but as we continue we find other equally important facts which group themselves with equal uniformity in another sense. The result produces compensation. Thus we find that the special liability of women to be affected by minor vital oscillations is balanced by a special resistance to more serious oscillations; that against the affectability of women we must place their disvulnerability. Again, the greater variability of men, while it

f    *Paedagogus*, Bk. II., Chap. xii.

produces many brilliant and startling phenomena, also produces a greater proportion of worthless or even harmful deviations, and the balance is thus restored with the more equable level of women. In the intellectual region men possess greater aptitude for dealing with the more remote and abstract interests of life; women have, at the least, as great an aptitude in dealing with the immediate practical interests of life. Women, it is true, remain nearer than men to the infantile state; but, on the other hand, men approach more nearly than women to the ape-like and senile state. The more clearly and broadly we investigate the phenomena the more emphatically these compensations stand out. It could scarcely be otherwise. A species in which the maternal half exhibited a general inferiority of vital functions could scarcely survive; still less could it attain the somewhat special and peculiar position which – however impartially we may look at the matter – can scarcely be denied to the human species.

From many groups of facts, it is true, one may conclude that the world, as it is naturally made, is a better world for women than for men. Nature, as Humboldt put it,[7] has taken women under her special protection. But so far as this is a fact it is zoological and not a merely human fact. The female animal everywhere is more closely and for a longer period occupied with that process of reproduction which is Nature's main concern. This is, indeed, more than a zoological fact; it is a biological fact; among plants we find that the stamens soon fall away while the pistil remains. The female retains her youthfulness for the sake of possible offspring; we all exist for the sake of our possible offspring, but this final end of the individual is more obviously woven into the structure of women. The interests of women may therefore be said to be more closely identified with Nature's interests. Nature has made women more like children in order that they may better understand and care for children, and in the gift of children Nature has given to women a massive and sustained physiological joy to which there is nothing in men's lives to correspond. Nature has done her best to make women healthy and glad, and has on the whole been content to let men run somewhat wild.

Men have had their revenge on Nature and on her *protégée*. While women have been largely absorbed in that sphere of sexuality which is Nature's, men have roamed the earth, sharpening their aptitudes and energies in perpetual conflict with Nature. It has thus come about that the subjugation of Nature by Man has often practically involved the subjugation, physical and mental, of women by men. The periods of society most favourable for women appear, judging from the experiences of the past, to be somewhat primitive periods in which the militant tendency is not strongly marked. Very militant periods, and those so-called advanced periods in which the complicated and artificial products of the variational tendency of men are held in chief honour, are not favourable to the freedom and expansion of women. Greece and Rome, the favourite types of civilisation bring before us emphatically masculine states of culture. The lust of power and knowledge, the research for artistic perfection, are usually masculine characters; and so most certainly are the suppression of natural emotion and the degradation of sexuality and maternity. Morgan[8] has remarked that the fall of classical civilisation was due to the failure to develop women. But women never could have been brought into line with classic civilisation without transforming it entirely. As a matter of fact, when the feminine element at last came to the front with Christianity and the barbarians, classic civilisation went, and for a long time the masculine element in life also largely went – to reappear in monasteries, there to develop its most characteristic aberrations. The hope of our future civilisation lies in the development in equal freedom of both the masculine and feminine elements in life. The broader and more varied character of modern civilisation seems to render this more possible than did the narrow basis of classic civilisation, and there is much evidence around us that a twin movement of this kind is in progress. Still there is considerable advance yet to be made. So long as maternity under certain conditions is practically counted as a criminal act, it cannot be said that the feminine element in life has yet been restored to due honour.

It will be seen that a broad and general survey of the secondary sexual phenomena in humanity brings us at last into a very humble and conservative attitude before the facts of the natural world. It could scarcely be otherwise; the sexual adjustment has been proceeding for so vast a period of time, even if we can only take Man and his immediate ancestors into consideration, that the sexual balance has become as nearly perfect as possible, and every inaptitude is accompanied by some compensatory aptitude, even if it has not, as sometimes occurs, itself developed into an advantageous character. An open-eyed, child-like, yet patient study of the natural facts of life can only lead us to be reverent in the face of those facts.

This conclusion must not, however, be misunderstood. A cosmic conservatism does not necessarily involve a social conservatism. The wisdom of Man, working through a few centuries or in one corner of the earth, by no means necessarily corresponds to the wisdom of Nature, and may be in flat opposition to it. This is especially the case when the wisdom of Man merely means, as sometimes happens, the experience of our ancestors gained under other conditions, or merely the opinions of one class or one sex. Taking a broad view of the matter, it seems difficult to avoid the conclusion that it is safer to trust to the conservatism of Nature than to the conservatism of Man. We are not at liberty to introduce any artificial sexual barrier into the social concerns. The respective fitness of men and of women for any kind of work or any kind of privilege can only be ascertained by actual open experiment; and as the conditions for such experiment are never twice the same, it can never be positively affirmed that anything has been settled once and for all. When such experiment is successful, so much the better for the race; when it is unsuccessful, the minority who have broken natural law alone suffer. An exaggerated anxiety lest natural law be overthrown is misplaced. The world is not so insecurely poised. We may preserve an attitude of entire equanimity in the face of social readjustment. Such readjustment is either the outcome of wholesome natural instinct, in which case our social structure will be strengthened and broadened, or it is not; and if not, it is unlikely to become organically ingrained in the species.

Our investigation, therefore, shows us in what state of mind we ought to approach the whole problem; it can scarcely be said that it gives us the definite solution of definite problems. It is not on that account fruitless. There is distinct advantage in clearing away, so far as we can, the thick undergrowth of prepossession and superstition which flourishes in the region we have traversed to a greater extent than in any other region. It is something to have asked the right question, and to be set on the right road. It is something, also, to realise that we may disregard the assertions, or even the facts, of those who have not faced all the difficulties that must be encountered. At the very least it seems impossible to follow the paths we have here traversed without gaining a more vivid and tolerant insight into what for us must always be the two most interesting beings in the world.

# 11

# DEFINING WOMEN

## SARAH STICKNEY ELLIS, *THE WOMEN OF ENGLAND: THEIR SOCIAL DUTIES, AND DOMESTIC HABITS* (N.D. 1843?)

Sarah Stickney Ellis (1812–72) was the second wife of a missionary, William Ellis. Brought up as a Quaker, she later joined the Congregational Church, and with her husband was a zealous campaigner in the Temperance Movement. She was also a prolific writer, producing numerous volumes of conduct manuals, poems, stories and travel writing. *The Women of England*, first published in 1838, was one of her earliest and most successful works. In it Ellis set out an enduring and familiar image of Victorian femininity – in Coventry Patmore's well-known phrase, that of the 'angel in the house', to which she added the notion of practical or domestic (as opposed to academic) intelligence. *The Women of England* was quickly followed by *The Wives of England* (1843), *The Mothers of England* (1843) and *The Daughters of England* (1845). During this time Sarah Ellis found a further outlet for her ideas in Rawdon House – a school for young ladies which she founded in order to put into practice the prescriptions about character-formation and domestic duty which her works contained.

**From** Sarah Stickney Ellis, *The Women of England: Their Social Duties, and Domestic Habits* (London: The London Printing and Publishing Company, n.d. [1843?])[1]

*Chapter II: Influence of the Women of England*

It might form a subject of interesting inquiry, how far the manifold advantages possessed by England as a country, derive their origin remotely from the cause already described;[2] but the immediate object of the present work is to show how intimate is the connexion which exists between the *women* of England, and the *moral* character maintained by their country in the scale of nations. For a woman to undertake such a task, may at first sight appear like an act of presumption; yet when it is considered that the appropriate business of men is to direct, and expatiate upon, those expansive and important measures for which their capabilities are more peculiarly adapted, and that to women belongs the minute and particular observance of all those trifles which fill up the sum of human happiness or misery, it may surely be deemed pardonable for a woman to solicit the serious attention of her own sex, while she endeavours to prove that it is the minor morals of domestic life which give the tone to English character, and that over this sphere of duty it is her peculiar province to preside.

Aware that the word *preside*, used as it is here, may produce a startling effect upon the ear of man, I must endeavour to bespeak his forbearance, by assuring him, that the highest aim of the writer does not extend beyond the act of warning the women of England back to their domestic duties, in order that they may become better wives, more useful daughters, and mothers, who by their example shall bequeath a rich inheritance to those who follow in their steps.

On the other hand, I am equally aware that a work such as I am proposing to myself must be liable to the condemnation of all modern young ladies, as a homely, uninteresting book, and wholly unsuited to the present enlightened times. I must therefore endeavour also to conciliate their good will, by assuring them, that all which is most lovely, poetical, and interesting, nay, even *heroic* in women, derives its existence from the source I am now about to open to their view, with all the ability I am able to command; – and would it were a hundred-fold, for their sakes!

The kind of encouragement I would hold out to them is, however, of a nature so widely different from the compliments to which they are too much accustomed, that I feel the difficulty existing in the present day, of stimulating a laudable ambition in the female mind, without the aid of public praise, or printed records of the actual product of their meritorious exertions. The sphere of woman's happiest and most beneficial influence is a domestic one, but it is not easy to award even to her quiet and unobtrusive virtues that need of approbation which they really deserve, without exciting a desire to forsake the homely household duties of the family circle, to practise such as are more conspicuous, and consequently more productive of an immediate harvest of applause.

I say this with all kindness, and I desire to say it with all gentleness, to the young, the amiable, and the – *vain*; at the same time that my perception of the temptation to which they are exposed, enhances my value for the principle that *is* able to withstand it, and increases my admiration of those noble-minded women who *are* able to carry forward, with exemplary patience and perseverance, the public offices of benevolence, without sacrificing their home-duties, and who thus prove to the world, that the perfection of female character is a combination of private and public virtue, – of domestic charity, and zeal for the temporal and eternal happiness of the whole human race.

496

No one can be farther than the writer of these pages from wishing to point out as objects of laudable emulation those domestic drudges, who, because of some affinity between culinary operations and the natural tone and character of their own minds, prefer the kitchen to the drawing-room, – of their own free choice, employ their whole lives in the constant bustle of providing for mere animal appetite, and waste their ingenuity in the creation of new wants and wishes, which all their faculties again are taxed to supply. This class of individuals have, by a sad mistake in our nomenclature, been called *useful*, and hence, in some degree, may arise the unpopular reception which this valuable word is apt to meet with in female society.

It does not require much consideration to perceive, that these are not the women to give a high moral tone to the national character of England; yet so entirely do human actions derive their dignity or their meanness from the *motives* by which they are prompted, that it is no violation of truth to say, the most servile drudgery may be ennobled by the self-sacrifice, the patience, the cheerful submission to duty, with which it is performed. Thus a high-minded and intellectual woman is never more truly great, than when willingly and judiciously performing kind offices for the sick; and much as may be said, and said justly, in praise of the public virtues of women, the voice of nature is so powerful in every human heart, that could the question of superiority on these two points be universally proposed, a response would be heard throughout the world, in favour of woman in her private and domestic character.

Nor would the higher and more expansive powers of usefulness with which women are endowed, suffer from want of exercise, did they devote themselves assiduously to their domestic duties. I am rather inclined to think they would receive additional vigour from the healthy tone of their own minds, and the leisure and liberty afforded by the systematic regularity of their household affairs. Time would never hang heavily on their hands, but each moment being husbanded with care, and every agent acting under their influence being properly chosen and instructed, they would find ample opportunity to go forth on errands of mercy, secure that in their absence the machinery they had set in motion would still continue to work, and to work well.

But if, on the other hand, all was confusion and neglect at home – filial appeals unanswered – domestic comforts uncalculated – husbands, sons, and brothers, referred to servants for all the little offices of social kindness, in order that the ladies of the family might hurry away at the appointed time to some committee-room, scientific lecture, or public assembly; however laudable the object for which they met, there would be sufficient cause why their cheeks should be mantled with the blush of burning shame when they heard the women of England and their virtues spoken of in that high tone of approbation and applause, which those who aspire only to be about their Master's business will feel little pleasure in listening to, and which those whose charity has not begun at home ought never to appropriate to themselves.

It is a widely mistaken notion to suppose that the sphere of usefulness recommended here is a humiliating and degraded one. As if the earth that fosters and nourishes in its lovely bosom the roots of all the plants and trees which ornament the garden of the world, feeding them from her secret storehouse with supplies that never fail, were less important, in the economy of vegetation, than the sun that brings to light their verdure and their flowers, or the genial atmosphere that perfects their growth, and diffuses their perfume abroad upon the earth. To carry out the simile still farther, it is but just to give the preference to that element which, in the absence of all other favouring circumstances, withholds not its support; but when the sun is shrouded, and the showers forget to fall, and blighting winds go forth, and the hand of culture is withdrawn, still opens out its hidden fountains, and yields up its resources, to invigorate, to cherish, and sustain.

It would be an easy and a grateful task, thus, by metaphor and illustration, to prove the various excellencies and amiable peculiarities of woman, did not the utility of the present work demand a more minute and homely detail of that which constitutes her practical and individual duty. It is too much the custom with writers, to speak in these general terms of the *loveliness* of the female character; as if woman were some fragrant flower, created only to bloom, and exhale in sweets; when perhaps these very writers are themselves most strict in requiring that the domestic drudgery of their own households should each day be faithfully filled up. How much more generous, just, and noble it would be to deal fairly by woman in these matters, and to tell her that to be *individually*, what she is praised for being *in general*, it is necessary for her to lay aside all her natural caprice, her love of self-indulgence, her vanity, her indolence – in short, her very *self* – and assuming a new nature, which nothing less than watchfulness and prayer can enable her constantly to maintain, to spend her mental and moral capabilities in devising means for promoting the happiness of others, while her own derives a remote and secondary existence from theirs.

If an admiration almost unbounded for the perfection of female character, with a sisterly participation in all the errors and weaknesses to which she is liable, and a profound sympathy with all that she is necessarily compelled to feel and suffer, are qualifications for the task I have undertaken, these certainly are points on which I yield to none; but at the same time that I do my feeble best, I must deeply regret that so few are the voices lifted up in her defence against the dangerous influence of popular applause, and the still more dangerous tendency of modern habits, and modern education. Perhaps it is not to be expected that those who write most powerfully, should most clearly perceive the influence of the one, or the tendency of the other; because the very strength and consistency of their own minds must in some measure exempt them from participation in either. While, therefore, in the art of reasoning, a writer like myself must be painfully sensible of her own deficiency; in sympathy of feeling, she is perhaps the better qualified to address the weakest of her sex.

With such, it is a favourite plea, brought forward in extenuation of their own uselessness, that they have no influence – that they are not leading women – that society takes no note of them; – forgetting, while they shelter themselves beneath these indolent excuses, that the very feather on the stream may serve to warn the doubtful mariner of the rapid and fatal current by which his bark might be hurried to destruction. It is, moreover, from amongst this class that wives are more frequently chosen; for there is a peculiarity in men – I would fain call it *benevolence* – which inclines them to offer the benefit of their protection to the most helpless and dependent of the female sex; and therefore it is upon this class that the duty of training up the young most frequently devolves; not certainly upon the naturally imbecile, but upon the uncalculating creatures whose non-exercise of their own mental and moral faculties renders them not only willing to be led through the experience of life, but thankful to be relieved from the responsibility of thinking and acting for themselves.

It is an important consideration, that from such women as these, myriads of immortal beings derive that early bias of character, which under Providence decides their fate, not only in this world, but in the world to come. And yet they flutter on, and say they have no influence – they do not aspire to be leading women – they are in society but as grains of sand on the sea-shore. Would they but pause one moment to ask how will this plea avail them, when, as daughters without gratitude, friends without good faith, wives without consideration, and mothers without piety, they stand before the bar of judgment, to render an account of the talents committed to their trust! Have they not parents, to whom they might study to repay the debt of care and kindness accumulated in their childhood? – perhaps to whom they might overpay this debt, by assisting to remove such obstacles as apparently intercept the line of duty, and by endeavouring to alleviate the perplexing cares which too often obscure the path of life? Have they not their young friendships, for those sunny hours when the heart expands itself in the genial atmosphere of mutual love, and shrinks not from revealing its very weaknesses and errors; so that a faithful hand has but to touch its tender chords, and conscience is awakened, and then instruction may be poured in, and medicine may be administered, and the messenger of peace, with healing on his wings, may be invited to come in, and make that heart his home? Have they not known the secrets of some faithful bosom laid bare before them in a deeper and yet more confiding attachment, when, however insignificant they might be to the world in general, they held an influence almost unbounded over one human being, and could pour in, for the bane or the blessing of that bosom, according to the fountain from whence their own was supplied, either draughts of bitterness, or floods of light? Have they not bound themselves by a sacred and enduring bond, to be one fellow-traveller along the path of life, a companion on his journey, and, as far as ability might be granted them, a guide and a help in the doubts and the difficulties of his way? Under these urgent and serious responsibilities, have they not been appealed to, both in words and in looks, and in the silent language of the heart, for that promised help? And how has the appeal been answered? Above all, have they not, many of them, had the feeble steps of infancy committed to their care – the pure unsullied page of childhood presented to them for its first and most durable inscription? – and what have they written there? It is vain to plead their inability, and say they knew not what to write, and therefore left the tablet untouched, or sent away the vacant page to be filled up by other hands. Time will prove to them they *have* written, if not by any direct instrumentality, by their example, their conversation, and the natural influence of mind on mind. Experience will prove to them they have written; and the transcript of *what* they have written will be treasured up, either for or against them, amongst the awful records of eternity.

It is therefore not only false in reasoning, but wrong in principle, for women to assert, as they not unfrequently do with a degree of puerile satisfaction, that they have no influence. An influence fraught either with good or evil, they must have; and though the one may be above their ambition, and the other beyond their fears, by neglecting to obtain an influence which shall be beneficial to society, they necessarily assume a bad one: just in the same proportion as their selfishness, indolence, or vacuity of mind, render them in youth an easy prey to every species of unamiable temper, in middle age the melancholy victims of mental disease, and, long before the curtain of death conceals their follies from the world, a burden and a bane to society at large.

A superficial observer might rank with this class many of those exemplary women, who pass to and fro upon the earth with noiseless step, whose names are never heard, and who, even in society, if they attempt to speak, have scarcely the ability to command an attentive audience. Yet amongst this unpretending class are found striking and noble instances of women, who, apparently feeble and insignificant, when called into action by pressing and peculiar circumstances, can accomplish great and glorious purposes, supported and carried forward by that most valuable of all faculties – *moral power*. And just in proportion as women cultivate this faculty (under the blessing of heaven) independently of all personal attractions, and unaccompanied by any high attainments in learning or art, is their influence over their fellow-creatures, and consequently their power of doing good.

It is not to be presumed that women *possess* more moral power than men; but happily for them, such are their early impressions, associations, and general position in the world, that their moral feelings are less liable to be impaired by the pecuniary objects which too often constitute the chief end of man, and which, even under the limitations of better principle, necessarily engage a large portion of his thoughts. There are many humble-minded women, not remarkable for any particular intellectual endowments, who yet possess so clear a sense of the right and wrong of individual actions, as to be of essential service in aiding the judgments of their husbands, brothers, or sons, in those intricate affairs in which it is sometimes difficult to dissever worldly wisdom from religious duty.

To men belongs the potent – (I had almost said the *omnipotent*) consideration of worldly aggrandisement; and it is constantly misleading their steps, closing their ears against the voice of conscience, and beguiling them with the promise of peace, where peace was never found. Long before the boy has learned to exult in

500

the dignity of the man, his mind has become familiarized to the habit of investing with supreme importance, all considerations relating to the acquisition of wealth. He hears on the Sabbath, and on stated occasions, when men meet for that especial purpose, of a God to be worshipped, a Saviour to be trusted in, and a holy law to be observed; but he sees before him, every day and every hour, a strife, which is nothing less than deadly to the highest impulses of the soul, after another god – the mammon of unrighteousness – the moloch of this world;[3] and believing rather what men do, than what they preach, he learns too soon to mingle with the living mass, and to unite his labours with theirs. To unite? Alas! there is no union in the great field of action in which he is engaged; but envy, and hatred, and opposition, to the close of the day – every man's hand against his brother, and each struggling to exalt himself, not merely by trampling upon his fallen foe, but by usurping the place of his weaker brother, who faints by his side, from not having brought an equal portion of strength into the conflict, and who is consequently borne down by numbers, hurried over, and forgotten.

This may be an extreme, but it is scarcely an exaggerated picture of the engagements of men of business in the present day. And surely they now need more than ever all the assistance which Providence has kindly provided, to win them away from this warfare, to remind them that they are hastening on towards a world into which none of the treasures they are amassing can be admitted; and, next to those holier influences which operate through the medium of reve-lation, or through the mysterious instrumentality of Divine love, I have little hesitation in saying, that the society of woman in her highest moral capacity, is best calculated to effect this purpose.

How often has man returned to his home with a mind confused by the many voices, which, in the mart, the exchange, or the public assembly, have addressed themselves to his inborn selfishness, or his worldly pride; and while his integrity was shaken, and his resolution gave way beneath the pressure of apparent neces-sity, or the insidious pretences of expediency, he has stood corrected before the clear eye of woman, as it looked directly to the naked truth, and detected the lurking evil of the specious act he was about the commit. Nay, so potent may have become this secret influence, that he may have borne it about with him like a kind of second conscience, for mental reference, and spiritual counsel, in moments of trial; and when the snares of the world were around him, and temp-tations from within and without have bribed over the witness in his own bosom, he has thought of the humble monitress who sat alone, guarding the fireside comforts of his distant home; and the remembrance of her character, clothed in moral beauty, has scattered the clouds before his mental vision, and sent him back to that beloved home, a wiser and a better man.

The women of England, possessing the grand privilege of being better instructed than those of any other country, in the minutiae of domestic comfort, have obtained a degree of importance in society far beyond what their unobtru-sive virtues would appear to claim. The long-established customs of their country have placed in their hands the high and holy duty of cherishing and protecting the minor morals of life, from whence springs all that is elevated in purpose, and glorious in action. The sphere of their direct personal influence is central, and consequently small; but its extreme operations are as widely extended as the range of human feeling. They may be less striking in society than some of the women of other countries, and may feel themselves, on brilliant and stirring occasions, as simple, rude, and unsophisticated in the popular science of excitement; but as far as the noble daring of Britain has sent forth her adventurous sons, and that is to every point of danger on the habitable globe, they have borne along with them a generosity, a disinterestedness, and a moral courage, derived in no small measure from the female influence of their native country.

It is a fact well worthy of our most serious attention, and one which bears immediately upon the subject under consideration, that the present state of our national affairs is such as to indicate that the influence of woman in counteracting the growing evils of society is about to be more needed than ever.

In our imperfect state of being, we seldom attain any great or national good without its accompaniment of evil; and every improvement proposed for the general weal, has, upon some individual, or some class of individuals, an effect which it requires a fresh exercise of energy and principle to guard against. Thus the great facilities of communication, not only throughout our own country, but with distant parts of the world, are rousing men of every description to tenfold exertion in the field of competition in which they are engaged; so that their whole being is becoming swallowed up in efforts and calculations relating to their pecuniary success. If to grow tardy or indifferent in the race were only to lose the goal, many would be glad to pause; but such is the nature of commerce and trade, as at present carried on in this country, that to slacken in exertion, is altogether to fail. I would fain hope and believe with my countrymen, that many of the rational and enlightened would now be willing to reap smaller gains, if by so doing they could enjoy more leisure. But a business only half attended to, soon ceases to be a business at all; and the man of enlightened understanding, who neglects his, for the sake of hours of leisure, must be content to spend them in the debtor's department of a jail.[4]

Thus, it is not with single individuals that the blame can be made to rest. The fault is in the system; and happy will it be for thousands of immortal souls, when this system shall correct itself. In the mean time, may it not be said to be the especial duty of women to look around them, and see in what way they can counteract this evil, by calling back the attention of man to those sunnier spots in his existence, by which the growth of his moral feelings have been encouraged, and his heart improved?

We cannot believe of the fathers who watched over our childhood, of the husbands who shared our intellectual pursuits, of the brothers who went hand in hand with us in our love of poetry and nature, that they are all gone over to the side of mammon, that there does not lurk in some corner of their hearts a secret longing to return; yet every morning brings the same hurried and indifferent parting, every evening the same jaded, speechless, welcomeless return – until we almost fail to recognize the man, in the machine.

English homes have been much boasted of by English people, both at home and abroad. What would a foreigner think of those neat, and sometimes elegant residences, which form a circle of comparative gentility around our cities and our trading-towns? What would he think, when told that the fathers of those families have not time to see their children, except on the Sabbath-day? and that the mothers, impatient, and anxious to consult them about some of their domestic plans, have to wait, perhaps for days, before they can find them for five minutes disengaged, either from actual exertion, or from that sleep which necessarily steals upon them immediately after the over-excitement of the day has permitted them a moment of repose.

And these are rational, intellectual, accountable, and immortal beings, undergoing a course of discipline by which they are to be fitted for eternal existence! What women can look on without asking – 'Is there nothing I can do, to call them back?' Surely there is; but it never can be done by the cultivation of those faculties which contribute only to selfish gratification. Since her society is shared for so short a time, she must endeavour to make those moments more rich in blessing; and since her influence is limited to so small a range of immediate operation, it should be rendered so potent as to mingle with the whole existence of those she loves.

Will an increase of intellectual attainments, or a higher style of accomplishments, effect this purpose? Will the common-place frivolities of morning calls, or an interminable range of superficial reading, enable them to assist their brothers, their husbands, or their sons, in becoming happier and better men?

No: let the aspect of society be what it may, man is a social being, and beneath the hard surface he puts on, to fit him for the wear and tear of every day, he has a heart as true to the kindly affections of our nature, as that of woman – as true, though not as suddenly awakened to every pressing call. He has therefore need of all her sisterly services, and, under the pressure of the present times, he needs them more than ever, to foster in his nature, and establish in his character, that higher tone of feeling, without which he can enjoy nothing beyond a kind of animal existence – but with which, he may faithfully pursue the necessary avocations of the day, and keep as it were a separate soul for his family, his social duty, and his God.

There is another point of consideration by which this necessity for a higher degree of female influence is greatly increased, and it is one which comprises much that is interesting to those who aspire to be the supporters of their country's worth. The British throne being now graced by a female sovereign, the auspicious promise of whose early years seems to form a new era in the annals of our nation, and to inspire with brighter hopes and firmer confidence the patriot bosoms of her expectant people; it is surely not a time for the female part of the community to fall away from the high standard of moral excellence, to which they have been accustomed to look, in the formation of their domestic habits. Rather let them show forth the benefits arising from their more enlightened systems of education, by proving to their youthful sovereign, that whatever plan she may think it right to sanction for the moral advancement of her subjects, and the promotion of their true interests as an intelligent and happy people, will be welcomed by every female heart throughout her realm, and faithfully supported in every British home by the female influence prevailing there.

## JOHN RUSKIN, *SESAME AND LILIES* (1865)

### *From* John Ruskin, *Sesame and Lilies* (London: Smith, Elder & Co., 1865)[1]

From *Lecture II – Lilies: Of Queens' Gardens*

[ . . . ][2] I do not insist by any farther argument on this, for I think it should commend itself at once to your knowledge of what had been and to your feeling of what should be. You cannot think that the buckling on of the knight's armour by his lady's hand was a mere caprice of romantic fashion. It is the type of an eternal truth – that the soul's armour is never well set to the heart unless a woman's hand has braced it; and it is only when she braces it loosely that the honour of manhood fails. Know you not those lovely lines – I would they were learned by all youthful ladies of England: –

> 'Ah wasteful woman! – she who may
> On her sweet self set her own price,
> Knowing he cannot choose but pay –
> How has she cheapen'd Paradise!
> How given for nought her priceless gift,
> How spoiled the bread and spill'd the wine,
> Which, spent with due, respective thrift,
> Had made brutes men, and men divine!'[a]

Thus much, then, respecting the relations of lovers I believe you will accept. But what we too often doubt is the fitness of the continuance of such a relation throughout the whole of human life. We think it right in the lover and mistress, not in the husband and wife. That is to say, we think that a reverent and tender duty is due to one whose affection we still doubt, and whose character we as yet do but partially and distantly discern; and that this reverence and duty are to be withdrawn, when the affection has become wholly and limitlessly our own, and the character has been so sifted and tried that we fear not to entrust it with the happiness of our lives. Do you not see how ignoble this is, as well as how unreasonable? Do you not feel that marriage – when it is marriage at all, – is only the seal which marks the vowed transition of temporary into untiring service, and of fitful into eternal love?

But how, you will ask, is the idea of this guiding function of the woman reconcilable with a true wifely subjection? Simply in that it is a *guiding*, not a

---

a   Coventry Patmore [whose *The Angel in the House*, a sequence of poems in four parts, was published between 1854 and 1863; the exact reference is to Book I, canto vii, prelude i, ll. 13–20].

determining, function. Let me try to show you briefly how these powers seem to be rightly distinguishable.

We are foolish, and without excuse foolish, in speaking of the 'superiority' of one sex to the other, as if they could be compared in similar things. Each has what the other has not: each completes the other, and is completed by the other: they are in nothing alike, and the happiness and perfection of both depends on each asking and receiving from the other what the other only can give.

Now their separate characters are briefly these. The man's power is active, progressive, defensive. He is eminently the doer, the creator, the discoverer, the defender. His intellect is for speculation and invention; his energy for adventure, for war, and for conquest, wherever war is just, wherever conquest necessary. But the woman's power is for rule, not for battle, – and her intellect is not for invention or creation, but for sweet ordering, arrangement, and decision. She sees the qualities of things, their claims, and their places. Her great function is Praise: she enters into no contest, but infallibly adjudges the crown of contest. By her office, and place, she is protected from all danger and temptation. The man, in his rough work in open world, must encounter all peril and trial: – to him, therefore, the failure, the offence, the inevitable error: often he must be wounded, or subdued, often misled, and *always* hardened. But he guards the woman from all this; within his house, as ruled by her, unless she herself has sought it, need enter no danger, no temptation, no cause of error or offence. This is the true nature of home – it is the place of Peace; the shelter, not only from all injury, but from all terror, doubt, and division. In so far as it is not this, it is not home; so far as the anxieties of the outer life penetrate into it, and the inconsistently-minded, unknown, unloved, or hostile society of the outer world is allowed by either husband or wife to cross the threshold, it ceases to be home; it is then only a part of that outer world which you have roofed over, and lighted fire in. But so far as it is a sacred place, a vestal temple, a temple of the hearth watched over by Household Gods, before whose faces none may come but those whom they can receive with love, – so far as it is this, and roof and fire are types only of a nobler shade and light, – shade as of the rock in a weary land, and light as of the Pharos in the stormy sea;[3] – so far it vindicates the name, and fulfils the praise, of Home.

And wherever a true wife comes, this home is always round her. The stars only may be over her head; the glowworm in the night-cold grass may be the only fire at her foot: but home is yet wherever she is; and for a noble woman it stretches far round her, better than ceiled with cedar, or painted with vermilion,[4] shedding its quiet light far, for those who else were homeless.

This, then, I believe to be, – will you not admit it to be? – the woman's true place and power? But do not you see that, to fulfil this, she must – as far as one can use such terms of a human creature – be incapable of error? So far as she rules, all must be right, or nothing is. She must be enduringly, incorruptibly good; instinctively, infallibly wise – wise, not for self-development, but for self-renunciation: wise, not that she may set herself above her husband, but that she

506

may never fail from his side: wise, not with the narrowness of insolent and love-less pride, but with the passionate gentleness of an infinitely variable, because infinitely applicable, modesty of service – the true changefulness of woman. In that great sense – 'La donna e mobile,' not 'Quam piùm' al vento;' no, nor yet 'Variable as the shade, by the light quivering aspen made;'[5] but variable as the *light*; manifold in fair and serene division, that it may take the colour of all that it falls upon, and exalt it.

II. I have been trying, thus far, to show you what should be the place, and what the power of woman. Now, secondly, we ask, What kind of education is to fit her for these?

And if you indeed think this a true conception of her office and dignity, it will not be difficult to trace the course of education which would fit her for the one, and raise her to the other.

The first of our duties to her – no thoughtful persons now doubt this, – is to secure for her such physical training and exercise as may confirm her health, and perfect her beauty; the highest refinement of that beauty being unattainable without splendour of activity and of delicate strength. To perfect her beauty, I say, and increase its power; it cannot be too powerful, nor shed its sacred light too far: only remember that all physical freedom is vain to produce beauty without a corresponding freedom of heart. There are two passages of that poet who is distinguished, it seems to me, from all others – not by power, but by exquisite *right*ness – which point you to the source, and describe to you, in a few syllables, the completion of womanly beauty. I will read the introductory stanzas, but the last is the one I wish you specially to notice: –

'Three years she grew in sun and shower,
Then Nature said, a lovelier flower
      On earth was never sown.
This child I to myself will take;
She shall be mine, and I will make
      A lady of my own.

'Myself will to my darling be
Both law and impulse; and with me
      The girl, in rock and plain,
In earth and heaven, in glade and bower,
Shall feel an overseeing power
      To kindle, or restrain.

'The floating clouds their state shall lend
To her, for her the willow bend;
      Nor shall she fail to see
Even in the motions of the storm,
Grace that shall mould the maiden's form
      By silent sympathy.

'And *vital feelings of delight*
Shall rear her form to stately height, –
    Her virgin bosom swell.
Such *thoughts* to Lucy I will give,
While she and I together live,
    Here in this happy dell.'[6]

'*Vital* feelings of delight,' observe. There are deadly feelings of delight; but the natural ones are vital, necessary to very life.

And they must be feelings of delight, if they are to be vital. Do not think you can make a girl lovely, if you do not make her happy. There is not one restraint you put on a good girl's nature – there is not one check you give to her instincts of affection or of effort – which will not be indelibly written on her features, with a hardness which is all the more painful because it takes away the brightness from the eyes of innocence, and the charm from the brow of virtue.

This for the means: now note the end. Take from the same poet, in two lines, a perfect description of womanly beauty –

'A countenance in which did meet
Sweet records, promises as sweet.'[7]

The perfect loveliness of a woman's countenance can only consist in that majestic peace, which is founded in the memory of happy and useful years, – full of sweet records; and from the joining of this with that yet more majestic childishness, which is still full of change and promise; – opening always – modest at once, and bright, with hope of better things to be won, and to be bestowed. There is no old age where there is still that promise – it is eternal youth.

Thus, then, you have first to mould her physical frame, and then, as the strength she gains will permit you, to fill and temper her mind with all knowledge and thoughts which tend to confirm its natural instincts of justice, and refine its natural tact of love.

All such knowledge should be given her as may enable her to understand, and even to aid, the work of men: and yet it should be given, not as knowledge, – not as if it were, or could be, for her an object to know; but only to feel, and to judge. It is of no moment, as a matter of pride or perfectness in herself, whether she knows many languages or one; but it is of the utmost, that she should be able to show kindness to a stranger, and to understand the sweetness of a stranger's tongue. It is of no moment to her own worth or dignity that she should be acquainted with this science or that; but it is of the highest that she should be trained in habits of accurate thought; that she should understand the meaning, the inevitableness, and the loveliness of natural laws, and follow at least some one path of scientific attainment, as far as to the threshold of that bitter Valley of Humiliation,[8] into which only the wisest and bravest of men can descend, owning themselves for ever children, gathering pebbles on a boundless shore.[9] It is of little consequences how many positions of cities she knows, of how many dates of events, or how many names of celebrated persons – it is not the object of education to turn a woman into a dictionary; but it is deeply necessary that she should be taught to enter with her whole personality into the history she reads; to picture the passages of it vitally in her own bright imagination; to apprehend, with her fine instincts, the pathetic circumstances and dramatic relations, which the historian too often only eclipses by his reasoning, and disconnects by his arrangement: it is for her to trace the hidden equities of divine reward, and catch sight, through the darkness, of the fateful threads of woven fire that connect error with retribution. But, chiefly of all, she is to be taught to extend the limits of her sympathy with respect to that history which is being for ever determined, as the moments pass in which she draws her peaceful breath; and to the contemporary calamity which, were it but rightly mourned by her, would recur no more hereafter. She is to exercise herself in imagining what would be the effects upon her mind and conduct, if she were daily brought into the presence of the suffering which is not the less real because shut from her sight. She is to be taught somewhat to understand the nothingness of the proportion which that little world in which she lives and loves, bears to the world in which God lives and loves; – and solemnly she is to be taught to strive that her thoughts of piety may not be feeble in proportion to the number they embrace, nor her prayer more languid than it is for the momentary relief from pain of her husband or her child, when it is uttered for the multitudes of those who have none to love them, – and is 'for all who are desolate and oppressed.'[10]

Thus far, I think, I have had your concurrence; perhaps you will not be with me in what I believe is most needful for me to say. There *is* one dangerous science for women – one which let them indeed beware how they profanely touch – that of theology. Strange, and miserably strange, that while they are modest enough to doubt their powers, and pause at the threshold of sciences where every step is demonstrable and sure, they will plunge headlong, and without one thought of incompetency, into that science in which the greatest men have trembled, and the wisest erred. Strange, that they will complacently and pridefully bind up whatever vice or folly there is in them, whatever arrogance, petulance, or blind incomprehensiveness, into one bitter bundle of consecrated myrrh. Strange, in creatures born to be Love visible, that where they can know least, they will condemn first, and think to recommend themselves to their Master by scrambling up the steps of His judgement-throne, to divide it with Him. Most strange, that they should think they were led by the Spirit of the Comforter into habits of mind which have become in them the unmixed elements of home discomfort; and that they dare to turn the Household Gods of Christianity into ugly idols of their own – spiritual dolls, for them to dress according to their caprice; and from which their husbands must turn away in grieved contempt, lest they should be shrieked at for breaking them.

I believe, then, with this exception, that a girl's education should be nearly, in its course and material of study, the same as a boy's; but quite differently directed. A woman, in any rank of life, ought to know whatever her husband is likely to know, but to know it in a different way. His command of it should be foundational and progressive, hers, general and accomplished for daily and helpful use. Not but that it would often be wiser in men to learn things in a womanly sort of way, for present use, and to seek for the discipline and training of their mental powers in such branches of study as will be afterwards fittest for social service; but, speaking broadly, a man ought to know any language or science he learns, thoroughly – while a woman ought to know the same language, or science, only so far as may enable her to sympathise in her husband's pleasures, and in those of his best friends.

Yet, observe, with exquisite accuracy as far as she reaches. There is a wide difference between elementary knowledge and superficial knowledge – between a firm beginning, and a feeble smattering. A woman may always help her husband by what she knows, however little; by what she half-knows, or mis-knows, she will only teaze him.

And indeed, if there were to be any difference between a girl's education and a boy's, I should say that of the two the girl should be earlier led, as her intellect ripens faster, into deep and serious subjects; and that her range of literature should be, not more, but less frivolous, calculated to add the qualities of patience and seriousness to her natural poignancy of thought and quickness of wit; and also to keep her in a lofty and pure element of thought. I enter not now into any question of choice of books; only let us be sure that her books are not heaped up in her lap as they fall out of the package of the circulating library, wet with the last and lightest spray of the fountain of folly.

Or even of the fountain of wit; for with respect to that sore temptation of novel reading, it is not the badness of a novel that we should dread, but its over-wrought interest. The weakest romance is not so stupefying as the lower forms of religious exciting literature, and the worst romance is not so corrupting as false history, false philosophy, or false political essays. But the best romance becomes dangerous, if, by its excitement, it renders the ordinary course of life uninter-esting, and increases the morbid thirst for useless acquaintance with scenes in which we shall never be called upon to act.

I speak therefore of good novels only; and our modern literature is particu-larly rich in types of such. Well read, indeed, these books have serious use, being nothing less than treatises on moral anatomy and chemistry; studies of human nature in the elements of it. But I attach little weight to this function: they are hardly ever read with earnestness enough to permit them to fulfil it. The utmost they usually do is to enlarge somewhat the charity of a kind reader, or the bitter-ness of a malicious one; for each will gather, from the novel, food for her own disposition. Those who are naturally proud and envious will learn from Thackeray to despise humanity; those who are naturally gentle, to pity it; those who are naturally shallow, to laugh at it. So, also, there might be a serviceable power in novels to bring before us, in vividness, a human truth which we had before dimly conceived; but the temptation to picturesqueness of statement is so

510

great, that often the best writers of fiction cannot resist it; and our views are rendered so violent and one-sided, that their vitality is rather a harm than good.

Without, however, venturing here on any attempt at decision how much novel reading should be allowed, let me at least clearly assert this, that whether novels, or poetry, or history be read, they should be chosen, nor for what is *out* of them, but what is *in* them. The chance and scattered evil that may here and there haunt, or hide itself in, a powerful book, never does any harm to a noble girl; but the emptiness of an author oppresses her, and his amiable folly degrades her. And if she can have access to a good library of old and classical books, there need be no choosing at all. Keep the modern magazine and novel out of your girl's way: turn her loose into the old library every wet day, and let her alone. She will find what is good for her; you cannot: for there is just this difference between the making of a girl's character and a boy's – you may chisel a boy into shape, as you would a rock, or hammer him into it, if he be of a better kind, as you would a piece of bronze. But you cannot hammer a girl into anything. She grows as a flower does, – she will wither without sun; she will decay in her sheath, as a narcissus does, if you do not give her air enough; she may fall, and defile her head in dust, if you leave her without help at some moments of her life; but you cannot fetter her; she must take her own fair form and way, if she take any, and in mind as in body, must have always

'Her household motions light and free
And steps of virgin liberty.'[11]

Let her loose in the library, I say, as you do a fawn in a field. It knows the bad weeds twenty times better than you; and the good ones too, and will eat some bitter and prickly ones, good for it, which you had not the slightest thought were good.

Then, in art, keep the finest models before her, and let her practice in all accomplishments be accurate and thorough, so as to enable her to understand more than she accomplishes. I say the finest models – that is to say, the truest, simplest, usefullest. Note those epithets; they will range through all the arts. Try them in music, where you might think them the least applicable. I say the truest, that in which the notes most closely and faithfully express the meaning of the words, or the character of intended emotion; again, the simplest, that in which the meaning and melody are attained with the fewest and most significant notes possible; and, finally, the usefullest, that music which makes the best words most beautiful, which enchants them in our memories each with its own glory of sound, and which applies them closest to the heart at the moment we need them.

And not only in the material and in the course, but yet more earnestly in the spirit of it, let a girl's education be as serious as a boy's. You bring up your girls as if they were meant for sideboard ornaments, and then complain of their frivolity. Give them the same advantages that you give their brothers – appeal to the same grand instincts of virtue in them; teach *them* also that courage and truth are the pillars of their being: do you think that they would not answer that appeal, brave and true as they are even now, when you know that there is hardly a girl's school in this Christian kingdom where the children's courage or sincerity would be thought of half so much importance as their way of coming in at a door; and when the whole system of society, as respects the mode of establishing them in life, is one rotten plague of cowardice and imposture – cowardice, in not daring to let them live, or love, except as their neighbours choose; and imposture, in bringing, for the purposes of our own pride, the full glow of the world's worst vanity upon a girl's eyes, at the very period when the whole happiness of her future existence depends upon her remaining undazzled?

And give them, lastly, not only noble teachings, but noble teachers. You consider somewhat before you send your boy to school, what kind of a man the master is; – whatsoever kind of a man he is, you at least give him full authority over your son, and show some respect to him yourself: if he comes to dine with you, you do not put him at a side table; you know also that, at his college, your child's immediate tutor will be under the direction of some still higher tutor, for whom you have absolute reverence. You do not treat the Dean of Christ Church or the Master of Trinity as your inferiors.

But what teachers do you give your girls, and what reverence do you show to the teachers you have chosen? Is a girl likely to think her own conduct, or her own intellect, of much importance, when you trust the entire formation of her character, moral and intellectual, to a person whom you let your servants treat with less respect than they do your housekeeper (as if the soul of your child were a less charge than jams and groceries), and whom you yourself think you confer an honour upon by letting her sometimes sit in the drawing-room in the evening?

Thus, then, of literature as her help, and thus of art. There is one more help which she cannot do without – one which, alone, has sometimes done more than all other influences besides, – the help of wild and fair nature. Hear this of the education of Joan of Arc;

> 'The education of this poor girl was mean according to the present standard; was ineffably grand, according to a purer philosophic standard; and only not good for our age, because for us it would be unattainable.
>
> Next after her spiritual advantages, she owed most to the advantages of her situation. The fountain of Domrémy was on the brink of a boundless forest; and it was haunted to that degree by fairies, that the parish priest (*curé*) was obliged to read mass there once a year, in order to keep them in any decent bounds.
>
> But the forests of Domrémy – those were the glories of the land; for in them abode the mysterious powers and ancient secrets that towered into tragic strength. "Abbeys there were, and abbey windows," – "like Moorish temples of the Hindoos," that exercised even princely power both in Lorraine and in the German Diets.[12] These had their sweet

bells that pierced the forests for many a league at matins or vespers, and each its own dreamy legend. Few enough, and scattered enough, were these abbeys, so as in no degree to disturb the deep solitude of the region; yet many enough to spread a network or awning of Christian sanctity over that else might have seemed a heathen wilderness.'b

Now, you cannot, indeed, have here in England, woods eighteen miles deep to the centre; but you can, perhaps, keep a fairy or two for your children yet, if you wish to keep them. But *do* you wish it? Suppose you had each, at the back of your houses, a garden, large enough for your children to play in, with just as much lawn as would give them room to run, – no more – and that you could not change your abode; but that, if you chose, you could double your income, or quadruple it, by digging a coal shaft in the middle of the lawn, and turning the flower-beds into heaps of coke. Would you do it? I think not. I can tell you, you would be wrong if you did, though it gave you income sixty-fold instead of four-fold.

Yet this is what you are doing with all England. The whole country is but a little garden, not more than enough for your children to run on the lawns of, if you would let them *all* run there. And this little garden you will turn into furnace-ground, and fill with heaps of cinders, if you can; and those children of yours, not you, will suffer for it. For the fairies will not be all banished; there are fairies of the furnace as of the wood, and their first gifts seem to be 'sharp arrows of the mighty;' but their last gifts are 'coals of juniper.'[13]

And yet I cannot – though there is no part of my subject that I feel more – press this upon you; for we made so little use of the power of nature while we had it that we shall hardly feel what we have lost. Just on the other side of the Mersey you have your Snowdon, and your Menai Straits, and that mighty granite rock beyond the moors of Anglesea,[14] splendid in its heathery crest, and foot planted in the deep sea, once thought of as sacred – a divine promontory, looking westward; the Holy Head or Headland, still not without awe when its red light glares first through storm. These are the hills, and these the bays and blue inlets, which, among the Greeks, would have been always loved, always fateful in influence on the national mind. That Snowdon is your Parnassus; but where are its Muses? That Holyhead mountain is your Island of Aegina; but where is its Temple to Minerva?[15]

Shall I read you what the Christian Minerva had achieved under the shadow of our Parnassus, up to the year 1848? – Here is a little account of a Welsh school, from page 261 of the Report on Wales, published by the Committee of Council on Education.[16] This is a school close to a town containing 5000 persons: –

---

b    'Joan of Arc: in reference to M Michelet's *History of France.*' De Quincey's Works. Vol. iii. p. 217.

'I then called up a larger class, most of whom had recently come to the school. Three girls repeatedly declared they had never heard of Christ, and two that they had never heard of God. Two out of six thought Christ was on earth now' (they might have had a worse thought perhaps), 'three knew nothing about the crucifixion. Four out of seven did not know the names of the months, nor the number of days in a year. They had no notion of addition beyond two and two, or three and three; their minds were perfect blanks.'

Oh, ye women of England! from the Princess of that Wales to the simplest of you, do not think your own children can be brought into their true fold of rest, while these are scattered on the hills, as sheep having no shepherd.[17] And do not think your daughters can be trained to the truth of their own human beauty, while the pleasant places, which God made at once for their school-room and their playground, lie desolate and defiled. You cannot baptize them rightly in those inch-deep fonts of yours, unless you baptize also in the sweet waters which the great Lawgiver strikes forth for ever from the rocks of your native land[18] – waters which a Pagan would have worshipped in their purity, and you worship only with pollution. You cannot lead your children faithfully to those narrow axe-hewn church altars of yours, while the dark azure altars in heaven – the mountains that sustain your island throne, – mountains on which a Pagan would have seen the powers of heaven rest in every wreathed cloud – remain for you without inscription; altars built, not to, but by, an Unknown God.[19]

III. Thus far, then, of the nature, thus far of the teaching, of woman, and thus of her household office, and queenliness. We now come to our last, our widest question, – What is her queenly office with respect to the state?

Generally, we are under an impression that a man's duties are public, and a woman's private. But this is not altogether so. A man has a personal work or duty, relating to his own home, and a public work or duty, which is the expansion of the other, relating to the state. So a woman has a personal work or duty, relating to her own home, and a public work or duty, which is also the expansion of that.

Now the man's work for his own home is, as has been said, to secure its maintenance, progress, and defence; the woman's to secure its order, comfort, and loveliness.

Expand both these functions. The man's duty, as a member of a commonwealth, is to assist in the maintenance, in the advance, in the defence of the state. The woman's duty, as a member of the commonwealth, is to assist in the ordering, in the comforting, and in the beautiful adornment of the state.

What the man is at his own gate, defending it, if need be, against insult and spoil, that also, not in a less, but in a more devoted measure, he is to be at the gate of his country, leaving his home, if need be, even to the spoiler, to do his more incumbent work there.

And, in like manner, what the woman is to be within her gates, as the centre of order, the balm of distress, and the mirror of beauty: that she is also to be without her gates, where order is more difficult, distress more imminent, loveliness more rare.

And as within the human heart there is always set an instinct for all its real duties, – an instinct which you cannot quench, but only warp and corrupt if you withdraw it from its true purpose; – as there is the intense instinct of love, which, rightly disciplined, maintains all the sanctities of life, and, misdirected, undermines them; and *must* do either the one or the other; – so there is in the human heart an inextinguishable instinct, the love of power, which, rightly directed, maintains all the majesty of law and life, and, misdirected, wrecks them.

Deep rooted in the innermost life of the heart of man, and of the heart of woman, God set it there, and God keeps it there. Vainly, as falsely, you blame or rebuke the desire of power! – For Heaven's sake, and for Man's sake, desire it all you can. But *what* power? That is all the question. Power to destroy? the lion's limb, and the dragon's breath? Not so. Power to heal, to redeem, to guide, and to guard. Power of the sceptre and shield; the power of the royal hand that heals in touching, – that binds the fiend, and looses the captive; the throne that is founded on the rock of Justice, and descended from only by steps of Mercy. Will you not covet such power as this, and seek such throne as this, and be no more housewives, but queens?

It is now long since the women of England arrogated, universally, a title which once belonged to nobility only; and, having once been in the habit of accepting the simple title of gentlewoman, as correspondent to that of gentleman, insisted on the privilege of assuming the title of 'Lady,'[c] which properly corresponds only to the title of 'Lord'.

I do not blame them for this; but only for their narrow motive in this. I would have them desire and claim the title of Lady, provided they claim, not merely the title, but the office and duty signified by it. Lady means 'bread-giver' or 'loaf-giver,' and Lord means 'maintainer of laws,'[20] and both titles have reference, not to the law which is maintained in the house, nor to the bread which is given to the household; but to law maintained for the multitude, and to bread broken among the multitude. So that a Lord has legal claim only to his title in so far as he is the maintainer of the justice of the Lord of Lords; and a Lady has legal claim to her title only so far as she communicates that help to the poor representatives of her Master, which women once, ministering to Him of their substance,

---

c   I wish there were a true order of chivalry instituted for our English youth of certain ranks, in which both boy and girl should receive, at a given age, their knighthood and ladyhood by true title; attainable only by certain probation and trial both of character and accomplishment; and to be forfeited, on conviction, by their peers, of any dishonourable act. Such an institution would be entirely, and with all noble results, possible, in a nation which loved honour. That it would not be possible among us, is not to the discredit of the scheme.

were permitted to extend to that Master Himself; and when she is known, as He Himself once was, in breaking of bread.[21]

And this beneficent and legal dominion, this power of the Dominus, or House-Lord, and of the Domina, or House-Lady, is great and venerable, not in the number of those through whom it has lineally descended, but in the number of those whom it grasps within its sway; it is always regarded with reverent worship wherever its dynasty is founded on its duty, and its ambition co-relative with its beneficence. Your fancy is pleased with the thought of being noble ladies, with a train of vassals. Be it so; you cannot be too noble, and your train cannot be too great; but see to it that your train is of vassals whom you serve and feed, not merely of slaves who serve and feed *you*; and that the multitude which obeys you is of those whom you have comforted, not oppressed, – whom you have redeemed, not led into captivity.

And this, which is true of the lower or household dominion, is equally true of the queenly dominion; – that highest dignity is open to you, if you will also accept that highest duty. Rex et Regina – Roi et Reine – '*Right*-doers;' they differ but from the Lady and Lord, in that their power is supreme over the mind as over the person – that they not only feed and clothe, but direct and teach. And whether consciously or not, you must be, in many a heart, enthroned: there is no putting by that crown; queens you must always be: queens to your lovers; queens to your husbands and your sons; queens of higher mystery to the world beyond, which bows itself, and will for ever bow, before the myrtle crown,[22] and the stainless sceptre, of womanhood. But, alas! you are too often idle and careless queens, grasping at majesty in the least things, while you abdicate it in the greatest; and leaving misrule and violence to work their will among men, in defiance of the power, which, holding straight in gift from the Prince of all Peace, the wicked among you betray, and the good forget.

'Prince of Peace.'[23] Note that name. When kings rule in that name, and nobles, and the judges of the earth, they also, in their narrow place, and mortal measure, receive the power of it. There are no other rulers than they: other rule than theirs is but *mis*rule; they who govern verily 'Dei Gratiâ'[24] are all princes, yes, or princesses of peace. There is not a war in the world, no, nor an injustice, but you women are answerable for it; not in that you have provoked, but in that you have not hindered. Men, by their nature, are prone to fight; they will fight for any cause, or for none. It is for you to choose their cause for them, and to forbid them when there is no cause. There is no suffering, no injustice, no misery, in the earth, but the guilt of it lies lastly with you. Men can bear the sight of it, but you should not be able to bear it. Men may tread it down without sympathy in their own struggle; but men are feeble in sympathy, and contracted in hope; it is you only who can feel the depths of pain; and conceive the way of its healing. Instead of trying to do this, you turn away from it; you shut yourselves within your park walls and garden gates; and you are content to know that there is beyond them a whole world in wilderness – a world of secrets which you dare not penetrate; and of suffering which you dare not conceive.

I tell you that this is to me quite the most amazing among the phenomena of humanity. I am surprised at no depths to which, when once warped from its honour, that humanity can be degraded. I do not wonder at the miser's death, with his hands, as they relax, dropping gold. I do not wonder at the sensualist's life, with the shroud wrapped about his feet. I do not wonder at the single-handed murder of a single victim, done by the assassin in the darkness of the railway, or reed-shadow of the marsh. I do not even wonder at the myriad-handed murder of multitudes, done boastfully in the daylight, by the frenzy of nations, and the immeasurable, unimaginable guilt heaped up from hell to heaven, of their priests, and kings. But this is wonderful to me – oh, how wonderful! – to see the tender and delicate woman among you, with her child at her breast, and a power, if she would wield it, over it, and over its father, purer than the air of heaven, and stronger than the seas of earth – nay, a magnitude of blessing which her husband would not part with for all that earth itself, though it were made of one entire and perfect chrysolite:[25] – to see her abdicate this majesty to play at precedence with her next-door neighbour! This is wonderful – oh, wonderful! – to see her, with every innocent feeling fresh within her, go out in the morning into her garden to play with the fringes of its guarded flowers, and lift their heads when they are drooping, with her happy smile upon her face, and no cloud upon her brow, because there is a little wall around her place of peace: and yet she knows, in her heart, if she would only look for its knowledge, that, outside of that little rose-covered wall, the wild grass, to the horizon, is torn up by the agony of men, and beat level by the drift of their life-blood.

Have you ever considered what a deep under meaning there lies, or at least, may be read, if we choose, in our custom of strewing flowers before those whom we think most happy? Do you suppose it is merely to deceive them into the hope that happiness is always to fall thus in showers at their feet? – that wherever they pass they will tread on herbs of sweet scent, and that the rough ground will be made smooth for them by depths of roses? So surely as they believe that, they will have, instead, to walk on bitter herbs and thorns; and the only softness to their feet will be of snow. But it is not thus intended they should believe; there is a better meaning in that old custom. The path of a good woman is indeed strewn with flowers; but they rise behind her steps, not before them. 'Her feet have touched the meadows, and left the daisies rosy.'[26] You think that only a lover's fancy; – false and vain! How if it could be true? You think this also, perhaps, only a poet's fancy –

'Even the light harebell raised its head
Elastic from her airy tread.'[27]

But it is little to say of a woman, that she only does not destroy where she passes. She should revive; the harebells should bloom, not stoop, as she passes. You think I am rushing into wild hyperbole! Pardon me, not a whit – I mean what I say in calm English, spoken in resolute truth. You have heard it said – (and I believe there is more than fancy even in that saying, but let it pass for a fanciful one) – that flowers only flourish rightly in the garden of some one who loves them. I know you would like that to be true; you would think it a pleasant magic if you could flush your flowers into brighter bloom by a kind look upon them: nay, more, if your look had the power, not only to cheer, but to guard them – if you could bid the black blight turn away, and the knotted caterpillar spare – if you could bid the dew fall upon them in the drought, and say to the south wind, in frost – 'Come, thou south, and breathe upon my garden, that the spices of it may flow out.'[28] This you would think a great thing? And do you think it not a greater thing, that all this, (and how much more than this!) you *can* do, for fairer flowers than these – flowers that could bless you for having blessed them, and will love you for having loved them; – flowers that have eyes like yours, and thoughts like yours, and lives like yours; which, once saved, you save for ever? Is this only a little power? Far among the moorlands and the rocks, – far in the darkness of the terrible streets, – these feeble florets are lying, with all their fresh leaves torn, and their stems broken – will you never go down to them, nor set them in order in their little fragrant beds, nor fence them in their shuddering, from the fierce wind? Shall morning follow morning, for you, but not for them; and the dawn rise to watch, far away, those frantic Dances of Death;[d] but no dawn rise to breathe upon these living banks of wild violet, and woodbine, and rose; nor call to you, through your casement, – call, (not giving you the name of the English poet's lady, but the name of Dante's great Matilda, who, on the edge of happy Lethe, stood, wreathing flowers with flowers),[29] saying: –

'Come into the garden, Maud,
For the black bat, night, has flown,
And the woodbine spices are wafted abroad
And the musk of the roses blown?'[30]

Will you not go down among them? – among those sweet living things, whose new courage, sprung from the earth with the deep colour of heaven upon it, is starting up in strength of goodly spire; and whose purity, washed from the dust, is opening, bud by bud, into the flower of promise; – and still they turn to you, and for you, 'The Larkspur listens – I hear, I hear! And the Lily whispers – I wait.'[31]

Did you notice that I missed two lines when I read you that first stanza; and think that I had forgotten them? Hear them now: –

d  [At this point Ruskin refers his readers to an earlier note which describes a Parisian ball that ended with a 'châine diabolique' (devilish chain) and a 'cancan d'enfer' (diabolical can-can) which were danced at seven in the morning; Ruskin refers to an article in the *Morning Post*, 10 March 1865 as the source of the anecdote.]

'Come into the garden Maud,
For the black bat, night, has flown;
Come into the garden, Maud,
I am here at the gate, alone.'

Who is it, think you, who stands at the gate of this sweeter garden, alone, waiting for you? Did you ever hear, not of a Maud, but a Madeleine, who went down to her garden in the dawn, and found One waiting at the gate, whom she supposed to be the gardener?[32] Have you not sought Him often; – sought Him in vain, all through the night; – sought Him in vain at the gate of that old garden where the fiery sword is set? He is never there; but at the gate of *this* garden He is waiting always – waiting to take your hand – ready to go down to see the fruits of the valley, to see whether the vine has flourished, and the pomegranate budded. There you shall see with Him the little tendrils of the vines that His hand is guiding – there you shall see the pomegranate springing where His had cast the sanguine seed; – more: you shall see the troops of the angel keepers that, with their wings, wave away the hungry birds from the pathsides where He has sown, and call to each other between the vineyards rows. 'Take us the foxes, the little foxes, that spoil the vines, for our vines have tender grapes.' Oh – you queens – you queens! among the hills and happy greenwood of this land of yours, shall the foxes have holes, and the birds of the air have nests; and in your cities, shall the stones cry out against you, that they are the only pillows where the Son of Man can lay His head?[33]

## JOHN STUART MILL, *THE SUBJECTION OF WOMEN* (1869)

### *From* John Stuart Mill, *The Subjection of Women* (London: Longmans, Green, Reader and Dyer, 1869)[1]

### From *Chapter I*

The object of this essay is to explain as clearly as I am able, the grounds of an opinion which I have held from the very earliest period when I had formed any opinions at all on social or political matters, and which, instead of being weakened or modified, has been constantly growing stronger by the progress of reflection and the experience of life: That the principle which regulates the existing social relations between the two sexes – the legal subordination of one sex to the other – is wrong in itself, and now one of the chief hindrances to human improvement; and that it ought to be replaced by a principle of perfect equality, admitting no power of privilege on the one side, nor disability on the other. [ ... ][2]

The generality of a practice is in some cases a strong presumption that it is, or at all events once was, conducive to laudable ends. This is the case, when the practice was first adopted, or afterwards kept up, as a means to such ends, and was grounded on experience of the mode in which they could be most effectually attained. If the authority of men over women, when first established, had been the result of a conscientious comparison between different modes of constituting the government of society; if, after trying various other modes of social organization – the government of women over men, equality between the two, and such mixed and divided modes of government as might be invented – it had been decided, on the testimony of experience, that the mode in which women are wholly under the rule of men, having no share at all in public concerns, and each in private being under the legal obligation of obedience to the man with whom she has associated her destiny, was the arrangement most conducive to the happiness and well being of both; its general adoption might then be fairly thought to be some evidence that, at the time when it was adopted, it was the best: though even then the considerations which recommended it may, like so many other primeval social facts of the greatest importance, have subsequently, in the course of ages, ceased to exist. But the state of the case is in every respect the reverse of this. In the first place, the opinion in favour of the present system, which entirely subordinates the weaker sex to the stronger, rests upon theory only; for there never has been trial made of any other: so that experience, in the sense in which it is vulgarly opposed to theory, cannot be pretended to have pronounced any verdict. And in the second place, the adoption of this system of inequality never was the result of deliberation, or forethought, or any social ideas, or any notion whatever of what conduced to the benefit of humanity or the good order of society. It arose simply from the fact that from the very earliest twilight of human society, every woman (owing to the value attached to her by men, combined with her inferiority in muscular strength) was found in a state of bondage to some man. Laws and systems of polity always begin by recognising the relations they find already existing between individuals. They convert what was a mere physical fact into a legal right, give it the sanction of society, and principally aim at the substitution of public and organized means of asserting and protecting these rights, instead of the irregular and lawless conflict of physical strength. Those who had already been compelled to obedience became in this manner legally bound to it. Slavery, from being a mere affair of force between the master and the slave, became regularized and a matter of compact among the masters, who, binding themselves to one another for common protection, guaranteed by their collective strength the private possessions of each, including his slaves. In early times, the great majority of the male sex were slaves, as well as the whole of the female. And many ages elapsed, some of them ages of high cultivation, before any thinker was bold enough to question the rightfulness, and the absolute social necessity, either of the one slavery or of the other. By degrees such thinkers did arise: and (the general progress of society assisting) the slavery of the male sex has, in all the countries of Christian Europe at least (though, in one of them, only within the last few years) been at length abolished, and that of the female sex has been gradually changed into a milder form of dependence. But this dependence, as it exists at present, is not an original institution, taking a fresh start from considerations of justice and social expediency – it is the primitive state of slavery lasting on, through successive mitigations and modifications occasioned by the same causes which have softened the general manners, and brought all human relations more under the control of justice and the influence of humanity. It has not lost the taint of its brutal origin. No presumption in its favour, therefore, can be drawn from the fact of its existence. The only such presumption which it could be supposed to have, must be grounded on its having lasted till now, when so many other things which came down from the same odious source have been done away with. And this, indeed, is what makes it strange to ordinary ears, to hear it asserted that the inequality of rights between men and women has no other source that the law of the strongest. [ . . . ][3]

There was a time when the division of mankind into two classes, a small one of masters and a numerous one of slaves, appeared, even to the most cultivated minds, to be a natural, and the only natural, condition of the human race. No less an intellect, and one which contributed no less to the progress of human thought, than Aristotle, held this opinion without doubt or misgiving; and rested it on the same premises on which the same assertion in regard to the dominion of men over women is usually based, namely that there are different natures among mankind, free natures, and slave natures; that the Greeks were of a free nature, the barbarian races of Thracians and Asiatics of a slave nature. But why need I go back to Aristotle?[4] Did not the slave owners of the Southern United States maintain the same doctrine, with all the fanaticism with which men cling to the theories that justify their passions and legitimate their personal interests?

Did they not call heaven and earth to witness that the dominion of the white man over the black is natural, that the black race is by nature incapable of freedom, and marked out for slavery? some even going so far as to say that the freedom of manual labourers is an unnatural order of things anywhere. Again, the theorists of absolute monarchy have always affirmed it to be the only natural form of government; issuing from the patriarchal, which was the primitive and spontaneous form of society, framed on the model of the paternal, which is ante- rior to society itself, and, as they contend, the most natural authority of all. Nay, for that matter, the law of force itself, to those who could not plead any other, has always seemed the most natural of all grounds for the exercise of authority. Conquering races hold it to be Nature's own dictate that the conquered should obey the conquerors, or, as they euphoniously paraphrase it, that the feebler and more unwarlike races should submit to the braver and manlier. The smallest acquaintance with human life in the middle ages, shows how supremely natural the dominion of the feudal nobility over men of low condition appeared to the nobility themselves, and how unnatural the conception seemed, of a person of the inferior class claiming equality with them, or exercising authority over them. It hardly seemed less so to the class held in subjection. The emancipated serfs and burgesses, even in their most vigorous struggles, never made any pretension to a share of authority; they only demanded more or less of limitation to the power of tyrannizing over them. So true is it that unnatural generally means only uncustomary, and that everything which is usual appears natural. The subjection of women to men being a universal custom, any departure from it quite naturally appears unnatural. But how entirely, even in this case, the feeling is dependent on custom, appears by ample experience. Nothing so much aston- ishes the people of distant parts of the world, when they first learn anything about England, as to be told that it is under a queen: the thing seems to them so unnatural as to be almost incredible. To Englishmen this does not seem in the least degree unnatural, because they are used to it; but they do feel it unnatural that women should be soldiers or members of Parliament. In the feudal ages, on the contrary, war and politics were not thought unnatural to women, because not unusual; it seemed natural that women of the privileged classes should be of manly character, inferior in nothing but bodily strength to their husbands and fathers. The independence of women seemed rather less unnatural to the Greeks than to other ancients, on account of the fabulous Amazons (whom they believed to be historical), and the partial example afforded by the Spartan women;[5] who, though no less subordinate by law than in other Greek states, were more free in fact, and being trained to bodily exercises in the same manner with men, gave ample proof that they were not naturally disqualified for them. There can be little doubt that Spartan experience suggested to Plato,[6] among many other of his doctrines, that of the social and political equality of the two sexes.

But, it will be said, the rule of men over women differs from all these others in not being a rule of force: it is accepted voluntarily; women make no complaint, and are consenting parties to it. In the first place, a great number of women do not accept it. Ever since there have been women able to make their sentiments known by their writings (the only mode of publicity which society permits to them), an increasing number of them have recorded protests against their present social condition: and recently many thousands of them, headed by the most eminent women known to the public, have petitioned Parliament for their admission to the Parliamentary Suffrage.[7] The claim of women to be educated as solidly, and in the same branches of knowledge, as men, is urged with growing intensity, and with a great prospect of success; while the demand for their admission into professions and occupations hitherto closed against them, becomes every year more urgent. Though there are not in this country, as there are in the United States, periodical Conventions and an organized party to agitate for the Rights of Women, there is a numerous and active Society organized and managed by women, for the more limited object of obtaining the political franchise. Nor is it only in our own country and in America that women are beginning to protest, more or less collectively, against the disabilities under which they labour. France, and Italy, and Switzerland, and Russia now afford examples of the same thing. How many more women there are who silently cherish similar aspirations, no one can possibly know; but there are abundant tokens how many *would* cherish them, were they not so strenuously taught to repress them as contrary to the proprieties of their sex. It must be remembered, also, that no enslaved class ever asked for complete liberty at once. When Simon de Montfort[8] called the deputies of the commons to sit for the first time in Parliament, did any of them dream of demanding that an assembly, elected by their constituents, should make and destroy ministries, and dictate to the king in affairs of state? No such thought entered into the imagination of the most ambitious of them. The nobility had already these pretensions; the commons pretended to nothing but to be exempt from arbitrary taxation, and from the gross individual oppression of the king's officers. It is a political law of nature that those who are under any power of ancient origin, never begin by complaining of the power itself, but only of its oppressive exercise. There is never any want of women who complain of ill usage by their husbands. There would be infinitely more, if complaint were not the greatest of all provocatives to a repetition and increase of the ill usage. It is this which frustrates all attempts to maintain the power but protect the woman against its abuses. In no other case (except that of a child) is the person who has been proved judicially to have suffered an injury, replaced under the physical power of the culprit who inflicted it. Accordingly wives, even in the most extreme and protracted cases of bodily ill usage, hardly ever dare avail themselves of the laws made for their protection: and if, in a moment of irrepressible indignation, or by the interference of neighbours, they are induced to do so, their whole effort afterwards is to disclose as little as they can, and to beg off their tyrant from his merited chastisement.

All causes, social and natural, combine to make it unlikely that women should be collectively rebellious to the power of men. They are so far in a position different from all other subject classes, that their masters require something more from them than actual service. Men do not want solely the obedience of women, they want their sentiments. All men, except the most brutish, desire to have, in the woman most nearly connected with them, not a forced slave but a willing one, not a slave merely, but a favourite. They have therefore put everything in practice to enslave their minds. The masters of all other slaves rely, for maintaining obedience, on fear; either fear of themselves, or religious fears. The masters of women wanted more than simple obedience, and they turned the whole force of education to effect their purpose. All women are brought up from the very earliest years in the belief that their ideal of character is the very opposite to that of men; not self-will, and government by self-control, but submission, and yielding to the control of others. All the moralities tell them that it is the duty of women, and all the current sentimentalities that it is their nature, to live for others; to make complete abnegation of themselves, and to have no life but in their affections. And by their affections are meant the only ones they are allowed to have – those to the men with whom they are connected, or to the children who constitute an additional and indefeasible tie between them and a man. When we put together three things – first, the natural attraction between opposite sexes; secondly, the wife's entire dependence on the husband, every privilege or pleasure she has being either his gift, or depending entirely on his will; and lastly, that the principal object of human pursuit, consideration, and all objects of social ambition, can in general be sought or obtained by her only through him, it would be a miracle if the object of being attractive to men had not become the polar star of feminine education and formation of character. And, this great means of influence over the minds of women having been acquired, an instinct of selfishness made men avail themselves of it to the utmost as a means of holding women in subjection, by representing to them meekness, submissiveness, and resignation of all individual will into the hands of a man, as an essential part of sexual attractiveness. Can it be doubted that any of the other yokes which mankind have succeeded in breaking, would have subsisted till now if the same means had existed, and had been as sedulously used, to bow down their minds to it? If it had been made the object of the life of every young plebeian to find personal favour in the eyes of some patrician, of every young serf with some seigneur; if domestication with him, and a share of his personal affections, had been held out as the prize which they all should look out for, the most gifted and aspiring being able to reckon on the most desirable prizes; and if, when this prize had been obtained, they had been shut out by a wall of brass from all interests not centring in him, all feelings and desires but those which he shared or inculcated; would not serfs and seigneurs, plebeians and patricians, have been as broadly distinguished at this day as men and women are? and would not all but a thinker here and there, have believed the distinction to be a fundamental and unalterable fact in human nature?

The preceding considerations are amply sufficient to show that custom, however universal it may be, affords in this case no presumption, and ought not to create any prejudice, in favour of the arrangements which place women in social and political subjection to men. But I may go farther, and maintain that the course of history, and the tendencies of progressive human society, afford not only no presumption in favour of this system of inequality of rights, but a strong one against it; and that, so far as the whole course of human improvement up to this time, the whole stream of modern tendencies, warrants any inference on the subject, it is, that this relic of the past is discordant with the future, and must necessarily disappear.

For, what is the peculiar character of the modern world – the difference which chiefly distinguishes modern institutions, modern social ideas, modern life itself, from those of times long past? It is, that human beings are no longer born to their place in life, and chained down by an inexorable bond to the place they are born to, but are free to employ their faculties, and such favourable chances as offer, to achieve the lot which may appear to them most desirable. Human society of old was constituted on a very different principle. All were born to a fixed social position, and were mostly kept in it by law, or interdicted from any means by which they could emerge from it. As some men are born white and others black, so some were born slaves and others freemen and citizens; some were born patricians, others plebeians; some were born feudal nobles, others commoners and *roturiers*.[9] A slave or serf could never make himself free, nor, except by the will of his master, become so. In most European countries it was not till towards the close of the middle ages, and as a consequence of the growth of regal power, that commoners could be ennobled. Even among nobles, the eldest son was born the exclusive heir to the paternal possessions, and a long time elapsed before it was fully established that the father could disinherit him. Among the industrious classes, only those who were born members of a guild, or were admitted into it by its members, could lawfully practise their calling within its local limits; and nobody could practise any calling deemed important, in any but the legal manner – by processes authoritatively prescribed. Manufacturers have stood in the pillory for presuming to carry on their business by new and improved methods. In modern Europe, and most in those parts of it which have participated most largely in all other modern improvements, diametrically opposite doctrines now prevail. Law and government do not undertake to prescribe by whom any social or industrial operation shall or shall not be conducted, or what modes of conducting them shall be lawful. These things are left to the unfettered choice of individuals. Even the laws which required that workmen should serve an apprenticeship, have in this country been repealed: there being ample assurance that in all cases in which an apprenticeship is necessary, its necessity will suffice to enforce it. The old theory was, that the least possible should be left to the choice of the individual agent; that all he had to do should, as far as practicable, be laid down for him by superior wisdom. Left to himself he was sure to go wrong. The modern conviction, the fruit of a thousand years of experience, is, that things in which the individual is the person directly interested, never go right but as they are left to his own discretion; and that any regulation of them by authority, except to protect the rights of others, is sure to be mischievous. This conclusion, slowly arrived at, and not adopted until almost every possible application of the contrary theory had been made with disastrous result now (in the industrial department) prevails universally in the most advanced countries, almost universally in all that have pretensions to any sort of advancement. It is not that all processes are supposed to be equally good, or all persons to be equally qualified for everything; but that freedom of individual choice is now known to be the only thing which procures the adoption of the best processes, and throws each operation into the hands of those who are best qualified for it. Nobody thinks it necessary to make a law that only a strong-armed man shall be a blacksmith. Freedom and competition suffice to make blacksmiths strong-armed men, because the weak-armed can earn more by engaging in occupations for which they are more fit. In consonance with this doctrine, it is felt to be an overstepping of the proper bounds of authority to fix beforehand, on some general presumption, that certain persons are not fit to do certain things. It is now thoroughly known and admitted that if some such presumptions exist, no such presumption is infallible. Even if it be well grounded in a majority of cases, which it is very likely not to be, there will be a minority of exceptional cases in which it does not hold: and in those it is both an injustice to the individuals, and a detriment to society, to place barriers in the way of their using their faculties for their own benefit and for that of others. In the cases, on the other hand, in which the unfitness is real, the ordinary motives of human conduct will on the whole suffice to prevent the incompetent person from making, or from persisting in, the attempt.

If this general principle of social and economical science is not true; if individuals, with such help as they can derive from the opinion of those who know them, are not better judges than the law and the government, of their own capacities and vocation; the world cannot too soon abandon this principle, and return to the old system of regulations and disabilities. But if the principle is true, we ought to act as if we believed it, and not to ordain that to be born a girl instead of a boy, any more than to be born black instead of white, or a commoner instead of a nobleman, shall decide the person's position through all life – shall interdict people from all the more elevated social positions, and from all, except a few, respectable occupations. Even were we to admit the utmost that is ever pretended as to the superior fitness of men for all the functions now reserved to them, the same argument applies which forbids a legal qualification for members of Parliament. If only once in a dozen years the conditions of eligibility exclude a fit person, there is a real loss, while the exclusion of thousands of unfit persons is no gain; for if the constitution of the electoral body disposes them to choose unfit persons, there are always plenty of such persons to choose from. In all things of any difficulty and importance, those who can do them well are fewer than the need, even with the most unrestricted latitude of choice: and any limitation of the field of selection deprives society of some chances of being served by the competent, without ever saving it from the incompetent.

At present, in the more improved countries, the disabilities of women are the only case, save one, in which laws and institutions take persons at their birth, and ordain that they shall never in all their lives be allowed to compete for certain things. The one exception is that of royalty. Persons still are born to the throne; no one, not of the reigning family, can ever occupy it, and no one even of that family can, by any means but the course of hereditary succession, attain it. All other dignities and social advantages are open to the whole male sex: many indeed are only attainable by wealth, but wealth may be striven for by any one, and is actually obtained by many men of the very humblest origin. The difficulties, to the majority, are indeed insuperable without the aid of fortunate accidents; but no male human being is under any legal ban: neither law nor opinion superadd artificial obstacles to the natural ones. Royalty, as I have said, is excepted: but in this case every one feels it to be an exception – an anomaly in the modern world, in marked opposition to its customs and principles, and to be justified only by extraordinary special expediences, which, though individuals and nations differ in estimating their weight, unquestionably do in fact exist. But in this exceptional case, in which a high social function is, for important reasons, bestowed on birth instead of being put up to competition, all free nations contrive to adhere in substance to the principle from which they nominally derogate; for they circumscribe this high function by conditions avowedly intended to prevent the person to whom it ostensibly belongs from really performing it; while the person by whom it is performed, the responsible minister, does obtain the post by a competition from which no full-grown citizen of the male sex is legally excluded. The disabilities, therefore, to which women are subject from the mere fact of their birth, are the solitary examples of the kind in modern legislation. In no instance except this, which comprehends half the human race, are the higher social functions closed against any one by a fatality of birth which no exertions, and no change of circumstances, can overcome; for even religious disabilities (besides that in England and in Europe they have practically almost ceased to exist) do not close any career to the disqualified person in case of conversion.

The social subordination of women thus stands out an isolated fact in modern social institutions; a solitary breach of what has become their fundamental law; a single relic of an old world of thought and practice exploded in everything else, but retained in the one thing of most universal interest; as if a gigantic dolmen, or a vast temple of Jupiter Olympius,[10] occupied the site of St Paul's and received daily worship, while the surrounding Christian churches were only resorted to on fasts and festivals. This entire discrepancy between one social fact and all those which accompany it, and the radical opposition between its nature and the progressive movement which is the boast of the modern world, and which has successively swept away everything else of an analogous character, surely affords, to a conscientious observer of human tendencies, serious matter for reflection. It raises a primâ facie presumption on the unfavourable side, far outweighing any which custom and usage could in such circumstances create on the favourable; and should at least suffice to make this, like the choice between republicanism and royalty, a balanced question.

The least that can be demanded is, that the question should not be considered as prejudged by existing fact and existing opinion, but open to discussion on its merits, as a question of justice and expediency: the decision on this, as on any of the other social arrangements of mankind, depending on what an enlightened estimate of tendencies and consequences may show to be most advantageous to humanity in general, without distinction of sex. And the discussion must be a real discussion, descending to foundations, and not resting satisfied with vague and general assertions. It will not do, for instance, to assert in general terms, that the experience of mankind has pronounced in favour of the existing system. Experience cannot possibly have decided between two courses, so long as there has only been experience of one. If it be said that the doctrine of the equality of the sexes rests only on theory, it must be remembered that the contrary doctrine also has only theory to rest upon. All that is proved in its favour by direct experience, is that mankind have been able to exist under it, and to attain the degree of improvement and prosperity which we now see; but whether that prosperity has been attained sooner, or is now greater, than it would have been under the other system, experience does not say. On the other hand, experience does say, that every step in improvement has been so invariably accompanied by a step made in raising the social position of women, that historians and philosophers have been led to adopt their elevation or debasement as on the whole the surest test and most correct measure of the civilization of a people or an age. Through all the progressive period of human history, the condition of women has been approaching nearer to equality with men. This does not of itself prove that the assimilation must go on to complete equality; but it assuredly affords some presumption that such is the case.

Neither does it avail anything to say that the *nature* of the two sexes adapts them to their present functions and position, and renders these appropriate to them. Standing on the ground of common sense and the constitution of the human mind, I deny that any one knows, or can know, the nature of the two sexes, as long as they have only been seen in their present relation to one another. If men had ever been found in society without women, or women without men, or if there had been a society of men and women in which the women were not under the control of the men, something might have been positively known about the mental and moral differences which may be inherent in the nature of each. What is now called the nature of women is an eminently artificial thing – the result of forced repression in some directions, unnatural stimulation in others. It may be asserted without scruple, that no other class of dependants have had their character so entirely distorted from its natural proportions by their relation with their masters; for, if conquered and slave races have been, in some respects, more forcibly repressed, whatever in them has not been crushed down by an iron heel has generally been let alone, and if left with any liberty of development, it has developed itself according to its own laws; but in the case of women, a hot-house and stove cultivation has always been carried on of some of the capabilities of their nature, for the benefit and pleasure of their masters. Then, because certain products of the general vital force sprout luxuriantly and reach a great development in this heated atmosphere and under this active nurture and watering, while other shoots from the same root, which are left outside in the wintry air, with ice purposely heaped all round them, have a stunted growth, and some are burnt off with fire and disappear; men, with that inability to recognise their own work which distinguishes the unanalytic mind, indolently believe that the tree grows of itself in the way they have made it grow, and that it would die if one half of it were not kept in a vapour bath and the other half in the snow.

Of all difficulties which impede the progress of thought, and the formation of well-grounded opinions on life and social arrangements, the greatest now is the unspeakable ignorance and inattention of mankind in respect to the influences which form human character. Whatever any portion of the human species now are, or seem to be, such, it is supposed, they have a natural tendency to be: even when the most elementary knowledge of the circumstances in which they have been placed, clearly points out the causes that made them what they are. Because a cottier[11] deeply in arrears to his landlord is not industrious, there are people who think that the Irish are naturally idle. Because constitutions can be overthrown when the authorities appointed to execute them turn their arms against them, there are people who think the French incapable of free government. Because the Greeks cheated the Turks, and the Turks only plundered the Greeks, there are persons who think that the Turks are naturally more sincere: and because women, as is often said, care nothing about politics except their personalities, it is supposed that the general good is naturally less interesting to women than to men. History, which is now so much better understood than formerly, teaches another lesson: if only by showing the extraordinary susceptibility of human nature to external influences, and the extreme variableness of those of its manifestations which are supposed to be most universal and uniform. But in history, as in travelling, men usually see only what they already had in their own minds; and few learn much from history, who do not bring much with them to its study.

Hence, in regard to that most difficult question, what are the natural differences between the two sexes – a subject on which it is impossible in the present state of society to obtain complete and correct knowledge – while almost everybody dogmatizes upon it, almost all neglect and make light of the only means by which any partial insight can be obtained into it. This is, an analytic study of the most important department of psychology, the laws of the influence of circumstances on character. For, however great and apparently ineradicable the moral and intellectual differences between men and women might be, the evidence of there being natural differences could only be negative. Those only could be inferred to be natural which could not possibly be artificial – the residuum, after deducting every characteristic of either sex which can admit of being explained from education or external circumstances. The profoundest knowledge of the laws of the formation of character is indispensable to entitle any one to affirm even that there is any difference, much more what the difference is, between the two sexes considered as moral and rational beings; and since no one, as yet, has that knowledge, (for there is hardly any subject which, in proportion to its importance, has been so little studied), no one is thus far entitled to any positive opinion on the subject. Conjectures are all that can at present be made, conjectures more or less probable, according as more or less authorized by such knowledge as we yet have of the laws of psychology, as applied to the formation of character.

Even the preliminary knowledge, what the differences between the sexes now are, apart from all question as to how they are made what they are, is still in the crudest and most incomplete state. Medical practitioners and physiologists have ascertained, to some extent, the differences in bodily constitution; and this is an important element to the psychologist: but hardly any medical practitioner is a psychologist. Respecting the mental characteristics of women; their observations are of no more worth than those of common men. It is a subject on which nothing final can be known, so long as those who alone can really know it, women themselves, have given but little testimony, and that little, mostly suborned. It is easy to know stupid women. Stupidity is much the same all the world over. A stupid person's notions and feelings may confidently be inferred from those which prevail in the circle by which the person is surrounded. Not so with those whose opinions and feelings are an emanation from their own nature and faculties. It is only a man here and there who has any tolerable knowledge of the character even of the women of his own family. I do not mean, of their capabilities; these nobody knows, not even themselves, because most of them have never been called out. I mean their actually existing thoughts and feelings. Many a man thinks he perfectly understands women, because he has had amatory relations with several, perhaps with many of them. If he is a good observer, and his experience extends to quality as well as quantity, he may have learnt something of one narrow department of their nature – an important department, no doubt. But of all the rest of it, few persons are generally more ignorant, because there are few from whom it is so carefully hidden. The most favourable case which a man can generally have for studying the character of a woman, is that of his own wife: for the opportunities are greater, and the cases of complete sympathy not so unspeakably rare. And in fact, this is the source from which any knowledge worth having on the subject has, I believe, generally come. But most men have not had the opportunity of studying in this way more than a single case: accordingly one can, to an almost laughable degree, infer what a man's wife is like, from his opinions about women in general. To make even this one case yield any result, the woman must be worth knowing, and the man not only a competent judge, but of a character so sympathetic in itself, and so well adapted to hers, that he can either read her mind by sympathetic intuition, or has nothing in himself which makes her shy of disclosing it. Hardly anything, I believe, can be more rare than this conjunction. It often happens that there is the most complete community of interests as to all external things, yet the one has as little admission into the internal life of the other as if they were common acquaintance. Even with true affection, authority on the one side and subordination on the other prevent perfect confidence. Though nothing may be intentionally withheld, much is not shown. In the analogous relation of parent and child, the corresponding phenomenon must have been in the observation of every one. As between father and son, how many are the cases in which the father, in spite of real affection on both sides, obviously to all the world does not know, nor suspect, parts of the son's character familiar to his companions and equals. The truth is, that the position of looking up to another is extremely unpropitious to complete sincerity and openness with him. The fear of losing ground in his opinion or in his feelings is so strong, that even in an upright character, there is an unconscious tendency to show only the best side, or the side which, though not the best, is that which he most likes to see: and it may be confidently said that thorough knowledge of one another hardly ever exists, but between persons who, besides being intimates, are equals. How much more true, then, must all this be, when the one is not only under the authority of the other, but has it inculcated on her as a duty to reckon everything else subordinate to his comfort and pleasure, and to let him neither see nor feel anything coming from her, except what is agreeable to him. All these difficulties stand in the way of a man's obtaining any thorough knowledge even of the one woman whom alone, in general, he has sufficient opportunity of studying. When we further consider that to understand one woman is not necessarily to understand any other woman; that even if he could study many women of one rank, or of one country, he would not thereby understand women of other ranks or countries; and even if he did, they are still only the women of a single period of history; we may safely assert that the knowledge which men can acquire of women, even as they have been and are, without reference to what they might be, is wretchedly imperfect and superficial, and always will be so, until women themselves have told all that they have to tell.

And this time has not come; nor will it come otherwise than gradually. It is but of yesterday that women have either been qualified by literary accomplishments, or permitted by society, to tell anything to the general public. As yet very few of them dare tell anything, which men, on whom their literary success depends, are unwilling to hear. Let us remember in what manner, up to a very recent time, the expression, even by a male author, of uncustomary opinions, or what are deemed eccentric feelings, usually was, and in some degree still is, received; and we may form some faint conception under what impediments a woman, who is brought up to think custom and opinion her sovereign rule, attempts to express in books anything drawn from the depths of her own nature. The greatest woman who has left writings behind her sufficient to give her an eminent rank in the literature of her country, thought it necessary to prefix as a motto to her boldest work, 'Un homme peut braver l'opinion; une femme doit s'y soumettre.'[a] The greater part of what women write about women is mere sycophancy to men. In the case of unmarried women, much of it seems only intended to increase their chance of a husband. Many, both married and unmarried, overstep the mark, and inculcate a servility beyond what is desired or relished by any man, except the very vulgarest. But this is not so often the case as, even at a quite late period, it still was. Literary women are becoming more freespoken, and more willing to express their real sentiments. Unfortunately, in this country especially, they are themselves such artificial products, that their sentiments are compounded of a small element of individual observation and consciousness, and a very large one of acquired associations. This will be less and less the case, but it will remain true to a great extent, as long as social institutions do not admit the same free development of originality in women which is possible to men. When that time comes, and not before, we shall see, and not merely hear, as much as it is necessary to know of the nature of women, and the adaptation of other things to it.

I have dwelt so much on the difficulties which at present obstruct any real knowledge by men of the true nature of women, because in this as in so many other things 'opinio copiae inter maximas causas inopiae est;'[12] and there is little chance of reasonable thinking on the matter, while people flatter themselves that they perfectly understand a subject of which most men know absolutely nothing, and of which it is at present impossible that any man, or all men taken together, should have knowledge which can qualify them to lay down the law to women as to what is, or is not, their vocation. Happily, no such knowledge is necessary for any practical purpose connected with the position of women in relation to society and life. For, according to all the principles involved in modern society, the question rests with women themselves – to be decided by their own experience, and by the use of their own faculties. There are no means of finding what either one person or many can do, but by trying – and no means by which any one else can discover for them what it is for their happiness to do or leave undone.

One thing we may be certain of – that what is contrary to women's nature to do, they never will be made to do by simply giving their nature free play. The anxiety of mankind to interfere on behalf of nature, for fear lest nature should not succeed in effecting its purpose, is an altogether unnecessary solicitude. What women by nature cannot do, it is quite superfluous to forbid them from doing. What they can do, but not so well as the men who are their competitors, competition suffices to exclude them from; since nobody asks for protective duties and bounties in favour of women; it is only asked that the present bounties and protective duties in favour of men should be recalled. If women have a greater natural inclination for some things than for others, there is no need of laws or

a    Title-page of Mme de Staël's 'Delphine' [1802; the quotation translates as: 'A man can defy opinion; a woman must submit to it'].

social inculcation to make the majority of them do the former in preference to the latter. Whatever women's services are most wanted for, the free play of competition will hold out the strongest inducements to them to undertake. And, as the words imply, they are most wanted for the things for which they are most fit; by the appointment of which to them, the collective faculties of the two sexes can be applied on the whole with the greatest sum of valuable result.

The general opinion of men is supposed to be, that the natural vocation of a women is that of a wife and mother. I say, is supposed to be, because, judging from acts – from the whole of the present constitution of society – one might infer that their opinion was the direct contrary. They might be supposed to think that the alleged natural vocation of women was of all things the most repugnant to their nature; insomuch that if they are free to do anything else – if any other means of living, or occupation of their time and faculties, is open, which has any chance of appearing desirable to them – there will not be enough of them who will be willing to accept the condition said to be natural to them. If this is the real opinion of men in general, it would be well that it should be spoken out. I should like to hear somebody openly enunciating the doctrine (it is already implied in much that is written on the subject) – 'It is necessary to society that women should marry and produce children. They will not do so unless they are compelled. Therefore it is necessary to compel them.' The merits of the case would then be clearly defined. It would be exactly that of the slaveholders of South Carolina and Louisiana. 'It is necessary that cotton and sugar should be grown. White men cannot produce them. Negroes will not, for any wages which we choose to give. *Ergo* they must be compelled.' An illustration still closer to the point is that of impressment. Sailors must absolutely be had to defend the country. It often happens that they will not voluntarily enlist. Therefore there must be the power of forcing them. How often has this logic been used! and, but for one flaw in it, without doubt it would have been successful up to this day. But it is open to the retort – First pay the sailors the honest value of their labour. When you have made it as well worth their while to serve you, as to work for other employers, you will have no more difficulty than others have in obtaining their services. To this there is no logical answer except 'I will not:' and as people are now not only ashamed, but are not desirous, to rob the labourer of his hire,[13] impressment is no longer advocated. Those who attempt to force women into marriage by closing all other doors against them, lay themselves open to a similar retort. If they mean what they say, their opinion must evidently be, that men do not render the married condition so desirable to women, as to induce them to accept it for its own recommendations. It is not a sign of one's thinking the boon one offers very attractive, when one allows only Hobson's choice, 'that or none.'[14] And here, I believe, is the clue to the feelings of those men, who have a real antipathy to the equal freedom of women. I believe they are afraid, not lest women should he unwilling to marry, for I do not think that any one in reality has that apprehension; but lest they should insist that marriage should be on equal conditions; lest all women of spirit and capacity should prefer doing almost anything else, not in their own eyes degrading, rather than marry, when marrying is giving themselves a master, and a master too of all their earthly possessions. And truly, if this consequence were necessarily incident to marriage, I think that the apprehension would be very well founded. I agree in thinking it probable that few women, capable of anything else, would, unless under an irresistible *entraînement*,[15] rendering them for the time insensible to anything but itself, choose such a lot, when any other means were open to them of filling a conventionally honourable place in life: and if men are determined that the law of marriage shall be a law of despotism, they are quite right, in point of mere policy, in leaving to women only Hobson's choice. But, in that case, all that has been done in the modern world to relax the chain on the minds of women, has been a mistake. They never should have been allowed to receive a literary education. Women who read, much more women who write, are, in the existing constitution of things, a contradiction and a disturbing element: and it was wrong to bring women up with any acquirements but those of an odalisque,[16] or of a domestic servant.

# 12

# DEFINING MEN

## EDWARD CARPENTER, *HOMOGENIC LOVE AND ITS PLACE IN A FREE SOCIETY* (1894)

The varied career of Edward Carpenter (1844–1929) was aptly summed up by E. M. Forster as that of 'a poet, prose writer, a prophet, a socialist, a mystic, a manual labourer, an anti-vivisectionist, an art-critic, etcetera'. Carpenter's early life began conventionally. Born into a respectable family in Brighton, he was educated at Cambridge where, after taking holy orders, he was elected in 1868 to a clerical fellowship. He was ordained deacon in 1869 and became curate of the Church of St Edward (which was under the patronage of Trinity Hall, Cambridge). Carpenter, however, quickly felt dissatisfied with life as a clerical don. Depressed and debilitated he travelled to Italy in 1872 to recover his health and spirits. The long holiday proved a turning point in his life, both emotionally and intellectually. On returning to England he resigned his fellowship to become a peripatetic teacher for the University Extension Scheme, spending the next few years living among, and lecturing to, working men in Leeds, Nottingham and Sheffield. In the early 1880s Carpenter gave up teaching and took over a small farm in Derbyshire which he later shared with his lover George Merrill – a working-class man from Sheffield. This period also saw the beginning of Carpenter's involvement in the Labour movement (as a founder-member of the Sheffield Socialist Society). He also began campaigning for socialism, homosexuality, women's liberation, and animal rights, causes which for him were all closely bound together. Among his first published works were *Towards Democracy* (1883), published anonymously, and a pamphlet, *Modern Money-lending and the Meaning of Dividends* (1883). These political themes were continued in works such as *England's Ideal* (1885) – influenced by H.

M. Hyndman's *England for All* (1881) – and *Civilisation, Its Cause and Cure* (1889). A controversial series of pamphlets issued by the Manchester Labour Press in 1894 – *Sex-Love and Its Place in a Free Society*, *Woman and Her Place in a Free Society* and *Marriage in Free Society* – marked Carpenter's interest in sex and gender. They were followed in 1895 by *Homogenic Love and Its Place in a Free Society* which although privately circulated caused a considerable controversy. Carpenter offered the first three pamphlets, together with some new material, to the publisher, Fisher Unwin. However, the conviction and imprisonment of Oscar Wilde in 1895 made the proposed book (to be titled, *Love's Coming-of-Age*) virtually unpublishable, and Unwin refused to honour the contract, at the same time withdrawing *Towards Democracy* (by now in its third edition). *Love's Coming-of-Age* was eventually published by the Manchester Labour Press in 1896 (the material from *Homogenic Love* was discreetly left out). Despite the change in public mood caused by Wilde's conviction, Carpenter continued to write openly about homosexuality: in July 1897 'An Unknown People' was published in the *Reformer* magazine and as a separate pamphlet; and in 1899 the *International Journal of Ethics* published 'Affection in Education'. In 1902 Carpenter produced a collection of poems and essays on homogenic love entitled *Ioläus: an Anthology of Friendship*. In 1908 he collected his own writings on the subject in *The Intermediate Sex*. Later works included an ethnographic study of homosexuality, *Intermediate Types Among Primitive Folk* (1914), *Pagan and Christian Creeds* (1920), and in 1916, a frank autobiography, *My Days and Dreams*.

*From* **Edward Carpenter,** *Homogenic Love and Its Place in a Free Society* **(Manchester: Manchester Labour Press, 1894)**[1]

### *II*

We have now I think said enough to show from the testimony of History, Literature, Art and even of Modern Science, that the homogenic passion is capable of splendid developments;[2] and that a love and capacity of love of so intimate, penetrating and inspiring a kind – and which has played so important a part in the life-histories of some of the greatest races and individuals – is well worthy of respectful and thoughtful consideration. And I think it has become obvious that to cast a slur upon this kind of love because it may in cases lead to aberrations and extravagances would be a most irrational thing to do – since exactly the same charges, of possible aberration and extravagance, might be brought, and the same conclusion enforced, against the ordinary sex-love.

It is however so often charged against the sentiment in question that it is essentially unnatural and *morbid* in character, that it may be worth while, though we have already touched on this point, to consider it here at greater length. I therefore propose to devote a few more pages to the examination of the scientific position on this subject, and then to pass on to a consideration of the general place and purpose of the homogenic or comrade-love (its sanity being granted) in human character and social life.

It might be thought that the testimonies of History, Literature and Art, above referred to, would be quite sufficient of themselves to dispose of the charge of essential morbidity. But as mankind in general is not in the habit of taking bird's eye views of History and Literature, and as it finds it easy to assume that anything a little exceptional is also morbid, so it is not difficult to see how this charge (in countries where the sentiment *is* exceptional) has arisen and maintained itself. Science, of course, is nothing but common observation organized and systematized, and so we naturally find that with regard to this subject it started on its investigations from the same general assumptions that possessed the public mind. It may safely be said that until the phenomena of homogenic Love began to be calmly discussed by the few scientific men already mentioned, the subject had never since classical times been once fairly faced in the arena of literature or public discussion, and had as a rule been simply dismissed with opprobrious epithets well suited to give an easy victory to prejudice and ignorance. But the history of even these few years of scientific investigation bears with it a memorable lesson. For while at the outset it was easily assumed that the homogenic instinct was thoroughly morbid in itself, and probably always associated with distinct disease, either physical or mental, the progress of the inquiry has – as already pointed out – served more and more to dissipate this view; and it is noticeable that Krafft-Ebing and Moll[3] – the latest of the purely scientific authorities – are the least disposed to insist upon the theory of morbidity. It is true that Krafft-Ebing clings to the opinion that there is generally some *neurosis*, or degeneration of a nerve-centre, or *inherited tendency in that direction*, associated with the instinct; see p. 190 (seventh ed.), also p. 227, where he speaks, rather vaguely, of 'an hereditary neuropathic or psychopathic tendency' – *neuro(psycho)pathische Belastung*. But it is an obvious criticism on this that there are few people in modern life, perhaps none, who could be pronounced absolutely free from such a Belastung! And whether the Dorian Greeks or the Polynesian Islanders or the Kelts (spoken of by Aristotle, *Pol.*, ii. 7) or the Normans or the Albanian mountaineers, or any of the other notably hardy races among whom the passion has been developed, were particularly troubled by nervous degeneration we may well doubt![a]

---

a    It is interesting, too, to find that Walt Whitman [see note 11, page 545], who certainly had the homogenic instinct highly developed, was characterized by his doctor, W. B. Drinkard, as having 'the most natural habits, bases, and organization he had ever met with or ever seen' in any man. *In re Walt Whitman*, p. 115.

As to Moll, though he speaks[b] of the instinct as morbid (feeling perhaps in duty bound to so do), it is very noticeable that he abandons the ground of its association with other morbid symptoms – as this association, he says, is by no means always to be observed; and is fain to rest his judgement on the *dictum* that the mere failure of the sexual instinct to propagate the species is itself patholog-ical – a *dictum* which in its turn obviously springs from that pre-judgement of scientists that generation is the sole object of love,[c] and which if pressed would involve the good doctor in awkward dilemmas, as for instance that every worker-bee is a pathological specimen.

With regard to the nerve-degeneration theory, while it may be allowed that sexual inversion is not uncommonly found in connection with the specially nervous temperament, it must be remembered that its occasional association with nervous troubles or disease is quite another matter; since such troubles ought perhaps to be looked upon as the *results* rather than the causes of the inversion. It is difficult of course for outsiders not personally experienced in the matter to realize the great strain and tension of nerves under which those persons grow up from boyhood to manhood – or from girl to womanhood – who find their deepest and strongest instincts under the ban of the society around them; who before they clearly understand the drift of their own natures discover that they are somehow cut off from the sympathy and understanding of those nearest to them; and who know that they can never give expression to their tenderest yearnings of affection without exposing themselves to the possible charge of actions stigmatized as odious crimes.[d] That such a strain, acting on one who is perhaps already of a nervous temperament, should tend to cause nervous prostration or even mental disturbance is of course obvious; and if such disturbances are really found to be commoner among homogenic lovers than among ordinary folk we have in these social causes probably a sufficient explana-tion of the fact.

Then again in this connection it must never be forgotten that the medico-scientific enquirer is bound on the whole to meet with those cases that *are* of a morbid character, rather than with those that are healthy in their manifestation, since indeed it is the former that he lays himself out for. And since the field of his research is usually a great modern city, there is little wonder if disease colours his conclusions. In the case of Dr Moll, who carried out his researches largely under the guidance of the Berlin police (whose acquaintance with the subject would naturally be limited to its least satisfactory sides), the only marvel is that

b    *Conträre Sexual-empfindung*, second ed., p. 269.
c    See *Sex-Love*, p. 23. [i.e. a reference to Carpenter's own pamphlet of 1894.]
d    'Though then before my own conscience I cannot reproach myself, and though I must certainly reject the judgement of the world about us, yet I suffer greatly. In very truth I have injured no one, and I hold my love in its nobler activity for just as holy as that of normally disposed men, but under the unhappy fate that allows us neither sufferance nor recognition I suffer often more than my life can bear.' – (Extract from a letter given by Krafft-Ebing.)

his verdict is so markedly favourable as it is. As Krafft-Ebing says in his own preface 'It is the sad privilege of medicine, and especially of Psychiatry, to look always on the reverse side of life, on the weakness and wretchedness of man.'

Having regard then to the direction in which science has been steadily moving in this matter, it is not difficult to see that the epithet 'morbid' will probably before long be abandoned as descriptive of the homogenic bias – that is, of the general sentiment of love towards a person of the same sex. That there are excesses of the passion – cases, as in ordinary sex-love, where mere physical desire becomes a mania – we may freely admit; but as it would be unfair to judge of the purity of marriage by the evidence of the Divorce courts, so it would be monstrous to measure the truth and beauty of the attachment in question by those instances which stand most prominently perhaps in the eye of the modern public; and after all deductions there remains, we contend, the vast body of cases in which the manifestation of the instinct has on the whole the character of normality and healthfulness – sufficiently so in fact to constitute this *a distinct variety of the sexual passion*. The question, of course, not being whether the instinct is *capable* of morbid and extravagant manifestation – for this can easily be proved of any instinct – but whether it is capable of a healthy and sane expression. And this, we think, it has abundantly shown itself to be.

Anyhow the work that Science has practically done has been to destroy the dogmatic attitude of the former current opinion from which itself started, and to leave the whole subject freed from a great deal of misunderstanding, and much more open than before. Its labours – and they have been valuable in this way – have been chiefly of a negative character. While unable on the one hand to characterize the physical attraction in question as definitely morbid or the result of morbid tendencies, it is unable on the other hand to say positively at present what physiological or other purpose is attained by the instinct.

This question of the physiological basis of the homogenic love – to which we have more than once alluded – is a very important one; and it seems a strange oversight on the part of Science that it has hitherto taken so little notice of it. The desire for corporeal intimacy of some kind between persons of the same sex existing as it does in such force and so widely over the face of the earth, it would seem almost certain that there must be some physiological basis for the desire: but until we know more than we do at present as to what this basis may be, we are necessarily unable to understand the desire itself as well as we might wish. It may be hoped that this is a point to which attention will be given in the future. Meanwhile, though the problem is a complex one, it may not be amiss here to venture a suggestion or two.

In the first place it may be suggested that an important part of *all* love-union, mental or physical, is its influence personally on those concerned. This influence is, of course, subtle and hard to define; and one can hardly be surprised that Science, assuming hitherto in its consideration of ordinary sexual relations that the mutual actions and reactions were directed solely to the purpose of generation and the propagation of the species, has almost quite neglected the question of the direct influences on the lovers themselves. Yet everyone is sensible practically that there is much more in an intimacy with another person than the question of children alone; that even setting aside the effects of actual sex-intercourse there are subtle elements passing from one to another which are indispensable to personal well-being, and which make some such intimacy almost a necessary condition of health. It may be that there are some persons for whom these necessary reactions can only come from one of the same sex. In fact it is obvious there are such persons. 'Successful love,' says Moll (p. 125) 'exercises a helpful influence on the Urning.[4] His mental and bodily condition improves, and capacity of work increases – just as it often happens in the case of a normal youth with *his* love.' And further on (p. 173) in a letter from a man of this kind occur these words: 'The passion is I suppose so powerful, just because one looks for everything in the loved man – Love, Friendship, Ideal, and Sense-satisfaction. . . . As it is at present I suffer the agonies of a deep unresponded passion, which wake me like a nightmare from sleep. And I am conscious of physical pain in the region of the heart.' In such cases the love, in some degree physically expressed, of another person of the same sex, is clearly as much a necessity and a condition of healthy life and activity, as in more ordinary cases is the love of a person of the opposite sex.

It has probably been the arbitrary limitation of the function of love to child-breeding which has (unconsciously) influenced the popular mind against the form of love which we are considering. That this kind of union was not concerned with the propagation of the race was in itself enough to make people look askance at it; that any kind of love-union could exist in which the sex-act might possibly *not* be the main object was an incredible proposition. And, in enforcing this view, no doubt the Hebraic and Christian tradition has exercised a powerful influence – dating, as it almost certainly does, from far-back times when the multiplication of the tribe was one of the very first duties of its members, and one of the first necessities of corporate life; though nowadays when the need has swung round all the other way it is not unreasonable to suppose that a similar revolution will take place in people's views of the place and purpose of the non-child-bearing love. We find in some quarters that even the most naïve attachments between youths are stigmatized as 'unnatural' (though, inconsistently enough, not those between girls) – and this can only well be from an assumption that all familiarities are meant by Nature to lead up to generation and race-propagation. Yet no one – if fairly confronted with the question – would seriously maintain that the mutual stimulus, physical, mental and moral, which flows from embrace and endearment is nothing, and that because these things do not lead to actual race propagation therefore they must be discountenanced. If so, must even the loving association between man and wife, more than necessary for the breeding of children, or after the period of fertility has passed, be also discountenanced? Such questions might be multiplied indefinitely. They only serve to show how very crude as yet are all our theories on these subjects, and how necessary it is in the absence of more certain knowledge to suspend our judgement.[e]

Summarizing then some of our conclusions on this rather difficult question we may say that the homogenic love, as a distinct variety of the sex-passion, is in the main subject to the same laws as the ordinary love; that it probably demands and requires some amount of physical intimacy; that a wise humanity will quite recognize this; but that the degree of intimacy, in default of more certain physiological knowledge than we have, is a matter which can only be left to the good sense and feeling of those concerned; and that while we do not deny for a moment that excesses of physical appetite exist, these form no more reason for tabooing all expression of the sentiment than they do in the case of the more normal love. We may also say that if on the side of science much is obscure, there is no obscurity in the principles of healthy morality involved; that there is no exception here to the law that sensuality apart from love is degrading and something less than human; or to the law that love – true love – seeks nothing which is not consistent with the welfare of the loved one; and that here too the principle of Transmutation applies[f] – the principle that Desire in man has its physical, emotional and spiritual sides, and that when its outlet it checked along one channel, it will, within limits, tend to flow with more vehemence along the other channels – and that reasonable beings, perceiving this, will (again within limits) check the sensual and tend to throw the centre of their love-attraction upwards.

Probably in this, as in all love, it will be felt in the end by those who devote themselves to each other and to the truth, to be wisest to concentrate on the *real thing*, on the enduring deep affection which is the real satisfaction and outcome of the relation, and which like a young sapling they would tend with loving care till it grows into a mighty tree which the storms of a thousand years cannot shake; and those who do so heartily and truly can leave the physical to take care of itself. This indeed is perhaps the only satisfactory touchstone of the rightness and fitness of human relations generally, in sexual matters. People, not unnaturally, seek for an absolute rule in such matters, and a *fixed* line between the right and the wrong; but may we not say that there is no rule except that of Love – Love making use, of course, of whatever certain knowledge Science may from time to time be able to provide?

And speaking of the law of Transmutation and its importance, it is clear, I think, that in the homosexual love – whether between man and man or between woman and woman – the physical side, from the very nature of the case, can never find expression quite so freely and perfectly as in the ordinary heterosexual

---

e  'The truth is that we can no more explain the inverted sex-feeling than we can the normal impulse; all the attempts at explanation of these things, and of Love, are defective.' (Moll, second ed. p. 253.)

f  See *Sex-Love*, p. 8.

love; and therefore that there is a 'natural' tendency for the former love to run rather more along emotional channels.[g] And this no doubt throws light on the fact that love of the homogenic type has inspired such a vast amount of heroism and romance – and is indeed only paralleled in this respect (as J. Addington Symonds[5] has pointed out in his paper on 'Dantesque and Platonic ideals of Love')[h] by the loves of Chivalry, which of course owing to their special character, were subject to a similar transmutation.

It is well-known that Plato in many passages in his dialogues gives expression to the opinion that the love which at that time was common among the Greek youths had, in its best form, a special function in education, social and heroic work. I have already quoted a passage from the *Symposium*, in which Phaedrus speaks of the inspiration which this love provides towards an honourable and heroic life. Pausanias in the same dialogue says:[i]

> 'In Ionia and other places, and generally in countries which are subject to the barbarians, the custom is held to be dishonourable; loves of youths share the evil repute of philosophy and gymnastics *because they are inimical to tyranny*, for the interests of rulers require that their subjects should be poor in spirit, and that there should be no strong bond of friendship or society between them – which love above all other motives, is likely to inspire, as our Athenian tyrants learned by experience.'

This is a pretty strong statement of the political significance of this kind of love.

Richard Wagner[6] in his pamphlet *The Art-work of the Future*[j] has some interesting passages to the same effect – showing how the conception of the beauty of manhood became the formative influence of the Spartan State.[7] He says:

> 'This beauteous naked man is the kernel of all Spartanhood; from genuine delight in the beauty of the most perfect human body – that of the male – arose that spirit of comradeship which pervades and shapes the whole economy of the Spartan State. This love of man to man, in its primitive purity, proclaims itself as the noblest and least selfish utterance of man's sense of beauty, for it teaches man to sink and merge his entire self in the object of his affection;' and again: 'The higher element of that love of man to man consisted even in this: that it excluded the motive of egoistic[k] physicalism. Nevertheless it not only included a purely spiritual bond of friendship, but this spiritual friend-

g   See *Marriage*, p. 7. [Again a reference to Carpenter's own pamphlet of 1894.]
h   See *In the Key of Blue* by J. A. Symonds. (Published by Elkin Matthews, 1893).
i   [Benjamin] Jowett's *Plato*, second ed. vol. ii. p. 33.
j   Prose-works of Richard Wagner, translated by W. A. Ellis.
k   The emphasis is on the word *egoistic*.

ship was the blossom and the crown of the physical friendship. The latter sprang directly from delight in the beauty, aye in the material bodily beauty of the beloved comrade; yet this delight was no egoistic yearning, but a thorough stepping out of self into unreserved sympathy with the comrade's joy in himself; involuntarily betrayed by his life-glad beauty-prompted bearing. This love, which had its basis in the noblest pleasures of both eye and soul – not like our modern postal correspondence of sober friendship, half businesslike, half sentimental – was the Spartan's only tutoress of youth, the never-ageing instructress alike of boy and man, the ordainer of common feasts and valiant enterprises; nay the inspiring helpmeet on the battle-field. For this it was that knit the fellowship of love into battalions of war, and fore-wrote the tactics of death-daring, in rescue of the imperilled or vengeance for the slaughtered comrade, by the infrangible law of the soul's most natural necessity.'

The last sentence in this quotation is well illustrated by a passage from a 'privately printed' pamphlet entitled *A Problem in Greek Ethics*,[8] in which the author endeavours to reconstruct as it were the genesis of comrade-love among the Dorians in the early Greek times. Thus:

'Without sufficiency of women, without the sanctities of established domestic life, inspired by the memory of Achilles and venerating their ancestor Herakles,[1] the Dorian warriors had special opportunity for elevating comradeship to the rank of an enthusiasm.[9] The incidents of emigration into a distant country – perils of the sea, passages of rivers and mountains, assaults of fortresses and cities, landings on a hostile shore, night vigils by the side of blazing beacons, foragings for food, picquet service in the front of watchful foes – involved adventures capable of shedding the lustre of romance on friendship. These circumstances, by bringing the virtues of sympathy with the weak, tenderness for the beautiful, protection for the young, together with corresponding qualities of gratitude, self-devotion, and admiring attachment into play, may have tended to cement unions between man and man no less firm than that of marriage. On such connections a wise captain would have relied for giving strength to his battalions, and for keeping alive the flames of enterprise and daring.'

---

1    Whose tomb on account of this attachment to Ioläus was a place where Comrades swore troth to each other (Plutarch on *Love*, section xvii). [Ioläus was the son of Iphicles, Hercules' twin-brother; he became Hercules' charioteer and faithful companion.]

The author then goes on to suggest that though in such relations as those indicated the physical probably has its share, yet it did not at that time overbalance the emotional and spiritual elements, or lead to the corruption and effeminacy of a later age.

At Sparta the lover called *Eispnêlos*, the inspirer, and the younger beloved *Aïtes*, the hearer. This alone would show the partly educational aspects in which comradeship was conceived; and a hundred passages from classic literature might be quoted to prove how deeply it had entered into the Greek mind that this love was the cradle of social chivalry and heroic life. Finally it seems to have been Plato's favourite doctrine that the relation if properly conducted led up to the disclosure of true philosophy in the mind, to the divine vision or mania, and to the remembrance or rekindling within the soul of all the forms of celestial beauty. He speaks of this kind of love as causing a 'generation in the beautiful'[m] within the souls of the lovers. The image of the beloved one passing into the mind of the lover and upward through its deepest recesses reaches and unites itself to the essential forms of divine beauty there long hidden – the originals as it were of all creation – and stirring them to life excites a kind of generative descent of noble thoughts and impulses, which thenceforward modify the whole cast of thought and life of the one so affected.

I have now said enough I think to show that though Science has not as yet been able to give any decisive utterance on the import of the physical and physiological side of the homogenic passion (and it must be remembered that its real understanding of this side of the ordinary sex-love is very limited), yet on its ethical and social sides – which cannot of course, in the last resort, be separated from the physiological – the passion is pregnant with meaning, and has received at various times in history abundant justification. And in truth it seems the most natural thing in the world that just as the ordinary sex-love has a special function in the propagation of the race, so the other love should have its special function in social and heroic work, and in the generation – not of bodily children – but of those children of the mind, the philosophical conceptions and ideals which transform our lives and those of society. This without limiting too closely. In each case the main object may be said to be union. But as all love is also essentially creative, we naturally look for the creative activities of different kinds of love in different directions – and seem to find them so.

If there is any truth – even only a grain or two – in these speculations, it is easy to see that the love with which we are specially dealing is a very important factor in society, and that its neglect, or its repression, or its vulgar misapprehension, may be matters of considerable danger or damage to the common-weal. It is easy to see that while on the one hand the ordinary marriage is of indispensable importance to the State as providing the workshop as it were for the breeding and rearing of children, another form of union is almost equally indis-

m  *Symposium*: speech of Socrates.

544

pensable to supply the basis for social activities of other kinds. Every one is conscious that without a close affectional tie of some kind his life is not complete, his powers are crippled, and his energies are inadequately spent. Yet it is not to be expected (though it may of course happen) that the man or woman who have dedicated themselves to each other and to family life should leave the care of their children and the work they have to do at home in order to perform social duties of a remote and less obvious, though may-be more arduous, character. Nor is it to be expected that a man or woman single-handed, without the counsel of a helpmate in the hour of difficulty, or his or her love in the hour of need, should feel equal to these wider activities. If – to refer once more to classic story – the love of Harmodius[10] had been for a wife and children at home, he would probably not have cared, and it would hardly have been his business, to slay the tyrant. And unless on the other hand each of the friends had had the love of his comrade to support him, the two could hardly have nerved themselves to this audacious and ever-memorable exploit. So it is difficult to believe that anything except that kind of comrade-union which satisfies and invigorates the two lovers and yet leaves them free from the responsibilities and *impedimenta* of family life can supply the force and liberate the energies required for social and mental activities of the most necessary kind.

For if the slaughter of tyrants is not the chief social duty nowadays, we have with us hydra-headed monsters at least as numerous as the tyrants of old, and more difficult to deal with, and requiring no little courage to encounter. And beyond the extirpation of evils we have solid work waiting to be done in the patient and life-long building up of new forms of society, new orders of thought, and new institutions of human solidarity – all of which in their genesis will meet with opposition, ridicule, hatred, and even violence. Such campaigns as these – though different in kind from those of the Dorian mountaineers described above – will call for equal hardihood and courage and will stand in need of a comradeship as true and valiant. It may indeed be doubted whether the higher heroic and spiritual life of a nation is ever quite possible without the sanction of this attachment in its institutions; and it is not unlikely that the markedly materialistic and commercial character of the last age of European civilized life is largely to be connected with the fact that the *only* form of love and love-union that it has recognized has been one founded on the quite necessary but comparatively materialistic basis of matrimonial sex-intercourse and child-breeding.[n]

Walt Whitman,[11] the inaugurator, it may almost be said, of a new world of

---

n   It is interesting in this connection to notice the extreme fervour, almost of romance, of the bond which often unites lovers of like sex over a long period of years, in an unfailing tenderness of treatment and consideration towards each other, equal to that shown in the most successful marriages. The love of many such men, says Moll (p. 119), 'developed in youth lasts at times the whole life through. I know of such men, who had not seen their first love for years, even decades, and who yet on meeting showed the old fire of their first passion. In other cases a close love-intimacy will last unbroken for many years.'

democratic ideas and literature, and – as one of the best of our critics° has remarked – the most Greek in spirit and in performance of modern writers, insists continually on this social function of 'intense and loving comradeship, the personal and passionate attachment of man to man.' 'I will make,' he says, 'the most splendid race the sun ever shone upon, I will make divine magnetic lands. . . . I will make inseparable cities with their arms about each others necks, by the love of comrades.' And again, in *Democratic Vistas*,[12]

> 'It is to the development, identification, and general prevalence of that fervid comradeship (the adhesive love at least rivalling the amative love hitherto possessing imaginative literature, if not going beyond it), that I look for the counterbalance and offset of materialistic and vulgar American Democracy, and for the spiritualization thereof. . . . I say Democracy infers such loving comradeship, as its most inevitable twin or counterpart, without which it will be incomplete, in vain, and incapable of perpetuating itself.'

Yet Whitman could not have spoken, as he did, with a kind of authority on this subject, if he has not been fully aware that through the masses of the people this attachment was already alive and working – though doubtless in a somewhat suppressed and unselfconscious form – and if he had not had ample knowledge of its effects and influence in himself and others around him. Like all great artists he could but give form and light to that which already existed dim and inchoate in the heart of the people. To those who have dived at all below the surface in this direction it will be familiar enough that the homogenic passion ramifies widely through all modern society, and that among the masses of the people as among the classes, below the stolid surface and reserve of British manners, letters pass and enduring attachments are formed, differing in no very obvious respect from those correspondences which persons of opposite sexes knit with each other under similar circumstances; but hitherto while this passion has occasionally come into public notice through the police reports, etc., in its grosser and cruder forms, its more sane and spiritual manifestations – though really a moving force in the body politic – have remained unrecognized.

It is hardly needful in these days when social questions loom so large upon us to emphasize the importance of a bond which by the most passionate and lasting compulsion may draw members of the different classes together, and (as it often seems to so) none the less strongly because they are members of different classes. A moment's consideration must convince us that such a comradeship may, as Whitman says, have 'deepest relations to general politics.' It is noticeable, too, in this deepest relation to politics that the movement among women towards their own liberation and emancipation which is taking place all over the civilized

o   J. A. Symonds.

world has been accompanied by a marked development of the homogenic passion among the female sex. It may be said that a certain strain in the relations between the opposite sexes which has come about owing to a growing conscious-ness among women that they have been oppressed and unfairly treated by men,[p] and a growing unwillingness to ally themselves unequally in marriage – that this strain has caused the womankind to draw more closely together and to cement alliances of their own. But whatever the cause may be it is pretty certain that such comrade-alliances – and of a quite passionate kind – are becoming increas-ingly common, and especially perhaps among the more cultured classes of women, who are working out the great cause of their sex's liberation; nor is it difficult to see the importance of such alliances in such a campaign. In the United States where the battle of women's independence has been fought more vehemently perhaps than here, the tendency mentioned is even more strongly marked.

In conclusion there are a few words to be said about the legal aspect of this important question. It has to be remarked that the present state of the Law – arising as it does partly out of some of the misapprehensions above alluded to, and partly out of the sheer unwillingness of legislators to discuss the question – is really quite impracticable and unjustifiable, and will no doubt have to be altered.

The Law, of course, can only deal, and can only be expected to deal, with the outward and visible. It cannot control feeling; but it tries – in those cases where it is concerned – to control the expression of feeling. It has been insisted on in this essay that the Homogenic Love is a valuable social force, and, in cases, an indis-pensable factor of the noblest human character; also that it has a necessary root in the physical and sexual organism. This last is the point where the Law steps in. 'We know nothing' – it says – 'of what may be valuable social forces or factors of character, or of what may be the relation of physical things to things spiritual; but when you speak of a sexual element being present in this kind of love, we can quite understand that; and that is just what we mean to suppress. That sexual element is nothing but gross indecency, *any form of which by our Act of 1885 we make criminal.*'[13]

Whatever substantial ground the Law may have had for previous statutes on this subject – dealing with a specific act (sodomy) – it has surely quite lost it in passing so wide-sweeping a condemnation on all relations between male persons.[q] It has undertaken a censorship over private morals (entirely apart from social results) which is beyond its province, and which – even if it were its province – it could not possibly fulfil; it has opened wider than ever before the door to a real social evil and crime – that of blackmailing; and it has thrown a

p   See *Woman*, p. 11, etc.
q   Though, inconsistently enough, making no mention of females.

547

shadow over even the simplest and most natural expressions of an attachment which may, as we have seen, be of the greatest value in national life.[r]

That the homosexual passion may be improperly indulged in, that it may lead, like the heterosexual, to public abuses of liberty and decency we of course do not deny; but as, in the case of persons of opposite sex, the law limits itself on the whole to the maintenance of public order, the protection of the weak from violence and insult[s] and, of the young from their inexperience: so it should be here. Whatever teaching may be thought desirable on the general principles of morality concerned must be given – as it can only be given – by the spread of proper education and ideas, and not by the clumsy bludgeon of the statute-book.[t]

We have shown the special functions and really indispensable import of the homogenic or comrade love, in some form, in national life, and it is high time now that the modern States should recognize this in their institutions – instead of (as is also done in schools and places of education) by repression and disallowance perverting the passion into its least satisfactory channels. If the dedication of love were a matter of mere choice or whim, it still would not be the business of the State to compel that choice; but since no amount of compulsion can ever change the homogenic instinct in a person, where it is innate, the State in trying to effect such a change is only kicking vainly against the pricks of its own advantage – and trying, in view perhaps of the conduct of a licentious few, to cripple and damage a respectable and valuable class of its own citizens.

r  Dr Moll maintains (second ed., pp. 314, 315) that if familiarities between those of the same sex are made illegal, as immoral, self-abuse ought much more to be so made.

s  Though it is doubtful whether the marriage-laws even do this!

t  In France, since the adoption of the Code Napoléon, sexual inversion is tolerated under the same restrictions as normal sexuality; and according to Carlier, formerly Chief of the French Police, Paris is not more depraved in this matter than London. Italy in 1889 also adopted the principles of the Code Napoléon on this point.

# JOHN ADDINGTON SYMONDS, *A PROBLEM IN MODERN ETHICS* (1896)

The career of John Addington Symonds (1840–93) began in a model way. Educated at Harrow and then Balliol College, Oxford, he obtained a first-class degree, won the Newdigate prize for poetry, was offered an open fellowship at Magdalen, and in 1863 won one of the Chancellor's prizes for an essay on the Renaissance. There was, however, a price to be paid for this success; a few months later Symonds broke down. Exhausted and suffering from impaired sight he went abroad to recover his health. While in Switzerland Symonds met Catherine North whom he married in November 1864. The couple settled in London and in 1865 the first of four daughters was born. Symonds attempted to pursue a career in law but was forced to give it up because of his continued ill-health. In the late 1860s he decided to devote himself to a literary career. His first published works included some travel pieces for various periodicals which were later published as *Sketches in Italy and Greece* (1874); other works in this genre included *Sketches and Studies in Italy* (1879) and *Italian Byways* (1883). A period of teaching at Clifton College in the early 1870s produced two critical works: *Introduction to the Study of Dante* (1872) and *Studies of the Greek Poets* (two series: 1873 and 1876). In 1875 the first volume of the work for which he is best known, *History of the Renaissance in Italy* appeared (the seventh and final volume was published in 1886). In 1877, plagued once more by illness and exhaustion, Symonds travelled to Switzerland in the hope that the alpine air might refresh him. Impressed by the improvement in his health experienced while staying at Davos Platz, he decided to settle there permanently. From Davos Symonds continued his writing career, producing a number of commissioned works, including lives of Shelley (1878), Sidney (1886) and Jonson (1886) for the English Men of Letters series; several minor studies for the *Mermaid* series; translations of the sonnets of Michelangelo and Campanella (1878) and the autobiography of Benvenuto Cellini (1888); and in 1892 a life of Michelangelo. Symonds also produced several volumes of his own poetry as well as a book of critical essays, *In the Key of Blue*, published in 1893. On his death a study of Walt Whitman appeared. Indeed it is Whitman who provides a clue to the other side of Symonds' life in Davos, for Switzerland liberated him not only from ill-health, but also from frustration and anxiety over his homosexuality. In the more tolerant European climate, Symonds had a number of lovers, including an Italian gondolier, Angelo Fusato, whom he installed in his household as a man-in-waiting. Symonds had been writing about his homosexuality for some time, but always surreptitiously. One of his projects was a 'Uranian' epic about a London newsboy; it was unpublished in his lifetime and only two sections have survived. Many of his published poems were also written to men (although the pronouns were conventionally feminine). Symonds also produced two privately printed pamphlets on 'sexual inversion' which are regarded today as among the first serious works to have been produced on homosexuality in Britain. They are *A Problem in Greek Ethics*, written as early as 1873 but not published (in ten copies) until 1883; and *A Problem in Modern Ethics*, of which fifty copies were published in 1891. One of Symonds' last projects was a collaboration with Havelock Ellis on *Sexual Inversion*, the projected first volume of *Studies in the Psychology of Sex*. However, when the volume was finally published (after Symonds' death) his contribution was suppressed.

### *From* John Addington Symonds, *A Problem in Modern Ethics: Being an Inquiry into the Phenomenon of Sexual Inversion* (London, 1896)[1]

#### *IX: Epilogue*[2]

The conclusion to which I am led by this enquiry into sexual inversion are that its several manifestations may be classified under the following categories: (1) Forced abstinence from intercourse with females, or *faute de mieux*;[3] (2) Wantonness and curious seeking after novel pleasure; (3) Pronounced morbidity; (4) Inborn instinctive preference for the male and indifference to the female sex; (5) Epochs of history when the habit has become established and endemic in whole nations.

Under the first category we group the phenomena presented by schools, prisons, convents, ships, garrisons in solitary stations, nomadic tribes of marauding conquerors.[a]

To the second belong those individuals who amuse themselves with experiments in sensual pleasure, men jaded with ordinary sexual indulgence, and indifferent voluptuaries. It is possible that something morbid or abnormal usually marks this class.

To the third we assign clear cases of hereditary malady, in which a want of self-control is prominent, together with sufferers from nervous lesion, wounds,

---

a    Kelts [i.e. Celts], Scythians, Dorians, Tartars, Normans.

epilepsy, senile brain-softening, in so far as these physical disturbances are complicated with abnormal passions.[b]

The fourth includes the whole class of Urnings, who have been hitherto ignored by medical investigators, and on whose numerical importance Ulrichs has perhaps laid exaggerated stress.[4] These individuals behave precisely like persons of normal sexual proclivities, display no signs of insanity, and have no morbid constitutional diathesis to account for their peculiarity.

Under the existing conditions of European Society, these four categories exist sporadically. That is to say, the members of them are found scattered through all communities, but are nowhere recognised except by the penal code and the medical profession. In the fifth category we are brought face to face with the problem offered by ancient Hellas, by Persia, by Afghan, by the peoples of what Burton calls the Sotadic Zone.[5] However we may account for the origin of sexual inversion, the instinct has through usage, tradition, and social toleration passed here into the nature of the race; so that the four previous categories are confounded, or, if distinguished, are only separable in the same way as the vicious and morbid affections of the ordinary sexual appetite may be differentiated from its healthier manifestations.

Returning to the first four categories, which alone have any importance for a modern European, we perceive that only one of them, the third, is positively morbid, and only one, the second, is *ipso facto* vicious. The first is immoral in the same sense as all incontinence, including self-abuse, fornication, and so forth, practised *faute de mieux*, is immoral; but it cannot be called either morbid or positively vicious, because the habit in question springs up under extra-social circumstances. The members of the fourth category are abnormal through their constitution. Whether we refer that abnormality to atavism, or to some hitherto unapprehended deviation from the rule in their sexual conformation, there is no proof that they are the subjects of disease. At the same time it is certain that they are not deliberately vicious.

The treatment of sexual inversion by society and legislation follows the view taken of its origin and nature. Ever since the age of Justinian,[6] it has been regarded as an unqualified crime against God, the order of the world, and the State. This opinion, which has been incorporated in the codes of all the Occidental races, sprang originally from the conviction that sterile passions are injurious to the tribe by checking propagation. Religion adopted this view, and, through the legend of Sodom and Gomorrah,[7] taught that God was ready to punish whole nations with violent destruction if they practised the 'unmentionable vice.' Advancing civilisation, at the same time, sought in every way to limit and regulate the sexual appetite; and while doing so, it naturally excluded those

---

b    It ought to be borne in mind that they are by no means invariably complicated with abnormal sexuality, but quite as often with normal sexuality in some extravagant shape, as well as with other kinds of moral aberration.

forms which were not agreeable to the majority, which possessed no obvious utility, and which *prima facie* seemed to violate the cardinal laws of human nature.

Social feeling, moulded by religion, by legislation, by civility, and by the persistent antipathies of the majority regards sexual inversion with immitigable abhorrence. It does not distinguish between the categories I have indicated, but includes all species under the common condemnation of crime.

Meanwhile, of late years, we have come to perceive that the phenomena presented by sexual inversion, cannot be so roughly dealt with. Two great nations, the French and the Italian, by the 'Code Napoléon' and the 'Codice Penale' of 1889, remove these phenomena from the category of crime into that of immorality at worst. That is to say, they place the intercourse of males with males upon the same legal ground as the normal sexual relation. They punish violence, protect minors, and provide for the maintenance of public decency. Within these limitations, they recognise the right of adults to deal as they choose with their persons.

The new school of anthropologists and psychological physicians study sexual inversion partly on the lines of historical evolution, and partly from the point of view of disease. Mixing up atavism[8] and heredity with nervous malady in the individual, they wish to substitute medical treatment for punishment, lifelong sequestration in asylums for terms of imprisonment differing in duration according to the offence.

Neither society nor science entertains the notion that those instincts which the laws of France and Italy tolerate, under certain restrictions, can be simply natural in a certain percentage of male persons. Up to the present time the Urning has not been considered as a sport of nature in her attempt to differentiate the sexes. Ulrichs is the only European who has maintained this view in a long series of polemical and imperfectly scientific works. Yet facts brought daily beneath the notice of open-eyed observers prove that Ulrichs is justified in his main contention. Society lies under the spell of ancient terrorism and coagulated errors. Science is either wilfully hypocritical or radically misinformed.

Walt Whitman,[9] in America, regards what he calls 'manly love' as destined to be a leading virtue of democratic nations, and the source of a new chivalry. But he does not define what he means by 'manly love.' And he emphatically disavows any 'morbid inferences' from his doctrine as 'damnable.'

This is how the matter stands now. The one thing which seems clear is that sexual inversion is no subject for legislation, and that the example of France and Italy might well be followed by other nations. The problem ought to be left to the physician, the moralist, the educator, and finally to the operation of social opinion.

*Suggestions on the Subject of Sexual Inversion in Relation to Law and Education*

## I.

The laws in force against what are called unnatural offences derive from an edict of Justinian, AD 538. The Emperor treated these offences as criminal, on the ground that they brought plagues, famines, earthquakes, and the destruction of whole cities, together with their inhabitants, upon the nations who tolerated them.

## II.

A belief that sexual inversion is a crime against God, nature, and the State pervades all subsequent legislation on the subject. This belief rests on (1) theological conceptions derived from the Scriptures; (2) a dread of decreasing the population; (3) the antipathy of the majority for the tastes of the minority; (4) the vulgar error that antiphysical desires are invariably voluntary, and the result either of inordinate lust or of satiated appetites.

## III.

Scientific investigation has proved in recent years that a very large proportion of persons in whom abnormal sexual inclinations are manifested possess them from their earliest childhood, that they cannot divert them into normal channels, and that they are powerless to get rid of them. In these cases, then, legislation is interfering with the liberty of individuals, under a certain misconception regarding the nature of their offence.

## IV.

Those who support the present laws are therefore bound to prove that the coercion, punishment, and defamation of such persons are justified either (1) by any injury which these persons suffer in health of body or mind, or (2) by any serious danger arising from them to the social organism.

## V.

Experience, confirmed by scientific observation, proves that the temperate indulgence of abnormal sexuality is no more injurious to the individual than a similar indulgence of normal sexuality.

## VI.

In the present state of over-population, it is not to be apprehended that a small minority of men exercising sterile and abnormal sexual inclinations should seriously injure society by limiting the increase of the human race.

## VII.

Legislation does not interfere with various forms of sterile intercourse between men and women: (1) prostitution, (2) cohabitation in marriage during the period of pregnancy, (3) artificial precautions against impregnation, and (4) some abnormal modes of congress with the consent of the female. It is therefore in an illogical position, when it interferes with the action of those who are naturally sterile, on the ground of maintaining the numerical standard of the population.

## VIII.

The danger that unnatural vices, if tolerated by the law, would increase until whole nations acquired them, does not seem to be formidable. The position of women in our civilisation renders sexual relations among us occidentals different from those of any other country – ancient Greece and Rome, modern Turkey and Persia – where antiphysical habits have hitherto become endemic.

## IX.

In modern France, since the promulgation of the Code Napoléon, sexual inversion has been tolerated under the same restrictions as normal sexuality. That is to say, violence and outrages to public decency are punished, and minors are protected, but adults are allowed to dispose as they like of their own persons. The experience of nearly a century shows that in France, where sexual inversion is not criminal *per se*, there has been no extension of it through society. Competent observers, like agents of police, declare that London, in spite of our penal legislation, is no less notorious for abnormal vice than Paris.

## X.

Italy, by the Penal Code of 1889, adopted the principles of the Code Napoléon on this point. It would be interesting to know what led to this alteration of the Italian law. But it cannot be supposed that the results of the Code Napoléon in France were not fully considered.

## XI.

The severity of the English statutes render them almost incapable of being put into force. In consequence of this the law is not unfrequently evaded, and crimes are winked at.

## XII.

At the same time our laws encourage blackmailing upon false accusation; and the presumed evasion of their execution places from time to time a vile weapon in the hands of unscrupulous politicians, to attack the Government in office.

554

Examples: the Dublin Castle Scandals of 1884, the Cleveland Street Scandals of 1889.[10]

## XIII.

Those who hold that our penal laws are required by the interests of society must turn their attention to the higher education. This still rests on the study of the Greek and Latin classics, a literature impregnated with paederastia. It is carried on at public schools, where young men are kept apart from females, and where homo-sexual vices are frequent. The best minds of our youth are therefore exposed to the influences of a paederastic literature at the same time that they acquire the knowledge and experience of unnatural practices. Nor is any trouble taken to correct these adverse influences by physiological instruction in the laws of sex.

## XIV.

The points suggested for consideration are whether England is still justified in restricting the freedom of adult persons, and rendering certain abnormal forms of sexuality criminal, by any real dangers to society: after it has been shown (1) that abnormal inclinations are congenital, natural, and ineradicable in a large percentage of individuals; (2) that we tolerate sterile intercourse of various types between the two sexes; (3) that our legislation has not suppressed the immorality in question; (4) that the operation of the Code Napoléon for nearly a century has not increased this immorality in France; (5) that Italy, with the experience of the Code Napoléon to guide her, adopted its principles in 1889; (6) that the English penalties are rarely inflicted to their full extent; (7) that their existence encourages blackmailing, and their non-enforcement gives occasion for base political agitation; (8) that out higher education is in open contradiction to the spirit of our laws.[c]

---

c It may not be superfluous to recapitulate the main points of English legislation on this topic. (1) Sodomy is a felony, defined as the carnal knowledge (per anum) of any man or of any woman by a male person; punishable with penal servitude for life as a maximum, for ten years as a minimum. (2) The attempt to commit sodomy is punishable with ten years' penal servitude as a maximum. (3) The commission, in public or private, by any male person with another male person, of 'any act of gross indecency,' is punishable with two years' imprisonment and hard labour.

# NOTES

## INTRODUCTION

1 Modern arguments about the essentialist nature of literary value largely derive from post-Kantian, late nineteenth-century idealist aesthetics. The best known examples in literary criticism are the work in the 1940s and 1950s of the Cambridge critic, F. R. Leavis, and the American school of 'new criticism' associated with figures such as Cleanth Brooks, W. K. Wimsatt and Yvor Winters.

2 This kind of approach is most closely associated with the various kinds of Marxist criticism. Its earliest proponents in Britain included Raymond Williams, Arnold Kettle and John Lucas; more recently the work of Catherine Belsey (particularly her *Critical Practice* [London: Methuen, 1983]) and Terry Eagleton (*Literary Theory: An Introduction* [Oxford: Blackwell, 1983]) have gone a long way to popularising this view among a student audience.

3 This kind of argument is most closely associated with new historicism. See, for example, Aram Veeser, ed., *The New Historicism* (London: Routledge, 1989); for a recent and trenchant critique of some of the assumptions of new historicism, see John Lee, 'The Man Who Mistook his Hat: Stephen Greenblatt and the Anecdote', *Essays in Criticism*, XLV (1995), pages 285–300.

4 Discussion of this view can be found in Janet Wolff, *Aesthetics and the Sociology of Art* (London: Macmillan, 1983). In philosophy it is often referred to as the 'institutional theory of art', and is most closely associated with the work of George Dickie and his account of institutionalised aesthetic judgements (see *Art and the Aesthetic: An Institutional Analysis* [London: Cornell University Press, 1974]); see also Richard Wollheim, *Art and its Objects* (1968; second edn, Cambridge: Cambridge University Press, 1980).

5 See in particular Michel Foucault, *The Order of Things* (London: Tavistock Publications, 1970) and *The Archaeology of Knowledge* (London: Tavistock Publications, 1972). It is worth noting that Foucault's work is complex and obscure, and interpretations of it are contested (see, for example, the discussion in Charles C. Lemert and Garth Gillan, *Michel Foucault: Social Theory and Transgression* [New York: Columbia University Press, 1982]). Indeed Foucault's reputation is currently being reassessed, as social historians – such as Roy Porter and Leslie Hall in *The Facts of Life* (London: Yale University Press, 1995) – question the details of his research.

6 Ideology is an immensely complex concept, and it is used by critics in a whole variety of ways. For a useful discussion of the issues involved, see David McLellan, *Ideology* (Milton Keynes: Open University Press, 1986), and Raymond Geuss, *The Idea of a Critical Theory* (Cambridge: Cambridge University Press, 1981).

557

7 For a discussion of the social mechanisms of authority in the nineteenth century, see Ian Small, *Conditions for Criticism: Authority, Knowledge, and Literature in the Late Nineteenth Century* (Oxford: Clarendon Press, 1991).

8 See, for example, John Sutherland, *Victorian Novelists and Publishers* (London: Athlone Press, 1978) and Allan C. Dooley, *Author and Printer in Victorian England* (Charlottesville: University of Virginia, 1992).

9 This line of argument is most strongly associated with D. F. MacKenzie and Jerome J. McGann. See D. F. MacKenzie, *Bibliography and the Sociology of Texts* (London: The British Library, 1986) and Jerome J. McGann, *The Textual Condition* (Princeton, NJ: Princeton University Press, 1991). The importance of such considerations is most easily seen in the 'luxury' publishing of the 1890s.

## PART I: DEFINING SOCIETY

### Introduction

1 See Philip Abrams, *The Origins of British Sociology* (Chicago: University of Chicago Press, 1968).

2 The description is by P. Bairoch, and is cited in François Crouzet, *The Victorian Economy*, trans. A. S. Forster (London: Routledge, 1982), page 1.

3 See Peter Mathias, *The First Industrial Nation: An Economic History of Britain, 1700–1914* (1969; London: Methuen, 1983).

4 These figures are taken from Crouzet, op. cit. There is some dispute about the precise details of the economic performance of Victorian Britain, but none about the orders of magnitude involved.

5 See, for example, David Roberts, *Victorian Origins of the British Welfare State* (New Haven: Yale University Press, 1960).

6 See, for example, Dorothy Thompson, *The Chartists: Popular Politics in the Industrial Revolution* (Hounslow: Temple Smith, 1984).

7 Henry Sidgwick, 'Bentham and Benthamism in Politics and Ethics', *Fortnightly Review*, 21 n.s. (May 1877), pages 627–52; reprinted in *Miscellaneous Essays and Addresses* (London: Macmillan & Co., 1904), page 135 and page 137.

8 In fact the novel was conceived with a view to boosting the flagging sales of *Household Words*.

9 A useful introduction to utilitarianism is provided by John Plamenatz, *The English Utilitarians* (1958; Oxford: Basil Blackwell, 1966).

10 For an account of Owen's thought and influence, see J. F. C. Harrison, *Robert Owen and the Owenites in Britain and America* (London: Routledge and Kegan Paul, 1969).

11 The emergence of marginal utility theory is referred to by economic historians as the 'marginal revolution'; however, the precise nature and causes of that revolution are contested. For a useful account of some of the issues involved, see R. D. Collinson Black, A. W. Coats and D. W. Craufurd Goodwin, eds., *The Marginal Revolution in Economics: Interpretation and Evaluation* (Durham NC: Duke University Press, 1973); for an introductory description of the marginal revolution see the relevant chapters in T. W. Hutchinson, *Review of Economic Doctrines 1870–1919* (Westport CN: Greenwood Press, 1975).

12 For example, *Das Kapital* (*Capital*) was first translated into English (in two volumes) by Samuel Moore and Edward Aveling under the editorship of Friedrich Engels in 1887; a third volume appeared in 1896. Similarly *The Communist Manifesto* did not become widely available in Britain until 1888, when the first authorised English version appeared – once again translated by Moore and edited by Engels. (In fact

there had been one previous English translation by Helen MacFarlane; published in 1850 in the Chartist journal, *The Red Republican*, it remained relatively obscure. Many historians have commentated that *The Communist Manifesto* was largely unnoticed in Britain at the time of its publication in 1848).

## Bentham, *An Introduction to the Principles of Morals and Legislation*

1 *An Introduction to the Principles of Morals and Legislation* was first printed (but not published) as early as 1780. The first published edition appeared in 1789 and had a very restricted circulation, attracting little attention. A version of the first six chapters of the first edition formed the basis of the opening section of Etienne Dumont's *Traité de législation civile et pénale* (1802), and it was through Dumont's chapters that Bentham first obtained a wide reputation; as J. H. Burns and H. L. A. Hart argue, Bentham was 'almost certainly read more widely' in the chapters of the *Introduction* used by Dumont than the original from which they derived. (See J. H. Burns and H. L. A. Hart, eds, *An Introduction to the Principles of Morals and Legislation. Collected Works of Jeremy Bentham* [London: Athlone Press, 1970]; my account of the textual history is indebted to their edition.) The influence of Dumont's text was reinforced when it was retranslated into English by Richard Hildreth whose *Theory of Legislation, by Jeremy Bentham, Translated from the French of Etienne Dumont* was published in Boston in 1840 and then in London by Kegan Paul in 1864 (the first American translation of Dumont by John Neal had appeared as early as 1830). A second edition of *An Introduction to the Principles of Morals and Legislation*, with extensive corrections, addenda and supplementary notes by Bentham, was produced in 1823. A third version of the work (based on the 1823 text but with further corrections and addenda together with some passages from Dumont's *Traité de législation civile et pénale*) appeared as the first volume of *The Works of Jeremy Bentham*, ed. John Bowring (Edinburgh: William Tait, 1838). It is clear, then, that Bentham's work was mediated to Victorian readers in a variety of ways. Although he was probably best known through Dumont's version of the *Introduction*, to reproduce a nineteenth-century French text would be of little value for a modern reader. The extract therefore reproduces Bowring's text. His edition, however, is particularly user-unfriendly. It contains not only Bentham's (and aspects of Dumont's) text, but also Bentham's notes and additions, including material omitted from the 1823 edition. Furthermore, on some occasions Bowring provides his own explanatory notes. Although Bowring's and Bentham's notes are not formally marked off from each other, the context makes the distinction clear. I have reproduced all notes and commentary in order to approximate the text which a Victorian reader would have encountered.

## Mill, 'Utilitarianism'

1 *Utilitarianism* was first published in 1861 in three instalments in separate numbers of *Fraser's Magazine*: Chapters i–ii in the October number (pp. 391–406), Chapters iii–iv in the November number (pp. 525–34) and Chapter v in the December number (pp. 658–73). The essays were reprinted with very minor revisions in book form by Parker, Son and Bourn in 1863. Three further editions appeared in Mill's lifetime: a second edition, published by Longmans, in 1864, a third in 1867 and a fourth in 1871, both also by Longmans. Once again there are only very minor variations between the editions – most of Mill's revisions were minor verbal changes.

2 For Bentham, see headnote, page 27. The ethical teachings of the Athenian philosopher, Epicurus (d. 270 BC), argued that the highest good is pleasure; Epicurus further identified pleasure with virtue. Used in a derogatory sense, the term 'epicureanism' denoted the love of sensuous enjoyment, or pleasure for its own sake. Later writers such as Walter Pater, in his novel *Marius the Epicurean* (1885), emphasised the importance of refining the concept of pleasure to include the emotions and the intellect.

3 Stoicism was a school of Greek philosophy founded by Zeno and known for the austerity of its ethical doctrines which emphasised the repression of emotion, indifference to pleasure and pain, and patient endurance. In the second half of the nineteenth century there was a wide interest in Stoicism and particularly in its most celebrated formulation, the *Meditations* of Marcus Aurelius Antoninus. Aurelius was the subject of works by Matthew Arnold and Ernest Renan.

4 Mill may have had in mind Plato's *Republic*, Book IX, where Socrates argues that only the philosopher who in is possession of all three aspects of the soul (as Plato defines them) – intelligence, sensation and aggression – is competent to judge the different types of pleasures associated with those aspects.

5 For Carlyle, see headnote, page 155; Mill has in mind Carlyle's *Sartor Resartus* (1836), Book II, chap. 9, where the narrator challenges the reader to 'Love not Pleasure, love God.'

6 Novalis was the pseudonym of Friedrich von Hardenberg (1772–1801), a German poet much influenced by German Romanticism and German idealist philosophy. The reference is to his best known work, *Lehrlinge zu Saïs* (1798), a philosophical and allegorical account of the natural world. In it Novalis explains how an epoch will arrive when, no longer consoled by the natural world, the human race will seek to redeem itself from its current sorrow and imprisonment by an act of mass suicide.

7 i.e. a follower of transcendental philosophy as associated with the German philosopher, Immanuel Kant (1724–1804). In the second half of the nineteenth century there was a revival of interest in Kant and German idealist philosophy.

8 An astronomical ephemeris, or table of predicted positions of the stars, first published in 1767, and then annually in advance for navigators and astronomers.

## Grote, *An Examination of the Utilitarian Philosophy*

1 There was only one edition of *An Examination of the Utilitarian Philosophy*. The footnotes to the text are both Grote's and those of his editor, J. B. Mayor: they are, however, clearly distinguishable from each other. In the extract Grote's notes are marked off from those of Mayor by the addition of an asterisk.

2 i.e. John Stuart Mill, *Utilitarianism*. Grote read Mill's views on utilitarianism as they first appeared in *Fraser's Magazine* – hence the reference to 'papers'. Mayor's page references are to the book edition.

3 For Bentham, see headnote, page 27; William Paley (1743–1805), Archdeacon of Carlisle and author of many works on moral and theological subjects. The most influential in the nineteenth century included: *Principles of Moral and Political Philosophy* (1785), *A View of the Evidences of Christianity* (1794) and *Natural Theology* (1802).

4 See above, page 45.

5 See note 2 above.

## Owen, *Report to the County of Lanark*

1 *Report to the County of Lanark* was commissioned by the Lanarkshire magistrates who were concerned at rising poor rates. It was presented to them on 1 May 1820, and then separately to the House of Commons and the House of Lords. In both cases the motion to examine Owen's Plan was defeated. An attempt to implement the Report at an estate in Motherwell (offered by Archibald Hamilton) was abandoned through lack of funds. In the meantime Owen published the Report in Glasgow in 1821. A further edition, published in London, appeared in 1832. Owen reprinted the original edition (reproduced here) as an appendix to his *Autobiography* (1858).

2 The chapter is organised under six headings, each of which is concerned with a different aspect of Owen's model community. Part I describes the optimum number of people for each agricultural community; Part II gives the amount of land given over to cultivation; Part III (reproduced here) outlines the living arrangements; Part IV describes the government of the communities; Part V documents the relationships between communities; and Part VI covers the relationship between the new communities and the government of 'old society'.

3 Under the restoration of the monarchy in France, the liberals were opposed to both the republicans and supporters of Bonaparte; the Royalists were supporters of the king under the republican regime. 'Illuminati' is a translation of the German term, 'Illuminaten' – the name given to a celebrated secret society founded in 1776 at Ingolstadt in Bavaria by Adam Weishaupt, upholding republican principles and with an organisation similar to freemasonry. The term 'Illuminati' was also used generally to refer to freethinkers and atheists.

4 Owen is of course referring to himself.

5 Owen's reference is to the division of labour into specialised tasks which was a feature of early industrialisation and which was discussed by early political economists. A clodhopper was someone who followed behind the plough; more generally, the term refers to an unskilled agricultural labourer and so to a lout or boor.

## Spencer, 'Art IV. – The Social Organism'

1 'Art IV. – The Social Organism' took the form of a review article of editions of *The Works of Plato* and *The Works of Thomas Hobbes*. However, like many nineteenth-century reviews, the essay only refers glancingly to the works in question. The review was reprinted with minor revisions as an essay entitled 'The Social Organism' in *Essays: Scientific, Political, and Speculative. Second Series* (1864). In 1874 the complete series of *Essays* (the first, second and third series) was issued in three volumes. A library edition of the *Essays* with additional material was published in 1891; this edition was revised and reprinted with further new material in 1901. The substance of the argument in 'The Social Organism' was reproduced in the section entitled 'A Society is an Organism' in Part II, chap. 2 of the first volume of *The Principles of Sociology*.

2 The publication details of the books nominally under review have been omitted.

3 Sir James Mackintosh (1765–1832) was a philosopher and historian, and in 1818 was made Professor of Law and General Politics at Haileybury College. In 1791 he published *Vindiciae Gallicae* in support of the French Revolution. After meeting Edmund Burke, however, he became converted to Burke's conservative, anti-revolutionary polemic, and in 1798 published *Introductory Discourse*, a repudiation of his

earlier work. He produced several other works of history and philosophy including the posthumous *History of the Revolution in England in 1688* (1834).

4 After the failure of the 1745 Jacobite rebellion, an attempt was made to dissolve the power structures of the clan system. An act was passed in 1747 which deprived the Highlanders of their jurisdiction and judicial powers. It was followed by further measures which proscribed the wearing of Highland dress and made it an offence for Highlanders to possess arms.

5 Cromwell ruled England as Lord Protector and Head of State between December 1653 and September 1658; the monarchy was restored unconditionally eighteen months later in 1660.

6 See Plato, *The Republic*, Book IV.

7 Thomas Hobbes (1588–1679) wrote many works on science and political philosophy. He was famous for his atheism and his pessimistic view of human nature, and in his best known work, *Leviathan* (1651), he advocated the need for a strong or totalitarian state to subdue human failings. The quotation is from the opening of the Introduction to *Leviathan*.

8 Any form of lower animal life such as corals and sponges; zoophytes were originally thought to constitute a distinct phylum between plants and animals.

9 The terms refer to various classes of protozoa which are single cell organisms of microscopic size and the most primitive type of animal life.

10 A class of marine animals of gelatinous substance which includes jelly-fish.

11 A mass of undifferentiated tissue – the primitive substance from which cells are formed – collected about a nucleus. The OED records that the term 'nucleated cell' was first used in 1843.

## Ricardo, *On the Principles of Political Economy, and Taxation*

1 *On the Principles of Political Economy, and Taxation* was first published in 1817. A review by J. R. McCulloch in the *Edinburgh Review* in June 1818 brought it to wide public attention and a revised second edition followed in 1819. A third edition, with further revisions and an additional chapter ('On Machinery') appeared in 1821. The revisions made to the second edition are relatively minor; some historians have seen the more substantial revisions to the third edition (particularly to the chapter on value) as representing a partial retreat from Ricardo's first views. The present extracts are taken from this edition for it was the version best known to Ricardo's Victorian readers. My notes draw upon *The Works and Correspondence of David Ricardo*, ed. Piero Sraffa with the collaboration of M. H. Dobb (Cambridge: Cambridge University Press, 1951–73).

2 Adam Smith (1723–90), Scottish philosopher and founder of political economy; the reference is to the *Wealth of Nations* (1776), Book I, chap. 4.

3 See *Wealth of Nations*, Book I, chap. 5; the quotation is inaccurate and the italics are Ricardo's.

4 *Wealth of Nations*, Book I, chap. 6.

5 Thomas Malthus (1766–1834), curate and political economist, and from 1805 Professor of History and Political Economy at Haileybury College. He is best known for his controversial *An Essay on the Principle of Population* (1798) which claimed that the population increased faster than the rate of subsistence – an argument which strongly influenced Ricardo. In this instance, however, Ricardo has in mind Malthus's *Principles of Political Economy* (1820), chap. 2, sect. vii.

6 See *Wealth of Nations*, Book I, chap. 5 (once again, the quotation is not accurate).

7  Such a calculation had been made by Malthus in his *Essay on the Principle of Population* (1798), Book I, chap. 1.

8  Sraffa notes that the argument of this passage derives from John Weyland's *The Principles of Population and Production* (1815).

9  As Sraffa comments, in the first edition of the *Principles*, Ricardo had included a reference to Ireland as one of those 'poor countries' where poverty was the result of 'idleness'. He rewrote the passage as a result of criticism from George Ensor in *Inquiry Concerning the Population of Nations* (1818).

10  Ricardo's figure of an annual agricultural labourer's wage of £24–5 is, if anything, slightly generous.

11  i.e. in the next chapter in the *Principles*.

12  At this point Ricardo, as is his practice in the *Principles*, gives detailed figures to support his argument; these have been omitted.

## Mill, 'On the Definition of Political Economy'

1  The article was written in the autumn of 1831; it was then rewritten in the summer of 1833, and published in the *London and Westminster Review* in 1836. It was reprinted with minor revisions as 'Essay V' in *Essays on Some Unsettled Questions of Political Economy* (London: Parker, 1844), pages 120–64. A second edition of *Essays on Some Unsettled Questions* (probably prepared by Helen Taylor) was published by Longmans after Mill's death in 1874. As the title suggests, the article rehearses Mill's views on the method and scope of political economy. Mill defends political economy's reliance on 'a priori' reasoning, and he attempts to define the limits of its enquiry; that is, he emphasises that the concept of 'economic man' is merely an abstraction, and that for all practical purposes the findings of political economy must constantly be tested against specific experience and supplemented by knowledge from other sciences. (Only a small section from the middle of the essay has been reproduced.) There is some debate among historians about how far Mill's later and highly influential *Principles of Political Economy* actually fulfilled these prescriptions, although as J. M. Robbins suggests, the full title of that work – *The Principles of Political Economy with Some of Their Applications to Social Philosophy* – suggests Mill's intention so to do. See *Collected Works of John Stuart Mill. Volume IV: Essays on Economics and Society*, ed. J. M. Robson (London: Routledge and Kegan Paul, 1967).

2  Omitted is a discussion of the accessibility of political economy to experimental confirmation.

## Bagehot, 'The Postulates of English Political Economy No. I.'

1  'The Postulates of English Political Economy No. I' first appeared in the *Fortnightly Review* in February 1876; the companion essay, 'The Postulates of English Political Economy No. II', was published in May. Both essays were reprinted in 1880 in *Economic Studies*, edited by Richard Holt Hutton. A second edition of *Economic Studies* appeared in 1888. A student's edition of 'The Postulates of English Political Economy' edited by Alfred Marshall (Professor of Political Economy at the University of Cambridge) was published in 1885.

2  For Adam Smith, see note 2, page 562. Sir James Stewart (1712–80), Lord Denham, was a political economist. His *Inquiry into the Principles of Political Economy* was published in 1767.

3  Bagehot relates an anecdote from the memoirs of 'le bon Mollien' which has been
   omitted. François Nicolas, Count Mollien (1758–1850) was employed in the French
   Ministry of Finance from 1778; he was also the teacher and financial adviser to
   Napoleon Bonaparte.

4  For Ricardo, see headnote, page 93.

5  For Bentham, see headnote, page 27. John Austin (1790–1859) was a close friend of
   Bentham and James Mill; in 1826 he was appointed to the Chair of Jurisprudence
   at the University of London (now University College, London); his *The Providence of
   Jurisprudence Determined* (subtitled, *An Outline of a Course of Lectures of General
   Jurisprudence or the Philosophy of Positive Law*) was published in 1832 and went through
   several editions, the fourth appearing in 1873.

6  Louis Adolphe Thiers (1797–1877) was a French statesman, journalist and historian.
   Through his journal, *Le National*, Thiers helped to promote the July Revolution of
   1830, and was Minister of the Interior in Louis Philippe's administration; he was a
   leader of right-wing liberals under the Second Republic and the Second Empire,
   and a well-known protectionist. His conservative views are to be seen in his ten-
   volume history of the French Revolution (1823–7) and history of the Consulate and
   Empire (1840–55).

7  Richard Cobden (1804–65) was a member of the Philosophic Radicals and a
   vigorous campaigner for free trade and non-intervention. He was best known for his
   leading role in the Anti-Corn Law League. Founded in 1838, the League was a
   successful campaign for the repeal of the Corn Laws which taxed imports of grain
   into Britain. The issue split the Tory party.

8  i.e. a provisional certificate of money subscribed to a bank or a company which enti-
   tles the holder to a formal certificate, dividends, etc. in due time.

9  i.e. consolidated stock – that is, securities without a maturity date.

10 Belfort was an ancient fortress town commanding the territory between Vosges and
   the Jura; in the nineteenth century it successfully withstood three sieges – in 1814,
   1815 and between November, 1870 and February, 1871. Metz, a town in Lorraine,
   was also besieged in the Franco-Prussian war in August 1870. In October a large
   French force, which had retreated to the fort, surrendered unconditionally after a
   period of negotiation.

11 i.e. Gustav Cohn (1840–1919), German economist and Professor of Political
   Economy at Göttingen University, Hanover. The article to which Bagehot refers is
   'The History and Present State of Political Economy in Germany', *Fortnightly Review*,
   LXXXI n.s. (September 1873), pages 337–50.

12 Francis Bacon (1561–1626); his correct title was Baron Verulam and Viscount St
   Albans, not 'Lord Bacon'. His *Novum Organum* (1620) was widely read in the nineteenth century, and his discussion of methodology attracted the attention of
   economists such as W. S. Jevons, as well literary figures such as Walter Pater and
   Oscar Wilde.

13 For Jevons, see headnote, page 129. The opening chapters of Jevons' *Theory of
   Political Economy* explicitly connected the scientific status of economics with his new
   mathematically based methodology.

14 Sir Isaac Newton (1642–1727), mathematician and discoverer of gravity, whose
   *Principia Mathematica* was published in 1687.

15 For Lyell, see headnote, page 213.

16 For Darwin, see headnote page 227. In fact, Darwin could only loosely be described
   as a disciple of Lyell, who found the most radical aspects of Darwin's work uncongenial.

17 For the Nautical Almanac, see note 8, page 560.

18 John Flamsteed (1646–1719) was the first Astronomer Royal at the Royal Greenwich Observatory.

19 The reference is to banking and the City of London.

20 Jevons taught at Owen's College, Manchester (later the University of Manchester); Léon Walras (1834–1910), a Swiss economist, was with Jevons and Carl Menger the co-originator of marginal utility theory. See the Introduction to this section.

21 James Mill (1773–1836), utilitarian philosopher and father of John Stuart Mill; Nassau William Senior (1790–1864), political economist and first holder of the Chair of Political Economy at the University of Oxford (from 1825 to 1830 and from 1847 to 1852), was a member of the Poor Law Commission and the author of the report which formed the basis of the 1834 Poor Law; for Robert Torrens see note d, page 102; John Ramsay McCulloch (1789–1864), statistician and political economist, held the first Chair of Political Economy at the University of London (now University College, London).

22 For Mill, see headnote, page 39.

23 Literally, 'in the clouds' and 'an unknown land'.

## Jevons, *The Theory of Political Economy*

1 The first edition of *The Theory of Political Economy* was published in 1871; a second edition with revisions and additions by Jevons appeared in 1879. A third posthumous edition with a Preface by Jevons' wife, Harriet, appeared in 1888. This edition was a reprint of the second with the exception of the first Appendix – a bibliography of books on mathematical economics – which Harriet, with the help of advice from Jevons' friends and colleagues, brought up to date. A fourth edition prepared by Jevons' son was published in 1911; it contains several additional appendices.

2 For Smith, see note 2, page 562; for Senior, see note 21, above; for Ricardo and Mill, see headnotes, page 93 and page 39 respectively; for Malthus, see note 5, page 562. James Anderson (1739–1808) was the founder of the Edinburgh paper, *The Bee* (which ran from 1790–4); he was also the author of many tracts and of the multi-volume *Recreations in Agriculture, Natural History, Arts, and Miscellaneous Literature* (1799–1802). He was best known, however, for his pamphlet, *An Inquiry into the Nature of the Corn Laws* (1777) which anticipated Ricardo's theory of rent.

3 I have omitted the page number of Jevons' cross-references to other parts of the book; the omission on page 131 is for the same reason.

4 William Whewell (1794–1866) was elected to a fellowship at Trinity College, Cambridge in 1817, and was appointed Knightbridge Professor of Moral Philosophy in 1838. He published widely on science, philosophy and mathematics, and was active in attempts to reform the University, taking a particular interest in the teaching of mathematics. In his *An Elementary Treatise on Mechanics*, published in 1819 (and subsequently running to many editions) he helped promote the analytical methods of Continental mathematics which at the time were neglected at Cambridge; in 1835 he published the controversial pamphlet, *Thoughts on the Study of Mathematics*. Jevons' term 'Memoirs' appears to be a reference to this last work.

5 Clément Joseph Garnier was the author of *Traité d'économique politique*, a work which had reached its fourth edition by 1860. Jevons' references are unusually wide in range and include continental writers as well as minor British theorists. In a speech delivered to the Political Economy Club in 1876 (and reprinted in the November issue of the *Fortnightly Review*) Jevons deprecated British intellectual parochialism and the oppressive authority of orthodox economic circles in Britain.

6 Jean-Baptiste Say (1767–1832), a political economist whose *Traité d'économie politique* (1803) went through many editions and was translated into many languages. In it Say systematised and organised economic principles into the broad categories of production, distribution and consumption; he was pre-eminent for his 'law of markets' ('Say's law') which argued that supply creates its own demand. The quotation translates as: 'the faculty which things possess of serving men, in any way whatsoever.'

7 For the context of the quotation, see pages 28–9.

8 Lord Lauderdale (James Maitland) (1759–1839) published his *Inquiry into the Nature and Origin of Public Wealth* in 1804; the work attracted considerable attention and led to a public disagreement with Lord Brougham (later Lord Chancellor) after the latter's critical notice of it in the *Edinburgh Review*.

9 Claude Frédéric Bastiat (1801–50) was a critic of socialist economics and protectionism, but unlike most classical theorists, Bastiat argued in his *Harmonies économiques* (1850) for the existence of providential economic laws.

10 Jean Gustave Courcelle-Seneuil (1813–92) published three main works of political economy: *Traité théorique et pratique des entreprises industrielles* (1857); *Traité théorique et pratique d'économie politique* (1858); *Traité sommaire d'économie politique* (1865). He also co-translated John Stuart Mill's *Principles of Political Economy*. The quotations from Courcelle-Seneuil translate as: 'economic need is a desire which has for its end the possession and the enjoyment of a material object' and 'to satisfy our needs with the least possible amount of work possible'.

11 William Hearn (1826–88) was the first Professor of Modern History, Modern Literature, Law, Logic and Political Economy at the University of Melbourne. As well as *Plutology, or the Theory of the Efforts to Satisfy Human Wants* (1864), he also published *The Government of England, its Structure and Development* (1867), together with works on jurisprudence and education.

12 Jevons' reference is probably to Thomas C. Banfield who gave a course of lectures at Cambridge in 1844 which were published in 1845 as *Four Lectures on the Organization of Industry*. A second edition appeared in 1848 with the shorter title, *The Organization of Industry*. Banfield was also the author of two books on the *Industry of the Rhine* (1846 and 1848) and *The Economy of the British Empire* (1849).

13 Here Jevons gives a mathematical illustration of the law by using graphs. Indeed the mathematical aspect of Jevons' *Theory* – his translation of the laws of production and consumption into mathematical equations – was one of its most distinctive features. While of importance to the economic specialist, these details are less relevant to the general reader (as Jevons himself admits in the Preface); they have consequently been omitted. All subsequent ellipses are of this nature.

14 Richard Jennings was a minor writer on political economy; he published *The Natural Elements of Political Economy* in 1855 and *Social Delusions Concerning Wealth and Want* in 1856.

15 Literally, 'in equal steps'.

16 i.e. 'golden mean'.

17 Iron-puddling was a skilled (and dangerous) part of iron production; interestingly the development of mechanised puddlers began only a few years after Jevons' *Theory* was published.

## Hyndman, *England for All*

1 *England for All: The Text-Book of Democracy* was published in June 1881; a cheap reprint was issued in September of the same year.

2 The opening pages of the chapter (omitted here) give a general description of the labour theory of value as it had been proposed by Adam Smith and especially David Ricardo. The critique of this theory by William Stanley Jevons is acknowledged in a footnote, but only in order to dismiss it. Hyndman comments: 'this is not the place to discuss this theory which is of course turned to account at once by capitalists. The cloud of differentiations and metaphysics which Mr Jevons throws up as he goes along does not, however, obscure the fact that without labour there would be no value at all.'

3 i.e. John Stuart Mill in his *Principles of Political Economy*.

4 See David Ricardo, 'Chapter V: On Wages' in *Principles of Political Economy, and Taxation*. See page 100.

5 An Employer's Liability Act was introduced in 1880; it began the process by which employers were increasingly held responsible for injuries incurred on their premises. At the time it was seen as establishing an important precedent, that the state had the right to interfere in the law of contract between employer and employee.

6 William Cobbett (1762–1835), essayist, politician and agriculturist, began as a loyalist and anti-Jacobin sympathiser, but in the early 1800s became interested in popular politics, actively taking up the cause of reform through his journal, *Cobbett's Weekly Political Register*. Begun in 1802, the *Political Register* continued (with intermittent interruptions) until his death; when Cobbett lowered the price, the journal achieved a large circulation among the working classes.

7 Hyndman gives a further and more complex example which takes account of the cost of machinery. It has been omitted.

8 i.e. the system of collective labour in France (reduced from 180 to 12 days a year under the *ancien régime*) which peasants were obliged to give free of charge to the 'seigneur' or lord of the manor; typically it involved harvesting and transporting the harvest. In the seventeenth century the introduction of the *corvée royale* obliged peasants to give between eight and forty days free labour to the king mainly in order to construct roads. The *corvée* system was abolished in 1789–90 after the French Revolution.

9 There was a long series of Factory Acts throughout the century. The first was in 1802, but the most important were the 1833 and 1847 Acts, which progressively limited the employment of women and children to ten hours a day. An act in 1878 consolidated previous legislation.

10 Throughout the Victorian period there were numerous enquiries into the state of public health. These produced a considerable body of legislation on matters of health which culminated in the 1875 Public Health Act. In this instance Hyndman is probably referring to the Report by the Charity Organisation Society into 'The Dwellings of the Poor'. Four members of the government helped to draft the report which led to the 1875 Artisan's Dwelling Act (which Hyndman mentions later in the chapter). The Act empowered local authorities to make compulsory purchases of land for the purposes of building new dwellings to rehouse those most in need. The Act was permissive only – that is, it granted powers, but did not enjoin their use. The result was that most local authorities, unable to meet compensation costs for compulsory purchases, simply ignored it. The notable exception was the corporation of Birmingham under the interventionist guidance of Joseph Chamberlain.

11 Dr James Fraser (1818–85), Bishop of Manchester from 1870 to 1885. During that time, Fraser was actively involved in issues of social reform and participated in a whole variety of social movements, often attending several meetings a day. He gave regular public addresses and was renowned for the frankness of his speeches. He acted as umpire in several strikes and lockouts, including the North East Lancashire cotton strike of 1876 and 1878.

12 W. E. Forster, the Irish Secretary, introduced a Coercion Act in 1881 which gave the Lord Lieutenant extensive powers of arrest. The Act was a response to the violent unrest over the Ground Game Act passed earlier that year which had given tenants the right to take rabbits and hares from the land they rented.

13 The term 'sweating' refers to those who work in very hard conditions for very low wages. It was particularly associated with the tailoring trade and conditions in work-rooms above tailors' shops. The horrors of the 'sweating' system were first brought to public attention by Henry Mayhew in his series of reports in the *Morning Chronicle* on 'London Labour and the London Poor', and by Charles Kingsley's condemna-tion of the system in his pamphlet, *Cheap Clothes and Nasty* (1849), and in his novel, *Alton Locke* (1850). The terms 'sweating' and 'sweated labour' are common in critiques of work-practices in the 1880s.

## Carlyle, *Chartism*

1 Written in 1839, *Chartism* was initially offered as an essay to the radical *Westminster Review* and then to the Tory *Quarterly Review*. Both refused, and it was finally published in its own right in December of that year (although it carries the date of 1840). A second edition appeared later in 1840; it was reissued by Chapman and Hall in 1842.

2 Carlyle several times refers to a 'Reformed House' or 'Reform Ministry'. He seems to be alluding to the way Whig MPs dominated the Commons after the 1832 Reform Bill; they held power (with the exception of a few months in 1834) for the next nine years.

3 The Chartist Movement, active in the 1830s and 1840s, was a radical campaign to improve the political rights of the working classes. Those rights were set out in the People's Charter as 'six points': universal (but, in fact, universal male) suffrage, secret ballots, equal electoral districts, payment of MPs, abolition of property qualifica-tions for MPs and annual parliamentary elections. The Charter, with around two million signatures, was presented to Parliament in 1839. It was debated and rejected – a failure which led to outbursts of rioting and unrest in several areas of the country.

4 Attempts to quell riots associated with Chartist protests sometimes involved bringing in troops; one of the most notable of such cases was during the 'Bull Ring' riots in Birmingham in July 1839. The Bull Ring (in the centre of the city) had become a regular meeting-place for Chartists, and on 4 July the Birmingham magistrates brought in a body of London policemen to break up a Chartist gathering. A riot ensued, the police fled, and troops were called in to restore order. The phrase 'money to Birmingham' refers to the controversy which surrounded a motion tabled in the House of Commons later that month to fund a new Birmingham police force. A Bill was tabled proposing a sum of £10,000 for the purpose; after much debate it was given Royal Assent on 26 August. The middle years of the century saw the establishment of urban (although not initially rural) police forces.

5 Vitriol is a generic term for various acids, particularly sulphuric acid; Carlyle has in mind the use of acid as a weapon. Pikes were traditionally the weapon of infantry militia.

6 The reference is to alleged misconduct among trade unions during the Glasgow Cotton-Spinners' strike of 1837. A Select Committee Report on the strike exposed examples of intimidation by union officials at clandestine meetings.

7 i.e. the penal settlements in Australia; the practice of transporting felons was abol-ished in the late 1860s and the last convict ship sailed on 10 January 1868.

8 'Swing riots' was the term given to the machine-breaking and rick-burning protests by agricultural labourers in the 1830s; letters warning of such protests were signed by 'Captain Swing'.

9 The reference is to the Houses of Parliament.

10 i.e. the official report of the proceedings and debates in the Houses of Parliament.

11 Carlyle has in mind a number of general and specific foreign and domestic policy issues in the late 1830s. The Canada question refers to the 1837 rebellions in the French and English speaking provinces which had been separated by the 1791 Canada Act. The rebellions were easily suppressed, but an inquiry led by Lord Durham recommended (in the Durham Report) reuniting the provinces, a proposition which was effected in 1840. The Irish Appropriation question concerned the attempts in 1836 and 1838 to revise the Irish poor laws to bring them in line with the 1834 Poor Law Amendment Act in Britain (see note 15). The 'appropriation' clause (which wrecked the 1836 Bill) proposed that tithes be converted to a rent-charge, and where the tithe exceeded the rent, some of the excess should be allocated to education for all religious groups. The Bill was finally passed in 1838 when all surplus funds were reserved for the Catholic Church only. The West India question concerned objections made in 1838 to protective duties on imported sugar from the British West Indies; it was claimed that the black population (freed by the 1833 Emancipation Act) was enjoying a high standard of living at the expense of the hard-pressed working classes in Britain. The 'Bedchamber plot' of 1839 centred on Queen Victoria's refusal to concede to Peel's demand that she make changes to the female members of her Household in order to demonstrate confidence in Peel's proposed new government. Victoria's stubbornness was widely interpreted as a demonstration of political allegiance to the former Prime Minister, Lord Melbourne, who had resigned. Peel eventually declined the Queen's Commission, and Melbourne resumed power for a further two years. The more general issues which Carlyle alludes to include the Game Laws (dating from the reign of Charles II) which restricted shooting rights to peers and particular landowners – the prevalence of poaching and the violence associated with it made the Game Laws a constant source of controversy in the early nineteenth century. Other references – to Usury Laws, Hill Coolies and Smithfield Market – are also to matters of contemporary legislation.

12 See Heroditus, *Histories*, iv, where an African tribe, holding the South Wind responsible for a drought, march against it into the desert and are buried in a sand storm.

13 A hot dry suffocating sand wind which sweeps across the African deserts in spring and summer.

14 Oedipus fled from Thebes in order to protect his kingdom from plague, a punishment which resulted from his incestuous marriage to his mother.

15 The reference is to the 1834 Poor Law Amendment Act which replaced the local parish system of outdoor relief with a centralised bureaucracy administered by Poor Law Commissioners. The 'New Poor-Law' is the subject of the third chapter of *Chartism*. 'Laissez-faire' (literally, 'leave-to-do') was the shorthand term for the non-interventionist economic policy advocated by political economists which underwrote the reforms to the Poor Laws.

16 i.e. a suicide.

17 Generally Carlyle's references are to legislation aimed at coercing the working classes. Tread-mills were widely used in the nineteenth century as a form of punishment for convicts; gibbets exhibited the bodies of executed prisoners in public places; poor rates were a levy raised for the relief or support of the poor.

18 Lucifers were an early (and non-safety) match.

19  J. N. Thom, a religious fanatic, attracted a following among Kentish labourers, and in May 1838 was killed along with a dozen of his men in a battle with militia near Canterbury. The 'fifth-monarchy men' were a seventeenth-century radical millenarian sect who believed that Christ's return to earth was imminent. Bedlam (or 'St Mary's of Bethlehem') was a London hospital for the insane, and became a metaphor for madness.

20  Fustian is a coarse cloth of cotton and flax, and is used by Carlyle to denote the working classes. Femgericht, or Vehmgericht, refers to the Vehmic or 'free' Courts which grew up in Germany in the first half of the fifteenth century in order to punish individuals who were seen to have eluded common justice. Dependent for their authority on the emperor alone, they became increasingly secretive and were suppressed in 1461. Glasgow was a centre for Chartist activity. The allusion appears to be to trade union activities in the Glasgow cotton-spinners' strike, and particularly to local, non-judicial ('kangaroo') courts.

21  The allusion is to Carlyle himself, or rather to 'Sauerteig' (literally 'sour-dough') – a fictional persona he uses in chapter 8 of *Chartism*. A similar device is used in *Sartor Resartus*.

22  For Adam Smith, see note 2, page 562.

23  An ironic reference to the conduct of parliamentary debates.

24  The Peterloo massacre refers to events in Manchester in 1819 when a crowd of over 50,000, assembled to listen to the radical Henry Hunt, was fired on by militia. There were eleven deaths and four hundred wounded. The Place de Grève in Paris, originally the site of public executions, was a gathering point for revolutionary crowds during the early stages of the French Revolution.

25  The allusion is to revolutionary politics of the eighteenth century concerning the inviolability of the rights of the individual, and in particular to Tom Paine's *Rights of Man* (1791).

26  i.e. the governing body of France in the revolutionary period.

27  The reference is to the Bayezid Ottoman sultans and princes. 'Bajazet' is a French rendering of 'Bayezid' which Carlyle perhaps adopted from Racine's tragedy, *Bajazet*.

28  The Girondins were a moderate Republican party and the opponents of the Jacobins; they were expelled from the National Convention in 1793. The Comité de Salut was established that same year by the Revolutionary Convention. Effectively it was the government of France during the Reign of Terror in which many Girondins were guillotined.

29  Henri de Saint-Simon (1760–1825), an influential French social theorist who had a significant following in early nineteenth-century Britain. Robert Macaire was a fictitious confidence trickster invented by the French artist, Daumier; Daumier's cartoons were very popular in the 1830s and the term Macairism became synonymous with roguery.

30  See Daniel v. 5: at Belshazzar's feast mysterious writing appeared on a wall warning him of his fate.

31  In the nineteenth century Quarter Sessions were courts presided over by the county or district magistrate who was generally a member of the local gentry. Soup kitchens were establishments which prepared and supplied soup to the poor; the OED records the first use of the term in 1839.

32  i.e. *The Republic*, one of Plato's *Dialogues*, and Sir Thomas More's *Utopia* (1516), both of which attempt to describe perfect societies.

33  Toussaint L'Ouverture was born a slave, but later became an important black leader who brought about the liberation of Haiti and led the black opposition to Napoleon when the French tried to restore slavery in the West Indies.

34 The reference is to Robert Burns (1759–96); the second edition of Burns' *Poems, Chiefly in the Scottish Dialect* (1787) was prefaced by a dedication to its subscribing readers, the 'Noblemen and Gentlemen of the Caledonian Hunt'. Burns worked as an Excise Officer in 1789, hence Carlyle's reference to a 'gauger of beer barrels'.

35 i.e. a musical setting of one of the Penitential Psalms (number fifty-five) beginning 'Miserere mei Deus' – part of the Mass.

36 Mahometanism was the nineteenth-century term for Islam; Carlyle may be referring to the fact that in Islam the prophet Mohammad was a real person. The reference to 'Dalai-Lamaism' appears to be to the Tibetan Buddhists' traditional reliance for their support on voluntary donations of food.

## Arnold, 'Anarchy and Authority'

1 'Anarchy and Authority' was revised and reprinted as 'Chapter II: Doing As One Likes' of *Culture and Anarchy* (1869); a second edition of *Culture and Anarchy* appeared in 1875, a third edition in 1882 and a popular edition in 1889.

2 Arnold has in mind two pieces in the *Saturday Review* – 'Mr Matthew Arnold on Culture,' XXIV (July 1867), pages 78–9 and 'Culture and Action,' XXIV (November 1867), pages 591–3 – both of which referred to his definition of culture as a kind of religion. (For this note and many others I am indebted to the critical editions of *Culture and Anarchy* by J. Dover Wilson and by R. H. Super; see Wilson, ed., *Matthew Arnold: Culture and Anarchy* [Cambridge: Cambridge University Press, 1935], and Super, ed., *The Complete Words of Matthew Arnold. Volume 5* [Ann Arbor: University of Michigan Press, 1965].)

3 The allusion is to I *Henry IV*, I, iii, l. 58, where the foppish courtier, addressing Hotspur, proposes parmaceti as the remedy for 'an inward bruise'. The term was a popular corruption of spermaceti, a fatty substance found in the head of sperm whales and used in medicinal preparations.

4 Alcibiades (450–404 BC) was a pupil and intimate friend of Socrates; he assumed the leadership in 420 of the extreme democrats. The allusion is used as an ironic reference to Samuel Lucas, the brother-in-law of the radical MP John Bright (see note, page 150), and editor of the *Morning Star* – a cheap paper which had been founded in 1856 to promote the radical cause, and which had been bitterly critical of Arnold.

5 Arnold has in mind a critique of himself in the *Daily Telegraph* (2 July 1887), page 6; the offices of the paper were in Fleet Street.

6 The allusion is to E. L. Godkin, 'Sweetness and Light', *Nation*, V (September 1867), pages 212–13.

7 Frederick Harrison (1831–1923), a disciple of the French social theorist, Auguste Comte, and between 1880 and 1905 President of the English Positivist Committee. With Richard Congreve and other Comtists, Harrison founded a chapel inspired by the Comtean religion of positivism; faith was in 'common humanity' rather than the supernatural. The article Arnold refers to is Harrison's 'Culture: A Dialogue,' *Fortnightly Review*, VIII (November 1867), pages 603–14. (See also note 10, page 575.)

8 i.e. the name was used by Arnold for the protagonist of *Friendship's Garland* (1871). The speakers in Harrison's 'Culture: A Dialogue' were Harrison himself and Arminius (who represented Arnold).

9 A small box with a perforated lid for perfume; the allusion is once again to I *Henry IV*, I, iii, l. 37: 'And 'twixt his finger and his thumb he held / A pouncet-box'.

10 At this point Arnold gives a long digression on Harrison and Comte; he omitted the passage when the essay was reprinted in *Culture and Anarchy*, and it has been omitted here.

11 Super comments that Arnold may have in mind a speech Bright gave on the Elective Franchise Bill when he repeatedly claimed to be 'unwilling to depart from the ancient practice of the Constitution of this country'.

12 The lord-lieutenancy was the chief executive authority and head of the magistracy appointed by the sovereign; under this office was the deputy lord-lieutenancy. Established in the sixteenth century, the office held extensive powers with regard to the militia until 1871 when control reverted to the crown. The *posse comitatus* was the body of men which the Sheriff was entitled to call out in order to aid the enforcement of law.

13 i.e. the membership of a parochial vestry; guardians were members of boards elected to administer poor laws in the parish or district.

14 Jules Michelet (1789–1874) was a French historian; his *Histoire de la Révolution française* (1847–53) was popular in England at this time.

15 Clay Cross, a colliery town, south of Chesterfield.

16 The allusion is to the Hyde Park riots of 1866. After the defeat of Gladstone's 1866 Reform Bill there were demonstrations all over the country. In one incident, the Reform League (see note 27, page 573) headed by Edmund Beales, Colonel Dickinson, G. J. Holyoake and Charles Bradlaugh, led marches to Hyde Park with the intention of holding a mass meeting there. The Home Secretary ordered the gates to be shut, and the leaders moved on to Trafalgar Square. A large rump, however, remained and proceeded to tear down the Park railings and vandalise the gardens; the rioting continued for several days.

17 Super notes that on 18 November 1867 a mob of sympathisers, protesting at the death sentence passed on some Fenians, forced their way into the outer office of the Home Secretary to demand a pardon. (See also note 21 below.)

18 William Murphy described himself as an 'agent of the London Protestant Electoral Union'; in Birmingham in the summer of 1867 he began a series of highly inflammatory anti-Catholic lectures which provoked social unrest and rioting. Murphy, however, insisted on his right to free speech, and continued his activities in other parts of the country in May and September 1868. Gathorne Hardy was the then Home Secretary.

19 Sir William Page Wood (1801–81), a distinguished Chancery judge and Lord Chancellor (1868–72) in the first Gladstone Administration. The incident Arnold refers to was first reported in the *Transactions of the National Association for the Promotion of Social Science* (1859); it was referred to again in a paper in the 1866 *Transactions* which was reprinted the same year as a pamphlet entitled, *A Scheme for General and Local Administration of Endowments*.

20 Originally the term 'Philistine' designated the opponents of the Israelites; the German term 'Philister', as defined by the nineteenth-century German social theorist, Wilhelm von Riehl, denoted selfish egotism and a love of material comforts. Arnold appears to have this latter meaning in mind, using the term 'Philistine' pejoratively to refer to the uncultured, prosaic materialism of the English middle classes.

21 The Fenians were an Irish-American revolutionary organisation dedicated to the overthrow of British government in Ireland. 1867 saw several outbursts of Fenian protest in Britain, including a bungled attempt to free some prisoners from Clerkenwell prison in London in which a dozen innocent bystanders were killed and many others injured.

22 i.e. Cole's Truss Manufactory in Trafalgar Square; the building was torn down in 1874.

23 Sir Daniel Gooch (1816–89) was a railway engineer and inventor. In 1837 he was made locomotive superintendent for the Great Western Railway (GWR), a post which he resigned in 1864 to supervise the laying of the Atlantic cable. From 1868–87 Gooch was chairman of the GWR; Swindon was where its headquarters were located.

24 Traditionally an area set aside for baiting bears and rough sport; figuratively, it means a scene of strife and tumult.

25 See headnote, page 155; the reference is to Carlyle's essay, 'Shooting Niagara: and After?', *Macmillan's Magazine*, XVI (August 1867), pages 319–36.

26 Robert Lowe (1811–92), politician. In 1859 Lowe was appointed vice-president of the Committee of the Council on Education. In office he was subjected to much criticism – particularly over his revised code regulations (which proposed that school grants should be funded via a system of payment by results) and over his proposal to return to School Inspectors reports the Committee considered unsatisfactory. Lowe also headed the campaign which led to the defeat of the 1866 Reform Bill.

27 The quotation is from Frederick Harrison, 'Our Venetian Constitution,' *Fortnightly Review*, VII (March 1867), pages 261–83. The Reform League was founded in 1864 by John Bright to press the case for adult male suffrage. Although its president, Edmund Beales, was a middle-class barrister, the League attracted widespread support among the working classes and its secretary, George Howell, was a former bricklayer. In 1866 the League held a rally which led to the Hyde Park Riots (see note 16, page 572).

28 Again the reference is to Carlyle's 'Shooting Niagara: and After?'.

29 i.e. the wife of the American president who, after her husband's assassination in 1865, became mentally unstable.

30 See Luke xvi. 19. In the parable of Dives and Lazarus, Dives is the 'certain rich man'.

31 The reference is to Harrison, 'Culture: A Dialogue'.

32 i.e. Oxford University before the series of mid-century reforms focused by the 1854 Oxford University Act.

33 Super comments that in November 1867, Lowe addressed the Philosophic Institute in Edinburgh on the need to reform education by breaking up the influence of classics; a revised version of his speech was published as a pamphlet, *Primary and Classical Education* (1867); the reference to Aristotle is to *Nicomachean Ethics* II. vi. 15–16.

34 Lord Elcho was a liberal conservative and supporter of Robert Lowe's opposition to the 1866 Reform Bill; Sir Thomas Bateson was MP for Devizes in 1867.

35 Edward Miall (1809–81) was a politician and congregational minister. He edited the *Nonconformist*, and in 1844 founded the British Anti-State Church Association. The terms 'dissenters' and 'nonconformists' refer to those Protestant Churches which had defined themselves in distinction to the Church of England.

36 An Act of 1868 relieved Nonconformists of the need to pay rates for the upkeep of parish churches; voluntaryism refers to the principle of leaving matters of religion and education to voluntary rather than state action. The right of a man to marry his deceased wife's sister was a topic which provoked much amusement in both the press and music-halls for half a century. It was consistently resisted on the grounds that it imperiled the virtue of the spinster sisters of married women, encouraging polygamy and even incest. The rejection of the proposal was almost an annual parliamentary event, until its success in 1906.

37 i.e. a disestablished church.

38 Thomas Wilson (1663–1753) was Bishop of Sodor and Mann (in the Isle of Man). The quotation is from his *Maxims of Piety and of Christianity*, published posthumously

in 1789 by Clement Cruttwell; in the nineteenth century Wilson's *Works* were edited by John Keble for the 'Library of Anglo-Catholic Theology' (1847–63).

39  i.e. E. L. Godkin; see note 6, page 571.

40  The reference is to an anonymous essay entitled 'A Plea for the Uncultivated', *Nation*, V (September 1867), page 215.

41  See note 4, page 571.

42  Jacob Bright (1821–99) was MP for Manchester from 1867 until 1874.

43  Sir Thomas Bazley, Liberal MP 1858–80, was a Manchester cotton-spinner and for a time Chairman of the Manchester Chamber of Commerce; the reference is to a speech he made in Manchester in November 1864.

44  i.e. the Revd. W. Cattle, a Wesleyan Minister. The reference was corrected to Cattle in later editions of the work.

45  A reference to the Irish potato famine of 1845–6.

46  i.e. followers of Philipp Melanchthon (1497–1560), a German reformer.

47  Super notes that in 1867 the City of London Militia – some 600 men – marched their regimental band into the West End; gangs attacked and robbed spectators along the line of the march. Later, in front of the Court of Aldermen, the Colonel of the regiment, Alderman Samuel Wilson, defended his decision not to use arms.

48  The reference is to Harrison's 'Our Venetian Constitution'; see note 27, page 573.

49  Honoré Gabriel, Comte de Mirabeau (1749–91), politician and orator, and one of the greatest figures in the National Assembly which governed France in the early stages of the Revolution. A moderate and an advocate of constitutional monarchy, in 1790 Mirabeau became the secret counsellor of Louis XVI. When he died, a national monument – the Panthéon in Paris – was created for the burial of great men. Mirabeau's remains were later removed when his relationship with Louis was discovered.

50  George Odger (1820–77), Secretary of the London Trades Council 1862–72, and one of the most influential union officials; Odger was a supporter of political activism and a member of the Reform League.

51  Charles Bradlaugh (1803–81), president of the Reform League; see also note 16, page 572.

52  The quotation is from Wilson's *Maxims*; see note 38, page 573.

53  Ibid.

54  The reference is to the Duke of Wellington's views on the 1832 Reform Bill.


## Mill, *On Liberty*

1  The success of the first edition of *On Liberty* (from which the above extract is taken) led to the publication of a second edition (again by Parker) later in 1859. A third and fourth edition, both published by Longman (which had taken over Parker's business) appeared in 1864 and 1869. However, the impact of these last two texts was eclipsed by a paperback 'People's Edition' published by Longman in 1865. In the next few years many thousands of these cheap copies were sold. *On Liberty* was the least revised of all Mill's major works, and variants between all its editions are minor.

2  The reference is presumably to the emergence of the United States of America as a world power.

3  The phrase comes from Alexis de Tocqueville's *De la démocratie en Amérique* (1835–40). Mill was deeply influenced by de Tocqueville's analysis of democracy and in 1835 he published a long essay in the *London Review* on the first volume of de Tocqueville's work. When the second volume appeared in 1840, Mill produced a further essay for

the *Edinburgh Review*. Both were reprinted in Mill's *Dissertations and Discussions* (1859–75).

4 The inhabitants of Sparta, a city state in ancient Greece, were renowned for their frugality, courage and stern discipline; the Helots were a class of serfs in Sparta, intermediate between ordinary slaves and free Spartans.

5 i.e. persons of low rank.

6 i.e. religious hatred.

7 i.e. the Roman Catholic Church; the allusion is to the Reformation.

8 Unitarianism developed in the late seventeenth century from a strain of Presbyterianism influenced by Enlightenment rationalism; its doctrines were formalised in the eighteenth century by Joseph Priestley, Theophilius Lindsey and Thomas Belsham. Unitarians rejected the mystical doctrines of the Trinity and the divinity of Christ; they also rejected the notion of original sin or the doctrine of atonement. They were popularly seen as embodying the opposite of Catholicism.

9 'Akbar' is an Arabic title meaning 'very great', but the term was especially associated with Jelaled-din-Mohammed, Akbar Khan, the powerful Mogul Emperor of India (1556–1605). Charlemagne (742–814), or Charles the Great, was king of the Franks in 771, and in 800, first Holy Roman Emperor. He ruled over most of Western Europe.

10 Auguste Comte (1798–1857), the French social theorist and founder of sociology. In general Comte used the methods of science to uncover what he held to be objective laws of social development; he argued that society progressed through three stages – theological, metaphysical and positivist. The work which Mill has in mind is in fact *Système de politique positive*; the correction was made in later editions.

### Morris *et al.*, 'The Manifesto of the Socialist League'

1 *The Commonweal* was the official journal of The Socialist League, and the 'Manifesto' appeared in the first issue. It was signed by the members of the League's 'Provisional Council': W. B. Adams, Edward Aveling, Eleanor Marx Aveling, Robert Banner, E. Belfort Bax, Thomas Binning, H. Charles, William J. Clark, J. Cooper, E. T. Craig, Charles Faulkner, W. Hudson, Frank Kitz, Joseph Lane, Frederick Lessner, Thomas Maguire, J. L. Mahon, S. Mainwaring, James Mavor, William Morris, C. Mowbray, Andreas Scheu, Edward Watson.

2 The *Communist Manifesto*, drafted by Marx and Engels, was presented at the second meeting of The League of Communists in December 1847; the League had been founded earlier that year. The *Communist Manifesto* was published in London in 1848.

3 The allusion is to the policies of the Social Democratic Federation, led by H. M. Hyndman; the Socialist League was formed by former members of the SDF who had become disaffected by Hyndman's views on social change (see also headnote, page 142).

## PART II: SCIENCE AND RELIGION

### Introduction

1 *Charles Darwin, Thomas Huxley: Autobiographies*, ed. Gavin de Beer (Oxford: Oxford University Press, 1974), page 109.

2 See Ernst Mayr, *One Long Argument* (1991; Harmondsworth: Penguin, 1992), page 20. Mayr's concise and authoritative account of Darwin and modern evolutionary

thought is one of the best introductions to this subject for the non-specialist reader. Tess Cosslett's Introduction to her anthology, *Science and Religion in the Nineteenth Century* (Cambridge: Cambridge University Press, 1984), provides a useful overview of some of the issues involved in the larger debate between science and religion.

3 For a detailed and authoritative study of the *Essays and Reviews* controversy, see Ieuan Ellis, *Seven Against Christ, A Study of 'Essays and Reviews'* (Leiden: Brill, 1980).

## Lyell, *Principles of Geology*

1 The first edition of Lyell's *Principles of Geology* (from which this extract is taken) comprised three volumes and was completed in 1833; by that time, however, a second edition of the first two volumes had already been published. The whole work subsequently went through many further editions in Lyell's lifetime. All were revised, some extensively so. Their popularity (the sixth appeared by 1840) combined with the sheer number of them (the twelfth was published in 1875) is a testimony both to the popularity of the work, and to Lyell's willingness to respond to his critics and to take account of new research in the field.

2 Lyell, adopting the views of the scientist, John Herschel, argued that only *verae causae* – that is, 'true causes' or causal agents which could be observed – had any place in scientific explanation; he further argued that present causes were the same both in kind and degree as those causes which had acted in the past. William Whewell later coined the term 'uniformitarianism' to describe Lyell's argument, and opposed it to what he termed 'catastrophism' – that is, the theory advocated by figures such as Buckland and Adam Sedgwick that the geological landscape was the result of occasional sudden and violent events.

3 Lyell argued that the origins of the earth were of no concern to the geologist, and that to maintain its scientific status geology must confine itself to the subsequent changes (i.e. secondary causes) which the earth had undergone.

4 Jacques Champollion-Figeac (1778–1867), a French archaeologist and Egyptologist, who later published his findings in *L'Egypt ancienne* (1839) and *L'Egypt et les cent-jours* (1844).

5 Manethos (or Manethon) was an Egyptian priest who, in 217 BC, wrote a history of Egypt dividing the pharaohs into thirty dynasties; his classification is still accepted today. Vulcan was a god of the ancients who presided over fire; the worship of Vulcan was particularly well established in Egypt where he was represented under the figure of a monkey. Hercules was a legendary hero who received divine honours on his death.

6 At this point Lyell includes (as a digression) a fanciful passage speculating on the origin of men; it has been omitted.

7 Gabriele Falloppio (1523–62), a celebrated Italian anatomist and surgeon; in 1551 he succeeded to the Chair of Anatomy and Botany in Padua.

8 i.e. Chile.

9 John Woodward (1665–1728) in his *Essay Toward a Natural History of the Earth* (1695) was the first to recognise the organic nature of fossils, but he attributed their origins to a universal flood.

10 The reference is to Alexander Pope, *The Rape of the Locke* (1714), Canto IV, ll. 13–18:

> *Umbriel*, a dusky melancholy Sprite,
> As ever sully'd the fair face of Light,
> Down to the Central Earth, his proper Scene,
> Repair'd to search the gloomy Cave of *Spleen*.

Swift on his sooty Pinions flitts the *Gnome,*
And in a Vapour reach'd the dismal Dome.

11 i.e. the imaginary 'Umbriel', see note 10, page 576.
12 Gottfried Wilhelm Leibniz (1646–1719), German philosopher and mathematician; the reference is to Leibniz' hypothesis that the earth was originally molten, and that its present formation was the result of a process of cooling.
13 The Pandects were a compendium of fifty books on Roman civil law made on the order of the Emperor Justinian in the sixth century.
14 The incident Lyell describes took place in 1750; his source was an historical essay by the Italian geologist, Giovanni Battista Brocchi (1772–1826). Brocchi's essay formed part of a monograph on the tertiary mollusks of the Sub-Apennine Hills – *Conchiologia fossile subapennina* (1814) – which at the time was considered a classic work.
15 i.e. invertebrate animals having shells.
16 Giovanni Arduino (1714–95), Professor of Mineralogy and Metallurgy at the University of Venice, was responsible for the classification of sedimentary rocks as Primary, Secondary and Tertiary; on the basis of his studies in northern Italy, he also distinguished them from volcanic rocks, such as lavas and tuffs.
17 Followers of James Hutton (1726–97), a Scottish geologist and agriculturist, whose *Theory of the Earth* (1798) laid down the principles of geology as a science. Hutton was the first to perceive the immensity of geological time and famously described geological processes as having 'no vestige of a beginning and no prospect of an end'.
18 A reference to Lyell himself, who had undertaken such a trip in 1828–9 in the company of the London geologist, Richard Murchison.
19 The term given to supporters of Hutton's thesis about the role played by subterranean heat and volcanic activity in the formation of rocks; Hutton's main opponent was Abraham Werner (1750–1817) who argued that rocks originated from a primeval ocean. Appropriately, Werner's supporters were called 'Neptunists'.
20 The 'law' of superposition holds that in any sequence of sedimentary rocks, where strata is not strongly folded or tilted, the youngest stratum is at the top and the oldest at the bottom.

## Darwin, *On the Origin of Species*

1 The first edition of *On the Origin of Species* appeared on 24 November 1859; a second printing with minor corrections (later considered a second edition) was published on 7 January 1860. In Darwin's lifetime six further editions were produced. All were revised by him, the fourth (1866) substantially so. The fifth edition (1869) saw the inclusion of Herbert Spencer's famous phrase, 'survival of the fittest'. During this period, in Britain and the USA, the book was printed thirty-five times in all and translated into eleven languages.
2 Andrew Jackson Downing (1815–52), American horticulturist and landscape gardener; the reference is probably to his *Fruit and Fruit Trees of America* (1845) written with his brother Charles. It was the first book of its kind and led to Downing's appointment as editor of a new periodical, the *Horticulturist* – a post he retained until he died.
3 Sir Robert Heron (1795–1854) was a politician; in 1850 a volume of his 'notes' was printed anonymously for private circulation, and in 1851, reprinted for sale under the title, *Notes by Sir R. H.* The book dealt mainly with politics and economics, but

included some comments on natural history drawn together from Heron's observations of his private collection of curious animals, known locally as the 'menagerie'.

4 Charles George William St John (1809–56), sportsman and naturalist; the reference is to his best-known work, *Short Sketches of the Wild Sports and Natural History of the Highlands* (1846).

5 I have been unable to identify this reference.

6 i.e. the family of nitrogen-fixing plants such as beans or peas.

7 Darwin's reference is to the French zoologist, Henri Milne-Edwards (1800–85), whose concept of the 'physiological division of labour' used the industrial analogy from political economy.

8 For Lyell, see headnote, page 213; the reference is to the controversy which greeted the publication of Lyell's *Principles of Geology* (1830–3).

9 At this point Darwin offers what he terms 'a short digression' on the intercrossing of individuals which he concludes by claiming that in no organic beings (including hermaphrodites) 'can self-fertilisation go on in perpetuity'. The digression has been omitted.

10 Oswald Heer (1809–83), a Swiss botanist, zoologist and palaeobotanist; Heer worked in Madeira in 1852 and published widely on botany and palaeobotany.

11 An order of fish with polished bony plates or scales.

12 Ornithorhynchus is otherwise known as the Australian duck-billed platypus; it is the only species of its genus and family in the order of Monotremata. Lepidosiren is a genus of fish with both gills and lungs.

13 Alphonse Pyrame de Candolle (1806–93), a Swiss botanist who introduced new methods of investigation and analysis into phylogeography – a branch of biology which deals with the geographic distribution of plants; in 1842 he succeeded his father, the eminent botanist, Augustin Candolle, to the Chair of Botany and Director of the Botanical Gardens at the University of Geneva.

14 Asa Gray (1810–88), an American botanist whose extensive study of North American flora did more than any other botanist to unify the taxonomic knowledge of plants. The work Darwin has in mind is in fact entitled *A Manual of the Botany of the Northern United States*; published in 1848 it became (and remains) the standard work in the field.

15 i.e. Henri Milne-Edwards; see note 7 above.

16 George Robert Waterhouse (1810–88), naturalist, co-founder (and later President) of the Entomological Society of London; Waterhouse also held posts in the British Museum and in 1836 was curator of the Zoological Society. His main works included: *The Natural History of Marsupialia or Pouched Animals* (1843) and *A Natural History of the Mammalia* (1846–8). On returning from his voyage on the Beagle, Darwin placed his mammal collection and his coleoptera (or beetles) in Waterhouse's hands for classification.

## Huxley, *Evidence as to Man's Place in Nature*

1 The first edition of *Evidence as to Man's Place in Nature* was published in 1863; the first one thousand copies sold quickly and the edition was reprinted in a matter of weeks. It was reissued in book form by Williams and Norgate in 1864 and 1883, and reprinted by Macmillan in 1894 as the seventh volume of Huxley's *Collected Essays: Man's Place in Nature and other Anthropological Essays*.

2 The title is followed by a long Latin quotation from Linnaeus (see note 19, page 579) which has been omitted.

3 i.e. the final form of an insect after all stages of metamorphosis.

4  i.e. the casting off of an outer skin or shell.

5  i.e. a natural covering such as a skin or husk.

6  Karl Ernst von Baer (1792–1876), a Prussian-Estonian embryologist who discovered the mammalian ovum and the notochord, and established the new science of comparative embryology; his *Über Entwickelungsgeschichte der Thiere* (1827–37) remains one of the most important books in embryology. Martin Heinrich Rathke (1793–1860), a German anatomist who first described the gill slits and gill arches in the embryos of mammals and birds; in 1839 he described the embryonic structure 'Rathke's pouch' from which the anterior lobe of the pituitary gland develops. Karl Bogislaus Reichert (1811–83), a German anatomist. Theodor Ludwig Wilhelm von Bischoff (1807–82), a German embryologist and anatomist, and the author of many works on these subjects; an English translation of his *The Periodical Maturation and Extrusion of the Ova* appeared in 1845. Robert Remak (1815–65), a German embryologist and neurologist who discovered and named (in 1842) the three germ layers of the early embryo: the ectoderm, mesoderm and endoderm.

7  i.e. soft and sticky.

8  Rudolf Albert Von Kölliker (or Koelliker) (1817–1905), a Swiss histologist and embryologist who in 1841 identified the true nature of spermatozoa; his *Entwickelungsgeschichte der Cephalopoden* (1844) is a classic description of the early stages of cell division in ontogeny; his *Entwickelungsgeschichte des Menschenund der Löhoren Thiere* (1861) was the first comparative study of embryology written from the viewpoint of cell theory.

9  i.e. flat and circular shaped.

10  i.e. birds.

11  Saturnians were a sect of Gnostic heretics of the second century, but Huxley seems to have in mind simply an inhabitant of Saturn.

12  i.e. belonging to the earth.

13  A member of an aboriginal people of South Africa; the term derives from the Dutch 'bosjesman' or 'boschjesman' meaning 'bushman' – a term applied by Dutch colonists to the native population of Southern Africa.

14  i.e. a long-armed ape or gibbon.

15  i.e. the largest and most ferocious of the baboons, and a native of Western Africa.

16  i.e. another name for the babacoote – a lemurine animal of Madagascar which lives in trees and has soft woolly hair, very long hind legs and a short tail.

17  Huxley goes on to give a whole series of anatomical comparisons: of the vertebral column, backbone, and ribs, followed by the teeth and skull, hand and foot, and ending with the brain. He concludes that 'whatever the system of the organs be studied, the comparison of their modifications in the ape series leads to one and the same result – that the structural differences which separate Man from the Gorilla and the Chimpanzee are not so great as those which separate the Gorilla from the lower apes.' These details have been omitted.

18  i.e. a genus of anthropoid ape such as a gorilla or chimpanzee.

19  Carolus Linnaeus (1707–78), a Swedish botanist and explorer who was the first to frame principles for defining genera and species of organisms, and the first to create a uniform system for naming them.

20  An allusion to a Roman custom in which a slave, riding behind a triumphant general through the streets of the city, would whisper 'remember that you are mortal'.

21  i.e. an order of monkey distinguished by a flattened nose and widely separated nostrils facing outwards.

22  Jean-Baptiste Lamarck (1744–1829), a pioneer French biologist, known for his thesis that acquired traits are heritable – a view which was rejected by Darwin. Lamarck

imagined life as a vast sequence of forms extending like a staircase from the most simple to the most complex; in his *Philosophie zoologique* (1809) he argued that the ascent of life was governed by two laws: that organs are improved with repeated use and weakened by disuse, and that such environmentally acquired acquisitions or losses of organs were 'preserved by reproduction to the new individuals which arise'.

23  The allusion is to *Vestiges of the Natural History of Creation* published anonymously in 1844 by Robert Chambers (1802–83), a Scottish publisher and amateur geologist. *Vestiges* was the first systematic theory of the evolutionary development of species in English. Chambers, working in the tradition of natural theology, argued that the 'progress of organic life' was determined by an intrinsic 'Law of Development' in which the 'effect of an Almighty Will' could be traced; his famous summary of his thesis stated that 'the simplest and most primitive type, under a law to which that of like-production is subordinate, gave birth to the type next above it, that this again produced the next higher, and so on to the very highest, the stages of advance being in all cases very small – namely from one species to another; so that the phenomenon has always been of a simple and modest character.' When the tenth edition of *Vestiges* appeared in 1854 Huxley wrote a savage review in which he objected that Chambers' 'Law', even if proved, 'would not be, in any intelligible sense, an *explanation* of creation', but simply 'an orderly miracle'.

24  In 1543 Nicolaus Copernicus formulated the model of the solar system with the sun at its centre and the earth and planets moving around it.

25  i.e. the wave theory of light. In the early nineteenth century, the work of a number of physicists, including Thomas Young (1773–1829) in England, revived interest in the wave theory. It was argued that a universal medium, an 'ether', or an elastic solid, pervading all space made it possible for the transmission of light through a vacuum. However the nature of the 'ether' was unexplained; neither was there any satisfactory account of the way light is modified by transparent materials such as glass. The need for such an 'ether' disappeared, however, in the early 1860s when James Maxwell (1831–79) proposed an electromagnetic theory of light; his two seminal papers on this subject were published between 1860–5.

26  Interest in atomic theory was stimulated in the early 1860s by the Russian and German chemists, Dimitri Mendeleyen and Lothar Meyer, who were independently investigating the relationship between the properties of elements and their atomic weights – work which later led to the formulation of the periodic table.

27  The reference is to the Linnaean system of classification (see note 19, page 579). The systematic study of embryology dates from the nineteenth century when scientists began to use analytical and experimental approaches to determine how body organs and tissues acquired their forms and functions. Prior to this, in the seventeenth and eighteenth centuries, embryology was based on descriptive and comparative studies.

28  See notes 2 and 3, page 576.

29  The Hippocampus minor and major are two elongated areas on the floor of each lateral ventricle of the brain; they are named after their supposed resemblance to the sea-horse. The allusion is to Richard Owen (1804–92), London's leading comparative anatomist, and the holder of many public posts including, in 1858, the Presidency of the British Association for the Advancement of Science. Owen was bitterly opposed to the idea of transmutation of species and in 1858 he published a paper in which he denied the existence of the posterior lobe and the hippocampus minor in apes, proposing a classification in which man and apes were widely separated. Two years later, in the Reade Lecture at Cambridge University, Owen repeated the substance of his argument, but left out the dangerous caveat which Huxley quotes in note 'c' (see page 269). The lecture marked the beginning of a celebrated controversy between Owen and Huxley which culminated in a long letter

to the *Athenaeum* where Huxley provided a devastating critique of Owen's position; *Evidences* continues Huxley's argument with Owen.

## Wilberforce, 'Art VII. – *On the Origin of Species*'

1 Wilberforce's review is long and detailed, containing point by point refutations of the most conjectural parts of Darwin's thesis; only a small section from his concluding remarks has been reproduced here.
2 Lorenz Oken (1779–1851), a German anatomist and naturalist and the author of several works on anatomy, zoology and natural history, including *Lehrbuch der Naturphilosophie* (1809–11) and *Lehrbuch der Naturgeschicte* (1813–26).
3 For Milne-Edwards, see note 7, page 578.
4 All quotations from Darwin are from *On the Origin of Species*.
5 For protozoa, see note 9, page 562.
6 i.e. small, winged, parasitic insects which deposit their eggs on or in the larva of another insect.
7 In Greek mythology Pan was a god associated with sexuality, fecundity and music; the term 'panic' takes its meaning from the pandemonium brought about by the actions of Pan.
8 Lucretius was a first-century Latin poet best known for his long poem, *De rerum natura*, which sets out the physical theories of the Greek philosopher, Epicurus (see note 2, page 560); in it Lucretius argues that though the gods exist, they neither made nor manipulate the world.
9 Here Wilberforce provides as examples of this view of scientific inquiry long quotations from the work of the anatomist, Ricard Owen (see note 29, page 580) and the geologist, Adam Sedgwick (see note 2, page 576); they have been omitted.
10 For Lamarck, see note 22, page 579.
11 Benoît de Maillet (1656–1738), French scientist and philosopher; the work Wilberforce has in mind is probably *Telliamed* (1748) which was translated into English in 1750. Its full English title is *Telliamed: or, Discourses between an Indian philosopher and a French missionary, on the diminution of the sea, the formation of the earth, the origin of men and animals, and other curious subjects, relating to natural history and philosophy.* Jean Baptiste Bory de Saint Vincent (1778–1846) was the author of many works on natural history, and one of the contributors to *Dictionaire classique d'histoire naturelle* (1822–31). Julien Joseph Virey (1775–1846), French zoologist and natural historian; Wilberforce may have had in mind his *Philosophie de l'histoire naturelle* (1835).
12 i.e. the work of Owen and Sedgwick (see note 9 above).
13 For Lyell, see headnote, page 213.
14 Wilberforce's use of Lyell is rather misleading; although it is true that Lyell always retained misgivings about the more radical aspects of Darwin's thesis, he was in fact instrumental in gaining a publisher for *On the Origin of Species*, using his influence to convince his own publisher, John Murray, to accept it.
15 For *Vestiges*, see note 23, page 580.
16 i.e. mythical creatures: a centaur is a horse with a human body, arms and head in place of its neck; a hippogriff has an eagle's head with a body and hindquarters of a horse.
17 The term 'mephitic' refers to a gas with anaesthetic properties. Wilberforce probably has in mind nitrous oxide or 'laughing gas' which has intoxicating effects when inhaled.

18  David Livingstone (1813–73), the Scottish missionary and explorer whose explorations of Africa took place from 1841 to 1856, from 1858 to 1864 and from 1866 to 1873.

## Spencer, 'The Study of Sociology. XIV'

1  'Preparation in Biology' was one of a group of essays serialised in the *Contemporary Review* in 1872–3, and subsequently reprinted with minor revisions as volume five of the International Scientific Series, entitled *The Study of Sociology* (London: Henry S. King, 1873). In this form, the essay was reproduced many times – *The Study of Sociology* reached its sixteenth edition by 1892.

2  The opening section of the essay rehearses Spencer's argument about the possible analogies between the 'social organism' and the 'biological organism' made earlier in 'The Social Organism' (see pages 83–91); it has been omitted.

3  Spencer appears to be referring to Germanic languages only; most modern (and some nineteenth-century) linguists locate these languages in a larger group (called Indo-European) which as well as most European languages includes others such as Sanskrit.

4  When used in relation to causation, the term 'proximate' means results coming next to each other.

5  i.e. inhabitants of the Tierra del Fuego in South America.

6  i.e. natives of Central Asia east of the Caspian Sea, including Mongolia.

7  At this point Spencer gives a short digression in which he dissociates his argument from contemporary controversies over the policy of 'laissez-faire' (see note 15, page 569). Spencer's argument is that it is only 'the biological point of view' which can provide appropriate criteria for deciding when the state should intervene to control individual activities. The passage has been omitted.

## Jowett, 'On the Interpretation of Scripture'

1  *Essays and Reviews*, edited by Parker, comprised seven essays in all; it ran to many editions – reaching its tenth in 1862 and its twelfth in 1865.

2  Jowett's essay was by far the longest contribution; it contains five sections – only the first, which introduces the argument, is reproduced here.

3  i.e. the term given to representatives of the Roman Catholic Church north of the Alps (as opposed to the Church in Italy).

4  The 'Nicene period' refers to the two Ecclesiastic Councils held at Nicaea in 325 and 787 to discuss respectively the 'Arian Controversy' (that is, the growing influence of the doctrines of Arius, a fourth-century presbyter of Alexandra who denied that Christ was of the same essence or substance as God) and the question of images. 'Pelagian' is the name of a British monk of the fourth and fifth centuries whose doctrines were opposed by St Augustine and Pope Zosimus as heretical; they suggested that man took the initial and fundamental steps towards salvation by his own efforts apart from the assistance of Divine Grace.

5  Martin Luther (1483–1546), the German preacher, biblical scholar and linguist, whose 'Ninety-five theses' – an attack on various Roman Catholic ecclesiastical abuses – precipitated the Protestant Reformation. John Calvin (1509–64), a French theologian and ecclesiastical statesman, and one of the most important Protestant reformers of the sixteenth century; the basis of his theology was Holy Scripture, and

he placed particular stress on the doctrine of salvation and the importance of the Word and of Faith.

6 From Thomas Gray, *The Progress of Poesy* (1757), l. 110.

7 See *A Midsummer-Night's Dream*, II, i, l. 164: 'In maiden meditation, fancy-free'.

8 i.e. the four sacred books of the Hindu religion.

9 The passages which Jowett refers to are: Matthew v. 34 – 'But I say unto you, Swear not at all; neither by heaven; for it is God's throne'; ix. 13 – 'But go ye and learn what that meaneth, I will have mercy, and not sacrifice: for I am not come to call the righteous, but sinners to repentance'; xix. 21 – 'Jesus said unto him, If thou wilt be perfect, go and sell that thou hast, and give to the poor, and thou shalt have treasure in heaven: and come and follow me'; Acts v. 29 – 'Then Peter and the other apostles answered and said, We ought to obey God rather than men'; Matthew xxii. 21 – 'They say unto him, Caesar's. Then saith he unto them, Render therefore unto Caesar the things which are Caesar's; and unto God the things that are God's'; xxviii. 20 – 'Teaching them to observe all things whatsoever I have commanded you; and, lo, I am with you alway, even unto the end of the world. Amen.'; Romans xiii. 1, begins 'Let every soul be subject unto the higher powers. For there is no power but of God: the powers that be are ordained of God'; the verse proceeds to list various commandments.

10 i.e. the sacred writings of the Persians.

11 Aldus was the name of a small Italian publishing firm founded in Venice in 1495 which specialised in small-sized editions of Greek and Latin classics that it published until 1515. 'Stephens' may be a reference to George Stephens (1813–95), a runic archaeologist, Fellow of the Society of Antiquaries, and one of the founders in 1843 of the Society for the Publication of Ancient Swedish Texts, for which he edited from manuscript several important works of early Swedish literature. Alternatively Jowett may be referring to 'Stephanus', the name adopted by the Estienne family of scholar-printers in the sixteenth and seventeenth centuries. The house was known in particular for the *Thesaurus Linguae Graeca* (1572) which was republished twice during the nineteenth century.

12 For *Novum Organum*, see note 12, page 564.

13 Origen, or Oregenes Adamantius (185–254), was the most important theologian and biblical scholar of the early Greek Church; his most significant work was the *Hexapla*, a synopsis of the six versions of the Old Testament. Quintus Septimus Florens Tertullian (155/60–220) was an important early Christian theologian; he was instrumental in shaping the thought and vocabulary of Western Christianity. St Jerome (347–419/20), a biblical translator and monastic leader, was traditionally regarded as the most learned of the Latin fathers; his writings, particularly his Latin translation of the Bible, known as the 'Vulgate', had a profound influence on the Middle Ages. St Augustine (354–430) was Bishop of Hippo in Roman Africa and the major Christian theologian of the early Western Church: his best known works are *Confessions* and *The City of God*. Pierre Abélard (1079–1142) was a French theologian and philosopher best known for his solution to the 'problem of universals' and his original use of dialectics. St Thomas Aquinas (1224/5–74) was an Italian Dominican theologian and the founder of medieval scholasticism (see note 15, page 584); his *Summa Theologica* and *Summa contra Gentiles* form the classic systematisation of Roman Catholic theology.

14 Desiderius Erasmus (1469–1536) was the greatest humanist scholar of the Northern Renaissance and the first editor of the New Testament (1516). Theodore Beza (1519–1605) was a French theologian who assisted and later succeeded John Calvin as a leader of the Protestant Reformation centred in Geneva. Hugo Grotius (1583–1645) was a Dutch jurist and scholar who was best known for his *De Jure*

*Belliac Pacis* in which he argued that man was bound by natural law, independent of God and based in man's own nature. Henry Hammond (1605–60), an Anglican divine who was best known for his *Practical Catechism* (1644), a seminal work of biblical criticism in England. Wilhelm Martin Leberecht De Wette (1780–1849) was a German theologian and the author of several works on the New Testament. The reference to Meier is probably to the classical scholar, Moritz Herman Eduard Meier (1796–1855).

15 i.e. the educational tradition of the Medieval Schools which practised a method of philosophical and theological investigation, centred on analogy and on systematising the data of faith, in order to gain a better understanding of the revealed truths of Christian doctrine.

16 i.e. Thucydides (460?–404 BC), the greatest of ancient Greek historians and the author of a history of the Peloponnesian War which Jowett later translated into English; the incident referred to concerns a prophecy that 'a Dorian war will come and a plague with it' which was seen to be fulfilled when in 430 BC a plague descended on Athens following the invasion of the Peloponnesians.

17 Joseph Mede (1586–1638) was a biblical scholar whose fame rested on his *Clavis Apocalyptica* (1627) in which he argued that the visions of the Apocalypse formed a chronological sequence which provided the key to interpreting events in Revelation xvii. 18.

18 The passages to which Jowett refers to are: Jeremiah xxxvi. 30 – 'Therefore thus saith the Lord of Jehoiakim king of Judah; He shall have none to sit upon the throne of David: and his dead body shall be cast out in the day to the heat, and in the night to the frost'; Isiah xxiii. – 'And it shall come to pass in that day, that Tyre shall be forgotten seventy years, according to the days of one king; after the end of seventy years shall Tyre sing as an harlot' (15); Amos vii. 10–17 – 'Therefore thus saith the Lord; Thy wife shall be an harlot in the city, and thy sons and thy daughters shall fall by the sword, and thy land shall be divided by line; and thou shalt die in a polluted land: and Israel shall surely go into captivity forth of his land' (17); Isiah xlv. 1 – 'Thus saith the Lord to his anointed, to Cyrus, whose right hand I have holden, to subdue nations before him; and I will lose the loins of kings, to open before him the two leaved gates; and the gate shall not be shut'.

19 A system of natural religion developed in England in the seventeenth and eighteenth centuries which separated the Creator from his creation, thus undermining all personal religion.

## Colenso, *The Pentateuch and Book of Joshua Critically Examined*

1 *The Pentateuch and Book of Joshua Critically Examined* was frequently reprinted over a short period of time; by 1863, for example, it had already reached its fifth edition, and an abridged 'People's Edition' appeared in 1865.

2 John Henry Pratt (1809–71) was Archdeacon of Calcutta; his *Scripture and Science not at Variance* proved a successful work – first published in 1856, it had reached its seventh edition by 1872.

3 Arthur West Haddan (1816–73), Rector of Barton-on-Heath in Warwickshire and an ecclesiastical historian, was best known for his defence of apostolic succession. His contribution to *Replies to Essays and Reviews* (1862), a collection of seven essays with a Preface by the Bishop of Oxford, was entitled 'Rationalism'. It was directed specifically at Mark Pattison's 'Tendencies of Religious Thought in England

1688–1750' in *Essays and Reviews*. The emphasis in the quotation (as in most others) is by Colenso.

4  Andrew Bruce Davidson (1831–1902), a Scottish Old Testament scholar, was one of the first to introduce historical methods of exegesis into Scotland.

5  John William Burgon (1813–88) was made a fellow of Oriel in 1846, became Vicar of St Mary's in Oxford in 1863 and Dean of Chichester in 1876. An old-fashioned Oxford High Churchman, he became famous for his support of a series of lost causes. His *Inspiration and Interpretation* (1861) is subtitled: *Seven Sermons preached before the University of Oxford with preliminary remarks; being an answer to a volume entitled 'Essays and Reviews'*.

6  Edward Harold Browne (1811–91) was made Professor of Divinity at Cambridge in 1854, became Bishop of Ely in 1864 and succeeded Samuel Wilberforce as Bishop of Winchester in 1873; his main work was *Exposition of the Thirty-Nine Articles* (1850–3). He was generally seen as a moderating influence in the fierce conflicts aroused by *Essays and Reviews* and by Colenso's work. *Aids to Faith* (1861), another collection of essays written as a response to *Essays and Reviews*, was edited by William Thompson. A former associate of Benjamin Jowett and supporter of the Broad Church movement at Oxford, Thompson severed the relationship when *Essays and Reviews* was published. Browne's contribution to *Aids to Faith* was entitled 'Inspiration'.

7  i.e. those undergoing training and instruction preparatory to Christian baptism.

8  Leviticus, the third book of the Pentateuch, consists almost entirely of legislation relating to sacrifice, ritual purification and holiness, vows and tithes.

9  Henry Longueville Mansel (1820–71) an Anglican divine who in 1859 became the first Waynflete Professor of Moral and Metaphysical Philosophy at Oxford; in his highly influential Bampton lectures of 1858, entitled 'The Limits of Religious Thought', he had argued that the human intellect acquired its knowledge of the nature of God from supernatural revelation alone. At the time he was the subject of much criticism from F. D. Maurice and John Stuart Mill.

10  Joseph Butler (1692–1752), Bishop of Durham and an exponent of natural theology and ethics; his writings, particularly his *Analogy of Religion* (1736), were widely studied in the nineteenth century by candidates for Anglican Ordination.

11  In the early chapters of Part II of *Analogy of Religion*, Butler, while stressing the importance of Revelation, nevertheless argued that its supernatural character did not rule out theological speculation, and that it was in the competence of human reason to judge the meaning and the morality of the evidence of Revelation.

## PART III: ART AND CULTURE

### Introduction

1  See George Moore, *Literature at Nurse: Or, Circulating Morals* (London: Vizetelley & Co., 1885).

2  See John Ruskin, 'Lecture III' in E. T. Cook and Alexander Wedderburn, eds., *The Complete Works of John Ruskin. Volume XX* (London: George Allen, 1904), page 79.

3  See John Stuart Mill, 'Thoughts on Poetry and Its Varieties' in John M. Robson and Jack Stillinger eds., *Collected Works of John Stuart Mill. Volume I* (London: University of Toronto Press, 1981), page 346.

4  See, for example, R. V. Johnson, *Aestheticism* (London: Methuen, 1969).

5  The length of time that it appeared to take a fairly simple idea to cross the Channel suggests the importance of local factors; the nature of the influence of French ideas

on British culture in the nineteenth century is commented upon by Ian Small in the 'Introduction' to Ceri Crossley and Ian Small, eds., *The French Revolution and British Culture* (Oxford: Oxford University Press, 1989), pages ix-xvii.

6 See Ian Small, *Conditions for Criticism* (Oxford: Clarendon Press, 1991), pages 64–88.

7 See John Campbell Shairp, 'English Poets and Oxford Critics', *Quarterly Review*, 153 (1882), page 431.

8 See, for example, Regenia Gagnier, *Idylls of the Market Place* (Aldershot: Scolar Press, 1987), and 'On the Insatiability of Human Wants: Economic and Aesthetic Man', *Victorian Studies*, 36 (1993), pages 125–53. See also Jonathan Freedman, *Professions of Taste: Henry James, British Aestheticism, and Commodity Culture* (Stanford: Stanford University Press, 1990).

## Ruskin, *The Stones of Venice*

1 A second edition of the second volume of *The Stones of Venice* appeared in 1867; further editions of the complete three-volume work appeared in 1874, 1886 and 1898. (A 'Traveller's Edition' of 1879–81, which contained selections by Ruskin from the three-volume work, excluded 'The Nature of Gothic'.) Ruskin seems never to have revised the second volume of *The Stones of Venice* and the small number of variants which exist between editions are mainly printers' errors. 'The Nature of Gothic' was reprinted as a separate essay entitled 'On the Nature of Gothic Architecture: and herein of the True Functions of the Workman in Art' in a cheap format in 1854; because the plates in the original were omitted, some passages in the text were altered. A second edition of the separate essay, with additional material from the third volume of *The Stones of Venice*, also appeared in 1854. In 1892, as a tribute to Ruskin, William Morris produced an expensive 'Kelmscott' edition of the essay; it too was reissued in a cheaper format in 1899.

2 Although there is no formal division in the text, 'The Nature of Gothic' has two clear sections: §I-LXXII define the distinguishing features of the Gothic style and temperament, and §LXXX-CXIV make use of many illustrations and plates to describe its 'outward form'. Only the 'first' section has been reproduced. Ruskin's practice of numbering his paragraphs has been retained.

3 The first volume of *The Stones of Venice* divides Venetian architecture into three periods – Byzantine, Gothic and Renaissance – which are then surveyed in volumes two and three. The labels, however, are no more than loose heuristic devices, and do not accurately describe separate historical developments. For example, Ruskin argues that the Byzantine (or eastern Romanesque) period includes western Romanesque buildings, and that even those most eastern Romanesque in character possesses Islamic influences. In general terms he points to the eclectic nature of Venetian architecture.

4 A flying buttress is a prop or stay, usually carried by a segment of an arch, springing from a pier (or other support) and leaning against another structure to strengthen it.

5 Ruskin's editors, E. T. Cook and Alexander Wedderburn (*The Works of John Ruskin. Volume X* [London: George Allen, 1904]), note that the application of the term Gothic to architecture derives from the French phrase 'les siècles gothiques' which referred to the Middle or Dark Ages; the first use of the term in England, they argue, was in the mid-seventeenth century, where it was sometimes employed critically to denote any style or building not Greek or Roman.

6 i.e. the name given to Germanic tribes who in the third, fourth and fifth centuries invaded the Eastern and Western Empires and founded kingdoms in Italy, France and Spain.

7 i.e. the hot wind which blows from the North Coast of Africa over the Mediterranean to affect parts of Southern Europe.

8 An architectural term meaning swelling into rounded or knob-like bumps.

9 i.e. a beautiful hard rock quarried in Egypt; usually understood as a highly polished purple stone.

10 i.e. of Nineveh, an ancient city of the Assyrian empire.

11 i.e. Gothic ornament; Ruskin, like many nineteenth-century art historians, saw Gothic as a uniquely Christian style.

12 Cook and Wedderburn identify here an allusion to George Herbert's 'The Church Porch', a poem which Ruskin knew by heart: 'Sink not in spirit; who aimeth at the sky / Shoots higher much than he that means a tree'.

13 i.e. a serf; see note 4, page 575.

14 i.e. without anatomy; the term is of Ruskin's own coining.

15 An allusion to Matthew viii. 9.

16 As Cook and Wedderburn note, in the early 1850s agrarian crime in Ireland was rife: in 1850 the Irish Tenant-Right League was formed; that year also saw (according to official reports) 'several landlords murdered by discontented tenants'.

17 At the battle of Inverkeithing in 1651 Cromwell defeated the Royalist supporters of Charles II. Ruskin's allusion is to the description of the battle in Walter Scott's historical novel, *Saint Valentine's Day, or The Fair Maid of Perth* (1828), where a foster-father and his seven sons sacrifice themselves for their chief, Sir Hector Maclean of Duart; as each boy dies, the foster-father pushes forward another son with the cry 'Another for Sir Hector!'.

18 The reference is to Adam Smith (see note 2, page 562), who first coined the phrase, and to the subsequent use of it by political economists. (See also H. M. Hyndman's criticism of the concept, pages 142–54; and Darwin's use of it in formulating his theory of natural selection, pages 235–7.)

19 Cook and Wedderburn note that Ruskin's description is probably based on the Venetian glass works he visited in Murano in Italy.

20 The slave-trade was abolished so far as Britain was concerned in 1807, and in the British colonies in 1833. Cook and Wedderburn comment that Ruskin probably has in mind the efforts by the anti-slavery movement to encourage the suppression of the slave-trade in other countries.

21 i.e. Michelangelo (1475–1564), Leonardo da Vinci (1452–1519) and Perugino (Pietro di Cristoforo Vannucci) (1450–1523) – Italian Renaissance artists; Phidias or Pheidias (490–430 BC), an Athenian sculptor, was the director of the construction of the Parthenon.

22 Doric, Ionic and Corinthian are the names given to the three 'orders' of classical architecture identified by their 'capitals' (that is, the ornamentation at the top of a column): the Corinthian capital, the highest and most ornate, is decorated with formalised acanthus leaves; the Doric is the oldest and simplest; and the Ionic is characterised by two lateral spirals. Ruskin saw Gothic as deriving its character from Corinthian largely because of the latter's natural analogy between the column and a tree.

23 Titian (1487/90–1567), Italian painter of the Venetian school.

24 Picturesque was an English architectural and pictorial style of the late eighteenth and early nineteenth centuries which predated the Gothic revival. It evolved as a reaction against eighteenth-century formalism and abstraction, and valued variety and irregularity over order and proportion.

25 The shaft is the main portion of a column between the base and capital; in Gothic churches the piers (or arch supports) and columns tend to be made up of clusters of

shafts with a main shaft supporting the wall directly above it, and more slender shafts reaching above to support the roof vaulting on either side.

26 Tracery is the term given to the intersecting ribwork in the upper pointed part of a Gothic window; it is also used to refer to the interlacing work in the vault and the walls and panels in tabernacle work and screens.

27 At this point Ruskin refines his argument by distinguishing between a healthy and a diseased love of change which he describes in terms of the relationship between monotony and change; this digression has been omitted.

28 The quotation is from Genesis i. 31, where God surveys his creation.

29 i.e. a Doric ornament consisting of a block or tablet with three vertical groves repeated at regular intervals along a frieze; Ruskin's point is that it is formal and unvarying, in contrast to the variety of the naturally based designs of Gothic ornament.

30 An allusion to I Thessalonians v. 10.

31 At this point Ruskin includes a long digression on Naturalism; it has been omitted.

32 In his account of Naturalism, Ruskin identified three moral classes of artists: the 'Purists', who 'perceive, and pursue, the good, and leave the evil'; 'Naturalists', who 'perceive and pursue the good and evil together'; and the 'Sensualists', who 'perceive and pursue the evil, and leave the good'. He argues that only the Naturalists are capable of the highest forms of art.

33 At this point Ruskin has a footnote referring the reader to an illustration earlier in the volume; it has been omitted.

34 Torcello is an island in the Lagoon of Venice; Ruskin's reference is to the mosaic of the last judgement which covers the west wall of its western Romanesque cathedral. It is discussed in detail in the second chapter of the volume.

35 St Maclou is a tiny fifteenth-century church with elaborate decorations in the 'French Flamboyant' style; it had been praised by Ruskin in his earlier work, *The Seven Lamps of Architecture* (1849).

36 Hades is the underworld in classical mythology.

37 i.e. gaps or spaces.

38 An image taken from Revelation xix and xx.

39 i.e. a scrupulous insistence on purity or correctness in style; see note 32 above.

40 Ruskin goes on to discuss the Gothic fondness for vegetation which he sees as a manifestation of Naturalism peculiar to this school; the discussion has been omitted.

41 i.e. small ornaments placed on the inclined side of pinnacles (see note 42), pediments and canopies in Gothic architecture which usually take the form of a bud, curled leaves or small bird.

42 A small ornamental turret ending in a pyramid or cone which crowns a buttress or rises above the roof or coping of a building.

43 A reference to Matthew xx. 3.

### Arnold, 'Art VIII. – The Functions of Criticism at the Present Time'

1 Arnold delivered 'The Functions of Criticism at the Present Time' as a lecture at Oxford University (where he was Professor of Poetry) a month before it was published in the *National Review*. The following year it was revised and reprinted as 'The Function of Criticism at the Present Time' in Arnold's collection of essays – *Essays in Criticism* (London: Macmillan and Co., 1865). A second edition of *Essays in Criticism* appeared in 1869 and a third in 1875; in 1883 Macmillan published an American edition, and in 1884 a 'new' English edition was produced. All were

revised by Arnold. Several further editions appeared after his death; and in 1888 the words 'First Series' were appended to the title. The following notes are once again indebted to the scholarship of R. H. Super in *The Complete Works of Matthew Arnold. Volume 3.*

2 See Lecture II in *On Translating Homer* (1861).

3 See [John Campbell Shairp] 'Wordsworth: the Man and the Poet,' *North British Review*, XLI (August 1864), pages 1–54; Shairp (1819–85) had been a friend of Arnold's when they were undergraduates, and in 1877 he was made Professor of Poetry at Oxford. The biography Arnold refers to is that of Christopher Wordsworth, *Memoirs of William Wordsworth* (1851).

4 A letter to Bernard Barton dated 12 January 1816 in *Memoirs of William Wordsworth*, II, page 53.

5 i.e. Lady Richardson; the source is her 'notes' for November 1843 in ibid., page 439.

6 Samuel Johnson's tragedy *Irene* was written in 1736 and produced by David Garrick in 1749; *The Lives of the English Poets* was published from 1779–81. Wordsworth's sequence of sonnets on religious themes, *Ecclesiastical Sketches* (1822) became known as the *Ecclesiastical Sonnets* from 1837; the 'Preface' refers to the critical essay which Wordsworth added as a Preface to the second edition of the *Lyrical Ballads* (1800); it was revised and lengthened for the third edition of 1802. Johann Wolfgang von Goethe (1759–1832), German poet, novelist, playwright and philosopher.

7 Super comments here that Arnold's account of the Romantic movement is indebted to the French critic, Charles-Augustin Sainte-Beuve (1804–69), particularly to a passage in his *Chateaubriand et son groupe littéraire sous l'Empire* (1861) which Arnold had copied into one of his 'general note-books'.

8 Pindar (518–438 BC) was a Greek lyric poet famous for his choral odes; Sophocles (496–406 BC) was a Greek dramatist best known in the nineteenth century for his *Oedipus Rex*.

9 Pericles (495–429 BC), an Athenian statesman responsible for the development of Athenian democracy in the late fifth century BC.

10 On 23 July 1637 in St Giles Church, Edinburgh, Jenny Geddes flung a stool at the head of Bishop David Lindsay to protest against his attempt to read Laud's service book on a Sunday. William Laud (1573–1645), Archbishop of Canterbury from 1633, was an advocate of liturgical uniformity; he had aroused great hostility among Puritans (particularly in Scotland) when he tried to implement his reforms.

11 Super notes that decimal coinage and the metric system were established in France in 1799–1803 and the Decimal Association was established in London in 1854. A bill for changing weights and measures passed a second reading in the Commons in July 1863 but was later withdrawn; *The Times* carried a long discussion of the problem (in favour of the English system) on 15 and 17 September 1863.

12 Super comments that whether or not the reference was to a real person and a real question, the idea had become common-place; a leading article in *The Times*, 6 May 1863, remarked that 'Englishmen are so accustomed to anomaly that they attach a constitutional virtue to it'.

13 The French critic, Joseph Joubert (1754–1824), was the subject of a lecture by Arnold at Oxford. It was published in the *National Review* in 1864 and reprinted the same year in an American journal, *Littell's Living Age*, and in 1865 in *Essays in Criticism*; the quotation is from Paul de Raynal's edition of Joubert's *Pensées* (1842), II, Titre xv, no. 2.

14 Edmund Burke (1729–97), statesman, historian and political theorist; his *Reflections on the Revolution in France* (1790) was seen as championing conservatism.

15 Richard Price (1723–91), a Protestant Dissenter, whose sermon of 4 November 1789 in praise of the French Revolution goaded Burke into writing on the subject.

16 See Oliver Goldsmith (1730–74), 'Retaliation. A Poem' (1774), l. 32.

17 'Thoughts on French Affairs' was in fact the title of one of the pieces in Burke's *Three Memorials on French Affairs* (1797).

18 See Numbers xxii–xxiii, and especially xxii. 38: Balaam, a non-Israelite diviner, is asked by the King of Moab to curse the people of Israel who are camped on the Moab plains, but when the Angel of God appears to Balaam's ass, his eyes are opened and he changes his mind, blessing the Israelites instead.

19 William Eden, first Baron Auckland (1744–1814) and a close friend and supporter of Pitt, was ambassador extraordinary to the Hague from 1791–93 – that is, during the early period of the wars which followed the French Revolution. Super quotes a letter of 6 January 1793 from Auckland to Lord Loughborough (reprinted in *Journal and Correspondence of William, Lord Auckland* [1861]), as a possible source for the sentiments Arnold attributes to Auckland.

20 The allusion is to the phrase 'man is by nature a political animal' in Aristotle's *Politics*, I. i. 9.

21 An allusion to Aesop's fable of the wind and the sun.

22 Super notes that Arnold's use of the word 'disinterested' was once again indebted to Sainte-Beuve; for a full discussion of this issue see Super, op. cit., page 477.

23 *Revue des deux mondes* was a fortnightly journal of the arts published in Paris. It had been founded in 1829 following the suspension of censorship in France in 1828.

24 For Dissenters, see note 35, page 573.

25 The *Home and Foreign Review* was a liberal Catholic quarterly published from 1862–4 under the editorship of the liberal historian, Lord Acton (1843–1902); it was closed down by Acton when he was threatened with censure by the ecclesiastical authorities.

26 Charles Adderley (later Sir Charles and Baron Norton) was a Conservative MP for North Staffordshire; Super notes that the incident Arnold alludes to was a speech given to the Warwickshire Agricultural Association at Leamington Spa on 16 September 1863; Adderley's speech was reported in *The Times* the following day.

27 John Arthur Roebuck (1801–79) was a Benthamite MP, a friend of John Stuart Mill and a popular orator; Super notes that the quotation comes from a speech given at a dinner at Cutlers' Hall in Sheffield on 18 August 1864; it was reported in *The Times* the following day and was the subject of an article on 20 August.

28 See Goethe, *Iphigenie auf Tauris* (1781), I, ii, ll. 91–2.

29 References to issues of contemporary legislation. In 1860 Palmerstone's government introduced (and later withdrew) a £6 borough franchise. Church rates were taxes upon property levied by the vestry for the maintenance of the church; a series of bills had been introduced from the late 1830s to abolish them, but all were unsuccessful until Gladstone's attempt in 1868. The difficulties involved in collecting agricultural statistics was the subject of a parliamentary debate in 1864.

30 i.e. a festive song.

31 The incident, reported in *The Times* on 15 March 1865, concerned Elizabeth Wragg's manslaughter of her baby for which she was sentenced to twenty years' penal servitude; Super comments that in her defence Wragg claimed, 'I should never have done it if I had had a home for him'. The Mapperly Hills are to the north of Nottingham.

32 Ionia was a confederacy of twelve cities which formed one of the three branches of the Hellenic race, the others being Attica (a region in the eastern extremity of central Greece) and Achaia; Ilissus is a small river in Attica rising on the northern slopes of Mt Hymettus.

33 Lord John Somers (1651–1716), a distinguished statesman and constitutional lawyer, was elected to Parliament in 1689 where he was appointed chairman of the committe which drew up the Bill of Rights following the abdication of James II.

34 For Philistine, see note 20, page 572.

35 For Cobbett, see note 6, page 567.

36 For Ruskin and Carlyle, see headnotes, pages 325 and 155 respectively; the reference to 'pugnacious political economy' is almost certainly to Ruskin's *Unto this Last* (1862) which was withdrawn from serialisation in the *Cornhill Magazine* because of its controversial nature.

37 The phrase (literally translated as 'sons of the soil') more colloquially means 'nobodies'. It was used by the Stoic Latin poet, Persius (34–62) in *Satires*, vi. 59: 'terrae est iam filius'.

38 See Goethe, *Wilhelm Meisters Lehrjahre* (1795–6), VII, chap. ix, 'Lehrbrief'.

39 *Obermann* (1804) was a novel about a reclusive suffering hero by the French writer, Etienne Pivert de Senancour (1770–1846). The quotation, from Letter XC, ninth paragraph, translates literally as: 'let us perish while resisting'.

40 For Colenso, see headnote, page 299; the reference is to Arnold's essay, 'The Bishop and the Philosopher', *Macmillan's Magazine*, VII (January 1863), pages 241–56, which unfavourably contrasted Colenso's method of criticism (and that of the writers in *Essays and Reviews*) with the practice of the philosopher Benedict Spinoza (see note 9, page 604).

41 Joubert, *Pensées*, II, Titre xxiii, no. 54.

42 Arthur Penrhyn Stanley (1815–81), Regius Professor of Ecclesiastical History at Oxford, and from 1864 Dean of Westminster, was a close friend of the Arnold family; a Broad Churchman, he consistently advocated toleration during the doctrinal disputes of the period. The reference is to his *Lectures on the History of the Jewish Church* (1863) which Arnold had discussed in 'Dr Stanley's Lectures on the Jewish Church', *Macmillan's Magazine*, VII (February 1863), pages 327–36; the essay was largely a reply to the controversy which had been stirred up by 'The Bishop and the Philosopher'.

43 *The Church and State Review*, a High Church periodical edited by Archdeacon George Anthony Denison, was founded in June 1862 to counteract *Essays and Reviews*; it had attacked both Colenso and Stanley. High Churchmen stressed historical continuity with Catholic Christianity, upholding the authority of the episcopacy and the nature of the Sacraments; their position was reasserted in the nineteenth century by the Oxford Movement (see page 202). *The Record*, begun in 1828, was the first Anglican weekly newspaper; its sympathies were strongly Evangelical. The Evangelicals stressed the importance of verbal inspiration and Scripture as the sole form of Divine authority, denying that the Church had the power to impose its interpretation upon the individual; they were strongly opposed to both Roman Catholicism and High Churchmen.

44 Joseph-Ernest Renan (1823–92), French philosopher and religious scholar, was famous for his *Vie de Jésus* (1863) which presented a mythical account of the creation of Christianity which was violently denounced by the Church.

45 The reference is to *Broken Lights: an Inquiry into the Present Condition and Future Prospects of Religious Faith* (1864) by Frances Power Cobbe (1822–1904); it contained appendices on Colenso and Renan.

46 For Luther, see note 5, page 582.

47 David Friedrich Strauss (1808–74), a German theologian, known for his *Leben Jesu* (1835–6) which applied the 'myth-theory' to the life of Christ; Arnold's reference is probably to the revised and more positive version of the work published in 1864: *Leben Jesu für das deutsche Volk*.

48 Claude Fleury (1640–1725), an ecclesiastical historian known for his twenty-volume *Histoire ecclésiastique* (1691–1720), the first large-scale history of the Church; the quotation, from the Preface, translates as: 'whoever imagines the authority to write better, does not understand it'.

49 The quotation is from a review of 'Les Historiens critiques de Jésus' in *Etudes d'histoire religieuse* (1857); Renan's *Vie de Jésus* was written after a visit to the Holy Land in 1860–1.

50 Arnold appears to have in mind the following line from Cicero's *Ad Atticum*, XVI, vii. 3: 'Nemo doctus umquam ... mutationem consilii inconstantiam dixit esse' – 'no philosopher ever called a change of plan inconsistency'. The *Essays in Criticism* version of 'The Functions of Criticism' gives the exact quotation.

51 Super identifies the reference as Samuel Taylor Coleridge, *Confessions of an Inquiring Spirit* (1840), the end of letter I, beginning of letter II: 'In the Bible there is more that *finds* me than I have experienced in all other books put together.'

52 Super comments that the aim of *Religious Duty* (1864) was 'the development of Theism as a Religion for Life no less than a Philosophy for the Intellect'.

53 The British College of Health for the dispensing of vegetable pills was founded in 1828 by a self-styled 'Hygeist' James Morison (1770–1840) – Arnold misspells his surname. The College was located in Hamilton Place, New Road (now King's Cross Road).

54 A reference to the Court for Divorce and Matrimonial Causes established by the 1857 Divorce Law.

55 Luther's theory of grace taught that faith alone, without works, entails the certitude of salvation for every Christian.

56 Jacques-Bénigne Bossuet (1627–1704), French historian, whose *Discours sur l'histoire universelle* (1681) argued that history was ruled by Divine Providence.

57 The Bishop of Durham was Charles Thomas Baring (1807–79), a strong Evangelical; Pius IX, Pope from 1846–78, was responsible for re-establishing a Roman Catholic hierarchy in England in 1850.

58 See Virgil, *Eclogues*, iv. 5; literally, 'the line of the centuries begins anew'.

59 Aeschylus (525/4–455/6 BC), the first of classical Athens' great tragic dramatists, best known for his trilogy, the *Orestia*.

## Swinburne, *Notes on Poems and Reviews*

1 A second edition of *Notes on Poems and Reviews* was published by John Camden Hotten the same year without Swinburne's knowledge; it was also brought out in 1866 by G. W. Carleton, the American publisher of *Poems and Ballads*. These editions have few variants. In 1899 another American publisher, Thomas B. Mosher, published *Notes on Poems and Reviews* in an edition with *Poems and Ballads*. In preparing the following notes I have found useful Clyde Hyder's edition of *Notes on Poems and Reviews* in his *Swinburne Replies* (New York: Syracuse University Press, 1966).

2 Of these anonymous reviews, the most significant were those by John Morley in the *Saturday Review*, XXII (August 1866), pages 145–7; and Robert Buchanan in the *Athenaeum*, 4 August 1866, pages 137–8.

3 A quotation from John Webster's *The White Devil* (1612), III, ii, ll. 449–50.

4 The reference is to I Corinthians xv. 32.

5 A quotation from 'To the Reader', ll. 8–10, at the conclusion of *The Poetaster* (1600–1) by Ben Jonson.

6 Animalcules are tiny vertebrate and invertebrates animals; infusoria are a class of tiny unicellular organisms so named because they are usually found in infusions of decaying animal or vegetable matter.

7 The phrase was taken from an unsigned review of *Poems and Ballads* in the *London Review*, XIII (August 1866), pages 130–1.

8 From Shelley's 'The Witch of Atlas' (1820), xi, ll. 7–8.

9 I have been unable to find a source for this phrase; it translates as 'My depravity would blush at their modesty'.

10 Sappho (610–580 BC), a Greek lyric poet famous for her love poems about women; her work survives only in fragments. She is frequently referred to in *Poems and Ballads*.

11 Gaius Valerius Catullus (84–54 BC) was a Roman lyric poet best known for the twenty-five poems which speak of his love for a woman called Lesbia; his version of Sappho's famous ode (Catullus, LI) is both darker and more personal that the original.

12 The reference is to Sappho's address and invocation to Aphrodite.

13 The references are to 'A Fragment on Sappho' in *Pastorals, Epistles, Odes and other original poems, with translations from Pindar, Anacreon, and Sappho* (1748) by Ambrose Philips (1675–1749); and to chap. VIII of *Traité du sublime* (1694), a translation of the treatise attributed to Longinus by the French poet and critic, Nicholas Boileau-Despréaux (1636–1711).

14 A quotation from Homer's *Iliad*, iv. 43; Hyder notes that Swinburne translates the phrase as 'of mine own will, yet with reluctant mind'.

15 In classical mythology the three Fates controlled the birth, life and death of mortals. Swinburne is referring to the arbitrary survival of some manuscripts.

16 A quotation from the poem 'To My Most Dearly-Loved Friend Henry Reynolds Esquire' (1627), ll. 107–8, by Michael Drayton (1563–1631): 'his raptures were, / All ayre, and fire, which made his verses deere'.

17 A quotation from *Romeo and Juliet*, II, vi, ll. 9–11: 'Thy violent delights have violent ends / And in their triumph die, like fire and powder / Which as they kiss consume'.

18 A quotation from Matthew Arnold's 'To a Gypsy Child by the Seashore' (1849), l. 18.

19 Cotytto was a Thracian goddess worshipped with orgiastic rights; she is often identified with the goddess Cybele, whose worship was also associated with ecstatic states and prophetic rapture.

20 Nero (37–68), Roman emperor from 54–68, was in the late nineteenth century a by-word for personal debauchery and extravagance.

21 Swinburne uses the epithet to describe Dolores in *Poems and Ballads*.

22 For Origen, see note 13, page 583; the mythical Atys, driven mad by Cybele, castrated himself; Dindymus, a mountain in Phrygia was the site of an early sanctuary to Cybele; Loreto, a church in central Italy, was reputed to contain the Virgin's house brought there from Nazareth by angels.

23 'Hesperia' was the title of a poem in *Poems and Ballads*; Hespere was the name of one of the mythical sisters who guarded the tree of golden apples in the garden of Hesperides. 'Islands of the blest' is an allusion to Byron's *Don Juan*, III, l. 700 where it refers to the Cape Verde or Canary Islands.

24 A French proverb which translates as 'who has drunk will drink'.

25 An allusion to Milton, *Paradise Lost*, XI, ll. 413–15: 'Which that false fruit that promised clearer sight / Had bred; then purged with euphrasy and rue / The visual nerve'. Euphrasy (or eyebright) was a herb used for poultices for the eyes; rue was a herb also believed to improve eyesight.

26 See *The Book of Common Prayer* and Psalm cxxxix. 6.

27 A quotation from Chapter XCVIII of Théophile Gautier's *Albertus* (1832). It translates as 'I warn the mothers of families that I am not writing for little girls, for whom one cuts bread into slices; my verses are a young man's verse.'

28 Characters in *Le Malade imaginaire* (1673) by the French comic playwright, Molière.

29 Literally, 'buyer beware'. A feature of English law is the responsibility placed on the purchaser of goods or services. Swinburne's point is that it is the reader who should censor what he or she reads.

30 *Faustine* was published in the *Spectator* in May that year.

31 Faustina was the name of the wives of the Roman emperors Antoninus Pius and Marcus Aurelius (see also note 82, page 602). Antoninus' wife (Faustina the elder) was noted for her moral integrity; less moral behaviour was often attributed to Faustina the younger. The Maenads (or Bacchae) were women inspired to ecstatic frenzy in the worship of Dionysus.

32 The reference is to Swinburne's 'Laus Veneris', an interpretation of the Tannhäuser legend – a sixteenth-century German ballad which tells how a lyric poet becomes enamoured of a beautiful woman who beckons him into the grotto of Venus where he spends the next seven years. On emerging he travels to Rome to ask for absolution from the Pope, and is told that it is as impossible as for the Pope's dry staff to blossom. Three days later the staff does indeed break into flower and the Pope calls for the poet's return, but he has already gone back to the grotto of Venus.

33 An allusion to the parable of the foolish and wise virgins in Matthew xxv.

34 Charles Baudelaire was best known in Britain for his volume of poems, *Les Fleurs du mal* (1857); the reference is to 'Richard Wagner', first published in April 1861 in *Revue Européens*, and revised and reprinted the same year as a separate pamphlet entitled *Richard Wagner et Tannhäuser*. Richard Wagner's opera *Tannhäuser* was first produced in 1845.

35 A reference to Swinburne's drama, *Chastelard* (1865).

36 i.e. a member of a schismatic or heretical sect.

37 Hermaphroditus was a bisexual Greek god; in the art of the fourth century BC he is represented as a beautiful youth with developed breasts. In later art (which Swinburne has in mind) he is Aphrodite with male genitalia; Swinburne is probably thinking of the well-known statue of Hermaphroditus at the Louvre in Paris.

38 The references are to Shakespeare's *Othello* and *A Midsummer Night's Dream*, and to Keats' *Hyperion* (1820).

39 An allusion to Plato's *Symposium*.

40 Hyder suggests a possible allusion to Shelley's 'The Witch of Atlas' and 'Lines Connected with Epipsychidion' which both refer to 'that sweet marble monster of both sexes'.

41 According to Greek legend, the weeping Niobe, inconsolable following the death of her children, was turned into a stone from which water ran. The context suggests that Swinburne has in mind the Greek sculpture, *Dying Niobid* (c. 450–440 BC) at the Museo delle Terme in Rome; alternatively the reference may be to the flower-shaped vase at the Louvre in Paris by the 'Niobid painter' (475–50 BC) which represents the death of Niobe and her children. Simonides (556–468 BC) was a minor Greek lyric and elegiac poet. For Aeschylus see note 59, page 592. Correggio (Antonio Allegri, 1494–1534) was a painter of the Parma school; for Titian, see note 23, page 587.

42 A quotation from the first line of Keats' *Endymion* (1818): 'A thing of beauty is a joy for ever'.

43 The reference is to John Morley's review (see note 2, page 592).

44 The quotation is from 'Appended to the *Hellenics*' (1859), ll. 48–9 by Walter Savage Landor (1775–1864).
45 The poem is Swinburne's own.
46 Ludovico Ariosto (1474–1533), the Italian poet best known for his epic *Orlando Furioso* (1516); Pietro Aretino (1492–1556) was an Italian poet, dramatist and writer known for his satirical writings and his collection of 'lewd sonnets', *Sonetti lussuriosi* (1524). The quotation translates as 'Ariosto laughs at the sun; Aretino sniggers in the shade'. Successive critics have been unable to identify the source.
47 i.e. white lead which at the time was used as a cosmetic.
48 An allusion to the song in Ben Jonson's *Epicoene, or The Silent Woman* (1609–10), I, i, ll. 90–92: 'Lady, it is to be presumed, / Though art's hid causes are not found, / All is not sweet, all is not sound.'
49 For gibbet, see note 17, page 569.
50 The OED traces the first pejorative use of the term 'gig-man' (meaning a narrow-minded person who belongs to the middle classes and is chiefly concerned with respectability) to an article by Thomas Carlyle in the *Quarterly Review* (1828). A trull is a prostitute.
51 A quotation from Landor, 'Wearers of Rings and Chains' (1853), ll. 5–6. Sunium was a promontory in Attica crowned by a marble temple of Poseidon.

### Pater, *Studies in the History of the Renaissance*

1 *Studies in the History of the Renaissance* was made up of eight essays – five of which had already been published in the periodical press – together with a Preface and Conclusion; the Conclusion used material from a review essay, 'Poems by William Morris', *Westminster Review*, XXXIV (October 1868), pages 300–12. A second edition of the work (with the Conclusion omitted) appeared in 1877, a third edition (with the Conclusion reinstated and with the addition of a new essay, 'The School of Giorgione') in 1888 and a fourth edition in 1893. All were revised by Pater. The following notes are indebted to Donald Hill, ed., *Walter Pater: The Renaissance* (London: University of California Press, 1980).
2 One such attempt in Britain was John Ruskin's highly successful *Modern Painters* (see page 325); but Pater also has in mind the treatises on aesthetics which had been produced by German philosophers (and particularly by Hegel [see note 18, page 596]) since the mid-eighteenth century.
3 An allusion to the phrase used by Matthew Arnold in *On Translating Homer* and 'The Functions of Criticism at the Present Time'; see pages 351–68.
4 i.e. a reference to the 'Mona Lisa', Leonardo da Vinci's famous painting in the Louvre. Carrara in Tuscany is renowned for its white marble hills. Giovanni Pico della Mirandola (1463–95), a Florentine Platonist and classical scholar, was the first Christian to use Kabbalistic doctrine in support of Christian theology – ideas which were heretical and for which he was forced to flee to Florence; he was the subject of an essay by Pater first published in the *Fortnightly Review*, X (October 1871), pages 377–86, and reprinted in *The Renaissance*.
5 For Sainte-Beuve, see note 7, page 589; Donald Hill notes that the quotation is in fact from Sainte-Beuve himself – from a passage in his review of Charles Marty-Laveaux, ed., *Oeuvres françoises de Joachim du Bellay* (1866–7) in *Journal des savants* (June 1867), pages 345–6; it translates as 'to confine themselves to knowing beautiful things at first hand, and to nourishing themselves on these things as discriminating amateurs, as accomplished humanists'.

6 A reference to Blake's annotations to volume I of the second edition of *The Works of Joshua Reynolds* (1789): 'Ages are All Equal. But Genius is Always Above the Age.' The book is held in the British Library, but Hill comments that Pater's phrasing suggests that he took the quotation from volume I of Alexander Gilchrist's *Life of William Blake* (1863) where it appears as: 'Ages are all equal, but genius is always above its Age.'

7 For Goethe, see note 6, page 589.

8 i.e. Wordsworth's 'Resolution and Independence' (1807) and 'Ode: Intimations of Immortality from Recollections of Early Childhood' (1807).

9 Hill comments that the phrase 'Christian art' had gained currency from two well-known works: Alexis-François Rio, *De l'Art chrétien* (1861–7) and Alexander William Crawford, *Sketches of the History of Christian Art* (1847).

10 An allusion to Matthew Arnold's essay, 'Pagan and Mediaeval Religious Sentiment', first published in the *Cornhill Magazine*, IX (April 1864), pages 422–35, and reprinted in *Essays in Criticism* (1865); Arnold used the phrase to describe the 'mediaeval spirit' which he contrasted with 'the senses and the understanding' of the 'later pagan spirit'.

11 Joachim du Bellay (1522–60), French poet and critic, and leader (with Pierre de Ronsard) of the literary group known as La Pléiade; du Bellay was also the author of La Pléiade's manifesto, *La défense et illustration de la langue françoise* (1549), which asserted that the French language was capable of producing a modern literature at least equal to that of the Italians. He is the subject of one of the chapters in *The Renaissance*.

12 i.e. asceticism.

13 For Pericles, see note 9, page 589; Lorenzo de Medici (1449–92), or 'Lorenzo the Magnificent', governed Florence (with his brother) from 1469–78 and alone from 1478–92; under him Florence achieved its artistic and cultural pre-eminence.

14 Johann Joachim Winckelmann (1717–68), German archaeologist and art historian, known chiefly for his essay, *Gedanken über die Nachahmung der griechischen Werke in der Malerei und Bildhauerkunst* (1755), which argued that greatness in art entailed imitating the Greeks; and his *Geschichte der Kunst des Altertums* (1764) which defined ancient art in terms of an organic development of growth, maturity and decline, and which attempted a definition of ideal beauty. He was the subject of an essay by Pater in the *Westminster Review*, XXXI (January 1867), pages 80–110, reprinted in *The Renaissance*.

15 A saying attributed to Heraclitus and uttered by Socrates in Plato's *Cratylus*; in *Plato and Platonism* (1893) Pater translates it as: 'All things give way: nothing remaineth.' Ingram Bywater, one of Pater's closest friends at Brasenose, was a distinguished editor of Heraclitus.

16 Perhaps an allusion to Laertes' command as Ophelia is buried, in *Hamlet*, V, i, l. 262: 'Lay her i' th' earth; / And from her fair and unpolluted flesh / May violets spring!'.

17 For Novalis, see note 6, page 560; the quotation, from Novalis' 'Fragmente II', translates as 'to philosophise is to cast off inertia, to make oneself alive'.

18 For Comte see note 7, page 571; Georg Wilhelm Friedrich Hegel (1770–1831), German idealist philosopher, influential in late nineteenth-century Britain, who emphasised the progress of history and ideas from thesis to antithesis, and thence to a new and richer synthesis.

19 The quotation is from Victor Hugo's *Les Misérables* (1862), part 5, vol. I, book 2, chap. 2; it translates as: 'philosophy is the microscope of thought'.

20 Jean-Jacques Rousseau (1712–94), French philosopher whose social writings strongly influenced the principles behind the French Revolution and inspired the Romantics; *Confessions*, his autobiography, was published posthumously in 1782.
21 Voltaire, the pseudonym of the French critic and writer, François-Marie Arouet (1694–1778), was renowned for his wit and his tireless crusade against bigotry; his best known work is *Candide* (1758) – a satire on philosophical optimism.
22 See Hugo, *Le Dernier jour d'un condamné* (1832); in later editions of the *Renaissance* Pater translates the quotation as 'we are all under sentence of death but with a sort of indefinite reprieve'.

## Wilde, 'The Decay of Lying: A Dialogue'

1 'The Decay of Lying: A Dialogue' was revised and reprinted as 'The Decay of Lying: An Observation' in *Intentions* (London: James Osgood, McIlvaine & Co., 1891); a second edition of *Intentions*, also published by Osgood, McIlvaine & Co., appeared in 1894. The best critical edition is an unpublished PhD thesis by Jacqueline Evans: *A Critical Edition of Oscar Wilde's Intentions* (PhD thesis, University of Birmingham, 1987).
2 Cyril and Vyvyan (later Cyril and Vyvyan Holland) were the names of Wilde's sons.
3 Jean-Baptiste Corot (1796–1875), French landscape painter who was much admired for his realistic depictions of nature when his work was exhibited in London in the 1860s; John Constable (1776–1837), English landscape painter, again celebrated in the late nineteenth century for his detailed depictions of the English countryside.
4 i.e. a furniture store; in the book version of the essay Wilde changed the reference to the hand-made products of William Morris and the address to Oxford Street.
5 Ralph Waldo Emerson (1803–82), American writer and poet, whose work advocated self-sufficiency. The allusion is to his 1841 essay, 'Self-Reliance', in which he comments: 'I shun father and mother and wife and brother when my genius calls me. I would write on the lintels of the doorpost, *Whim*.'
6 Wilde had argued for such a possibility in his lecture, 'The English Renaissance of Art' (January 1882).
7 The original *Retrospective Review*, founded in 1820 and running until 1828, dealt with historical and antiquarian subjects; a second *Retrospective Review* was briefly revived in 1853–4.
8 Roses formed a motif in Walter Pater's *Marius the Epicurean* (1885), and were associated with Aestheticism more generally by W. H. Mallock in his satirical portrait of Pater as 'Mr Rose' in *The New Republic* (1876–7). Domitian (51–96), a Roman emperor renowned for his cruelty and his decadent behaviour. Wilde later wrote to George Ives describing Lord Alfred Douglas as the 'young Domitian'.
9 i.e. to be banned or excluded from a club.
10 i.e. government publications of official reports so-called because of their blue binding.
11 An allusion to the French novelist Emile Zola (1840–1902). 'Les documents humains' was the title of one of the articles in Zola's *Le Roman expérimental* (1880); in *Mes haines* (1866) he describes a work of art as 'un coin de la création vu à travers un temperament'.
12 Perhaps an allusion to Wilde's quarrels with the American painter, James Abbott MacNeill Whistler (1834–1903), who had publicly accused Wilde of plagiarism.
13 See *The Republic*, Book II; Wilde is of course misrepresenting Plato whose connection between poetry and lying is made in the context of an argument that poetry misrepresents the ideal truth of things.

14 *The Black Arrow* by Robert Louis Stevenson (1850–94) was serialised in 1883 and published in book form in 1888; Stevenson's *The Strange Case of Dr Jekyll and Mr Hyde* appeared in 1886 and has some themes in common with Wilde's own *The Picture of Dorian Gray*. *The Lancet* is a leading British medical journal (founded in 1823).

15 Henry Rider Haggard (1856–1925), an author of popular adventure stories, particularly *King Solomon's Mines* (1885) and *She* (1887).

16 The later work of the American novelist Henry James (1843–1916) was distinguished by the sophistication and complexity of its narrative techniques. James, whose work only ever enjoyed limited popularity, was envious of Wilde's later success.

17 Margaret Oliphant (1828–97), a prolific and successful Scottish novelist and historical writer, best known for her *Chronicles of Carlingford* (1863–6).

18 Francis Marion Crawford (1854–1909) was a popular and prolific American author and historian, known for his minute attention to detail. Isobel Murray (*The Writings of Oscar Wilde* [Oxford: Oxford University Press, 1989]) comments that the reference to 'le beau ciel d'Italie' is a misremembered anecdote told by the Italian actress Adelaide Ristori (in her *Etudes et Souvenirs*) about a Veronese censor so sensitive to politics that he insisted that the phrase 'Beautiful sky of Italy' be changed to 'Beautiful sky of Lombardy Venetia'.

19 *Robert Elsmere* (1888) by Mary (Mrs Humphrey) Ward (1851–1920), a highly successful Victorian novel describing a crisis of faith experienced by a young clergyman. The phrase 'genre ennuyeux' means literally 'boring genre'.

20 The East End of London, the product of rapid urban immigration, and associated with overcrowding and poverty, was becoming the subject of a variety of novels; Wilde himself later used the theme of the East End in *A Woman of No Importance*.

21 Guy de Maupassant (1850–93), a French writer of short stories of the naturalist school, became famous in the early 1880s following the publication of 'Boule de suif'.

22 The quotation is from Zola's comments on 'Le Naturalisme au théâtre' in Chapter III of *Le Roman expérimental*; his novel *Germinal* was published in 1885.

23 The allusion is to Caliban, a character in *The Tempest*; Wilde also used the phrase in the 'Preface' to *The Picture of Dorian Gray*: 'The nineteenth-century dislike of Realism is the rage of Caliban seeing his own face in a glass.'

24 *L'Assommoir* (1877), *Nana* (1880) and *Pot-Bouille* (1882) are all works in Zola's Rougon-Macquart cycle.

25 The reference is to Ruskin's comments on *The Mill on the Floss* in his essay, 'The Two Servants', *The Nineteenth Century*, X (October 1881), pages 516–31.

26 Alphonse Daudet (1840–97) was a popular French novelist, dramatist and short story writer associated with the naturalist school. Dolobelle is the broken-down actor in his *Fromont jeune et Risler aîné* (1874); Valmajour is a simple-minded tambourine player in *Numa Roumestan* (1881); d'Argenton, the self-centred, fraudulent poet in *Jack*, is ridiculed for repeating the 'cruel words' he claims to have addressed to those who refused his work. *Vingt ans de ma Vie littéraire* conflates two volumes of Daudet's memoirs published in 1888: *Souvenirs d'un homme de lettres* and *Trente ans de Paris*.

27 Paul Bourget (1852–1935), a French poet and critic, was noted for his interest in psychology in general and mental abnormalities in particular.

28 i.e. the Faubourg St Germain, a quarter of Paris on the Left Bank traditionally associated with aristocratic society.

29 The reference is to *Hamlet* and the *Henry IV* plays, particularly Part II.

30 For Arnold, see headnote, page 167; for Paley, see note 3, page 560; for Colenso, see headnote, page 299.

31  T. H. Green (1836–82), Professor of Moral Philosophy at Oxford from 1878, was an idealist philosopher of the neo-Kantian school who exercised a large influence on late nineteenth-century philosophy in England. He was thought to have been the model for Mary Ward's Robert Elsmere.

32  Honoré de Balzac (1799–1850), French novelist, was known for his vast collection of novels, *La Comédie humaine*. Balzac is generally credited with establishing the techniques of realism. George Meredith (1828–1909), novelist and poet, was frequently criticised for the obscurity of his work.

33  See *As You Like It*, II, iv, ll. 54–5: 'Nay, I shall ne'er be ware of mine own wit / till I break my shins against it'.

34  The term 'Baal' was used of Semitic deities; the debased rights which were used in connection with Baal were condemned by Hebrew prophets. Here Wilde is using the name to denote a false god – that of realism.

35  See Charles Baudelaire's essay, 'Théophile Gautier', in *L'Artiste* (March, 1859); Wilde is in fact paraphrasing Baudelaire. Scullions are the lowest rank of domestic servants.

36  i.e. the impoverished young journalist and poet in Balzac's *Les Illusions perdues* (1837–43) who kills himself in a fit of remorse after falling in love with a courtesan.

37  Hans Holbein the younger (1497–1543), German court painter to Henry VIII, was admired for the realism of his portraits.

38  All the references are to historical novels: *Salammbô* (1862), by Gustave Flaubert (1821–80), is set in Carthage after the First Punic War; William Thackeray's *Henry Esmond* (1852) is set in the eighteenth century; *The Cloister and the Hearth* (1861), by the novelist and poet Charles Reade (1814–85), is a historical romance about the father of Erasmus; *Le Vicomte de Bragelonne* (1848–50), by the French novelist Alexander Dumas the elder (1802–70), is set in the seventeenth century and is a sequel to his better known, *Les trois mousquetaires* (1844).

39  An allusion to the players in Hamlet, II, ii, ll. 552–3: 'For Hecuba! / What's Hecuba to him, or he to Hecuba, / That he should weep for her?' Hecuba, the wife of King Priam of Troy, was the subject of a tragedy by Euripides (see note 94, page 602).

40  i.e. novels by George Eliot: *Romola* (1862–3) is an historical novel; *Daniel Deronda* (1876) is concerned with contemporary life, and particularly with Jewish immigrants.

41  Reade's *Christie Johnstone* (1853) was concerned with prison reform and his *Hard Cash* (1863) was directed against abuses in private lunatic asylums.

42  For the 'poor-law', see note 15, page 569; Wilde has in mind Dickens' *Oliver Twist* (1837–9).

43  Apollo, the Greek god of poetry and music, was attended on Mount Parnassus by the nine muses.

44  An allusion to *As You Like It*, II, i, ll. 14–17: 'And this our life, exempt from public haunt, / Finds tongues in trees, books in running brooks, / Sermons in stones, and good in everything.'

45  i.e. Wordsworth's poems 'Laodamia' (1815), 'Ode: Intimations of Immortality' (1807), 'The Idiot Boy' (1798), in which Martha Ray appears, and 'Peter Bell' (1819).

46  An allusion to Wordsworth's 'The Tables Turned' (1798), l. 21: 'One impulse from a vernal wood / May teach you more of man; / Of moral evil and of good, / Than all the sages can.

47  i.e. the earliest generation of gods, the sons of Heaven and Earth, who were eventually overthrown by the Olympians.

48  An allusion to *Antony and Cleopatra*, II, ii, ll. 191–5.

49  For Goethe, see note 6, page 589; the quotation is from his short poem, 'Natur und Kunst'. Wilde's translation is accurate.

50  i.e. an ode or piece of writing in which an author retracts something said in an earlier poem or work – a recantation. The idea that Shakespeare's late plays represent Shakespeare's increasing disillusion with the drama was something of a commonplace in late nineteeth-century Shakespeare criticism.

51  For Philistine, see note 20, page 572.

52  For Mahomedan, see note 36, page 571.

53  Herodotus (480–425 BC), Greek historian whom Cicero referred to as 'the father of history' because of his realistic (rather than poetic) account of war and politics; Cicero (106–43 BC), orator and statesman; Suetonius (70–160), Roman historian best known for his *Lives of the Caesars*; Tacitus (55–120), Roman historian known for his biography of Agricola and his *Annals* of the Julian emperors; Pliny the elder (23–79), Roman historian and author of *Naturalis Historia*; Hanno, a fifth to sixth century Carthaginian navigator – *Periplus* was the title of a Greek translation of his account (in Phoenecian) of a voyage around the West Coast of Africa; Jean Froissart (1333–1405), French chronicler and poet whose history of Europe, *Chronique*, was popular in the nineteenth century; Sir Thomas Malory (Wilde's spelling is not unusual in the nineteenth century), fifteenth-century author of the prose romance, *Le Morte D'Arthur*; Marco Polo (1254–1324) Venetian explorer, famous for his marvellous account of his travels in Asia; Olaus Magnus (1490–1558), a Swedish historian, known for his history of Sweden and Scandinavian customs; Ulissi Aldrovandi (1522–1605), an Italian naturalist; Conrad Lycosthenes (1518–61), a Swiss philologist and theologian, known for his Latin catalogue of strange prodigies, translated into English in 1581 as *The Doome Warning all Men to Judgement*; Benvenuto Cellini (1500–71) an Italian sculptor and goldsmith, noted for his autobiography; Giovanni Casanova (1752–98), an Italian adventurer famed for the sexual exploits recorded in his *Memoirs*; Daniel Defoe (1660–1731), author, adventurer and spy, whose *A Journal of the Plague Year* (1722) was written as if an eye-witness account; James Boswell (1740–95) published *The Life of Samuel Johnson* in 1791; the source for Napoleon's 'Despatches' may have been D. A. Bingham, ed., *A Selection from the Letters and Despatches of the First Napoleon* (1884); Carlyle's *The French Revolution* (see headnote, page 155) was a 'poetic' rather than historically accurate account of events.

54  A reference to the popular legend that as a 6-year-old George Washington cut down a cherry tree, and when asked by his father who had destroyed it, replied: 'I can't tell a lie, Pa; I cut it down with my hatchet.' 1889 was the centenary of Washington's inauguration as President.

55  i.e. an extinct genus of a huge herbivorous animal resembling the sloth whose fossil remains were found in South Africa.

56  Isobel Murray suggests an allusion to the 'Society of Authors' which had been founded in 1884 by Walter Besant to protect writers' financial interests.

57  For Spencer, see headnote, page 83.

58  Wilde is alluding to an unsigned critical review of his own *The Happy Prince and Other Tales* (1888) which appeared in the *Saturday Review* in October that year.

59  John Mandeville (1300–72) was the author of a supposedly autobiographical account of journeys in the east which were in fact compiled from other works; Walter Raleigh (1555–1618) wrote and published the first part of his *A History of the World* (1614) when imprisoned for conspiracy during the reign of James I.

60  i.e. references to events in *The Tempest*, *A Midsummer Night's Dream* and *Macbeth*.

61  See *Hamlet*, III, ii, ll. 23–9.

62  i.e. the villain in *Othello*.

63  See Shelley, *Prometheus Unbound*, I, l. 748.

64 Winged lions are griffins; the Lydian hills are in Greece; dryads are nymphs of the trees; for centaurs, see note 16, page 581.

65 Wilde has in mind paintings by Dante Gabriel Rossetti (1821–82) such as 'Beata Beatrix' and 'Proserpine'.

66 The works which Wilde probably has in mind are 'The Golden Stairs' (1880), 'Laus Veneris' (1873–5) and 'The Beguiling of Merlin' (1877) – all paintings by Edward Burne-Jones (1833–98); 'Andromeda Chained to a Rock' is by Whistler.

67 Sir Anthony van Dyck (1599–1614), Flemish court painter to Charles I of England.

68 Greek gods represented in statuary as idealised images of male beauty.

69 For Pheidias, see note 21, page 587. Praxiteles (370–330 BC) was a famous Greek sculptor; the statue of 'Hermes Carrying the Infant Dionysus' is the only surviving example of his work.

70 i.e. legendary criminals: Sheppard (1701–24) was renowned for his escapes from Newgate; Turpin was a noted highwayman, executed in 1739.

71 Artur Schopenhauer (1788–1860), German 'philosopher of pessimism' whose ideas came to be associated with the English decadence. His work, which argued that relief from suffering required an extinction of the will, was popularised by Helen Zimmern's translation in 1876.

72 Nihilism was a philosophy of scepticism which originated in nineteenth-century Russia during the early years of the reign of Alexander II; by the 1860s it was associated with unruly men who rebelled against tradition and the social order. The regicide of Alexander, and the political terror employed by those opposed to absolutism were attributed (erroneously) to the Nihilists; this topic forms the subject of Wilde's play, *Vera; or, the Nihilist*. The Russian novelists, Fydor Dostoyevsky (1821–81) and Ivan Turgenev (1818–83) both wrote works with Nihilist heroes: Raskolnikov in Dostoyevsky's *Crime and Punishment* (1866) and Bazarov in Turgenev's *Fathers and Sons* (1862). Wilde had anonymously translated Turgenev's 'A Fire at Sea' for *Macmillan's Magazine* (May, 1886).

73 Maximilien Robespierre (1818–83), French Revolutionary leader who dominated the Committee of Public Safety during the Reign of Terror (see note 28, page 570); for Jean-Jacques Rousseau, see note 20, page 597; the 'People's Palace' is a reference to the Crystal Palace built in Hyde Park for the Great Exhibition of 1851.

74 Rastignac, Henri de Marsay, and Lucien de Rubempré are all ambitious young men who appear in more than one novel in Balzac's cycle of novels, *La Comédie humaine*.

75 Becky Sharp (Mrs Rawdon Crawley) is a character in Thackeray's *Vanity Fair* (1847–8). The death of Colonel Newcome in Thackeray's *The Newcomes* (1853–5) is described in the final chapter, five paragraphs from the end.

76 Proteus was a minor sea-god in Greek mythology. In the *Odyssey* he has the power to change shape; when detained by Odysseus he resumes his true shape and answers questions.

77 Rolla is the eponymous hero of a work by the French poet, Alfred de Musset (1810–57); Werther, the hero of Goethe's *Die Leiden des jungen Werthers* (1774), commits suicide because of unrequited love.

78 For Pater, see headnote, page 383; the allusion is to Pater's essay, 'The School of Giorgione', published in the *Fortnightly Review* in 1877 and included in the 1888 edition of *The Renaissance*, where he argues that 'all art constantly aspires towards the condition of music'.

79 In Greek mythology Marsyas was the flute player who challenged Apollo to a musical contest and was flayed alive after being judged by the gods to be the loser.

80 An allusion to Plato's allegory of the caves in *The Republic*, Book VII.

81 For porphyry, see note 9, page 587; jasper is a variety of quartz.

82 Tiberius (14–37) was a Roman emperor who, like Domitian, was a byword for cruelty and lust; the Antonines (Antoninus Pius who ruled from 138–61 and Marcus Aurelius Antoninus, from 161–80) were associated with a period of tolerant, beneficent government. The Roman civilisation of the second century AD was the setting for Pater's novel *Marius the Epicurean*.

83 i.e. the Sistine Chapel in the Vatican Palace; Wilde probably has in mind the frescoes by Michelangelo on the Sistine ceiling which depict incidents and personages from the Old Testament. Sybils are mythical female prophets in Roman history; they are frequently depicted in Renaissance statuary.

84 i.e. an allusion to Pieter Breugel ('Breugel the Elder': 1522–69) who was from the Netherlands.

85 i.e. the Japanese artists, Katsushika Hokusai (1760–1849) and Toyota Hokkei (1780–1850), who became popular in Britain in the late nineteenth century; they had a particular influence on Whistler.

86 An allusion to the Australian painter and disciple of Whistler, Mortimer Menpes (1859–1938), who became famous following his Japanese exhibition at the Dowdeswell Gallery in 1888. Diego Velásquez (1599–1660), Spanish Court painter to Philip II, made a series of paintings of court dwarfs; Lilliput is the island of miniature people in Jonathan Swift's *Gulliver's Travels* (1726). I have supplied 'his' from the book edition of Wilde's essay to make sense of the sentence.

87 Aristophanes (448–380 BC) was an Athenian comic writer.

88 i.e. in Greek mythology, the gates from which true and fictitious dreams issue; the allusion is to the *Odyssey*, xix. 559ff: 'For two are the gates of shadowy dreams, and one is fashioned of horn and one of ivory. Those dreams that pass though the gate of sawn ivory deceive men, bringing words that find no fulfilment. But those that come forth through the gate of polished horn bring true things to pass, when any mortal sees them.'

89 Frederick Myers (1843–1910), poet and essayist, was President of the Society for Psychical Research, founded in 1882; his publications included *Science and a Future Life* (1893) and with Edmund Gurney and Frank Podmore, the two-volume *Phantasms of the Living* (1886) – the work Wilde appears to have in mind.

90 i.e. 'Doubting Thomas', the disciple who claimed he could not believe in the Resurrection in the absence of tangible proof; see John xx. 24–9.

91 i.e. Oxford or Cambridge.

92 For Balaam's ass, see note 18, page 590.

93 In Greek mythology Athena is the goddess of war; Odysseus is the wandering hero of the *Odyssey* whom Homer presented on occasions as a cunning and fluent liar. The book edition of the essay indicates that Wilde has in mind William Morris' translation of the *Odyssey* (1887), XIII, l. 295, where Athena smiles at Odysseus' 'words of sly devising'. The Cambridge professor (if he ever existed) remains lost to literary history.

94 Euripides (?485–406 BC) was the last of classical Athens' great tragic dramatists; the allusion is to *Ion*. Wilde is also alluding to Horace's *Odes*, III, xi. 36–7, where Hypermnestra is described as 'a maiden noble for all time to come'.

95 Thomas Sanchez (1551–1610), a Jesuit casuist; the reference is to his *A Treatise on the Noble and High Science of Nescience* (1581).

96 District School Boards, established by the 1870 Forster Education Act, had powers to levy an education rate, and to compel attendance at school for children from 5–12.

97 i.e. the name of the school where Plato and his followers taught philosophy.

98 An allusion to the seventh section of Flaubert's dramatic prose-poem, *La Tentation de Saint Antoine* (1874), which contains a dialogue between the Sphinx (who embodies

secrecy, immobility and sadness) and the Chimera (who embodies fantasy, light and caprice).

99　i.e. gigantic beasts described in the Book of Job.

100　For hippogriff, see note 16, page 581; 'L'Oiseau Bleu' is the title of a classic French fairy tale by Madame d'Aulnoy; it appears in her *Contes des Fées* (1697).

101　A misquotation from Tennyson's *The Princess*, VII, l. 165 – 'Now droops the milk white peacock like a ghost'; and a quotation from Blake's 'To the Evening Star,' l. 10 – 'speak silence with thy glimmering eyes, / And wash the dusk with silver'.

## Symons, *The Symbolist Movement in Literature*

1　The work which we know as *The Symbolist Movement in Literature* was planned and announced in 1896 as *The Decadent Movement in Literature*. The *Symbolist Movement in Literature* bears the date of 1899 although in fact it appeared in 1900. A second edition, substantially revised, was published in 1908 by A. Constable & Co.; and a third, which included several new essays – some on writers who had little or no relation to the Symbolist movement – was produced in 1919.

2　For Carlyle, see headnote, page 155; this and subsequent quotations are from *Sartor Resartus* (1836), Book III. chap. iii, 'Symbols'.

3　Eugène Félicien Albert Goblet d'Alviella (1846–1925), a French writer whose main works were on religious and anthropological topics; *La Migration des symbols* (1891) had been translated into English in 1894.

4　Gérard de Nerval, pseudonym of Gérard Labrunie (1808–55), one of the first French symbolist poets; he saw dreams as a means of communication between the everyday and supernatural worlds. He is best known for his *Voyage en Orient* (1843–51), a travelogue which examines folk mythology, symbols and religion, and his sonnets, *Les Chimères* (1854).

5　For Baudelaire, see note 34, page 594. For Flaubert, see note 38, page 599. Edmond and Jules de Goncourt (1822–98 and 1830–70) were French brothers and writers who collaborated to produce a number of novels and works of art-criticism, of which *L'Art du dix-huitième siècle* (1859–75) is the best known. Hippolyte-Adolphe Taine (1828–93), French critic and historian, who attempted to apply the methods of positivism to the study of the arts; the most lucid exposition of his views is in the later chapters of *Les Philosophes français du XIXᵉ siècle* (1857). For Zola, see note 11, page 597. Charles-Marie-René Leconte de Lisle (1818–94) a French poet and leader of the 'Parnassians' – a group of poets who opposed Romanticism by attempting to represent the positivist and scientific spirit in poetry.

6　Impressionism was a movement in painting (and later music) which originated in late nineteenth-century France, and which attempted to record accurately the visual world in terms of the effects of light and colour. The history of the reception of Impressionist art in Britain is extraordinarily complex. Often – as here – its aims were conflated with those of Realism and Decadence.

7　Nirvana is the supreme goal of meditation in Eastern thought.

8　José-Maria de Heredia (1842–1905) was a Cuban-born poet, educated in France where he lived from 1861. His fame rested on the 118 sonnets of *Les Trophées*, published in book form in 1893.

9　Stéphane Mallarmé (1842–98), a French symbolist poet whose work was noted for its obscurity.

10　Symons is translating the phrase 'épater la bourgeoisie', by 1890 a hackneyed ambition of most French art or writing with any pretensions to being avant-garde.

11 Paul Verlaine (1844–98), a French lyric poet who was associated first with the Parnassians and the Decadents; on the publication in 1884 of his collection of essays, *Les Poètes maudits*, he became the leader of the early Symbolists.

12 Philippe-Auguste Villiers de l'Isle-Adam (1838–89) was a French novelist, dramatist and symbolist poet whose verse was marked by the ornateness of its language; he was also later known for his vagabond existence. Maurice Maeterlinck (1862–1949) a Belgian-born poet, dramatist and essayist, who lived mainly in France, and was an important figure in the Symbolist movement in both countries; he was best known for his allegorical and romantic plays produced at the *Théâtre de l'Oeuvre*.

## Nordau, *Degeneration*

1 The English translation of *Entartung* was taken from the second edition of the German work; *Entartung* was also translated into Italian (1893), French (1894) and Russian (1894). Heinemann brought out a popular edition of *Degeneration* in 1913. In the text and in Nordau's notes I have replaced his occasional use of square brackets – thus '[ ]' – with swung brackets – thus '{ }' – in order to distinguish between his editorial emendations and my own explanatory notes.

2 The opening sentences refer back to the previous chapter. They have been omitted.

3 Benedict Augustin Morel (1809–73), an Austrian-born French psychologist who was known for his work on the hereditary aspects of mental illness and for his *Traité de maladies mentales* (1860) in which he coined the term 'demence precoce' (dementia praecox) to describe mental and emotional deterioration.

4 Cesare Lombroso (1835–1909), criminologist and Professor of Psychiatry at the University of Turin, was also known for his hereditary theory of mental illness which he saw exhibited in various physical and mental stigmata. Charles Samson Féré (1852–1907), a French criminologist and psychologist, once more known for his views on the hereditary nature of mental abnormalities which he expounded in works such as *La Famille névropathique* (1894) and *Dégénérescence et criminalité* (1888); both works are cited by Nordau later in the chapter.

5 Henry Maudsley (1835–1918), after whom the Maudsley Hospital in London was named, was an English psychologist best known for his Gulstonian lectures (delivered to the Royal College of Physicians in 1870), *Body and Mind*, which examined the relationships between mental degeneracy and disorders of the nervous system, and between morbid bodily states and disordered mental functions; he also edited *The Journal of Mental Science*. Benjamin Ball (1834?–93), a French psychologist best known for his *Leçons sur les malades mentales* (1880–3) and *La folie érotique* (1888).

6 Valentin Magnan (1835–1916), French psychologist who argued that mental troubles were caused by degeneration.

7 i.e. bombast.

8 For Philistine, see note 20, page 572.

9 In the nineteenth century there was a widespread interest in the Dutch-Jewish philosopher, Benedict Spinoza (1632–1677); in Britain, for example, George Eliot and Matthew Arnold were both influenced by his thought. Spinoza's discussion of the mind is to be found in Book II of the *Ethics*.

10 For Schopenhauer, see note 71, page 601. Edward von Hartmann (1842–1906), known as the 'philosopher of the unconscious', had a reputation for pessimism, based mainly on his *Die Philosophie des Unbewussten* (1870) which ran to many editions.

11 A mattoid is a person of erratic mind, a mixture of a genius and a fool; a graphomaniac is a compulsive writer. I have been unable to trace Guérinsen.

12 For Goethe, see note 6, page 589.

13 i.e. a trick of nature.

14 i.e. trinkets or curios.

15 Nordau is referring to the technique of using small dots or flecks of paint which characterised the work of some Impressionist painters (see note 6, page 603). Jean-Martin Charcot (1825–1893), the founder of modern neurology, opened in 1882 a neurological clinic at the Salpêtrière Hospital in Paris. It became famous throughout Europe, later attracting visitors such as Sigmund Freud.

16 *Fliegende Blätter* was a non-political humorous journal founded in Munich in 1844; the comic illustrations which Nordau refers to (by draftsmen such as E. Harburger, A. Hengeler, A. Oberländer and E. Reinicke) were later reproduced in a separate work.

17 Pierre Puvis de Chavannes (1824–98), a French mural painter, decorated many of France's public buildings in a style which imitated the effects of fresco paintings. His works were characterised by pale non-naturalistic colours and simplified forms intended to evoke moods; he was much admired by the symbolists. The context suggests that the reference to 'Besnard' is a confusion (by Nordau, or by his translator or printer) of the French painters Albert Besnard (1849–1934) and Emile Bernard (1868–1941). Bernard, a friend of Van Gogh and Gaugin (both of whom were known for their use of bright colour) was the pioneer of 'cloisonnism' – a style characterised by dark outlines enclosing areas of bright flat colours in the manner of stained glass or cloisonné enamels.

18 Once again the context suggests that Nordau (or the translator or printer) may have confused the work of Edouard Manet (1832–83) with his contemporary Claude Monet (1840–1926). Monet was one of the founders of the Impressionist movement; his post-1870 works concentrated on rendering the harmonies of colour in varying light conditions with results which broadly fit Nordau's description.

19 The reference is to St Bernadette (1844–79); her visions were the origin of the pilgrimages to Lourdes.

20 i.e. the Paris Stock Exchange.

## Morris, 'Art Under Plutocracy'

1 'Art Under Plutocracy' was originally delivered as a lecture entitled 'Art and Democracy' at University College, Oxford on 14 November 1883 to a meeting chaired by John Ruskin. It was reprinted in *Architecture, Industry and Wealth* (London: Longman, Green & Co., 1902).

2 A reference to the famous cathedral, the Hagia (or Santa) Sophia, built in Constantinople under the direction of the Byzantine Emperor, Justinian I; and to the San Marco Basilica in Venice, a Byzantine church famous for the richness of its interior – in particular its mosaics of coloured marble on gold ground and its inlaid marble and glass floor which glow in subdued light. Both had been written about by John Ruskin and Walter Pater. The monumental qualities of northern French cathedrals had also been noted by Pater.

3 Pericles (see note 9, page 589) commissioned the Parthenon and many other buildings in Athens.

4 For laissez-faire, see note 15, page 569.

5 For Ruskin, see headnote, page 325; the sentiments Morris attributes to Ruskin are to be found in his chapter 'The Nature of Gothic' in *The Stones of Venice, Volume II* (see pages 325–50).

6 For division of labour, see note 5, page 561.

7 The allusion is to the first and second century AD, and the reference is almost certainly to Pliny the younger (61–112) who was known for his books of literary letters on contemporary social, political and domestic events. The second implied date is to the fifteenth and sixteenth centuries in Britain; for Thomas More, see note 32, page 570.

8 A quern is a simple apparatus consisting of two circular stones for grinding corn; I have been unable to locate the reference to the Sicilian poet.

9 For Mill, see headnote, page 39.

10 For Cobbett, see note 6, page 567. A 'wen' is a wart or tumour; Cobbett's famous description of London as the 'Great Wen' is in *Rural Rides* (1830).

11 Morris uses the remainder of the lecture for what he terms 'Socialist propaganda'; he argues that it is only under socialist organisation that the conditions for a successful or non-exploitiative art can occur. The general political position underlying this part of the essay is similar to that outlined in the Socialist League Manifesto (see pages 193–6); for this reason it has been omitted.


## Courthope, *Life in Poetry: Law in Taste*

1 The volume comprised the two series of lectures which were delivered in Oxford between 1895 and 1900 when Courthope was Professor of Poetry.

2 In the election of 1895 (called after the defeat in the Lords of the second Home Rule Bill) the minority Liberal government, with Rosebery (see note 28, page 607) as Prime Minister, was defeated by the Conservative and Unionist party under Salisbury. In 1900 Parliament was dissolved over the issue of the War in South Africa; known as the 'Khaki election' (after the new uniform adopted by British troops), the Conservatives were returned with a convincing majority. The war was concluded in 1902.

3 The Balance of Power refers to the overriding principle of British foreign policy in Europe in the nineteenth century – to bring about a series of alliances so that no single state would be in a position to interfere with the independence of the others.

4 See Aristotle's *Poetics*, xviii. 1. The term 'δέσις' translates literally as 'tying' and is contrasted with 'λύσις' which means 'loosing'; Loeb gives 'complication' and 'dénouement' as the nearest modern equivalent.

5 For laisser-faire (or laissez-faire), see note 15, page 569.

6 i.e. Mill's *On Liberty* (1859); see above pages 183–93.

7 *The Prelude*, X, ll. 689–94; Courthope is either misquoting slightly or using an inaccurate edition.

8 Ibid., ll. 818–38.

9 For Schopenhauer, see note 71, page 601.

10 The Manchester School was the term given to Richard Cobden (see note 7, page 564) and his followers; its philosophy, which derived from the most radical political economy, was based on free trade and laissez-faire economic policy.

11 Pierre Waldeck-Rousseau (1846–1904) was asked in 1899 to form a 'government of republican defence' following the threat to public order provoked by the controversy over the Dreyfus affair; his Cabinet, based on pro-Dreyfus moderates, also included members of both right and left.

12 i.e. Proverbial. In his opening lecture Courthope translates it as: 'There can be no established law in the sphere of Art and Taste' (see *Life in Poetry*, page 8).

13 For Impressionists see note 6, page 603; Naturalism was a movement in art and literature which (like Impressionism) originated in France, and stressed the importance of representing objects as they are empirically observed. It is interesting to

compare Courthope's sense of the relationship between Naturalism and Impressionism with that of Symons (see page 412).

14  See James i. 25.

15  See Aristotle's *Poetics* ix. 4 where he contrasts the particulars of sense (Τὰ καθ' ἕκαστα) with the universal truth (Τὰ καθόλου) represented by art.

16  The phrase translates as: 'always, everywhere, by everyone'.

17  Jean de la Fontaine (1621–95) French poet and fabulist best known for his *Fables* published in twelve books between 1688–94; Heinrich Heine (1797–1856), German poet and critic, and an important influence on English Decadent writing.

18  Samuel Henry Butcher (1850–1910), an Irish-born classical scholar and man of letters, was appointed in 1882 to the chair of Greek at the University of Edinburgh; his best-known work was *Aristotle's Theory of Poetry and Fine Art* (1895), a translation of the *Poetics* together with a commentary analysing Aristotle's views in relation to modern philosophy.

19  Courthope is alluding to a number of famous works of criticism: Quintilian's *Institutio Oratoria*, especially Book 9 which contains a discussion of artistic structure and rhythm; Dante's Latin treatise on poetic language, *De vulgari eloquentia*; Nicholas Boileau-Despréaux's *L'Art poétique* (1674), a didactic poem in four cantos modelled on Horace's *Ars Poetica*; Gotthold Lessing's essay on poetry and the plastic arts, *Laocoön* (1766); Johnson's *The Lives of the English Poets* (1779–81).

20  George Saintsbury (1845–1933), critic and writer, from 1895 held the Chair of Rhetoric and English Literature at the University of Edinburgh; the first part of his three-volume *The History of Criticism and Literary Taste in Europe* was published in 1900.

21  See Aristotle's *The Art of Rhetoric*, especially Book I which was also discussed by Courthope in his lecture on Aristotle.

22  Sir Richard Claverhouse Jebb (1841–1905), Regius Professor of Greek at Cambridge University, was a member of several Royal Commissions on education as well as a member (from 1900) of the Consultative Committee of the Board of Education; 'Humanism in Education' was delivered at Oxford in 1899 as the Romanes Lecture.

23  James Anthony Froude (1818–94), critic and historian, and from 1892 Regius Professor of Modern History at Oxford.

24  An allusion to *Culture and Anarchy* (1869) by Matthew Arnold, Professor of Poetry at Oxford from 1857–67. See headnote, page 167.

25  Dr Pangloss is the Leibniz-like philosopher in Voltaire's *Candide*, who holds that all is for the best in the best of all possible worlds.

26  Bernard Bosanquet (1848–1923); his formidable *A History of the Aesthetic* was published in 1892.

27  See Aristotle, *Politics* I. i. 11.

28  Archibald Philip Primrose (Lord Rosebery: 1847–1929), statesman and Prime Minister from March 1894–June 1895; the reference is to Rosebery's rectorial address on imperial questions delivered at Glasgow University on November 1899 and which he used to mark his return to active politics in the House of Lords.

29  *Literae Humaniores*, a degree which encompassed the study of classical literature, philosophy and history.

30  Literally, 'training in the art of government'.

31  Ignaz von Döllinger (1799–1890), Roman Catholic Professor of Ecclesiastical History at Munich (1826–73) and from 1873 President of the Bavarian Royal Academy of Sciences.

32  The quotation is from *King John*, V, vii, ll. 117–18.

## PART IV: SEX AND GENDER

### Introduction

1 See Roy Porter and Lesley Hall, *The Facts of Life* (London: Yale University Press, 1995), page 132.

2 See Michel Foucault, *History of Sexuality: An Introduction*, trans. Robert Hurley (London: Allen Lane, 1978).

3 See *The Facts of Life*, page 147; and Ann Dally, *Women under the Knife: A History of Surgery* (London: Hutchinson Radius, 1991), pages 162–81.

4 Sarah Lewis's immensely popular *Women's Mission* (1839) also made use of Martin's book.

5 See Montgomery Hyde, *The Trials of Oscar Wilde* (London: William Hodge, 1948), pages 141–4.

6 *The Facts of Life*, page 132.

7 One of the most systematic studies of this topic is Richard Jenkyns' *The Victorians and Ancient Greece* (Oxford: Blackwell, 1980); a more recent and controversial account is Linda Dowling's *Hellenism and Homosexuality in Victorian Oxford* (London: Cornell University Press, 1994).

8 See *The Trials of Oscar Wilde*, page 236.

### Acton, *The Functions and Disorders of the Reproductive Organs*

1 A second edition of *The Functions and Disorders of the Reproductive Organs* was printed in 1858; it was followed by further editions in 1862, 1865, 1871 and 1875. It was also published in several American editions. The work was still in print twenty years after Acton's death.

2 *The Functions and Disorders of the Reproductive Organs* is divided into two parts: the first is concerned with 'normal functions' in youth, adult age and advanced life; and the second with 'functional disorders'. The extract is taken from the introduction to the second chapter in Part I; the opening paragraphs which examine evidence for the 'sex-passion' in animals have been omitted.

3 The reference is to George Drysdale (1825–1904). The work Acton quotes from is his *Elements of Social Science: or Physical, Sexual and Natural Religion* (1854), which was published anonymously in its early editions.

4 The reference is to the French surgeon, Jean Parise; I have been unable to trace the work to which Acton refers, both here and his footnote on page 483.

5 William Benjamin Carpenter (1813–85), Professor of Forensic Medicine at University College, London and editor of the *British and Foreign Medico-Chirurgical Review*. The reference is to Carpenter's most important work, *The Principles of General and Comparative Physiology*, published in 1839. It was the first book in English to consider biology as a science.

6 Robert Brudenell Carter (1828–1918); the reference is to *On the Pathology and Treatment of Hysteria* (1853).

7 i.e. the breasts.

8 I have omitted a page reference to a passage from Parise which Acton later quotes and which claims that 'semen is life itself under a fluid form – the vital principle, condensed and perceptible' and that 'nothing costs the economy so much as the production of semen, and its forced ejaculation'.

9  For Newton see note 14, page 564; William Pitt the younger (1759–1806), Prime Minister in 1783–1801 and 1804–6; for Kant see note 7, page 560. Minerva is a Roman goddess, usually of handicrafts; she is associated with medicine in Ovid, *Fasti*, iii. 827. For Apollo and the Muses see note 43, page 599. I have been unable to trace Acton's source for his account of Minerva.

10  Claude François Lallemand, French surgeon; the reference is to his *A Practical Treatise on the Causes, Symptoms, and Treatment of Spermatorrhoea*, trans. and ed. H. J. MacDougal (1847).

11  i.e. general well-being.

12  Omitted is a page reference to the anecdote by a patient described a few paragraphs earlier in the chapter.

13  William Farr (1807–83), statistician, and from 1871–72, President of the Statistical Society; the reference is to the *Census of Great Britain, 1851*, put together by Farr and published in 1852.

14  For Bacon, see note 12, page 564.

15  The reference is to the *Cyclopaedia of Anatomy and Physiology* edited by Robert B. Todd (1835–59).

16  The allusion is probably to George Mathew, Vicar of Greenwich, who published a number of exhortatory sermons on contemporary social ills, including *The Religious Improvement of the Present Awful Time Considered* (1803).

17  Omitted is a page reference to a quotation from Pittard earlier in the chapter.

18  A further reference to a quotation from Pittard earlier in the chapter has been omitted.

19  Charles Varnell, editor of the *Veterinarian*.

20  i.e. a laxative.

21  'Young England' was the name given to a group of Tory MPs in the middle of the nineteenth century who, led by Benjamin Disraeli, challenged the conservatism of the Prime Minister, Robert Peel. Acton appears to be using the term to refer simply to young men.

22  In Greek mythology a rapacious monster with a woman's face and body and the wings and claws of a bird.

23  Acton goes on to discuss at length some statistics from the 1851 census. These details have been omitted. Of interest, however, are Acton's calculations that the average age of marriage for men is 26 and for women 24.5, and that there are about '1,407,225 "young" and 359,969 "old" maids' and '1,413,912 "young" and 275,204 "old" bachelors', where 'young' means between 20 and 40 and 'old' means above 40.

24  Omitted is a page reference to a later passage in the book where Acton claims that the consequence of excessive sexual activity by newly-weds is ill-formed spermatozoa which in turn prevent pregnancy.

25  The reference is to Aubrey de La Mottraye (1674?–1743); his *Voyages* was translated into English in three volumes as *A. de la Mottraye's Travels* (1732).

26  i.e. the excretory duct of the testes which forms part of the ejaculatory duct.

27  Omitted is a page reference to a later passage in the book in which this observation is discussed in more detail.

### Ellis, *Man and Woman: A Study of Human Secondary Sexual Characters*

1  *Man and Woman* was Ellis's most popular work. It went through six editions between 1894 and 1926.

2 Ellis lists a series of examples including asthma (allegedly common in children and men and rare in women); diabetes, contraction of the fingers, hay-fever and aneurism (allegedly more common in men than women, and rare in children); and scarlet fever, scleroderma and herpes zoster (allegedly common in children and women and rare in men); these details have been omitted.

3 For Spencer, see headnote, page 83.

4 A page reference to an earlier part of the book has been omitted.

5 St Clement of Alexandria (150–215) was a theologian who attempted to combine Christianity with Greek philosophy; Ellis is referring to his *Paedagogus*.

6 Ellis has in mind the closing four lines of *Faust: Part II*. John Auster's 1864 edition translates them as follows:

> Love, whose perfect type is Woman,
> The divine and human blending,
> Love for ever and for ever
> Wins us onward, still ascending.

7 A reference to Alexander Freiherr von Humboldt (1769–1859), the younger brother of the humanist, Wilhelm Freiherr von Humboldt; Ellis has in mind Alexander's most widely read work, *Ansichten der Natur* (1808).

8 Henry Lewis Morgan (1818–81) was an American ethnologist and the principal founder of scientific anthropology. Ellis is referring to his comprehensive theory of social and cultural evolution set out in *Ancient Society; or Researches in the Lines of Human Progress from Savagery through Barbarism to Civilisation* (1877), which argued that human society advanced from an initial stage of promiscuity through to the development of family life and monogamy.

## Ellis, *The Women of England: Their Social Duties, and Domestic Habits*

1 *The Women of England* was an immediate best-seller, running to sixteen editions in Britain and America in less than three years. The text above has been taken from perhaps the widest-known edition, that produced for the 'Englishwoman's Family Library'. Several of Ellis's other works, including (in 1846) *The Wives of England*, were also in the series.

2 In Chapter I Ellis attributes the advantages possessed by England to the superiority of the country's 'moral characteristics' which in turn derive from 'her domestic character – the home comforts, and fireside virtues for which she is so justly celebrated'.

3 Mammon is a term of Aramaic origin; it refers to the regarding of wealth as an idol. Moloch was the name of a Cannanite idol to whom children were sacrificed as burnt-offerings; see Leviticus xviii. 21. Both terms were commonly used in the nineteenth century to denote idolatry.

4 Imprisonment for debt was abolished in 1868.

## Ruskin, *Sesame and Lilies*

1 'Of Queens' Gardens' was first delivered as a lecture in Manchester Town Hall on 14 December 1864; it was published in *Sesame and Lilies*, together with a second lecture, 'Of Kings' Treasuries', in 1865. The most popular of all Ruskin's works,

*Sesame and Lilies* was reprinted many times and in several different forms. A second edition of *Sesame and Lilies* with an identical text to the first edition but with an added preface was also published in 1865; it was reprinted in 1866 and 1867. In 1871, Ruskin revised both lectures for the first volume of his *Collected Works*, wrote a new Preface and included a third lecture, entitled 'The Mystery of Life and its Arts'. This version of *Sesame and Lilies* was reprinted in 1876, 1880, 1883, 1887 and 1891. The three-lecture volume next appeared in the form known as the 'Small Complete Edition', first published in 1893 and subsequently reissued many times, reaching its thirteenth edition by 1898. In the meantime (in 1882) another edition of only the first two lectures (that is, 'Of Queens' Gardens' and 'Of Kings' Treasuries') with a new Preface and using the text of the *Collected Works* was issued. This too was reprinted many times, reaching its thirteenth edition by 1892. A popular edition of this version of the two-lecture volume, printed from the same plates, was issued in 1894, and reached its eighteenth edition by 1898. The textual history of 'Of Queens' Gardens', then, reveals how topical many of its concerns were. A case can be made for reprinting one of a number of versions. The text of the following extract is, though, from the first (1865) version of the lecture which perhaps made the strongest impression on the reading public. (The following notes are again indebted to the scholarship of E. T. Cook and Alexander Wedderburn, *The Works of John Ruskin. Volume XVIII.*)

2 The opening pages of the lecture are mainly concerned with a series of literary examples of ideal female behaviour taken from Shakespeare, Walter Scott, Dante, Aeschylus, Homer and Chaucer; these have been omitted.

3 An allusion to Isiah xxxii. 2. The Pharos was the lighthouse on the Mediterranean coast at Alexandria built in the third century BC.

4 An allusion to Jeremiah xxii. 14.

5 The quotations are from the famous aria 'La donna e mobile' in Act III of Verdi's opera *Rigoletto*; and from Walter Scott's *Marmion* (1808), canto vi, verse 30, ll. 3–4.

6 One of Wordsworth's 'Lucy' poems, 'Three years she grew in sun and shower' (1800); Ruskin omits the second, third, fifth and seventh stanzas.

7 A quotation from Wordsworth's 'She was a phantom of delight' (1807), ll. 15–16.

8 An allusion to John Bunyan's *Pilgrim's Progress* (1684) in which the hero, Christian, has to pass through such a valley.

9 An allusion to Milton's *Paradise Regained*, IV, l. 330: 'As Children gathering pebbles on the shore'.

10 A quotation from the Litany in the *Book of Common Prayer*.

11 Another quotation from Wordsworth's 'She was a phantom of delight'.

12 i.e. the national assemblies or parliaments of the German Empire.

13 The quotations are from Psalms cxx. 4.

14 i.e. the island of Anglesey.

15 Parnassus was a mountain near Delphi with two summits, one consecrated to Apollo and the nine Muses, the other to Bacchus; through the connection with the Muses Parnassus came to be regarded as the seat of poetry and music. Aegina was a Greek island thought to have inspired the poetry of the Greek lyric poet, Pindar. Minerva was the Roman goddess of wisdom and patroness of the arts.

16 Cook and Wedderburn comment that Ruskin's reference is incorrect; the passage in fact comes from *Reports of the Commissioners of Inquiry into the State of Education in Wales* (1846–7), Part II, pages 38 and 133.

17 An allusion to Matthew ix. 36.

18 An allusion to Exodus xvii. 6.

19 An allusion to Acts xvii. 23.

20 As Cook and Wedderburn note, Ruskin assumes that 'lord' derives from the Old English *lágu* (meaning law). They point out that contemporary etymologists (and indeed modern editors of the OED) identified the origin of 'lord' with the Old English noun *hláford* ('loaf-keeper') and the origin of 'lady' with the Old English noun *hláefdíge* ('loaf-kneader').

21 An allusion to Luke xxiv. 30, 31, 35.

22 Cook and Wedderburn comment that in Virgil's *Eclogues* vii. 61, myrtle is sacred to Venus, the Roman goddess of beauty and sensual love.

23 For the origin of the epithet, see Isaiah ix. 6.

24 i.e. by the grace of God.

25 i.e. a precious stone whose colour varies from pale yellowish green to dark bottle-green. Cook and Wedderburn identify an allusion to *Othello*, V, ii, l. 146: 'Had she been true, / If heaven would make me such another world, / Of one entire and perfect chrysolite, / I'd not have sold her for it'.

26 Tennyson's *Maud* (1855), part I, canto xii, verse 6, ll. 3–4.

27 A slight misquotation from Walter Scott, *Lady of the Lake* (1810), i. l. 18.

28 Song of Solomon iv. 16.

29 An allusion to Dante's *Purgatorio*, xxviii; in Greek mythology Lethe is the river of forgetfulness in the Underworld.

30 *Maud*, part I, canto xxii, verse 1, ll. 1–2 and 5–6.

31 Ibid., verse 10, ll. 7–8.

32 A Madeleine is a type of faithful, grieving woman. Ruskin's allusion is to John xx. 15.

33 In the remainder of the paragraph Cook and Wedderburn identify allusions to Genesis iii. 24; Song of Solomon vii. 12 and ii. 15; and Matthew vii. 20.

## Mill, *The Subjection of Women*

1 *The Subjection of Women* sold well and a second edition (without variants) was produced in a matter of months: in the same year, 1869, there were also two American editions. In 1870 a third edition (again with very few variants) appeared, to be followed by a fourth edition in 1878 and a fifth in 1883. The work was also translated almost immediately into French, Danish, German, Italian, Polish and Russian.

2 In the opening pages of the essay Mill explains the difficulties involved in presenting an argument which runs counter to general opinion; these details have been omitted.

3 Mill proceeds to fill out this history of slavery by force followed by slavery by legal sanction with a number of detailed examples (both historical and contemporary). As several of them are reiterated at later points in the chapter, their mention at this stage in the argument has been omitted.

4 The reference is to the *Politics* VII. vi. 1. The Thracians, who inhabited what is today Bulgaria and parts of Turkey, were colonised by the Greeks in the eighth century BC.

5 In Greek mythology the Amazons were a race of female warriors in Scythia living in a society without any men; any sons born through unions with their neighbours were either killed or sent to live with their fathers. Spartan women like Spartan men (see note 4, page 575) were known for their strength and courage.

6 The reference is to Book V of *The Republic*.

7 A reference to 'The Petition for Extension (of the Elective Franchise) to All Householders without Distinction of Sex' – Public Petition no. 8501 – which was presented to the House of Commons by Mill on 7 June 1866.

8 Simon de Montfort, Earl of Leicester (1208–65), was the leader of the baronial revolt against King Henry III; although he ruled England for less that a year, he is remembered as an early advocate for a limited monarchy to rule (as Mill suggests) through elected councils and responsible officials.

9 See note 5, page 575.

10 A dolmen is a prehistoric structure consisting of a large flattish stone supported on two or more smaller upright stones. Jupiter is the supreme God in Roman mythology; his main temple was on the Capitoline Hill.

11 i.e. a peasant renting and cultivating a smallholding under a system of cottier tenure; in 1860 an Act of Parliament defined cottier tenure as tenancy of a cottage with not more that half an acre of land at a rent not exceeding five pounds a year.

12 A quotation from the opening paragraph of the preface to the 'Instaurato Magna' in Francis Bacon's *Novum Organum. Vol. I* (1620); James Spedding (*The Works of Francis Bacon. Vol. IV: Translations of the Philosophical Works* [1858]) translates it as: 'opinion of store is one of the chief causes of want'.

13 An allusion to Luke x. 7.

14 Hobson's choice is the option of either taking what is offered or nothing at all.

15 i.e. impulse or driving force.

16 i.e. a female slave or concubine in a harem.

## Carpenter, *Homogenic Love*

1 Although dated 1894, *Homogenic Love* in fact appeared in January 1895; it was reprinted in *The Intermediate Sex* (1908).

2 In the first part of the pamphlet Carpenter was concerned with providing evidence of homogenic love drawn from classical sources, literary sources (the work of Shakespeare and Michelangelo, Melville, Whitman, Tennyson and Pater), anthropological evidence from the Polynesian Islanders and African tribes such as the Balonda as well as a variety of contemporary scientific sources.

3 Richard Freiheer von Krafft-Ebing (1840–1902), a German neuropsychiatrist and pioneer in the area of sexual psychopathology; he was known for his *Psychopathia Sexualis* which is cited by Carpenter several times. Albert Moll (1862–?), a German psychologist who wrote prolifically on hypnotism and sexology; his best known work was *Die konträre Sexualempfindung* (1893) which is again cited by Carpenter. Moll also produced an edition of Krafft-Ebing's *Psychopathia Sexualis*.

4 i.e. a homosexual. The term 'Urning' or 'Uranian' was coined by the German writer Karl Heinrich Ulrichs who wrote prolifically on homosexuality from the 1860s to the 1890s. He argued that homosexuality was congenital, resulting from 'a feminine soul enclosed in a male body'; his ideas greatly influenced Carpenter and John Addington Symonds.

5 For Symonds, see headnote, page 549.

6 Richard Wagner (1813–83), German composer and dramatist; his prose works (from which Carpenter quotes) were translated into English by W. Ashton Ellis in eight volumes between 1892 and 1899.

7 For Sparta, see note 4, page 575.

8 Ten copies of *A Problem in Greek Ethics* by John Addington Symonds were privately printed in 1883.

9 Herakles (Hercules) and Achilles are both heroes in Greek mythology; in some sources Achilles is reputed to be the lover of Patroclus and Troilus. The Dorians were the last of the northern invaders of Greece. Carpenter is referring to the social organisation in Sparta (and Crete) where the subject-population were serfs and the enfranchised Dorians constituted a ruling military class with a special organisation of men's clubs.

10 In Greek mythology the tyrant slain by Harmodius and his lover, Aristogeiton, was Hipparchus who, disappointed in his love for Harmodius, had publicly insulted Harmodius' sister.

11 Walt Whitman (1819–92), American poet, journalist and essayist; his *Leaves of Grass* (1855) which celebrated the beauty, physical health and sexuality of the human body, made him a revolutionary figure in American literature. The third edition of *Leaves of Grass* (1860) contained what were known as the 'Calamus' poems – seemingly a record of a homosexual love affair. Whitman's apparent propagandising of male–male desire made him something of a celebrity with British gay writers. Oscar Wilde, for example, went to meet him in Camden, New Jersey in January 1882.

12 Whitman's *Democratic Vistas* was published in 1871.

13 An allusion to the 1885 Criminal Law Amendment Act; see page 472.

## Symonds, *A Problem in Modern Ethics*

1 The text is taken from a pirated edition of *A Problem in Modern Ethics* which was printed in one hundred copies in 1896. The volume contains no publisher's name and is subtitled, 'Addressed especially to Medical Psychologists and Jurists'.

2 Symonds' slim book comprises a discussion of the origins of the hostility towards homosexuality (which he dates from the time of the Emperor Justinian), followed by a review of the literature on the subject which he divides into six groups: 'Pornographic and Descriptive', 'Medico-Forensic', 'Medico-Psychological', 'Historical and Anthropological', 'Polemical' and 'Idealistic'. The Epilogue, reprinted here, summarises his findings and sets out some proposals for the future treatment of homosexuals.

3 i.e. 'for want of anything better'.

4 For 'Urnings' and 'Ulrichs', see note 4, page 613.

5 Richard Burton (1821–90), writer, linguist and explorer, published over forty volumes of travel writing; he was known in particular for his translation of the *Karma Sutra* (1883) and his works on Arabian erotica which included an unexpurgated version of the *Arabian Nights* (1885–8). The term 'Sotadic' derives from 'Sotades', a minor Greek poet noted for the coarseness and scurrility of his writing.

6 Justinian, Roman Emperor at Constantinople from AD 527–65, is remembered for his systematic reorganisation of Roman law. The 'Corpus Juris' of Justinian consisted of four parts: the Institutes, The Digests or Pandects (see note 13, page 577), the Code and the Novels. There is a long discussion of Justinian in Chapter I of *A Problem in Modern Ethics*.

7 In Genesis xix. 24 ff, Sodom and Gomorrah are the two cities destroyed by a fire from heaven for their wickedness.

8 i.e. the recurrence of a disease or the constitutional symptoms of an ancestor after the space of one or more generations. Atavism, manifesting at a social or racial level, was a topic of considerable anxiety among Victorian social scientists in that it seemed to threaten their notions of progress.

9  See note 11, above; in Chapter VIII of *A Problem in Modern Ethics* Symonds devotes several pages to a discussion of Whitman, particularly the 'Calamus' poems in *Leaves of Grass*.

10  Two famous homosexual scandals, both of which involved senior public figures who were perceived at the time to have escaped prosecution while others were brought to trial. The Dublin Castle scandal centred on alleged homosexual activities involving Gustavus Cornwall (Secretary of the General Post Office), Detective Inspector James Ellis French (Head of the Criminal Investigation Department) and Captain Martin Kirwan (of the Royal Dublin Fusiliers). The journalist responsible for publishing the allegations, William O'Brien, was the subject of several unsuccessful libel actions; nevertheless, the main protagonists largely escaped censure. The Cleveland Street scandal concerned a male brothel which was allegedly frequented by MPs and members of the aristocracy.

# INDEX

*a posteriori* method 111, 112–13, 114
*a priori* method 111–13, 114
abstinence: sexual 476, 477–8, 482; utilitarianism 50
abstract science, political economy as 111–14, 117–18, 123, 126
academic institutions 201–2
Academies, art 453–4
Acton, William 465, 466, 467, 468, 473–85
adaptation *see* natural selection
Adderley, Charles 360
Aestheticism 317–21; conservative critique of 449; as degeneracy 416–32; Pater 384–9; Swinburne 370–82; Wilde 391–409; *see also* English Decadent Movement
aesthetics: aesthetic value 314–16, 318–19, 321, 322–3, 450–9; criticism 384–9; schools 428–31, 449; *see also* Aestheticism
age, mortality 281–2
agricultural production 96–7, 103–4, 147
*Aids to Faith* 303, 305
Aldrovandi, Ulissi 400, 600*n*53
alienation, homosexuality 538
'All-case' method of investigation 121–4
Allbutt, H.A. 465
allegory 291
*Analogy of Religion* (Butler) 309
anarchy 170
*Anarchy and Authority* (Arnold) 168–82
anatomy, human/ape comparison 265–6, 489–90
ancient Greece: art 331, 402, 406–7; homosexuality 470–1, 542–4; literature 292–4; poetry 378–9; women 522

Anglican Church *see* Church of England
animals *see* biology
*Annals of the Parish* (Galt) 41
anthropology, sexual 470
Anti-Corn Law League 118, 564*n*7
'Anti-scrape' *see* Society for the Protection of Ancient Buildings
apes *see* primates
*Appreciations* (Pater) 383–4
archaeology 215–16
architecture, Gothic 326–50
Arduino, Giovanni 221
aristocracy 160, 163, 164, 170, 174–6
Aristotle 176, 451, 453, 456, 521
*Arithmetic designed for the use of schools* (Colenso) 299
Arnold, Matthew: art 315, 455; criticism 5, 351–68, 396; politics 24, 26, 167–82; religion 203
art 313–459; aesthetic schools 428–31, 449; aesthetic value 314–16, 318–19, 321, 322–3, 450–9; Aestheticism 317–21, 370–409; conservatism 321, 446–59; criticism 351–68, 391–409; Decadence 410, 412–13; decline under capitalism 434–45; Gothic elements 326–50; life relationship 397–400, 402–5, 409; Naturalism 344–6; nature relationship 391–2, 397–8, 401–2, 438; as pathology 320, 415–32; social function of 314–15, 320–3; socialism 321–2, 434–45; state relationship 455–6; symbolism 411–13; women's education 511; *see also* aesthetics; literature; poetry
'Art IV. – The Social Organism' (Spencer) 83–91

'Art VII. – On the Origin of Species' (Wilberforce) 272, 273–7
'Art VIII. – The Functions of Criticism at the Present Time' (Arnold) 351–68
'Art Under Plutocracy' (Morris) 434–45
*The Art-work of the Future* (Wagner) 542–3
astronomy 220–1
*Atalanta in Calydon* (Swinburne) 369
Auckland, Lord 357
'authorial process' 4
authoritarianism: Arnold 24, 167–82; Carlyle 24, 155–66
authority: art and culture 450–1, 452–3; church 202–3; force 522; liberty conflict 183–92; *see also* authoritarianism

BAAS *see* British Association for the Advancement of Science
Bacon, Francis 122, 479
Baer, Karl Ernst von 257, 579n6
Bagehot, Walter 21, 115–28
Ball, Benjamin 418, 604n5
*The Ballad of Reading Gaol* (Wilde) 391
Balzac, Honoré de 396, 403
Banfield, Thomas C. 133–4, 137
banking 121–2, 123
Bastiat, Claude Frédéric 133
Bateson, Thomas 176
Baudelaire, Charles 317, 377–8, 396, 412
Bax, E. 434
Bazley, Thomas 178
beauty: female 507–8; loss of 435, 437–8, 445; *see also* aesthetics
'Bedborough trial' 487
'Bedchamber plot' 158, 569n11
Bellay, Joachim du 386
Bentham, Jeremy 15–16, 27–38, 39, 57, 64, 132
Bible: geological interpretation 204–5; historicised interpretation 210–11, 289–309; literary criticism 364–5
Binet, Alfred 427–8
biology: developments in 200; embryology 257–62; evolutionary 206, 227–71; sex 468–70, 476–7; sociology analogy 86–91, 278–88; *see also* evolutionary theory; natural selection; physiology
Bischoff, Theodor Ludwig Wilhelm von 257, 579n6
*The Black Arrow* (Stevenson) 394, 598n14
*Blackwood's Magazine* 390

Blake, William 385
blasphemy 371, 374
Boileau-Despréaux, Nicholas 373, 453, 607n19
*Book of the New Moral World* (Owen) 18, 68
Bory de Saint Vincent, Jean Baptiste 276, 581n11
Bosanquet, Bernard 456
Bossuet, Jacques-Bénigne 366
Boswell, James 400, 600n53
*Bothwell* (Swinburne) 370
Bourget, Paul 395
Bradlaugh, Charles 180
breeding: intercrossing 237–8; selective 243, 268
Bright, Jacob 178
Bright, John 149–50, 169, 178
British Association for the Advancement of Science (BAAS) 199, 272
British College of Health 365
*British Quarterly Review* 359
Brown, Isaac Baker 465
Browne, Edward Harold 303, 305–6
Browning, Elizabeth Barrett 349
Buchanan, Robert 370
Buddhism 421
'Bull Ring' riots 568n4
Burdach, Karl Friedrich 489
Burgon, John William 302, 303, 309
Burke, Edmund 356–7
Burns, Robert 165, 571n34
Burton, Richard 470, 551
business 117–18, 127; *see also* capitalism; political economy
Butcher, Samuel Henry 453
Butler, Joseph 307, 309
Byron, George Gordon Lord 353
Byzantine architecture 326, 344

Calculus of Economy 131
Canada question 158, 569n11
Candolle, Alphonse Pyrame de 244
capital, political economy 101–4
capitalism: art relationship 322, 439–40, 442–5; labour exploitation 142–4, 145, 146–53; socialist critique of 23, 193–6
Carlyle, Thomas: aristocracy 174, 176; happiness 45; literature 400, 600n53; politics 14–15, 24, 26, 155–66, 362; symbolism 411
Carpenter, Edward 469, 470, 535–48
Carpenter, William Benjamin 476, 478–9

Carter, Robert Brudenell 476–7
Casanova, Giovanni 400, 600n53
Cassel, Revd W. *see* Cattle, Revd W.
Catullus, Gaius Valerius 373
'catastrophism' 205, 224
Cattle, Revd W. 178–9
causation: geology 214–15; scientific method 205
celibacy 479–80, 482
Cellini, Benvenuto 400, 600n53
cells, embryology 257–62
censorship 5, 380–1
Chamberlain, Joseph 149–50
Chambers, Robert 206–7
Champollion-Figeac, Jacques 215, 576n4
changefulness, Gothic architecture 340–4
Charcot, Jean-Martin 421, 429
charity 283–4
Chartism 14, 23; critique of 156–7
*Chartism* (Carlyle) 155, 156–66
*Chastelard* (Swinburne) 369
chastity 477–8, 482
chemistry 200
children: eugenics 282–3; exploitation at work 149, 151; human evolution 490; Owenite education 78–82; women comparison 488–9
*La Chimère* (Flaubert) 408
chivalry 515
Christianity: artistic imperfection 332; Bible interpretation 210–11, 289–309; creation 204–5; evolutionary theory conflict 272–7; French Revolution 163; religous toleration 187–8; sex and gender 468, 480–1; utilitarianism 52, 53; *see also* Bible; Protestantism; Roman Catholicism; theology
Church of England: decline of 211; Dissenters 203; Nonconformism 177; Oxford Movement 202; scepticism 407; social guidance 160; *see also* Protestantism
Cicero, Marcus Tullius 65, 400, 600n53
cities: poor housing 153; ugliness of 438–9
*Civilisation, Its Cause and Cure* (Carpenter, E.) 536
class *see* social class
class conflict 23, 24, 193–6
classical literature 292–4, 457–8
classification, biological 251, 252–3, 263–4, 266–7
climate, natural selection 229

*The Cloister and the Hearth* (Reade) 396, 397, 599n38
clothing, communitarianism 76–7
co-operation: art 436, 438; communitarianism 68–82
*The Coal Question* (Jevons) 129
Cobbe, Francis Power 364, 365
Cobbett, William 146, 362, 445
Cobden, Richard 118, 450
Code Napoléon 548, 554, 555
*Codification Proposal* (Bentham) 27
coercion: authoritarianism 157; moral repression 191–2; state intervention 189–90; of women 533
Coercion Act 1881 151, 568n12
Cohn, Gustav 121–2, 123, 564n11
Colenso, John William 210–11, 299–309, 363–4, 396
Coleridge, Samuel Taylor 119
Colin, Henri 419, 422, 425
colonies, West India question 158, 569n11
colour, perception of 427–8
commercialism: art relationship 322–3, 442–5; political economy 117–18, 127
commodities: definition 131; exchangeable value 143; prices 119–20; utility 134–8; value 94–100, 139–41; wage values 100–7
*The Commonweal* (Socialist League) 434
communism 23
*Communist Manifesto* 194
communitarianism 17–18, 68–82
community, utilitarianism 29
competition: art relationship 322, 439–40, 442–3; between the sexes 472, 532–3; class conflict 194; in nature 208–9, 240, 241–2, 244, 248; political economy 19–20, 106, 108
*A Complete Practical Treatise on Venereal Diseases* (Acton) 473
Comte, Auguste 21, 39, 192
*Confessions* (Rousseau) 389
conscience, liberty of 190
conscription 170
conservatism: art 321, 446–59; organicism 18–19; political economy 19–21; religious 272
*Considerations on Representative Government* (Mill, J. S.) 39
constitutional checks 169, 183–4
*Constitutional Code* (Bentham) 28
consumerism: art 322–3; origins of 22

consumption, marginal utility theory 22, 132–4, 135–8
*Contemporary Review* 370
contraception 465
*Conventional Lies of Our Civilisation* (Nordau) 415
Corn Laws 564*n*7
*corvée* (collective labour) system 148
Courcelle-Seneuil, Jean Gustave 133
Courthope, William John 320–1, 446–59
craftsmanship 332–3, 336–9, 437, 440–4
Crawford, Francis Marion 394
creation 204–5; anti-evolutionism 273–6
creativity: Aestheticism 317–18; criticism comparison 351–3, 367–8
crime, degeneracy 418–19
*The Criminal* (Havelock Ellis) 486
criticism: aesthetic 384–9; Arnold 351–68; biblical 289–309; critics 313–14, 351–2, 367; poetry 370–82; taste 453; Wilde 391–409
Cromwell, Oliver 85, 162
*The Crown of Wild Olive* (Ruskin) 326
cultural specificity, biblical interpretation 290–1, 293–4
culture: cultural decay 319–20; Law of National Character 452; mass vs elite 322–3; as perfection 168–9, 173, 174, 177, 181; relativism 315, 318, 319; Renaissance 386–7; *see also* art; literature; poetry
*Culture and Anarchy* (Arnold) 5, 167, 203, 316
custom: sexual inequality 522, 524–5; social rules 186
*Cyclopedia of Anatomy and Physiology* (ed. Todd) 480

*Daily Telegraph* 168
Dante Alighieri 453, 607*n*19
Darwin, Charles 122–3, 202, 203, 207–10, 227–53; Huxley defence of 254, 267–8; Wilberforce critique of 273–7
Daudet, Alphonse 395
*The Daughters of England* (Ellis) 495
Davidson, Andrew Bruce 301–2
*Days and Nights* (Symons) 410
death, mortality rates 280–1
Decadence *see* English Decadent Movement
'The Decay of Lying: A Dialogue' (Wilde) 391–409

Decorative Art 435–6, 437–8
*The Defence of Guenevere and Other Poems* (Morris) 433
Defoe, Daniel 400, 600*n*53
degeneracy 320, 416–32
*Degeneration* (Nordau) 320, 415, 416–32
demand 132–3; wages 104, 106
democracy 23–5, 162–3, 185
*Democracy in America* (De Tocqueville) 24
*Democratic Vistas* (Whitman) 546
demographics, economy relationship 12
*The Descent of Man* (Darwin) 228
*Descriptive Sociology* (Spencer) 83
desire: economic consumption 133–4; English Decadent Movement 319; sexual 464–5, 474–9, 482, 484–5
despotism 85, 110–11; primitive societies 189
deviance, degeneracy 416–32
Dickens, Charles 16, 397
*Discourses in America* (Arnold) 167
diseases, sex relationship 464–5, 474, 481–2
disinterestedness 358–9, 366–7
Dissenters 176, 177, 178, 203, 573*n*36
distribution of wealth 13, 20, 21, 106–7
divergence of character, natural selection 242–51, 252
diversification *see* divergence of character
divine creation 204–5
divine intervention, evolution 207
division of labour 23, 74, 81, 84, 335–6, 443
Döllinger, Ignaz von 458
domestic life, women's roles 465–6, 496–504, 506
Dostoyevsky, Fydor 403, 601*n*72
Downing, Andrew Jackson 231
drama, Wilde critique 398–9
Drysdale, George 465, 474–6, 608*n*3
*Dublin Review* 359
duty: moral theory 49, 57; women 497, 498, 514

earth, history of 217–26
*The Earthly Paradise* (Morris) 433
earthquakes 217, 219, 224
*Economic Studies* (Bagehot) 115
economics: art relationship 439–40, 442–5; industrialisation 12–13; marginal utility theory 21–2, 129–41; Marxism 22–3;

political economy 19–21, 93–141; socialism 142–54

*Economist* 115

*Edinburgh Review* 155, 359

education: aesthetic taste 456; anti-classical view 457; classical 458; communitarianism 17, 68, 78–82; homosexuality 555; humanism 454–5, 458; literature 321; middle class 178; public health 47; sex 484; socialism 195; of women 465–6, 507–14, 524, 534

*Education* (Spencer) 83

*The Education of Women* (Lee) 466

Egypt: archaeology 215–16; art 331, 347

Elcho, Lord 176

*An Elementary Grammar of the Zulu-Kafir Language* (Colenso) 300

*The Elements of Algebra* (Colenso) 299

*The Elements of Drawing* (Ruskin) 325

*Elements of Geology* (Lyell) 214

*Elements of Social Science* (Drysdale) 465

Eliot, George 11, 19, 26, 395

élitism, artistic 321, 322

Ellis, Sarah Stickney 465, 468, 495–504

embryology 257–62

emotions: degeneracy 419–20; hysteria 425; influence on physical health 477

*Empedocles on Etna, and Other Poems* (Arnold) 167

empiricism: scientific 201, 203, 209–10; *see also a posteriori*

Employer's Liability Act (1880) 145

employment: communitarianism 77, 81–2; working hours 148–9, 152; *see also* labour

enfranchisement: democracy 24, 25; economic empowerment 14; suffrage movement 523

*England for All: The Text-Book of Democracy* (Hyndman) 22, 142–54, 535–6

*England and the Italian Question* (Arnold) 167

*England's Ideal* (Carpenter, E.) 535–6

*The English Constitution* (Bagehot) 115

English Decadent Movement 318–19, 320, 410, 412–13

Enumerative method of investigation 121–4

Epicureanism 41–2

*The Epistles of St Paul* (Jowett) 289

equality, socialism 196

*The Erotic Rights of Women* (Havelock Ellis) 487

*An Essay on the External Corn Trade* (Torrens) 102

*Essay on the Influence of a Low Price of Corn on the Profits of Stock* (Ricardo) 93

*Essay on the Principle of Population* (Malthus) 12

*Essays in Criticism* (Arnold) 167

*Essays and Reviews* 210, 272, 289, 290–8

*Essays on Some Unsettled Questions of Political Economy* (Mill, J. S.) 39

*Essays and Studies* (Swinburne) 370

*Essays Upon Some Controverted Questions* (Huxley) 255

essentialism: evolutionary theory 207; human nature 15; literary value 1

ethics: communitarianism 17–18, 68–82; utilitarianism 15–17, 27–67; *see also* morality

*The Ethics of the Dust* (Ruskin) 326

eugenics 209, 279, 282–4, 286–8

*Evidence as to Man's Place in Nature* (Huxley) 209, 254, 255–71

*Evidences* (Paley) 396

*Evolution and Ethics* (Huxley) 255

evolutionary theory: Christian critique of 272–7; Darwin 207–10, 227–53; development of 204; Huxley 254–71; 'saltationist' view 205–6, 207, 208; society analogy 19, 83–91, 278–88; transformational theory 206, 207, 208; *see also* natural selection

*An Examination of the Utilitarian Philosophy* (Grote) 56–67

exchangeable value 94–9, 139, 143

exegesis, biblical 289–309

experience: aesthetic 317, 384–5, 387–9; theory conflict 110–11; *see also* empiricism

expertise, scientific 201–2

*Exploratio Philosophica* (Grote) 56

*Expression of the Emotions in Man and Animals* (Darwin) 228

extinction 241–2, 248–9, 251

factories: mechanisation 443–4; poor working conditions 148–9, 151–2

Factory Acts 149, 151

facts, scientific method 121–3

Falret, Jules Philippe 423

famine 104

Faraday, Michael 200
Farr, William 479–80
*Felix Holt, the Radical* (Eliot) 11
femininity, evolutionary tendency towards 490–1
feminism, scientific investigation 469–70
Fenianism 172
Féré, Charles Samson 418
feudalism 439, 441–2, 522, 525
*First Steps in Zulu* (Colenso) 300
Flamsteed, John 123
Flaubert, Gustave 408, 412, 599n38
*Fliegende Blätter* 427
food production: communitarianism 74–5; labour value 96
foreign loans 121
*The Formation of Vegetable Mould, through the Action of Worms* (Darwin) 228
Forster, W. E. 151, 568n12
*Fortnightly Review* 40, 121, 383, 390–1
fossils 204–5, 221
Foucault, Michel 3, 464, 465
*Fragment on Government* (Bentham) 27
France: conscription 170; homosexuality 548, 552, 554, 555; hysteria 424–5; religious liberty 450; Renaissance 386; Revolution 162, 163–4, 316, 354–7; social instability 12; Symbolist literature 411–12
Fraser, James, Bishop of Manchester 150
*Fraser's Magazine* 39, 155
free trade *see* political economy
freedom: artistic 333, 334–5, 340–1, 449; authoritarianism 169–73; of speech 25, 171, 190–1, 370–82; *see also* liberty
*A French Eton* (Arnold) 167
*The French Revolution: A History* (Carlyle) 155, 400, 600n53
friendship, homosexuality 542–4
*Friendship's Garland* (Arnold) 167
Froissart, Jean 400, 600n53
Froude, James Anthony 454
*The Functions and Disorders of the Reproductive Organs* (Acton) 466, 473–85

Galt, John 41
Game Laws 158, 569n11
Garnier, Clément Joseph 131
Gaskell, Elizabeth 26, 467
*Gaston de Latour* (Pater) 383, 384
Gautier, Théophile 317
gender: clichés 463; differences 470, 487–94; equality 471–2; roles 496–504, 506; science influence 468–70; social class 466–7; social and political equality 520–34; women's education 465–6; *see also* men; women
*Genio e Follia* (Lombroso) 415
genius 422–3
geography: geology 225–6; natural selection 237–40
*The Geological Evidences of the Antiquity of Man* (Lyell) 214
geology: catastrophism 205; Darwin 271; literalism 204; Lyell 205–6, 213–26, 237; scientific method 122
geometry, *a priori* method 111–12
*George Chapman* (Swinburne) 370
Germany, biblical interpretation 296
*Germinal* (Zola) 394–5
*Ghosts* (Ibsen) 465
Gibbon, Edward 471
Gissing, George 467
Goblet d'Alviella, Eugène Félicien Albert 411
God: anti-evolutionism 273–6; scientific justification of 203; utilitarian conception of 51–2; *see also* Bible
*God and the Bible* (Arnold) 167
Goethe, Johann Wolfgang von 352, 353, 354, 360, 363, 399, 423
Goncourt, Edmond de 412, 431, 603n5
Goncourt, Jules de 412, 603n5
Gooch, Daniel 172
Gothic architecture 325, 326–50
government: democracy 23–5, 162–3; laissez-faire policy 160–2; liberty/authority conflict 183–5; national will 85; Platonic conception of 86; political economy conflict 117; social class 180–1; utilitarianism 31; *see also* Parliament; state
gradualism, evolutionary theory 208–9
Gray, Asa 244
greatest happiness principle *see* utilitarianism
Greeks, ancient *see* ancient Greece
Green, T. H. 396, 599n31
gross domestic product 13
Grote, George 16
Grote, John 56–67
grotesque, Gothic architecture 346–7
guilds, craftsman 442

Haddan, Arthur West 301
Haggard, Henry Rider 394
Hake, Alfred Egmont 416
Hall, Lesley 463, 468
handiwork *see* craftsmanship
Hanno 400, 600*n*53
happiness 28–9, 41–50, 56–66, 135; *see also* pleasure
*The Happy Prince and Other Tales* (Wilde) 390
*Hard Times* (Dickens) 16
Hardy, Thomas 26, 467
harm: principle 24–5, 189–90
*Harmonies of Political Economy* (Bastiat) 133
*Harper's Monthly Magazine* 410
Harrison, Frederick 168, 175, 180
Havelock Ellis, Henry 470, 486–94
health: communitarianism 76–7; mortality 280–2; working classes 150, 567*n*10
Hearn, William 133
Heer, Oswald 240
*Henry Esmond* (Thackeray) 396, 599*n*38
heredity: eugenics 278–9, 282–3; homosexuality 550–1; natural selection 231–2
Herodotus 400, 600*n*53
*On Heroes, Hero Worship and the Heroic in History* (Carlyle) 155
Heron, Robert 233
*The Historical Basis of Socialism in England* (Hyndman) 142
Historical method 124
history: knowledge of 114; women's education 509
*A History of the Aesthetic* (Bosanquet) 456
*History of Criticism* (Saintsbury) 453, 456
*History of English Poetry* (Courthope) 446
*History of Friedrich II of Prussia, called Frederick the Great* (Carlyle) 155–6
*History of the Plague* (Defoe) 400, 600*n*53
*History of the Renaissance in Italy* (Symonds) 549
Hobbes, Thomas 15, 86–7
*Home and Foreign Review* 359
*Homogenic Love and Its Place in a Free Society* (Carpenter, E.) 536–48
homosexuality 467, 469, 470–1, 472, 486, 536–55
*A House of Pomegranates* (Wilde) 390
housing: communitarianism 69, 75–6; working-class deprivation 153
Hugo, Victor 389, 596*n*19
human evolution 255–71

human nature: communitarianism 71, 72–3, 79; desires 133–4; essentialism 15; gender differences 468, 506, 528–30; happiness 41–2, 43–4; political economy 19–20, 108, 117–18; power 515; utilitarianism 34–5, 61, 62–3
Humanism, education 454–5, 458
Humboldt, Alexander Freiheer von 492
Hume, David 15
humility, Gothic architecture 346, 349–50
Hutton, James 222, 576*n*17
Huxley, Thomas Henry 199–200, 209, 254–71
Hyde Park riots 170, 572*n*16
Hyndman, Henry Mayers 22–3, 142–54, 434, 535–6
hysteria 425–8, 431–2

Ibsen, Henrik Johan 465
idealism, positivism conflict 58
ideas: creativity 352–3; disinterestedness 358–9, 366–7; politics relationship 355–7
ideology 1–2, 4
idyllic poetry 381–2
*Illusions Perdues* (Balzac) 396
*Illustrations of the Huttonian Theory* (Playfair) 222
*Imaginary Portraits* (Pater) 383
imperfection: artistic 331–3, 337–40, 343; in nature 275
impotence 478
Impressionism 412, 450
impressment, naval 533
*In the Key of Blue* (Symonds) 549
*In Memoriam* (Tennyson) 204
individualism: artistic 428–9, 436–7; communitarian critique of 17–18, 70–1; liberty 447–9, 525–6; political economy 20, 21; protection from tyranny 185; religion 187–8
induction 111
industrial action 145
industrialisation: critique of 513–14; economic change 12–13; economic organisation 84–5; effect on craftsmanship 443–4; social stability 12
inequality, sexual 463, 471–2, 520–34
*Inquiry into the Principles of Political Economy* (Stewart) 116
insanity *see* degeneracy
*Inspiration and Interpretation* (Burgon) 302

institutions: academic 201–2; art and cultural 313, 316, 321–2, 453–4
Intellectual art 435–6, 440
intelligence: sexual appetite relationship 478; social Darwinism 282–4, 287; utilitarianism 42–4
*Intentions* (Wilde) 5, 390
intercrossing, natural selection 237–8
interests: individual vs public 15, 23–4, 70–1, 74, 90–1, 190; utilitarianism 29, 48–9, 50
*The Intermediate Sex* (Carpenter, E.) 536
*Intermediate Types Among Primitive Folk* (Carpenter, E.) 536
*International Journal of Ethics* 536
intertextuality 3
interventionism 13–14
intimacy, homosexuality 540, 541
*An Introduction to the Classification of Animals* (Huxley) 254
*An Introduction to the Principles of Morals and Legislation* (Bentham) 15–16, 27, 28–38
*An Introduction to the Study of Browning* (Symons) 410
*Introduction to the Study of Dante* (Symonds) 549
*Ioläus: an Anthology of Friendship* (Carpenter, E.) 536
Ireland: Fenianism 172; Irish Appropriation question 158, 569n11; religious conflict 178–9
*Irish Essays* (Arnold) 167
'iron law of wages' 20
*Italian Byways* (Symonds) 549
Italy: geology 221; homosexuality 548, 552, 554, 555; Renaissance 386–7

James, Henry 394
Japanese art 313, 406
Jebb, Richard Claverhouse 454–5
Jennings, Richard 137
Jevons, William Stanley 21–2, 122, 124, 129–41
Johnson, Samuel 61, 453, 607n19
Joubert, Joseph 356, 363
Jowett, Benjamin 210, 289–98
*Jude the Obscure* (Hardy) 467
judgement: aesthetic 451–9; critical 367; *see also* criticism
jurisprudence 116–17
Justinian, Emperor 551, 552–3

*A Key to Algebra* (Colenso) 299
knowledge: Owenite education 78–82; scientific 200–2; women's education 508–10
Krafft-Ebing, Richard Freiheer von 537, 538–9

labour: artistic freedom 340–1; commodity value 116; craftsmanship 322, 333, 336–9, 437, 440–4; division of 23, 74, 81, 84, 335–6, 443; mechanisation 444; political economy 20; social class 334–5; socialism 142–54, 193–5; value 139–41; wages 100–7
labour theory of value 20, 22, 94–107, 116, 142–4
Labrunie, Gérard *see* Nerval, Gérard de
laissez-faire 20, 160–3, 440, 448, 449–50
Lallemand, Claude François 479
Lamarck, Jean-Baptiste 206, 267, 276–7
La'mert, Samuel 466
landlords, rent increases 105
language: education 458; poetic 315
*L'Assommoir* (Zola) 396
*Latter-day Pamphlets* (Carlyle) 155, 362
law: homosexuality 547–8, 552–5; punishment 34; *see also* jurisprudence
Law of National Character 452, 453, 456
'Law of the Subordination of Wants' 137
Law of the Universal 451–2, 453
Law of Variety 133, 136–8
leadership, authoritarianism 163
Leconte de Lisle, Charles-Marie-René 412, 603n5
Lee, Edwin 466
legislation: gender issues 472; homosexuality 552–5; social evolution 85; utilitarianism 16, 29–35, 37–8, 57
Legrain, Paul Maurice 419, 421, 422, 424, 430
Leibniz, Gottfried Wilhelm 219–20
Lessing, Gotthold 453, 607n19
*Lessons on Elementary Physiology* (Huxley) 254
Lewes, George Henry 19
liberal democracy 25
*The Liberal Movement in English Literature* (Courthope) 446
liberalism 24–5, 170–1, 176–7, 183–92, 363–4, 365
liberty: individual 24–5, 169–70, 171–3, 447–9, 458, 525–6; liberalism 183–92; of taste 454; *see also* freedom

life, art relationship 397–400, 402–5, 409
*Life of Alexander Pope* (Courthope) 446
*The Life and Death of Jason* (Morris) 433
*The Life of Frederick Schiller* (Carlyle) 155
*The Life of John Sterling* (Carlyle) 156
*Life in Poetry: Law in Taste* (Courthope)
    446–59
*The Life of Samuel Johnson* (Boswell) 400,
    600n53
*Lippincott's Monthly Magazine* 390
literalism, challenges to 204–5, 210–11
literature: classical 292–4, 454, 457–8;
    criticism 351–68, 391–409; education
    321; homosexuality in 555; sexual 466;
    Symbolist Movement 411–13; taste
    315; women in 531–2; women's
    education 510–11
*Literature and Dogma* (Arnold) 167, 396
Livingstone, David 277
loans, foreign 121
Lombroso, Cesare 415, 418, 422, 423, 424
London Militia 179
*London and Westminster Review* 39
*Lord Arthur Savile's Crime and Other Stories*
    (Wilde) 390
L'Ouverture, Toussaint 165
love 478–9, 505; homosexual 536–48
*Love is Enough* (Morris) 433
*Love's Coming of Age* (Carpenter, E.) 536
Lowe, Robert 174, 176
*Ludibria Lunae* (Courthope) 446
Lycosthenes, Conrad 400, 600n53
Lyell, Charles 122, 123, 205–6, 213–26,
    237, 276–7

Macaire, Robert 164, 570n29
McCulloch, John Ramsay 93, 126
Macintosh, James 83–4
*Macmillan's Magazine* 383
Maeterlinck, Maurice 413, 604n12
magazines 5
Magnan, Valentin 418, 422, 426
Magnus, Olaus 400, 600n53
Maillet, Benoît de 276, 581n11
Maitland, James (Lord Lauderdale) 132–3
majoritarianism 24–5, 185
Mallarmé, Stéphane 413, 603n9
Mallock, W. H. 383
Mallory, Thomas 400, 600n53
Malthus, Thomas 12, 93, 98
mammals 263–4; *see also* primates
*The Man Versus the State* (Spencer) 83

*Man and Woman: A Study of Human Secondary
    Sexual Characters* (Havelock Ellis) 470,
    486, 487–94
Manchester School 449–50
Mandeville, John 401, 600n59
*The Manifesto of the Socialist League* (Morris *et
    al.*) 193–6
Mansel, Henry Longueville 305
*A Manual of the Anatomy of Invertebrated
    Animals* (Huxley) 254
*A Manual of the Anatomy of Vertebrated Animals*
    (Huxley) 254
*A Manual of the Botany of the Northern United
    States* (Gray) 244, 578n14
manuals, sex 465
'marginal revolution' 129
marginal utility theory 21–2, 129–41
*Marius the Epicurean* (Pater) 383
market: art industry 322; marginal utility
    theory 129–41; Marxist critique of
    22–3; political economy 19–21,
    93–141; social issues 15
marriage: coercion of women 472, 524,
    533–4; sex 478–9, 481, 483–4
*Marriage in Free Society* (Carpenter, E.) 536
Martin, Aimé 466
martyrdom 47–8
Marx, Karl 22–3, 142
Marxism 22–3, 142
*Mary Barton* (Gaskell) 467
masturbation 468
mathematics, economic theory analogy
    130–1
Mathias, Peter 12
Maudsley, Henry 418, 419, 604n5
Maupassant, Guy de 394
Maxwell, James 200
means of production 23, 143–4, 193,
    194–5
mechanisation, craftsmanship 443–4
Mede, Joseph 297
men: character of 506; competitive world
    of 500–1, 502, 503; homosexuality
    536–55; repression of women 523–4;
    variational tendencies of 488, 491–2
Menger, Carl 21–2
mental cultivation 46–7, 62, 65
mental pathology, degeneracy 416–32
Meredith, George 396
method: *a priori/a posteriori* 111–14; 'All-
    case' (Enumerative) 121–4; Historical

124; practice/theory conflict 110;
single-case 124
Miall, Edward 176–7
Michelet, Jules 170
Middle Ages: art 406, 441–2; feudalism
525
middle classes: art 313, 315;
authoritarianism 170, 175, 176–9; sex
and gender 466–7
*The Migration of Symbols* (Goblet d'Alviella)
411
militias 179
Mill, James 16, 28, 93, 126
Mill, John Stuart: art 316; gender 464,
471–2; liberalism 183–92; liberty 448;
mechanisation 444; political economy
20–1, 108–14, 126–7, 129–30, 132,
144; state 24–5; utilitarianism 16, 17,
39–55, 58–62, 64–7; women 520–34
miracles 304, 305
misogyny 468
model communities, Owenite 18, 68, 82
*Modern Money-lending and the Meaning of
Dividends* (Carpenter, E.) 535
*Modern Painters* (Ruskin) 313–14, 325
modernity 323, 396–7, 409
Moll, Albert 537, 538–9, 540, 541, 545
monarchy: absolute 522; women 503–4,
527
*A Monograph on the Fossil Balanidae and
Verrucidae of Great Britain* (Darwin) 227
Montfort, Simon de 523
Moore, George 315
morality: art relationship 314–15, 325–68;
class influence on 186–7; degeneracy
418–19; homosexuality 544, 547–8,
551; lying 407–8; religious coercion
191–2; sex relationship 465; state
intervention 191; taste relationship 456;
women 500, 503–4; *see also* ethics
More, Thomas 165, 570n32
Morel, Benedict Augustin 416–18, 419,
420
Morgan, Henry Lewis 493
*Morning Chronicle* 39
*Morning Star* 168, 571n4
Morris, William 23, 26, 193–6, 320–2,
433–45
mortality rates, social evolution 280–2
'Mosaic' geologists 204, 205
*The Mothers of England* (Ellis) 495
motivation, utilitarianism 49–50

Murphy, William 171
music, women's education 511
*My Days and Dreams* (Carpenter, E.) 536
Myers, Frederick 407
mysticism, degeneracy 422

*Natal Sermons* (Colenso) 299
*Nation* 168
National Character, Law of 452, 453, 456
*National Review* 115, 446
national will 85
nationalisation 195
*The Nationalisation of Health* (Havelock Ellis)
486
*The Natural Elements of Political Economy*
(Jennings) 137
*Natural History* (Pliny) 400, 600n53
natural phenomena *see* earthquakes;
volcanic activity
natural price of labour 101–3, 144–5
natural selection 207, 208–9, 228–53,
267–8; Christian critique of 273–7;
divergence of character 242–51;
extinction 241–2; illustrations 234–7;
sexual selection 232–4, 252
natural theology 203, 204
*Natural Theology* (Paley) 203
Naturalism: artistic taste 450, 606n13;
Gothic architecture 344–6
naturalisation of plants 244–5
nature: art relationship 391–2, 397–8,
401–2, 438; Christian conception of
273–7; geology 213–26; Gothic art
analogy 329–31; human evolution
254–71; imperfection in 340; natural
selection 207, 227–53, 267–8; scientific
vs religion explanations 203–4; women
492, 512–13
nature–nurture problem, gender 528–30
Nerval, Gérard de 412
nervousness, homosexuality 538
*Neue Freie Presse* 415
neurosis, homosexuality relationship 537,
538
New Lanark Mills 18, 68, 69–82
*The New Republic* (Mallock) 383
*A New View of Society* (Owen) 18, 68
*The Newcomes* (Thackeray) 403
*News from Nowhere* (Morris) 434
Newton, Isaac 122
*The Nigger Question* (Carlyle) 156
Nihilism 403

Nonconformism 176, 177, 203, 573*n*35, 36
Nordau, Max 320, 415–32
the North, Gothic architecture 329–31, 347–8
*North British Review* 351
*Notes on Poems and Reviews* (Swinburne) 369, 370–82
novels, women's education 510–11
*Novum Organum* (Bacon) 122

*The Odd Women* (Gissing) 467
Odger, George 180
Oken 276
old age 281–2
*Old Studies and New* (Grote) 56
Old Testament *see* Pentateuch
Oliphant, Margaret 394
*Oliver Cromwell's Letters and Speeches* (Carlyle) 155
'On the Definition of Political Economy; and on the Method of Philosophical Investigation in that Science' (Mill, J. S.) 108–14
*On the Genius of Spenser* (Courthope) 446
*On the Interpretation of Scripture* (Jowett) 290–8
*On Liberty* (Mill, J. S.) 24–5, 39, 183–92, 448
*On the Origin of Species* (Darwin) 207–10, 227–53
*On the Principles of Political Economy, and Taxation* (Ricardo) 93–107
oniomania 426
opinion *see* public opinion
order, artistic freedom 341–2
organicism 18–19, 83–91
organisms: embryology 257–62; natural selection 228–53
Orientalism 399
ornament, architectural 331–2
Owen, Richard 269–70
Owen, Robert 17–18, 68–82
Owenism 18, 22, 68
*Oxford and Cambridge Magazine* 433
Oxford Movement 202, 272
Oxford University 455–6

*Pagan and Christian Creeds* (Carpenter, E.) 536
Paget, James 468
painting 406–7; degeneracy 426–8
Paley, William 27, 57, 60–1, 63–4, 203, 396

*Panopticon; or, The Inspection House* (Bentham) 27
parallelism, organicist political philosophy 86–8
Parise, Jean 475, 477–8, 479, 483–4
Parliament: authoritarian critique of 158; eligibility for 526; *see also* democracy; government
*Past and Present* (Carlyle) 155
Pater, Walter 317, 318, 383–9
pathology: art as 320, 415–32; homosexuality 537–9, 550–1
Patmore, Coventry 505
Pentateuch 297, 300–9; *see also* Bible
*The Pentateuch and the Book of Joshua Critically Examined* (Colenso) 210–11, 299, 300–9
perception, visual 426–8
perfection: artistic 332, 334; *see also* imperfection
*Periplus* (Hanno) 400, 600*n*53
pessimism 420; economic 12
Peterloo Massacre 161, 570*n*24
Philips, Ambrose 373
philosophic method, political economy 110–14
Philosophic Radicals 16
*Philosophie zoologique* (Lamarck) 206
philosophy: aesthetic judgement 453; communitarianism 68–82; utilitarianism 27–67; *see also* philosophic method
physics 200
*Physics and Politics* (Bagehot) 115
'physiological division of labour' 236, 245
physiology: degeneracy 417–18; gender differences 489–90; homosexuality 537–9; human/ape comparison 265–6, 489–90; sex 468–70, 476–7, 480, 482
*The Picture of Dorian Gray* (Wilde) 317, 390
the picturesque 342
*The Pilgrims of Hope* (Morris) 434
Pinero, Arthur Wing 467
*Plan of Parliamentary Reform, in the Form of a Catechism* (Bentham) 28
plants *see* biology
Plato: homosexuality 542, 544; interpretation 293–4; sexual equality 522, 570*n*32; society 86, 87, 165
*Plato and Platonism* (Pater) 384
*The Play-Function of Sex* (Havelock Ellis) 487
Playfair, John 222
pleasure: aesthetic 384–5; craftsmanship

440–1; marginal utility theory 130, 131–2, 135, 136–7; utilitarianism 16–17, 28–9, 32–8, 40–6, 58–9; *see also* happiness

Pliny the Elder 400, 600*n*53

*Plutology, or the Theory of Efforts to supply Human Wants* (Hearn) 133

*Poems* (Wilde) 390

*Poems and Ballads* (Swinburne) 369–70

*Poetics* (Aristotle) 453

poetry 315; Courthope 446; Decadence 318–19; freedom of expression 370–82; idyllic 381–2; life relationship 353–4; Morris 433; Wilde 393

police, civil disorder 157

political economy 19–21; Bagehot 115–28; critique of communitarianism 18; individual interest 70; marginal utility theory 129–41; Mill 108–14; radical 450, 606*n*10; Ricardo 93–107

*The Political Economy of Art* (Ruskin) 325

politics: anti-democratic 24; art relationship 316; authoritarianism 155–82; gender equality 520–34; Hobbes 86–7; homosexual scandals 554; ideas relationship 355–7; liberal democracy 24–5; liberalism 183–92; local factors 14; Plato 86, 87; representation 23–4; socialism 25–6, 193–6; *see also* democracy; government; Parliament; state

pollination 235–6

Polo, Marco 400, 600*n*53

poor countries 104

poor houses 75

Poor Laws 106–7, 160

*The Popular Education of France* (Arnold) 167

population: control 47, 66; economy relationship 12; eugenics 282–4, 286–8; mortality rates 280–2; production relationship 103–4

Porter, Roy 463, 468

positivism 56, 58

'The Postulates of English Political Economy No.1' (Bagehot) 115–28

poverty: communitarianism 70, 71; population control 47, 66; social protests 14; wealth inequalities 13; working classes 150–1

power, human desire for 515

practice, theory conflict 110–11

*Praeterita* (Ruskin) 326

Pratt, John Henry 300–1

Pre-Raphaelites 319, 325, 369

preaching 292

prices: natural vs market 20; statistical tables 119–20

primates, human evolution 261, 262, 264–7, 269–70, 489–90

primitive societies 88, 103–4, 189

Primrose, Archibald *see* Rosebery, Lord

*The Principles of Economics* (Jevons) 129

*Principles of Geology* (Lyell) 205, 206, 213, 214–26

*Principles of Moral and Political Philosophy* (Paley) 27

*Principles of Political Economy* (Malthus) 93

*Principles of Political Economy* (Mill, J.S.) 20–1, 39

*Principles of Political Economy, and Taxation* (Ricardo) 20

*Principles of Sociology* (Spencer) 19

prisons 27

*A Problem in Greek Ethics* (Symonds) 486, 543, 550–5

*A Problem in Modern Ethics* (Symonds) 550–5

*Prodigiorum et Ostentorum Chronicon* (Lycosthenes) 400, 600*n*53

production: agricultural 96–7, 103–4, 147; capitalism 146–7; craftsmanship 336–9, 439–40, 442–4; economic growth 13; labour value 94–9; means of 23, 143–4, 193, 194–5; wages 100–7

profit, capitalism 193–4

property: authoritarianism 164–5; capitalism 108; communitarianism 18; utilitarian value 38

prophecy 296, 297

prostitution 474

*Prostitution Considered in its Moral, Social and Sanitary Aspects in London and Other Large Cities* (Acton) 474

protest, social 156–7, 170–1, 182

Protestantism: biblical interpretation 290–1, 297; Catholicism conflict 178–9; criticism 366; sex 481; *see also* Church of England

protests 14

*Protoplasm; The Physical Basis of Life* (Huxley) 254

psychology: degeneracy 320, 416–32; gender differences 529–30; scientific method 202

puberty 475

public health, working classes 150, 567n10
public hysteria 431–2
public opinion: homosexuality 552; moral
    sanctions 34–5; tyranny of the majority
    185–8; women writers 531–2
publishing 4–5, 7–8, 322
Pugin, Augustus 322
*Punch* 383
punishment: Benthamism 34; biblical 305
*Pure Logic* (Jevons) 129

Quarter Sessions 164, 570n31
*Quarterly Review* 272, 359
*The Queen-Mother and Rosamond* (Swinburne)
    369
Quintilian 453, 607n19

racism 156, 522
radicalism 7
Raleigh, Walter 401, 600n59
Rathke, Martin Heinrich 257, 579n6
*Rationale of Judicial Evidence* (Bentham) 39
rationalism *see a priori* method
Reade, Charles 397
realism: artistic 314–15, 402, 406–7, 409;
    dramatic 399; Gothic 344–6; literary
    396; Romanticism 412
redundance, Gothic architecture 349–50
reform, social 13–14
Reform League 174
Reformation 290–1
*Reformer* 536
*Regeneration: A Reply to Max Nordau* (Hake)
    416
regional loyalty, political activity 14
Reichert, Karl Bogislaus 257, 579n6
relative value 97–8, 99–100, 106
relativism, cultural 315, 318, 319
religion: Bible interpretation 289–309;
    Darwinism impact on 209–10; decline
    of 199, 316; French Revolution 163–4;
    homosexuality 540, 551, 553; literary
    criticism 364–5; moral repression 187,
    191–2; political exclusion 450; science
    conflict 199–200, 272–7; sex and
    gender 468; toleration 187–8, 448;
    university secularisation 201;
    utilitarianism 51–2; voluntaryism 177,
    573n36; women's education 509
*Religious Duty* (Cobbe) 365
Remak, Robert 257, 579n6

*Remarks on the Proper Treatment of Cases of
    Polygamy* (Colenso) 299
*Reminiscences* (Carlyle) 156
Renaissance 332, 386–7, 442, 444, 453
Renan, Joseph-Ernest 364–5
rent, wages relationship 105
*Replies to Essays and Reviews* (Haddan) 301
*Report to the County of Lanark* (Owen) 18, 68,
    69–82, 561n1
Reports on Artisans' Dwellings 153
representation, political 23–4
repression: moral 191–2; sexual 463,
    464–5, 469, 473–85; social unrest 13; of
    women 520–34
reproduction: pollination 235–6; sexual
    selection 232–4, 252
*Retrospective Review* 393
Revolutionary Socialism 193–6
revolutionism: degeneracy 422; socialism
    23
*Revue des Deux Mondes* 359
rhetoric: biblical interpretation 292, 294;
    Symbolism 413
Ricardo, David 20, 93–107, 126, 139–40,
    144–5
rights: liberalism 25, 183; womens' 471–2,
    523
rigidity, Gothic architecture 347–9
riots 157, 170–1, 568n4
*Robert Elsmere* (Ward) 394, 395–6, 598n19
Robespierre, Maximilien 403, 601n73
Roebuck, John Arthur 360, 361
roles, gender 465–6, 471–2, 496–504, 506
Roman Catholicism: biblical interpretation
    290–1, 297; criticism 366;
    Protestantism conflict 171, 178–9; sex
    481
romance *see* love
romantic novels 510
Romanticism 317–18, 319, 412
Rosebery, Lord (Archibald Primrose) 457
Roubinovitch, Jacques 419, 420, 423
Rousseau, Jean-Jacques 389, 403
rules, social 186–7
Ruskin, John: art 313–14, 315, 325–50,
    440; criticism 362, 395; gender 466,
    468; women 505–19

St Clement of Alexandria 491
St John, Charles George William 234
*St Paul and Protestantism* (Arnold) 167
Saint-Simon, Henri de 39, 164, 570n29

Saintsbury, George 453, 456
*Salammbô* (Flaubert) 396, 599*n*38
*Salomé* (Wilde) 390
'saltationist' view of evolution 205–6, 207, 208
Sanchez, Thomas 408
*The Sanity of Art: An Exposure of the Current Nonsense about Artists Being Degenerate* (Shaw) 416
Sappho 373–4
*Sartor Resartus* (Carlyle) 155, 411
*Saturday Review* 401
savageness, Gothic architecture 329–40
Say, Jean-Baptiste 132
scandals, homosexual 554
scarcity: marginal utility theory 137–8, 139; political economy 94
scholarship, biblical 289–309
schools, communitarianism 79
Schopenhauer, Artur 403, 423–4, 449
science 199–288; abstract 111–14, 117–18, 123, 126; Darwinism impact on 209–10; evolutionary theory 227–77; gender roles 468–70; geology 213–26; homosexuality research 537–9, 553; human development 73; human evolution 254–71; religion conflict 199–200, 272–7; scientific method 110–14, 122–3, 200, 202, 205, 210; Social Darwinism 278–88; women's education 508
*Science and Culture* (Huxley) 255
*Science and Scripture not at Variance* (Pratt) 300–1
'Scriptural' geologists 204, 205
Scripture *see* Bible
sculpture 378–9
*The Second Mrs Tanqueray* (Pinero) 467
*A Second Visit to the United States of North America* (Lyell) 214
secularism 199
Sedgwick, Adam 205
self-culture 455–7
self-government *see* democracy
self-interest, political economy 20, 21
*Self-Preservation: A Medical Treatise on Nervous and Physical Debility, Spermatorrhoea, Impotence and Sterility* (La'mert) 466
self-protection: liberalism 189; *see also* harm
Senior, Nassau William 126, 133, 134, 136–7, 139
senses, visual 427–8

*Sermons* (Grote) 56
servility, architectural ornament 331–2, 334
*Sesame and Lilies* (Ruskin) 326, 505–19
*The Seven Lamps of Architecture* (Ruskin) 325, 343
sex 463–94; English Decadent Movement 319; homosexuality 467, 469, 470–1, 472, 486, 536–55; moral repression 473–85; socialism 195; *see also* gender
*Sex-Love and Its Place in a Free Society* (Carpenter, E.) 536
sex socialism 195
sexual inversion *see* homosexuality
*Sexual Inversion* (Havelock Ellis/Symonds) 487, 550
sexual selection 232–4, 252
sexual virtue 76
Shairp, John Campbell 321
Shakespeare, William 354, 398–9, 401
Shaw, George Bernard 416
Shelley, Percy Bysshe 378
'Shooting Niagara: and After?' (Carlyle) 156
Sidgwick, Henry 16
*Silhouettes* (Symons) 410
single-case method 124
*Sketches in Italy and Greece* (Symonds) 549
*Sketches and Studies in Italy* (Symonds) 549
slavery 336, 521–2, 533, 587*n*20
Smith, Adam 19–20, 94–9, 115–16, 126
sociability 11, 15
social alienation, homosexuality 538
social class: art and culture 321–2, 436, 441–2; authoritarianism 159, 164, 170, 173, 180–1; homosexuality 546; influence on morality 186–7; labour 334–5; Marxism 23; organicism 85, 90; sex and gender 466–7, 481; *see also* aristocracy; class conflict; middle classes; working classes
social cohesion, art as 315, 316
Social Darwinism 209, 278–88, 320, 416–32
Social Democratic Federation (SDF) 23, 142, 195, 575*n*3
social disorder 12, 13–14, 156–7, 160–1, 170–3, 182
social engineering *see* Social Darwinism
social evolution 278–88
social good: political authority 24; socialism 26

social reform 13–14
social rules 186–7
*Social Statics* (Spencer) 83
social theory 11–196; art 320–3, 434–45;
  authoritarianism 24, 155–82;
  communitarianism 17–18, 68–82;
  economics 93–154; ethics 27–82;
  gender 520–34; liberalism 24–5,
  183–92; marginal utility theory 21–2,
  129–41; organicism 18–19, 68–91;
  political economy 19–21, 93–141;
  politics 155–96; Social Darwinism
  278–88; socialism 21, 22–3, 25–6,
  142–54, 193–6; utilitarianism 15–17,
  27–67
social tyranny 185
social-problem novels 11, 21
*Socialism: Its Growth and Outcome*
  (Bax/Morris) 434
socialism: abolishment of the state 25–6;
  art 321–2, 434–45; economics 21,
  22–3, 142–54; Morris 193–6
Socialist League 23, 142, 193–6, 434
Society for the Protection of Ancient
  Buildings 433
sociology: evolutionary theory analogy
  83–91, 278–88; founding of 83; of
  reading 5
sodomy 555; *see also* homosexuality
*Songs Before Sunrise* (Swinburne) 370
Sophocles 293–4
soup kitchens 164, 570n31
Sparta: homosexuality 542–3; women 522
specialisation, intellectual 201–2
speciation 206, 208, 227, 228–53, 268, 274
Spencer, Herbert 19, 83–91, 209, 278–88,
  401
*The Sphinx* (Wilde) 391
Spinoza, Benedict de 420
stability, social 12–13
Stanley, Arthur Penrhyn 364
state: abolition of 25–6; art relationship
  456; authoritarianism 169–70, 174,
  180–2; church relationship 202;
  Hobbesian 86–7; individual
  relationship 23–5, 90–1, 183–92;
  universities relationship 455–6; *see also*
  state intervention
state intervention: homosexuality 547–8;
  individual liberty 447–8, 525–6;
  liberalism 25, 188; political economy
  20, 21, 117; reform 13–14

State Socialism 195–6
statistics, business 119–20
'steady-state' theory of geological
  development 205, 213–26
Stevenson, Robert Louis 394, 403
Stewart, James 116
stockbroking 119–20
Stoicism 42, 43, 50
*The Stones of Venice. Volume II* (Ruskin) 325,
  326–50
*The Strange Case of Dr Jekyll and Mr Hyde*
  (Stevenson) 394, 403–4, 598n14
Strauss, David Friedrich 364
*The Strayed Reveller, and Other Poems* (Arnold)
  167
strikes 145
*The Student's Elements of Geology* (Lyell) 214
*Studies of the Greek Poets* (Symonds) 549
*Studies in the History of the Renaissance* (Pater)
  383, 384–9
*Studies in the Psychology of Sex* (Havelock
  Ellis) 470, 486
'The Study of Sociology. XIV. –
  Preparation in Biology' (Spencer)
  278–88
*The Subjection of Women* (Mill, J. S.) 40, 464,
  471–2, 520–34
Suetonius 400, 600n53
suffering: overcoming 47; sexual 480–1
suffrage, women's movement 523
*A Summary of the Principles of Socialism*
  (Hyndman/Morris) 434
supply: marginal utility theory 134–7;
  wages 104, 106
surplus value 145, 146, 147; art industry
  313
'survival of the fittest' 208, 209; *see also*
  natural selection; Social Darwinism
sweating system 151–2
Swinburne, Algernon Charles 318, 369–82
symbolism: Decadent vs Romantic notions
  319; literary 411–13
Symbolist Movement 411–13
*The Symbolist Movement in Literature* (Symons)
  410, 411–13
Symonds, John Addington 469, 486–7,
  542, 543, 549–55, 613n8
Symons, Arthur 319, 410–13
*Symposium* (Plato) 542
*System of Logic* (Mill, J. S.) 39
*System of Synthetic Philosophy* (Spencer) 83

Tacitus 400, 600n53
tailoring industry 151–2
Taine, Hippolyte-Adolphe 412, 603n5
Tarabaud 424
taste 314, 315, 450–9; *see also* aesthetics
taxonomy 251, 252–3, 263–4, 266–7
technology: industrialisation 12–13;
    innovations 199, 200
teleology, evolutionary theory 204, 206–7
*telos* 58
*Ten Weeks in Natal* (Colenso) 299
Tennyson, Alfred 204
Thackeray, William 403, 599n38
theology: biblical interpretation 298–309;
    natural 203, 204; women's education
    509
theory, practice conflict 110–11
*The Theory of Political Economy* (Jevons)
    21–2, 129–41
Thiers, Louis Adolphe 117
Thom, J. N. 161, 570n19
*Thoughts on French Affairs* (Burke) 357
*Time and Tide* (Ruskin) 326
*The Times* 359
timescale, geological 216–18, 223–4
Tocqueville, Alexis de 24
toleration, religious 188, 448
Topinard, Paul 489
Torrens, Robert 93, 102, 126
Tourette, Gilles de la 427
Tourgénieff, Ivan *see* Turgenev
*Towards Democracy* (Carpenter, E.) 535
Tractarianism 202
tradition, artistic 321
tranquillity 46
transformational theory of evolution 206,
    207, 208
*On Translating Homer* (Arnold) 167
*Travels in North America* (Lyell) 214
*A Treatise on the Moral Ideals* (Grote) 56
truth, beauty relationship 345–6
Turgenev, Ivan 403, 601n72
typography 7–8
tyranny of the majority 185

Ulrichs, Karl Heinrich 469, 551, 552,
    613n4
*Under the Microscope* (Swinburne) 370
uniformitarianism, geological development
    205, 213, 214–15, 221–6, 576n2
United States of America: artistic dullness
    of 400; slavery 521–2, 533

universities: aesthetic taste 455–8; scientific
    development 201–2
*Unto This Last* (Ruskin) 326
urban decay 438–9
utilitarianism 15–17; Bentham 27–38;
    Grote 56–67; Mill 39–55
*Utilitarianism* (Mill, J. S.) 39, 40–55
utility: definition 130, 132; marginal utility
    theory 21–2; nature of 134–6; political
    economy 94; value 139–40

value: aesthetic 314–16, 317–19, 321,
    322–3; labour theory of 20, 22,
    94–107, 116, 142–4; marginal utility
    theory 129, 130, 138–41; surplus 145,
    146, 147; wages 100–7
*Vanity Fair* (Thackeray) 403
*The Vanity of Human Wishes* (Johnson) 61
variation *see* natural selection
variety, Gothic architecture 340–4
Varnell, Charles 482
venereal diseases 464–5, 474, 481–2
Venetian architecture 326–7
Verlaine, Paul 413, 604n11
*Vestiges of the Natural History of Creation*
    (Chambers) 206–7
vice, homosexuality 551–2
*Vicomte de Bragelonne* (Dumas) 396, 599n38
villages, agricultural 74–8
Villiers de l'Isle-Adam, Philippe-Auguste
    413, 604n12
*Vingt ans de ma Vie littéraire* (Daudet) 395
Virey, Julien Joseph 276, 581n11
virtue, utilitarianism 50
volcanic activity 217, 218, 219, 223–4
voting *see* enfranchisement
Vulcanists 225

wages: 'iron law of' 20; labour exploitation
    145; value of 98–9, 100–7; Wage Fund
    Theory 130
Wagner, Richard 542
Waldeck-Rousseau, Pierre 450
Wallace, Alfred Russel 227
Walras, Léon 21–2, 124
war, female responsibility for 516
Ward, Mary 598n19
Waterhouse, George Robert 245
wealth: consumption 132; distribution of
    13, 20, 21; marginal utility theory 130;
    pursuit of 108–9

*Wealth of Nations* (Smith) 19, 99, 100
Wedderburn, Alexander 30–1
welfare policies, social Darwinism 282, 284
welfare state, origins of 13
West India question 158, 569*n*11
*Westminster Review* 19, 383
Whewell, William 131
Whitman, Walt 537, 545–6, 549, 552
*Wife's Handbook* (Allbutt) 465
Wilberforce, Samuel 199, 272–7
Wilde, Oscar: Aestheticism 317, 318;
    consumerism 322–3; criticism 5,
    390–409; homosexuality 467, 470–1;
    individualism 26
Wilson, Alderman 179
Wilson, Thomas (Bishop of Sodor and
    Mann) 177, 181
Winckelmann, Johann Joachim 387
wisdom, female 506–7
*The Wives of England* (Ellis) 495
*Woman and Her Place in a Free Society*
    (Carpenter, E.) 536
*The Woman's World* (Wilde) 390
women 495–534; character of 498, 506;
    children comparison 488–9, 490; class
    issues 466–7; discrimination against
    463; domestic roles 465–6, 496–504,
    506; education of 465–6, 507–14, 524,

534; equality 471–2, 520–34; as
    evolutionary leaders 490–2;
    exploitation at work 149, 151, 152;
    feminism 469–70; homosexuality
    546–7; men's knowledge of 529–31,
    532; moral power 500, 503–4; sexual
    desire 465
*The Women of England: Their Social Duties, and
    Domestic Habits* (Ellis) 495–504
Wood, William Page 171
Woodward, John 218, 576*n*9
Wordsworth, William: criticism 351–2,
    354; poetry 398, 448–9, 507–8, 611*n*6
working classes: authoritarian view of
    156–66, 170–3, 179–80; capitalist
    exploitation of 142–4, 145–54;
    communitarianism 69, 74, 77, 82; poor
    countries 104; sex and gender 467;
    socialism 193–6
working hours 148–9, 152
workshop-system, craftsmanship 443

Yeats, W. B. 410

Zionism 416
Zola, Emile 394–5, 396, 412
zoology, taxonomy 263–4, 266–7
Zulu culture 300

Printed in the United Kingdom
by Lightning Source UK Ltd.
134969UK00003B/32/A